HUGH JOHNSON'S

Pocket Encyclopedia of Wine

1997

A FIRESIDE BOOK
PUBLISHED BY SIMON & SCHUSTER

FIRESIDE
Rockefeller Center
1230 Avenue of the Americas
New York, New York 10020

© Mitchell Beazley International Ltd 1977–1996
Text © Hugh Johnson 1977–1996
Maps © Reed International Books Limited 1977–1996

First edition published 1977
Revised editions published 1978, 1979, 1980, 1981, 1982, 1983, 1984, 1985,
1986, 1987, 1988, 1989, 1990, 1991, 1992, 1993, 1994, 1995, 1996

Editor: Susan Keevil
Design: Neil Wadsworth
Commissioning Editor: Sue Jamieson
Executive Art Editor: Fiona Knowles
Production: Juliette Butler, Christina Quigley

Produced by Mandarin Offset
Printed and bound in China

10 9 8 7 6 5 4 3 2 1

ISBN 0-684-83061-2
ISSN 0893-259X

Contents

Foreword

This 20th annual edition of my micro-encyclopedia has put on weight – and I hope regained a little of the elegance of design, if not language – which my shoe-horning technique has eroded over the years. It should be easier to read. It is certainly more up to date than ever, bringing news not just of new vintages but of the continuing headlong expansion of the good-wine world.

So much expansion indeed that I have instigated a new feature for the impatient: here and there you will find little national or regional selections as suggestions of wines to try. Don't run away with the idea that these are my 100-pointers. Old readers will know that I don't give points: rushing to judgement is not my scene. For the Johnson System of scoring turn to page 279.

For those who pay any attention to the official pronouncements of government nannies about drinking and health, 1996 was a milestone year. In January the US Department of Agriculture issued new Dietary Guidelines for Americans which gave cautious backing to what wine-drinkers – doctors especially – have known all along: that alcohol in moderation is moderately good for you. Most of the benefit seems to be in reducing the risk of coronary heart disease. Nutritionists are still reluctant to endorse the idea that cheerfulness, good company and good digestion are healthy in themselves.

Coincidentally the British government also revised its official view of the risks and benefits of moderate drinking at the same time. Ten years of research in many countries (Denmark must get an honourable mention here) has made it impossible either medically or morally to hold the prohibitionist line. It is the French government, absurdly and uncharacteristically, that remains out on a limb with its 'Loi Evin' against the advertising of alcohol. Whether wine comes out of all the current medical research as being different from any other form of alcohol is less clear – though beer certainly gives you a different-shaped tummy.

There have been other things to raise wine-lovers morale, too. A splendid Bordeaux vintage in 1995 was the headline-maker, but a huge one in Australia will add just as much to the sum of human pleasure. Chile and Argentina moved perceptibly up in the quality stakes, Germany took serious first steps towards an inevitable classification of its vineyards, Italy made masses of seriously good wine… wine-growing is steadily moving from tentative to confident in more parts of the USA and Canada. Round the world, in fact, the science of wine made progress and its appreciation more than kept pace.

As always, my aim in this book is to compress the essentials of this ever-changing world into your pocket. My information is gleaned from many sources, through visits, tastings and never-ending correspondence. Revision is constant. I shall have a much-scribbled on proof for 1998 before you even read this.

The book is designed to take the panic out of buying. You are faced with a daunting restaurant wine list, or mind-numbing shelves of bottles in a store. Your mind goes blank. Out comes your little book. You can start with what you propose to eat, by turning to the wines for food section on pages 14–27, or where you are by turning up a national section, or a grape variety you like. Just establish which country a wine comes from, then look up the principal words on the label in that country's section. You should find enough information to guide your choice – and often a great deal more: the cross-references are there to help you delve further. Even after 19 editions I find I can browse for hours...

...and my thanks

This store of detailed recommendations comes partly from my own notes and partly from those of a great number of kind friends. Without the generous help and cooperation of innumerable winemakers, merchants and critics, I could not attempt it. I particularly want to thank the following for help with research or in the areas of their special knowledge.

Burton Anderson
Colin Anderson MW
Fritz Ascher
Martyn Assirati
Jean-Claude Berrouet
Paul Robert Blom
Michael Broadbent MW
Jim Budd
John Cossart
Stelios Damianou
Marc Dubernet
Len Evans
Dereck Foster
Howard G Goldberg
Grahame Haggart
James Halliday
Russell Hone
Shirley Jones

Susan Keevil
Andreas Keller
Gabriel Lachmann
Tony Laithwaite
Miles Lambert-Gócs
Christopher Lindlar
John Livingstone-
    Learmonth
Giles MacDonogh
Andreas März
Richard Mayson
Maggie McNie MW
Eszter Molnár
Jasper Morris MW
Vladimir Moskvan
Christian Moueix
Douglas Murray
Richard Neill

Nobuko Nishioka
Judy Peterson-Nedry
Stuart Pigott
John and Erica Platter
Carlos Read
Jan and Maite Read
Michael, Prinz zu Salm
Peter A Sichel
Stephen Skelton
Steven Spurrier
Charles & Philippa Sydney
Paul Symington
Bob Thompson
Peter Vinding-Diers
Rebecca Wassermann-
    Hone
Julia Wilkinson

How to use this book

The top line of most entries consists of the following information:

Aglianico del Vulture Bas | r dr (s/sw sp) | ★★★ | 86 87 88 90 91 92 (93) (94) (95)

❶ Wine name and the region the wine comes from.

❷ Whether it is red, rosé or white (or brown/amber), dry, sweet or
sparkling, or several of these (and which is most important):

r	red
p	rosé
w	white
br	brown
dr	dry*
sw	sweet
s/sw	semi-sweet
sp	sparkling

( ) brackets here denote a less important wine
*assume wine is dry when **dr** or **sw** are not indicated

❸ Its general standing as to quality: a necessarily rough and ready
guide based on its current reputation as reflected in its prices:

★	plain, everyday quality
★★	above average
★★★	well known, highly reputed
★★★★	grand, prestigious, expensive

So much is more or less objective. Additionally there is a subjective rating:

★ etc Stars are coloured green for any wine which in my experience is
usually especially good within its price range. There are good everyday
wines as well as good luxury wines. This system helps you find them.

❹ Vintage information: which of the recent vintages that may still
be available can be recommended; of these, which are ready to
drink this year, and which will probably improve with keeping.
Your choice for current drinking should be one of the vintage years
printed in **bold** type. Buy light-type years for further maturing.

95 etc recommended years which may be currently available

90'etc vintage regarded as particularly successful for the
property in question

87 etc years in **bold** should be ready for drinking (the others should
be kept)

89 etc vintages in colour are the ones to choose first for drinking in '97–
they should be à point. (See also Bordeaux introduction, page 78.)

(93) etc provisional rating

The German vintages work on a different principle again: see page 136.

Other abbreviations

DYA drink the youngest available

NV vintage not normally shown on label; in Champagne,
means a blend of several vintages for continuity

CHABLIS properties, areas or terms cross-referred within the section

A quick-reference vintage chart appears on page 280

Grape Varieties

In the past ten years a radical change has come about in all except the most long-established wine countries. Suddenly the names of a handful of grape varieties have become the ready reference to wine. In the senior wine countries, above all France and Italy (which between them still produce nearly half the world's wine), more complex traditions prevail. Wine is known by its origin, not just the particular fruit-juice that fermented.

For the present the two notions are in rivalry. Eventually the primacy of place over fruit will become obvious, at least for wines of quality. But for now, for most people, grape tastes are the easy reference-point – despite the fact that they are often confused by the added taste of oak. If grape flavours were really all that mattered this would be a very short book.

But of course they do matter, and a knowledge of them both guides you to flavours you enjoy and helps comparisons between regions. Hence the originally Californian term 'varietal wine' – meaning, in principle, one grape variety.

At least seven varieties – Cabernet, Pinot Noir, Riesling, Sauvignon Blanc, Chardonnay, Gewürztraminer and Muscat – have tastes and smells distinct and memorable enough to form international categories of wine. To these you can add Merlot, Syrah, Sémillon, Chenin Blanc, Pinots Blanc and Gris, Sylvaner, Nebbiolo, Sangiovese, Tempranillo… The following are the best and/or commonest wine grapes. Abbreviations used in the text are in brackets.

Grapes for white wine

Albariño
The Spanish name for N Portugal's Alvarinho, emerging as excellently fresh and fragrant wine in Galicia.

Aligoté
Burgundy's second-rank white grape. Crisp (often sharp) wine, needs drinking in 1–3 yrs. Perfect for mixing with cassis (blackcurrant liqueur) to make a 'Kir'. Widely planted in E Europe, esp Russia.

Arinto
White central Portuguese grape for crisp, fragrant dry whites.

Blanc Fumé
Alias of SAUV BL, referring to its reputedly 'smoky' smell, particularly from the Loire (Sancerre and Pouilly). In California used for oak-aged Sauv and reversed to 'Fumé Blanc'. But the smoke is oak.

Bual
Makes top quality sweet Madeira wines.

Chardonnay (Chard)
The white burgundy grape, the white champagne grape, and the best white grape of the New World, partly because it is one of the easiest to grow and vinify. All regions are trying it, mostly aged (or, better, fermented) in oak to reproduce the flavours of burgundy. Australia and California make classics. Those of Italy, Spain, New Zealand, South Africa, New York State, Chile, Hungary and the Midi are all coming on strong. Called Morillon in Austria.

Chasselas
A prolific early-ripening grape with little aroma, mainly grown for eating. Best known as Fendant in Switzerland (where it is supreme), Gutedel in Germany.

Chenin Blanc (Chenin Bl)
Great white grape of the middle Loire (Vouvray, Layon etc). Wine can be dry or sweet (or very sweet), but always retains plenty of acidity – hence its long life and use in California, where it can make fine wine, but is rarely so used. See also Steen.

Clairette
A low-acid grape formerly widely used in the S of France as a vermouth base. Being revived.

Colombard
Slightly fruity, nicely sharp grape, hugely popular in California, now gaining ground in SW France, South Africa, California etc.

Fendant See Chasselas.

Folle Blanche
High acid/little flavour make this ideal for brandy. Called Gros Plant in Brittany, Picpoul in Armagnac. Respectable in California.

Fumé Blanc (Fumé Bl) See Blanc Fumé.

Furmint
A grape of great character: the trademark of Hungary both as the principal grape in Tokay and as vivid vigorous table wine with an appley flavour. Called Sipon in Slovenia. Some grown in Austria.

Gewürztraminer, alias Traminer (Gewürz)
One of the most pungent grapes, distinctively spicy with aromas like rose petals and grapefruit. Wines are often rich and soft, even when fully dry. Best in Alsace; also good in Germany, E Europe, Australia, California, Pacific NW, New Zealand.

Grauburgunder See Pinot Gris.

Grechetto or Greco
Ancient grape of central and S Italy: vitality and style.

Grüner Veltliner
Austria's favourite (planted in almost half her vineyards). Around Vienna and in the Wachau and Weinviertel (also in Moravia) it can be delicious: light but dry and lively. The best age 5 years or so.

Italian Riesling
Grown in N Italy and E Europe. Much inferior to Rhine RIES, with lower acidity, best in sweet wines. Alias Welschriesling, Olaszrizling (no longer legally labelled simply 'Riesling').

Kéknyelü
Low-yielding, flavourful grape giving one of Hungary's best whites. Has the potential for fieriness and spice. To be watched.

Kerner
The most successful of many recent German varieties, mostly made by crossing RIES and SILVANER, but in this case Ries x (red) Trollinger. Early-ripening flowery (but often too blatant) wine with good acidity. Popular in Pfalz, Rheinhessen etc.

Loureiro
The best and most fragrant Vinho Verde variety in Portugal.

Macabeo
The workhorse white grape of N Spain, widespread in Rioja
(alias Viura) and in Catalan cava country.

Malvasia
Known as Malmsey in Madeira, Malvasia in Italy, Malvoisie in France.
Alias Vermentino (esp in Corsica). Also grown in Greece, Spain,
W Australia, E Europe. Makes rich brown wines or soft whites,
ageing magnificently with superb potential not often realized.

Marsanne
Principal white grape (with Roussanne) of the N Rhône (eg in
Hermitage, St-Joseph, St-Péray). Also good in Australia, California
and (as Ermitage Blanc) the Valais. Soft full wines that age v well.

Müller-Thurgau (Müller-T)
Dominant in Germany's Rheinhessen and Pfalz and too common on
the Mosel; a cross between RIESLING and SILVANER. Ripens early to make
soft aromatic wines for drinking young. Makes good sweet wines but
usually dull, often coarse, dry ones.

Muscadelle
Adds aroma to many white Bordeaux, esp Sauternes.

Muscadet, alias Melon de Bourgogne
Makes light, very dry wines with a seaside tang round Nantes in Brittany.
They should not be sharp, but faintly salty and very refreshing.
(California 'Pinot Bl' is this grape.)

Muscat
(Many varieties; the best is Muscat Blanc à Petits Grains.) Universally
grown, easily recognized, pungent grapes, mostly made into perfumed
sweet wines, often fortified (as in France's vins doux naturels). Superb
in Australia. Rarely (eg Alsace) made dry.

Palomino, alias Listan
Makes all the best sherry but poor table wine.

Pedro Ximénez, alias PX
Makes very strong wine in Montilla and Málaga. Used in blending
sweet sherries. Also grown in Argentina, the Canaries, Australia,
California, South Africa.

Pinot Blanc (Pinot Bl)
A cousin of PINOT N; not related to CHARD, but with a similar, milder
character: light, fresh, fruity, not aromatic, to drink young; eg good
for Italian spumante. Grown in Alsace, N Italy, S Germany, E Europe.
Weissburgunder in Germany. See also Muscadet.

Pinot Gris (Pinot Gr)
At best makes rather heavy, even 'thick', full-bodied whites with a
certain spicy style. Known (formerly) as Tokay in Alsace; Ruländer
(sweet) or Grauburgunder (dry) in Germany; Tocai or Pinot Grigio in
Italy and Slovenia (but much thinner wine).

Pinot Noir (Pinot N)
Superlative black grape (See Grapes for red wine) used in Champagne
and occasionally elsewhere (eg California, Australia) for making white,
sparkling, or very pale pink 'vin gris'.

9

Riesling (Ries)
Germany's great grape, and at present the world's most underrated.
Wine of brilliant sweet/acid balance, either dry or sweet,
flowery in youth but maturing to subtle oily scents and flavours.
Unlike CHARD it does not need high alcohol for character. Very good
(usually dry) in Alsace (but absurdly nowhere else in France),
Austria, Australia (widely grown), Pacific NW, Ontario, California,
South Africa. Often called White-, Johannisberg- or Rhine-Riesling.
Subject to 'noble rot'.

Ruländer
German name for PINOT GRIS used for sweeter wines.

Sauvignon Blanc (Sauv Bl)
Makes v distinctive aromatic grassy – or gooseberry – sometimes
rank-smelling wines; best in Sancerre. Blended with SEM in Bordeaux.
Can be austere or buxom. Pungent success in New Zealand,
now overplanted everywhere. Also called Fumé Blanc or vice versa.

Scheurebe
Spicy-flavoured German RIES X SYLVANER, very successful in Pfalz,
esp for Auslesen. Can be weedy in dry wines.

Sémillon (Sém)
Contributes the lusciousness to Sauternes; subject to 'noble rot' in the
right conditions but increasingly important for Graves and dry white
Bordeaux, too. Grassy if not fully ripe, but can make soft dry wine of
great ageing potential. Formerly called 'Riesling' in parts of Australia.
Old Hunter Valley Sem can be great wine.

Sercial
Makes the driest Madeira (where myth says it is really RIESLING).

Seyval Blanc (Seyval Bl)
French-made hybrid of French and American vines. V hardy and
attractively fruity. Popular and reasonably successful in eastern States
and England but banned by EC from 'quality' wines.

Steen
South Africa's most popular white grape: good lively fruity wine.
Said to be the CHENIN BL of the Loire.

Silvaner, alias Sylvaner
Germany's former workhorse grape: wine rarely fine except in Franken
where it is savoury and ages admirably, and in Rheinhessen and Pfalz,
where it is enjoying a renaissance. Good in the Italian Tyrol and useful
in Alsace. Very good (and powerful) as 'Johannisberg'
in the Valais, Switzerland.

Tokay
See Pinot Gris. Also a table grape in California and a supposedly
Hungarian grape in Australia. The wine Tokay is made of FURMINT.

Traminer See Gewürztraminer.

Trebbiano
Important but mediocre grape of central Italy, used in Orvieto, Chianti,
Soave etc. Also grown in S France as Ugni Bl, and Cognac as St-Emilion.
Mostly thin, neutral wine; really needs blending.

Ugni Blanc (Ugni Bl) See Trebbiano.

Verdejo
The grape of Rueda in Castile, potentially fine and long-lived.

Verdelho
Madeira grape making excellent medium-sweet wine; in Australia, fresh soft dry wine of great character.

Verdicchio
Gives its name to good dry wine in central-eastern Italy.

Vermentino See Malvasia.

Vernaccia
Grape grown in central and S Italy and Sardinia for strong smooth lively wine, sometimes inclining towards sherry.

Viognier
Rare grape of the Rhône, grown at Condrieu for v fine fragrant wine. Much in vogue in the Midi, California etc, but still only a trickle.

Viura See Macabeo.

Weissburgunder See Pinot Blanc.

Welschriesling See Italian Riesling.

Grapes for red wine

Aleatico
Dark Muscat variety, alias Aglianico, used the length of W Italy for fragrant sweet wines.

Baga
The standard red of Bairrada in central Portugal. Dark, tannic – potentially vg.

Barbera
Most popular of many productive grapes of N Italy, esp Piedmont, giving dark, fruity, often sharp wine. Gaining prestige in California.

Brunello
South Tuscan form of SANGIOVESE, splendid at Montalcino.

Cabernet Franc, alias Bouchet (Cab F)
The lesser of two sorts of Cab grown in Bordeaux but dominant (as 'Bouchet') in St-Emilion. The Cab of the Loire, making Chinon, Saumur etc, and rosé.

Cabernet Sauvignon (Cab S)
Grape of great character: spicy, herby, tannic, with characteristic 'blackcurrant' aroma. The first grape of the Médoc; also makes most of the best California, S American and E European reds. Vies with Shiraz in Australia. Its wine almost always needs ageing; usually benefiting from blending with eg MERLOT, CAB F or SYRAH. Makes very aromatic rosé.

Cannonau
Grenache in its Sardinian manifestation: can be v fine, potent.

Carignan
By far the commonest grape of France, covering hundreds of thousands of acres. Prolific with dull but harmless wine. Best from old vines in Corbières. Also common in N Africa, Spain, California.

Cinsaut
Common bulk-producing grape of S France; in S Africa crossed with
PINOT N to make PINOTAGE. Pale wine, but quality potential.

Dolcetto
Source of soft seductive dry red in Piedmont. Now high fashion
(though low budget).

Gamay
The Beaujolais grape: light, very fragrant wines, at their best young.
Makes even lighter wine on the Loire, in central France, and in
Switzerland and Savoie. Known as 'Napa Gamay' in California.

Gamay Beaujolais
Not GAMAY but a poor variety of PINOT N in California.

Grenache, alias Garnacha, Alicante, Cannonau
Useful grape for strong fruity but pale wine: good rosé and vin doux
naturel. Esp in S France, Spain, California. Old-vine versions are currently
prized in S Australia. Usually blended (eg in Châteauneuf-du-Pape).

Grignolino
Makes one of the good everyday table wines of Piedmont.

Kadarka, alias Gamza
Makes healthy, sound, agreeable reds in Hungary, Bulgaria etc.

Kékfrankos
Hungarian Blaufränkisch, said to be related to Gamay and producing
similar light red wines.

Lambrusco
Productive grape of the lower Po Valley, giving quintessentially Italian,
cheerful sweet and fizzy red.

Malbec, alias Cot
Minor in Bordeaux, major in Cahors (alias Auxerrois) and esp Argentina.
Dark, dense and tannic wine capable of real quality.

Merlot
Adaptable grape making the great fragrant and plummy wines of
Pomerol and (with CAB F) St-Emilion, an important element in Médoc
reds, soft and strong (and à la mode) in California, Washington,
a useful adjunct in Australia, lighter but often good in N Italy, Italian
Switzerland, Slovenia, Argentina etc.

Montepulciano
Confusingly, a major central-eastern Italian grape of high quality,
as well as a town in Tuscany.

Mourvèdre, alias Mataro
Excellent dark aromatic tannic grape used mainly for blending in
Provence (but solo in Bandol) and the Midi. Enjoying new interest in eg
S Australia, California.

Nebbiolo, alias Spanna and Chiavennasca
One of Italy's best red grapes; makes Barolo, Barbaresco, Gattinara,
Valtellina. Intense, nobly fruity and perfumed wine but very tannic,
taking years to mature.

Periquita
Ubiquitous in Portugal for firm-flavoured reds. Often blended with
Cabernet Sauvignon and also known as Castelão Francês.

Petit Verdot
Excellent but awkward Médoc grape now largely superseded.

Pinot Noir (Pinot N)
The glory of Burgundy's Côte d'Or, with scent, flavour, and texture
unmatched anywhere. Less happy elsewhere; makes light wines
rarely of much distinction in Germany, Switzerland, Austria, Hungary.
The great challenge to California and Australia (and recently S Africa).
Shows exciting promise in California's Carneros and Central Coast,
Oregon, Ontario, Yarra Valley, Adelaide Hills, Tasmania and NZ.

Pinotage
Singular S African grape (PINOT N x CINSAUT). Can be very fruity and age
interestingly, but often jammy.

Saint-Laurent
Dark, smooth and full-flavoured Austrian speciality. Also a little
in the Pfalz.

Sangiovese (or Sangioveto)
The main red grape of Chianti and much of central Italy. BRUNELLO is the
Sangiovese Grosso.

Saperavi
Makes good sharp very long-lived wine in Georgia, Ukraine etc.
Blends very well with CABERNET (eg in Moldova).

Spätburgunder
German for PINOT N, but a very pale shadow of burgundy.

Syrah or Petite Sirah, alias Shiraz
The great Rhône red grape, giving tannic purple peppery wine
which can mature superbly. Very important as Shiraz in Australia,
increasingly successful in the Midi, S Africa and California.
Has a growing fan club.

Tannat
Raspberry-perfumed, highly tannic force behind Madiran, Tursan and
other firm-structured reds from southwest France. Also for rosé.

Tempranillo
The pale aromatic fine Rioja grape, called Ull de Lebre in Catalonia,
Cencibel in La Mancha. Early ripening.

Touriga Nacional
Top port and Douro grape, travelling further afield in Portugal for
full-bodied reds.

Zinfandel (Zin)
Fruity adaptable grape peculiar to California with blackberry-like,
and sometimes metallic, flavour. Can be gloriously lush, but also
makes 'blush' white wine.

Wine & Food

Critics are at last beginning to discuss this long-neglected (or at least avoided) field of human endeavour. It is fertile ground for experiment. Few combinations can be dismissed outright as 'wrong', but generations of tradition and error have produced certain working conventions that certainly do no harm.

The following are ideas intended to help you make quick decisions. Any of the groups of recommended wines could be extended at will. In general I have stuck to wines that are widely available, at the same time trying to ring the changes so that the same wines don't come up time and time again – as they tend to do in real life. Remember that in a restaurant that is truly regional (Provençal, Basque, Tuscan, Catalan, Austrian…) there is a ready-made answer – the wine of the region in question.

Before the meal – aperitifs

The conventional aperitif wines are either sparkling (epitomized by champagne) or fortified (epitomized by sherry in Britain, port in France, vermouth in Italy etc). A glass of white or rosé (or in France red) table wine before eating is presently in vogue. It calls for something light and stimulating, fairly dry but not acid, with a degree of character; rather Riesling or Chenin Blanc than Chardonnay.

Warning: Avoid peanuts; they destroy wine flavours.

Olives are also too piquant for most wines; they need sherry or a Martini. Eat almonds, pistachios or walnuts, plain crisps or cheese straws instead.

First courses

Aïoli
A thirst-quencher is needed for its garlic heat. Rhône (★→★★), Provence rosé, Minervois, Verdicchio. And marc, too, for courage.

Antipasto in Italy
Dry or medium white (★★): Italian (Arneis, Soave, Pinot Grigio, Greco di Tufo or try Muscadet sur lie); light red (Dolcetto, Franciacorta or ★★ young Chianti).

Artichoke vinaigrette
Young red (★): Bordeaux, Côtes du Rhône; or a rather blunt white, eg Côtes du Rhône or one from Greece.
hollandaise Full-bodied slightly crisp dry white (★ or ★★): Pouilly Fuissé, Pfalz Spätlese, or a Carneros or Yarra Valley Chardonnay (★★).

Asparagus
A difficult flavour for wine, so the wine needs plenty of its own. Sémillon beats Chardonnay, esp from Australia. Alsace Pinot Gris, even dry Muscat can be good, or Jurançon Sec. Or try similarly flavoured Cabernet Franc red: Chinon or Bourgueil.

Avocado with prawns, crab etc
Dry to medium or slightly sharp white (★★→★★★★): Rheingau or Pfalz Kabinett, Sancerre, Pinot Grigio; Sonoma or Australian Chard or Sauvignon, Cape Steen, or dry rosé.
vinaigrette Light red (★), N Italian Enfer d'Arvier, or manzanilla sherry.

Bisques
Dry white with plenty of body (★★): Pinot Gris, Chardonnay. Fino or dry
amontillado sherry, or Montilla. West Australian Semillon.

Boudin (blood sausage)
Local Sauvignon or Chenin – esp in the Loire.

Bouillabaisse
Herby dry white (★→★★), Roussette de Savoie or Provence or Corsica
rosé, or Cassis, Verdicchio, California Blanc Fumé.

Caesar Salad
California (Central Coast) Chardonnay.

Carpaccio, beef
Seems to work well with the flavour of most wines, incl ★★★ reds.
Top Tuscan vino da tavola is appropriate, but fine Chards are good.
So is vintage champagne. (See also Carpaccio under fish.)
salmon Chardonnay (★★→★★★), or champagne.

Caviar
Iced vodka. Champagne, if you must, full-bodied (eg Bollinger, Krug).

Ceviche
Australian Riesling or Verdelho (★★), NZ Sauvignon Blanc.

Chabrot
The end of a bowl of vegetable soup; add equal quantity of young red.

Charcuterie
Young Beaujolais-Villages or ★★ Bordeaux Blanc, Loire reds such as
Bourgueil, Swiss or Oregon Pinot N.

Cheese fondue
Dry white (★★): Valais Fendant or any other Swiss Chasselas,
Grüner Veltliner, Alsace Riesling or Pinot Gris.

Chowders
Big-scale white (★★), not necessarily bone dry: Pinot Gris, Rhine Spätlese,
Australian Semillon. Or fino sherry, dry Madeira or Marsala.

Clams As for Oysters.

Consommé
Medium-dry amontillado sherry (★★→★★★), Sercial Madeira.

Crostini
Morellino di Scansano, Montepulciano d'Abruzzo, Valpolicella.

Crudités
Light red or rosé (★→★★, no more): Côtes du Rhône, Minervois, Chianti
Okanagan Pinot Noir; or fino sherry.

Dim-Sum
Classically, tea: Oolong or Bo-Li. For fun: fried Dim-Sum: Pinot Grigio or
Riesling; steamed: light red (Bardolino or Beaujolais-Villages).

Eggs See also Soufflés.
These present difficulties: they clash with most wines and spoil good
ones. So ★→★★ of whatever is going. Try straightforward, not too oaky
Chardonnay. As a last resort I can bring myself to drink champagne
with scrambled eggs.

Escargots
Rhône reds such as Gigondas or Vacqueyras, or St-Véran. In the Midi,
vg Petits-Gris go with local white or red. In Alsace, Pinot Bl or Muscat.

Fish terrine
Pfalz Riesling Spätlese Trocken, Chablis, Washington Sémillon,
Clare Valley Riesling, Sonoma Chardonnay; or fino sherry.

Foie gras
White (★★★→★★★★★). In Bordeaux they drink Sauternes. Others prefer
a late-harvest Riesling (incl New World) or Gewürz. Tokay Aszú is the
new choice. Old dry amontillado can be sublime. But not Chard.

Gazpacho
A glass of fino before and after.

Goat's cheese, grilled or fried (warm salad)
Chilled Chinon or Saumur-Champigny or Provence rosé. Or strong red:
Château Musar, Greek, Turkish.

Grapefruit
If you must start a meal with grapefruit, try contrasting with port,
Madeira or sweet sherry with (or in) it.

Gravlax
Akvavit or iced sake. Or Grand Cru Chablis, or ★★★ California, Washington
or Margaret River Chardonnay, or Mosel Spätlese (not Trocken).

Guacamole
California Chardonnay (★★), Riesling Kabinett or Mexican beer.

Haddock, smoked, mousse of
A wonderful dish for showing off any stylish full-bodied white,
incl Grand Cru Chablis or New Zealand Chardonnay.

Ham, raw or cured See also Prosciutto.
Alsace Grand Cru Pinot Gris or good, crisp Italian Collio white.

Herrings, raw or pickled
Dutch gin (young, not aged) or Scandinavian akvavit, and cold beer.
If wine essential, try Muscadet.

Hors d'oeuvres See also Antipasto.
Clean, fruity, sharp white (★→★★): Sancerre or any Sauvignon, Grüner
Veltliner, Vinho Verde, Cape Steen; or young light red Bordeaux,
Rhône or Corbières. Or fino sherry.

Houmous
Pungent, spicy dry white, eg Gewürztraminer or Retsina.

Mackerel, smoked
An oily wine-destroyer. Manzanilla sherry, or schnapps, peppered or
bison-grass vodka. Or good lager.

Mayonnaise
Adds richness that calls for a contrasting bite in the wine.
Côte Chalonnaise whites (eg Rully) are good. Try NZ Sauvignon Blanc,
Verdicchio or a Spätlese Trocken from the Pfalz.

Melon
Strong sweet wine (if any): port (★★), Bual Madeira, Muscat de
Frontignan or vin doux naturel; or dry, perfumed Viognier or
Australian Marsanne.

Minestrone
Red (★): Grignolino, Chianti, Zinfandel, Rhône Syrah etc. Or fino.

Mushrooms à la Grecque
Greek Verdea or Mantinia, or any hefty dry white, or fresh young red.

Omelettes See Eggs.

Oyster stew
California, Long Island or S Australian ★★ Chardonnay.

Oysters
White (★★→★★★): NV champagne, Chablis or (better) Chablis Premier
Cru, Muscadet, white Graves, Sancerre. Guinness or Scotch and water.

Pasta
Red or white (★→★★) according to the sauce or trimmings:
cream sauce Orvieto, Frascati, Alto Adige Chardonnay.
meat sauce Montepulciano d'Abruzzo, Salice Salentino, Merlot.
pesto (basil) sauce Barbera, Sicilian Torbato, NZ Sauvignon Blanc.
seafood sauce (eg vongole) Verdicchio, Soave, Pomino, Sauv Bl.
tomato sauce Barbera, S Italian red, Zinfandel, S Australian Grenache.

Pâté
According to constituents and quality:
chicken livers Call for pungent white (Alsace Pinot Gris or Marsanne),
a smooth red like a light Pomerol or Volnay, or even amontillado sherry.
with simple pâté A dry white ★★: Good vin de pays, Graves, Fumé Blanc.
with duck pâté Châteauneuf-du-Pape, Cornas, Chianti Classico
or Franciacorta.

Pimentos, roasted
NZ Sauvignon, Spanish Chardonnay, or Valdepeñas.

Pizza
Any dry Italian red ★★ or Rioja ★★, Australian Shiraz or California
Sangiovese. Corbières, Coteaux d'Aix-en-Provence or red Bairrada.

Prawns or shrimps
Fine dry white (★★→★★★): burgundy, Graves, New Zealand Chard,
Washington Riesling – even fine mature champagne.
Indian-, Thai- or Chinese-style rich Australian Hunter Valley
Chardonnay. ('Cocktail sauce' kills wine, and I suspect, in time, people.)

Prosciutto (also with melon, pears or figs)
Full-bodied dry or medium white (★★→★★★): Orvieto, Gambellara,
Pomino, Fendant or Grüner Veltliner, Alsace or California
Gewürztraminer, Australian Semillon or Jurançon Sec.

Quiches
Dry white with body (★→★★): Alsace, Graves, a Sauvignon, or dry
Rheingau; or try young red (Beaujolais-Villages, Chilean Pinot Noir),
according to the ingredients. Never a fine-wine dish.

Ravioli See pasta.
with wild mushrooms Dolcetto or Nebbiolo d'Alba, Oregon Pinot Noir.

Saffron sauces (eg on fish)
Pungent or full-bodied white (esp Chardonnay) or Provence rosé.

Salade niçoise
Very dry, ★★, not too light or flowery white or rosé: Provençal,
Rhône or Corsican; Catalan white; Fernão Pires, California Sauv Bl.

Salads
As a first course, especially with blue cheese dressing, any dry and
appetizing white wine. After a main course: no wine.
NB Vinegar in salad dressings destroys the flavour of wine. If you want
salad at a meal with fine wine, dress the salad with wine or a little
lemon juice instead of vinegar.

Salami
Very tasty red or rosé (★→★★): Barbera, top Valpolicella, young Zinfandel, Tavel or Ajaccio rosé, Vacqueyras, young Bordeaux or Chilean Cabernet Sauvignon.

Salmon, smoked
A dry but pungent white: fino sherry, Alsace Pinot Gris, Chablis Grand Cru, Pouilly-Fumé, Pfalz Riesling Spätlese, vintage champagne. Lighter red or vodka, schnapps or akvavit.

Seafood salad
Fresh N Italian Chardonnay or Pinot Grigio. Australian Verdelho or Clare Riesling.

Shark's fin soup
Add a teaspoon of cognac. Sip amontillado.

Soufflés
As show dishes these deserve ★★→★★★ wines.
fish Dry white: ★★★ burgundy, Bordeaux, Alsace, Chardonnay etc.
cheese ★★★ Red burgundy or Bordeaux, Cabernet Sauvignon etc.
spinach (tougher on wine) Mâcon-Villages, St-Véran, Valpolicella.

Taramasalata
A rustic southern white with personality; not necessarily Retsina. Fino sherry works well. Try Arbois or white Rioja. The bland supermarket version goes well with fine delicate whites or champagne.

Terrine
As for pâté, or equivalent red: Mercurey, St-Amour or Beaujolais-Villages, fairly young St-Emilion (★★), California Syrah or Sangiovese, Bulgarian or Chilean Cabernet.

Thai-style dishes (seasoned with lemon-grass, coconut milk, ginger etc)
Riesling Spätlese (Pfalz or Austrian), Gewürz or pungent Sauvignon.

Tortilla
Rioja crianza.

Trout, smoked
Sancerre, California or NZ Fumé Blanc. Rully or Bourgogne Aligoté.

Vegetable terrine
Not a great help to fine wine, but California, Chilean or South African Chardonnays make a fashionable marriage.

Fish

Abalone
Dry or medium white (★★→★★★): Sauvignon Blanc, Côte de Beaune blanc, Pinot Grigio, Muscadet sur lie.

Anchovies
A robust wine: red, white or rosé – try Rioja.

Bass, striped or sea
Weissburgunder from Baden or Pfalz. Vg for any fine/delicate white, eg Coonawarra dry Riesling, Chablis.

Beurre blanc, fish with
A top-notch Muscadet sur lie, a Sauvignon/ Sémillon blend, or a Rheingau Charta wine.

Carpaccio of salmon or tuna See also First courses.
Puligny-Montrachet, Condrieu or (★★★) Australian Chardonnay.

Cod
Good neutral background for fine dry/medium whites: ★★→★★★
Chablis, Meursault, Corton-Charlemagne, cru classé Graves, dry Vouvray;
German Kabinett or dry Spätlesen, or a good light red, eg Beaune.

Coquilles St Jacques See Scallops.

Crab, cioppino
Sauvignon Blanc; but West Coast friends say Zinfandel.
cold, with salad Alsace Riesling or Muscat, dry California or Australian
Riesling, or Viognier from Condrieu.
softshell ★★★ Chardonnay or top quality German Riesling Spätlese.

Chinese, baked with ginger and onion
Hungarian Furmint, Gewürz.
with Black Bean sauce A big Barossa Shiraz or Syrah.

Eel, jellied
NV champagne or a nice cup of (Ceylon) tea.
smoked Strong/sharp wine: fino sherry, Bourgogne Aligoté. Schnapps.

Fish and chips, fritto misto (or tempura)
Chablis, ★★ white Bordeaux, Sauvignon Blanc, Arneis, Fino, Montilla,
Koshu, tea...

Fish pie (with creamy sauce)
Napa Chardonnay, Pinot Gris d'Alsace.

Haddock
Rich dry white (★★→★★★): Meursault, California or NZ Chard, Marsanne.

Hake
Sauv Bl or any freshly fruity white: Pacherenc, Tursan, white Navarra.

Herrings
Need a white with some acidity to cut their richness. Bourgogne Aligoté,
Gros Plant from Brittany, dry Sauvignon Blanc. Or cider.

Kedgeree
Full white, still or sparkling: Mâcon-Villages or champagne.

Kippers
A good cup of tea, preferably Ceylon (milk, no sugar). Scotch?

Lamproie à la Bordelaise
5-yr-old St-Emilion or Fronsac: ★★→★★★.

Lobster, richly sauced
Vintage champagne, fine white burgundy, cru classé Graves,
California Chard or Australian Ries, Pfalz Spätlese.
salad White (★★→★★★★): NV champagne, Alsace Riesling,
Chablis Premier Cru, Condrieu, Mosel Spätlese, Penedès Chard.

Mackerel
Hard or sharp white (★★): Sauvignon Blanc from Bergerac or Touraine,
Gros Plant, Vinho Verde, white Rioja. Or Guinness.

Mullet, red
A chameleon, adaptable to good white or red (but avoid the liver).

Mussels
Muscadet sur lie, Chablis Premier Cru, ★★★ Chardonnay.
stuffed, with garlic See Escargots.

Perch, Sandre
Exquisite fishes for finest wines: Bâtard-Montrachet Premiers Crus or noble Mosels. Top Swiss Fendant or Johannisberg.

Salmon, fresh
Fine white burgundy (★★★): Puligny- or Chassagne-Montrachet, Meursault, Corton-Charlemagne, Chablis Grand Cru; Condrieu, California, Idaho or New Zealand Chard, Rheingau Kabinett/Spätlese, Australian Riesling or equivalent. Young Pinot Noir can be perfect, too – and claret not bad.

Sardines, fresh grilled
Very dry white (★→★★): Vinho Verde, Soave, Muscadet.

Sashimi
If you are prepared to forego the wasabi, sparkling wines (incl California's) will go, or Washington or Tasmanian Chardonnay, Chablis Grand Cru, Rheingau Riesling Halbtrocken. Otherwise, iced sake or beer.

Scallops
An inherently slightly sweet dish, best with medium-dry whites.
in cream sauces German Spätlese (★★★) a -Montrachet or top Australian Chardonnay.
grilled or fried Hermitage Blanc, Gewürztraminer, Grüner Veltliner, ★★ Entre-Deux-Mers, Australian Riesling or champagne.

Shad
White Graves (★★→★★★) or Meursault or Hunter Semillon.

Shellfish
Dry (★★★) white with plain boiled shellfish, richer wines with richer sauces.

Shrimps, potted
Fino sherry, (★★★) Chablis, Gavi or Long Island Chardonnay.

Skate with black butter
White (★★) with some pungency (eg Menetou-Salon), or a clean straightforward one like Muscadet or Arneis.

Snapper
Serious Sauvignon Blanc country.

Sole, plaice etc: plain, grilled or fried
An ideal accompaniment for fine wines: ★★★→★★★★ white burgundy, or its equivalent.
with sauce Depending on the ingredients: sharp dry wine for tomato sauce, fairly rich for sole véronique etc.

Sushi
Hot wasabi is usually hidden in every piece. German QbA trocken wines or simple Chablis are good enough. Or, of course, sake or beer.

Swordfish
Dry (★★) white of whatever country you are in. Nothing grand.

Trout
Delicate white wine, eg ★★★ Mosel (esp from Saar), Alsace Pinot Bl.
smoked A full-flavoured ★★→★★★ white: Gewürztraminer, Alsace Pinot Gr, Rhine Spätlese, Swiss Amigne or Australian Hunter white.

Tuna, grilled
White, red or rosé (★★) of fairly fruity character; a top St-Véran or white Hermitage, or Côtes du Rhône would be fine.

Turbot
Your best rich dry white: ★★★ Meursault or Chassagne-Montrachet or
its California, Australian or NZ equivalent. Condrieu. Mature Rheingau,
Mosel or Nahe Spätlese or Auslese (not trocken).

Whitebait
Crisp dry whites: Muscadet, Touraine Sauvignon or Verdicchio.

Meat, poultry etc

Barbecues
Red (★★) with a slight rasp, therefore young: Shiraz, Chianti, Navarra,
Zinfandel, Turkish Buzbag. Bandol for a real treat.

Beef, boiled
Red (★★): Bordeaux (Bourg or Fronsac), Roussillon, Australian Shiraz.
Gevrey-Chambertin, Côte Rôtie. Or top-notch beer.
roast An ideal partner for fine red wine: ★★→★★★★ red of any kind.

Beef stew
Sturdy red (★★→★★★): Pomerol or St-Emilion, Hermitage, Cornas,
Barbera, Shiraz, Napa Cabernet, Torres Gran Coronas.

Beef Stroganoff
Dramatic red (★★→★★★): Barolo, Valpolicella Amarone, Cahors,
Hermitage, late-harvest Zin – even Moldovan Negru de Purkar.

Warning notice:
Tomatoes (with anything): the acidity of tomatoes is no friend to
fine wines. Red (★★) will do. Try Chianti. Try skipping tomatoes.

Cabbage, stuffed
Hungarian Cabernet Franc/Kadarka, Bulgarian Cabernet.

Cajun food
Fleurie or Brouilly. With gumbo: amontillado or Mexican beer.

Cassoulet
Red (★★) from SW France (Madiran, Corbières), or Barbera or Zinfandel
or Australia's Great Western Shiraz.

Chicken/turkey/guinea fowl, roast
Virtually any wine, incl very best bottles of dry/medium white and finest
old reds (esp burgundy). The meat of fowl can be adapted with sauces
to match almost any fine wine (eg coq au vin: with red burgundy). Avoid
sauces which include tomato if you want to taste any good bottles.

Chicken casserole
Lirac, St-Joseph, or ★★ Bordeaux or Chilean Pinot Noir.

Kiev Alsace Riesling, Collio, Bergerac Rouge.

Chilli con carne
Young red (★→★★): Gattinara, Beaujolais, Navarra, Zinfandel.

Chinese food, Canton or Peking style
Dry to medium-dry white (★★→★★★) – Sauvignon Blanc or (better)
Riesling – can be good throughout a Chinese banquet. Many like
Gewürztraminer. Dry sparkling (esp cava) is good for cutting the oil.
Eschew sweet/sour dishes but try an 89/90 St-Emilion ★★ or St-Estèphe
cru bourgeois, or Châteauneuf-du-Pape with duck. I often serve both
white and red wines concurrently through Chinese meals.
Szechuan style Muscadet, Alsace Pinot Blanc or v cold beer.

Choucroute garni
Alsace, Pinot Blanc, Pinot Gris or Riesling or beer.

Cold meats
Generally taste better with full-flavoured white wine than red.
Mosel Spätlese or Hochheimer are very good. And so is Beaujolais.

Confit d'oie
Young tannic red Bordeaux Cru Bourgeois (★★→★★★) helps cut the
richness. Alsace Tokay-Pinot Gris or Gewurztraminer matches it.

Coq au vin
Red burgundy (★★→★★★★). In an ideal world one bottle of Chambertin
in the dish, two on the table.

Corned beef hash
Zinfandel, Rioja crianza, Côtes du Rhône red: (★★).

Curry
Medium-sweet white (★→★★★), very cold: Orvieto abboccato, California
Chenin Bl, Slovenian Traminer, Indian sparkling. Or emphasize the heat
with a tannic Barolo or Barbaresco, or deep-flavoured reds such as
St-Emilion, Cornas, Shiraz-Cabernet or Valpolicella Amarone.

Duck or goose
Rather rich white (★★★): Pfalz Spätlese or Alsace réserve
exceptionelle; or mature gamey red: Morey-St-Denis or
Côte-Rôtie, or ★★★ Bordeaux or burgundy. With oranges or
peaches, the Sauternais propose drinking Sauternes, others
Monbazillac or Auslese.

Peking See Chinese food.
wild duck Big-scale red (★★★): Hermitage, Châteauneuf-du-Pape,
Bandol, California or S African Cabernet, Australian Shiraz –
Grange if you can find it.
with olives Top-notch Chianti or Tuscan VdT.

Frankfurters
German (★→★★), New York Riesling, Beaujolais. Or Budweiser.

Game birds, young birds plain roasted
The best red wine you can afford.
older birds in casseroles ★★→★★★ Red (Gevrey-Chambertin,
Pommard, Santenay or Grand Cru St-Emilion, Napa Valley
Cabernet Sauvignon).
well-hung game Vega Sicilia, great red Rhône, Château Musar.
cold game Mature vintage champagne.

Game pie
hot Red (★★★): Oregon Pinot Noir.
cold Equivalent white or champagne.

Goulash
Flavoursome young red (★★): Zinfandel, Bulgarian Cabernet or
Mavrud, Hungarian Kadarka, young Australian Shiraz.

Grouse See Game birds – but push the boat right out.

Haggis
Fruity red, eg young claret, New World Cabernet. Or of course
malt whisky.

For key to grape variety abbreviations, see pages 7–13.

Ham
Softer red burgundies (★★→★★★): Volnay, Savigny, Beaune; Chinon or
Bourgueil; slightly sweet German white (Rhine Spätlese); Czech Müller-
Thurgau; lightish Cabernet (eg Chilean), or California Pinot Noir.

Hamburger
Young red (★→★★): Beaujolais or Bulgarian Cabernet, Chianti,
Zinfandel, Kadarka from Hungary. Or Coke or Pepsi.

Hare
Jugged hare calls for ★★→★★★ flavourful red: not-too-old burgundy
(try Vosne-Romanée) or Bordeaux, Rhône (eg Gigondas), Bandol,
or a fine Rioja reserva. The same for saddle. Australia's Grange would
be an experience.

Heart, stuffed
Full-bodied tannic red: Shiraz-Cabernet, Dão, Cornas.

Kebabs
Vigorous red (★★): Greek Nemea or Naoussa, Turkish Buzbag,
Chilean Cabernet, Zinfandel or Barossa Shiraz.

Kidneys
Red (★★→★★★): St-Emilion or earthier versions: Nuits-St-Georges, Cornas,
Barbaresco, Rioja, Spanish or Australian Cabernet, Portuguese Bairrada.

Lamb, cutlets or chops
As for roast lamb, but a little less grand.
roast One of the traditional and best partners for very good red
Bordeaux – or its Cabernet equivalents from the New World.
In Spain, the partner of the finest old Rioja reservas.

Liver
Young red (★★): Beaujolais-Villages, St-Joseph, Médoc, Italian Merlot,
Breganze Cabernet, Zinfandel, Portuguese Bairrada.

Meatballs
Tangy medium-bodied red (★★→★★★): Mercurey, Crozes-Hermitage,
Madiran, Rubesco, Dão, Zinfandel or Cabernet.

Mixed grill
A fairly light, easily swallowable red: ★★ Bordeaux from Bourg,
Fronsac or Premières Côtes; Côtes de Buzet; Coteaux du Languedoc;
Chianti; Chilean Cabernet; or a Cru Beaujolais such as Juliénas.

Moussaka
Red or rosé (★→★★): Naoussa from Greece, Chianti, Corbières,
Côtes de Provence, Ajaccio or Patrimonio, Chilean Pinot Noir.

Oxtail or osso bucco
Rather rich red (★★→★★★): St-Emilion, Pomerol, Pommard,
Nuits-St-Georges, Barolo or Rioja reserva, California or
Coonawarra Cabernet; or a dry Rheingau Riesling Spätlese.

Paella
Young Spanish red (★★), dry white or rosé: Penedès or Rioja.

Pigeons or squab
Lively red burgundy (★★→★★★): Savigny, Chambolle-Musigny;
Chianti Classico or California Pinot. Silvaner Spätlese from Franken.

Pork, roast
A good rich neutral background to a fairly light red or rich white.
It deserves ★★★ treatment – Médoc is fine. Portugal's famous sucking
pig is eaten with Bairrada garrafeira, Chinese is good with Beaujolais.

Quail As for pigeon. But does not harm finer reds.

Rabbit
Lively medium-bodied young Italian red (★→★★★), or Chiroubles,
Chinon, Saumur-Champigny or Rhône rosé.

Risotto
Pinot Gr from Friuli, Gavi, youngish Sém, Dolcetto or Barbera d'Alba.
with mushrooms Cahors, Madiran, Barbera.
with fungi porcini Finest mature Barolo or Barbaresco.

Satay
Australia's McLaren Vale Shiraz or Alsace or
New Zealand Gewürztraminer.

Sauerkraut
Lager or stout. (But see also Choucroute garni.)

Sausages See also Frankfurters, Salami.
The British banger requires a 2½-yr-old NE Italian Merlot
(or a red wine, anyway).

Shepherd's pie
Rough and ready red (★→★★) seems most appropriate, eg Barbera,
but beer or dry cider is the real McCoy.

Spare ribs
Vacqueyras or St-Joseph, or Australian old-vine Grenache, or Zinfandel.

Steak, au poivre
A fairly young ★★★ Rhône red or Cabernet.
tartare Vodka or ★★ light young red: Beaujolais, Bergerac, Valpolicella.
Korean Yuk Whe (the world's best steak tartare) Sake.
filet or tournedos Any ★★★ red (but not old wines with
béarnaise sauce).
T-bone Reds of similar bone structure (★★→★★★): Barolo, Hermitage,
Australian Cabernet or Shiraz.
fiorentina (bistecca) Chianti Classico Riserva or Brunello.

Steak and kidney pie or pudding
Red Rioja reserva or mature ★★→★★★ B'x.

Stews and casseroles
★★★ Burgundy such as Chambolle-Musigny or Bonnes-Mares if fairly
simple; otherwise lusty full-flavoured red: young Côtes du Rhône,
Corbières, Barbera, Shiraz, Zinfandel etc.

Sweetbreads
A grand dish, so grand wine: Rhine Riesling (★★★) or Franken Silvaner
Spätlese, Alsace Grand Cru Pinot Gris or Condrieu, depending on sauce.

Tandoori chicken
Sauvignon Blanc, or young ★★ red Bordeaux.

Thai food
Ginger and lemon grass call for Gewürztraminer.
coconut curries Hunter Valley Chard; Alsace Pinot Bl for refreshment.

Tongue
Good for any red or white of abundant character, esp Italian.

Tripe
Red (★→★★★), eg Corbières, Roussillon or rather sweet white
(eg German Spätlese). Better: W Australian Semillon-Chardonnay.

Veal, roast
A good neutral background dish for any fine old red which may have faded with age (eg a Rioja reserva) or a ★★★ German or Austrian Riesling.

Venison
Big-scale red (★★★): Rhône, Bordeaux or California Cab of a mature vintage; or rather rich white (Pfalz Spätlese or Alsace Tokay-Pinot Gr).

Vitello tonnato
Light red (Valpolicella, Beaujolais) served cool.

Vegetarian dishes

Bean salad
Red Rioja reserva.

Bean stew
Bairrada from Portugal, Toro from Spain.

Broccoli mornay
Crisp aromatic white: Sancerre, Riesling Spätlese, Muscat.

Urgent notice: sherry, port, Madeira and food
By a quirk of fashion the wines of Jerez, Madeira and to some extent the ports of the Douro Valley are currently being left on the sidelines by a world increasingly hypnotized by a limited range of 'varietal' wines. Yet all three regions include wines of every quality of 'greatness', and far more gastronomic possibilities than anyone seems to remember. It is notorious that for the price of eg a bottle of top-class white burgundy you can buy three of the very finest fino sherry, which with many dishes (see above) will make an equally exciting accompaniment. Mature Madeiras give the most lingering farewell of any wine to a splendid dinner. Tawny port is a wine of many uses, especially wonderful at sea. Perhaps it is because the New World cannot rival these Old World classics that they are left out of the headlines.

Cabbage (including 'bubble-and-squeak')
Beer, stout, or Beaujolais Nouveau.

Choucroute See also Sauerkraut.
Alsace Pinot Gris or Sylvaner.

Couscous
Young red with a bite: Shiraz, Corbières, Minervois etc.

Fennel-based dishes
Sauvignon: Pouilly-Fumé or one from NZ; Beaujolais.

Marrow, stuffed
Fruity dry white: S African Chenin or Australian Marsanne.

'Meaty' aubergine, lentil or mushroom bakes
Corbières, Zinfandel.

Mushrooms (in most contexts)
Fleshy red; eg ★★★ Pomerol, California Merlot, Rioja reserva or Vega Sicilia.
on toast Your best claret.
wild mushrooms (ceps are best for wine) Barolo or Chianti Rufina, or top claret: Pauillac or St-Estèphe.

Onion/leek tart
Fruity off-dry or dry white (★→★★★): Alsace Pinot Gr or Gewurz.
Jurançon, Australian Ries. Or Beaujolais or Loire red.

Peppers or aubergines (eggplant), stuffed
Vigorous red wine(★★): Italian Chianti or Dolcetto, California
Zinfandel, Bandol, Vacqueyras.

Ratatouille
Vigorous young red (★★): Chianti, Bulgarian Cabernet or Merlot, young
red Bordeaux or Gigondas or Coteaux du Languedoc.

Spinach/pasta bakes
Valpolicella (its bitterness helps); Greco di Molise,
or Sicilian/Sardinian white.

Desserts

Apple pie or strudel
Sweet (★★→★★★) German, Austrian, Hungarian white.

Apples, Cox's Orange Pippins
Vintage port (55 60 63 66 70 75 82).

Banoffi Pie
Very sweet fortified wine such as Australian liqueur Muscat or the
sweetest of sherries.

Bread and butter pudding
10-yr-old Barsac from a good château.

Cakes
Bual or Malmsey Madeira, oloroso or cream sherry.

Cheesecake
Sweet white: Vouvray or Anjou, refreshing but nothing special.

Chocolate cake, mousse, soufflés
Bual Madeira, Huxelrebe Auslese, California orange Muscat, Beaumes-
de-Venise. Or a tot of good rum.

Christmas pudding, mince pies
Tawny port, cream sherry, Asti or Banyuls.

Creams, custards, fools
Sauternes, Loupiac, Ste-Croix-du-Mont, Monbazillac.

Crème brûlée
★★★→★★ Sauternes or Rhine Beerenauslese, best Madeira or Tokay.
(With concealed fruit, a more modest sweet wine.)

Crêpes Suzette
Sweet champagne or Asti spumante.

Fruit, fresh
Sweet Coteaux du Layon, light sweet or liqueur Muscat.
stewed, ie apricots, pears etc Sweet Muscatel: try serving
Muscat de Beaumes-de-Venise, Moscato di Pantelleria or Spanish
dessert Tarragona.

Fruit flans
Sauternes, Monbazillac or sweet Vouvray or Anjou: ★★★.

Fruit salads, orange salad
A fine sweet sherry, or any Muscat-based wine.

Ice-cream
Fortified wine (eg Banyuls) or sparkling sweet Asti spumante.

Mille Feuille
Delicate medium-dry sparkling white such as Moscato d'Asti or demi-sec champagne.

Nuts
Oloroso sherry, Bual Madeira, vintage or tawny port, Vin Santo.

Oranges, caramelized
Experiment with old Sauternes or California Orange Muscat.

Pears in red wine
A pause before the port or other fortified reds: Rivesaltes, Banyuls.

Raspberries (no cream, little sugar)
Excellent with fine reds that themselves taste of raspberries: young Juliénas, Regnié.

Rice Pudding
Liqueur Muscat, Moscatel de Valencia or Loupiac.

Sorbets, ice-creams
Asti, or (better) Moscato d'Asti Naturale. Amaretto liqueur with vanilla; rum with chocolate.

Strawberries, wild (no cream)
Serve with ★★★ red B'x poured over them.

Strawberries and cream
Sauternes (★★★) or similar sweet Bordeaux, or Vouvray Moelleux (1990).

Summer pudding
Fairly young Sauternes of a good vintage (82 83 85 86).

Sweet soufflés
Sauternes or Vouvray moelleux. Sweet champagne.

Tiramisú
Vin Santo, young tawny port, Beaumes-de-Venise.

Trifle
Should be sufficiently vibrant with its internal sherry.

Walnuts
Nature's match for finest port, madeira, oloroso sherry.

Zabaglione
Light gold Marsala or Australian botrytised Semillon.

Wine & Cheese

The notion that wine and cheese were married in heaven is not born out by experience. Fine red wines are slaughtered by strong cheeses: only sharp or sweet white wines survive.

Principles to remember, despite exceptions, are first: the harder the cheese the more tannin the wine can have. And the creamier it is the more acidity is needed in the wine. The main exception constitutes a third principle: wines and cheeses of a region usually go together.

Cheese is classified by its texture and the nature of its rind, so its appearance is a guide to the type of wine to match it. Individual cheeses mentioned below are only examples taken from the hundreds sold in good cheese shops.

Fresh, no rind – cream cheese, crème fraîche, Mozzarella, Mascarpone (not layered with blue)
Light crisp white – Côtes de Duras, Bergerac, Vinho Verde;
or pink – Anjou, Rhône; or very light, v young, v fresh red Bordeaux, Bardolino or Beaujolais.

Hard cheeses, waxed or oiled, often showing marks from cheesecloth – Gruyère family, Manchego and many other Spanish cheeses, Parmesan, Cantal, old Gouda, Cheddar and most 'traditional' English cheeses
Particularly hard to generalize here; Gouda, Gruyère, some Spanish and a few English cheeses complement fine claret or Cab and great Shiraz/Syrah wines, but strong cheeses need less refined wines, preferably local. Sugary, granular old Dutch red Mimolette is perhaps the best of all for finest mature Bordeaux.

Blue cheeses
Roquefort is wonderful with Sauternes, but don't extend the idea to other blues. It is the sweetness of Sauternes, especially old, which complements the saltiness of the cheese. Stilton and port, preferably tawny, is a classic. Intensely flavoured old oloroso, dry amontillado, Madeira, dry Marsala and other fortified wines, go with most blues.

Natural rind (mostly goat's cheese) with bluish-grey mould (the rind becomes wrinkled when mature, s'times dusted with ash – St-Marcellin
Sancerre, Valençay, light fresh Sauv, Jurançon, Savoy, Soave, Italian Chard.

Bloomy rind soft cheeses, pure white rind if pasteurized, or dotted with red: Brie, Camembert, Chasource, Bougon (goat's milk 'Camembert')
Full dry white burgundy or Rhône if cheese is white, immature; powerful, fruity St-Emilion, E European Pinot, young Australian (or Rhône) Shiraz/Syrah if mature.

Washed-rind soft cheeses, with rather sticky orange-red rind – Langres, mature Epoisses, Maroilles, Carré de l'Est, Milleens
Local reds, especially for Burgundy cheeses; vigorous Languedoc, Cahors, Côtes du Frontonnais, Corsican, southern Italian, Sicilian, Bairrada.

Semi-soft cheeses, grey pink thickish rind – Livarot, Pont l'Evêque, Reblochon, Tomme de Savoie, St-Nectaire
Powerful white Bordeaux, Chardonnay, Alsace Pinot Gris, dryish Riesling, southern Italian and Sicilian white, aged white Rioja, dry oloroso sherry. But the strongest of these cheeses kill most wines.

Food & Finest Wine

With very special bottles the wine sometimes guides the choice of food rather than the usual way round. The following suggestions are largely based on the gastronomic conventions of the wine regions producing these treasures, plus diligent research. They should help bring out the best in your best wines.

Red wines

Red Bordeaux
and other Cabernet Sauvignon-based wines

(very old, light and delicate: eg pre-59, with exceptions such as 45)
Leg or rack of young lamb, roast with a hint of herbs (but not garlic); entrecôte; roast partridge or grouse, sweetbreads; or cheese soufflé after the meat has been served.

Fully mature great vintages (eg Bordeaux 59 61)
Shoulder or saddle of lamb, roast with a touch of garlic, roast ribs or grilled rump of beef.

Mature but still vigorous (eg 78 70 66)
Shoulder or saddle of lamb (incl kidneys) with rich sauce, eg béarnaise. Fillet of beef marchand de vin (with wine and bone-marrow). Avoid Beef Wellington: pastry dulls the palate.

Merlot-based Bordeaux (Pomerol, Saint-Emilion)
Beef as above (fillet is richest) or venison.

Côte d'Or red burgundy

(Consider the weight and texture, which grow lighter/more velvety with age. Also the character of the wine: Nuits is earthy, Musigny flowery, great Romanées can be exotic, Pommard renowned for its four-squareness etc.) Roast chicken, or better, capon, is safe standard with red burgundy; guinea-fowl for slightly stronger wines, then partridge, grouse or woodcock for those progressively more rich and pungent. Hare and venison (chevreuil) are alternatives.

Great old reds
The classic Burgundian formula is cheese: Epoisses (unfermented). It is a terrible waste of fine old wines.

Vigorous younger burgundy
Duck or goose roasted to minimize fat.

Great Syrahs: Hermitage, Côte Rôtie, Grange; or Vega Sicilia

Beef, venison, well-hung game; bone-marrow on toast; English cheese (esp best farm Cheddar).

Rioja Gran Reserva, Pesquera...

Richly flavoured roasts: wild boar, mutton.

Barolo, Barbaresco

Cheese risotto with white truffles; pasta with game sauce (eg pappardelle alle lepre); porcini mushrooms; Parmesan.

White wines

Very good Chablis, white burgundy, other top quality Chardonnays

White fish simply grilled or meunière with Doria garnish of sautéed cucumber. Dover sole, turbot, Rex sole are best. (Seabass is too delicate; salmon passes but does little for fine wine.)

Supreme white burgundy (Le Montrachet, Corton-Charlemagne) or equivalent Graves

Roast veal, capon or sweetbreads; richly sauced white fish or scallops as above. Or lobster or wild salmon.

Condrieu, Château Grillet or Hermitage Blanc

Very light pasta scented with herbs and tiny peas or broad beans.

Grand Cru Alsace, Riesling

Truite au bleu, smoked salmon or choucroute garni.
Pinot Gris Roast or grilled veal.
Gewurztraminer Cheese soufflé (Munster cheese).
Vendange Tardive Foie gras or Tarte Tatin.

Sauternes

Simple crisp buttery biscuits (eg Langue-de-Chat), white peaches, nectarines, strawberries (without cream). Not tropical fruit. Pan-fried foie-gras. Experiment with cheeses.

Supreme Vouvray moelleux etc

Buttery biscuits, apples, apple tart.

Beerenauslese/TBA

Biscuits, peaches, greengages.

Finest old amontillado/oloroso

Pecans.

Great vintage port or Madeira

Walnuts or pecans.

Old vintage champagne (not Blanc de Blancs)

As aperitif, or with cold partridge, grouse or woodcock.

The 1995 Vintage

To say that a vintage was 'saved by the rain' sounds like a contradiction. But that was the story in Bordeaux in 1995 – as it was in that most memorable vintage of '45, 50 years before. The hot dry summer had almost 'shut down' the vines and stopped grapes ripening until rain came, in September, to save the day. The result: many rich, ripe, concentrated wines – the best since 1990. Reds, dry whites and Sauternes all have a good chance of being excellent.

What happens in Bordeaux tends to colour the reputation of the vintage everywhere. But homogeneity (as in '90) is extremely rare. Burgundy was less lucky: poor flowering conditions and vintage rain meant a reduced crop of wine which will vary widely from grower to grower. Potentially, though, the whites will be better than the reds, with good acidity and body.

The Loire had an excellent year, from Muscadet to Sancerre, with good reds, some honeyed whites in Anjou and Touraine. Alsace also produced some late-harvest wines affected by botrytis, but the early-ripening grapes were affected by the rain. A Riesling year therefore.

A very wet winter and heavy spring rains in the Rhône, followed by excessive summer heat causing the vines to 'shut down', meant quality was dependent on whether rains fell in the run up to harvest. Where they did, the vintage was good and concentrated (like '90).

The Midi fared well, despite vine stress in the very hot dry summer. Quality and quantity were the result, and Provence especially made wines for good mid-term keeping.

A wet September in Germany again meant selection and early harvesting was necessary to avoid rot. But conditions brightened for late-ripening Riesling. Wines emerged with significant ageing potential: many were QmP (Kabinett and Spätlese). Also Eiswein.

A rainy spring and wet August in Italy – with hailstorms in Piedmont – meant some producers lost as much as 70 percent of their crop. This was the smallest vintage since 1920. A return to better weather in September gave fine dry whites with good acidity and sweet passitos; for red wines from Piedmont to the south '95 was good to excellent.

Frosts in northern Spain in May and June reduced the crop, but warm weather up to the harvest meant Rioja and Navarra made better wines than in '94. In the south there was drought but good quality. Ideal conditions and scorching August heat across Portugal resulted in a Douro vintage as splendid as '94.

Across the Atlantic there was a poor fruit-set in California (winter and spring had rain, cold and hail) and reduced yields, then a warm, dry ripening season making harvest easy. There are reds of fine concentration: good fruit and firm tannins, and balanced whites.

Australia suffered drought. Rich concentrated wines are the result – the best will stand long-term cellaring. (The first signs of '96 suggest a very large vintage of near record quantities which should go some way towards satisfying the international demand for Australian wines.) South Africa's vintage in 1995 paralleled Australia's: reduced by heat-stress but of great concentration.

France

Heavily shaded areas are the
wine growing regions

The following abbreviations
of regional names
are used in the text:

Al   Alsace
Beauj   Beaujolais
Burg   Burgundy
B'x   Bordeaux
Champ   Champagne
Lo   Loire
Prov   Provence
Pyr   Pyrenees
N/S Rh North/South Rhône
SW   Southwest

Le Havre

Caen

Brest

LOIRE

Loire

Nantes
Muscadet   Anjou-
              Saumur

La Rochelle

BORDEA

Médoc
Bordeaux   Pomero
              St-Emili
Graves   Entre-
           Deux-M
Sauternes
          Bu
Côtes du
Marmandais
          Côtes
Tursan   St-Mo
Biarritz   Madir
Jurançon

Each year hears louder voices challenging France's pole position in
the wine world. In 1996 they were even raised in France itself
when the director of the Institut National des Appellations d'Origine
admitted that disgraceful wines were being sold under certified
AOC labels. (He lost his job). It is a healthy sign – and may come just in
time. For as yet still no-one has displaced France by definitively
bettering even one of her many wine styles. Tens of thousands of
properties make wine of all complexions over a large part of her
surface. This is a guide to the names, types, producers and vintages.

Appellations still remain the key. All France's best wine regions
have them. They may apply to a single small vineyard or to a large
district: the system varies. Burgundy on the whole has the smallest
and most precise appellations, Bordeaux the widest and most
general. In between lies an infinity of variations.

Calais
Lille

Reims
CHAMPAGNE

Paris

Seine

Strasbourg

Marne

ALSACE

Tours

Loire

Chablis

Pouilly-Fumé

Sancerre

uraine

Cher

Côte d'Or

Dijon

BURGUNDY

JURA

Saône

Côte Chalonnaise

Geneva

Mâconnais

Bugey

Beaujolais

Lyon

SAVOIE

RHONE

Côte Rôtie

Condrieu

St-Joseph

Grenoble

Cornas

Hermitage

Crozes Hermitage

erac

Dordogne

Cahors

OUTHWEST

Tarn

Côtes du Rhône-Villages

Beaumes-de-Venise

Châteauneuf-du-Pape

Gaillac

Côtes du Frontonnais

LANGUEDOC

Toulouse

St-Chinian

PROVENCE

Nice

Minervois

Montpellier

Bandol

Corbières

Marseille

USSILLON

Fitou

Rivesaltes

Perpignan

Banyuls

Mediterranean Sea

Bastia

CORSICA

Ajaccio

FRANCE

An appellation contrôlée is a guarantee of origin, production method, grape varieties and quantities produced, but not one of quality. The AC is the first thing to look for on a label. But more important is the name of the maker. The best growers' and merchants' names are a vital ingredient of these pages. Regions without the overall quality and traditions required for an appellation can be ranked as vins délimités de qualité supérieure (VDQS), a shrinking category as its members gain AC status. Their place is being taken by the relatively new and highly successful vins de pays. Vins de pays are almost always worth trying. They include some brilliant originals and often offer France's best value for money – which still (and even with an over-valued franc) means the world's.

33

Recent vintages of the French classics

Red Bordeaux

Médoc/red Graves For some wines bottle-age is optional: for these it is indispensable. Minor châteaux from light vintages need only 2 or 3 yrs, but even modest wines of great years can improve for 15 or so, and the great châteaux of these years need double that time.

1995 Heatwave and drought; saved by rain. Good to excellent. 1999–2020.

1994 Hopes of a supreme vintage; then heavy rain. At least good; some v fine. 1998–2010.

1993 Ripe grapes but a drenching vintage. Some tannic long-stayers. Vg Graves. 1998–2015.

1992 Rain at flowering, in August and at vintage. A huge crop; some good early drinking. Now–2005.

1991 Frost in April halved crop and rain interrupted vintage. Difficult; but keep an open mind. Now–2010?

1990 A paradox: a drought year with a threat of over-production. Self-discipline was essential. Its results are magnificent. To 2020.

1989 Early spring and splendid summer. The top wines will be classics of the ripe dark kind with elegance and length. Small ch'x are uneven. To 2020.

1988 Generally excellent; ripe, balanced, for long keeping. To 2020.

1987 Much more enjoyable than seemed likely. Not for long keeping. Now or soon.

1986 Another splendid, huge, heatwave harvest. Superior to 85 in Pauillac and St-Julien. Now–2020.

1985 Vg vintage, in a heatwave. V fine wines already accessible. Now–2010.

1984 Poor. Little Merlot but good ripe Cabernet. No charm. Originally overpriced. Drink up.

1983 A classic vintage, esp in Margaux: abundant tannin with fruit to balance it. To 2010.

1982 Made in a heatwave. Huge, rich, strong wines which promise a long life but are developing unevenly. Most châteaux are now ready. Now–2010.

1981 Admirable despite rain. Not rich, but balanced and fine. Now–2005.

1980 Small late harvest: ripe but rained-on. Some delicious light wines. Drink up.

1979 Abundant harvest of above average quality. Now–2000.

1978 A miracle vintage: magnificent long warm autumn. Some excellent wines. Now–2000.

1976 Excessively hot, dry summer; rain just before vintage. Generally vg; now ready.

1975 A v fine vintage. For long keeping, but some may not improve now; many have lost their fruit.

1970 Big, excellent vintage with scarcely a failure. Now–2005.

Older fine vintages: 66 62 61 59 55 53 52 50 49 48 47 45 29 28.

St-Emilion/Pomerol

1995 Perhaps even better than Médoc/Graves.

1994 Less compromised by rain than Médoc. Very good, especially Pomerol. 1999–2015.

1993 As in the Médoc, but probably better, esp in Pomerol; good despite terrible vintage weather.

1992 Exceptionally dilute but some charming wines to drink quickly. Drink now or soon.

1991 A sad story. Terrible frost and little chance to recover. Many wines not released.

1990 Another chance to make great wine or a lot of wine. Now–2020.

1989 Large, ripe, early harvest; an overall triumph. To 2020.

1988 Generally excellent; ideal conditions. But some overproduced. Now–2000+.

1987 Some v adequate wines (esp in Pomerol). For drinking soon.

1986 A prolific vintage; but top St-Emilions have long life ahead.

1985 One of the great yrs, with a long future. To 2010.

1984 A sad story. Most of the crop wiped out in spring. Avoid.

1983 Less impressive than it seemed. Drink soon.

1982 Enormously rich and concentrated wines, most excellent. Now–2000+.

1981 A vg vintage, if not as great as it first seemed. Now or soon.

1979 A rival to 78, but not developing as well as hoped. Now or soon.

1978 Fine wines, but some lack flesh. Drink soon.

1976 V hot, dry summer, but vintage rain. Some excellent. Drink soon.

1975 Most St-Emilions good, the best are superb. Pomerol made splendid wine. Now–2000.

1971 On the whole better than Médocs, but now ready.

1970 Beautiful wines with great fruit and strength. V big crop. Now.

Older fine vintages: 67 66 64 61 59 53 52 49 47 45.

Red burgundy

Côte d'Or Côte de Beaune reds generally mature sooner than the bigger wines of the Côte de Nuits. Earliest drinking dates are for lighter commune wines, eg Volnay, Beaune; latest for the biggest wines of eg Chambertin, Romanée. But even the best burgundies are much more attractive young than the equivalent red Bordeaux.

1995 Small, v promising crop, despite vintage rains. Grapes were very ripe.

1994 Ripe grapes compromised by vintage rain. Uneven, not for long keeping. Côte de Nuits better.

1993 Emerging as an excellent vintage – in the right hands. 1998–2010.

1992 Ripe, plump, pleasing. No great concentration. Start to drink. Now–2005.

1991 Very small harvest; some wines v tannic. Côte de Nuits best. 1998–2010.

1990 A great vintage: perfect weather compromised only by drought on some slopes and over-production in some vineyards. Long life ahead but start to enjoy.

1989 A year of great charm, not necessarily for very long maturing, but will age. Now–2015.

1988 Very good but tannic. Now–2020.

1987 Small crop with ripe fruit flavours, esp in Côte de Beaune. Now–2010.

1986 A very mixed bag – aromatic but rather dry wines: generally lack flesh. Drink now–2000.

1985 At best a great vintage. Concentrated wines are splendid. Now–2010.

1984 Lacks natural ripeness; tends to be dry and/or watery. Now – if at all.

1983 Powerful, vigorous, tannic and attractive vintage, compromised by rot. The best are splendid, but be careful. Now–2000.

1982 Big vintage, pale but round and charming. Côte de Beaune best. Drink up.

1981 A small crop, ripe but picked in rain.

1980 A wet yr, but v attractive wines from best growers who avoided rot. Côte de Nuits best. Drink.

1979 Big, generally good, ripe vintage with weak spots. Drink up.

1978 A small vintage of outstanding quality. The best will live to 2000+.

Older fine vintages: 71 69 66 64 62 61 59 (all mature).

White burgundy

Côte de Beaune Well-made wines of good vintages with plenty of acidity as well as fruit will improve and gain depth and richness for some years – anything up to 10. Lesser wines from lighter vintages are ready for drinking after 2 or 3 years.

1995 A potentially great vintage, diluted in places.

1994 Patchy; top growers made v fine potent wines – but not for long keeping. 1998–2005.

1993 September rain on ripe grapes. Easy wines, high potential but v variable. Now–2005.

1992 Ripe, aromatic and charming. Will develop beautifully. Now–2010.

1991 Mostly lack substance. Frost problems. For early drinking. Now.

1990 Very good, even great, but with a tendency to fatness. Now–2000+.

1989 Revealing itself as a model. At best ripe, tense, structured and long. Now–2005.

1988 Extremely good, some great wines but others rather dilute. Now–2000.

1987 V disappointing, though a few exceptions have emerged. Now. Avoid.

1986 Powerful wines; most with better acidity/balance than 85. Now–2000.

1985 V ripe; those that still have balance are ageing v well. Now–2000.

1984 Most lean or hollow. Avoid.

1983 Potent wines; some exaggerated, some faulty, but the best splendid. Drink soon.

1982 Fat, tasty but delicate whites of low acidity. Drink up.

1981 A sadly depleted crop with great promise. But time to drink up.

The white wines of the Mâconnais (Pouilly-Fuissé, St-Véran, Mâcon-Villages) follow a similar pattern, but do not last as long. They are more appreciated for their freshness than their richness.

Chablis Grand Cru Chablis of vintages with both strength and acidity can age superbly for up to 10 years; Premiers Crus proportionately less.

1995 Potentially an outstanding vintage. 1998–2010.

1994 Downpours on a ripe vintage. Delicious easy wines to 2000+.

1993 Fair to good quality; nothing great. Now–2001.

1992 Ripe and charming wines. Grands Crus splendid. Now–2005 at least.

1991 Generally better than Côte d'Or. Useful wines. Now.

1990 Grands Crus will be magnificent; other wines may lack intensity and acidity. Now–2000.

1989 Excellent vintage of potent character. Now–2000.

1988 Almost a model: great pleasure now in store. Now–2000.

1987 Rain at harvest. wines for the short term. Drink up.

1986 A splendid big vintage. Now or soon.

Beaujolais 95 is excellent. 94 is vg; drink or keep. 93: Crus to keep. 92: good primeur wines; not keepers. 91: small crop, Crus excellent, now. 90 was a lusciously ripe vintage; drink top Crus. 89 was v fine, drink up. 88, 87 and 86 wines should be finished.

Alsace 95 has mixed results – late-harvest Riesling best. 94 was a general success, if not a triumph. 93 was good, fruity, not for long keeping. 92 was splendid; 91 admirable. 90 was the third outstanding vintage in succession. 89 and 88 both made wines of top quality (though rain spoiled some 88s). 87s should be drunk soon and 86s finished. Top 85s and 83s may be drunk or kept even longer.

Abel-Lepitre Brut NV; Brut 85 86 88 90; Cuvée 134 Bl de Blancs NV; Réserve Crémant Bl de Blancs Cuvée 'C' 83 85 86 88 90; Rosé 83 85 86 88 90 CHAMPAGNE house, also owning GOULET, PHILIPPONNAT and St-Marceaux. Luxury Cuvée: Cuvée Reserve Abel-Lepitre 85.

Abymes Savoie w ★ DYA Hilly little area nr Chambéry; light mild Vin de Savoie AC from the Jacquère grape has alpine charm.

Ackerman-Laurance Classic method sparkling house of the Loire, oldest in SAUMUR. Improving still wines under guidance of Jacques Lurton.

Ajaccio Corsica r p w ★→★★ 89' 90' 91 92 93 94 95 The capital of CORSICA. AC for some vg SCIACARELLO reds. Top grower: Peraldi.

Aligoté Second-rank burgundy white grape and its wine. Should be pleasantly tart and fruity with local character when young. BOUZERON is the one commune to have an all-Aligoté appellation. Its wine is richer, but try others from good growers. NB PERNAND-VERGELESSES.

Aloxe-Corton Burg r w ★★→★★★ 78' 85' 87 88' 89' 90' 91 92 93' 94 95 Village at N end of CÔTE DE BEAUNE famous for its two GRANDS CRUS: CORTON (red), CORTON-CHARLEMAGNE (white). Village wines much lighter but can be good value.

Alsace Al w (r sp) ★★→★★★ 85' 88 89 90' 91 93 94 Aromatic, fruity, often strong rather Germanic dry white from eastern foothills of Vosges Mts, bordering the River Rhine. Generally dry but increasingly made sweet (see Vendange Tardive and Sélection des Grains Nobles). Sold by grape variety (Pinot Bl, Ries, GEWURZ etc). Matures well (except Pinot Bl) up to 5, even 10 yrs; GRAND CRU even longer. Also good quality and value CREMANT, but red wines (Pinot N) offer little to non-natives. (See below.)

Alsace Grand Cru W ★★★→★★★★ 76 83 85 86 88 89' 90 91 92 93 94 AC restricted to 50 of the best named v'yds (1,400 acres) and noble grapes (Ries, Pinot Gr ('Tokay'), GEWURZ and MUSCAT). Not without controversy but all the region's best wines are GRANDS CRUS.

Twelve good Alsace producers
Among many good growers offering reliability, value for money and tastes varying from scintillating to sumptuous, NB Marcel Deiss, Dopff 'Au Moulin', Hugel (Special cuvées), Marc Kreydenweiss, Kuentz-Bas, Albert Mann, Meyer-Fonné, Muré-Clos St-Landelin, Rolly-Gassmann, Charles Schleret, Domaine Schoffit, Domaine Trimbach, Domaine Weinbach, Zind-Humbrecht.

Ampeau, Robert Exceptional grower and specialist in VOLNAY; also POMMARD etc. Perhaps unique in only releasing long matured bottles.

André, Pierre Négociant with growing reputation at Ch Corton-André, ALOXE-CORTON; 95 acres of v'yds in CORTON, SAVIGNY, GEVREY-CHAMBERTIN etc. Also owns REINE PEDAUQUE.

d'Angerville, Marquis Top burgundy grower with immaculate 30-acre estate in VOLNAY. Top wines: Champans and Clos des Ducs.

Anjou Lo p r w (sw dr sp) ★→★★★ Both region and Loire AC embracing wide spectrum of styles – light reds incl AC Anjou Gamay, improving dry whites. Esp good red (Cab) ANJOU-VILLAGES, strong dry SAVENNIERES, luscious COTEAUX DU LAYON Chenin Bl whites.

Anjou-Coteaux de la Loire Lo w s/sw sw ★★→★★★ 89' 90' 93 94 95' AC for some forceful Chenin Bl whites. Only 100 acres; demi-sec or sweet not as rich as COTEAUX DU LAYON, esp Musset-Roullier, Dom du Fresche.

France entries also cross-refer to Châteaux of Bordeaux section, pages 78–103.

Anjou-Villages Lo r ★→★★★ 89 90 93 95 Superior AC for red wines (majority Cab F, some Cab S) from central ANJOU. Potentially juicy, quite tannic young but good value esp Bablut, RICHOU, Rochelles and Pierre-Bise.

Appellation Contrôlée (AC or AOC) Government control of origin and production of all the best French wines (see France Introduction).

Apremont Savoie w ★★ DYA One of the best villages of SAVOIE for pale delicate whites, mainly from Jacquère grapes, but recently incl CHARD.

Arbin Savoie r ★★ Deep-coloured lively red from MONDEUSE grapes, rather like a good LOIRE Cabernet. Ideal après-ski wine. Drink at 1–2 yrs.

Arbois Jura r p w (sp) ★★→★★★ Various good and original light but tasty wines; speciality is VIN JAUNE. On the whole DYA.

l'Ardèche, Coteaux de Central France r p (w) ★→★★ DYA Area W of Rhône given impetus by GEORGES DUBOEUF (of BEAUJOLAIS). Viognier, Chard in whites. Bargain fresh country reds; best from pure Syrah, also Gamay and recently Cab. Powerful, almost burgundy-like CHARD 'Ardèche' from LOUIS LATOUR (keep 1–3 yrs). (Choose this rather than its too-oaky 'Grand Ardèche'.)

l'Arlot, Domaine de Outstanding producer of supreme NUITS-ST-GEORGES, esp Clos de l'Arlot, red and white. Owned by AXA Insurance.

Armagnac Region of SW France and its often excellent brandy, a fiery spirit of rustic character. The outstanding red wine of the area is MADIRAN. See Côtes de Gascogne for region's other still wines.

Aube Southern extension of CHAMPAGNE region. See Bar-sur-Aube.

Aujoux, J-M Substantial grower/merchant of BEAUJOLAIS. Swiss-owned.

Auxey-Duresses Burg r w ★★ →★★★ 78 85 87 88 89 90' 91 92 93 94 95 Second-rank (but v pretty) CÔTE DE BEAUNE village: affinities with VOLNAY, MEURSAULT. Best estates: Diconne, HOSPICES DE BEAUNE (Cuvée Boillot), LEROY, M Prunier, R Thévenin. Drink whites in 4–5 yrs. Top white: Leroy's Les Boutonniers.

Avize Champ ★★★★ One of the top Côte des Blancs villages. All CHARDONNAY.

Aÿ Champ ★★★★ One of the best Pinot N-growing villages of CHAMPAGNE.

Ayala NV; Demi-Sec NV; Brut 89 90; Château d'Aÿ 82 83 85; Grande Cuvée 82 83 85 88 90; Blanc de Blancs 82 83 88 92; Brut Rosé NV Once-famous Ay-based old-style CHAMPAGNE firm. Deserves more notice for its fresh appley wines.

Bahuaud, Donatien Leading Loire wine merchant. Le Master de Donatien is the top MUSCADET Ch de la Cassemichère also vg.

Bandol Prov r p (w) ★★★ 73 79 82 83 85' 86 87' 88 89 90 91 92 93 94 95 Little coastal region near Toulon producing Provence's best wines; splendid vigorous tannic reds from the Mourvèdre grape; esp DOM OTT, Dom de Pibarnon, Ch Pradeaux, Mas de la Rouvière, DOM TEMPIER, Ch Vannières.

Banyuls Pyr br sw ★★→★★★★ One of the best VINS DOUX NATURELS, made chiefly of Grenache (a Banyuls GRAND CRU is made from over 75% Grenache, aged for 2 yrs+). Technically a distant relation of port. The best wines are RANCIOS eg those from Domaine des Hospices, Domaine du Mas Blanc (★★★), Domaine Vial Magnères (Blanc), at 10–15 yrs old. There are also cheap NV wines for bars.

Bar-sur-Aube Champ w (p) ★★ Important secondary CHAMPAGNE region 100 miles SE of R Marne, Epernay etc – ie, half-way to CHABLIS. Some good lighter wines and excellent ROSE DES RICEYS.

Barancourt Brut Réserve NV; Rosé NV; Bouzy Grand Cru 81 83 85; Rosé GC 85 Grower at BOUZY making full-bodied CHAMPAGNE. New owners Champagne Vranken; now esp Bouzy Rouge and Rosé Grand Cru.

Barrique The Bordeaux (and Cognac) term for an oak barrel holding 225 litres (eventually 300 bottles). Barrique-ageing to flavour almost any wine with oak was the craze of the late '80s, with some sad results.

Barsac B'x w sw ★★→★★★★ 70 71' 75 76' 78 79' 80' 81 82 83' 85 86' 88' 89' 90' 91 93 95 Neighbour of SAUTERNES with similar superb golden wines, generally less rich and more racy. Richly repays ageing. Top ch'x: CLIMENS, COUTET, DOISY-DAENE, DOISY-VEDRINES.

Barton & Guestier BORDEAUX shipper since 18th C, now owned by Seagram.

Bâtard-Montrachet Burg w ★★★★ 78 79 85 86' 88 89' 90' 91 92 93 94 95 Larger (55-acre) neighbour of MONTRACHET. Should be v long-lived with intense flavours and rich texture. Bienvenues-Bâtard-M is a separate adjacent 9-acre GRAND CRU with 15 owners, thus no substantial bottlings and very rare. Top growers include BOUCHARD PERE, J-M Boillot, CARILLON, DROUHIN, Gagnard, LOUIS LATOUR, LEFLAIVE, Lequin-Roussot, MOREY, RAMONET, SAUZET.

Baumard, Domaine des Leading grower of ANJOU wine, especially SAVENNIERES, COTEAUX DU LAYON (Clos Ste-Catherine) and QUARTS DE CHAUME.

Baux-en-Provence, Coteaux des Prov r p ★→★★★ Neighbour of COTEAUX D'AIX-, also gathering speed. NB the excellent DOMAINE DE TREVALLON (Cab and Syrah) and Mas de Gourgonnier.

Béarn SW France r p w ★→★★ DYA Wide-spread low-key AC of growing local (Basque) interest, esp wines of coop Sallies de Béarn-Bellocq. Rosés began post-war as instant Paris hit. Also the AC covering red JURANCON, white and rosé MADIRAN.

> Confusingly, the best wines of the Beaujolais region are not identified as Beaujolais at all on their labels. They are known simply by the names of their 'crus': Brouilly, Chénas, Chiroubles, Côte de Brouilly, Fleurie, Juliénas, Morgon, Moulin-à-Vent, Regnié, Saint-Amour. See entries for each of these. The Confrérie des Compagnons du Beaujolais offers a 'Beaujolais Grumé' label to selected wines from the region with ageing potential.

Beaujolais Beauj r (p w) ★ DYA Simple AC of the v big Beaujolais region: light short-lived fruity red of Gamay grapes. Beaujolais Supérieur is little different.

Beaujolais de l'année The BEAUJOLAIS of the latest vintage, until the next.

Beaujolais Primeur (or Nouveau) Same as above, made in a hurry (often only 4–5 days fermenting) for release at midnight on the third Wednesday in November. Ideally soft, pungent, fruity and tempting; often crude, sharp, too alcoholic. BEAUJOLAIS-VILLAGES should be a better bet.

Beaujolais-Villages Beauj r ★★ 93 94 95 Wines from better (N) half of BEAUJOLAIS; should be much tastier than plain BEAUJOLAIS. The 10 (easily) best 'villages' are the 'CRUS': FLEURIE etc (see note above). Of the 30 others the best lie around Beaujeu. Crus cannot be released EN PRIMEUR before December 15th. Best kept until spring (or longer).

Beaumes-de-Venise S Rh br (r p) ★★→★★★ DYA Regarded as France's best dessert MUSCAT, from S COTES DU RHONE; can be high-flavoured, subtle, lingering (eg from CHAPOUTIER, Dom de Coyeux, Dom Durban, JABOULET, VIDAL-FLEURY). Red and rosé from Ch Redortier and the coop are also good.

Beaune Burg r (w) ★★★ 78' 83 85' 88 89' 90' 91 92 93 94 95 The historic wine capital of Burgundy, a walled town, hollow with cellars. Wines are middle-rank classic burgundy. Many fine growers. Négociants' CLOS wines (usually PREMIER CRU) are often best; eg DROUHIN's superb Clos des Mouches, JADOT's Clos des Ursules. Beaune du Château is a BOUCHARD PERE brand. Best v'yds: Bressandes, Fèves, Grèves, Marconnets, Teurons.

Becker, Caves J Proud old family firm at Zellenberg, ALSACE. Classic RIESLING Hagenschlauf and GRAND CRU Froehn MUSCAT. Second label: Gaston Beck.

Bellet Prov p r w ★★★ Fashionable much above average local wines from nr Nice. Serious producers: ch'x de Bellet and CREMAT. Pricey.

Bergerac Dordogne r w dr sw ★★→★★★ 90' 92 93 94 95' Lightweight, often tasty, BORDEAUX-style. Drink young, the white v young. See also Monbazillac, Côtes du Montravel, Pécharmant, Saussignac. Top growers include Dom Bosredon, Dom de la Colline, Courts-les-Muts, JAUBERTIE, CH DE MONTAIGNE, Ch de Panisseau, Tiregand.

Besserat de Bellefon Grande Tradition NV; Cuvée des Moines Brut and Rosé NV; Grande Cuvée NV; Brut and Rosé 82 85 89 Reims CHAMPAGNE house for light wines. Owned by MARNE ET CHAMPAGNE.

Beyer, Léon Ancient ALSACE family firm at Eguisheim making forceful dry wines that need ageing at least 3–5 yrs. Comtes d'Eguisheim GEWURZ is renowned, and 'Cuvée Particulière' Ries of GRAND CRU Pfersigberg is esp fine. Beyer is militant against Grand Cru restrictions.

Bichot, Maison Albert One of BEAUNE's biggest growers and merchants. V'yds (32-acre Domaine du Clos Frantin is excellent) are in CHAMBERTIN, RICHEBOURG, CLOS DE VOUGEOT, etc, and Dom Long-Depaquit in CHABLIS; also with many other brand names.

Billecart-Salmon NV; Rosé NV; Brut 85 86 88; Bl de Blancs 83 85 86 88; Grande Cuvée 82 85 One of the best small CHAMPAGNE houses, founded in 1818, still family-owned. Fresh-flavoured wines incl a v tasty rosé. CUVÉES: Nicolas François Billecart (88), Elisabeth Salmon Rosé (88 89).

Bize, Simon Admirable red burgundy grower with 35 acres at SAVIGNY-LES-BEAUNE. Usually model wines, racy and elegant.

Blagny Burg r w ★★→★★★ (w) 85 86' 88 89 90' 91 92 93 94 95 Hamlet between MEURSAULT and PULIGNY-MONTRACHET: whites have affinities with both (sold under each AC), reds with VOLNAY (sold as AC Blagny). Good ones need age; esp AMPEAU, Jobard, LATOUR, LEFLAIVE, Matrot, G Thomas.

Blanc de Blancs Any white wine made from white grapes only, esp CHAMPAGNE (usually both red and white). Not an indication of quality.

Blanc de Noirs White (or slightly pink or 'blush') wine from red grapes.

Blanck, Marcel Versatile ALSACE grower at Kientzheim. Good Pinot Bl, and GRANDS CRUS Furstentum (GEWURZ, Pinot Gr, esp Ries), Schlossberg (Ries).

Blanquette de Limoux Midi w sp ★★ Good bargain sparkler from near Carcassonne with long local history. V dry and clean; increasingly tasty as more CHARD and Chenin Bl are added, esp in new AC Crémant de Limoux. Normally NV.

Blaye B'x r w ★ 88 89 90 93 94 95 Your daily BORDEAUX from E of the Gironde. PREMIERES COTES DE BLAYE is the AC of the better wines.

Boisset, Jean-Claude Far and away the biggest burgundy merchant and grower, based in NUITS-ST-GEORGES. Owner of Bouchard-Aîné, Lionel Bruck, F Chauvenet, Delaunay, JAFFELIN, Morin Père et Fils, de Marcilly, Pierre Ponnelle, Thomas-Bassot, VIENOT. Generally high commercial standards.

Bollinger NV 'Special Cuvée'; Grande Année 76 79 82 83 85 88 89; Rosé 81 82 83 85 88 Top CHAMPAGNE house, at AY. Dry, very full-flavoured style, needs ageing. Luxury wines: RD (73 75 76 79 81 82 85), Vieilles Vignes Françaises (75 79 80 81 82 85 88 89) from ungrafted Pinot vines. Pioneered Charter of Quality ('91). Investor in Petaluma, Australia.

Bonneau du Martray, Domaine Biggest grower (with 27 acres) of CORTON-CHARLEMAGNE of the highest quality; also red GRAND CRU CORTON which has been much better since '90. Cellars at PERNAND-VERGELESSES. White wines have often outlived reds.

NB Vintages in colour are those you should choose first for drinking in 1997.

Bonnes-Mares Burg r ★★★→★★★★★ 78' 79 80 85' 87 88 89 90' 91 92 93 94 95
37-acre GRAND CRU between CHAMBOLLE-MUSIGNY and MOREY-ST-DENIS. V sturdy long-lived wines, less fragrant than MUSIGNY; can rival CHAMBERTIN. Top growers: DUJAC, Groffier, JADOT, MUGNIER, ROUMIER, DOM DES VAROILLES, DE VOGUE.

Bonnezeaux Lo w sw ★★★ 76' 78 81 83 85' 86 88' 89' 90' 91 92 93' 94 95'
Unusual rich tangy wine from Chenin Bl grapes, potentially the best of COTEAUX DU LAYON. Esp Angeli, Ch de Fesles, Dom du Petit Val. Ages well – but v tempting young.

Bordeaux B'x r w (p) ★ 88 89 90 92 93 94 95 (for ch'x see pages 78–103)
Catch-all AC for low-strength B'x wine. Not to be despised: it may be light but its flavour cannot be imitated. If I had to choose one daily wine this would be it.

Bordeaux Supérieur ★→★★ As above, with slightly more alcohol.

Borie-Manoux Admirable BORDEAUX shippers and château-owners, owned by the Castéja family. Ch'x incl BATAILLEY, BEAU-SITE, DOMAINE DE L'EGLISE, HAUT-BAGES-MONPELOU, TROTTEVIEILLE.

Bouchard Père et Fils Important burgundy shipper (est 1731) and grower with 209 acres of excellent v'yds, mainly in the COTE DE BEAUNE, and cellars at the Château de Beaune. Controlled by HENRIOT since '95, who have taken radical steps to upgrade quality and image.

Bouches-du-Rhône Prov r p w ★ VINS DE PAYS from Marseille environs. Robust reds from southern varieties, Cab S, Syrah and Merlot.

Bourg B'x r (w) ★★ 85' 86' 88' 89' 90' 93 94 Un-fancy claret from E of the Gironde. For châteaux see Côtes de Bourg.

Bourgeois, Henri Leading SANCERRE growers/merchants in Chavignol; owners of Laporte. Also POUILLY-FUME. Top wines: MD de Bourgeois, La Bourgeoise.

Bourgogne Burg r w (p) ★★ 90' 91 92 93 94 95 Catch-all Burgundy AC, with higher standards than basic B'x. Light, often gd flavour, best at 2–4 yrs. Top growers make bargain beauties from fringes of Côte d'Or villages; do not despise. BEAUJOLAIS CRUS can also be labelled Bourgogne.

Bourgogne Grand Ordinaire Burg r (w) ★ DYA Lowest B AC, also allowing GAMAY. Rare. White may incl ALIGOTE, Pinot Bl, Melon de Bourgogne.

Bourgogne Passe-Tout-Grains Burg r (p) ★ Age 1–2 yrs Junior burgundy: minimum 33% Pinot N, the balance GAMAY, mixed in the vat. Often enjoyable. Not as heady as BEAUJOLAIS.

Bourgueil Lo r (p) ★★★ 76' 83' 85 86' 88 89' 90' 91 92 93' 95' Normally delicate fruity Cab red from TOURAINE. Deep-flavoured, long-lasting in best yrs, ageing like Bordeaux. ST-NICOLAS-DE-BOURGUEIL often lighter. Esp from Amirault, Audebert, Billet, Caslot, Cognard, Druet, Gambier, Jamet, Lamé-Delille-Boucard, Mailloches.

Bouvet-Ladubay The major producer of sparkling SAUMUR, controlled by TAITTINGER. Excellent CREMANT DE LOIRE. 'Saphir' is over-sweet vintage wine. Oak-fermented deluxe 'Trésor' (white, rosé), with 2 yrs age, is much better.

Bouzeron Village of the COTE CHALONNAISE distinguished for the only single-village AC ALIGOTE. Top grower: de Villaine. Also NB BOUCHARD PERE.

Bouzy Rouge Champ r ★★★ 85 88 89 90 91 Still red of famous red-grape CHAMPAGNE village. Like v light burgundy, ageing early but can last well.

Brand ALSACE GRAND CRU hot spot nr Turkheim. Tokay-Pinot Gris does extremely well here; also excellent GEWURZ from ZIND-HUMBRECHT.

Brédif, Marc One of the most important growers and traders of VOUVRAY, owned by LADOUCETTE.

Bricout Brut NV (Réserve, Prestige, Cuvée Spéciale Arthur Bricout); Rosé NV; Brut 82 85 86 Small CHAMPAGNE house at AVIZE making light wines. Owned by Kupferberg of Mainz.

Brouilly Beauj r ★★ **92 93 94** Biggest of the 10 CRUS of BEAUJOLAIS: fruity, round, refreshing wine, can age 3–4 yrs. CH DE LA CHAIZE is largest estate. Top growers: Michaud, Dom de Combillaty, Dom des Grandes Vignes.

Bruno Paillard Brut Première Cuvée NV; Rosé Première Cuvée NV; Chard Réserve Privée NV, Brut **85 89** Small but prestigious young CHAMPAGNE house: excellent silky vintage and NV; fair prices.

Brut Term for the driest wines of CHAMPAGNE.

Buisse, Paul Quality merchant in Montrichard with range of Loire, especially TOURAINE wines.

Bugey Savoie r p w sp ★→★★ DYA VDQS district for light sparkling, still or half-sparkling wines. Grapes incl Roussette (or Roussanne) and good CHARD. Best from Cerdon and Montagnieu.

Buxy Burg w ★★ Village in AC MONTAGNY with good coop for CHARD.

Buzet SW France r (w) ★★ **86 88 89' 90' 92' 93 94** Good BORDEAUX-style wines, reputedly 'pruney', from just southeast of Bordeaux. Good value area with well-run cooperative: best are barrel-aged Tradition, Carte d'Or, Cuvée Baron d'Ardeuil and firm, ageable Ch de Gueyze. Also ch'x de Frandat, Matelot and Sauvagnères, and Dom de Versailles.

Cabardès Midi r (p w) ★→★★ **85 86 88 89 90 91 92 93 94 95** Newcomer VDQS region north of Carcassonne, CORBIÈRES, etc. MIDI and BORDEAUX grapes show promise at Ch Rivals, Ch Rayssac, Ch Ventenac, Coop de Conques sur Orbiel.

Cabernet See Grapes for red wine (pages 11–13).

Cabernet d'Anjou Lo p s/sw ★→★★ DYA Delicate, grapey, medium-sweet rosé. Traditionally a sweet rosé for ageing; a few venerable bottles survive. Especially from Bablut.

Cabrières Midi p (r) ★★ DYA COTEAUX DU LANGUEDOC.

Cahors SW France r ★→★★ **82 83 85 86' 88 89' 90' 92' 93 94** Historically 'black' and tannic from Malbec grapes, now made like BORDEAUX: full-bodied and distinct or much lighter. Top growers: Clos Triguedina (esp 'Prince Probus'), ch'x de Caïx, La Caminade, de Cayrou, de Chambert, Latuc, Pech de Jammes; Clos la Coutale, Dom Eugénie (v traditional), Clos de Gamot, Jouffreau, Vigouroux (esp Ch de Haute-Serre). Lighter wines from coop Caves d'Olt.

Cairanne S Rh r p w ★★ **86 88 89 90' 92 93 94 95** One of best COTES DU RHONE-VILLAGES: solid, robust esp from doms Brusset, l'Oratoire St-Martin, Rabasse-Charavin, Richaud. Some improving whites.

Calvet Famous old shippers of BORDEAUX and burgundy, now owned by Allied-Domecq. Some reliable standard wines, esp from Bordeaux.

Canard-Duchêne Brut NV; Demi-Sec NV; Rosé NV; Charles VII NV; Brut **83 85 88 90** Quality CHAMPAGNE house connected with VEUVE-CLICQUOT, ie, the same group as MOET-Hennessy. Fair prices for lively, Pinot N-tasting wines.

Canon-Fronsac B'x r ★★→★★★ **82 83' 85' 86 88 89' 90' 92 93 94** Full tannic reds of increasing quality from small area W of POMEROL. Need less age than formerly. Eg Châteaux: CANON, CANON DE BREM, CANON-MOUEIX, Coustolle, La Dauphine, La Fleur Caillou, Junayme, Mazeris-Bellevue, Moulin-Pey-Labrie, Toumalin, La Truffière, Vraye-Canon-Boyer. See also Fronsac.

Cantenac B'x r ★★★ Village of HAUT-MEDOC entitled to the AC MARGAUX. Top châteaux include BRANE-CANTENAC, PALMER etc.

Cap Corse Corsica w br ★★→★★★ CORSICA's wild N cape. Splendid MUSCAT from Clos Nicrosi, Rogliano, and rare soft dry Vermentino white. Vaut le détour, if not le voyage.

Caramany Pyr r (w) ★ **88 89 90 91 92 93 94 95** Notionally superior new AC for part of COTES DU ROUSSILLON-VILLAGES.

Carillon, Louis Leading PULIGNY-M domaine now in top league. Esp PREMIER CRU Referts, Perrières and a tiny amount of GRAND CRU Bienvenues-Bâtard.

Cassis Prov w (r p) ★★ DYA Seaside village E of Marseille known for lively dry white wine – one of the best in PROVENCE (eg Domaine du Paternel). Not to be confused with cassis, a blackcurrant liqueur made in Dijon.

Cave Cellar, or any wine establishment.

Cave coopérative Wine-growers' cooperative winery. Coops now account for 55% of all French production (4 out of 10 growers are members). Almost all now well-run, well-equipped and their wine is good value.

Cellier des Samsons BEAUJOLAIS/MACONNAIS coop at Quincié with 2,000 grower-members. Widely distributed.

Cépage Variety of vine, eg CHARDONNAY, Merlot.

Cérons B'x w dr sw ★★ 83' 85' 86' 88' 89' 90 91 92 93 94 Neighbour of SAUTERNES with some good sweet wine châteaux, eg de Cérons et de Calvimont, Grand Enclos, Haura. Ch Archambeau makes vg dry GRAVES.

Chablis

There is no better expression of the all-conquering Chardonnay than the full but tense, limpid but stony wines it makes on the heavy limestone soils of Chablis. Chablis terroir divides cleanly into 3 quality levels with remarkable consistency. Best makers use v little or no new oak to mask the precise definition of variety and terroir. They include: Billand-Simon, J-M Brocard, J Collet, D Dampt, R Dauvissat, B, D et E, and J Defaix, Droin, Drouhin, Durup, Fèvre, Geoffroy, J-P Grossot, Lamblin, Laroche, Long-Depaquit, Dom des Malandes, Michel, Pic, Pupillon, Raveneau, G Robin, Tribut. Simple unqualified 'Chablis' may be thin; best is premier or grand cru (see below). Coop, La Chablisienne, has high standards and many different labels (it makes 1 in every 3 bottles).

Chablis Burg w ★★→★★★ 90 92 93 94 95 Unique full-flavoured dry minerally wine of N Burgundy, CHARD only, from 10,000 acres (doubled since '85).

Chablis Grand Cru Burg w ★★★→★★★★ 78 83 85 86 88 89 90 91 92 93 94 95 In maturity a match for greatest white burgundy: forceful but often dumb in youth, at best almost SAUTERNES-like with age. 7 v'yds: Blanchots, Bougros, Clos, Grenouilles, Preuses, Valmur, Vaudésir. See also Moutonne.

Chablis Premier Cru Burg w ★★★ 85 86 88 89 90 91 92 93 94 95 Technically second-rank but at best excellent, more typical of CHABLIS than its GRANDS CRUS. Often outclasses more expensive MEURSAULT and other COTE DE BEANES. Best vineyards include Côte de Léchet, Fourchaume, Mont de Milieu, Montée de Tonnerre, Montmains, Vaillons. See above for producers.

Chai Building for storing and maturing wine, esp in BORDEAUX.

Chambertin Burg r ★★★★ 78' 79 80 83 85' 87 88 89 90' 91 92 93 94 95 32-acre GRAND CRU for some of the meatiest, most enduring, best red burgundy, 15 growers, incl BOUCHARD, Camus, Damoy, DROUHIN, MORTET, PONSOT, Rebourseau, Rossignol-Trapet, ROUSSEAU, Tortochot, TRAPET.

Chambertin-Clos de Bèze Burg r ★★★★ 78' 79 80 83 85 87 88 89 90' 91 92 93 94 95 37-acre neighbour of CHAMBERTIN. Similarly splendid wines. May legally be sold as Chambertin. 10 growers incl B CLAIR, CLAIR-DAU, Damoy, DROUHIN, Drouhin-Laroze, FAIVELEY, JADOT, ROUSSEAU.

Chambolle-Musigny Burg r (w) ★★★→★★★★ 78' 85' 87 88 89 90' 91 92 93 94 95 420-acre COTE DE NUITS village with fabulously fragrant, complex, never heavy wine. Best v'yds: Les Amoureuses, part of BONNES-MARES, Les Charmes, MUSIGNY. Growers to note: Barthod, DROUHIN, FAIVELEY, Hudelot-Noëllat, JADOT, Moine-Hudelot, Mugneret, MUGNIER, RION, ROUMIER, Serveau, DE VOGUE.

Champagne Sparkling wine of Pinots N and Meunier and/or CHARD, and its region (70,000+ acres 90 miles E of Paris); made by METHODE CHAMPENOISE. Wines from elsewhere, however good, cannot be champagne.

Champy Père et Cie Oldest Burgundy négociant, in BEAUNE, rejuvenated by Meurgey family (also brokers 'DIVA'). Range of v well chosen wines.

Chandon de Briailles, Domaine Small burgundy estate at SAVIGNY. Makes wonderful CORTON (and Corton Blanc) and vg PERNAND-VERGELESSES.

Chanson Père et Fils Old grower-négociant family co at BEAUNE (125 acres). Esp BEAUNE Clos des Fèves, SAVIGNY, PERNAND-VERGELESSES, CORTON. Fine quality.

Chapelle-Chambertin Burg r ★★★ 78' 85 87 88 89' 90' 91 92 93 94 95 13-acre neighbour of CHAMBERTIN. Wine more 'nervous', not so meaty. Top producers: Damoy, JADOT, Rossignol-Trapet, TRAPET.

Chapoutier Long-est'd growers and traders of top-quality, full-bodied Rhônes. Best are special CUVEES CHATEAUNEUF Barbe Rac (100% Grenache), red HERMITAGE Le Pavillon, white Hermitage Cuvée d'Orée (100% Marsanne, late-picked), also CROZES red Les Varonniers (since '94).

Charbaut, A et Fils Brut NV; Bl de Blancs Brut NV; Brut Rosé NV; Brut 79 82 85 87 88 90; Certificate Bl de Blancs 82 85; Certificate Rosé 79 82 85 Substantial Epernay CHAMPAGNE house. Clean light wines. Good rosé. New CUVEE launched '93: Grand Evénement Brut NV.

Chardonnay See Grapes for white wine (pages 7–11). Also the name of a MACON-VILLAGES commune. Hence Mâcon-Chardonnay.

Charmes-Chambertin Burg r ★★★ 78' 85' 87 88 89' 90' 91 92 93 94 95 76-acre CHAMBERTIN neighbour, incl AC MAZOYERES-CHAMBERTIN. Wines 'suppler', rounder; esp from Bachelet, Castagnier, DROUHIN, DUJAC, LEROY, ROTY, ROUMIER, ROUSSEAU.

Chartron & Trebuchet Young co (founded '84): some delicate harmonious white burgundies, esp Dom Chartron's PULIGNY-MONTRACHET, Clos de la Pucelle. Also BATARD- and CHEVALIER-MONTRACHET. Good ALIGOTE too.

Chassagne-Montrachet Burg r ★★★→★★★★ r (★★★) 78' 85 87 88 89' 90' 91 92 93 94; w 78' 83 85 86 88 89' 90 91 92 93 94 95 750-acre COTE DE BEAUNE village with excellent rich dry whites and sterling hefty reds. Whites rarely have the extreme finesse of PULIGNY next door but often cost less. Best vineyards include part of MONTRACHET, BATARD-MONTRACHET, Boudriottes (r w), Caillerets, CRIOTS-BATARD-MONTRACHET, Morgeot (r w), Ruchottes, CLOS ST-JEAN (r). Growers include Amiot-Bonfils, Blain-Gagnard, Colin-Deleger, Delagrange-Bachelet, DROUHIN, J-N Gagnard, GAGNARD-DELAGRANGE, Lamy-Pillot, MAGENTA, Ch de la Maltroye, MOREY, Niellon, RAMONET-PRUDHON.

Chasseloir, Dom du HQ of the firm of Chéreau-Carré: makers of several excellent AC-leading domaine MUSCADETS (esp Ch du Chasseloir).

Château
Means an estate, big or small, good or indifferent, particularly in Bordeaux (see pages 78–103). Elsewhere in France château tends to mean, literally, castle or great house, as in most of the following entries. In Burgundy 'Domaine' is the usual term.

Château d'Arlay Major JURA estate; 160 acres in skilful hands with wines incl vg VIN JAUNE, VIN DE PAILLE, Pinot N and MACVIN.

Château de Beaucastel S Rh r w ★★★ 78' 79 81' 83 85 86' 87 88 89' 90' 92 93 94' 95 One of the biggest (173 acres), best-run CHATEAUNEUF-DU-PAPE estates. Deep-hued, complex wines from unusual varietal mix incl ⅓ Mourvèdre. Small amount of wonderful Roussanne white to keep 5–10 yrs. Also leading COTES DU RHONE Coudoulet de Beaucastel (red and white). New interest: Beaucastel Estate, California.

Château de la Chaize Beauj r ★★★ 93 94 95 Best-known BROUILLY estate.

Château Corton-Grancey Burg r ★★★ 78 85 88 89 90 91 92 93 95 Famous ALOXE-CORTON estate; property of LOUIS LATOUR: benchmark wines.

Château de Crémat Prov r p w ★★→★★★ Prestigious little estate in BELLET, nr Nice. Light but long-lived reds, adequate rosés, excellent original whites.

Château Fortia S Rh r (w) ★★★ 78' 79 81 83 84 85 86 88 89 90 93 94 95 Trad 72-acre CHATEAUNEUF property. Owner's father, Baron Le Roy, also fathered the APPELLATION CONTROLEE system in the '20s. Good, but not at v top today.

Château Fuissé Burg w ★★★ The ultimate POUILLY-FUISSE estate. Its Pouilly-F VIEILLES VIGNES is ★★★★, and sumptuous with age; though recent wines have needed less time.

Château de la Jaubertie English- ('Rystone'-) owned top BERGERAC estate. Sumptuous luxury Sauv, Cuvée Mirabelle. Equally fine Réserve red.

Château de Meursault Burg r w ★★★ 100-acre estate owned by PATRIARCHE, with good v'yds and wines in BEAUNE, MEURSAULT, POMMARD, VOLNAY. Splendid cellars open to the public for tasting.

Château de Mille Prov r p w ★★ Leading star of advancing COTES DU LUBERON AC.

Château de Montaigne Dordogne w (sw) ★★ Home of the great philosopher Michel de M (outside HAUT-MONTRAVEL), now making sweet COTES DE MONTRAVEL, also sharing a part-owner with CH PALMER (MARGAUX).

Château La Nerthe S Rh r (w) ★★★ 78' 79 81' 85 86 88 89' 90' 93 94 95 Renowned imposing 222-acre CHATEAUNEUF estate. Solid modern-style wines, esp special CUVEES Cadettes (r) and Beauvenir (w).

Château du Nozet Lo w ★★★ 90 91' 92' 93' 94 95 Biggest and best-known estate of POUILLY (FUME) -SUR-LOIRE. Luxury Baron de L wines, can be wonderful (but at a price).

Château Rayas S Rh r (w) ★★★ 78' 79 81' 83 85 86 88' 89 90' 91 92 93 Famous old-style property of only 37 acres in CHATEAUNEUF-DU-PAPE. Concentrated wines (crops kept to half legal maximum) entirely Grenache, yet can age superbly. Pignan is second label. Also vg Ch Fonsalette, COTES DU RHONE (NB Cuvée Syrah and long-lived whites).

Château Routas Prov r p w ★★ Recent blends incl Syrah, Cab S, Chard-Viognier have been outstanding for the Var region.

Château de Selle Prov r p w ★★→★★★ 100-acre estate of OTT family nr Cotignac, Var. Pace-setters for PROVENCE. Cuvée Spéciale is largely Cab.

Château Simone Prov r p w ★★ Age 2–6 yrs. Famous old property in Palette; the only one with a name in this AC nr Aix-en-Provence. The red is best: smooth but herby and spicy. White is catching up.

Château Val-Joanis Prov r p w ★★★ Impressive estate making outstanding full-blooded COTES DU LUBERON. Don't miss them.

Château Vignelaure Prov r ★★★ 82' 83' 85 86 87 88 89 90 91 92 93 94 95 135-acre Provençal estate nr Aix: exceptional more-or-less B'x-style wine with Cab, Syrah and Grenache grapes. Bought in '94 by Rystone Co.

Château-Chalon Jura w ★★★ Not a CHATEAU but an area/appellation with unique strong dry yellow wine, like sharpish fino sherry. Usually ready when bottled (at about 6 yrs). A curiosity.

Château-Grillet N Rh w ★★★★ 89' 90 92 94 9-acre v'yd: one of France's smallest ACs. Intense, fragrant, absurdly over-expensive, but showing signs of revival in the '90s. Drink young; any oxidation spoils it.

Châteaumeillant Lo r p ★ DYA Tiny VDQS area nr SANCERRE. Gamay, Pinot Gris and Pinot N for light reds and rosés. Don't bother.

To decipher codes, please refer to 'Key to symbols' on front flap of jacket, or to 'How to use this book' on page 6.

Châteauneuf-du-Pape S Rh r (w) ★★★ 78' 79 81' 83 85 86 88 89' 90' 93 94 95' 8,200 acres near Avignon with core of 30 or so domaines for very fine wines (quality more variable over remaining 90). The best of them are dark, strong, exceptionally long-lived. Whites either fruity and zesty or rather heavy: mostly now 'DYA'. Top growers incl châteaux DE BEAUCASTEL, FORTIA, MONT-REDON, LA NERTHE, RAYAS; doms de Beaurenard, Le Bosquet des Papes, Les Cailloux, Font-de-Michelle, Grand Tinel, VIEUX TELEGRAPHE; Henri Bonneau, Clos du Mont-Olivet, Clos des Papes etc.

Châtillon-en-Diois Rh r p w ★ DYA Small AC of mid Rhône. Adequate largely Gamay reds; white (some ALIGOTE) mostly made into CLAIRETTE DE DIE.

Chave, Gérard To many the superstar grower (with his son Jean-Louis) of HERMITAGE, with 25 acres red, 12 acres white – spread over 9 hillside v'yds. V long-lived red and white (esp vg red ST-JOSEPH), and also VIN DE PAILLE.

Chavignol Village of SANCERRE with famous v'yd, Les Monts Damnés. Chalky soil gives vivid wines that age 4–5 yrs; esp from BOURGEOIS and Cotat. Also fromage de chèvre.

Chénas Beauj r ★★★ 90 91 92 93 94 95 Smallest BEAUJOLAIS CRU and one of the weightiest; neighbour to MOULIN-A-VENT and JULIENAS. Growers incl Benon, Champagnon, Charvet, Ch Chèvres, DUBOEUF, Lapièrre, Robin, Trichard, coop.

Chenin Blanc See Grapes for white wine (pages 7–11).

Chenonceau, Ch de Lo ★★ Architectural jewel of Loire now makes excellent AC Touraine Sauv, Cab, Cot (Malbec) and ★★★ Chenin, still and sparkling.

Chevalier-Montrachet Burg ★★★★ 78 83 85 86 88 89' 90 91 92 93 95 17-acre neighbour of MONTRACHET making similar luxurious wine, perhaps less powerful. Incl 2.5-acre Les Demoiselles. Growers incl LATOUR, JADOT, BOUCHARD PERE, CHARTRON, Deleger, LEFLAIVE, Niellon, PRIEUR.

Cheverny Lo r p w ★→★★ DYA Loire AC nr Chambord. Dry crisp whites from Sauv Bl and Chard. Also Gamay, Pinot N or Cab reds; generally light but tasty. 'Cour Cheverny' uses the local Romorantin grape. Sparkling wines use CREMANT DE LOIRE AC. Esp Cazin, Huards, OISLY ET THESEE, Salvard, Tue Boeuf.

Chevillon, R 32-acre estate at NUITS-ST-GEORGES; outstanding winemaking.

Chignin Savoie w ★ DYA Light soft white from Jacquère grapes for alpine summers. Chignin-Bergeron is best and liveliest.

Chinon Lo r (p w) ★★★ 76 83' 85 86' 88 89' 90' 91' 92 93' 95' Juicy, variably rich Cab F from TOURAINE. Drink cool, young; treat exceptional yrs like B'x. Small quantity of crisp dry white from Chenin. Growers: Alliet, Baudry, COULY-DUTHEIL (Clos de l'Echo), Druet, Joguet, Mabileau, Noblaie, Raffault. Cave Rabelais coop is prolific with wine to drink young.

Chiroubles Beauj r ★★★ 94 95 Good but tiny BEAUJOLAIS CRU next to FLEURIE; freshly fruity silky wine for early drinking (1–3 yrs). Growers incl Bouillard, Cheysson, DUBOEUF, Fourneau, Passot, Raousset, coop.

Chorey-lès-Beaune Burg r (w) ★★ 85 87 88 89 90' 91 92 93 94 95 Minor AC on flat land N of BEAUNE: 3 fine growers: Arnoux, Germain (Ch de Chorey), TOLLOT-BEAUT.

Chusclan S Rh r p w ★→★★ 89 90 92 93 94 95 Village of COTES DU RHONE-VILLAGES with able coop. Labels incl Cuvée de Marcoule, Seigneurie de Gicon. Also special CUVEES from André Roux, incl pure Syrah and good white.

Cissac HAUT-MEDOC village just west of PAUILLAC.

Clair, Bruno Recent domaine at MARSANNAY. Vg wines from there and GEVREY-CHAMBERTIN (esp CLOS DE BEZE), FIXIN, MOREY-ST-DENIS, SAVIGNY.

Clairet Very light red wine, almost rosé. Bordeaux Clairet is an AC.

Clairette Traditional white grape of the MIDI. Its low-acid wine was a vermouth base. Revival by Terrasses de Landoc is full and zesty.

Clairette de Bellegarde Midi w ★ DYA AC nr Nîmes: plain neutral white.

Clairette de Die Rh w dr s/sw sp ★★ NV Popular dry or (better) semi-sweet MUSCAT-flavoured sparkling wine from E Rhône; or straight dry CLAIRETTE white, surprisingly ageing well 3–4 yrs. Worth trying.

Clairette du Languedoc Midi w ★ DYA Neutral white from nr Montpellier, but watch for improvements. Ch La Condamine Bertrand looking good.

Clape, La Midi r p w ★→★★ AC to note of COTEAUX DU LANGUEDOC. Full-bodied wines from limestone hills between Narbonne and the sea. Red gains character after 2–3 yrs, Bourboulenc white after even longer. Vg rosé. Esp from ch'x Rouquette-sur-Mer, Pech-Redon, Dom de l'Hospitalet.

Claret Traditional English term for red BORDEAUX.

Climat Burgundian word for individually named v'yd, eg BEAUNE Grèves.

Clos A term carrying some prestige, reserved for distinct, usually walled, v'yds, often in one ownership. Frequently found in Burgundy and ALSACE. Les Clos is CHABLIS' Grandest Cru.

Clos de Bèze See Chambertin-Clos de Bèze.

Clos des Lambrays Burg r ★★★ 15-acre GRAND CRU vineyard at MOREY-ST-DENIS. Changed hands *again* in '96.

Clos des Mouches Burg r w ★★★ Splendid PREMIER CRU BEAUNE v'yd, largely owned by DROUHIN. White and red, spicy and memorable – and consistent.

Clos de la Roche Burg r ★★★ 78' 82 85' 86 87 88 89' 90 91 92 93' 94 95 MOREY-ST-DENIS GRAND CRU (38-acres). Powerful complex, like CHAMBERTIN. Especially BOUCHARD PERE, BOUREE, CASTAGNIER, DUJAC, Lignier, PONSOT, REMY, ROUSSEAU.

Clos du Roi Burg r ★★★ Part of GRAND CRU CORTON. Also a BEAUNE PREMIER CRU.

Clos St-Denis Burg r ★★★ 78 79 82 85' 87 88 89' 90' 91 92 93' 94 95 16-acre GRAND CRU at MOREY-ST-DENIS. Splendid sturdy wine growing silky with age. Growers incl DUJAC, Lignier, PONSOT.

Clos Ste Hune Al w ★★★★ V fine austere Ries from TRIMBACH; perhaps ALSACE'S best. Needs 5+ yrs age; doesn't need GRAND CRU status.

Clos St-Jacques Burg r ★★★ 78' 82 83 85' 86 87 88 89' 90' 91 92 93' 94 95 17-acre GEVREY-CHAMBERTIN PREMIER CRU. Excellent powerful velvety long ager, often better (and dearer) than some GRANDS CRUS. The main growers are Esmonin and ROUSSEAU.

Clos St-Jean Burg r ★★★ 78 85' 88 89' 90' 91 92 93 94 95 36-acre PREMIER CRU of CHASSAGNE-MONTRACHET. Vg red, more solid than subtle, from eg Ch de la Maltroye. NB Domaine RAMONET.

Clos de Tart Burg r ★★★ 85' 87 88' 89' 90' 92 93 94 95 GRAND CRU at MOREY-ST-DENIS, owned by MOMMESSIN. At best wonderfully fragrant, young or old.

Clos de Vougeot Burg r ★★★ 78 85' 87 88 89' 90' 91 92 93 94 95 124-acre COTE DE NUITS GRAND CRU with many owners. Variable, occasionally sublime. Maturity depends on the grower's philosophy, technique and position on hill. Top growers incl CLAIR-DAU, DROUHIN, ENGEL, FAIVELEY, GRIVOT, GROS, Hudelot-Noëllat, JADOT, LEROY, Chantal Lescure, MEO-CAMUZET, Mugneret, ROUMIER.

Coche-Dury 16-acre MEURSAULT domaine (and 1 acre+ of CORTON-CHARLEMAGNE) with high reputation for oak-perfumed wines. Also vg ALIGOTE.

Cognac Town and region of the Charentes, W France, and its brandy.

Collines Rhodaniennes S Rh r w p ★ Popular Rhône VIN DE PAYS. Mainly reds: Merlot, Syrah, Gamay. Some VIOGNIER and CHARD in white.

Collioure Pyr r ★★ 85 86 88 89 90 91 92 93 94 95' Strong dry red from BANYULS area. Tiny production. Top growers include Cellier des Templiers, Les Clos de Paulilles, Cave L'Etoile, Dom du Mas Blanc, Dom de la Rectorie, La Tour Vieille, Vial-Magnères.

Comté Tolosan SW r p w Regional VDP for Midi and Pyrenees. Mostly red from traditional varieties. Esp from Dom du Ribonnet and Coop de Fronton (COTES DU FRONTONNAIS).

Condrieu N Rh w ★★★★ DYA Soft fragrant white of great character (and price) from the VIOGNIER grape. Can be outstanding but rapid growth of v'yd (now 222 acres) has made quality outside top names variable. Increased use of young oak (eg GUIGAL's Doriane CUVÉE) is a doubtful move. Best growers: Y Cuilleron, DELAS, Dumazet, GUIGAL, André Perret, Niéro-Pinchon, Vernay (esp Coteau de Vernon). CHATEAU-GRILLET is similar. Don't try ageing it.

Corbières Midi r (p w) ★★→★★★ 88 89 90 91 92 93 94 95' Vigorous bargain red wines. Best growers include châteaux Aiguilloux, Lastours, des Ollieux, Les Palais, de la Voulte Gasparet, Dom de Fontsainte, Dom du Vieux Parc, Dom de Villemajou, and Coops de Embrès et Castelmaure, Camplong, St-Laurent-Cabrerisse etc.

Cordier, Ets D Important BORDEAUX shipper and château-owner with wonderful track-record, now owned by Groupe Suez. Over 600 acres. Incl châteaux CANTEMERLE, CLOS DES JACOBINS, GRUAUD-LAROSE, LAFAURIE-PEYRAGUEY, MEYNEY etc.

Cornas N Rh r ★★→★★★ 78' 79 80 81 83' 85' 86 88 89' 90' 91 93 94 95 Sturdy v dark Syrah wine of unique quality, from steep-sloping granite v'yds S of HERMITAGE, on W bank of Rhône. Needs 5–15 yrs' ageing. Top are Allemand, de Barjac, J-L Colombo, Clape, DELAS, Juge, Lionnet, JABOULET, Noël Verset.

Corsica (Corse) Strong wines of all colours. Better ACs incl AJACCIO, CAP CORSE, PATRIMONIO, Sartène. VIN DE PAYS: ILE DE BEAUTE.

Corton Burg r ★★★→★★★★ 78' 85' 87 88 89' 90' 91 92 93 94 95 The only GRAND CRU red of the COTE DE BEAUNE. 200 acres in ALOXE-C incl CLOS DU ROI, Les Bressandes. Rich and powerful, should age well. Many good growers.

Corton-Charlemagne Burg w ★★★★ 78' 79 82 83 85' 86' 87 88 89' 90' 91 92 93 94 95 The white section (one-third) of CORTON. Rich spicy lingering wine, behaves like a red and ages magnificently. Top growers: BONNEAU DU MARTRAY, Chapuis, COCHE-DURY, Delarche, Dubreuil-Fontaine, FAIVELEY, HOSPICES DE BEAUNE, JADOT, LATOUR, Rapet.

Costières de Nîmes Midi r p w ★→★★ DYA Large new AC of improving quality from the Rhône delta. Formerly Costières du Gard. NB Ch de Nages, Ch de la Tuilerie ('Dinettes et Croustilles').

Côte(s)
Means hillside; generally a superior v'yd to those on the plain.
Many ACs are prefixed by either 'Côtes' or 'Coteaux',
meaning the same. In St-Emilion distinguishes valley slopes
from higher plateau.

Côte de Beaune Burg r w ★★→★★★★ Used geographically: the southern half of the COTE D'OR. Applies as an AC only to parts of BEAUNE itself.

Côte de Beaune-Villages Burg r w ★★ 85 88 89' 90' 91 92 93 94 95 Regional APPELLATION for secondary wines of classic area. Cannot be labelled 'Côte de Beaune' without either '-Villages' or village name appended.

Côte de Brouilly Beauj r ★★ 91 93 94 95 Fruity rich vigorous BEAUJOLAIS CRU. One of best. Esp from: Dom de Chavanne, G Cotton, Ch Delachanel, J-C Nesme, Ch Thivin.

Côte Chalonnaise Burg r w sp ★★→★★★ V'yd area between BEAUNE and MACON. See also Givry, Mercurey, Montagny, Rully. Alias 'Région de Mercurey'.

Côte de Nuits Burg r (w) ★★→★★★★ N half of COTE D'OR. Mostly red wine.

Côte de Nuits-Villages Burg r (w) ★★ 88 89 90 91 92 93 94 95 A junior AC for extreme N and S ends of Côte; well worth investigating for bargains.

Côte d'Or Département name applied to the central and principal Burgundy v'yd slopes, consisting of the COTE DE BEAUNE and COTE DE NUITS. The name is not used on labels.

Côte Rôtie N Rh r ★★★→★★★★ 78 79 80 82 83' 85' 86 87 88' 89' 90' 91 94 95
Potentially the finest Rhône red, from S of Vienne; can achieve rich, complex softness and finesse with age. Top growers incl Barge, Burgaud, Champet, CHAPOUTIER, Clusel-Roch, DELAS, J-M Gérin, GUIGAL (long oak-ageing, different and fuller in style), JABOULET, Jamet, Jasmin, Rostaing (elegant, cask-influenced wine), VIDAL-FLEURY.

Coteaux d'Aix-en-Provence Prov r p w ★→★★★ AC on the move. Est'd CH VIGNELAURE now challenged by ch'x Commanderie de la Bargemone and Fonscolombe. See also Baux-en-Provence.

Coteaux d'Ancenis Lo r p w (sw) ★ DYA VDQS E Of Nantes for light Gamay reds and rosés, sharpish dry whites from Chenin, and semi-sweet from Malvoisie (ages well). Esp Guidon (Malvoisie).

Coteaux de l'Ardèche See l'Ardèche.

Coteaux de l'Aubance Lo w sw ★★ 88' 89' 90' 93' 94' 95 Similar to COTEAUX DU LAYON, improving sweet wines from Chenin Bl. A few SELECTION DES GRAINS NOBLES. Esp from Bablut, Montgilet, RICHOU.

Coteaux des Baronnies S Rh r p w ★ Rhône VIN DE PAYS. Syrah, Merlot, Cab, CHARD, plus trad grapes. Promising. Dom du Rieu-Frais (incl good Viognier) worth noting.

Coteaux Champenois Champ r w (p) ★★★ DYA (whites) The AC for non-sparkling CHAMPAGNE. Vintages (if mentioned) follow those for Champagne. Do not pay inflated prices.

Champagne: a handful of good small houses

Jacques Selosse – in Avize, specializes in Blanc de Blancs

Ployez Jacquemart – excellent NV and vintage, based in Ludes on the Montagne de Reims

Vilmart – in the centre of Rilly-la-Montagne, tiny amounts, high quality

Napoléon – exceptionally fine vintage wines

R & I Legras – Chouilly house with complete range, incl Blanc de Blancs and a Coteaux Champenois

Boizel – Epernay house; champagnes noted for their fruit

Gardet & Cie – rich well-aged wines with high Pinot Noir element

---

Coteaux du Giennois Lo r p w ★ DYA Small VDQS north of POUILLY about to become AC. Light Gamay and Pinot, Sauv à la SANCERRE. Top growers: Balland-Chapuis, Gitton.

Coteaux du Languedoc Midi r p w ★★ Scattered well-above-ordinary MIDI AC areas. Best reds (eg CABRIERES, LA CLAPE, FAUGERES, St-Georges-d'Orques, Quatourze, ST-CHINIAN, St-Saturnin) age for 2–4 yrs. Now also some good whites. Standards rising dizzily.

Coteaux du Layon Lo w s/sw sw ★★ 79 82 85' 86 88' 89' 90' 91 92 93' The heart of ANJOU, S of Angers: sweet Chenin with admirable acidity, ageing almost forever, excellent aperitif, or goes with rich creamy main courses or fruit dessert. Since '93 new AC SELECTION DES GRAINS NOBLES; cf ALSACE. 7 villages can add name to AC. Top ACs: BONNEZEAUX, C du Layon-Chaume. Growers incl esp Dom d'Ambinos, Baudouin, BAUMARD, Bidet, Cady, Delesvaux, des Forges, Maurières, Ogereau, Papin, Pithon, Robineau, SOULEZ, Tomaze.

Coteaux du Loir Lo r p w dr sw ★★ 78 82 83 85 86 88' 89' 90' 92 93' 95 Small region N of Tours. Occasionally fine Chenin Bl, Gamay, Pineau d'Aunis, Cab. Best v'yd: JASNIERES. Top growers: Aubert de Rycke, Fresneau, Gigou. The Loir is a tributary of the Loire.

Coteaux de la Loire See Anjou-Coteaux de la Loire.

Coteaux du Lyonnais Beauj r p (w) ★ DYA Junior BEAUJOLAIS. Best EN PRIMEUR.

Coteaux de Peyriac Midi r p ★ DYA One of the most-used VIN DE PAYS names of the Aude département. Huge quantities.

Coteaux de Pierrevert S Rh r p w sp ★ DYA Minor southern VDQS nr Manosque. Well-made coop wine, mostly rosé, with fresh whites.

Coteaux de Saumur Lo w sw ★★→★★★ 89 90 93 95' Rare potentially fine s/sw Chenin. Creamy-sweet (MOELLEUX) best. Esp Drouineau, Clos Rougeard, Vatan.

Coteaux du Tricastin S Rh r p w ★★ 88 89 90 92 93 94 Fringe COTES DU RHONE of increasing quality. Attractive red can age 8 yrs. Dom de Grangeneuve, Dom St-Luc and Ch La Décelle among the best.

Coteaux Varois Prov r p w ★→★★ Substantial new AC zone: California-style Dom de St-Jean de Villecroze makes vg red.

Coteaux du Vendômois Lo r p w ★ DYA Fringe Loire VDQS west of Vendôme. Reds, incl Cab, increasing.

Côtes d'Affreux Centre r ★ Aspiring to VDP. Shd perhaps use grapes as base.

Côtes d'Auvergne Central France r p (w) ★ DYA Flourishing small VDQS. Red (at best) like light BEAUJOLAIS. Chanturgues is best known. Corent is rosé.

Côtes de Blaye B'x w ★ DYA Run-of-the-mill BORDEAUX white from BLAYE.

Côtes de Bordeaux Saint-Macaire B'x w dr sw ★ DYA Everyday BORDEAUX white from E of SAUTERNES.

Côtes de Bourg B'x r ★→★★ 82' 83 85' 86' 88' 89' 90 92 93 94 95 Appellation used for many of the better reds of BOURG. Ch'x incl DE BARBE, La Barde, DU BOUSQUET, Brûlesécaille, La Croix de Millorit, Falfas, Font Guilhem, Grand-Jour, de la Grave, La Grolet, Guerry, Guionne, Haut-Maco, Lalibarde, Lamothe, Mendoce, Peychaud, Rousset, Tayac, de Thau.

Côtes de Castillon B'x r ★→★★ 86' 88' 89' 90' 92 93 94 95 Flourishing region just E of ST-EMILION. Similar but lighter wines. Ch'x incl Beauséjour, La Clarière-Laithwaite, Fonds-Rondes, Haut-Tuquet, Lartigue, Moulin-Rouge, PITRAY, Rocher-Bellevue, Ste-Colombe, Thibaud-Bellevue.

Côtes de Duras Dordogne r w ★ 90' 92 93 94 95 BERGERAC neighbour: similar light wines. Dominated by two v competent coops (Landerrouat, Berticot).

Côtes de Forez Lo r p (sp) ★ DYA Uppermost Loire VDQS (Gamay), around Boën, N of St-Etienne: juicy easy-drinking wines. Esp Vignerons Foreziens, P Noire.

Côtes de Francs B'x r w ★★ 85 86' 88' 89' 90' 92 93 94 95 Fringe BORDEAUX from E of ST-EMILION. Increasingly attractive tasty wines, esp from ch'x de Belcier, La Claverie, de Francs, Lauriol, PUYGUERAUD, La Prade.

Côtes de Frontonnais SW France r p ★★ DYA Local wines of Toulouse, gaining admirers everywhere. Two distinct styles: CdF-Fronton good from coop, Ch du Roc and Ch Bellevue-la-Forêt (250 acres, outstanding silky red to age 2–4 yrs and rosé 'l'Allégresse'), CdF-Villaudric is bolder (esp from Ch La Colombière and Dom Caze).

Côtes de Gascogne SW W (r) ★→★★ DYA VIN DE PAYS branch of ARMAGNAC. Esp deliciously floral Sauv Bl whites, Ugni Bl, Colombard and Gros Manseng blends, all in bountiful supply; also full fruity reds. Top growers: Dom de Biau, Grassa, Dom de Papolle, Coop de Plaimont. Also Floc de Gascogne (red or white, like PINEAU DES CHARENTES).

Côtes du Haut-Roussillon SW France br sw ★→★★ NV Area for VINS DOUX NATURELS N of Perpignan.

Côtes du Jura Jura r p w (sp) ★ DYA Various light tints/tastes. ARBOIS is better.

Côtes du Lubéron S Rh r p w sp ★→★★ 88 89 90 93 94 95 Spectacularly improved country wines from N PROVENCE. Actors and media magnates among owners. Stars are CH DE MILLE, CH VAL-JOANIS, with vg largely Syrah red, and whites as well. Others incl good coop and Ch de la Canorgue.

For key to grape variety abbreviations, see pages 7–13.

Côtes de la Malepère Midi r ★ DYA Rising star VDQS on frontier of MIDI and SW, nr Limoux. Watch for fresh eager reds.

Côtes du Marmandais Dordogne r p w ★ DYA Light wines from southeast of BORDEAUX. The coops at Cocumont and Beaupuy make most of the best.

Côtes de Montravel Dordogne w dr sw ★ DYA Part of BERGERAC; traditionally medium-sweet, now often quite dry. Good from Ch Laroque and Dom de Libarde. Montravel Sec is dry, HAUT MONTRAVEL sweet.

Côtes de Provence Prov r p w ★→★★★ Wines of Provence; revolutionized by new attitudes and investment. Dom Bernarde, Castel Roubine, Commanderie de Peyrassol, Dom de la Courtade, DOM OTT, Dom des Planes, Dom Rabiéga, Dom Richeaume are leaders. 60% is rosé, 30% red. See also Coteaux d'Aix, COTES DU LUBERON, Bandol etc.

Côtes du Rhône S Rh r p w ★→★★★ 90' 93 94 95 Basic AC of the Rhône Valley. Best drunk young – even as PRIMEUR. Wide variations of quality due to grape ripeness: tending to rise with alcohol %. See Côte du Rhône-Villages.

> Top Côtes du Rhône producers: châteaux La Courançonne, l'Estagnol, Fonsalette, St-Esteve and Trignon (incl Viognier white); Clos Simian; Coops Chantecotes (Ste-Cécile-les-Vignes), Villedieu (esp white); doms Coudoulet de Beaucastel, Gramenon (Grenache, Viognier), Jaume, Réméjeanne, Vieux Chêne; Guigal, Jaboulet.

Côtes du Rhône-Villages S Rh r p w ★→★★ 88 89' 90' 93 94 95 Wine of the 17 best S Rhône villages. Substantial and, on the whole, reliable. S'times delicious. See Beaumes-de-Venise, Cairanne, Chusclan, Laudun, Rasteau, Séguret, St-Gervais etc.

Côtes Roannaises Central France r p ★→★★ DYA Recent ('94) AC for Gamay, between Lyon and the Loire. At best (from Montroussier, Plaisse, R Serol, Vial) like good BEAUJOLAIS.

Côtes du Roussillon Pyr r p w ★ →★★ 88 89 90 91 93 94 95 E Pyrenees AC. Hefty CARIGNAN reds best, can be very tasty (eg Gauby). Some whites are sharp VINS VERTS.

Côtes du Roussillon-Villages Pyr r ★★→★★★ 86 88 89 90 91 92 93 94 95 The region's best reds, from 28 communes including CARAMANY, LATOUR DE FRANCE, LESQUERDE. Best labels are Coop Baixas, Cazes Frères, Dom des Chênes, Gauby, Château de Jau, Coop Lesquerde, Dom Piquemal, Coop Les Vignerons Catalans. Some now choose to renounce AC status and make varietal VINS DE PAYS.

Côtes de St-Mont SW France r w p ★ Promising Gers VDQS, not unlike lighter MADIRAN. The same coop as COTES DE GASCOGNE: esp for Les Hauts de Bergelle range and Ch de Sabazan; Ch de Bergalasse also good.

Côtes de Thongue Midi r w ★ DYA Popular VIN DE PAYS from the HERAULT. Some good wines coming. Especially from doms Arjolle, COUSSERGUES, Croix Belle, Montmarin.

Côtes de Toul E France p r w ★ DYA Very light VDQS wines from Lorraine; mainly VIN GRIS (rosé).

Côtes du Ventoux S Rh r p (w) ★★ 90' 93 94 95 Booming (17,000-acre) AC between the Rhône and PROVENCE for tasty reds (from café-style to much deeper flavours) and easy rosés. La Vieille Ferme, owned by J-P Perrin of CH DE BEAUCASTEL, is top producer; Domaine Anges, ch'x Pesquié and Valcombe and Paul Jaboulet are good too.

Côtes du Vivarais Prov r p w ★ DYA Ardèche VDQS. 2,500 acres across several villages on W bank S of ST-PERAY. Improving, more substantial reds. Best producers: Boulle, Gallety, Dom de Belvezet.

Coulée de Serrant Lo w dr sw ★★★★ 73 76' 78 79' 81 82 83' 85' 86 88 89' 90'
91 92 93 95' 16-acre Chenin Bl v'yd on Loire's N bank at SAVENNIERES run on
ferociously organic principles. Intense strong fruity/sharp wine, good aperitif
and with fish. Ages almost for ever.

Couly-Dutheil Lo r p w ★★ Largest grower and merchant in CHINON; range of
reliable wines – Clos d'Olive and l'Echo are top quality.

Coussergues, Domaine de Midi r w p ★ DYA Large estate in formerly
notorious territory nr Beziers. CHARD, Syrah etc are bargains.

Crémant In CHAMPAGNE means 'creaming' (half-sparkling). Since '75 an AC for
quality classic method sparkling from ALSACE, Loire, BOURGOGNE and most
recently LIMOUX – often a bargain. Term phasing out in Champagne.

Crémant de Loire w sp ★★→★★★ NV High quality sparkling wine from ANJOU,
especially SAUMUR and TOURAINE. Esp Berger, de Grenelle, Lambert, LANGLOIS-
CHATEAU, Michaud, Nerleux, OISLY ET THESEE, Passavant and Pibaleau.

Crépy Savoie w ★★ DYA Light soft Swiss-style white from S shore of Lake
Geneva. 'Crépitant' has been coined for its faint fizz.

Criots-Bâtard-Montrachet Burg w ★★★ 78' 79 85 86 88 89 90 91 92 93 94 95
4-acre neighbour to BATARD-M. Similar wine without extreme pungency.

Crozes-Hermitage N Rh r (w) ★★ 85' 86 88 89 90' 91' 92 94 95 Nr HERMITAGE:
larger v'yds, wine with fewer dimensions. Some is fruity, early-drinking
(drink at 2+ yrs); some cask-aged (wait 5–8 yrs). Good examples from Belle,
Ch Curson, Dom du Colombier, Combier, Desmeure, Dom des Entrefaux
(US name Pierrelles), Fayolle et Fils, Alain Graillot, Dom du Pavillon, E Pochon,
Dom de Thalabert of JABOULET. Jaboulet's Mule Blanche is good white.

The Bourgeoisie and other classes

Cru
Growth, as in first growth/classed growth – meaning vineyard. In
Beaujolais, one of the top 10 villages.

Cru Bourgeois
General term for Médoc châteaux below Cru Classé. There are
250-odd in the Syndicat, covering 7,000 acres, with an annual
competition. Others who use the term are prosecuted. In '94
a Paris merchant was jailed for a year.

Cru Bourgeois Supérieur (Cru Grand Bourgeois)
One rank better than the last – must be barrel-aged. Being
phased out by typically unhelpful Brussels decree from '93.

Cru Classé
Classed growth. One of the first five official quality classes of
the Médoc, classified in 1855. Also any growth of another district
(eg Graves, St-Emilion, Sauternes) named in its local classification.

Cru Exceptionnel
Rank above Cru Bourgeois Supérieur, immediately below Cru
Classé. Cru Bourgeois divisions are being phased out as of '93.
Now officially suppressed by Brussels – but memories are long.

Cruse et Fils Frères Senior BORDEAUX shipper. Now owned by Pernod-Ricard.
The Cruse family (not the company) owns CH D'ISSAN.

Cussac Village S of ST-JULIEN. (AC HAUT-MEDOC.) Top ch'x: BEAUMONT, LANESSAN.

Cuve Close Short-cut method of making sparkling wine in a tank. Sparkle
dies away in glass much quicker than with METHODE TRADITIONELLE wine.

Cuvée Wine contained in a cuve or vat. A word of many uses, including for 'blend' (as in CHAMPAGNE); in Burgundy interchangeable with 'CRU'. Often just refers to a 'lot' of wine.

Dagueneau, Didier Top POUILLY-FUMÉ producer. Serge D is another.

De Castellane Brut NV; Brut 85 89 90; Cuvée Royale 82 88 89; Prestige Florens de Castellane 82 86 88; Cuvée Commodore Brut 85 88 89 Long-established Epernay CHAMPAGNE house, now part-owned by LAURENT-PERRIER. Good, rather light wines incl Maxim's house champagne.

De Luze, A & Fils BORDEAUX shipper owned by Rémy-Martin of COGNAC.

Degré alcoolique Degrees of alcohol, ie percent by volume.

Deiss, Marcel Fine ALSACE grower at Bergheim with 50 acres, wide range incl splendid Ries (GRAND CRU Schoenenberg), GEWURZ (Altenburg at Bergheim), good SELECTION DES GRAINS NOBLES and VIN DE PAILLE.

Delamotte Brut; Bl de Blancs (85); Cuvée Nicolas Delamotte Fine small CHARD-dominated CHAMPAGNE house at Le Mesnil, owned by LAURENT-PERRIER.

Delas Frères Old and worthy firm of Rhône wine specialists with vineyards at CONDRIEU, CÔTE RÔTIE, HERMITAGE. Top wines: Condrieu, Marquise de Tourette Hermitage (red and white). Owned by ROEDERER.

Delbeck Small fine CHAMPAGNE house reborn '91. Plenty of Pinot N in blend.

Delorme, André Leading CÔTE CHALONNAISE merchants and growers. Specialists in CRÉMANT DE BOURGOGNE and excellent RULLY etc.

Demi-Sec Half-dry: in practice more than half sweet. (Eg of CHAMPAGNE.)

Deutz Deutz Brut Classic NV; Rosé NV; Brut 79 81 82 85 88 90; Rosé 82 85 88; Bl de Bls 81 82 85 88 89 90 One of the best small CHAMPAGNE houses, bought in '95 by ROEDERER. Flavourful wines. Luxury brands: Cuvée William Deutz (79 82 85 88), Rosé (85). V successful branches in California, NZ. Also Sekt in Germany.

Dirler, Jean-Pierre ALSACE producer of Kessler, Saering and Spiegel GRAND CRUS: each esp for Ries.

Dom Pérignon, Cuvée 71 73 75 76' 78 82' 83 85' 88; Rosé 78 82 85 Luxury CUVÉE of MOËT & CHANDON (launched 1936), named after the legendary abbey cellarmaster who first blended (still) CHAMPAGNE. Astonishing consistent quality, esp with 10–15 yrs bottle-age.

Domaine Property, particularly in Burgundy and the south.

Dopff & Irion Another excellent Riquewihr (ALSACE) business. Esp MUSCAT les Amandiers, Ries de Riquewihr, Ries Les Murailles, GEWURZ Les Sorcières, Pinot Gr Les Maquisards: long-lived. Good Crémant d'Alsace.

Dopff au Moulin Ancient top-class family wine house at Riquewihr, ALSACE. Best: GEWURZ Eichberg, Ries Schoenenbourg, Sylvaner de Riquewihr. Pioneers of sparkling wine in Alsace; good CUVÉES: Bartholdi and Julien.

Doudet-Naudin SAVIGNY burgundy merchant and grower. V'yds incl BEAUNE-CLOS DU ROI, Redrescul. Dark long-lived wines, supplied to Berry Bros & Rudd of London, eventually come good. Lighter style recently.

Dourthe Frères B'X merchant with wide range: good CRUS BOURGEOIS, incl BELGRAVE, MAUCAILLOU, TRONQUOY-LALANDE. Beau-Mayne is well-made brand.

Doux Sweet.

Drappier, André Leading Aube region CHAMPAGNE house, esp for Bl de Noirs. Family-run. Tasty crisp NV, Signature Bl de Bl 88, Grande Sendrée 83 89.

DRC See Romanée-Conti, Domaine de la.

Drouhin, J & Cie Deservedly prestigious Burgundy grower (130 acres) and merchant with highest standards. Cellars in BEAUNE; v'yds in Beaune, CHABLIS, CLOS DE VOUGEOT, MUSIGNY, etc, and Oregon, USA. Top wines incl (esp) BEAUNE-CLOS DES MOUCHES, CHABLIS LES CLOS, CORTON-CHARLEMAGNE, GRIOTTE-CHAMBERTIN, PULIGNY-MONTRACHET-Les Folatières. Majority share now held by Tokyo co.

Duboeuf, Georges The Grand Fromage of BEAUJOLAIS. Top-class merchant at Romanèche-Thorin. Leader of the region in every sense, with a huge range of admirable wines. Also MOULIN-A-VENT untypically aged in new oak, and white MACONNAIS, etc.

Dubos High-level BORDEAUX négociant.

Duclot BORDEAUX négociant; top-growth specialist. Linked with J-P MOUEIX.

Dujac, Domaine Burgundy grower (Jacques Seysses) at MOREY-ST-DENIS with vineyards in that village and BONNES-MARES, ECHEZEAUX, GEVREY-CHAMBERTIN etc. Splendidly vivid and long-lived wines. Now also buying grapes in MEURSAULT, and new venture with Cab in COTEAUX VAROIS.

Dulong Highly competent BORDEAUX merchant. Breaking all the rules with unorthodox Rebelle blends. Also VIN DE PAYS.

Durup, Jean One of the biggest CHABLIS growers with 140 acres, including Domaine de l'Eglantière and admirable Ch de Maligny.

Duval-Leroy Coteaux Champenois r w; Brut; Bl de Blancs Brut NV; Fleur de Champagne Brut NV and Rosé NV; Cuvée des Rois Rosé NV; Fleur de Champagne Brut **88**; Cuvée des Rois Brut **86** Large progressive Vertus producer with high standards.

Echézeaux Burg r ★★★ 78' 82 85' 87 88 89' 90' 91 92 93 94 95 74-acre GRAND CRU between VOSNE-ROMANEE and CLOS DE VOUGEOT. Can be superlative, fragrant, without great weight, eg Confuron-Cotetidot, ENGEL, Gouroux, Grivot, A F GROS, MONGEARD-MUGNERET, Mugneret, DRC.

Edelzwicker Alsace w ★ DYA Modest blended light white: often fruity, good.

Eguisheim, Cave Vinicole d' Vg ALSACE coop: fine GRAND CRUS Hatchbourg, Hengst, Ollwiller and Spiegel. Owns WILLM. Top label: Wolfberger (65% of production). Grande Réserve and Sigillé ranges best. Good CREMANT.

Eichberg Eguisheim (ALSACE) GRAND CRU. Another warm patch, with the lowest rainfall in Colmar area: good for vg KUENTZ-BAS VENDANGE TARDIVE.

Engel, R Top-class grower of CL DE VOUGEOT, ECHEZEAUX, GRANDS ECH'X, VOSNE-ROM.

Entraygues le Fel SW p w VDQS ★ Fragrant sharp country wine. Esp F Avallon's.

Entre-Deux-Mers B'x w ★→★★ DYA Improving standard dry white BORDEAUX from between the Garonne and Dordogne rivers (aka E-2-M). Often a good buy as techniques improve. Esp ch'x BONNET, Gournin, Latour-Laguens, Moulin de Launay, Séguin, Thieuley, Turcaud etc.

L'Estandon The everyday wine of Nice (AC COTES DE PROVENCE) in all colours.

l'Etoile Jura w dr sp (sw) ★★ Subregion of the Jura known for stylish whites, incl VIN JAUNE, similar to CHATEAU-CHALON; good sparkling.

Faiveley, J Family-owned growers and merchants at NUITS-ST-GEORGES, with v'yds (150 acres) in CHAMBERTIN-CLOS DE BEZE, CHAMBOLLE-MUSIGNY, CORTON, MERCUREY, NUITS (44 acres). Consistent high quality rather than charm.

Faller, Théo Top ALSACE grower at Domaine Weinbach, Kaysersberg. Makes concentrated firm dry wines needing unusually long ageing, up to 10 yrs. Esp GRAND CRUS Geisburg (Ries), Kirchberg de Ribeauvillé (GEWURZ).

Faugères Midi r (p w) ★★★ 88 89 90 91 92 93 94 95 Isolated COTEAUX DU LANGUEDOC village with above-average wine and exceptional terroir. Gained AC status '82. Best growers: Dom Alquier, Dom des Estanilles, Ch La Liquière.

Fessy, Sylvain Dynamic BEAUJOLAIS merchant with wide range.

Fèvre, William Excellent CHABLIS grower with the biggest GRAND CRU holding (40 acres). But spoils some of his top wines with new oak. One whimsy wine he calls Napa Vallée de Paris. His label is Dom de la Maladière.

Fiefs Vendéens Lo r p w ★ DYA Up-and-coming VDQS for light wines from the Vendée, just S of MUSCADET on the Atlantic coast. Wines from Chenin, Colombard, Grolleau, Melon (whites), Cab and Gamay for reds and rosés. Esp Coirier, St-Nicolas.

Fitou Midi r ★★ 85 86 88 89 90 91 92 93 94 95 Superior CORBIERES red wines; powerful, ageing well. Best from coops at Cascastel, Paziols and Tuchan. Interesting experiments with Mourvèdre grapes in Leucate.

Fixin Burg r ★★ 78' 85' 88' 89' 90' 91 92 93 94 95 Worthy and under-valued northern neighbour of GEVREY-CHAMBERTIN. Often splendid reds. Best v'yds: Clos du Chapitre, Les Hervelets, Clos Napoléon. Growers incl Bertheau, R Bouvrier, CLAIR, FAIVELEY, Gelin, Gelin-Molin, Guyard.

Lah-la, lah-la, la-la-la-la-lah-la

The Confrèrie des Chevaliers du Tastevin is the wine fraternity of Burgundy: the world's most famous of its kind. It was founded in 1933 by a group of Burgundian patriots, led by Camille Rodier and Georges Faiveley, to rescue their beloved region from a period of slump by promoting its inimitable wines. Today it regularly holds banquets – with elaborate, sprightly song and ceremonies, for 600 guests – at its headquarters, the Cistercian château in the Clos de Vougeot, above all at 'Les Trois Glorieuses', the November weekend of the Hospices de Beaune auction (see page 58). The Confrèrie has branches in many countries and members among lovers of wine all over the world.
See also Tastevin, page 74.

Fleurie Beauj r ★★★ 90 91 92 93 94 95 The epitome of a BEAUJOLAIS CRU: fruity, scented, silky, racy wines. Esp from Chapelle des Bois, Chignard, Depardon, Després, DUBOEUF, Ch de Fleurie, the coop.

Fortant de France Midi r p w ★→★★ Brand (dressed to kill) of remarkable quality single-grape wines from the neighbourhood of Sète. See Skalli.

Frais Fresh or cool.

Frappé Ice-cold.

Froid Cold.

Fronsac B'x r ★→★★★ 82 83 85' 86' 88' 89' 90' 92 93 94 95 Picturesque area of increasingly fine tannic reds just W of ST-EMILION. Ch'x incl de Carles, DALEM, LA DAUPHINE, Fontenil, Mayne-Vieil, Moulin-Haut-Laroque, LA RIVIERE, La Rousselle, La Valade, La Vieille Cure, Villars. Give them time. See also smaller Canon-Fronsac.

Frontignan Midi br sw ★→★★ NV Strong sweet liquorous MUSCAT of ancient repute. Best growers: Châteaux Stony and La Peyrade.

Gagnard-Delagrange, Jacques Estimable small (13-acre) grower of CHASSAGNE-MONTRACHET, including some MONTRACHET. Look out also for his daughter's estate, Blain-Gagnard and Fontaine-Gagnard.

Gaillac SW France r p w dr sw sp ★→★★ mostly DYA Ancient area coming to life. Reds in three styles: DYA Classique, selected-grape/short aged and new-oak-aged. Slightly fizzy perlé is value. Méthode Gaillacoise trad sparkling. Ch Larroze is the best known; other good growers Dom des Hourtets, Dom de Labarthe, Dom de Perches, Mas d'Aurel and Robert Plageoles. Important coops: Labastide de Lévis (with fruity wines from local Mauzac grapes incl top Gaberlé perlé), La Cave Técou (quality, esp successful wood-aged 'Passion').

Gamay See Grapes for red wine (pages 11–13).

Gard, Vin de Pays du The Gard département at the mouth of the Rhône is a centre of good VINS DE PAYS; incl Coteaux Flaviens, Pont du Gard, SABLES DU GOLFE DU LION, Salaves, Uzège and Vaunage. Watch this area.

Geisweiler et Fils Big Burgundy merchant and grower. Now owned by the Rehs of the Mosel. Cellars and 50 acres at NUITS-ST-GEORGES, also 150 acres at Bevy in HAUTES-COTES DE NUITS and 30 in the COTE CHALONNAISE.

Gevrey-Chambertin Burg r ★★★ 78 85' 87 88 89' 90' 91 92 93 94 95 The village containing the great CHAMBERTIN and its GRAND CRU cousins and many other noble v'yds (eg PREMIERS CRUS Cazetiers, Combe aux Moines, CLOS ST-JACQUES, Clos des Varoilles), as well as much more commonplace land. Growers incl Boillot, Damoy, DROUHIN, Dugat, Esmonin, FAIVELEY, Dom Harmand-Geoffroy, JADOT, LECLERC, LEROY, MORTET, ROTY, Roumier, ROUSSEAU, Serafin, TRAPET, VAROILLES.

Gewurztraminer Speciality grape of ALSACE: one of 4 allowed for specified GRAND CRU wines. Perfumed like old roses, often tasting like grapefruit.

Gigondas S Rh r p ★★→★★★ 78 79 81' 83 85 86 88 89' 90' 93 94 95' Worthy neighbour to CHATEAUNEUF-DU-PAPE. Strong, full-bodied, sometimes peppery wine, largely Grenache; eg Dom du Cayron, Les Goubert, Gour de Chaule, Dom les Pallières, Les Pallieroudas, Dom du Pesquier, Dom Raspail-Aÿ, Dom Sta-Duc, Dom St-Gayan, Dom des Travers, Ch du Trignon.

Ginestet Long-established B'x négociant now owned by Jacques Merlaut, said to be second in turnover. Merlaut's empire incl ch'x CHASSE-SPLEEN, HAUT-BAGES-LIBERAL, LA GURGUE, FERRIERE.

Gisselbrecht, Louis High quality ALSACE shippers at Dambach-la-Ville. Ries and GEWURZ best. Cousin Willy Gisselbrecht's wines are v competitive.

Givry Burg r w ★★ 85' 88' 89' 90' 91 92 93 94 95 Underrated COTE CHALONNAISE village: light but tasty and typical burgundy from eg DELORME, Dom Joblot, L Latour, T Lespinasse, Clos Salomon, BARON THENARD.

Gosset Brut NV; Brut 81 82 83 85 86 88 90; Grande Réserve; Grand Millésime Brut 79 82 83 85; Grand Rosé 85 88 Small, v old CHAMPAGNE house at AY. Excellent full-bodied wine (esp Grand Millésime). Linked with PHILIPPONNAT. Gosset Celebris is prestige CUVEE, launched '95.

Goulaine, Château de The ceremonial showplace of MUSCADET; a noble family estate and its appropriate wine.

Goulet, George NV; Rosé NV High quality Reims CHAMPAGNE house. Luxury brand: Cuvée du Centenaire (79 82 83 85) now replaced by Cuvée Veuve Goulet (90).

Goût Taste, eg goût anglais: as the English like it (ie, dry, or, differently for CHAMPAGNE, well-aged).

Grand Cru One of top Burgundy vineyards with its own APPELLATION CONTROLEE. Similar meaning in recent ALSACE law, but more vague elsewhere. In ST-EMILION the third rank of ch'x incl about 200 properties.

Grande Champagne The AC of the best area of COGNAC.

Grande Rue, La Burg r ★★★ 89' 90' 91 92 93 94 Recently promoted GRAND CRU in VOSNE-ROMANEE, neighbour to ROMANEE-CONTI. Owned by Dom Lamarche (itself recently sold).

Grands-Echézeaux Burg r ★★★★ 78' 82 85' 87 88' 89' 90' 91' 92 93 94 95 Superlative 22-acre GRAND CRU next to CLOS DE VOUGEOT. Wines not weighty but aromatic. Viz: DROUHIN, ENGEL, MONGEARD-MUGNERET, DOM DE LA ROMANEE-CONTI.

Gratien, Alfred and Gratien & Meyer Brut NV; Cuvée Paradis Brut; Cuvée Paradis Rosé; Brut 79 82 83 85' Excellent smaller family CHAMPAGNE house with top traditional standards. Fine v dry long-lasting wine is made in barrels. Gratien & Meyer is counterpart at SAUMUR. (Vg Cuvée Flamme.)

Graves B'x r w ★★→★★★★ Region S of B'x city with excellent soft earthy reds, dry whites (Sauv-Sém) reasserting star status. PESSAC-LEOGNAN is inner zone.

Graves de Vayres B'x r w ★ DYA Part of ENTRE-D-M; no special character.

Griotte-Chambertin Burg r ★★★★ 78' 85' 87 88' 89' 90' 91 92 93 94 95 14-acre GRAND CRU adjoining CHAMBERTIN. Similar wine, but less masculine, more 'tender'. Growers incl DROUHIN, PONSOT.

NB Vintages in colour are those you should choose first for drinking in 1997.

Grivot, Jean 25-acre COTE DE NUITS domaine, in 5 ACs incl RICHEBOURG, NUITS PREMIERS CRUS, VOSNE-ROMANEE, CLOS DE VOUGEOT etc. Top quality.

Gros, Domaines An excellent family of vignerons in VOSNE-ROMANEE comprising (at least) Domaines Jean, Michel, Anne et François, Anne-François Gros and Gros Frère et Soeur.

Gros Plant du Pays Nantais Lo w ★ DYA Junior VDQS cousin of MUSCADET, sharper, lighter; from the COGNAC grape, aka Folle Blanche, Ugni Bl etc.

Guffens-Heynen Belgian POUILLY-FUISSE grower. Minute quantity, fine quality. Also heady Gamay and COTE D'OR wine from bought-in grapes under the Verget label. To follow.

Guigal, Ets E Celebrated growers and merchants of CONDRIEU, COTE ROTIE and HERMITAGE. Since '85 owners of VIDAL-FLEURY. By ageing single-vineyard Côte Rôtie (La Landonne, La Mouline and La Turque) for over 3 years in new oak Guigal breaks local tradition to please (esp) American palates. His standard wines are good value, especially the red COTES DU RHONE. Special CONDRIEU CUVEE La Doriane (since '95).

Guyon, Antonin Considerable domaine at ALOXE-CORTON with adequate wines from CHAMBOLLE-MUSIGNY, CORTON etc, and HAUTES-COTES DE NUITS.

Haut Poitou Lo w r ★→★★ DYA Up-and-coming VDQS S of ANJOU. Vg whites (CHARD, SAUV) from coop, now linked with DUBOEUF. Improving reds from Gamay and Cab, best will age 4–5 yrs. Has rejected restrictions of AC status for freedom of choice.

Haut-Benauge B'x w ★ DYA AC for a limited area in ENTRE-DEUX-MERS.

Haut-Médoc B'x r ★★→★★★ 70 75 78 81' 82' 83' 85' 86' 87 88' 89' 90' 92 93 94 95 Big AC including all the best parts of the MEDOC. Most of the zone has communal ACs (eg MARGAUX, PAUILLAC). Some excellent châteaux (eg LA LAGUNE) are simply AC HAUT-MEDOC.

Haut-Montravel Dordogne w sw ★ 90' 93 95 Rare BERGERAC sweet white; rather like MONBAZILLAC.

Hautes-Côtes de Beaune Burg r w ★★ 85 88 89' 90' 91 92 93 94 95 AC for a dozen villages in the hills behind the COTE DE BEAUNE. Light wines, worth investigating. Top growers: Cornu, Mazilly.

Hautes-Côtes de Nuits Burg r w ★★ 85 88 89' 90' 91 92 93 94 95 As above, for COTE DE NUITS. An area on the way up. Top growers: C Cornu, Jayer-Gilles, M GROS. Also has large BEAUNE coop; good esp from GEISWEILER.

Heidsieck, Charles Brut Réserve NV; Brut 79 81 83 85 89; Rosé 81 83 85 Major Reims CHAMPAGNE house, now controlled by Rémy Martin; also incl Trouillard, de Venoge. Luxury brands: Cuvée Champagne Charlie (81 82 83, then withdrawn), Bl des Millénaires (83 85). Fine quality recently; NV a real bargain. See also Piper-Heidsieck.

Heidsieck, Monopole Brut NV Important CHAMPAGNE merchant and Reims grower now owned by Seagram and wines made by MUMM. Luxury brands of note: Diamant Bleu (76 79 82 85 89), Diamant Rosé (82 85 88).

Hengst Wintzenheim (ALSACE) GRAND CRU. Excels with top-notch GEWURZ from Albert Mann; also Pinot Auxerrois, Chasselas (esp JOSMEYER'S) and Pinot Noir (esp A Mann's) with no GC status.

Henriot Brut Souverain NV; Blanc de Blancs de Chard NV; Brut 79 82 85 88 89; Brut Rosé 81 83 85 88; Cuvée des Enchanteleurs 85 Old family CHAMPAGNE house; regained independence in '94. V fine fresh creamy style. Luxury CUVEES (eg Baron Philippe de Rothschild) withdrawn. Also owns BOUCHARD PERE (since '95).

Hérault Midi Biggest vineyard département in France with 980,000 acres of vines. Chiefly VIN DE TABLE but some good AC COTEAUX DU LANGUEDOC and pioneering Vins de Pays de l'Hérault.

FRANCE

Hermitage N Rh r w ★★★ →★★★★★ 61 66 70 72 78' 79 80 82 83' 84 85 86 87 88 89 90' 91' 94 95 By tradition, the 'manliest' wine of France: dark powerful and profound. Truest example of the Syrah grape from 312 hillside acres on E bank of Rhône, largely granite. Needs long ageing. White is heady and golden; now usually made for early drinking, though best wines mature for up to 25 yrs; can be better than red (eg 93). Top makers: CHAPOUTIER, CHAVE, DELAS, Faurie, Grippat, GUIGAL, JABOULET, Sorrel. TAIN COOP also useful.

Hospices de Beaune Historic hospital in BEAUNE, with excellent v'yds (known by 'CUVÉE' names) in BEAUNE, CORTON, MEURSAULT, POMMARD, VOLNAY. Wines are auctioned on the third Sunday of each November.

Huet 47' 59' 76' 85' 88' 89' 90' 93 95 Leading top quality estate in VOUVRAY, now run on biodynamic principles; often austere wines needing long ageing.

Hugel et Fils The best-known ALSACE growers and merchants; founded at Riquewihr in 1639 and still in the family. 'Johnny' H (ret'd '94) is the region's beloved spokesman. Quality escalates with Cuvée Tradition and then Jubilée Réserve ranges. SELECTIONS DES GRAINS NOBLES: Hugel pioneered this style in Alsace. Many are sweet, but not all.

Hureau, Ch de Dynamic SAUMUR estate making quality SAUMUR-CHAMPIGNY, Saumur Blanc, Coteaux de Saumur.

Ile de Beauté Name given to VINS DU PAYS from CORSICA. Mostly red.

Impériale BORDEAUX bottle holding 8.5 normal bottles (6.4 litres).

Irancy ('Bourgogne Irancy') Burg r (p) ★★ 85 88 89 90 91 92 93 94 95 Good light red made nr CHABLIS from Pinot N and the best vintages are long-lived and mature well. To watch. Growers incl Colinot.

Irouléguy SW France r p (w) ★★ DYA Agreeable local wines of the Basque country. Mainly rosé; also dark dense Tannat/Cab reds to keep 5 yrs+. Good from domaines Ilarria, Brana and coop. A future MADIRAN?

Jaboulet-Aîné, Paul Old family firm at Tain, leading growers of HERMITAGE (esp La Chapelle ★★★★), Crozes Thalabert (vg value) and merchants of other Rhône wines – esp CORNAS, COTES DU RHONE Parallèle 45.

Jacquart Brut NV, Brut Rosé NV (Carte Blanche and Cuvée Spéciale); Brut 85 87 89 90 Relatively new ('62) coop-based CHAMPAGNE marque; in quantity the sixth largest. Fair quality. Luxury brands: Cuvée Nominée Blanc 85 86, CN Rosé 85 86. Vg Mosaïque Bl de Blancs 86 90, Mosaïque Rosé 86 90.

Jacquesson Small quality Epernay CHAMP house. Several good luxury CUVÉES.

Jadot, Louis Much-respected top quality Burgundy merchant house with v'yds (150 acres) in BEAUNE, CORTON etc. Incl former Clair-Dau. Wines to bank on.

Jaffelin Independent quality négociant, bought in '92 from DROUHIN by BOISSET.

Jardin de la France Lo w r p DYA One of France's four regional VINS DE PAYS. Covers Loire Valley: mostly single grape (esp Chard, Gamay, Sauv). Top vin de pays de zone: Marches de Bretagne.

Jasnières Lo w dr (sw) ★★★ 76 78 79 83 85 86 88' 89' 90' 92 93' 95' Rare and almost immortal dry VOUVRAY-like wine (Chenin) of N TOURAINE. Esp Aubert de Rycke, Boulay, Gigou.

Jayer, Henri See Rouget, Emmanuel.

Jeroboam In BORDEAUX a 6-bottle bottle (holding 4.5 litres) or triple magnum; in CHAMPAGNE a double magnum.

Joseph Perrier Cuvée Royale Brut NV; Cuvée Royale Bl de Blancs NV; Cuvée Royale Rosé NV; Brut 76 79 82 83 85 89 Family-run CHAMPAGNE house with considerable v'yds at Châlons-sur-Marne. Light fruity style, best in prestige Cuvée Joséphine 82 85.

JosMeyer Family house at Wintzenheim, ALSACE. Vg long-ageing wines, esp GEWURZ and Pinot Bl. Fine Ries from Hengst GRAND CRU. Wide range of grape varieties, labels and locations.

Juliénas Beauj r ★★★ 91 92 93 94 95 Leading CRU of BEAUJOLAIS: vigorous fruity wine to keep 2–3 yrs. Growers incl ch'x du Bois de la Salle, des Capitans, de Juliénas, des Vignes; Dom Bottière, Dom R Monnet, coop.

Jura See Côtes de Jura.

Jurançon SW France w sw dr ★★ →★★★ 78 82 83 85' 86 88' 89' 90' 91 93 94 95 Rare high-flavoured long-lived speciality of Pau in Pyrenean foothills, at best like wildflower SAUTERNES. Not to be missed. Both sweet and dry should age. Top growers: Dom du Bellegarde, Barrère, Dom Cauhapé, Gaillot, Guirouilh, Lamouroux, Lapeyre, Larredya, de Rousse, Jean Schaetzel. Also coop's dry Grain Sauvage, Brut d'Ocean and Peyre d'Or.

A warning to visitors to France

France's retail wine trade is one of the worst in Europe. Do not expect to find either good quality or value. Anyone shopping for wine even close to famous vineyards will find high prices and generally poor to awful quality. Most supermarkets buy purely on name and price and épiceries (sometimes the only local wine retailers) only on price. The destiny of fine wines is principally the restaurant trade (where they are outrageously marked-up).

The French buy largely direct from producers. Very many have a cousin whose wine, rightly or wrongly, they believe in. No country has a wine trade more on the ball than Great Britain.

Kaefferkopf Alsace w dr sw ★★★ Ammerschwihr v'yd famous for blends rather than single-grape wines; growers are not happy with restrictions of GRAND CRU status but wines are equivalent or more.

Kientzheim-Kaysersberg Important ALSACE coop for quality as well as style. Esp for GEWURZ, Ries (Schlossburg GRAND CRU) and Crémant d'Alsace.

Kientzler, André Fine ALSACE Riesling specialist in Geisburg GRAND CRU, esp the VENDANGE TARDIVE and SELECTION DES GRAINS NOBLES. Equally good from GCs Kirchberg de Ribeauvillé for GEWURZ and Osterberg for occasional 'vins de glaces' (Eisweins).

Kreydenweiss Fine ALSACE grower with 24 acres at Andlau, esp for Pinot Gr (vg from Moenchberg GRAND CRU), Pinot Bl and Ries. Top wine: Kastelberg (Ries ages 20 yrs+); also fine Auxerrois 'Kritt Klevner' and good VENDANGE TARDIVE. One of first in Alsace to use new oak. Good Ries-Pinot Gr blend 'Clos du Val d'Eléon'.

Kriter Popular sparkler processed in Burgundy by PATRIARCHE.

Krug Grande Cuvée; Vintage 79 81 82 85; Rosé; Clos du Mesnil (Bl de Blancs) 79 80 81 82 83 85; Krug Collection 62 64 66 69 71 73 76 Small but supremely prestigious CHAMPAGNE house. Dense full-bodied v dry wines, superlative quality. Owned by Rémy-Cointreau (but no one would know).

Kuentz-Bas Top-quality ALSACE grower/merchant at Husseren-les-Châteaux, esp for Pinot Gr (Tokay d'Alsace), GEWURZ. Also good VENDANGES TARDIVES.

Labouré-Roi Outstandingly reliable merchant at NUITS. Mostly whites. Many domaine wines, esp René Manuel's MEURSAULT, Chantal Lescure's Nuits, CLOS DE VOUGEOT. Vg CHABLIS. Also VOLNAY-SANTENOTS.

Ladoix-Serrigny Burg r (w) ★★ Northernmost village of COTE DE BEAUNE below hills of CORTON. To watch for bargains.

Ladoucette, de Leading producer of POUILLY-FUME, based at CH DE NOZET. Luxury brand: Baron de L. Also SANCERRE Comte Lafond and La Poussie (and PIC CHABLIS).

Lafarge, Michel 23-acre COTE DE BEAUNE estate with VOLNAYS.

Lafon, Domaine des Comtes 32-acre top-quality Burgundy estate in MEURSAULT, LE MONTRACHET, VOLNAY. Glorious intense white wines; extraordinary dark reds.

Laguiche, Marquis de Largest owner of LE MONTRACHET. Magnificent wines made by DROUHIN.

Lalande de Pomerol B'x r ★★ 82 83 85 86' 88' 89' 90' 92 93 94 95 Neighbour to POMEROL. Wines similar, but less mellow. Top ch'x: Les Annereaux, DE BELAIR, Belles-Graves, Bertineau-St-Vincent, La Croix Bellevue, La Croix-St-André, Hauts-Conseillants, Hauts-Tuileries, Moncets, SIAURAC, TOURNEFEUILLE. To try.

Langlois-Chateau The top SAUMUR sp house (esp CREMANT) controlled by BOLLINGER. Also range of Loire still wines, esp Saumur Bl VIEILLES VIGNES.

Lanson Père & Fils Black Label NV; Rosé NV; Brut 88 89 90 Imp't second-rank CHAMPAGNE house with cellars at Reims. Luxury brand: Noble Cuvée (81 85 88). Black Label is reliable fresh (s'times thin) NV. New CUVEE: Bl de Bls 83 89.

Laroche Important grower (238 acres) and dynamic CHABLIS merchant, incl Domaines La Jouchère and Laroche. Top wines: Blanchots and Clos Vieilles Vignes. Also blends good non-regional CHARD and now ambitious MIDI range.

Latour, Louis Famous Burgundy merchant and grower with v'yds (120 acres) in BEAUNE, CORTON, etc. Among the v best for white: CHEVALIER-MONTRACHET Les Demoiselles, CORTON-CHARLEMAGNE, MONTRACHET, good value MONTAGNY and ARDECHE CHARD etc. Developing Pinot N in the Var.

Latour de France r (w) ★→★★ 88 89 90 91 92 93 94 95 New AC in COTES DE ROUSSILLON-VILLAGES.

Latricières-Chambertin Burg r ★★★ 78' 83 85' 88' 89' 90' 91 92 93 94 95 17-acre GRAND CRU neighbour of CHAMBERTIN. Similar wine but lighter and 'prettier' eg from FAIVELEY, LEROY, PONSOT, TRAPET.

Laudun S Rh w (r p) ★ Village of COTES DU RHONE-VILLAGES (west bank). Attractive wines from the coop incl fresh whites. Dom Pelaquié is best, esp white.

Laugel, Michel One of the biggest ALSACE merchant houses at Marlenheim: esp good Cuvée Jubilaire range and CREMANT.

Laurent-Perrier Brut NV; Rosé NV; Brut 78 79 81 82 85 88 89 90 Dynamic highly successful family-owned CHAMPAGNE house at Tours-sur-Marne. Excellent luxury brands: Cuvée Grande Siècle (NV and 85 88), CGS Alexandra Brut Rosé (85 88). Ultra Brut is bone dry. Owns SALON, DELAMOTTE, DE CASTELLANE.

Leflaive, Domaine Sometimes considered the best of all the white burgundy growers, at PULIGNY-MONTRACHET. Best vineyards: Bienvenues- and Chevalier-Montrachet, Clavoillons, Pucelles and (since 91) Le Montrachet. Increasingly organic methods; ever-finer wines.

Leflaive, Olivier Négociant at PULIGNY-MONTRACHET since '84, nephew of the above, now with 22 acres of his own. Reliable whites and reds, incl less famous ACs, have upgraded seriously since '90. Now ★★★.

Léognan B'x r w ★★★→★★★★ Top village of GRAVES with its own AC: PESSAC-LEOGNAN. Best ch'x: DOM DE CHEVALIER, HAUT-BAILLY, MALARTIC-LAGRAVIERE.

Leroy The ultimate NEGOCIANT-ELEVEUR at AUXEY-DURESSES with a growing domaine and the finest stocks of old wines in Burgundy. Part-owners of DOM DE LA ROMANEE-CONTI. In '88 bought the 35-acre Noëllat estate in CLOS VOUGEOT, NUITS, ROMANEE-ST-VIVANT, SAVIGNY etc. Leroy's whole range (from AUXEY whites to CHAMBERTIN and neighbours) is simply magnificent. ★★★★ all round.

Lesquerde ★★ 90 91 92 93 94 95 New superior AC Village of COTES DU ROUSSILLON-VILLAGES.

Lichine, Alexis & Cie BORDEAUX merchants (once of the late Alexis Lichine). No connection with CH PRIEURE LICHINE.

Lie, sur On the lees. MUSCADET is often bottled straight from the vat, without racking or filtering, for maximum freshness and character.

Limoux Pyr r w ★★ Burgeoning AC, formerly for BLANQUETTE DE LIMOUX sparkling, now good for CHARD and Pinot N as well as traditional grapes. Also a good claret-like red from the coop: Anne des Joyeuses.

Liquoreux Term for a very sweet wine: eg SAUTERNES, top VOUVRAY, JURANCON etc.

Lirac S Rh r p (w) ★★ 89' 90' 91 93 94 95 Next to TAVEL. Approachable soft red (best needs 5 yrs age). Red is overtaking rosé, esp doms Maby (Fermade), André Méjan, de la Mordorée, Sabon, St-Roch, Ch de Ségriès. Gd whites too.

Listel Midi r p w ★→★★ DYA Vast (4,000-acre+) historic estate on sandy beaches of the Golfe du Lion. Owned by giant Salins du Midi salt co and VAL D'ORBIEU group. Pleasant light 'vins des sables' incl sparkling. Dom du Bosquet-Canet is a fruity Cab, Dom de Villeroy fresh BLANC DE BLANCS SUR LIE, and CHARD since '89. Also fruity almost non-alcoholic PETILLANT, Ch de Malijay COTES DU RHONE, Abbaye de Ste-Hilaire COTEAUX VAROIS, Ch La Gordonne COTES DE PROVENCE.

Listrac-Médoc B'x r ★★→★★★ Village of HAUT-MEDOC next to MOULIS. Best ch'x: CLARKE, FONREAUD, FOURCAS-DUPRE, FOURCAS-HOSTEN.

Livinière, La Midi r (p w) ★→★★ High quality MINERVOIS CRU. Best growers: Abbaye de Tholomies, Combe Blanche, Ch de Gourgazaud, Laville Bertrou, Dom Maris, Dom Ste Eulalie, Dom Vallière, Coop La Livinière.

Long-Depaquit Vg CHABLIS domaine (esp MOUTONNE), owned by BICHOT.

Lorentz Two small quality ALSACE houses at Bergheim: Gustave L and Jerome L, have same management. Esp GEWURZ and Ries from Altenberg de Bergheim and Kanzlerberg.

Loron & Fils Big-scale grower and merchant at Pontanevaux; specialist in BEAUJOLAIS and sound VINS DE TABLE.

Loupiac B'x w sw ★★ 76 79' 83 85 86' 88' 89 90 91 93 95 Across the River Garonne from SAUTERNES. Top châteaux: Clos-Jean, Haut-Loupiac, LOUPIAC-GAUDIET, RICAUD, Rondillon.

Lugny See Mâcon-Lugny.

Lussac-St-Emilion B'x r ★★ 82 85 86' 88' 89' 90' 92 93 94 95 NE neighbour to ST-EMILION. Top ch'x incl Barbe Blanche, Bel Air, DU LYONNAT, Tour de Grenat, Villadière. Coop (at PUISSEGUIN) makes pleasant Roc de Lussac.

Macération carbonique Traditional technique of fermentation with whole bunches of unbroken grapes in a closed vat. Fermentation inside each grape eventually bursts it, giving vivid fruity mild wine, not for ageing. Esp in BEAUJOLAIS; now much used in the MIDI and elsewhere.

The Mâconnais
The hilly zone just north of Beaujolais has outcrops of limestone where Chardonnay gives full, if not fine, wines. The village of Chardonnay here may (or may not) be the home of the variety. Granite soils give strong Gamay reds. The top Mâconnais AC is Pouilly-Fuissé, then St-Véran, then Mâcon-Villages with a village name. The potential is here to produce lower priced, richly typical Chardonnays to out-do the New World (and indeed the south of France). Currently most wines are less than extraordinary.

Mâcon Burg r w (p) ★★ 90' 91 92 93 94 95 Sound, usually unremarkable reds (Gamay best), tasty dry (CHARD) whites. Almost DYA.

Mâcon-Lugny Burg r w sp ★★ 90 91 92 93 95 Village next to VIRE with huge and vg coop (4M bottles). Les Genevrières is sold by LOUIS LATOUR.

Mâcon-Villages Burg w ★★→★★★ 90 91 92 93 94 95 Increasingly well-made typical white burgundies (when not over-produced). Named for their villages, eg M-CHARDONNAY, -Clessé, -Lugny, -Prissé, -Viré, -Uchizy. Best coop is probably Prissé, biggest Lugny. Top growers: Thevenet (Clessé) Bonhomme (Viré), Merlin (La Roche Vineuse).

Mâcon-Viré Burg w ★★ 90 91 92 93 94 95 One of the best white wine villages of MACON. Esp A Bonhomme, Clos du Chapitre, JADOT, Ch de Viré, coop.

Macvin Jura w sw ★★ AC for 'traditional' MARC and grape juice aperitif.

Madiran SW France r ★★★ 82 85' 86' 88 89' 90' 92 93 94 95 Dark vigorous red from ARMAGNAC, like hard but fruity MEDOC with a fluid elegance of its own. Ages 5–10 yrs, but 'barriques' are changing it, not necessarily for the better: now light and heavy schools. Top growers: ch'x d'Arricau-Bordes, d'Aydié, Barréjat, Bouscassé, Dom Capmartin, Laplace (esp Ch d'Aydie), Montus, Peyros. White is AC PACHERENC DU VIC BILH.

Magenta, Duc de Recently revamped Burgundy estate (30 acres) based at CHASSAGNE-MONTRACHET, managed by JADOT.

Magnum A double bottle (1.5 litres).

Mähler-Besse First-class Dutch négociants in B'X, with a share in CH PALMER and owners of Ch Michel de Montaigne. Brands incl Cheval Noir. (Total of 250 acres in all.)

Mailly-Champagne Top CHAMPAGNE coop. Luxury wine: Cuvée des Echansons.

Maire, Henri The biggest grower/merchant of JURA wines, with half of the entire AC. Some top wines, many cheerfully commercial. To visit.

Maranges Burg r ★★ New ('89) AC for 600-odd acres of S COTE DE BEAUNE, beyond SANTENAY: one-third PREMIER CRU. Top/first négociant: JAFFELIN.

Marc Grape skins after pressing; also the strong-smelling brandy made from them (see Italian 'Grappa').

Marcillac SW France r p ★→★★ DYA Promoted to AC in '90. Violet-hued with grassy red-fruit character. Good from coop Cave de Valady (rustic), Dom du Cros and J-M Revel.

Margaux B'x r ★★→★★★★ 70 78 79 81 82' 83' 85 86' 87 88' 89 90' 92 93 94 95 Village of HAUT-MEDOC. Some of most 'elegant' red BORDEAUX. AC incl CANTENAC and several other villages. Top ch'x incl MARGAUX, RAUSAN-SEGLA, LASCOMBES etc.

Marionnet, Henry Leading TOURAINE property specializing in Gamay and Sauv (Cuvée M in best yrs). Now making wine in Chile: Terra Noble.

Marne et Champagne, Ste Recent but huge-scale CHAMPAGNE house, owner (since '91) of LANSON and many smaller brands, incl BESSERAT DE BELLEFON.

Marque déposée Trademark.

Marsannay Burg p w (r) ★★★ 85 88' 89' 90' 91 92 93 95 (rosé DYA) Village with fine light red and delicate Pinot N rosé. Incl villages of Chenôve, Couchey. Growers: Charlopin, CLAIR, Dijon University, JADOT, ROTY, TRAPET.

Mas de Daumas Gassac Midi r w p ★★★ 82 83 85 86 87 88 89 90 91 92 93 94' 95 The one 'first-growth' estate of the LANGUEDOC, producing potent largely Cab on apparently unique soil. Sensational quality. Also Rosé Frisant and a sumptuous white of blended CHARD, Viognier, Petit Manseng etc to drink at 2–3 yrs. Now also a vg quick-drinking red, Les Terrasses de Guilhem, from a nearby coop and trad Languedoc varietals (Clairette, Cinsaut, Aramon etc) from v old vines under Terrasses de Landoc label. VIN DE PAYS status.

Maury Pyr r sw ★★ NV Red VIN DOUX NATUREL of Grenache from ROUSSILLON. Taste the terroir. Much recent improvement.

Mazis (or Mazy) Chambertin Burg r ★★★ 78' 83 85' 87 88 89' 90' 91 92 93 94 95 30-acre GRAND CRU neighbour of CHAMBERTIN, s'times equally potent. Best from FAIVELEY, HOSPICES DE BEAUNE, LEROY, Maume, ROTY.

Mazoyères-Chambertin See Charmes-Chambertin.

Médoc B'x r ★★ 82' 83 85 86' 88' 89' 90' 92 93 94 95 AC for reds of the less good (northern) part of BORDEAUX's biggest and best district. Flavours tend to earthiness. HAUT-MEDOC is much better. Top châteaux include LA CARDONNE, GREYSAC, LOUDENNE, LES ORMES-SORBET, POTENSAC, LA TOUR-DE-BY.

Meffre, Gabriel The biggest S Rhône estate, based at GIGONDAS. Variable quality. Often in French supermarkets. Also bottles and sells for small CHATEAUNEUF-DU-PAPE domaines, eg Guy Jullian, Dom de Baban.

Mellot, Alphonse Leading SANCERRE grower and merchant. Especially for La Moussière and wood-aged Cuvée Edmond; also MENETOU-SALON.

Menetou-Salon Lo r p w ★★ DYA Attractive similar wines from W of SANCERRE: Sauv Bl white, Pinot N red. Top growers: Clément, Henri Pellé, Jean-Max Roger.

Méo-Camuzet V fine domaine in CLOS DE VOUGEOT, NUITS, RICHEBOURG, VOSNE-ROMANEE. HENRI JAYER inspires winemaking. Esp: V-R Cros Parantoux.

Mercier & Cie, Champagne Brut NV; Brut Rosé NV; Brut 81 82 83 85 86 88 90 One of the biggest CHAMPAGNE houses at Epernay. Controlled by MOET & CHANDON. Good commercial quality, sold mainly in France. Bulle d'Or and Reserve de l'Empereur CUVEES no longer produced.

Mercurey Burg r w ★★ →★★★ 85 88' 89' 90' 91 92 93 94 95 Leading red wine village of COTE CHALONNAISE. Good middle-rank burgundy incl more and improving whites. Growers incl Ch de Chamirey, Chanzy, FAIVELEY, M Juillot, Dom de Suremain.

Mercurey, Région de The up-to-date name for the COTE CHALONNAISE.

Métaireau, Louis The ringleader of a group of top MUSCADET growers. Expensive well-finished wines.

Méthode champenoise The traditional laborious method of putting bubbles into CHAMPAGNE by refermenting the wine in its bottle. Must be referred to as 'classic method' or 'méthode traditionelle' when used outside the region. Not mentioned on champagne labels.

Méthode traditionelle See entry above.

Meursault Burg w (r) ★★★ →★★★★ 78' 83 85 86 88 89' 90' 91 92 93 94 95 COTE DE BEAUNE village with some of the world's greatest whites: savoury, dry but nutty and mellow. Best v'yds: Charmes, Genevrières, Perrières; also: Goutte d'Or, Meursault-Blagny, Poruzots, Narvaux, Tillets. Producers incl AMPEAU, J-M Boillot, M Bouzereau, Boyer-Martenot, CH DE MEURSAULT, COCHE-DURY, Fichet, Grivault, P Javillier, Jobard, LAFON, LATOUR, O Leflaive, LEROY, Manuel, Matrot, Michelot-Buisson, P MOREY, G ROULOT, Tesson. See also Blagny.

Meursault-Blagny See Blagny.

Meyer-Fonné ALSACE grower with fine GEWURZ GRAND CRU SCHLOSSBURG, RIES KAEFFERKOPF and easy tasty Pinots Blanc and Gris.

Michel, Louis CHABLIS domaine with model, unoaked, v long-lived wines, incl superb LES CLOS, vg Montmains, MONTEE DE TONNERRE.

Midi General term for the south of France west of the Rhône delta. Improving reputation, brilliant promise. Many top wines based on grape variety rather than APPELLATION. A melting-pot.

Minervois Midi r (p w) br sw ★ →★★ 85 86 88 89 90 91 92 93 94 95 Hilly AC region for good MIDI wines: lively, full of flavour, esp from Ch du Donjon, Fabas, Dom Laurent Fabre, LA LIVINIERE, de Peyriac, Coop Pouzols, La Tour Boisée, de Violet. See also St-Jean de Minervois.

Mis en bouteille au château/domaine Bottled at the château, property or estate. NB dans nos caves (in our cellars) or dans la région de production (in the area of production) are often used but mean little.

Moelleux 'With marrow': creamy sweet. Used of the sw wines of VOUVRAY etc.

Moët & Chandon Brut NV; Rosé 81 82 85 86 88 90 92; Brut Imperial 76 78 81 82 83 85 86 88 90 92 Much the biggest CHAMPAGNE merchant and grower, with cellars in Epernay, and branches in Argentina, Australia, Brazil, California, Germany and Spain. Consistent quality, esp in Vintage wines. Coteaux Champenois 'Saran' is still wine. Prestige CUVEE: DOM PERIGNON. Links with CLICQUOT, MERCIER, POMMERY, RUINART etc and Cognac Hennessy.

Moillard Big family firm (Domaine Thomas-Moillard) of growers and merchants in NUITS-ST-GEORGES, making full range incl dark and v tasty wines, eg CLOS DU ROI, CLOS DE VOUGEOT, CORTON etc.

Mommessin, J Major BEAUJOLAIS merchant, merged with THORIN. Owner of CLOS DE TART. White wines less successful than red.

Monbazillac Dordogne w sw ★★ 75 76 79 83' 85 86' 88' 89' 90' 92 93 95 Golden SAUTERNES-style wine from BERGERAC, gradually gaining typicité. Can age well. Ch Monbazillac and Ch Septy are best known; also good are La Borderie, Haut-Brie, La Fage. The peripatetic British winemaker Hugh Ryman operates at the Cave Coop de Monbazillac.

Mondeuse Savoie r ★★ DYA Red grape of SAVOIE. Good vigorous deep-coloured wine. Perhaps the same as NE Italy's Refosco.

Mongeard-Mugneret 50+ acre VOSNE-ROMANEE estate. Very fine ECHEZEAUX, RICHEBOURG, SAVIGNY, VOSNE PREMIER CRU, VOUGEOT etc.

Monopole V'yd under single ownership.

Mont-Redon, Ch de S Rh r (w) ★★★ 78' 81' 85 86 88 89 90 93' 94 95 Outstanding 235-acre CHATEAUNEUF-DU-PAPE estate. Fine complex reds and vg aromatic but substantial (94') whites.

Montagne-St-Emilion B'x r ★★ 82' 83 85 86' 88' 89' 90' 93 94 95 NE neighbour and largest 'satellite' of ST-EMILION: similar wines and AC regulations; becoming more important each year. Top ch'x: Calon, Faizeau, Haut-Gillet, Roudier, St-André-Corbin, Teyssier, DES TOURS, VIEUX-CH-ST-ANDRE.

Montagny Burg w (r) ★★ 89' 90 92 93 94 95 COTE CHALONNAISE village. Between MACON and MEURSAULT, both geographically and gastronomically. Top producers: Cave Coop de Buxy, LOUIS LATOUR, Michel, Ch de la Saule.

Montée de Tonnerre Burg w ★★★ 86 88 89 90 91 92 93 94 95 Famous excellent CHABLIS PREMIER CRU. Esp from Duplessis, L Michel, Raveneau, Robin.

Monthelie Burg r (w) ★★→★★★ 85 88' 89' 90' 91 92 93 94 95 Little-known VOLNAY neighbour, s'times almost equal. Excellent fragrant reds. Esp BOUCHARD PERE, COCHE-DURY, COMTE LAFON, DROUHIN, Garaudet, Ch de Monthelie (Suremain).

Montlouis Lo w dr sw (sp) ★★→★★★ 75 76 78 82 83' 85' 86 88' 89 90' 91 92 93' 95' Neighbour of VOUVRAY. Similar sweet or dry long-lived wine. Top growers: Berger, Deletang, Levasseur, Taille aux Loups.

Montrachet Burg w ★★★★ 71 78 79 82 83 85' 86' 88 89' 90 91 92 93 94 95 (Both 't's in the name are silent.) 19-acre GRAND CRU v'yd in both PULIGNY- and CHASSAGNE-MONTRACHET. Potentially the greatest white burgundy: strong, perfumed, intense, dry yet luscious. Top wines from LAFON, LAGUICHE (DROUHIN), LEFLAIVE, RAMONET, DOM DE LA ROMANEE-CONTI, THENARD.

Montravel See Côtes de Montravel.

Moreau & Fils CHABLIS merchant and grower with 187 acres. Also major table wine producer. Best wine: Clos des Hospices (GRAND CRU).

Morey, Domaines 50 acres in CHASSAGNE-MONTRACHET. Vg wines made by family members, esp Bernard, incl BATARD-MONTRACHET.

Morey-St-Denis Burg r ★★★ 78 85' 87 88 89' 90' 91 92 93 94 95 Small village with four GRANDS CRUS between GEVREY-CHAMBERTIN and CHAMBOLLE-MUSIGNY. Glorious wine often overlooked. Incl Amiot, Castagnier, DUJAC, Groffier, Lignier, Moillard-Grivot, Perrot-Minot, PONSOT, ROUSSEAU, Serveau.

Morgon Beauj r ★★★ 88 89 90 91 93 94 95 The 'firmest' CRU of BEAUJOLAIS, needing time to develop its rich, savoury flavour. Growers incl Aucoeur, Ch de Bellevue, Desvignes, Lapièrre, Ch de Pizay. DUBOEUF excellent.

Mortet, Denis The new kid on the GEVREY block. Super wines since '93 incl a range of village Gevreys.

Moueix, J-P et Cie Legendary leading proprietor and merchant of ST-EMILION, POMEROL and FRONSAC. Châteaux incl LA FLEUR-PETRUS, MAGDELAINE and part of PETRUS. Also in California: see Dominus.

France entries also cross-refer to Châteaux of Bordeaux section, pages 78–103.

Moulin-à-Vent Beauj r ★★★ 85 89 90 91 93 94 95 The 'biggest' and potentially best wine of BEAUJOLAIS; can be powerful, meaty and long-lived, eventually can even taste like fine Rhône or burgundy. Many good growers, esp Ch du Moulin-à-Vent, Ch des Jacques, Dom des Hospices, Janodet.

Moulis B'x r ★★→★★★ H-MEDOC village with several CRUS EXCEPTIONNELS: CHASSE-SPLEEN, MAUCAILLOU, POUJEAUX (THEIL) etc. Good hunting ground.

Mousseux Sparkling.

Mouton Cadet Popular brand of blended red and white BORDEAUX.

Moutonne CHABLIS GRAND CRU honoris causa (between Vaudésir and Preuses), owned by BICHOT.

Mugnier, J-F 10-acre Ch de Chambolle estate with first-class delicate CHAMBOLLE-MUSIGNY Les Amoureuses and MUSIGNY. Also BONNES-MARES.

Mumm, G H & Cie Cordon Rouge NV; Mumm de Cramant NV; Cordon Rouge 79 82 85 88 89; Rosé NV Major CHAMPAGNE grower and merchant owned by Seagram. Luxury brands: René Lalou (79 82 85), Grand Cordon (85; launched '91). Also in Napa, California; Chile ('96 first yr), Argentina, South Africa ('Cape Mumm').

Muré, Clos St-Landelin Fine ALSACE merchant at Rouffach with v'yds in GRAND CRU Vorbourg. Full-bodied wines: ripe (unusual) Pinot N, big Ries and MUSCAT VENDANGES TARDIVES.

Muscadet Lo w ★★ DYA Popular, good value, often delicious v dry wine from around Nantes. Should never be sharp but should have an iodine tang (like the bilge of a trawler). Perfect with fish dishes. The best are from zonal appellations: COTEAUX DE LA LOIRE, COTES DE GRAND LIEU, SEVRE ET MAINE. Choose a SUR LIE – on the lees.

Muscadet Côte de Grand Lieu New zonal AC ('95) for MUSCADET around the eponymous lake. Best are SUR LIE, from eg Bâtard, Bel-Air, Luc Choblet.

Muscadet Coteaux de la Loire Lo w Small MUSCADET zone E of Nantes, best are SUR LIE, esp Guindon and Luneau-Papin.

Muscadet de Sèvre-et-Maine Wine from the central (best) part of the area. Top growers include Bossard, Chereau-Carré, Frères Leroux, Luneau-Papin, METAIREAU, Saupin and SAUVION.

Muscat Distinctively perfumed grape and its (usually sweet) wine, often fortified as VIN DOUX NATUREL. Made dry in ALSACE.

Muscat de Beaumes-de-Venise See Beaumes-de-Venise.

Muscat de Frontignan Midi br sw ★★ DYA Sweet MIDI MUSCAT. Quality improving – esp from ch'x Gres St-Paul, Tour de Farges, Coop du MUSCAT DE LUNEL. See Frontignan.

Muscat de Lunel Midi br sw ★★ NV Ditto. A small area but good, making real recent progress. Look for Dom Clos Bellevue.

Muscat de Mireval Midi br sw ★★ NV Ditto, from nr Montpellier.

Muscat de Rivesaltes Midi br sw ★★ NV Sweet MUSCAT wine from large zone near Perpignan. Especially good from Cazes Frères, Château de Jau and Domaine Mas Amiel.

Musigny Burg r (w) ★★★★ 78 79 82 85' 86 87 88' 89'90' 91 92 93 94 95 25-acre GRAND CRU in CHAMBOLLE-MUSIGNY. Can be the most beautiful, if not the most powerful, of all red burgundies (and a little white). Best growers: DROUHIN, JADOT, LEROY, MUGNIER, ROUMIER, DE VOGUE.

Nature Natural or unprocessed – esp of still CHAMPAGNE.

Négociant-éleveur Merchant who 'brings up' (ie matures) the wine.

Nicolas, Ets Paris-based wholesale and retail wine merchants controlled by Castel Frères. One of the biggest in France and one of the best.

Noble Joué p ★★ Ancient but recently-revived rosé from three Pinots (Gris, Meunier, Noir) just S of Tours. Esp from ROUSSEAU and Sard.

Nuits-St-Georges Burg r ★★→★★★ 78' 82 83 85' 86 87 88' 89' 90' 91 92 93 94 95 Important wine town: wines of all qualities, typically sturdy and relatively tannic, needing time. Name often shortened to 'Nuits'. Best vineyards incl Les Cailles, Clos des Corvées, Les Pruliers, Les St-Georges, Vaucrains etc. Many growers and merchants esp DOM DE L'ARLOT, Ambroise, J Chauvenet, Chevillon, Confuron, FAIVELEY, GRIVOT, Lechemeaut, LEROY, MACHARD DE GRAMONT, Michelot, RION.

d'Oc Midi r p w ★→★★ Regional VIN DE PAYS for Languedoc and ROUSSILLON. Esp single-grape wines and VINS DE PAYS PRIMEURS. Tremendous technical advances recently. Top growers: VAL D'ORBIEU, SKALLI, Jeanjean.

Oisly & Thesée, Vignerons de Go-ahead coop in E TOURAINE (Loire), with good Sauv (esp Cuvée Excellence), Cab and CHARD. Blends labelled Baronnie d'Aignan. Value.

Orléanais, Vin de l' Lo r p w ★ DYA Small VDQS for light but fruity wines. Esp Clos St-Fiacre.

Ostertag Little ALSACE domaine at Epfig. Uses new oak for good Ries and makes the best Pinot Gr of GRAND CRU Muenchberg. GEWURZ from lieu-dit Frönholz is worth ageing.

Ott, Domaines Top high-quality producer of PROVENCE, incl CH DE SELLE (rosé, red), Clos Mireille (white), BANDOL and Ch de Romassan.

Pacherenc du Vic-Bilh SW France w dr sw ★→★★ DYA Rare minor speciality of ARMAGNAC region, traditionally from currently-shunned Arrufiac grape variety. Domaines Capmartin and Mauréou make some of the best. The red is MADIRAN AC.

Palette Prov r p w ★★ Near Aix-en-Provence. Aromatic reds and vg rosés from CHATEAU SIMONE.

Parigot-Richard Producer of vg CREMANT DE BOURGOGNE at SAVIGNY.

Pasquier-Desvignes V old firm of BEAUJOLAIS merchants nr BROUILLY.

Patriarche One of the bigger firms of burgundy merchants. Cellars in BEAUNE; also owns CH DE MEURSAULT (100 acres), sparkling KRITER etc.

Patrimonio Corsica r w p ★★→★★★ 90 91 92 93 94 95 Wide range from dramatic chalk hills in N CORSICA. Fragrant reds, crisp whites, fine VINS DOUX NATURELS. Top grower: Gentile.

Pauillac B'x r ★★→★★★★ 66' 70' 75 78' 79 81' 82' 83' 85' 86' 87 88' 89' 90' 91 92 93 94 95' The only BORDEAUX (HAUT-MEDOC) village with 3 first-growths (CHATEAUX LAFITE, LATOUR, MOUTON) and many other fine ones, famous for high flavour; v varied in style.

Pécharmant Dordogne r ★★ 90 93 94 95 Red wines: usually better-than-typical BERGERAC: more 'meat'. Best: domaines des Bertranoux and du Haut-Pécharmant, Ch de Tiregand.

Pelure d'oignon 'Onion skin' – tawny tint of certain rosés.

Perlant or Perlé Very slightly sparkling.

Pernand-Vergelesses Burg (w) ★★★ 78' 85 87 88' 89' 90 91 92 93 94 95 Village next to ALOXE-CORTON containing part of the great CORTON and CORTON-CHARLEMAGNE v'yds and one other top v'yd: Ile des Vergelesses. Growers incl BONNEAU DU MARTRAY, CHANDON DE BRIAILLES, CHANSON, Delarche, Dubreuil-Fontaine, JADOT, LATOUR, Rapet.

Perrier-Jouët Brut NV; Blason de France NV; Blason de France Rosé NV; Brut 76 79 82 85 86 88 90 Excellent CHAMPAGNE-growers at Epernay, the first to make dry CHAMPAGNE and once the smartest name of all, now owned by Seagram. Luxury brands: Belle Epoque (79 82 83 85 86 88 89) in a painted bottle. Also Belle Epoque Rosé (79 82 85 86 88).

Pessac-Léognan B'x Relatively recent AC for the best part of N GRAVES, incl the area of most of the GRANDS CRUS.

Pétillant Normally means slightly sparkling; but half sparkling speciality in TOURAINE and VOUVRAY.

Petit Chablis Burg w ★★ DYA Wine from fourth-rank CHABLIS vineyards. Not much character but can be pleasantly fresh. Best wines are from coop La Chablisienne.

Pfaffenheim Top ALSACE coop with 500 acres. Strongly individual wines of all varieties incl good Sylvaner and vg Pinots (N, Gr, Bl). GRANDS CRUS: Goldert, Steinert. Hartenberger Crémant d'Alsace is vg.

Pfersigberg Eguisheim (ALSACE) GRAND CRU with two parcels. GEWURZ does v well. Paul Ginglinger makes good RIES. Top grower: KUENTZ-BAS.

Philipponnat NV; Rosé NV; Réserve Spéciale 82 85 88; Grand Blanc Vintage 76 81 82 85 86 88 89; Clos des Goisses 76 78 79 82 85 86 Small family-run CHAMPAGNE house: well-structured, wines, esp remarkable single-v'yd Clos des Goisses, charming rosé. Owners: Marie Brizard. Since '92 also Le Reflet Brut NV.

Piat Père & Fils Big-scale merchants of BEAUJOLAIS and MACON wines at Mâcon, now controlled by Grand Met. V'yds in MOULIN-A-VENT, also CLOS DE VOUGEOT. BEAUJOLAIS, MACON-VIRE in special Piat bottles maintain a fair standard. Piat d'Or is something else.

Pic, Albert Fine CHABLIS producer, controlled by DE LADOUCETTE.

Picpoul de Pinet Midi w ★→★★ AC exclusively for the old variety Picpoul. Best growers: Dom Gaujal, Coop Pomérols.

Pineau des Charentes Strong sweet aperitif made from white grape juice and COGNAC.

Pinot See Grapes for white and red wine (pages 7–13).

Piper-Heidsieck Brut NV; Brut Rosé NV; Brut 76 79 82 85 CHAMPAGNE-makers of old repute at Reims, now owned by Rémy-Cointreau. Rare (76 79 85 88) and Brut Sauvage (79 82 85) are far ahead of their other, rather light wines. See also Piper Sonoma, California.

Pol Roger Brut White Foil NV; Brut 75 76 79 82 85 86 88 89; Rosé 75 79 82 85 86 88; Blanc de Chardonnay 79 82 85 86 88 Top-ranking family-owned CHAMPAGNE house at Epernay, much-loved in Britain. Esp good NV White Foil, Rosé, Réserve PR (86 88) and CHARD. Sumptuous luxury CUVEE: 'Sir Winston Churchill' (75 79 82 85 86).

Pomerol B'x r ★★→★★★★ 70 75' 81' 82' 83 85 86 88 89' 90' 92 93 94 95 Next village to ST-EMILION: similar but more plummy and creamy wines, often maturing sooner, reliable, delicious. Top ch'x: CERTAN-DE-MAY, L'EVANGILE, LA FLEUR, LA FLEUR-PETRUS, LATOUR-A-POMEROL, PETRUS, LE PIN, TROTANOY, VIEUX CH CERTAN etc.

Pommard Burg r ★★★ 78' 85' 86 87 88' 89' 90 91 92 93 94 95 The biggest COTE D'OR village. Few superlative wines, but many potent and distinguished ones to age 10 yrs+. Best v'yds: Epenots, HOSPICES DE BEAUNE CUVEES, Rugiens. Growers incl Comte Armand, G Billard, Billard-Gonnet, J-M Boillot, de Courcel, Gaunoux, LEROY, Machard de Gramont, de Montille, A Mussy, Ch de Pommard, Pothier-Rieusset.

Burgundy: growers and merchants
The image of Burgundy négociants' wines is the family car/ Detroit end of the business. In contrast, buying growers' wines can feel like driving a sports car. There are arguments for both.

Pommery Brut NV; Rosé NV; Brut 82 83 85 87 88 89 Very big CHAMPAGNE growers and merchants at Reims, bought by MOET-Hennessy in '91. Wines are much improved. The luxury Louise Pommery (81 82 83 85 87 88) is outstanding. Louise Pommery Rosé (82 83 85 88 89).

Ponsot, J M 25-acre MOREY-ST-DENIS estate. Growers in many GRANDS CRUS including CHAMBERTIN, CHAPELLE-C, LATRICIERES-C, CLOS DE LA ROCHE, CLOS ST-DENIS. V high quality.

Pouilly-Fuissé Burg w ★★→★★★★ 89' 90' 91 92 93 94 95 The best white of the MACON region. At its best (eg Ch Fuissé VIEILLES VIGNES) outstanding, but usually over-priced compared with (eg) CHABLIS. Good growers: Ferret, Forest, GUFFENS-HEYNEN, Luquet, Noblet, Valette, Vincent.

Pouilly-Fumé Lo w ★★→★★★★ 90' 91' 92' 93' 94 95 'Gun-flinty', fruity, often sharp white from upper Loire, nr SANCERRE. Grapes must be Sauv. Best CUVÉES can improve 5–6 yrs. Top growers incl Bailly, Blondelet, Coulbois, DAGUENEAU, Figeat, LADOUCETTE, Masson-Blondelet, Redde, Renaud, Saget, Tinel, Tinel Blondelet, Ch de Tracy.

Pouilly-Loché Burg w ★★ POUILLY-FUISSE's neighbour. Similar, much cheaper, but scarce.

Pouilly-sur-Loire Lo w ★ DYA Inferior wine from the same v'yds as POUILLY-FUME but different grapes (Chasselas). Rarely seen today.

Pouilly-Vinzelles Burg w ★★ 90 91 92 93 94 95 Neighbour of POUILLY-FUISSE. Similar wine, worth looking for. Value.

Pousse d'Or, Domaine de la 32-acre estate in POMMARD, SANTENAY and esp VOLNAY, where its MONOPOLES Bousse d'Or and Clos des 60 Ouvrées are powerful, tannic, and justly famous.

Premier Cru First-growth in BORDEAUX, but the second rank of vineyards (after GRAND CRU) in Burgundy incl CHABLIS.

Premières Côtes de Blaye B'x r w ★→★★★ 82 85 86 88' 89' 90' 92 93 94 95 Restricted AC for better wines of BLAYE; greater emphasis on reds. Ch'x incl Barbé, LE BOURDIEU, Charron, l'Escadre, Haut-Sociondo, Le Menaudat, La Rose-Bellevue, Segonzac, La Tonnelle.

Premières Côtes de Bordeaux B'x r w (p) dr sw ★→★★ Large hilly area east of GRAVES across the River Garonne: a good bet for quality and value, upgrading sharply. Largely Merlot. Châteaux incl Bertinerie (esp), Carsin, La Croix de Roche, Fayau, Fontenil, Gardera, HAUT-BRIGNON, du Juge, Laffitte (sic), Lamothe, Peyrat, Plaisance, REYNON, Tanesse. An area to watch, esp in good vintages.

Prieur, Domaine Jacques Splendid 35-acre estate all in top Burgundy sites, incl PREMIER CRU MEURSAULT, VOLNAY, PULIGNY- and even LE MONTRACHET. Now 50% owned by RODET and quality rejuvenated, esp since '89.

Primeur 'Early' wine for refreshment and uplift; especially from BEAUJOLAIS; VINS DE PAYS too. Wine sold 'En Primeur' is offered for sale still in barrel for future delivery.

Prissé See Mâcon-Villages.

Propriétaire-récoltant Owner-manager.

Provence See Côtes de Provence.

Puisseguin St-Emilion B'x r ★★ 82 85 86 88' 89' 90' 92 93 94 95 E neighbour of ST-EMILION, its smallest 'satellite'; wines similar – not so fine or weighty but often good value. Ch'x incl La Croix de Berny, LAURETS, Puisseguin, Soleil, Teyssier, Vieux-Ch-Guibeau. Also Roc de Puisseguin from coop.

Puligny-Montrachet Burg w (r) ★★★★ 85' 86' 88 89' 90' 91 92 93 94 95 Bigger neighbour of CHASSAGNE-MONTRACHET with potentially even finer, more vital and complex rich dry whites. Apparent finesse can also be the result of over-production. Best v'yds: BATARD-MONTRACHET, Bienvenues-Bâtard-Montrachet, Caillerets, Champ-Canet, CHEVALIER-MONTRACHET, Clavoillon, Les Combettes, MONTRACHET, Pucelles etc. Top growers incl Amiot-Bonfils, AMPEAU, J-M Boillot, BOUCHARD PERE, L CARILLON, CHARTRON, H Clerc, DROUHIN, JADOT, LATOUR, DOM LEFLAIVE, O LEFLAIVE, Pernot, SAUZET.

Quarts de Chaume Lo w sw ★★★→★★★★ 75 76 78' 79' 82 85' 86 88' 89' 90' 91 92 93' 94 95 Famous COTEAUX DU LAYON plot. Chenin Blanc grapes grown for immensely long-lived intense rich golden wine. Esp from BAUMARD, Bellerive, Papin, Suronde.

Quatourze Midi r w (p) ★ 90 91 92 93 94 95 Minor AC area nr Narbonne. Best wines from Dom Notre Dame du Quatourze.

Quincy Lo w ★★ DYA Small area: v dry SANCERRE-style wine of Sauv. Worth trying. Growers: Domaine Mardon, Cave Romane de Brinay, Sorbe.

Ramonet, Domaine Leading estate in CHASSAGNE-MONTRACHET with 34 acres, incl some MONTRACHET. Vg whites, and red CLOS ST-JEAN.

Rancio Term for the much-appreciated nutty tang of brown wood-aged fortified wine, esp BANYULS and other VDN. A fault in table wines.

Rangen V high class ALSACE GRAND CRU in Thann and Vieux Thann. Owes much of its reputation to ZIND-HUMBRECHT. Esp for Pinot Gr, GEWURZ, RIES.

Rasteau S Rh r br sw (p w dr) ★★ 85' 86 88 89 90' 93 94 95 Village for sound, robust reds, especially Beaurenard, Cave des Vignerons, Ch du Trignon, doms Charavin, Corinne Couturier, St-Gayan, Soumade. Strong sweet dessert wine is (declining) speciality.

Ratafia de Champagne Sweet aperitif made in CHAMPAGNE of 67% grape juice and 33% brandy. Not unlike PINEAU DES CHARENTES.

Récolte Crop or vintage.

Regnié Beauj r ★★ 91 93 94 95 BEAUJ village between MORGON and BROUILLY, promoted to CRU in '88. About 1,800 acres. Try DUBOEUF's or Aucoeur's.

Reine Pédauque, La Long-established Burgundy growers and merchants at ALOXE-CORTON with growing reputation, esp in duty-free. V'yds in ALOXE-CORTON, SAVIGNY etc, and COTES DU RHONE. Owned by PIERRE ANDRE.

Remoissenet Père & Fils Fine burgundy merchant (esp for whites) with a tiny BEAUNE estate. Give his reds time. Also broker for NICOLAS wine shops. Some of his best wines are from DOM THENARD.

Rémy Pannier Important Loire wine merchant at SAUMUR.

Reuilly Lo w (r p) ★★ DYA Neighbour of QUINCY with similar whites, gaining in reputation. Also rosés (Pinot Gris, Pinot Noir) and reds (PN). Esp from Beurdin, CORDIER, Sorbe and Vincent.

Riceys, Rosé des Champ p ★★★ DYA Minute AC in S CHAMPAGNE for a notable Pinot N rosé. Principal producer: A Bonnet.

Richebourg Burg r ★★★★ 78' 80' 82 83 85' 87 88' 89' 90' 91 92 93' 94 95 19-acre VOSNE-ROMANEE GRAND CRU. Powerful perfumed fabulously expensive wine, among Burgundy's very best. Top growers: BICHOT, GRIVOT, J GROS, LEROY, MEO-CAMUZET, DOM DE LA ROMANEE-CONTI.

Richou, Dom Long-est'd quality ANJOU estate for wide range of wines, esp ANJOU-VILLAGES VIEILLES VIGNES, COTEAUX DE L'AUBANCE Les Trois Demoiselles.

Riesling See Grapes for white wine (pages 7–11).

Rion, Daniel et Fils 36-acre domaine in Prémeaux (NUITS). Excellent VOSNE-ROMANEE (Les Chaumes, Les Beaumonts), Nuits PREMIER CRU Les Vignes Rondes and CHAMBOLLE-MUSIGNY-Les Charmes. NB Also Patrice Rion.

Rivesaltes Midi r w br dr sw ★★ NV Fortified wine of east Pyrenees. A tradition v much alive, if struggling these days. Top producers: Château de Calce, Dom Cazes, Château de Jau.

Roche-aux-Moines, La Lo w sw ★★★ 75 76' 78 79 82 83 85' 86 88' 89' 90' 91 92 93' 94 95' 60-acre v'yd in SAVENNIERES, ANJOU. Intense strong fruity/sharp wine, needs long ageing or drinking fresh.

To decipher codes, please refer to 'Key to symbols' on front flap of jacket, or to 'How to use this book' on page 6.

Rodet, Antonin Substantial quality burgundy merchant with large (375-acre) estate, esp in MERCURY (Ch de Chamirey). See also Prieur. Now owned by LAURENT-PERRIER.

Roederer, Louis Brut Premier NV; Rich NV; Brut 71 73 75 76 78 79 81 83 85 86 88 89 90; Blanc de Blancs 88 90; Brut Rosé 75 83 85 86 88 91 One of the best CHAMPAGNE-growers and merchants at Reims. Reliable non vintage with plenty of flavour. Luxury brands: velvety Cristal Brut (79 82 83 85 86 88 89 90) and Cristal Rosé (88) in white glass bottles need time. Also owns champagne house DEUTZ and CHATEAU DE PEZ in Bordeaux. See also California, Australia (Tasmania).

Romanée, La Burg r ★★★★ 78' 82 85' 87' 88' 89' 90' 91 92 93 94 95 2-acre GRAND CRU in VOSNE-ROMANEE, just uphill from ROMANEE-CONTI. Monopole of Liger-Belair, sold by BOUCHARD PERE.

Romanée-Conti Burg r ★★★★ 66' 76 78' 80' 82 83 85' 86 87 88' 89' 90' 91 92 93' 94 95 4.3-acre MONOPOLE GRAND CRU in VOSNE-ROMANEE; 450 cases pa. The most celebrated and expensive red wine in the world, with reserves of flavour beyond imagination. See next entry.

Romanée-Conti, Domaine de la (DRC) The grandest estate in Burgundy. Includes the whole of ROMANEE-CONTI and LA TACHE and major parts of ECHEZEAUX, GRANDS ECHEZEAUX, RICHEBOURG and ROMANEE-ST-VIVANT. Also v small parts of MONTRACHET and VOSNE-ROMANEE. Crown-jewel prices. Keep top DRC vintages for decades.

Romanée-St-Vivant Burg r ★★★★ 78' 80' 82 85' 87 88' 89' 90' 91 92 93' 95 23-acre GRAND CRU in VOSNE-ROMANEE. Similar to ROMANEE-CONTI but lighter and less sumptuous. Top growers: DRC and LEROY.

Ropiteau Burgundy growers at MEURSAULT. Merchant business was bought in '94 by BOISSET.

Rosé d'Anjou Lo p ★ DYA Pale slightly sw rosé. CAB D'ANJOU should be better.

Rosé de Loire Lo p ★→★★ DYA Wide-ranging appellation for dry Loire rosé (ANJOU is sweet).

Roty, Joseph Small grower of classic GEVREY-CHAMBERTIN, esp CHARMES- and MAZIS-CHAMBERTIN. Long-lived wines.

Rouget, Emmanuel Inheritor (nephew) of the legendary 13-acre estate of Henri Jayer in ECHEZEAUX, NUITS-SAINT-GEORGES and VOSNE-ROMANEE. Top wine: Vosne-Romanée-Cros Parantoux. Jayer (who retired '88) still consults here and at DOMAINE MEO-CAMUZET.

Roumier, Georges 35-acre domaine with exceptional wines from BONNES-MARES, CHAMBOLLE-MUSIGNY-Amoureuses, MUSIGNY etc. High standards. Long-lasting reds.

Rousseau, Domaine A Major burgundy grower famous for CHAMBERTIN etc, of v highest quality. Wines are intense, long-lived and mostly GRAND CRU.

Roussette de Savoie Savoie w ★★ DYA Tastiest of the fresh whites from S of Lake Geneva.

Roussillon Midi The largest producer of VINS DOUX NATURELS (often 'Grands Roussillons'). Lighter MUSCATS are taking over from darker heavier wines. See Côtes du Rhône.

Ruchottes-Chambertin Burg r ★★★ 78' 85' 87 88' 89' 90' 91 92 93' 94 95 7.5-acre GRAND CRU neighbour of CHAMBERTIN. Similar splendid lasting wine of great finesse. Top growers: LEROY, Mugneret, ROUMIER, ROUSSEAU.

Ruinart Père & Fils 'R' de Ruinart Brut NV; 'R' de Ruinart Rosé NV; 'R' de Ruinart Brut 86 88 90 The oldest CHAMPAGNE house, now owned by MOET-Hennessy, with notably fine crisp wines, esp the luxury brands: Dom Ruinart Blanc de Blancs (81 82 83 85 86 88), Dom Ruinart Rosé (81 82 83 85 86). NB the vg mature Rosé. Notable value.

Rully Burg r w (sp) ★★ 89' 90' 91 92 93 94 95 COTE CHALONNAISE village famous for CREMANT. Still white and red are light but tasty, good value, esp whites. Growers incl DELORME, FAIVELEY, Dom de la Folie, Jacquesson, A RODET.

Sables du Golfe du Lion Midi p r w ★ DYA VIN DE PAYS from Mediterranean sand-dunes: especially GRIS DE GRIS from Carignan, Grenache and Cinsaut. Dominated by LISTEL.

Sablet S Rh r w (p) ★★ 89 90' 93 94 95 Admirable, improving COTES DU RHONE village, esp Dom de Boissan, Piaugier, Ch du Trignon, Dom de Verquière. Whites to try too.

St-Amour Beauj r ★★ 93 94 95 Northernmost CRU of BEAUJOLAIS: light, fruity, irresistible. Growers to try: Janin, Patissier, Revillon.

St-André-de-Cubzac B'x r w ★→★★ 88' 89' 90' 92' 93 94 95 Town 15 miles NE of BORDEAUX, centre of the minor Cubzaguais region. Sound reds have AC BORDEAUX SUPERIEUR. Incl: Domaine de Beychevelle, Ch du Bouilh, CH DE TERREFORT-QUANCARD, CH TIMBERLAY.

St-Aubin Burg w (r) ★★ 85' 86' 88 89' 90 91 92 93 94 95 Little-known neighbour of CHASSAGNE-MONTRACHET, up a side-valley. Several PREMIERS CRUS for light firm quite stylish wines at fair prices. Also sold as COTE DE BEAUNE-VILLAGES. Top growers include Clerget, JADOT, J Lamy, LAMY-PILLOT, H Prudhon, Roux and Thomas.

St-Bris Burg w (r) ★ DYA Village west of CHABLIS known for fruity ALIGOTE, but chiefly for SAUVIGNON de ST-BRIS. Also good CREMANT.

St-Chinian Midi r ★→★★ 88 89 90 91 92 93 94 95 Hilly area of growing reputation in COTEAUX DU LANGUEDOC. AC since '82. Tasty southern reds, esp at Berlou and Roquebrun, and from Ch de Viranel.

St-Emilion B'x r ★★→★★★★ 70' 75 79' 81 82' 83' 85' 86' 88 89' 90' 92 93 94 95 The biggest top-quality BORDEAUX district (13,000 acres); solid rich tasty wines from hundreds of châteaux, incl AUSONE, CANON, CHEVAL BLANC, FIGEAC, MAGDELAINE etc. Also a good coop.

St-Estèphe B'x r ★★→★★★★ 75 78' 81 82' 83' 85' 86 87 88' 89' 90' 91 92 93 94 95' N village of HAUT-MEDOC. Solid, structured, sometimes superlative wines. Top châteaux: COS D'ESTOURNEL, MONTROSE, CALON-SEGUR, etc, and more notable CRUS BOURGEOIS than any other HAUT-MEDOC commune.

St-Gall Brut NV; Extra Brut NV; Brut Blanc de Blancs NV; Brut Rosé NV; Brut Blanc de Blancs 88; Cuvée Or Pale 85 The brand name used by Union-Champagne, the vg CHAMPAGNE-growers' coop at AVIZE. Style is usually softer than true BRUT.

St-Georges-St-Emilion B'x r ★★ 82 83' 85' 86' 88' 89' 90' 92 93 94 95 Part of MONTAGNE-ST-EMILION with high standards. Best ch'x: Belair-Montaiguillon, Marquis-St-G, ST-GEORGES, Tour du Pas-St-G.

St-Gervais S Rh r (w) ★ West bank S Rhône village. Sound coop, excellent Dom Ste-Anne reds (marked Mourvèdre flavours); whites incl a VIOGNIER.

St-Jean de Minervois Min w sw ★★→★★★ Perhaps the best French MUSCAT: sweet and fine, esp from Dom de Barroubio, Michel Sige, Coop St-Jean de Minervois. Much recent progress.

St-Joseph N Rh r (p w) ★★ 85 86 88' 89 90' 91 94' 95 AC stretching the whole length of N Rhône (40 miles). Delicious, fruit-packed wines at its core, around Tournon; elsewhere quality variable. Often better than CROZES-HERMITAGE, esp from CHAPOUTIER, CHAVE, Chèze, Coursodon, Gaillard, B Gripa, Grippat, JABOULET, Marsanne, Paret, Trollat. Good whites too.

St-Julien B'x r ★★★→★★★★ 70' 75 78' 79 81' 82' 83' 85' 86' 87 88' 89' 90' 91 92 93 94 95' Mid-MEDOC village with a dozen of BORDEAUX's best châteaux, incl three LEOVILLES, BEYCHEVELLE, DUCRU-BEAUCAILLOU, GRUAUD-LAROSE, etc. The epitome of well-balanced, fragrant and savoury red wine.

St-Nicolas-de-Bourgueil Lo r p ★★ 85' 86 88 89' 90' 92 93' 95' The next village to BOURGUEIL: the same lively and fruity Cab F red. Top growers: Amirault, Cognard, Jamet, Lorieux, Mabileau, Taluau.

St-Péray N Rh w sp ★★ NV Rather heavy Rhône white, much of it sparkling. A curiosity worth trying once. Top names are J-F Chaboud, B Gripa (still wine), J-L Thiers.

St-Pourçain-sur-Sioule Central France r p w ★→★★ DYA Light but venerable local wine of Vichy. Red and rosé made from GAMAY and/or Pinot, white from Tressalier and/or CHARD or SAUV. Recent vintages improved but too pricey. Top growers: Ray, Dom de Bellevue and good coop.

St-Romain Burg r w ★★ (w) 88 89' 90' 91 92 93 94 95 Overlooked village just behind the COTE DE BEAUNE. Value, especially for firm fresh whites. The reds have a clean 'cut'. Top growers: FEVRE, Jean Germain, Gras, LATOUR, LEROY, Thévenin-Monthélie.

St-Véran Burg w ★★ 90 91 92 93 94 95 Next-door AC to POUILLY-FUISSE. Similar wines but better value, with real character from the best slopes of MACON-VILLAGES. Try DUBOEUF's, Domaine des Deux Roches, Demessey, CH FUISSE and Dom des Valanges.

Ste-Croix-du-Mont B'x w sw ★★ 75 76' 82 83 86' 88' 89 90 91 92 93 95' Neighbour to SAUTERNES with similar golden wine. No superlatives but well worth trying, esp Clos des Coulinats, Ch Loubens, Ch Lousteau Vieil, Ch du Mont. Often a bargain, esp with age.

Salon 71 73 76 79 82 The original Blanc de Blancs CHAMPAGNE, from Le Mesnil in the Côte de Blancs. Superlative intense v dry wine with long keeping qualities in tiny quantities. Bought in '88 by LAURENT-PERRIER.

Sancerre Lo w (r p) ★★★ 89 90' 91 92' 93' 94 95' Very fragrant and fresh Sauv Bl, almost indistinguishable from POUILLY-FUME, its neighbour across the Loire. Top wines can age 5 yrs+. Also light Pinot N red (best drunk at 2–3 yrs) and rosé. Occasional vg VENDANGES TARDIVES. Top growers incl BOURGEOIS, Ch de Sancerre, Cotat, Crochet, Dezat, Gitton, Jolivet, Laporte, MELLOT, Natter, Neveu, Pinard, Roger, B Reverdy, Vacheron, Vatan.

Santenay Burg r (w) ★★★ 78' 85' 87 88' 89' 90 91 92 93 94 95 Sturdy reds from village S of CHASSAGNE. Best v'yds: La Comme, Les Gravières, Clos de Tavannes. Top growers: Lequin-Roussot, MOREY, POUSSE D'OR.

Saumur Lo r w p sp ★→★★ Fresh fruity whites plus a few more serious, vg CREMANT, GRATIEN ET MEYER and Saumur Mousseaux (producers incl BOUVET-LADUBAY, Cave de St-Cyr, GRATIEN ET MEYER, de Grenelle, Haut-Sanziers, Lambert, LANGLOIS-CHATEAU), pale rosés and increasingly good Cab F (see next entry).

Saumur-Champigny Lo r ★★ 82 85 86' 88 89' 90' 93' 94 95' Flourishing nine-commune AC for fresh Cab F ageing remarkably in sunny years. Look for CH DU HUREAU, domaines Filliatreau, Nerleux, Roches Neuves, Val Brun, Ruault; Clos Rougeard, coop St-Cyr.

Saussignac Dordogne w sw ★ AC ('82) for almondy sweet wines only, like MONBAZILLAC. Top grower Ch Court-les-Mûts.

Sauternes B'x w sw ★★→★★★★ 67' 71' 75 76' 78 79' 80 81 82 83' 85 86' 88' 89' 90' 91 92 95' District of 5 villages (incl BARSAC) which make France's best sweet wine, strong (14%+ alcohol), luscious and golden, demanding to be aged. Top châteaux are D'YQUEM, CLIMENS, COUTET, GUIRAUD, SUDUIRAUT etc. Dry wines cannot be sold as Sauternes.

Sauvignon Blanc See Grapes for white wine (pages 7–11).

Sauvignon de St-Bris Burg w ★★ DYA A baby VDQS cousin of SANCERRE, from nr CHABLIS. To try. 'Dom Saint Prix' from Dom Bersan is good.

Sauvion & Fils Ambitious and well-run MUSCADET house, based at the Ch de Cléray. Top wine: Cardinal Richard.

Sauzet, Etienne Top-quality white burgundy estate at PULIGNY-MONTRACHET. Clearly-defined, well-bred wines, at best superb.

Savennières Lo w dr sw ★★★ 75 76' 78' 82 83 85 86' 88 89' 90' 93 94 95' Small ANJOU district of pungent long-lived whites, incl Ch de Chamboureau, Clos du Papillon, Closel, COULEE DE SERRANT, Ch d'Epiré, ROCHE-AUX-MOINES.

Savigny-lès-Beaune Burg r (w) ★★★ 85' 87 88' 89' 90' 91 92 93 94 95 Important village next to BEAUNE, similar balanced mid-weight wines, often deliciously lively, fruity. Top v'yds: Dominode, Les Guettes, Marconnets, Serpentières, Vergelesses; growers: BIZE, Camus, CHANDON DE BRIAILLES, CLAIR, Ecard, Girard-Vollot, LEROY, Pavelot, TOLLOT-BEAUT.

Savoie E France r w sp ★★ DYA Alpine area with light dry wines like some Swiss or minor Loires. APREMONT, CREPY and SEYSSEL are best-known whites, ROUSSETTE is more interesting. Also good MONDEUSE red.

Schaller, Edgard ALSACE grower (dry style wines) in Mandelburg GRAND CRU, Mittelwihr; esp for Ries 'Mambourg Vieilles Vignes' (needs time) and 'Les Amandiers' (younger-drinking).

> **Apples into milk**
> Malolactic (or secondary) fermentation sometimes happens after the first (alcoholic) fermentation. It is the natural conversion of excess malic (sharp) acid in the wine into (milder) lactic acid.
> It is generally desirable in cool, high-acid wine regions, not in warm regions where a touch of sharpness is a balancing attribute.
> It can be encouraged or prevented. Where the acidity can be spared, 'malo' adds 'complexity' to flavours.

Schlossberg V successful ALSACE GRAND CRU for RIESLING. Divided into two: Kaysersberg and Kientzheim.

Schlumberger ALSACE grower-merchants at Guebwiller. Unusually rich wines incl luscious Kessler and Kitterlé GRAND CRU GEWURZ (also SGN and VT). Fine Kitterlé and Saering Ries. Also good Pinot Gr.

Schlumberger, Robert de SAUMUR sparkling wine made by Austrian method: fruity and delicate.

Schoffit, Domaine Colmar ALSACE house with GRAND CRU Rangen Pinot Gris, GEWURZ of top quality. Chasselas is unusual daily delight.

Schröder & Schÿler Old BORDEAUX merchants, co-owners of CH KIRWAN.

Schoenenbourg V rich successful Riquewihr GRAND CRU (ALSACE): RIESLING, Tokay-Pinot Gris, v fine VT and SGN. Esp from MARCEL DEISS and DOPFF AU MOULIN.

Sciacarello Red grape of CORSICA's best red and rosé, eg AJACCIO, Sartène.

Sec Literally means dry, though CHAMPAGNE so-called is medium-sweet (and better at breakfast, tea-time and weddings than BRUT).

Séguret S Rh r w ★ Good S Rhône Village nr GIGONDAS. Peppery, quite full red, rounded clean white. Esp Ch La Courançonne, Dom de Cabasse.

Sélection des Grains Nobles (SGN) Description coined by HUGEL for ALSACE equivalent to German Beerenauslese. Grains nobles are individual grapes with 'noble rot' (see page 100).

Sèvre-et-Maine The département containing the best v'yds of MUSCADET.

Seyssel Savoie w sp ★★ NV Delicate pale dry Alpine white, making very pleasant sparkling wine.

Sichel & Co Two famous merchant houses. In BORDEAUX Peter A Sichel runs Maison Sichel and owns CH D'ANGLUDET and part of CH PALMER, with interests in CORBIERES. In Germany, Peter M F Sichel (of New York) runs Sichel Söhne, makers of BLUE NUN and respected merchants.

Silvaner See Grapes for white wine (pages 7–11).

Sipp, Jean and Louis Ribeauvillé GRAND CRU ALSACE producers competing to make finest Ries (in Kirchberg): Jean's with youthful elegance (smaller v'yd, own vines only), Louis' finer when mature.

Sirius Serious oak-aged blended BORDEAUX from Maison SICHEL.

Skalli Revolutionary producer of top VINS DE PAYS D'OC from Cabernet, Merlot, CHARD etc, at Sète in the Languedoc. FORTANT DE FRANCE is standard brand. Style and value.

Sparr, Pierre Sigolsheim ALSACE grower/producer, as good at CUVEES of several grapes (eg Symphonie) as rich GRANDS CRUS.

Sur Lie See Lie and Muscadet.

Syrah See Grapes for red wine (pages 11–13).

Tâche, La Burg r ★★★★ 78' 80' 82 83 85' 86 87 88' 89' 90' 91 92 93' 94 95 15-acre (1,500 case) GRAND CRU of VOSNE-ROMANEE and one of best v'yds on earth: dark perfumed luxurious wine. See DOM DE LA ROMANEE-CONTI.

Tain, Cave Coopérative de, 450-members. Making increasingly good red HERMITAGE since '91.

Taittinger Brut NV; Rosé NV; Brut 73 75 76 78 79 80 82 83 85 86 88 89 90; Collection Brut 78 81 82 83 85 86 88 Fashionable Reims CHAMPAGNE growers and merchants making their wines with a silky flowery touch. Luxury brand: Comtes de Champagne Blanc de Blancs (79 81 82 83 85 86 88), also vg Rosé (79 83 85 86). Also owns Champagne Irroy. See also Domaine Carneros, California.

Tastevin, Confrérie des Chevaliers du Burgundy's colourful successful promotion society. Wine with their Tastevinage label has been approved by them and is usually of a fair standard. A tastevin is the traditional shallow silver wine-tasting cup of Burgundy. See also page 55.

Tavel Rh p ★★★ DYA France's most famous, though not her best, rosé: strong and dry. Best growers: Ch d'Aquéria, Bernard, Dom Corne-Loup, Maby, Dom de la Mordorée, Ch de Trinquevedel. Drink v young.

Tempier, Domaine Top grower of BANDOL, with noble reds and rosé.

Thénard, Domaine The major grower of the GIVRY appellation, but best known for his substantial portion (4+ acres) of LE MONTRACHET. Could still try harder with this jewel.

Thorin, J Grower and major merchant of BEAUJOLAIS, owner of the Château des Jacques, MOULIN-A-VENT.

Thouarsais, Vin de Lo w r p ★ DYA Light Chenin (20% Chard permitted), Gamay and Cab from tiny VDQS S of SAUMUR. Esp Gigon.

Tokay d'Alsace Old name for Pinot Gris. Will be banned as real (Hungarian) Tokay owns the name.

Tollot-Beaut Stylish burgundy grower with 50+ acres in the COTE DE BEAUNE, including v'yds at Beaune Grèves, CORTON, SAVIGNY- (Les Champs Chevrey) and at his CHOREY-LES-BEAUNE base.

Touchais, Moulin ANJOU grower and merchant with remarkable stocks of reasonably priced old COTEAUX DU LAYON. Vintages back to the '20s are like creamy honey and not over-priced.

Touraine Lo r p w dr sw sp ★→★★★ Big mid-Loire region with immense range, includes dry white Sauv, dry and sweet Chenin (eg VOUVRAY), red CHINON and BOURGUEIL. Also large AC with light red Cab F, Gamays, gutsy Cot, grassy Sauv and MOUSSEUX; often bargains. Amboise, Azay-le-Rideau and Mesland are sub-sections of the AC.

Trévallon, Domaine de Provence r ★★★ Highly fashionable estate at LES BAUX with rich intense Cab-Syrah blend to age.

For key to grape variety abbreviations, see pages 7–13.

Trimbach, F E Distinguished ALSACE grower and merchant at Ribeauvillé. Best wines include the austere Ries CLOS STE-HUNE, GRAND CRU Geisberg and Cuvée Frédéric-Emile (Ries from GC Osterberg). Also GEWURZ.

Turckheim, Cave Vinicole de Perhaps the best coop in ALSACE. Many fine wines incl GRANDS CRUS from 900+ acres, eg vg Pinot Gr from GC Hengst.

Tursan SW France r p w ★ DYA Emerging VDQS in Landes. Sound red (light, holiday-drinking) and white wines. Château de Bachen (★★★), owned by the ★★★ chef Michel Gérard, guarantees notoriety and suggests the region's own AC is on the way.

Vacqueyras S Rh r ★★ 85 86 88' 89' 90' 93 94 95 Neighbour to GIGONDAS and often cheaper. Try JABOULET's version, Ch de Montmirail, Ch des Tours, Dom des Amouriers, Archambaud-Vache, Pascal Frères or Ricard.

Val d'Orbieu, Vignerons du Association of some 200 top growers and coops in CORBIERES, COTEAUX DU LANGUEDOC, MINERVOIS, ROUSSILLON etc, marketing a first-class range of selected MIDI AC wines.

Valençay Lo r p w ★ DYA VDQS in E TOURAINE, S of Cher; light easy-drinking s'times sharpish wines.

Vallée du Paradis Midi r w p ★ Popular VINS DE PAYS of local red varieties.

Vallouit, Louis de N Rhône family co mixing v'yd ownership (biggest in COTE ROTIE: esp Les Roziers, ST-JOSEPH Les Anges) with négociant business.

Valréas S Rh r (p w) ★★ 88 90' 93 94 95 COTES DU RHONE village with big coop. Good mid-weight reds, improving whites. Esp Romain Bouchard, Dom des Grands Devers.

The vin de pays revolution

The junior rank of country wines. No one should overlook this category, the most dynamic in France today. More than 140 vins de pays names have come into active use recently, mainly in the Midi. They fall into three categories: regional (eg Vin de Pays d'Oc for the whole Midi); departmental (eg Vin de Pays du Gard for the Gard département near the mouth of the Rhône); and vins de pays de zone, the most precise, usually with the highest standards. Single-grape vins de pays and vins de pays primeurs (reds and whites, all released on the third Thursday in November) are especially popular. Well-known zonal vins de pays include Coteaux de l'Uzège, Côtes de Gascogne, Val d'Orbieu. Don't hesitate. There are some real gems among them, and many charming trinkets.

Varichon & Clerc Principal makers and shippers of SAVOIE sparkling wines.

Varoilles, Domaine des Burgundy estate of 30 acres, principally in GEVREY-CHAMBERTIN. Tannic wines with long keeping qualities.

Vaudésir Burg w ★★★★ 78' 83' 85' 86 88 89' 90 91 92 93 94 95 Arguably the best of seven CHABLIS GRANDS CRUS (but then so are the others).

VDQS Vin Délimité de Qualité Supérieure (see page 33).

Vendange Harvest.

Vendange Tardive Late harvest. In ALSACE equivalent to German Auslese, but stronger and frequently less fine.

Veuve Clicquot Yellow label NV; White Label Demi-Sec NV; Gold Label 76 78 79 82 83 (since '85 called Vintage Réserve: 85 88 89); Rosé Reserve 83 85 88 Historic CHAMPAGNE house of highest standing, now owned by LVMH. Full-bodied, almost rich: one of Champagne's surest things. Cellars at Reims. Luxury brands: La Grande Dame (79 83 85 88 89) and new Rich Réserve (89) released '95.

Vidal-Fleury, J Long-established shippers of top Rhône wines and grower of CÔTE RÔTIE. Bought in '85 by GUIGAL.

Vieille Ferme, La S Rh r w ★★ Vg brand of CÔTES DU VENTOUX made by the Perrins, owners of CH DE BEAUCASTEL.

Vieilles Vignes Old vines – therefore the best wine. Used by many, esp by BOLLINGER, DE VOGÜE and CH FUISSÉ.

Vieux Télégraphe, Domaine du S Rh r (w) ★★★ 78' 79 81' 82 83 85 86 88 89 90' 92 93 94 95 A leader in fine, vigorous, modern red CHATEAUNEUF-DU-PAPE, and fresh whites (age well in lesser yrs). New second wine: Vieux Mas des Papes. Second domaine: de la Roquette.

Vignoble Area of vineyards.

Some vins de pays for 1997

1. **Vin de Pays d'Oc** – A great diversity of grapes for some of the best value vins de pays: some traditional (Carignan, Grenache, Syrah), some new to the region (Chardonnay, Viognier, Cabernet, Merlot), and usually mentioned on label.

2. **Vin de Pays du Jardin de la France** – Loire Valley Sauvignon, Chardonnay and Chenin whites and Gamay, Groleau and Cabernet light reds.

3. **Vin de Pays du Comté Tolosan** – A wider area of the Southwest for red wine from Cabernets, Merlot, Tannat (and there are whites from Sauvignon, Sémillon and others).

4. **Vin de pays des Côtes du Tarn** – For crisp, dry white wine of the Tarn département in the Massif Central: made from the Mauzac grape and others; also a little rustic red.

5. **Vin de Pays de l'Ardèche** – Covers the Ardèche département in the Rhône Valley: Louis Latour's pioneer Chardonnay, and Gamay and Syrah single-variety reds are the ones to look for.

6. **Vin de Pays de l'Hérault** – Some of the best and worst vins de pays are from this large Midi wine area; a demonstration of the extremes of tradition and innovation both in grape varieties and technique. You may be lucky.

7. **Mas de Daumas Gassac** – The Grand Cru vin de pays: serious Cabernet Sauvignon red; also look for white Viognier-Chardonnay blend, and a lightly sparkling rosé.

8. **Vin de Pays des Côtes de Gascogne** – Decline in sales of armagnac has been to the benefit of the local table wines: fragrant dry Colombard and Ugni Blanc are refreshing but perhaps less interesting than experiments with the local Gros and Petit Manseng.

9. **Vin de Pays des Sables du Golfe de Lion** – Pioneering Salins du Midi is virtually the sole producer here on S coast, renowned for its rosé, Listel.

10. **Vin de Pays de l'Yonne** – A useful outlet for wine from young Chablis vines – good value Chardonnays.

Vin de l'année This year's wine. See Beaujolais, Beaujolais-Villages.

Vin Doux Naturel (VDN) Sweet wine fortified with wine alcohol, so the sweetness is 'natural', not the strength. The speciality of ROUSSILLON. A vin doux liquoreux is several degrees stronger.

Vin de garde Wine that will improve with keeping. The serious stuff.

Vin Gris 'Grey' wine is v pale pink, made of red grapes pressed before fermentation begins, unlike rosé which ferments briefly before pressing. Oeil de Perdrix means much the same; so does 'blush'.

Vin Jaune Jura w ★★★ Speciality of ARBOIS: odd yellow wine like fino sherry. Normally ready when bottled (at at least 7 yrs old). Best is CH-CHALON.

Vin nouveau See Beaujolais Nouveau.

Vin de paille Wine from grapes dried on straw mats, consequently v sweet, like Italian passito. Esp in the JURA. See also Chave.

Vin de Table Standard everyday table wine, not subject to particular regulations about grapes and origin. Choose VINS DE PAYS instead.

Vin Vert Very light acidic refreshing white wine, a speciality of ROUSSILLON (and v necessary in summer in those torrid parts).

Vinsobres S Rh r (p w) ★★ 85 86 88 89 90' 93 94 95 Contradictory name of good S Rhône village. Potentially substantial reds, but many ordinary. Best producers incl Dom les Aussellons, Dom du Moulin.

Viré See Mâcon-Viré.

Visan S Rh r p w ★★ 88 89 90' 93 94 95 Village for far better reds than whites.

Viticulteur Wine-grower.

Vogüé, Comte Georges de ('Dom les Musigny') First-class 30-acre domaine at CHAMBOLLE-MUSIGNY. At best the ultimate BONNES-MARES and MUSIGNY.

Volnay Burg r ★★★ 78 85' 87 88' 89' 90' 91 92 93 94 95 Village between POMMARD and MEURSAULT: often the best reds of the COTE DE BEAUNE, not dark or heavy but structured and silky. Best v'yds: Caillerets, Champans, Clos des Chênes, Clos des Ducs etc. Best growers: D'ANGERVILLE, J Boillot, HOSPICES DE BEAUNE, LAFARGE, LAFON, de Montille, POUSSE D'OR, M ROSSIGNOL.

Volnay-Santenots Burg r ★★★ Excellent red wine from MEURSAULT is sold under this name. Indistinguishable from other PREMIER CRU VOLNAY. Best growers: AMPEAU, LAFON, LEROY.

Vosne-Romanée Burg r ★★★→★★★★ 78' 85' 87 88' 89' 90' 91 92 93 94 95 Village with Burgundy's grandest CRUS (ROMANEE-CONTI, LA TACHE etc). There are (or should be) no common wines in Vosne. Many good growers include Arnoux, Castagnier, CHEVIGNY, DRC, ENGEL, GRIVOT, GROS, JAYER, LATOUR, LEROY, MEO-CAMUZET, MONGEARD-MUGNERET, Mugneret, RION.

Vougeot See Clos de Vougeot.

Vouvray Lo w dr sw sp ★★→★★★★★ 76' 78' 79 82 83 85' 86 88' 89' 90' 92 93 95' 4,350-acre AC just E of Tours with v variable wines, increasingly good, reliable. DEMI-SEC is classic style but in great years MOELLEUX can be intensely sweet, almost immortal. Good dry sparkling – look out for PETILLANT. Best producers: Allias, Bourillon-Dorleans, BREDIF, Brisebarre, Champalou, Delaleu, Foreau, Fouquet, Ch Gaudrelle, HUET, Poniatowski, Vaugondy.

Willm, A N ALSACE grower at Barr, with vg GEWURZ Clos Gaensbronnel.

'Y' (pronounced 'ygrec') 78' 79' 80' 84 85 86 87 88 89 Dry wine produced occasionally at CH D'YQUEM. Most interesting with age.

Ziltener, André Swiss burgundy grower/mail-order merchant with entertaining cellars at Ch Ziltener, CHAMBOLLE MUSIGNY. Wide range.

Zind-Humbrecht 64-acre ALSACE estate in Thann, Turckheim, Wintzenheim. First-rate single-v'yd wines (esp Clos St-Urbain Ries), and v fine from GRANDS CRUS Goldert (GEWURZ and MUSCAT), HENGST and RANGEN.

NB Vintages in colour are those you should choose first for drinking in 1997.

77

Châteaux of Bordeaux

The following abbreviations
of regional names
are used in the text:

B'x	Bordeaux
E-Deux-Mers	Entre-Deux-Mers
H-Méd	Haut-Médoc
Mar	Margaux
Méd	Médoc
Pau	Pauillac
Pessac-L	Pessac-Léognan
Pom	Pomerol
St-Em	St-Emilion
St-Est	St-Estèphe
St-Jul	St-Julien
Saut	Sauternes

Heavily shaded
areas are the wine
growing regions

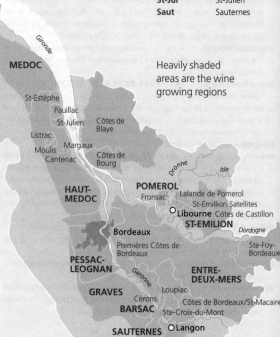

After the golden years of the 1980s, when eight vintages out of ten made excellent wines and five made great ones, 1991 began a decade that could be called morose, with a recurring pattern of rainy vintages. Bordeaux drinkers are now feeling the benefits of the glorious 1980s: bottles of '82, '83, '85, '86, '88, '89, '90 are all either appreciating assets or at least sweet memories. We are also picking our way gingerly through the very mixed offerings of '91, '92, '93 and '94 – finding that the frost reduced '91 vintage, when it came off at all (which was not in Pomerol and St-Emilion), made some very agreeable reds at reasonable prices, that '92, a huge diluted crop, offers bargains if not sensations, that '93s, which are rather tough and tannic, will need patience, and that the '94s are far better overall than the wet vintage suggested.

As for the '95, it was, as I have written elsewhere, saved by the rain. The most glorious of summers was not let down by September rain – on the contrary, it anointed a magnificent vintage.

As in last year's edition I have picked out in colour the vintages which proprietors themselves will be serving this year as first choices: their own wines in the state of maturity they prefer. Their choices remind us that there are no absolutes in wine – least of all in the glorious diversity of Bordeaux.

d'Agassac H-Méd r ★★ 82' 83' 85' 86 88 89' 90' 91 92 93 94 95 Sleeping Beauty 14th-C moated fort. 86 acres v nr Bordeaux suburbs. Lively wine popular in Holland. Same owners as CHATEAU CALON-SEGUR.

d'Alesme Mar r ★★ 81 82 83 85 86 88' 89 90 94 95 Tiny (17-acre) third-growth, formerly 'Marquis-d'Alesme.' A lost CRU CLASSE, once highly regarded. Potential.

Andron-Blanquet St-Est r ★★ 82 85' 86 88 89' 90 92 93 94 95 Sister château to COS-LABORY. 40 acres. Wines lack charm.

L'Angélus St-Em r ★★★ 81 82 83' 85' 86 87 88 89' 90' 91 92 93' 94' 95 57-acre classed-growth on ST-EMILION COTES. A recent star with fat showy wines.

d'Angludet Cantenac-Mar r ★★─★★★ 70' 76' 78' 79 80 81' 82 83 85 86 87 88' 89' 90 91 92 93 94 95 75-acre CRU EXCEPTIONNEL of classed-growth quality owned by PETER A SICHEL. Lively fragrant MARGAUX of great style. Value.

d'Archambeau Graves r w dr (sw) ★★ (r) 85 86 88 89 90 91 92 93 94 95 (w) 88 90' 92' 93 95 Up-to-date 54-acre property at Illats. Vg fruity dry white; since '85 fragrant barrel-aged reds (planned to be ¾ of v'yd).

d'Arche Saut w sw ★★ 81 82 83' 85 86' 88' 89' 90 93 94 95 Classed-growth of 88 acres rejuvenated since '80. Modern methods. Rich juicy wines.

d'Arcins Central Méd r ★★ 86 88 89 90 93 94 95 185-acre Castel family property (Castelvin is a famous VIN DE TABLE). Sister to next-door Barreyres (160 acres).

d'Armailhac Pau r ★★★ 78' 81 82' 83 85 86' 87 88 89 90' 91 92 93 94' 95 New name ('91) for CH MOUTON-BARONNE-PHILIPPE. Substantial fifth growth nurtured by the late Baron Philippe de Rothschild. 125 acres: wine less rich and luscious than MOUTON-ROTHSCHILD, but outstanding in its class.

Vintages shown in light type should only be opened now out of curiosity to gauge their future. Vintages shown in bold type are deemed (usually by their makers) to be ready for drinking. Remember though that the French tend to enjoy the vigour of young wines, and that many 82s, 83s, 85s and 86s have at least another decade of development in front of them. Vintages marked thus' are regarded as particularly successful for the property in question. Vintages in colour are the special selection for '97.

l'Arrosée St-Em r ★★★ 79 81 82 83 85' 86' 87 88 89' 90' 92 93 94' 95 24-acre COTES estate. Name means watered, but wine is top-flight: opulent, structured. Modern cuvier; 100% new barrels.

Ausone St-Em r ★★★★ 75 76 78' 79 81 82' 83' 85 86' 87 88 89 90 91 92 93 94 95 First growth with 17 acres (about 2,500 cases) in the best position on the COTES with famous rock-hewn cellars. The most expensive ST-EMILION, but far behind châteaux CHEVAL BLANC or FIGEAC in performance and appeal. See also Ch Belair.

Bahans-Haut-Brion Graves r ★★★ NV and 82 83 85 86' 87 88 89' 90 91 92 93 94 95 The second-quality wine of CH HAUT-BRION. Wine worthy of its noble origin; softly earthy yet intense.

Balestard-la-Tonnelle St-Em r ★★ 81 83 85 86' 87 88' 89 90' 92 93 94 95 Historic 30-acre classed growth on the plateau. Big flavour; more finesse since '85. New chai in '95.

de Barbe Côtes de Bourg r (w) ★★ 85 86 88 89 90 92 93 94 95 The biggest (148 acres), best-known château of BOURG. Light fruity Merlot.

Baret Pessac-L r w ★★ (r) 83 85 86 88 89' 90' 95 Famous name recovered from a lull. Now run by BORIE-MANOUX. White well-made too.

Bastor-Lamontagne Saut w sw ★★ 76 79 82 83 85 86 87 88' 89' 90' 94 95 Large Bourgeois Preignac château with same owners as CH BEAUREGARD. Classed-growth quality; excellent rich wines. Second label: Les Remparts de Bastor (92 93). Also Ch St-Robert at Pujols: red and white GRAVES. 10,000 cases.

Batailley Pau r ★★★ 70 75' 78' 79' 81 82' 83' 85' 86 87 88' 89' 90' 91 92 93 94 95 The bigger of the famous pair of fifth-growths (with HAUT-BATAILLEY) on the borders of PAUILLAC and ST-JULIEN. 110 acres. Fine, firm, strong-flavoured wine, to age. Home of the Castéja family of BORIE-MANOUX.

Beaumont Cussac (Haut-Méd) r ★★ 82 85 86' 88 89' 90' 91 92 93' 94 95 200-acre+ CRU BOURGEOIS, well-known in France for easily enjoyable and improving wines from maturing vines. Second label: Ch Moulin d'Arvigny. 35,000 cases. In the same hands as CH BEYCHEVELLE since '87.

Beauregard Pom r ★★★ 82' 83 85 86 87 88 89' 90' 92 93 94' 95 42-acre v'yd; fine 17th-C château nr LA CONSEILLANTE owned by a bank. Top-rank rich wines. Advice from M Rolland. Second label: Benjamin de Beauregard.

Beau-Séjour-Bécot St-Em r ★★→★★★ 75 82' 83 85 86' 88' 89' 90' 91 92 93 94 95 Other half of BEAUSEJOUR-DUFFAU-LAGAROSSE; 45 acres. Controversially demoted in class in '85 but much revved-up since. The Bécots also own CH GRAND-PONTET. Now also La Gomerie: 1,000 cases, 100% Merlot.

Beau-Site St-Est r ★★ 75' 78' 79 81 82 83 85 86' 87 88 89' 90 92 93 95 55-acre CRU BOURGEOIS EXCEPTIONNEL in same hands as CH BATAILLEY etc. Quality and substance typical of ST-ESTEPHE.

Beauséjour-Duffau-Lagarosse St-Em r ★★★ 82 83 85 86 88 89' 90' 93' 94 95 Part of the old Beau-Séjour Premier Grand Cru estate on W slope of the COTES. 17 acres in old family hands; firm-structured, concentrated.

de Bel-Air Lalande de Pom r ★★ 82' 85 86 88' 89' 90 92 93 94' 95 The best-known estate of L de P, just N of POMEROL. Pomerol-style wine. 37 acres.

Bel-Air-Marquis-d'Aligre Soussans-Mar r ★★ 79' 81 82' 85 86 88 89 90 95 Organically-run CRU EXCEPTIONNEL with 42 acres of old vines giving only 3,500 cases. The owner likes gutsy wine.

Bel-Orme-Tronquoy-de-Lalande St-Seurin-de-Cadourne (H-Méd) r ★★ 81 82 83 85 86 87 88 89 90 92 93 94 95 60-acre CRU BOURGEOIS N of ST-ESTEPHE. Old v'yd producing tannic wines. More effort since new manager.

Belair St-Em r ★★★ 75' 78 79' 82' 83' 85' 86' 88' 89' 90' 92 93 94 95 Sister château/neighbour of AUSONE. Wine considerably easier, less tight. High standard recently. Also NV Roc-Blanquant (magnums only).

Belgrave St-Laurent r ★★ 81 82 83 85 86' 87 88 89 90' 93 94 95 Obscure fifth growth in ST-JULIEN's back-country. 107 acres. Managed by DOURTHE since '79. Second label: Diane de Belgrave.

Bellegrave Listrac r ★★ 82 83 85 86 88 89 90 92 93 94 95 38-acre CRU BOURGEOIS making full-bodied wine with advice from PICHON-LALANDE.

Berliquet St-Em r ★★ 78 81 82 83 85 86 88 89' 90 91 92 93 94 95 23-acre Grand Cru Classé recently v well-run (sold by the ST-EMILION COOP).

Bertineau St-Vincent Lalande de Pom r ★★ 10 acres owned by top oenologist Michel Rolland (see also Le Bon Pasteur).

Beychevelle St-Jul r ★★★ →★★★★ 70' 78 81 82' 83 85 86' 87 88 89' 90 91 92 93 94' 95 170-acre fourth growth with MEDOC's finest mansion. Owned by an insurance company since '85. Wine of elegance and power, just below top-flight ST-JULIEN. Second wine: Amiral de Beychevelle.

Biston-Brillette Moulis r ★★ Another attractive MOULIS. 7,000 cases.

Le Bon Pasteur Pom r ★★★ 70 75 76 81 82 83 85 86' 87 88 89' 90' 92 93' 94' 95 Excellent small property on ST-EMILION boundary, owned by consultant oenologist Michel Rolland. Concentrated, s'times even creamy wines.

Bonalgue Pom r ★★ Ambitious 2,500-case estate to watch. Les Hautes-Tuileries is sister château. Wines built to age.

Bonnet E-Deux-Mers r w ★★ (r) 90 92 93 94 95 (w) DYA Big-scale producer (600 acres!) of some of the best ENTRE-DEUX-MERS.

Le Boscq St-Est r ★★ 82 83 85 86 87 88 89' 90 92 93 95 Leading CRU BOURGEOIS giving excellent value in tasty ST-ESTEPHE ('VIEILLES VIGNES').

Le Bourdieu-Vertheuil H-Méd r ★★ 81 82 83 85 86 88 89 90' 92 93' 94 95 Vertheuil CRU BOURGEOIS with sister château, Victoria, (134 acres in all); well-made ST-ESTEPHE-style wines. New owners, equipment and effort since '90.

Bourgneuf Pom r ★★ 81 82 83 85' 86 88 89' 90 92 95 22-acre v'yd on chalky clay soil, its best wines fairly rich with typically plummy POMEROL perfume. 5,000 cases. Alias Bourgneuf-Vayron.

Bouscaut Graves r w ★★ 81 82' 83 85 86' 88 89 90 92 93 95 Classed growth at Cadaujac bought in '80 by Lucien Lurton of BRANE-CANTENAC etc. 75 acres red (largely Merlot); 15 white. Never yet brilliant, but slowly getting there.

du Bousquet Côtes de Bourg r ★★ 82 83 85 86 88 89 90' 92 93 95 Reliable estate with 148 acres making attractive solid wine.

Boyd-Cantenac Mar r ★★★ 78' 81 82' 83' 85 86' 88 89 90 91 92 93 94' 95 44-acre third growth often producing attractive wine, full of flavour, if not of third-growth class. See also Ch Pouget.

Branaire-Ducru St-Jul r ★★★ 79' 81 82' 83 85 86 87 88 89' 90' 91 92 93 94 95 Fourth growth of 125 acres. Notably spicy and flavoury wine in the '70s. The late '80s saw a full-scale revival. New owners in '88. Second label: Duluc.

Brane-Cantenac Cantenac-Mar r ★★★ 78' 79 81 82' 83 85 86' 87 88 89 90 94 95 Big (211-acre) second growth. At best rich, even gamey wines of strong character. Same owners as CH'X BOUSCAUT, CLIMENS, DURFORT-VIVENS, VILLEGEORGE etc. Second labels: ch'x Baron de Brane, Notton.

du Breuil Cissac r ★★ 88 89 90 92 93 95 Abandoned historic château bought by owners of CISSAC and restored. To follow.

Brillette Moulis r ★★ 81' 82 83 85' 86 88 89' 90 91 92 93 95 70-acre CRU BOURGEOIS. Reliable and attractive. Second label: Berthault Brillette.

La Cabanne Pom r ★★ 79 81 82' 83 85 86 87 88' 89' 90' 92 93 94 95 Well regarded 25-acre property nr the great TROTANOY. Recently modernized. Second wine: Dom de Compostelle. See also CH HAUT-MAILLET.

Cadet-Piola St-Em r ★★ 75' 78 81 82 83' 85' 86 87 88 89' 90 92 93' 94' 95 Distinguished little property just N of the town of ST-EMILION. 3,000 cases of tannic wine. CH FAURIE-DE-SOUCHARD has same owner; less robust.

81

Caillou Saut w sw ★★ 75 76 78 81 **82 83 85 86 87** 88' 89' 90' 91 92 94 95 Well-run second-rank 37-acre BARSAC v'yd for firm fruity wine. Private Cuvée (**81 83 85** 86 88 89') is a top selection.

Calon-Ségur St-Est r ★★★ 78 79 81 82' **83 85**' **86 87** 88' 89' 90 91 93 94 95 Big (123-acre) third growth of great reputation for fruity hearty wines; less stylish than very top ST-ESTÈPHES but currently on good form. Second label: Marquis de Ségur.

Cambon-la-Pelouse H-Méd r ★★ 82 85 86 87 88 89 90 **92 93** 95 Big accessible CRU BOURGEOIS. A sure bet for fresh typical MEDOC without wood-ageing.

Camensac St-Laurent r ★★ 81 82' 85 86' **87 88** 89 90 91 **92 93** 94' 95 149-acre fifth growth. Good lively if not exactly classic wines. New vat-house in '94. Second label: La Closerie de Camensac.

Canon Canon-Fronsac r ★★ →★★★ 82 **83 85** 86' 88 89' 90 **92** 93 94 95 Tiny property of CHRISTIAN MOUEIX. Long-ageing wine.

Canon St-Em r ★★★ 79' 81 82' 83 85' **86 87** 88' 89' 90' 92 93' 94' 95 Famous first-classed-growth with 44+ acres on the plateau west of the town. Conservative methods, modern kit: v impressive wine, among ST-EMILION's best. Second label (in '91): Clos J Kanon.

Canon-de-Brem Canon-Fronsac r ★★ 81 82' **83 85 86** 88 89' 90 **92** 93 94 95 One of the top FRONSAC v'yds for vigorous wine. MOUEIX property.

Canon-la-Gaffelière St-Em r ★★★ 82 **83 85** 86' **87 88**' 89' 90' **92** 93' 94 95 47-acre classed-growth on lower slopes of CÔTES. German owners. Total renovation in '85. Stylish, up-front impressive wines.

Canon-Moueix Canon-Fronsac r ★★ 82 83 85 86 87 88 89' 90 91 **92** 93 94 95 The latest MOUEIX investment in this rising AC. V stylish wine. NB also sister-châteaux CANON-DE-BREM, Canon-Milary.

Cantegril Graves r ★★ 88 89 90 95 Good earthy red from CH DOISY-DAENE.

Cantemerle Macau r ★★★ 61 78 81 82 83' **85 87** 88 89' 90 91 **92** 93 94 95 Romantic southern MEDOC estate, a château in a wood with 150 acres of vines. Officially fifth growth; potentially much higher for its harmony of flavours. Problems in the late '70s, but a new broom (CORDIER) since '81 has restored to potential. New cellars and oak vats introduced in '90. Second label: Villeneuve de Cantemerle.

Cantenac-Brown Cantenac-Mar r ★★→★★★ 70 78 79 81 82 83 85 86' **87 88** 89 90' 91 92 93 94 95 Formerly old-fashioned 77-acre third growth. New owners (same as PICHON-LONGUEVILLE) investing heavily; direction from J-M Cazes and more promising recent vintages. Tannic wines. 2nd label: Canuet.

Cap-de-Mourlin St-Em r ★★ 79' 81 82' **83 85 86 87** 88 89 90 **92** 93 94 95 Well-known 37-acre property of the Cap-de-Mourlin family, owners of CH BALESTARD and CH ROUDIER, MONTAGNE-ST-EM. Rich tasty ST-EMILION.

Capbern-Gasqueton St-Est r ★★ 81 82 **83 85 86** 88 89 90 **92 93** 94 95 Good 85-acre CRU BOURGEOIS; same owner as CALON-SEGUR.

Carbonnieux Graves r w ★★★ 82 83 **85 86**' **87 88** 89' 90' 91 **92** 93 94 95 Historic estate at LEOGNAN for sterling red and white. The whites, 50% Sémillon (eg 87 88 89 90 91 92' 93 94'), have the structure to age 10 yrs. Ch'x Le Pape and Le Sartre are also in the family. Second label: La Tour-Léognan.

Cardaillan Graves r ★★ The trusty red wine of the distinguished CHATEAU DE MALLE (SAUTERNES).

La Cardonne Blaignan (Méd) r ★★ 86 **88** 89 90 91 **92 93** 94 95 Large (300-acre+) CRU BOURGEOIS of the northern MEDOC. Rothschild-owned 1973–90. Big changes since. Fairly simple fruity Médoc, best when young.

de Carles Fronsac r ★★ 90 **92 93** 94 95 Steadily well-made typical FRONSACS.

Châteaux entries also cross-refer to France section, pages 32–77.

Les Carmes-Haut-Brion Graves r ★★ 81' 82' 83 85 86 87 88' 89 90' 91 92 93' 94 95 Small (11-acre) neighbour of HAUT-BRION with higher than Bourgeois standards. Old vintages show its potential. Only 1,500 cases.

Caronne-Ste-Gemme St-Laurent r ★★→★★★ 81 82' 83 85 86 87 88 89' 90 91 92 93' 94' 95 CRU BOURGEOIS EXCEPTIONNEL (100 acres). Steady stylish quality repays patience. At minor CRU CLASSE level.

View from the Médoc...
'White wine is what you drink before you drink red wine.'
Bruno Prats, Château Cos d'Estournel.

Carteau-Côtes-Daugay St-Em ★★ Emerging 5,000-case GRAND CRU; to follow for full-flavoured wines maturing fairly early.

du Castéra Méd r ★★ 85 86 88 89 90' 91 92 93 94' 95 Historic property at St-Germain (N MEDOC). Recent investment; tasty but not tannic wine.

Certan-Giraud Pom r ★★ 75 81 82 83' 85 86 87 88 89' 90' 92 93' 94 95 Small (17-acre) property next to PETRUS. Good, but one expects more.

Certan-de-May Pom r ★★★ 75 78 79 81 82' 83' 85' 86 87 88' 89' 90' 91 92 93 94 95 Neighbour of VIEUX CHATEAU CERTAN. Tiny property (1,800 cases) with full-bodied, rich, tannic wine, consistently flying v high.

Chambert-Marbuzet St-Est r ★★ 70 76 78 79 81 82 83 85 86 87 88 89' 90' 92 93 94' 95 Tiny (20-acre) sister ch of HAUT-MARBUZET. Vg predominantly Cab wine, aged v tastily in new oak. Owner, M Duboscq, likes wines well hung.

Chantegrive Graves r w ★★★ 215-acre estate, half white, half red; modern GRAVES of high quality. Cuvée Caroline is top white selection (89 90 92 93 94), Cuvée Edouard top red (82 83 85 87 88 89 90). Other labels incl Mayne-Lévêque, Bon-Dieu-des-Vignes.

Chasse-Spleen Moulis r ★★★ 70 75' 78' 79 81' 82' 83' 85 86 87 88 89' 90' 91 92 93 94 95 180-acre CRU EXCEPTIONNEL of classed-growth quality. Consistently good, usually outstanding, long-maturing wine. Second label: Ermitage de C-S. One of the surest things in Bordeaux. See also La Gurgue.

Chéret-Pitres Graves r w ★→★★ Substantial estate in the up-and-coming village of Portets. Drink young or keep.

Cheval Blanc St-Em r ★★★★ 64 75' 76 78 79 81' 82' 83' 85' 86 87 88 89 90' 92 93 94' 95 This and AUSONE are the 'first growths' of ST-EMILION. Cheval Bl is consistently richer, more full-blooded, intensely vigorous and perfumed, from 100 acres. Delicious young; lasts a generation. 2nd wine: Le Petit Cheval.

Chevalier, Domaine de Graves r w ★★★★ 66' 70' 78' 79 81' 83' 85 86' 87 88' 89' 90' 91 92 93 94' 95 Superb small estate of 36 acres at LEOGNAN. The red is stern at first, richly subtle with age. The white matures slowly to rich flavours (81 82 83' 85' 87' 88 89 90' 91 92 93' 94). Also the little Domaine de la Solitude, PESSAC-LEOGNAN.

Cissac Cissac r ★★ 70' 75' 76 78' 79 81 82' 83' 85 86' 87 88 89 90 91 92 93 94' 95 Pillar of the bourgeoisie. 80-acre CRU GRAND BOURGEOIS EXCEPTIONNEL: steady record for tasty, v long-lived wine. Second wine: Les Reflets du Ch Cissac. Also, since '87, CH DU BREUIL.

Citran Avensan (H-Méd) r ★★ 82 85 86 87 88 89' 90' 91 92 93 94' 95 CRU GRAND BOURGEOIS EXCEPTIONNEL of 178 acres, bought by Japanese in '87. Major works. Recent good vintages turbo-charged. Second label is Moulins de Citran. To watch.

Clarke Listrac r (p w) ★★ 82 83 85' 86' 87 88 89' 90 91 92 93 94 95 Huge (350-acre) CRU BOURGEOIS Rothschild development, incl visitor facilities and neighbouring ch'x Malmaison and Peyrelebade. Also a unique sweet white 'Le Merle Blanc du Ch Clarke'.

Clerc-Milon Pau r ★★★ 78' 81 82' 83 85 86' 87 88 89' 90' 91 92 93 94 95
Once-forgotten fifth growth bought by the late Baron Philippe de Rothschild
in '70. Now 73 acres. Not thrilling in the '70s (except **70**), but vg 85, 86
(esp), and now a top performer, weightier than ARMAILHAC.

Climens Saut w sw ★★★★ 71' 75' 76 78 79 80' 81 82 83' 85' 86' 88' 89 90' 95
74-acre BARSAC classed growth making some of the world's most stylish
wine (but not the v sweetest) for a good 10 yrs' maturing. (Occasional)
second label: Les Cyprès. Same owner as CH BRANE-CANTENAC etc.

Clinet Pom r ★★★ 82 83 85 86 87 88' 89' 90' 91 92 93' 94 95 17-acre property
in central POMEROL making intense wines from old vines. Since '86 one of the
models for POMEROL.

Clos l'Eglise Pom r ★★★ 75 81 83 85 86 88 89 90' 92 93 94 95 14-acre v'yd
on one of the best sites in POMEROL. Fine wine without great muscle or flesh.
The same family owns CH PLINCE.

Clos Floridène Graves r w ★★ (r) 90' 91 92 93' 94 95 (w) 89' 90 92 93 94 95
A sure thing from one of the best white wine makers of Bordeaux, Denis
Dubourdieu. Oak-fermented Sauv-Sém to keep 5 yrs, and fruity red. See
also Ch Reynon.

Clos Fourtet St-Em r ★★★ 78 79 81 82' 83 85 86 88 89 90 92 93 94 95 Well-
placed 42-acre first growth on the plateau, cellars almost in town. Back on
form after a middling patch: André Lurton is now winemaker; more changes
to come. Same owners as BRANE-CANTENAC, CLIMENS etc. Second label: Dom
de Martialis.

Clos Haut-Peyraguey Saut w sw ★★ 75 76 79 80 83 85 86' 87 88' 89 90' 93
94 95 Tiny production of excellent medium-rich wine. Haut-Bommes is the
second label.

Clos des Jacobins St-Em r ★★ 75' 78 79 81 82' 83' 85 86 87 88' 89' 90' 92 93
94 95 Well-known and well-run little (18-acre) classed-growth owned by
the shipper CORDIER. Wines of notable depth and style.

Clos du Marquis St-Jul r ★★→★★★ 81 82 83 85 86' 87 88 89' 90 91 92 93
94 95 The second wine of LEOVILLE-LAS-CASES, cut from the same cloth and
regularly a match for many classed growths.

Clos René Pom r ★★ 75 81 82' 83 85 86 87 88 89 90 91 92 93 94 95 Leading
château west of POMEROL. 38 acres. Increasingly concentrated wines. Alias
Ch Moulinet-Lasserre.

La Closerie-Grand-Poujeaux Moulis r ★★ 85 86 88 89 90 91 92 93 94' 95
Small but respected middle-MEDOC property modernized in '92/'93. Also
owners of neighbouring ch'x Bel-Air-Lagrave and Haut-Franquet.

La Clotte St-Em r ★★ 82 83' 85 86 88 89 90' 92 93' 94 95 Tiny COTES GRAND
CRU: pungent supple wine. Drink at owners' restaurant, Logis de la Cadène,
in ST-EM. Second label: Clos Bergat Bosson (**91 93 93**).

Colombier-Monpelou Pau r ★★ 82 83 85 86' 87 88 89 90' 91 92 93 94 95
Reliable small CRU BOURGEOIS made to a fair standard.

La Conseillante Pom r ★★★★ 70' 75' 76 79 81' 82' 83 84 85 86 87 88 89 90'
91 92 93 94 95 29-acre historic property on the plateau between PETRUS
and CHEVAL BLANC. Some of the noblest and most fragrant POMEROL, worthy
of its superb position; drinks well, young or old.

Corbin (Giraud) St-Em r ★★ 75 79 81 82' 83 85 86 88 89 90' 92 93 94 95
28-acre classed-growth in N ST-EMILION where a cluster of Corbins occupy
the plateau edge. Top vintages are v rich. Same owner as CERTAN-GIRAUD.

Corbin-Michotte St-Em r ★★ 81 82 83 85 88 89' 90 93 94' 95 Well-run
modernized 19-acre property; 'generous' POMEROL-like wine.

Cordeillan-Bages Pau r ★★ A mere 1,000 cases of full-blooded PAUILLAC from
the château-hotel of J-M Cazes (see Lynch-Bages).

Cos-d'Estournel St-Est r ★★★★ 70 75' 76' 78' 79 81' 82' 83' 84 85' 86' 87 88' 89' 90' 91 92 93' 94 95 140-acre second growth with eccentric chinoiserie tower overlooking CH LAFITE. The most refined ST-ESTEPHE. Regularly one of best wines in the MEDOC. Second label: CH DE MARBUZET.

Cos-Labory St-Est r ★★ 82 83 85 86 87 88 89' 90' 91 92 93 94 95 Little-known fifth-growth neighbour of COS-D'ESTOURNEL with 37 acres. Efforts since '85 have raised it steadily to classed-growth form (esp since '90). ANDRON-BLANQUET is sister château.

Coufran St-Seurin-de-Cadourne (H-Méd) r ★★ 81 82' 83 85 86' 87 88 89 90 91 92 93 94 95 Coufran and CH VERDIGNAN, on the northernmost hillock of the HAUT-MEDOC, are co-owned. Coufran has mainly Merlot vines, giving soft supple wine. 148 acres. CH SOUDARS is another, smaller sister.

Couhins-Lurton Graves w ★★ 85 86' 88 89 90 91 92 93 94 95 Tiny quantity of v fine oaky Sauv for maturing. Classed-growth château being restored.

Coutet Saut w sw ★★★ 71' 75' 76 81' 82 83' 85 86' 87 88' 89' 90' (no 93 94) 95 Traditional rival to CH CLIMENS; 91 acres in BARSAC. Usually slightly less rich; at its best equally fine. Cuvée Madame is a v rich selection in the best vintages. A dry GRAVES is sold under the same name.

Couvent des Jacobins St-Em r ★★ 75 78 79' 81 82' 83 85 86 87 88 89 90 92 93 94 95 Well-known 22-acre v'yd on E edge of town. Among the best of its kind. Splendid cellars. Second label: Ch Beau-Mayne.

Le Crock St-Est r ★★ 79 81 82 83 85 86 87 88 89 90' 92 93 95 Outstanding CRU BOURGEOIS of 74 acres in the same family as CH LEOVILLE-POYFERRE. Among the best CRUS BOURGEOIS of the commune.

La Croix Pom r ★★ 75' 76 79' 81 82 83 85' 86 87 88 89 90 91 92 93 94 95 Well-reputed property of 32 acres. Appealing plummy POMEROL with a spine; matures well. Also La C-St-Georges, La C-Toulifaut, Castelot, Clos des Litanies and HAUT-SARPE (St-Em).

La Croix-de-Gay Pom r ★★★ 81 82' 83' 85 86 88' 89 90 91 92 93 94' 95 30 acres in best part of the commune. Recently on fine form. Has underground cellars (rare in POMEROL). LA FLEUR-DE-GAY is the best selection.

Croizet-Bages Pau r ★★ 82' 83 85 86 87 88 90' 91 92 93 94 95 52-acre fifth growth (lacking a château or a reputation). Same owners as CH RAUZAN-GASSIES. Only a flicker of life, but new manager in '94.

Croque-Michotte St-Em r ★★ 75 78 81 82' 83 85 86 87 88 89' 90' 93 94 95 35-acre classed growth on the POMEROL border. New equipment.

de Cruzeau Graves r w ★★ (r) 86 88 89 90 91 92 93 94 95 100-acre GRAVES-LEOGNAN v'yd recently developed by André Lurton of LA LOUVIERE etc. V high standards; to try. Oak-fermented white keeps 2–5 years.

Curé-Bon-la-Madeleine St-Em r ★★ 75 78 81 82' 83 85 86 88 89 90 94 95 Tiny little-known (12-acre) property between AUSONE and CANON.

Dalem Fronsac r ★★ 82 83 85 86 87 88 89 90 92 93 94 95 Leading full-blooded FRONSAC. 36 acres: 85% Merlot.

Dassault St-Em r ★★ 82 83 85 86 88 89 90 92 93 94 95 Consistent, early-maturing middle-weight GRAND CRU. 58 acres.

La Dauphine Fronsac ★★ 85 86 87 88 89' 90' 92 93 94 95 Old star rejuvenated by J-P MOUEIX.

Dauzac Labarde-Mar r ★★→★★★ 82' 83' 85' 86 87 88' 89' 90' 92 93' 94 95 120-acre fifth growth nr the river south of MARGAUX; underachiever for many years. New owner (insurance company) in '89; direction since '92 by André Lurton. New cuvier in '94. Second wine: La Bastide Dauzac.

To decipher codes, please refer to 'Key to symbols' on front flap of jacket, or to 'How to use this book' on page 6.

Desmirail Mar r ★★ 82 83' 85 86 88 89 90 94 95 Third growth, now 45 acres. A long-defunct name revived in '81 by Lucien Lurton of BRANE-CANTENAC. So far wines for drinking fairly young.

Doisy-Daëne Barsac w (r) sw dr ★★★ 76' 78 79 80 81 82 83 85 86 88' 89' 90' 91 94 95 Forward-looking, even experimental, 34-acre estate for crisp oaky dry white and red CH CANTEGRIL as well as notably fine (and long-lived) sweet BARSAC. L'Extravagance (90) was a super-cuvée.

Doisy-Dubroca Barsac w sw ★★ 75' 76 78 79 81 83 86 87 88' 89 90' 95 Tiny (8.5-acre) BARSAC classed growth allied to CH CLIMENS.

Doisy-Védrines Saut w sw ★★★ 70 75' 76' 78 79 80 81 82' 83' 85 86 88' 89' 90 92 93 95 50-acre classed growth at BARSAC, nr CLIMENS and COUTET, recently re-equipped. Delicious, sturdy, rich: for keeping. NB the 89.

La Dominique St-Em r ★★ 78 79 81 82' 83 86' 87 88' 89' 90' 92 93 94 95 45-acre classed growth next to CH CHEVAL BLANC for fruity, nose-catching wines. Second label: St Paul de Dominique (91).

Ducluzeau Listrac r ★★ Tiny sister property of DUCRU-BEAUCAILLOU. 10 acres, unusually 90% Merlot.

Ducru-Beaucaillou St-Jul r ★★★★ 61 62 66' 70' 75' 76 78' 79 80 81 82' 83' 84 85' 86' 87 88 89 90 91 92 93 94 95 Outstanding second growth; 120 acres overlooking the river in stone cellar under château. M Borie makes classic cedar-scented claret for long ageing. See also Grand-Puy-Lacoste, Haut-Batailley, Lalande-Borie.

Duhart-Milon-Rothschild Pau r ★★★ 78 79 80 81 82' 83 85 86 87 88 89 90 91 92 93 95 Fourth-growth neighbour of LAFITE, under same management. Maturing vines; increasingly fine quality and reputation. 110 acres. Second label: Moulin de Duhart.

Duplessis-Fabre Moulis r ★★ 82 83 85 86 87 88' 89 90 92 93 95 Former sister château of FOURCAS-DUPRE; since '89 owned by DOURTHE. To watch.

Durfort-Vivens Mar r ★★★ 78' 79' 81 82' 83 85' 86 87 88' 89' 90 95 Relatively small (49-acre) second growth owned by M Lurton of BRANE-CANTENAC. Recent wines have structure (lots of Cab S) and class.

Dûtruch-Grand-Poujeaux Moulis r ★★ 79 81 82' 83 85 86 87 88 89 90 91 92 93 94 95 One of the leaders of MOULIS making full-bodied and tannic wines. 60 acres.

de l'Eglise, Domaine Pom r ★★ 79' 81 82' 83 85 86 88 89 90 92 93 95 Small property: stylish resonant wine distributed by BORIE-MANOUX.

L'Eglise-Clinet Pom r ★★★ 70 71' 75 76 78 79 81 82' 83' 84 85' 86 87 88' 89 90' 91 92 93' 94 95 11 acres. Ranked v nr top; full fleshy wine. Changed hands in '82; 86 90 noble. 1,700 cases. Second label: La Petite Eglise.

L'Enclos Pom r ★★★ 47 59 70 75 79 82' 83 85 86 87 88 89' 90' 92 93 94 95 Respected 26-acre property on west side of POMEROL, nr CLOS RENE. Usually big well-made long-flavoured wine.

L'Evangile Pom r ★★★★ 75' 78 79 82' 83' 85' 86 87 88' 89' 90' 92 93 95 33 acres between PETRUS and CHEVAL BLANC. Deep-veined but elegant style in a POMEROL classic. In the same area and class as LA CONSEILLANTE. Bought in '90 by Domaines (LAFITE) Rothschild.

de Fargues Saut w sw ★★★ 70' 71' 75' 76' 78 79 80 81 83 85' 86 87 88 89 90 95 25-acre v'yd by ruined château in same ownership as CH D'YQUEM. Fruity and extremely elegant wines, maturing earlier than Yquem.

Faurie-de-Souchard St-Em r ★★ 82 83 85 86 88 89 90 91 92 93 94 Small GRAND CRU CLASSE château on the COTES, now tightening its grip. See also Château Cadet-Piola.

de Ferrand St-Em ★★→★★★ 85 86 87 88 89 90 92 93 95 Big (75-acre) plateau estate. Rich, oaky wines, sometimes too tannic.

Ferrand-Lartigue St-Em ★★ New perfectionist 5-acre property. First wine (93) v promising in dense rich style.

Ferrande Graves r (w) ★★ 81 82 83 **85** 86 **88** 89 90 91 **92** 93 94 95 Major estate of Castres: 100+ acres. Easy enjoyable red and good white wine, at their best at 1–4 yrs.

Ferrière Mar r ★★ 92 93 94 95 Until '92 a phantom third growth; only 10+ acres; part of LASCOMBES. Now in same capable hands as CHASSE-SPLEEN.

Feytit-Clinet Pom r ★★ 75' 79 81 82' 83 85' **86** 87 88' 89' 90' 92 93 94 95 Little property near LATOUR-A-POMEROL. Fine lightish wines. Managed by J-P MOUEIX.

Fieuzal Graves r (w) ★★★ 75 79 81 82' 83 85' 86' **87** 88 89' 90' 91 92 93 94 95 75-acre classed growth at LEOGNAN. Finely made, memorable wines of both colours esp since '84. Classic whites since '85 are 4–10-yr keepers (esp **85 90** 92 93). New owners took over in '94. Ch Le Bonnat is sister château vinified at Fieuzal.

Figeac St-Em r ★★★★ 59 64 70' 78 81 82' 83 84 85' 86' **87** 88 89' 90' **92** 93 94' 95 First growth neighbour of CHEVAL BLANC. 98-acre gravelly vineyard gives one of Bordeaux's most stylish, rich but elegant wines, lovely to drink relatively quickly but lasting indefinitely. Second label: Grangeneuve.

Filhot Saut w sw dr ★★ 75 76' 82' 83' 85 86' 87 88' 89 90' 91 92 93 94 95 Second-rank classed growth with splendid château, 148-acre v'yd. Lightish rather simple (Sauv) sweet wines for fairly early drinking, a little dry, and red. Vg 'Crème de Tête' (**90** extremely rich).

La Fleur St-Em r ★★ 75 78 81 82' 83 85 86 88 89' 90' 92 93 94 95 16-acre COTES estate; increasingly fruity wines. Now managed by J-P MOUEIX.

La Fleur-de-Gay 1,000-case super-CUVEE of CH LA CROIX DE GAY.

La Fleur-Pétrus Pom r ★★★★ 70 75' 78 79 81' 82 83' 85 86 87 88' 89' 90' 92 93 18-acre v'yd flanking PETRUS and under same management. Exceedingly fine plummy wines; POMEROL at its most stylish.

Fombrauge St-Em r ★★ 81 82' 83 85 86 87 88' 89 90 92 93 94' 95 120 acres at St-Christophe-des-Bardes, E of ST-EMILION; Danish connections. Reliable mainstream St-Emilion making great efforts. Second label: Ch Maurens.

Fonbadet Pau r ★★ 70 76 78 79 81' 82' 83 85 86 87 88 89 90' 91 92 93 94 95 CRU BOURGEOIS of solid reputation. 38 acres next to PONTET-CANET. Old vines; wine needs long bottle-age. Recent building work. Value.

Fonplégade St-Em r ★★ 75 78 81 82' 83 85 86 87 88 89 90' 93 94 95 48-acre Grand Cru Classé on the COTES W of ST-EMILION in the Armand Moueix group. Firm and long-lasting.

Fonréaud Listrac r ★★ 78' 79 81 82' 83 85' 86' **87** 88 89 90 91 92 93 94 95 One of the bigger (96 acres) and better CRUS BOURGEOIS of its area. New broom (and barrels) since '83. Now also 5 acres of white: Le Cygne, barrel-fermented. See also Ch Lestage.

Fonroque St-Em r ★★★ 70 75' 78 79 81 82 83' 85' 86 87 88 89' 90' 92 93 94 95 48 acres on the plateau N of ST-EMILION. J-P MOUEIX property. Big deep dark wine: drink or (better) keep.

Les Forts de Latour Pau r ★★★ 70' 75 78' 79 80 81 82' **83** 84 85 86' **87** 88 90' 91 92 93 94 95 The second wine of CH LATOUR; well worthy of its big brother. For long unique in being bottle-aged at least 3 yrs before release; since '90 offered EN PRIMEUR as well. Specially fine 82 and 90.

Fourcas-Dupré Listrac r ★★ 70' 75 78' 79 81 82' 83' 85' 86' 87 88 89' 90 91 92 93 95 Top-class 100-acre CRU BOURGEOIS EXCEPTIONNEL making consistent wine in the tight LISTRAC style. To follow. Second label: Ch Bellevue-Laffont.

Fourcas-Hosten Listrac r ★★→★★★ 70 75 78' 79 81 82' 83' 85 86' **87** 88 89 90 91 92 93 95 96-acre CRU BOURGEOIS currently considered the best of its (underestimated) commune. Firm wine with a long life.

Franc-Mayne St-Em r ★★ 85 86 87 88 89' 90' 91 92 93 94 95 '89 acquisition of AXA Insurance. 18 acres run by J-M Cazes (LYNCH-BAGES). Ch'x La Fleur-Pourret and Petit-Figeac (19 acres) are in same stable.

de France Pessac-L r w ★★ Well-known GRAVES property: 65 acres red, 10 white, recently replanted. Recent reds notable.

La Gaffelière St-Em r ★★★ 70 82' 83' 85 86' 87 88' 89' 90' 92 93 94 95 61-acre first growth at the foot of the COTES below CH BEL-AIR. Elegant, not rich wines; worth its rank since '82, after a bad patch.

Galius St-Em r ★★★ 85 86 88 89 90 92 93 94 95 Oak-aged selection from ST-EMILION coop, to a high standard. Formerly Haut Quercus.

La Garde Graves r (w) ★★ 81 82' 83' 84 85 86 88 89 90 91 92 93 94 95 Substantial property making reliably sound red.

Le Gay Pom r ★★★ 70 75' 76' 78 79 82' 83' 85 86 88 89' 90' 92 95 Fine 14-acre v'yd on N edge of POMEROL. Same owner as CH LAFLEUR; under J-P MOUEIX management since '85. Impressive tannic wines.

Gazin Pom r ★★★ 81 82 83 85 86 87' 88 89' 90' 92 93 94' 95 Large property (for POMEROL) with 58 acres next to PETRUS. Inconsistent up to '85; now back on top form. Distributed by J-P MOUEIX. Second label: Ch l'Hospitalet.

Gilette Saut w sw ★★★ 37 49 53 55 59 61 62 70 Extraordinary small Preignac château stores its sumptuous wines in cask to a great age. Only about 5,000 bottles of each. Ch Les Justices is the sister château (83 85 86).

Giscours Labarde-Mar r ★★★ 70 71' 75' 76 78' 79' 81' 82' 83' 85 86 87 88 89' 90 91 92 93 94 95 Splendid 182-acre third growth south of CANTENAC. Dynamically run with excellent vigorous wine in '70s; '80s less sure-footed; revival in '90s. Recently purchased by Mr Albada-Jelgersma. Second labels: ch'x Cantelaude, Grand Goucsirs(!). Ch La Houringue is baby sister.

du Glana St-Jul r ★★ 81 82' 83 85 86 88 89 90 91 92 93 94 95 Big CRU BOURGEOIS in ST-JULIEN centre. Undemanding; undramatic; value. Second wine: Ch Sirène.

Gloria St-Jul r ★★→★★★ 70' 75 76 81 82 83 85 86 88 89 90 92 93 94 95 CRU BOURGEOIS with wine of vigour and finesse. 110 acres. In '82 the owner bought ST-PIERRE. Recent return to long-maturing style. 2nd label: Peymartin.

Grand-Barrail-Lamarzelle-Figeac St-Em r ★★ 82' 83 85 86 88 89 90 91 92 93 94 95 48-acre property S of FIGEAC, incl Ch La Marzelle. Well-reputed and popular, if scarcely exciting. Now also a smart hotel.

Grand-Corbin-Despagne St-Em r ★★→★★★ 70 75 76 78 79 81 82' 83 85 86 88 89 90' 91 92 93 94 95 One of biggest and best GRANDS CRUS on CORBIN plateau. A new generation (of the founding Despagne family, since 1812) in '93. Also owns Ch Maison Blanche, MONTAGNE ST-EMILION.

Grand-Mayne St-Em ★★→★★★ 82 83 85 86 87 88 89' 90' 93 94 95 40-acre GRAND CRU CLASSE on W COTES. To follow for rich tasty wines.

Grand-Pontet St-Em r ★★ 82' 83 85 86' 87 88 89 90' 91 92 93 94 95 35 acres beside CH BEAU-SEJOUR-BECOT; both revitalized since '85. To follow.

Grand-Puy-Ducasse Pau r ★★★ 79 81 82' 83 85 86 87 88 89' 90 91 92 93 94 95 Fifth growth enlarged to 90 acres under expert management, but remains way behind the next entry. Second label: Ch Artigues-Arnaud.

Grand-Puy-Lacoste Pau r ★★★ 70' 75 78' 79' 81' 82' 83 85' 86' 87 88' 89' 90' 91 92 93 94 95 Leading fifth growth famous for excellent full-bodied vigorous PAUILLAC. 110 acres among the 'Bages' châteaux, owned by the Borie family of DUCRU-BEAUCAILLOU. Second label: Lacoste-Borie.

Gravas Saut w sw ★★ 83' 85 86 88 89' 90' 91 92 93 Small BARSAC property; impressive firm sweet wine. NB Cuvée Spéciale.

La Grave, Domaine Graves r w ★★ 89' 90' 91 92 93 94 95 Innovative little estate with lively reds and delicious oak-aged whites (w 91 92 93 94 95). Made at CH DE LANDIRAS by Peter Vinding-Diers.

La Grave-Trigant-de-Boisset Pom r ★★★ 75' 76' 78 79 81' 82' 83 85 86' 87 88 89' 90 92 93 94 95 Verdant château with small but first-class v'yd owned by CHRISTIAN MOUEIX. Beautifully structured lightish POMEROL.

Gressier-Grand-Poujeaux Moulis r ★★→★★★ 70 75' 78 79' 81 82 83' 85 86 87 88 89 90 91 92 93 94 95 Vg CRU BOURGEOIS, neighbour of CHASSE-SPLEEN. Fine firm wine with good track record for repaying patient cellaring.

Greysac Méd r ★★ 81' 82 83 85 86 88 89 90 91 92 93 94 95 Elegant 140-acre property. Easy early-maturing wines popular in US.

> Why do the Châteaux of Bordeaux have such a large section of this book devoted to them? The reason is simple: collectively they form by far the largest supply of high-quality wine on earth. A single typical Médoc château with 150 acres (some have far more) makes approximately 26,000 dozen bottles of identifiable wine each year – the production of two or three California 'boutique' wineries. Moreover between the extremes of plummy Pomerol, grainy Graves and tight, restrained Médocs – not to mention crisp dry whites and unctuous golden ones – Bordeaux offers a wider range of tastes than any other region.
>
> The tendency over the last two decades has been to buy more land. Many classed growths have expanded very considerably since their classification in 1855. The majority has also raised its sights and invested the good profits of the past decade in better technology.

Gruaud-Larose St-Jul r ★★★ 70 75 76 78' 79 81 82' 83 85 86' 87 88' 89 90' 91 92 93 94 95 One of the biggest and best-loved second growths. 189 acres. Smooth rich stylish claret, year after year ages for 20+ years. Bought '94 by Alcatel Co but same CORDIER management. New equipment '94. Vg second wine: Sarget de Gruaud-Larose.

Guadet-St-Julien St-Em ★★ 75 81 82 83 85 86 87 88 89 90' 92 93 95 Extremely well-made wines from v small GRAND CRU CLASSE.

Guiraud Saut w (r) sw (dr) ★★★ 67 79 80 81 82 83' 84 85 86' 87 88' 89' 90' 92 93 94 95 Restored classed growth of top quality. 250+ acres. At best excellent sweet wine of great finesse; also a small amount of red and dry white. The 88, 89 and 90 will be superb in time.

Guiteronde du Hayot Saut ★★ 75-acres in BARSAC; known for finesse, value.

La Gurgue Mar r ★★ 81 82 83' 85' 86 87 88 89' 90 91 92 93 94 95 Small, well-placed 30-acre property, for MARGAUX of the fruitier sort. From owners of CHASSE-SPLEEN and HAUT-BAGES-LIBERAL. To watch.

Hanteillan Cissac r ★★ 82' 83 85' 86 87 88' 89 90' 91 92 93 94 95 Huge vineyard: v fair Bourgeois wine, conscientiously made. Ch Laborde is the second quality.

Haut-Bages-Averous Pau r ★★ 81 82' 83 85' 86 87 88 89' 90 91 92 93 94 95 The second wine of CH LYNCH BAGES. Tasty drinking.

Haut-Bages-Libéral Pau r ★★ 78 82' 83 85 86' 87 88 89 90' 91 92 93 94' 95 Lesser-known fifth growth of 64 acres (next to LATOUR) in same stable as CHASSE-SPLEEN. Results are excellent, full of PAUILLAC vitality.

Haut-Bages-Monpelou Pauillac r ★★ 81 82' 83 85 86 88 89' 90 91 92 93 95 25-acre CRU BOURGEOIS stable-mate of CH BATAILLEY on former DUHART-MILON land. Good minor PAUILLAC.

Haut-Bailly Graves r ★★★ 70' 78 79' 81' 82 83 85' 86 87 88' 89' 90' 92 93' 94 95 70-acres+ at LEOGNAN, Belgian-owned. Since '79 some of the best savoury, round, intelligently-made red GRAVES have come from this château. Second label is La Parde de Haut-Bailly.

Haut-Batailley Pau r ★★★ 66 70' 75' 78 79 81 82' 83 85 86 87 88 89' 90' 91 92 93 94 95 Smaller part of divided fifth growth BATAILLEY: 49 acres. Often gentler than sister château, GRAND-PUY-LACOSTE. Second wine: La Tour-d'Aspic.

Haut-Bergey Pessac-L r ★★ 40 acres, largely Cab; fragrant delicate GRAVES.

Haut-Bommes See Clos Haut-Peyraguey.

Haut-Brion Pessac (Graves) r (w) ★★★★ 61 64 70' 71' 75' 76 78' 79' 80 81 82' 83' 84 85' 86' 87 88' 89' 90' 91 92 93 94 95 The oldest great château of BORDEAUX and the only non-MEDOC first growth of 1855. 108 acres. Deeply harmonious, never-aggressive wine with endless soft earthy complexity. Consistently great (and modestly priced) since '75. A little full dry white in 78 81 82 83 85 87 88 89' 90 91 92 93 94 95. See Bahans-Haut-Brion, La Mission-Haut-Brion.

Haut-Maillet Pom ★★ 82 83 85 86 88 89 90 91 92 93 95 12-acre sister château of LA CABANNE. Well-made gentle wines.

Haut-Marbuzet St-Est r ★★→★★★ 70 75' 76 78' 81 82' 83' 85' 86' 87 88 89' 90' 91 92 93' 94 95 The best of many good ST-ESTEPHE CRUS BOURGEOIS. Monsieur Dubosq has reassembled the ancient Dom de Marbuzet, in total 175 acres. Haut-M is 60% Merlot. See also CHAMBERT-MARBUZET, MACCARTHY, MacCarthy-Moula, Tour de Marbuzet. New oak gives them a distinctive, if not subtle, style of great appeal.

Haut-Pontet St-Em r ★★ Reliable 12-acre v'yd of the COTES deserving its GRAND CRU status. 2,500 cases.

Haut-Sarpe St-Em r ★★ 79 81 82 83' 85 86 87 88 89 90' 91 92 93 94 95 GRAND CRU CLASSE (6,000 cases) with elegant château and park, 70% Merlot. Same owner as CH LA CROIX, POMEROL.

Hortevie St-Jul r ★★ 81 82 83 85' 86 87 88 89' 90' 91 92 93 94 95 One of the few ST-JULIEN CRUS BOURGEOIS. This tiny v'yd and its bigger sister TERREY-GROS-CAILLOU are shining examples. Now hand-harvesting only.

Houissant St-Est r ★★ 82 83 85 86 87 88 89' 90' 91 92 93 94 95 Typical robust well-balanced ST-ESTEPHE CRU BOURGEOIS also called Ch Leyssac; well-known in Denmark.

d'Issan Cantenac-Mar r ★★★ 70 75' 78 79 81 82' 83' 85 86 87 88 89 90' 91 92 93 94 95 Beautifully restored moated château nr the Garonne with 75-acre third growth vineyard; wines recently flagging. Second label: Ch de Candale.

Kirwan Cantenac-Mar r ★★★ 70 78 81 82' 83' 85 86 87 88 89' 90' 91 92 93' 94 95 86-acre 3rd growth; majority owned by insurance co La Gan. Mature v'yds recently giving tastier wines. New consultant (M Rolland) since '92.

Labégorce Mar r ★★ 75' 78 79 81' 82' 83' 85 86 87 88 89' 90' 91 92 93 94 95 Substantial 69-acre property N of MARGAUX producing long-lived wines of true Margaux quality. New owner since '89.

Labégorce-Zédé Mar r ★★→★★★ 75' 78 81' 82' 83' 85 86' 87 88 89' 90' 91 92 93 94 95 Outstanding CRU BOURGEOIS on road N from MARGAUX. 62 acres. Typically delicate, fragrant; truly classic since '81. Same family as VIEUX CH CERTAN. Second label: Dom Zédé. Also 23 acres of AC Bordeaux: 'Z'.

Lacoste-Borie The second wine of CH GRAND-PUY-LACOSTE.

Lafaurie-Peyraguey Saut w sw ★★★ 78 80 81' 82 83' 85 86' 87 88' 89' 90 95 Fine classed growth of only 49 acres at Bommes, belonging to CORDIER. After a lean patch, good, rich and racy wines in late '80s.

Lafite-Rothschild Pau r ★★★★ 59 75' 76' 78 79 81 82' 83 84 85 86' 87 88' 89' 90' 91 92 93 94 95 First growth of famous elusive perfume and style in its great vintages, which keep for decades. Resplendent since '76. Amazing circular cellars opened '87. Joint ventures in Chile ('88), California ('89), Portugal ('92). Second wine: Carruades de Lafite. 225 acres. Also owns CH'X DUHART-MILON, L'EVANGILE, RIEUSSEC.

Lafleur Pom r ★★★★ 70' 75' 78 79' 81 82' 83 85' 86' 88' 89' 90' 92 93 94 95
Superb 12-acre property just N of PETRUS. Resounding wine of the turbo-charged tannic, less 'fleshy' kind for long maturing. Same owner as LE GAY.
Second wine: Les Pensées de Lafleur.

Lafleur-Gazin Pom r ★★ 75' 79 81 82' 83 85' 86 87 88' 89 90 92 93 94 95
Distinguished small J-P MOUEIX estate on the NE border of POMEROL.

Lafon-Rochet St-Est r ★★ 70' 79 81 82 83' 85 86 87 88' 89' 90' 91 92 93 94 95
Fourth-growth neighbour of COS D'ESTOURNEL, restored in '60s and again recently. 110 acres. Rather hard full-bodied ST-ESTEPHE, reluctant to 'give'. Same owner as CH PONTET-CANET. Second label: Numéro 2.

Lagrange Pom r ★★ 70' 75' 78 81 82' 83 85' 86 87 88' 89' 90' 92 93 94 95
20-acre vineyard in the centre of POMEROL run by the ubiquitous house of J-P MOUEIX. Rising profile for flavour/value.

Lagrange St-Jul r ★★★ 70 82 83 84 85' 86' 87 88' 89' 90' 91 92 93 94 95
Formerly run-down third growth inland from ST-JULIEN, bought by Suntory ('83). 280 acres now in tiptop condition with wines to match. Second wine: Les Fiefs de Lagrange (**83 85 86 87 88 89** 90 **91 92** 93 94 95).

La Lagune Ludon r ★★★ 70' 75' 76' 78' 79 81 82' 83' 85 86' 87 88' 89' 90' 91 92 93 94 95 Ultra-modern 160-acre 3rd growth in v S MEDOC. Attractively rich wines with marked oak; steadily v high quality. Owned by AYALA.

Lalande-Borie St-Jul r ★★ 81 82 83 85 86 87 88 89 90' 91 92 93 94 95 A baby brother of the great DUCRU-BEAUCAILLOU created from part of the former v'yd of CH LAGRANGE. Gracious, easy drinking.

Lamarque Lamarque (H-Méd) r ★★ 82 83' 85 86' 87 88 89 90' 91 92 93 94 95
Splendid medieval fortress in central MEDOC with 113 acres giving admirable wine of high Bourgeois standard. Second wine: Donjon de L.

Lamothe Bergeron H-Méd r ★★ 88 89 150 acres at CUSSAC making 25,000 cases of reliable claret. Run by GRAND-PUY-DUCASSE.

Landiras Graves w r ★★→★★★ (w) 90 91 92' 93' 94 95' Medieval ruin in S GRAVES replanted in '80s. 50 acres Sém, 15 red (**88 89 90' 91** 92 93 94 95). See also Domaine La Grave. Second label: Notre Dame de Landiras (AC B'x).

Lanessan Cussac (H-Méd) r ★★→★★★ 78' 79 81 82 83 85 86' 87 88' 89' 90' 91 92 93 94 95 Distinguished 108-acre CRU BOURGEOIS EXCEPTIONNEL just S of ST-JULIEN. Fine rather than burly but ages v well. Same family owns châteaux de Ste-Gemme, Lachesnaye, La Providence.

Langoa-Barton St-Jul r ★★★ 70' 75' 76 78' 79 81 82' 83 85 86' 87 88' 89' 90' 91 92 93 94' 95 49-acre third-growth sister château to LEOVILLE-BARTON. V old Barton-family estate with impeccable standards and generous value. Second wine: Lady Langoa.

Larcis-Ducasse St-Em r ★★ 66 78 79 81 82' 83 84 85 86 87 88' 89' 90' 91 92 93 94 95 Top property of St-Laurent, eastern neighbour of ST-EMILION, on COTES next to CH PAVIE. 30 acres in a fine situation.

Larmande St-Em r ★★★ 75' 78 79 81 82 83' 85 86 87 88' 89' 90' 91 92 93 94 95 Substantial 54-acre property related to CAP-DE-MOURLIN. Replanted, re-equipped and now making rich strikingly scented wine. Second label: Ch des Templiers.

Laroque St-Em r ★★ 75' 81 82' 83 85 86 88 89 90 91 92 93 94 95 Important 108-acre v'yd on the ST-EMILION COTES in St-Christophe.

Larose-Trintaudon St-Laurent r ★★ 82 85 86 87 88 89 90' 91 92 93 94' 95 The biggest v'yd in the MEDOC: 425 acres. Modern methods make reliable fruity and charming CRU BOURGEOIS wine to drink young. New management in '89 and second label Larose St-Laurent.

NB The vintages printed in colour are the ones you should choose first for drinking in 1997.

BORDEAUX

Laroze St-Em r ★★ 82 83 85 86 87 88' 89 90' 91 92 93 94 95 Big v'yd (74 acres) on western COTES. Fine lightish wines from sandy soil; soon enjoyable.

Larrivet-Haut-Brion Graves r (w) ★★ 75' 81 82' 83 85 86 87 88 89 90 91 92 93 94 95 Little LEOGNAN property with perfectionist standards. Also 500 cases of fine barrel-fermented white (87 88 89 90 91 92 93 94 95).

Lascombes Mar r (p) ★★★ 70' 75' 82 83 85 86 87 88' 89' 90' 91 92 93 94 95 240-acre second growth owned by British brewers Bass-Charrington; lavishly restored. Has reemerged as a serious contender since '86 with robust vigorous wines. Second wine: Ch Segonnes.

Latour Pau r ★★★★ 59 61 62 64 66 67 70' 71 73 75' 76 78' 79 81 82' 83 84 85 86 87 88' 89' 90' 91' 92 93 94' 95 First growth considered the grandest statement of MEDOC. Rich, intense, almost immortal wines in great yrs; classical, perfumed and pleasing even in weak ones. 150 acres sloping to R Gironde. Latour always needs time to show its hand. British-owned from '63 to '93, now again in (private) French hands. 2nd wine: LES FORTS DE LATOUR; 3rd, Pauillac.

Latour-Martillac Graves r w ★★ (r) 82' 83 85' 86 87 88' 89 90 91 92 93 94 95 Small but serious property at Martillac. 10 acres of white grapes; 37 of black. The white can age admirably (86 87 88 89 90 91 92 93' 94' 95). The owner is resurrecting the neighbouring Ch Lespault.

Latour-à-Pomerol Pom r ★★★★ 61 70' 71 75 76 78 79 81 82 83 85' 86 87 88' 89' 90' 92 93 94 95 Top growth of 19 acres under MOUEIX management. POMEROL of great power and perfume, yet also ravishing finesse.

des Laurets St-Em r ★★ 82 83 85 86 88 89' 90' 92 93 94 95 Major property in PUISSEGUIN-ST-EMILION and MONTAGNE-ST-EMILION (to the E) with 160 acres of v'yd on the COTES (40,000 cases). Sterling wines sold by J-P MOUEIX.

Laville-Haut-Brion Graves w ★★★★ 82 85' 86 87' 88 89' 90 92 93' 94 95 A tiny production of the v best white GRAVES for long succulent maturing, made at CH LA MISSION-HAUT-BRION. The '89 is off the dial.

Léoville-Barton St-Jul r ★★★ 70' 75' 76 78' 81 82' 83 85' 86' 87 88' 89' 90' 91 92 93 94' 95 90-acre portion of the great second growth LEOVILLE v'yd in Anglo-Irish hands of the Barton family for over 150 years. Powerful classic claret; traditional methods, v fair prices. Major investment has raised already v high standards 'to super-second'. See also Langoa-Barton.

Léoville-Las-Cases St-Jul r ★★★★ 66' 70 75' 76 78' 79 81' 82' 83' 84 85' 86' 87 88 89' 90' 91 92 93' 94 95 Largest LEOVILLE. Next to LATOUR; 210 acres. One of highest reputations in Bordeaux. Elegant complex powerful austere wines, for immortality. Second label CLOS DU MARQUIS outstanding.

Léoville-Poyferré St-Jul r ★★★ 81 82' 83' 84 85' 86' 87 88 89' 90' 91 92 93 94 95 For years the least outstanding of the LEOVILLES; since '80 again living up to the great name. Michel Rolland now makes the wine. 156 acres. Second label: Ch Moulin-Riche.

Lestage Listrac r ★★ 82' 83 85 86' 87 88 89' 90' 91 92 93 94 95 130-acre CRU BOURGEOIS in same hands as CH FONREAUD. Light, quite stylish wine aged in oak since '85. Second wine: Ch Caroline. Also white: La Mouette.

Lilian-Ladouys St-Est ★★ 89 90 91 92 93 94 95 Recent creation: a 50-acre CRU BOURGEOIS with high ambitions and real early promise. To watch.

Liot Barsac w sw ★★ 75' 76 82 83 85 86 88 89' 90' 92 94 95 Consistent fairly light golden wines from 50 acres.

Liversan St-Sauveur r ★★ 82' 83 85 86' 87 88' 89' 90' 91 92 93 94 95 116-acre Grand Cru Bourgeois inland from PAUILLAC. Since '84 the Polignac family has steadily high standards. Now managed by owners of PATACHE D'AUX. Second wine: Ch Fonpiqueyre.

Châteaux entries also cross-refer to France section, pages 32–77.

Livran Méd r ★★ 82' 83 85 86 88' 89' 90' 91 92 93 94' 95 Big CRU BOURGEOIS at St-Germain in the N MÉDOC. Consistent round wines (half Merlot).

Loudenne St-Yzans (Méd) r ★★ 82' 83 85 86' 87' 88 89' **90** 91 **92** 93 95 Beautiful riverside château owned by Gilbeys since 1875. Well-made CRU BOURGEOIS red and an increasingly delicious dry Sauvignon white from 120 acres. The white is best at 2–4 yrs (**90** 91 92' 93 94 95).

Loupiac-Gaudiet Loupiac w sw ★★ 85 86 87 88 89 90 91 **92** 93 94 95 Reliable source of value 'almost-SAUTERNES', just across R Garonne. 7,500 cases.

La Louvière Graves r w ★★ (r) 81 82' 83 85 86' 87 88' 89' **90'** 91 92 93' 94' 95 (w) 86 88 89' 90' 91 **92 93'** 94 95 Noble 135-acre LEOGNAN estate restored by the ubiquitous Lurton family. Excellent white, and red wine of classed-growth standard.

de Lussac St-Em r ★★ 82 83 85 86 88 89' 90 91 92 93 94 95 One of the best estates in LUSSAC-ST-EMILION (to the NE).

Lynch-Bages Pau r (w) ★★★ →★★★★ 61' 66 70 75' 78' 79 81 82' 83' **84 85'** 86' 87 88' 89' 90' 91 92 93 94' 95 Always popular, now a regular star. 200 acres. Rich robust wine: deliciously dense, brambly; aspiring to greatness. See also Haut-Bages-Averous. From '90, intense oaky white. Owner J-M Cazes also directs CH PICHON-LONGUEVILLE etc for AXA Insurance.

Lynch-Moussas Pau r ★★ 81 82 83 85 86 87 88 89 90' 91 92 93 94 95 Fifth growth restored by the director of CH BATAILLEY since '69. Now 60+ acres are making serious wine, gaining depth as the young vines age.

du Lyonnat Lussac-St-Em r ★★ 82 83 85 86' 88 **89** 90' 91 92 93 94 95 120-acre estate with well-distributed reliable wine.

MacCarthy St-Est r ★★ 88 89 **90** 91 92 93 94 95 The second label of CHATEAU CHAMBERT-MARBUZET.

Médoc: the class system

The Médoc has 60 crus classés, ranked in 1855 in five classes. In a separate classification it has 18 Crus Grands Bourgeois Exceptionnels, 41 Crus Grands Bourgeois (which must age their wine in barrels), and 68 Crus Bourgeois. (The terms Grand Bourgeois and Exceptionnel – like so many traditional and useful things – are not acceptable to the EC, and are therefore no longer used on labels.)

Apart from the first growths, the five classes of 1855 are now considerably jumbled in quality, with some second growths at fifth growth level and vice versa. They also overlap in quality with the Crus Exceptionnels. (Besides the official 18, another 13 châteaux are unofficially acknowledged as belonging to this category.) The French always do things logically.

Macquin-St-Georges St-Em r ★★ 85 86' 88 89 90' 91 92 93 94 95 Steady producer of delicious 'satellite' ST-EMILION at ST-GEORGES.

Magdelaine St-Em r ★★★ 70' 71' 75 78 82' 83' 85 86 88 89' 90' 92 93 94 95 Leading CÔTES first growth: 28 acres next to AUSONE owned by J-P MOUEIX. Beautifully balanced subtle wine: recently powerful and fine. Substantial rebuilding ('92) promises even better things.

Magence Graves r w ★★ Go-ahead 45-acre property in S GRAVES. Sauv Bl-flavoured dry white and fruity red. Both age well 2–6 yrs.

Malartic-Lagravière Graves r (w) ★★★ (r) 81 82' 83 85 86' 87 88 89 90' **91** 92 93' 94 95 (w) 85 87' 88 **89** 90 91 92 93 94 95 LEOGNAN classed growth of 53 acres. Well-structured rather hard red wine and a v little long-ageing Sauvignon Blanc white. Austere wines that need cellaring. New owners: LAURENT-PERRIER ('90).

Malescasse Lamarque (H-Méd) r ★★ 82 83 85 86 **88 89** 90 91 92 **93** 94 95 Renovated CRU BOURGEOIS with 100 acres in good situation. Second label is Le Tana de Malescasse. New (corporate) owners in '92 are the same as GRUAUD-LAROSE'S. To watch.

Malescot-St-Exupéry Mar r ★★★ 70 75 **82' 83'** 85 86 87 88 89 90' 91 92 93 94 95 Third growth of 84 acres. Often tough when young, eventually fragrant and stylish MARGAUX. New consultant from '90 augurs well.

de Malle Saut w r sw dr ★★★ (w sw) 75 76 78 79 80 81' **82'** 83 85 86' **87 88** 89' 90' 91 94 95 Beautiful château with Italian gardens at Preignac. 124 acres. Vg SAUTERNES (second label: Ste Hélène 93); also dry white (90 94 95) and red (GRAVES) CH DU CARDAILLAN (★★) **(88 89 90)**.

de Malleret H-Méd r ★★ 82 83 85 86 88 **89'** 90 92 93 94 95 An aristocrat's domaine. The Marquis du Vivier makes 25,000 cases of fine gentlemanly claret at Le Pian, among forests just N of Bordeaux.

de Marbuzet St-Est r ★★ Second label of COS-D'ESTOURNEL: equally reliable.

Margaux Mar r (w) ★★★★ 53 61' 78' 79 80 81' 82' 83' **84** 85' 86' 87 88' 89' 90' 91 92 93' 94 95 First growth (209 acres), the most penetrating and fabulously perfumed of all in its (v frequent) best vintages. Pavillon Rouge (81 82' 83 85 86 87 88 89 90' 91 92 93 94 95) is second wine. Pavillon Blanc is best white (Sauv) of MEDOC (85 86 87 88 89 90 91 92 93 94 95).

Marquis-d'Alesme See d'Alesme.

Marquis-de-Terme Mar r ★★→★★★ 81' 82 83' 85 86' 87 88' 89' 90' 91 92 93 95 Renovated fourth growth of 84 acres. Fragrant, fairly lean style has developed since '85, with more Cab S and more flesh.

Martinens Mar r ★★ 81 82 83 85 86 88 89 90 **91** 92 93 94' 95 Worthy 75-acre CRU BOURGEOIS of the mayor of CANTENAC; new barrels since '89.

Maucaillou Moulis r ★★ 75' 79 81 82 83' **85'** 86' 87 **88' 89'** 90' 91 92 93 94' 95 130-acre CRU BOURGEOIS with CRU CLASSE standards, property of DOURTHE family. Richly fruity Cap de Haut-Maucaillou is second wine.

Mazeyres Pom r ★★ Consistent, useful, improving lesser POMEROL. (50 acres.)

Méaume B'x Supérieur r ★★ An Englishman's domaine, N of POMEROL. Since '80 has built solid reputation for vg daily claret to age 4–5 yrs. 7,500 cases.

Meyney St-Est r ★★→★★★ 75' 78' 79 81 82' 83 85 86' 87 88' 89' 90' 91 92 93 94 95 Big (125-acre) riverside property next door to CH MONTROSE in a superb situation; one of the best of many steady CRUS BOURGEOIS in ST-ESTEPHE. Owned by CORDIER. Second label: Prieur de Meyney.

Millet Graves r w (p) ★★ (r) 82 83 85 86 88 89 90' 92 93 94 95 Useful GRAVES. Second label, Clos Renon: drink young. Cuvée Henri is new oak-aged white.

La Mission-Haut-Brion Graves r ★★★★ 59 61 64 66' 75' 78' 79 80 81 82' 83 84 85' 86 87 88 89' 90' 91 92 93 94' 95 Neighbour and long-time rival to CH HAUT-BRION; since '84 in same hands. New equipment in '87. Consistently grand-scale full-blooded wine for long maturing; even 'bigger' wine than H-B. 30 acres. Second label is La Chapelle de la Mission. White is LAVILLE-H-B.

Monbousquet St-Em r ★★ 78' 79' 81 82 83 85' 86 88' 89' 90' 93 94 95 Attractive early-maturing wine from deep gravel soil: lasts well. Second label: Ch Caperot 91 92'.

Monbrison Arsac-Mar r ★★→★★★ 81 82 83 84 85 86 87 88' 89' 90 91 92 93 94 95 A new name to watch. Top Bourgeois standards. 4,000 cases plus 2,000 of second label, Ch Cordet.

Montrose St-Est r ★★★ 61 64 66 70' 75' 76 78' 79 81 82' 83 84 85 86' 87 88 89' 90' 91 92 93 94 95 158-acre family-run second growth famous for deeply coloured forceful old-style claret. Vintages 79–85 (except 82) were lighter, but recent Montrose is almost ST-ESTEPHE'S answer to CH LATOUR. Second wine: La Dame de Montrose.

Moulin du Cadet St-Em r p ★★ 75' 81 82' 83 85 86 88 89' 90' 92 93 95 Little v'yd on the CÔTES, owned by J-P MOUEIX. Fragrant medium-bodied wines.

Moulin-à-Vent Moulis r ★★ 81 82' 83 85' 86 87 88 89 90' 91 92 93 94 95 60-acre property in the forefront of this booming AC. Lively forceful wine. LA TOUR-BLANCHE (MÉDOC) has the same owners.

Moulinet Pom r ★★ 82 83 85 86 87 88 89' 90 92 93 94 95 One of POMEROL's bigger châteaux; 45 acres on lightish soil, wine lightish too.

Mouton-Baronne-Philippe See d'Armailhac.

Mouton-Rothschild Pau r (w) ★★★★ 59 61 62' 66' 70' 75' 76 78 81 82' 83' 85' 86' 87 88' 89' 90' 91 92 93 94 95 Officially a first growth only since '73, though for 40 yrs worthy of the title. 175 acres (87% Cab S) make majestic rich wine, often MÉDOC's most opulent (also, from '91, white Aile d'Argent). Also the world's greatest museum of art relating to wine. Baron Philippe, the foremost champion of the MÉDOC, died in '88. His daughter Philippine now reigns. See also Opus One, California.

Nairac Saut w sw ★★ 73 75 76' 79 80 81 82 83' 85 86' 87 88 89 90' 91 92 93 94 95 Perfectionist BARSAC classed-growth château. Wines to lay down for a decade.

Nenin Pom r ★★ 70' 75' 76 78 82 83 85' 86 87 88' 89 90 93' 94 95 Well-known 66-acre estate; on a (v necessary) but slow upswing since '85 (esp 93).

d'Olivier Graves r w ★★★ (r) 82 83 84 85 86 87 88 89' 90' 91 92 93 94 95 (w) 87 88 89 90 91 92 93 94 95 90-acre classed growth, surrounding a moated castle at LÉOGNAN. 9,000 cases red, 6,000 white. New broom in '89 is upgrading flavour (with more oak).

Les Ormes-de-Pez St-Est r ★★→★★★ 75' 78 79 81' 82' 83' 85 86' 87 88 89' 90' 91 92 94 95 Outstanding 72-acre CRU BOURGEOIS owned by CH LYNCH-BAGES. Increasingly notable full-flavoured ST-ESTÈPHE.

Les Ormes-Sorbet Méd r ★★ 78 81 82' 83 85' 86' 87 88 89 90' 91 92 93 94 95 Emerging 10,000-case producer of grand stylish red aged in new oak at Couquèques. A leader of the N MÉDOC. Second label: Ch de Conques.

Palmer Cantenac-Mar r ★★★★ 61' 62 66' 70 71' 75' 76 78' 79' 80 81 82 83' 84 85 86' 87 88' 89 90 91 92 93 94 95 The star of CANTENAC: a third growth that can achieve first-growth quality. Wine of power, flesh, delicacy and much Merlot. New steel vat-room in '95. 110 acres with Dutch, British (PETER A SICHEL) and French owners. Second wine: Réserve du Général.

Pape-Clément Graves r (w) ★★★ 70 75' 82 83 85 86' 87 88' 89' 90' 92 93' 94' 95 Ancient v'yd at PESSAC with record of seductive, scented, not ponderous reds. Early '80s not so good: dramatic new quality (and more white) since '85.

de Parenchère r (w) ★★ 89 90 93 94 95 Steady supply of useful AC Ste-Foy Bordeaux from handsome château with 125 acres.

Patache d'Aux Bégadan (Méd) r ★★ 82' 83' 85 86 88 89' 90' 91 92 93 94 95 90-acre CRU BOURGEOIS of the N MÉDOC. Fragrant largely Cab wine with the earthy quality of its area.

Paveil (de Luze) Mar r ★★ 81 82' 83' 85 86' 87 88' 89' 90 91 92 93 94 95 Old family estate at SOUSSANS. Small but highly regarded.

Pavie St-Em r ★★★ 78 79' 81 82' 83' 85 86' 87 88' 89' 90' 92 93' 94 95 Splendidly-sited first growth; 92 acres mid-slope on the CÔTES. Rich and tasty and on top form since '82. PAVIE-DECESSE and La Clusière in same family.

Pavie-Decesse St-Em r ★★→★★★ 82 83 85 86 87 88 89 90 92 93 94 95 24 acres seriously challenging their big brother (above).

Pavie-Macquin St-Em r ★★→★★★ 82 83 85' 86 87 88 89 90 91 92 94 95 Another PAVIE challenge; this time the neighbours up the hill. 25-acre CÔTES v'yd E of ST-EMILION. Fine organic winemaking by a son of VIEUX CH CERTAN. Second label: Les Chênes.

Pavillon Rouge (Blanc) du Château Margaux See Ch Margaux.

Pedesclaux Pau r ★★ 81 82' 83 85 86 87 88 89 90' 91 92 93 94 95 50-acre fifth growth on the level of a good CRU BOURGEOIS. Solid strong wines that Belgians love. Second labels: Bellerose, Grand-Duroc-Milon.

Petit-Village Pom r ★★★ 75' 78 79 81 82' 83 85' 86 87 88 89' 90' 91 92 93 94 95 Top property revived. 26 acres next to VIEUX CHATEAU CERTAN, same owner (AXA) as CH PICHON-LONGUEVILLE since '89. Powerful plummy wine.

Pétrus Pom r ★★★★ 61 62 64 66 67 70' 71' 73 75' 76 78 79' 80 81 82' 83 84 85' 86 87 88' 89' 90' 92 93 94 95 The great name of POMEROL. 28 acres of gravelly clay giving (400 bottles of) massively rich and concentrated wine, on allocation to the world's millionaires. 95% Merlot vines. Each vintage adds lustre (NB no 91).

Peyrabon St-Sauveur r ★★ 79 81 82' 83 85 86' 87 88 89' 90' 91 92 93 94 95 Serious 132-acre CRU BOURGEOIS popular in the Low Countries. Also La Fleur-Peyrabon (only 12 acres).

Peyre-Labade r p Listrac ★★ Second label of CH CLARKE.

Peyreau St-Em r ★★ Sister château of Clos l'Oratoire.

de Pez St-Est r ★★★ 64 70' 75' 76 78' 79 81 82' 83 85 86' 87 88 89 90' 91 92 93' 94 95 Outstanding CRU BOURGEOIS of 60 acres. As reliable as any of the classed growths of the village if not as fine. Direction from CHAMPAGNE house ROEDERER in Reims.

Phélan-Ségur St-Est r ★★→★★★ 75' 81 82' 85 86 87 88' 89' 90' 91 92 93 94 95 Big and important CRU BOURGEOIS (125 acres): some fine old vintages. No 83 or 84, but from '86 has gone from strength to strength.

Pibran Pau r ★★ 87 88 89' 90' 91 92 93 94 95 Small CRU BOURGEOIS allied to PICHON-LONGUEVILLE. V classy wine with real PAUILLAC drive.

Pichon-Lalande (formerly Pichon-Longueville, Comtesse de Lalande) Pau r ★★★★ 61 62 66 70' 75' 76 78' 79' 81 82' 83' 84 85' 86' 87 88' 89' 90' 91 92 93 94 95 'Super-second'-growth neighbour to CH LATOUR. 148 acres. Consistently among v top performers; long-lived wine of fabulous breed for those who like it luscious, even in lesser yrs. Second wine: Réserve de la Comtesse. Rivalry across the road (next entry) is worth watching.

Pichon-Longueville (formerly Baron de Pichon-Longueville) Pau r ★★★★ 78 79' 81 82' 83 85 86' 87 88' 89' 90' 91 92 93 94' 95 77-acre second growth: wines have varied widely. Since '87 owned by AXA Insurance, run by J-M Cazes (LYNCH-BAGES). Revitalized winemaking matches aggressive new buildings. Second label: Les Tourelles de Longueville.

Le Pin Pom r ★★★★ 81 82 83 85 86 87 88 89 90' 92 93 94 95 A mere 500 cases of Merlot, with same owners as VIEUX CHATEAU CERTAN. A perfectionist miniature: Fabergé prices.

Pindefleurs St-Em r ★★ 82' 83 85 86 88 89 90' 92 93' 94 95 Steady 23-acre v'yd on light soil. Second label: Clos Lescure.

Pique-Caillou Graves r (w dr) ★★ 85' 86 88' 89' 90' 91 92 93 94 95 Refurbished property nr Bordeaux airport. Ripe seductive GRAVES, and white since '93. Also next-door Ch Chênevert.

de Pitray Castillon r ★★ 82 83 85 86 87 88 89 90 92 93 94 95 Large (62-acre) v'yd on COTES DE CASTILLON E of ST-EM. Good flavoursome chewy wines.

Plagnac Méd r ★★ 82 83 85 86 88 89' 90' 91 92 93 94 95 CRU BOURGEOIS at Bégadan in N MEDOC restored by CORDIER. To follow.

Plince Pom r ★★ 75 79 81 82 83 85 86 88 89' 90 92 93 94 95 Reputable 20-acre property nr Libourne. Attractive lightish wine from sandy soil.

La Pointe Pom r ★★→★★★ 82 83' 85 86 88 89' 90' 92 93 94 95 Prominent 63-acre estate; well-made wines, but relatively spare of flesh. LA SERRE is in the same hands.

Pontac-Monplaisir Graves r (w) ★★ 87 89 90 91 92 93 94 95 Another GRAVES property offering delicious white and fragrant light red.

Pontet-Canet Pau r ★★★ 81 82' 83 85 86' 87 88 89' 90' 91 92 93 94' 95 182-acre neighbour to MOUTON-ROTHSCHILD. Dragged its feet for many yrs. Owners (same as LAFON-ROCHET) have done better since '85. Should make v fine wines, but hardness (lack of selection in big v'yd?) is an old problem. '90 vintages promise well. Second label: Les Hauts de Pontet.

Pontoise-Cabarrus H-Méd r ★★ Useful and improving 60-acre CRU BOURGEOIS at ST-SEURIN. Wines need 5–6 yrs.

Potensac Méd r ★★ 78' 81' 82' 83 85' 86 87 88 89' 90' 91 92 93 94 95 Best-known CRU BOURGEOIS of N MEDOC. Neighbouring ch'x Lassalle, Gallais-Bellevue and super-second LEOVILLE-LAS-CASES all owned by Delon family. Class shows.

Pouget Mar ★★ 78 81 82' 83 85 86 87 88 89 90 91 92 93 94 95 19 acres attached to BOYD-CANTENAC. Sharing owners since 1906. Similar, lighter wines.

Poujeaux (Theil) Moulis r ★★ 70' 75' 76 78 79' 81 82' 83' 85' 86 87 88' 89' 90' 91 92 93' 94' 95 Family-run CRU EXCEPTIONNEL of 120 acres. 20,000-odd cases of characterful tannic and concentrated wine for a long life. Second label: La Salle de Poujeaux. Also Ch Arnauld.

Prieuré-Lichine Cantenac-Mar r ★★★ 70 75 78' 82' 83' 85 86' 87 88 89' 90' 91 92 93 94' 95 143-acre fourth growth brought to the fore by the late Alexis Lichine. Excellent full fragrant MARGAUX currently on form. Second wine: Clairefont. Now also excellent Bordeaux Blanc.

Puy-Blanquet St-Em r ★★ 75' 82' 83 85 86 88 89' 90' 92 93 95 The major property of St-Etienne-de-Lisse, E of ST-EMILION, with over 50 acres. Early-maturing in early '80s; now firming up well.

St-Emilion: the class system

St-Emilion has its own class system, revised in 1985. At the top are two Premiers Grands Crus Classés 'A': Châteaux Ausone and Cheval Blanc. Then come nine Premiers Grands Crus Classés 'B'. 63 châteaux were elected as Grands Crus Classés. Another 170-odd are classed simply as Grands Crus, a rank renewable each year after official tastings. St-Emilion Grand Cru is therefore the very approximate equivalent of Médoc Crus Bourgeois and Grand Bourgeois.

Puygueraud Côte de Francs r ★★ 85 86 88 89' 90 92 93 94 Leading château of this rising district. Wood-aged wines of surprising class. Ch Laclaverie and Les Charmes-Godard follow the same lines.

Rabaud-Promis Saut w sw ★★→★★★ 83' 85 86' 87 88' 89' 90 95 74-acre classed growth at Bommes. Since '86 near top rank.

Rahoul Graves r w ★★ (r) 82 83 85 86 88 89' 90' 91 92 93 94 95 37-acre v'yd at Portets making particularly good wine in the '80s from maturing vines; 80% red. White (90 91 94 95) also oak-aged.

Ramage-la-Bâtisse H-Méd r ★★ 82 83' 85 86 88 89' 90 91 92 93 94 95 Potentially outstanding CRU BOURGEOIS of 130 acres at ST-SAUVEUR, N of PAUILLAC. Increasingly good since '85. Ch Tourteran is second wine.

Rausan-Ségla Mar r ★★★ 70' 82 83' 84 85 86' 88' 89' 90' 91 92 93 94' 95 106-acre second growth famous for its fragrance; a great MEDOC name trying successfully to regain its rank since '82. New owners in '89 and again in '94. Second wine Ségla. This should be the top second growth of all. Ancient vintages can be superb.

Rauzan-Gassies Mar r ★★ 75' 79 82 83 85 86 88 89' 90' 91 92 93 94 95 75-acre second-growth neighbour of the last with little excitement to report for two decades.

Raymond-Lafon Saut w sw ★★★ 75' 76 78 79 80' 81 82 83' 85 86' 87 88 89' 90' 91 92 93 94 95 Serious SAUTERNES estate of 44 acres run by the ex-manager of YQUEM. Splendid wines for long ageing. Among the top Sauternes.

de Rayne-Vigneau Saut w sw ★★ 76' 83 85 86' 88' 89 90' 91 92 94 95 164-acre classed growth at Bommes. Standard sweet wine and dry Rayne Sec.

Respide-Médeville Graves w (r) ★★ (w) 87 88 89 90 91 92' 93 94 95 One of the better unclassified white wine châteaux. Full-flavoured wines for ageing. (NB Cuvée Kauffman.) Drink the reds at 4–6 yrs.

Reynon Premières Côtes r w ★★ 100 acres for fragrant white from old Sauv vines (VIEILLES VIGNES) (92 93' 94 95); serious red (85 86 88' 89 90 91 92 93 94 95). Second wine (red): Ch Reynon-Peyrat. See also Clos Floridène.

Reysson Vertheuil (H-Méd) r ★★ 82' 83 85 86 87 88 89' 90' 95 Recently replanted 120-acre CRU BOURGEOIS in Japanese hands.

Ricaud Loupiac w sw (r dr) ★★ (w) 81 82 83' 85 86' 88 89 90 91 92 94 95 Substantial grower of almost SAUTERNES-like wine just across the river. New owners are working hard. It ages well.

Rieussec Saut w sw ★★★★ 67 71' 75' 79 81 82 83' 85 86' 87 88' 89' 90' 91 92 93 94 95 Worthy neighbour of CH D'YQUEM with 136 acres in Fargues, bought in '84 by the (LAFITE) Rothschilds. Not the sweetest; can be exquisitely fine. Also dry 'R' and super-wine Crème de Tête.

Ripeau St-Em r ★★ 81 82 83 85 86 87 88 89 90 93 94 95 Steady GRAND CRU in the centre of the plateau. 40 acres.

La Rivière Fronsac r ★★ 82 83 85' 86 87 88' 89 90 95 The biggest and most impressive FRONSAC property with a Wagnerian castle. Tannic but juicy wines win prizes in youth and stay young for a decade.

de Rochemorin Graves r (w) ★★ 82 83 85 86 87 88 89' 90' 91 92 93 95 An important restoration at Martillac by CH LA LOUVIÈRE's owner: 165 acres of maturing vines promise great things. Oaky whites to keep 4–5 yrs.

Romer Saut w sw Classed-growth with its name under legal dispute.

de Roquetaillade-la-Grange Graves r w ★★ 86 88 89 90 91 92 93 94 95 Substantial estate: fine red (southern) GRAVES and well-made white. See Cap de Mourlin.

Rouget Pom r ★★ 75' 76' 78 79 81 82' 83 85' 86 88 89' 90 92 93 94 95 Attractive old estate on the northern edge of POMEROL. Good, without polish; needs age.

Royal St-Emilion Brand name of the important and dynamic growers' coop. See also Berliquet, Galius.

Ruat-Petit-Poujeaux Moulis r ★★ 82 85 86 88 89 90 91 92 93 94 95 45-acre v'yd gaining in reputation for vigorous wine, to drink in 5–6 yrs.

St-André-Corbin St-Em r ★★ 81 82' 83 85' 86 88 89 90 92 93 94 95 54-acre estate in MONTAGNE- and ST-GEORGES-ST-EMILION: above average wines.

St-Bonnet Méd r ★★ 82 85 86 88 89 90 91 92 93 94 95 Big N MEDOC estate at St-Christoly. V flavoury wine.

St-Estèphe, Marquis de St-Est r ★ 82 86 88 89 90 93 94 95 The growers' coop; bigger but not as interesting as formerly.

St-Georges St-Georges-St-Em r ★★ 82 83 85' 86 87 88' 89' 90' 92 93 94 95 Noble 18th-C château overlooking the ST-EMILION plateau from the hill to the north. 125 acres. Vg wine sold direct to the public.

St-Georges-Côte-Pavie St-Em r ★★ 82 83' 85' 86 88' 89' 90' 92 93 94 95 Perfectly placed little v'yd on the COTES. Run with dedication.

St-Pierre St-Jul r ★★★ 70' 78' 81' 82' 83' 85 86' 88' 89' 90' 91 92 93 94 95 Small (42-acre) fourth growth bought in '82 by the late Henri Martin of CH GLORIA. V stylish and consistent classic ST-JULIEN.

de St-Pierre Graves w (r) ★★ Main-line white of notable character and flavour to drink young or keep. Also red.

Smaller Bordeaux châteaux to watch for:
The detailed list of Bordeaux châteaux on these pages is limited to the prestigious classified parts of the vast Bordeaux region. But this huge vineyard by the Atlantic works on many levels. Standard Bordeaux appellation wine is claret at its most basic – but it is still recognizable. The areas listed on this page with some of their leading châteaux are a more important resource; they are potentially distinct and worthwhile variations on the claret theme to be investigated and enjoyed.

Bordeaux Supérieur Château Dôme Ile de Margaux

Canon Fronsac Châteaux Coustolle, La Dauphine, La Fleur Caillou, Junayme, Mazeris-Bellevue, Moulin-Pey-Labrie, Tournalin, La Truffière, Vraye-Canon-Boyer

Côtes de Bourg Châteaux La Barde, Brûlesécaille, Falfas (try 89 90 91 92 93 94 in '97, esp 89 90), Font Guilhem, Grand-Jour, de la Grave, La Grolet, Guerry, Guionne, Haut-Maco, Lalibarde, Lamothe, Mendoce, Peychaud (89 90 ready for '97 drinking), Roc des Combes, Rousset, Tayac, de Thau

Côtes de Castillon Châteaux Beauséjour, Belcier (92 90 89 are to try in '97), La Clarière-Laithwaite, Côte Montpezat (best in '97: 93 and 94), Fonds-Rondes, Haut-Tuquet, Lartigue, Moulin-Rouge, Rocher-Bellevue, Ste-Colombe, Thibaud-Bellevue

Côtes de Francs Châteaux de Belcier, Les Charmes Godard, La Claverie, de Francs, Lauriol, La Prade

Entre-Deux-Mers Châteaux Gournin, Latour-Laguens, Moulin de Launay, Séguin, Thieuley, Turcaud

Fronsac Châteaux de Carles, Fontenil, Mayne-Vieil, Moulin-Haut-Laroque, La Rousselle, La Valade, La Vieille Cure, Villars (82 85 86 89 best in '97)

Lalande de Pomerol Châteaux Les Annereaux, Belles-Graves, Bertineau-St-Vincent, La Croix Bellevue, La Croix-St-André, Les Hauts Conseillants (86 89 90 92 will be good in '97) and châteaux Les Hauts-Tuileries, Moncets

Lussac St-Emilion Châteaux Barbe Blanche, Bel Air, Du Courlat (89 90 92 ready in '97, also cuvée Jean-Baptiste), Tour de Grenat, Villadière

Montagne St-Emilion Châteaux Calon, Faizeau, Haut-Gillet, Maison Blanche, Roudier, St-André-Corbin, Teyssier

Premiers Côtes de Blaye Châteaux Bertinerie (88 89 90 reds, 89 90 91 Haut-Bertinerie white ready in '97), Barbé, Charron, l'Escadre, Haut-Sociando, Le Menaudat, Peybonhomme Les Tours (93 and prior for drinking in'97), La Rose-Bellevue, Segonzac (93 and 94 ready in '97), Sociando, La Tonnelle

Premiers Côtes de Bordeaux Châteaux Bertinerie (vg), Carsin, La Croix de Roche, Fayau, Fontenil, Gardera, du Juge, Laffitte (sic), Lamothe, Peyrat, Plaisance, Tanesse, Suau (91 93 94 will be ready for '97 drinking), Lafitte-Laguens

Sainte-Croix du Mont Châteaux Clos des Coulinats, Loubens, Lousteau-Vieil, du Mont

For key to grape variety abbreviations, see pages 7–13.

de Sales Pom r ★★★ 75' 82' 83 85 86 88 89' 90' 92 93 94 95 Biggest v'yd of POMEROL (116 acres), attached to grandest château. Rarely poetry, but good lucid prose. Second labels: ch'x Chantalouette, du Delias.

Saransot-Dupré Listrac r (w) ★★ 86 88 89 90 92 93 94 95 Small property performing well since '86. Also one of LISTRAC'S growing band of whites.

Sénéjac H-Méd r (w) ★★ 78 81 82' 83' 85 86' 87 88 89' 90' 91 92 93 94 95 60-acre CRU BOURGEOIS in S MEDOC. All-Sém white, to age (90 91 92 93 94 95). Second label: Artigue de Sénéjac.

La Serre St-Em r ★★ 75 81 82 83 85 86 88' 89 90 92 93 94 95 Small GRAND CRU, same owner as LA POINTE. Reliably tasty.

Siaurac Lalande de Pom r ★★ Substantial, consistent; nr POMEROL. 57 acres.

Sigalas-Rabaud Saut w sw ★★★ 76' 79 80 81 82 83 85 86 87 88' 89' 90' 91 92 95 The smaller part of the former RABAUD estate: 34 acres in Bommes making first-class sweet wine in a rich grapey style.

Siran Labarde-Mar r ★★ 70 75' 78' 81 82' 83 85 86 88 89' 90' 93 94 95 74-acre property approaching CRU CLASSE quality. Recent investment. To follow.

Smith-Haut-Lafitte Graves r (w p) ★★→★★★ (red) 82' 85 86 89' 90' 91 92 93 94 95, (white) 92 93 94 95 Classed growth at Martillac: 122 acres (14 acres planted to white grape varieties). New ambitious owners in '90 putting in huge investment. Formerly light wines are now much more concentrated. Second label: Les Hauts de Smith.

Sociando-Mallet H-Méd r ★★ 82' 83 85' 86' 88' 89' 90' 91 92 93 94 95 Splendid CRU GRAND BOURGEOIS at ST-SEURIN. 65 acres. Conservative big-boned wines to lay down for yrs. Second wine: Demoiselles de Sociando.

Soudars H-Méd r ★★ 86 89 90 93 94 95 Sister to COUFRAN; new CRU BOURGEOIS doing v well.

Soutard St-Em r ★★★ 70' 71 78' 79 81 82' 83 85' 86 87 88' 89' 90' 91 92 93 94 95 Excellent 48-acre classed growth, 60% Merlot. Potent wines: long-lived for Anglo-Saxon drinking; exciting young to French palates. Second label: Clos de la Tonnelle.

Suduiraut Saut w sw ★★★★ 67 70 75 76' 78 79' 81 82' 83' 84 85 86 88' 90' 94 95 One of the best SAUTERNES, in its best vintages supremely luscious. 173 acres potentially of top class. Now in AXA control. See Pichon-Longueville. Sélection Cuvée Madame (82 83 86 89).

Rotting with style

Botrytis cinerea (French pourriture noble, German Edelfäule, English noble rot) is a form of mould that attacks the skins of ripe grapes in certain vineyards in warm and misty autumn weather.

Its effect, instead of rotting the grapes, is to wither them. The skin grows soft and flaccid, the juice evaporates through it, and what is left is a super-sweet concentration of everything in the grape except its water content.

The world's best sweet table wines are all made of 'nobly rotten' grapes. They occur in good vintages in Sauternes, the Rhine and the Mosel (where wine made from them is called Trockenbeerenauslese), in Tokaji in Hungary, in Burgenland in Austria, and elsewhere – California and Australia included. The danger is rain on pulpy grapes already far gone in botrytis. All too often the growers' hopes are dashed by the weather.

---

du Tailhas Pom r ★★ 5,000 cases. POMEROL of the lighter kind, near FIGEAC.

Taillefer Pom r ★★ 82 83 85 86 88' 89 90 92 93 94 95 28-acres on the edge of POMEROL in the Armand Moueix family (see also Fonplégade).

Talbot St-Jul r (w) ★★★ 78' 79 81 82' 83' 84 85' 86' 87 88' 89' 90 91 92 93 94 95 Important 240-acre fourth growth, sister to GRUAUD-LAROSE. Wine similarly attractive: rich, satisfying, reliable and gd value. Vg second label: Connétable Talbot. White is 'Caillou Blanc'. Thierry Rustmann also oversees winemaking at TOUR DE MONS.

Tayac Soussans-Mar r ★★ 82 83 85 86 87 88 89 90 92 93 94 95 MARGAUX'S biggest CRU BOURGEOIS. Reliable if not noteworthy.

de Terrefort-Quancard B'x r w ★★ Huge producer of good value wines at ST-ANDRE-DE-CUBZAC on the road to Paris. Rocky subsoil contributes to very drinkable quality. 33,000 cases. Drink at 5–10 yrs. Several other châteaux owned by Cheval-Quancard.

Terrey-Gros-Caillou St-Jul ★★ 82' 83 85 86' 88 89 90 91 92 93 94 95 Sister-château to HORTEVIE; at best equally noteworthy and stylish.

du Tertre Arsac-Mar r ★★ 70' 79' 81 82' 83' 85 86 88' 89' 90' 91 92 93 94 95 Fifth growth isolated S of MARGAUX; restored by the owner of CALON-SEGUR. Formerly fragrant and long-lived. To watch.

Tertre-Daugay St-Em r ★★★ 82' 83' 85 86 88' 89' 90' 92 93 94 95 Small, spectacularly sited GRAND CRU. Restored to proper rank by owner of LA GAFFELIERE.

Le Tertre-Rôteboeuf St-Em ★★★ 85 86 87 88' 89' 90' 91 92 93 94 95 A new star making concentrated, even dramatic, largely Merlot wine since '83. The 'roast beef' of the name gives the idea.

Thieuley E-Deux-Mers r p w ★★ Substantial supplier esp of clairet (rosé) and grapey Sauv. But reds are aged in oak.

Timberlay B'x r (w) ★ 185 acres at ST-ANDRE-DE-CUBZAC. Pleasant light wines to age 2–5 yrs. Same owners as VILLEMAURINE.

Toumilon Graves r w ★★ Little château in St-Pierre-de-Mons to note. Fresh and charming red and white.

La Tour-Blanche Saut w (r) sw ★★★ 81' 82 83' 85 86 87 88' 89' 90' 91 92 93 94 95 Historic leader of SAUTERNES, now a gov't wine college. Coasted in '70s; hit historic form again in '88.

La Tour-de-By Bégadan (Méd) r ★★ 81 82' 83 85' 86 87 88' 89' 90' 91 92 93 94 95 V well-run 182-acre CRU BOURGEOIS in N MEDOC steadily increasing its reputation for sturdy, yet instantly appealing wine.

La Tour-Carnet St-Laurent r ★★ 82 83 85 86 88 89' 90 91 92 93' 94' 95 Fourth growth with medieval fortress, long neglected. Light wine; slightly bolder since '86. Second wine: Sire de Comin.

La Tour-Figeac St-Em r ★★ 79 81 82' 83 85 86 87 88 89' 90' 93 94' 95 34-acre GRAND CRU CLASSE between CH FIGEAC, POMEROL. California-style ideas since '94.

La Tour-Haut-Brion Graves r ★★★ 70 78 79 81 82' 83 85 86 87 88 89 90 91 92 93 94 95 Formerly second label of CH LA MISSION-HAUT-BRION. Up to '83 a plainer, v tannic wine for long life. Now a separate v'yd: serious wines.

La Tour-Haut-Caussan Méd r ★★ Ambitious small (23-acre) estate at Blaignan attracting admiration.

La Tour-du-Haut-Moulin Cussac (H-Méd) r ★★ 75 76 81 82' 83 84 85' 86' 87 88' 89' 90' 91 92 93 94 95 Conscientious grower: intense top CRU BOURGEOIS.

La Tour-de-Mons Soussans-Mar r ★★ 70' 82' 83 85 86' 88' 89' 90' 91 92 93 94 95 Famous CRU BOURGEOIS of 87 acres, 3 centuries in the same family. A long dull patch but new ('95) TALBOT-influence means wines look better.

Tour du Pas St-Georges St-Em r ★★ Wine from 40 acres of ST-GEORGES-ST-EMILION made by AUSONE winemaker. V stylish; to follow.

La Tour-du-Pin-Figeac St-Em r ★★ 26-acre GRAND CRU worthy of restoration.

La Tour-du-Pin-Figeac-Moueix St-Em r ★★ 81 82 83 85 86 88' 89' 90' 92 93 94 95 Another 26-acre section of the same old property, owned by the Armand Moueix family. Splendid site; powerful wines.

La Tour-St-Bonnet Méd r ★★ 82' 83 85 86 87 88 89' 90' 91 92 93 94 95 Consistently well-made potent N MEDOC from St-Christoly. 100 acres.

Tournefeuille Lalande de Pom r ★★ 81' 82' 83' 85 86 88 89 90' 91 92 93 94 95 Best-known château of NEAC. 43 acres; sound wine. Also Ch de Bourg.

des Tours Montagne-St-Em r ★★ 82 85 86 88 89 90 92 93 94 95 Spectacular château with modern 170-acre v'yd. Sound easy wine.

Toutigeac, Domaine de E-Deux-Mers r (w) ★ 89 90' 91 92 93 94' 95 Enormous producer of useful Bordeaux at Targon.

Tronquoy-Lalande St-Est r ★★ 70 79 81 82' 83 85 86 88 89 90 92 93 94 95 40-acre CRU BOURGEOIS estate: typical high-coloured, ageable ST-ESTEPHE wines. DOURTHE-distributed.

Troplong-Mondot St-Em r ★★→★★★ 82' 83 85' 86 87 88' 89' 90' 92 93 94 95 70 acres well-sited on the COTES above CH PAVIE (and in same family). Now run with passion and new barrels. To follow. Second wine: Mondot.

Trotanoy Pom r ★★★★ 61' 70' 71' 75' 76' 78 79 81 82 83 84 85' 86 87 88 89 90' 92 93 94 95 Potentially the second POMEROL, after PETRUS, from the same stable. Only 27 acres; but at best (eg **82**) a glorious fleshy perfumed wine.

Trottevieille St-Em r ★★★ 79' 81 82' 83 85' 86 87 88 89' 90 92 93 94 95 GRAND CRU of 27 acres on the COTES. Dragged its feet for yrs. Same owners as BATAILLEY have raised their sights since '85. To watch.

Le Tuquet Graves r w ★★ (r) 93 94 95 (w) 93 94 95 Big estate at Beautiran. Light fruity wines to drink young; the white better. (Cuvée Spéciale oak-aged.)

Valandraud St-Em r ★★ 91 92 93 94 Brand new micro-château with aspirations to glory.

Verdignan Méd r ★★ 81 82 83 85 86 87 88 89' 90 91 92 95 Substantial Bourgeois sister to CH COUFRAN. More Cab than Coufran.

Vieux Château Certan Pom r ★★★ 70 78 79 81 82' 83' 85 86' 87 88' 89 90' 92 93 94 95 Traditionally rated close to PETRUS in quality, but totally different in style; almost HAUT-BRION build. 34 acres. Same (Belgian) family owns LABEGORCE-ZEDE and tiny POMEROL, LE PIN. See also Château Puygueraud.

Vieux-Château-St-André St-Em r ★★ 82' 83 85' 86 87 88' 89' 90' 91 92 93' 94' 95 Small v'yd in MONTAGNE-ST-EMILION owned by the winemaker of PETRUS. To follow. 2,500 cases.

Villegeorge Avensan r ★★ 82 83' 85 86 87' 88 89 90 92 93 94 95 24-acre CRU BOURGEOIS N of MARGAUX; same owner as BRANE-CANTENAC. Enjoyable rather tannic wine. Sister château: Duplessis (Hauchecorne).

Villemaurine St-Em r ★★ 82' 83 85' 86 87 88 89 90 91 92 93 94 95 Small GRAND CRU with splendid cellars well-sited on the COTES by the town. Firm wine with a high proportion of Cab.

Vray-Croix-de-Gay Pom ★★ 75' 82' 83 85 86 87 88 89 90 92 93 94 95 V small ideally situated v'yd in the best part of POMEROL. Needs devotion.

Yon-Figeac St-Em r ★★ 81 82 83 85 86 88 89 90 92 93 94 95 59-acre GRAND CRU to follow for savoury supple wine.

d'Yquem Saut w sw (dr) ★★★★ 67' 71' 73 75' 76' 77 78 79 80' 81' 82' 83' 84 85 86' 87 88' 89' (90' 91 93 94 95 to come) The world's most famous sweet-wine estate. 250 acres; only 500 bottles per acre of v strong intense luscious wine, kept 4 yrs in barrel. Most vintages improve for 15 yrs+. Also make dry Ygrec ('Y') in 78 79 80 84 85 (86 v little) 87 88 89 91 92 95.

More Bordeaux châteaux are listed under Canon-Fronsac, Côtes de Bourg, Côtes de Castillon, Côtes de Francs, Fronsac, Lalande de Pomerol, Loupiac, Premières Côtes de Blaye, Premières Côtes de Bordeaux, St-André-de-Cubzac, Ste-Croix-du-Mont in the A–Z of France, pages 32–77.

Bordeaux's 'second wines'

Bordeaux's top châteaux have for centuries offered a Grand Vin and a second selection. The practice was revived in the 1960s by Château Latour with its remarkable Les Forts de Latour. Increasing yields and prosperity, especially in the 1980s, made the need for strict selection obvious. Most top châteaux started 'second wines', usually very good value. The following is a list of those worth looking out for (big brothers listed alongside).

Amiral de Beychevelle – CH BEYCHEVELLE
Artiges-Arnaud – CH GRAND-PUY-DUCASSE
Bahans Haut-Brion – CH HAUT-BRION
Baron de Brane/Notton – CH BRANE-CANTENAC
La Bastide Dauzac – CH DAUZAC
Beau-Mayne – CH COUVENT DES JACOBINS
Benjamin de Beauregard – CH BEAUREGARD
Le Bonnat – CH FIEUZAL
de Candale – CH D'ISSAN
Cantelaude – CH GISCOURS
Canuet – CH CANTENAC-BROWN
Cap de Haut-Maucaillou – CH MAUCAILLOU
Caroline – CH LESTAGE
Carruades de Lafite – CH LAFITE-ROTHSCHILD
Chambert-Marbuzet – CH HAUT-MARBUZET
Chantalouette and du Delias – CH DE SALES
Château Caperot – CH MONBOUSQUET
Château Grand Goucsirs – CH GISCOURS
Château Roquefort – CH TERTRE-DAUGAY
Château des Templiers – CH LARMANDE
Les Chênes – PAVIE-MACQUIN
Clairefont – CH PRIEURE-LICHINE
Le Clémentin du Pape-Clément – CH P-CLEMENT
Clos de la Gravette – VIEUX CHATEAU CERTAN
Clos J Kanon – CH CANON
Clos Labère – CH RIEUSSEC
Clos Lescure – CH PINDEFLEURS
Clos du Marquis – CH LEOVILLE-LAS-CASES
Clos de la Tonnelle – CH SOUTARD
La Closerie de Camensac – CH CAMENSAC
Connétable de Talbot – CH TALBOT
de Conques – CH LES ORMES-SORBET
Cordet – CH MONBRISON
La Croix-Beaucaillou – CH DUCRU-BEAUCAILLOU
Les Cyprès – CH CLIMENS
La Dame de Montrose – CH MONTROSE
Diane de Belgrave – CH BELGRAVE
Dom de l'Artigue – CH SENEJAC
Dom de Compostelle – CH LA CABANNE
Dom de Martialis – CH CLOS FOURTET
Dom Zédé – CH LABEGORCE-ZEDE
Duluc – CH BRANAIRE-DUCRU
Ermitage de Chasse-Spleen – CH CH SPLEEN
Les Fiefs de Lagrange – CH LAGRANGE
Fonpiqueyre – CH LIVERSAN
Les Forts de Latour – CH LATOUR
Franck Phélan – CH PHELAN-SEGUR
Grand Parc – CH LEOVILLE-LAS-CASES
Grangeneuve – CH FIGEAC
Haut-Bages-Averous – CH LYNCH-BAGES

Haut-Bommes – CH CLOS HAUT-PEYRAGUEY
Les Hauts de Pontet – CH PONTET-CANET
Les Hauts de Smith – CH SMITH-HAUT-LAFITTE
l'Hospitalet – CH GAZIN
L de Louvière – CH LA LOUVIERE
Lacoste-Borie – CH GRAND-PUY-LACOSTE
Lady Langoa – CH LANGOA-BARTON
Lamouroux – CH RAUSAN-SEGLA
Larose St-Laurent – CH LAROSE-TRINTAUDON
Lartigue-de-Brochon – CH SOCIANDO-MALLET
Ludon-Pomiès-Agassac – CH LA LAGUNE
MacCarthy – CH CHAMBERT-MARBUZET
Mademoiselle de St-Marc – CH LA TOUR BLANCHE
de Marbuzet – CH COS-D'ESTOURNEL
Marquis de Ségur – CH CALON-SEGUR
Maurens – CH FOMBRAUGE
Mayne-Lévêque – CH CHANTEGRIVE
Mondot – CH TROPLONG-MONDOT
Moulin d'Arvigny – CH BEAUMONT
Moulin de Duhart – CH D-MILON-ROTHSCHILD
Moulin-Riche – CH LEOVILLE-POYFERRE
Moulinet-Lasserre – CH CLOS RENE
Moulins de Citran – CH CITRAN
Notre Dame de Landiras – CH LANDIRAS
Numéro 2 – CH LAFON-ROCHET
La Parde de Haut-Bailly – CH HAUT-BAILLY
Pavillon Rouge – CH MARGAUX
Pensées de Lafleur – CH LAFLEUR
Le Petit Cheval – CH CHEVAL BLANC
La Petite Eglise – CH L'EGLISE-CLINET
Peymartin – CH GLORIA
Peyre-Labade – CH CLARKE
Prieur de Meyney – CH MEYNEY
Les Reflets du Ch Cissac – CH CISSAC
Réserve de la Comtesse – CH PICHON-LALANDE
Réserve du Général – CH PALMER
Reynon-Peyrat – CH REYNON
St-Paul de Dominique – CH LA DOMINIQUE
Ste-Hélène – CH DE MALLE
La Salle de Poujeaux – CH POUJEAUX-THEIL
Sarget de Gruaud-Larose – CH G-LAROSE
Ségla – CH RAUSAN-SEGLA
Segonnes – CH LASCOMBES
Sire de Comin – CH LA TOUR-CARNET
Le Tana de Malescasse – CH MALESCASSE
La Tour-d'Aspic – CH HAUT-BATAILLEY
La Tour-Léognan – CH CARBONNIEUX
Les Tourelles de Longueville – CH PICHON-L
Tourteran – CH RAMAGE-LA-BATISSE
Villeneuve de Cantemerle – CH CANTEMERLE

Italy

Heavily shaded areas are
the wine growing regions

The following abbreviations are used in the text:

Ab	Abruzzi	Pie	Piedmont
Ap	Apulia	Sar	Sardinia
Bas	Basilicata	Si	Sicily
Cal	Calabria	T-AA	Trentino-
Cam	Campania		Alto Adige
E-R	Emilia-Romagna	Tus	Tuscany
F-VG	Friuli-	Umb	Umbria
	Venezia Giulia	VdA	Valle d'Aosta
Lat	Latium	Ven	Veneto
Lig	Liguria		
Lom	Lombardy	fz	frizzante
Mar	Marches	pa	passito

VALLE
D'AOSTA

L Como

L Maggiore

Milan
○
LOMBAR

Turin ○
PIEDMONT

Genoa ○

Po

LIGURIA

Ligurian Sea

The genius of Italy is private and idiosyncratic. It reveals itself in
beauty amongst ugliness, kindness and wit among people with
little to spare – and in the steadily stubborn way in which wine
growers raise their personal stakes despite the floundering
legislation around them.

Five years ago I was writing here that the new 1992 Wine Law
was eventually going to make everything orderly and intelligible.

I described its 'pyramid' system with the (officially) humble vino
da tavola at the bottom, narrowing to the lofty and exclusive Vigna
wine from a DOCG zone at the top. In reality the law seems to have
changed almost nothing.

It never was going to increase the skill and dedication of the best
growers and makers – and they have predictably followed their own
stars, in many cases with wonderful results. The best Italian red wines
now belong with the world's best.

Italians will quibble, but Italy is not, on the whole, a country to
look to for fine white wines. I can immediately think of dozens of
exceptions, starting in the northeast in Friuli and scattered through
the peninsula down to Campania and even Sicily. It is more to the
point, perhaps, to say that the average Italian's taste in white wine
remains devoted to desert dryness, avoiding those lovely hints of
fruit that would be there if they didn't strip them out. Neither of the
two greatest wine regions, Piedmont or Tuscany, have any typical
white wines remotely worthy of their reds.

But their reds are glorious, and tend to distract attention from
many other regions with original and memorable tastes to offer. For
example, value-seekers should look closer and closer at the eastern

side of the country – especially from the Abruzzi down to Apulia, Italy's heel. Altogether this may be the world's biggest vineyard – and yet it has remained virtually anonymous until the past few years; its wines leaving home in tankers to unknown destinies in the north.

Sloppy wine-growers in the famous regions have the luxury of a name to ride on. You have to go to a trattoria in Florence to find out how appalling Chianti can be. Emerging regions have different ethos. Montepulciano d'Abruzzo, Salice Salentino... these and many other emerging Adriatic DOCs are worth careful study.

Abbazia di Rosazzo ★★★ Major estate of COLLI ORIENTALI. White Ronco delle Acacie and Ronco di Corte and red Ronco dei Roseti are vg single-v'yd wines.

Abboccato Semi-sweet.

Adami ★★→★★★ Producers of top PROSECCO DI CONEGLIANO-VALDOBBIADENE (Vigneto Giardino).

Adanti ★★→★★★ Umbrian maker of pleasant red SAGRANTINO DI MONTEFALCO, VINO DA TAVOLA BIANCO D'ARQUATA and Rosso d'Arquata (a very good blend of BARBERA, Canaiolo and MERLOT). Also produces good CABERNET SAUVIGNON reds. Value for money.

Aglianico del Vulture Bas DOC r dr (s/sw sp) ★★★ 85 86 87 88 90 91 92 (93) (94) (95) Among the best wines of S Italy. Ages well to rich aromas. Called VECCHIO after 3 yrs, RISERVA after 5. Top growers: D'ANGELO (also makes vg pure Aglianico VDT Canneto) and PATERNOSTER.

Alba Major wine city of PIEDMONT, on River Tanaro, S of Turin.

Albana di Romagna E-R DOCG w dr s/sw (sp) ★★(★) DYA Italy's first DOCG for white wine, though it is hard to see why. Albana is the (undistinguished) grape. FATTORIA PARADISO makes some of the best. AMABILE is usually better than dry. ZERBINA's botrytis-sweet PASSITO is outstanding. Also try Romandiola.

Alcamo Si DOC w ★ Soft neutral whites. Rapitalà is the best brand.

Aleatico Excellent red Muscat-flavoured grape for sweet aromatic strong dessert wines, chiefly of the south of Italy. Aleatico di Puglia DOC (best grower is CANDIDO) is better and more famous than Aleatico di Gradoli (Latium) DOC.

Alezio Ap DOC p (r) ★★ DYA Recent DOC at Salento, especially for delicate rosé. Top grower is Calò Michele (who also makes good barrel-aged NEGROAMARO VDT, Vigna Spano).

Allegrini ★★★ Top quality producer of Veronese wines, incl fine VALPOLICELLA from prime new v'yds and vg AMARONE.

Altare, Elio ★★★ Small producer of good, v modern BAROLO. Look for Barolo Vigna Arborina and BARBERA VDT Vigna Larigi.

Altesino ★★ Producer of BRUNELLO DI MONTALCINO and VDT Palazzo Altesi.

Alto Adige T-AA DOC r p w dr sw sp ★→★★★ DOC covering 20 different wines, usually named by their grapes, in 33 German-speaking villages around Bolzano. Whites are best. Region often called Südtirol.

Ama, Castello di, (or Fattoria di Ama) ★★★★ One of the best, most consistent modern CHIANTI CLASSICO estates, nr Gaiole. La Casuccia and Bellavista are top single-v'yd wines. Also good VDTS, CHARD, SAUV, MERLOT (Vigna L'Apparita), PINOT N (Il Chiuso).

Amabile Means semi-sweet, but usually sweeter than ABBOCCATO.

Amaro Bitter. When prominent on label, content are not wine but 'bitters'.

Amarone della Valpolicella (alias Recioto della Valpolicella Amarone) Ven DOC r ★★★→★★★★ 83 84 85 86 88 90 (91) (93) (94) 95 Dry version of RECIOTO DELLA VALPOLICELLA, potent, concentrated, long-lived and very impressive; from air-dried grapes. Best from the following growers: Serègo Alighieri, ALLEGRINI, BERTANI, BRIGALDARA, Brunelli, Corte Sant Alda, Aleardo Ferrari, Fornaser, DAL FORNO, GUERRIERI-RIZZARDI, LE RAGOSE, MASI, QUINTARELLI, SAN RUSTICO, LE SALETTE, Speri, TEDESCHI, Villa Spinosa. NB watch the high alcohol content.

Anghelu Ruju ★★★ ('Red Angel') Port-like version of Sardinian CANNONAU wine from SELLA & MOSCA. Well worth trying.

Anselmi, Roberto ★★★ A leader in SOAVE with his single-vineyard Capitel Foscarino and exceptional sweet dessert RECIOTO dei Capitelli.

NB Vintages in colour are those you should choose first for drinking in 1997.

Antinori, Marchesi L & P ★→★★★ Immensely influential long-established Florentine house of the highest repute, now wholly owned by Piero A, producing first-rate CHIANTI CLASSICO (esp PEPPOLI, Tenute Marchese Antinori, Villa Antinori and Badia a Passignano), Umbrian (CASTELLO DELLA SALA) and PIEDMONT (PRUNOTTO) wines. The first pioneer of new VDT, eg TIGNANELLO, SOLAIA (Tuscany), CERVARO DELLA SALA (Umbria). Marchese Piero A was the Voice of Italy in world wine circles in the '70s and '80s. His daughters are now managing. Recent acquisitions in MONTEPULCIANO (Fattoria La Braccesca for VINO NOBILE), MONTALCINO (Castello di Carmigliano for BRUNELLO), nr Pitigliano (southern Italy) and in ASTI (for BARBERA). See also Prunotto.

Apulia Puglia. Italy's heel, producing a fifth of all Italian wine, but mostly bottled in North Italy/France. Best DOC: SALICE SALENTINO. Producers are: Botromagno, Calò Michele, CANDIDO, Coop Copertino, Coppi, LEONE DE CASTRIS, Masseria Monaci, RIVERA, ROSA DEL GOLFO, TAURINO, Vallone.

Aquileia F-VG DOC r w ★★ (r) 88 90 93 94 12 single-grape wines from around the town of Aquileia on the Slovenian border. Good REFOSCO.

Argiano ★★★ Top MONTALCINO producer.

Argiolas, Antonio ★★ Important Sardinian producer making wines of astonishing quality. Very good: CANNONAU, NURAGUS, VERMENTINO and red VINO DA TAVOLA Turriga.

Arneis Pie w ★★ DYA At last a fairly good white from BAROLO country: the revival of an ancient grape to make fragrant light wine. Now DOC as Roero Arneis, a zone N of Alba, and Langhe Arneis. Good from Almondo, Bel Colle, Correggia, Deltetto, BRUNO GIACOSA, Malvirà, Negro, Rabino and Gianni Voerzio (Roero A); Castello di Neive (Langhe A).

Artimino Tusc r ★★★ Ancient hill-town W of Florence. Fattoria di Artimino produces top DOCG CARMIGNANO.

Assisi Umb r (w) ★★ DYA VDT Rosso and Bianco di Assisi: v attractive. Try drinking them cool.

Asti Major wine centre of PIEDMONT.

Asti (Spumante) Pie DOCG w sp ★→★★ NV Immensely popular sweet and v fruity Muscat sparkling wine, now updated to DOCG, but no perceptible improvement yet. V low in alcohol; can be delicious with dessert. Top producers include BERA WALTER, Dogliotti-Caudrina, Cascina Fonda, Vignaioli di Santo Stefano.

Attems, Conti Famous old COLLIO estate with wide range of good typical wines (esp PINOT GRIGIO). Now run by Collavini.

Avignonesi ★★★→★★★★ Noble MONTEPULCIANO house with very fine range: VINO NOBILE, blended red Grifi, top CHARDONNAY, SAUVIGNON, MERLOT and superlative VIN SANTO.

Azienda agricola/agraria A farm producing crops, often incl wine.

Azienda/casa vinicola Wine firm using bought-in grapes and/or wines.

Azienda vitivinicola A (specialized) wine estate.

Badia a Coltibuono ★★★ Fine CHIANTI-maker in an old abbey at Gaiole with a restaurant and collection of old vintages. Also VDT SANGIOVETO.

Banfi (Castello or Villa) ★★→★★★ Space-age CANTINA of biggest US importer of Italian wine. Huge plantings at MONTALCINO, mostly SANGIOVESE, but also Syrah, PINOT NOIR, CABERNET SAUVIGNON, CHARDONNAY, SAUVIGNON etc, are part of a drive for quality plus quantity. BRUNELLO is good but 'Poggio all'Oro' is ★★★★. Centine is ROSSO DI MONTALCINO. In PIEDMONT Banfi produces vg sparkling Banfi Brut, Principessa GAVI, BRACCHETO D'ACQUI, PINOT GRIS. See also Eastern States USA.

Barbacarlo Lom r dr sw sp ★★ Traditional light wines with typical bitter-almond taste, from OLTREPO PAVESE.

Barbaresco Pie DOCG r ★★★→★★★★ 85' 86 87 88' 89' 90' 93' (94) (95) Neighbour of BAROLO; the other great NEBBIOLO wine. Perhaps marginally less sturdy. At best palate-cleansing, deep, subtle and fine. At 4 yrs becomes RISERVA. Producers incl CERETTO, CIGLIUTI, GAJA, BRUNO GIACOSA, Marchesi di Gresy, MOCCAGATTA, Fiorenzo Nada, Giorgio Pelissero, PIO CESARE, Produttori del B, PRUNOTTO, Alfredo Roagna, BRUNO ROCCA, Sottimano.

Barbatella, Cascina La ★★★ Top producer of BARBERA D'ASTI: excellent single-v'yd Sonvico and dell'Angelo.

Barbera
Dark acidic red grape, the second most planted in Italy after SANGIOVESE; a speciality of PIEDMONT also used in Lombardy, Emilia-Romagna and other northern provinces. Its best wines follow...

Barbera d'Alba Pie DOC r ★★→★★★ 85' 86 87 88' 89' 90' 91 92 93' 94 95 Tasty tannic fragrant red. SUPERIORE can age 7+ yrs. Round ALBA, NEBBIOLO is sometimes added to make a VDT (some barrique-aged 100% BARBERA is also vdt). Top producers: CIGLIUTI, CLERICO, Elvio Cogno, A and G CONTERNO, CONTERNO-FANTINO, E GRASSO, Silvio Grasso, Manzone, G MASCARELLO, OBERTO, PARUSSO, Pianpolvere Soprana, PRUNOTTO, BRUNO ROCCA, Scavino, Aldo Vajra, Eraldo Viberti, VIETTI, Gianni Voerzio, R VOERZIO.

Barbera d'Asti Pie DOC r ★★→★★★ 85' 86 87 88' 89' 90' 91 92 93' 94 95 For real BARBERA-lovers: Barbera alone, tangy and appetizing, drunk young or aged up to 7–10 yrs or longer. Top growers incl La Barbatella, Bava, Bertelli, BOFFA, BRAIDA, Brema, Bricco Mondalino, CASCINA CASTLET, CHIARLO, Colle Manora, COPPO, Livio Pavese, Marchesi Alfieri, Occhetti, Rovero, SCARPA, TERRE DA VINO, Trinchero, Viarengo.

Barbera del Monferrato Pie DOC r ★→★★ DYA Easy-drinking BARBERA from Alessandria and ASTI. Pleasant, slightly fizzy, s'times sweetish.

Barberani ★★→★★★ Leading ORVIETO producer; Calcaia is botrytis-sweet wine.

Barbi, Fattoria dei ★★ Traditional producer of BRUNELLO DI MONTALCINO.

Barco Reale Tus DOC r ★★ DOC for junior wine of CARMIGNANO; same grapes.

Bardolino Ven DOC r (p) ★★ DYA Pale summery slightly bitter red from E shore of Lake Garda. Bardolino CHIARETTO is even paler and lighter. Top makers: GUERRIERI-RIZZARDI, Le Vigne di San Pietro, Villabella, Zenato, Fratelli Zeni.

Barolo Pie DOCG r ★★★→★★★★ 82' 85' 86 88' 89' 90' 93' (95) Small area S of ALBA with one of Italy's supreme reds: rich, tannic, alcoholic (min 13%), dry but wonderfully deep and fragrant (also crisp and clean) in the mouth. From NEBBIOLO grapes. Ages for up to 15 yrs (RISERVA after 5).

A Barole of honour
The giants of Barolo: Bruno Giacosa, Aldo Conterno, Giacomo Conterno, Bartolo Mascarello, Giuseppe Mascarello, Vietti.
A promising new generation of classic Barolos: Renato Corino, Elio Grasso, Rocche dei Manzoni, G D Vajra, Gianni Voerzio, Roberto Voerzio.
Successful experimental/fashionable Barolos: Elio Alterno, Domenico Cerico, Conterno-Fantino, Angelo Gaja, Luciano Sandrone, Paolo Scavino.

Bellavista ★★→★★★ FRANCIACORTA estate with brisk SPUMANTE (Gran Cuvée Franciacorta is top). Also Crémant. Good VDT reds from CAB and PINOT N.

Bera, Walter ★★ Small family estate nr BARBARESCO. Vg MOSCATO D'ASTI and ASTI.

Berlucchi, Guido ★ Italy's biggest producer of sparkling METODO CLASSICO, at FRANCIACORTA. Quality steady.

Bertani ★★ Well-known producers of quality Veronese wines (VALPOLICELLA, AMARONE, SOAVE, etc).

Bertelli ★★ Good small PIEDMONT producer: BARBERA D'ASTI, VDT CAB, CHARD.

Biancara, La ★★★ Top quality GAMBELLARAS (vg RECIOTO and late-harvest VENDEMMIA TARDIVA). (ZONIN is number one in quantity.)

Bianco White.

Bianco d'Arquata Umb w ★★ DYA See Adanti.

Bianco di Custoza Ven DOC w (sp) ★→★★ DYA Twin of SOAVE from the other side (west) of Verona. Good from Corte Sant'Arcadio, Le Tende, Le Vigne di San Pietro, MONTRESOR.

Bianco di Pitigliano Tus DOC w ★ DYA Dull dry white from nr Grosseto.

Biancolella ISCHIA's best white. A VDT from D'AMBRA.

Bigi Famous producer of ORVIETO and other wines of Umbria and TUSCANY. Their TORRICELLA v'yd produces vg dry Orvieto.

Biondi-Santi ★★→★★★★ The original producer of BRUNELLO DI MONTALCINO, from 45-acre Il Greppo v'yd. Prices are absurd, but the v old vintages are unique.

Boca Pie DOC r ★★ 85 88 89 90 93 95 Another NEBBIOLO from N of PIEDMONT. Look for Poderi ai Valloni (Vigneto Cristiana ★★★).

Boffa, Alfiero ★★→★★★ Small property for top BARBERA D'ASTI. Especially single-v'yd wines.

Bolgheri Tus DOC r p w (sw) ★★→★★★★ On the coast south of Livorno. Incl 7 types of wine: BIANCO, VERMENTINO, SAUVIGNON BLANC, ROSSO, ROSATO, VIN SANTO OCCHIO DI PERNICE and (since '94) SASSICAIA (★★★★). Top producers are Le Macchiole (Il Paleo ★★★★), ORNELLAIA (Masseto and Ornellaia, both ★★★★), SAN GUIDO (Sassicaia ★★★★). Also: Michele Satta.

Bolla Famous Verona firm for VALPOLICELLA, SOAVE, etc. Top wines: Castellaro (one of the v best SOAVES), Creso (red and white), Jago.

Bonarda Minor red grape (alias Croatina) widely grown in PIEDMONT, Lombardy, Emilia-Romagna and blended with BARBERA.

Bonarda (Oltrepò Pavese) Lom DOC r ★★ Soft fresh often FRIZZANTE red from S of Pavia.

Borgo del Tiglio ★★★ FRIULI estate for one of NE Italy's top MERLOTS: VDT Rosso della Centa; also good are COLLIO CHARD, TOCAI and BIANCO.

Boscaini Ven ★★ Verona producer of VALPOLICELLA, AMARONE, SOAVE.

Boscarelli, Poderi ★★★ Small estate with vg VINO NOBILE DI MONTEPULCIANO, barrel-aged VDT Boscarelli and good ROSSO DI M.

Brachetto d'Acqui Pie r sw (sp) ★★ DYA Sweet sparkling red with enticing Muscat scent. Much better than it sounds.

Braida ★★★ Estate for top BARBERA D'ASTI (Bricco della Bigotta and Barbera VDT BRICCO DELL'UCCELLONE).

Bramaterra Pie DOC r ★★ 85 88 89 90 93 95 Neighbour to GATTINARA. NEBBIOLO grapes predominate in a blend. Good producers: Perazzi, SELLA.

Breganze Ven DOC r ★→★★★ (r) 88 89 90 91 93 94 95 A catch-all for many varieties around Vicenza. CABERNET and PINOT BL are best. Top producers: B Bartolomeo, MACULAN.

Bricco Term for a high (and by implication vg) ridge v'yd in PIEDMONT.

Bricco del Drago Pie vdt Original long-lived blend of DOLCETTO and NEBBIOLO from Cascina Drago.

Bricco Manzoni Pie r ★★★ 82' 85' 88' 89' 90' 91 92 93' (94) 95 V successful blend of NEBBIOLO and BARBERA from Monforte d'Alba.

Bricco dell'Uccellone Pie r ★★★ 88' 89' 90' 91 92 93' 94 95 Barrique-aged BARBERA from the firm of the late Giacomo Bologna. Bricco della Bigotta and Ai Suma are others.

Brigaldara ★★★ Small producer in VALPOLICELLA with top AMARONE and RECIOTO.

Brindisi Ap DOC r ★★ Strong NEGROAMARO. Esp Patriglione (★★★) from TAURINO.

Brolio, Castello di ★★→★★★ After a sad period in foreign hands, the Ricasoli family has taken this legendary estate in hand again. The first results are very promising. More to come...

Brunello di Montalcino Tus DOCG r ★★★→★★★★ 82' 85' 86 88' 90' 91 93 94 95' With BAROLO, Italy's most celebrated red: strong, full-bodied, high-flavoured, tannic and long-lived. 4 yrs' ageing, after 5 becomes RISERVA. Quality ever-improving. Montalcino is 25 miles S of Siena.

Good Brunello di Montalcino producers include: Altesino, Argiano, Banfi, Barbi, Biondi-Santi, Campogiovanni, Capanna-Cencioni, Caparzo, Casanova di Neri, Case Basse, Castelgiocondo, Cerbaiona, Col d'Orcia, Costanti, Eredi Fuligni, Gorelli, Lisini, Marchesato degli Aleramici, Mastrojanni, Siro Pacenti, Pacenti Franco e Rosildo, Il Palazzone, Ciacci Piccolomini, Pieve di Santa Restituta, Poggio Antico, Poggione, Salvioni-Cerbaiola, San Giorgio, Talenti. See also Rosso di Montalcino (value).

Brusco dei Barbi Tus r ★★ 88 89 90 91 92 93 94 95 Lively variant on BRUNELLO using old CHIANTI GOVERNO method.

Bukkuram Si br ★★★ Celebrated MOSCATO DI PANTELLERIA from De Bartoli.

Ca'del Bosco ★★★ FRANCIACORTA estate making some of Italy's v best sparkling wine, CHARD, and excellent reds (see Zanella).

Cabernet Sauvignon Much used in NE Italy and now (esp in VDT) in TUSCANY, PIEDMONT and the south.

Cacchiano, Castello di ★★★ First-rate CHIANTI CLASSICO estate at Gaiole, owned by RICASOLI cousins. Outstanding RISERVA 'Millennio'.

Cafaggio, Villa ★★→★★★ CHIANTI CLASSICO estate. Solid red VDT: Solatio Basilica.

Caldaro (Lago di Caldaro) T-AA DOC r ★→★★ DYA Alias KALTERERSEE. Light soft bitter-almond red from SCHIAVA grapes. From a huge area. CLASSICO from a smaller area is better.

Caluso Passito Pie DOC w sw (fz) ★★ Made from Erbaluce grapes; delicate scent, velvety taste. Tiny production. Best from Bianco, Ferrando.

Candido, Francesco ★★ Top grower of Salento, APULIA; good reds: Duca d'Aragona, Cappello del Prete, SALICE SALENTINO; also vg dessert wine: ALEATICO DI PUGLIA.

Canevel ★★→★★★ Vg producer of PROSECCO DI CONEGLIANO-VALDOBBIADENE.

Cannonau di Sardegna Sar DOC r (p) dr s/sw ★★ 90 91 92 93 94 95 Cannonau (Grenache) is Sardinia's basic red grape. Wines range from v potent to fine and mellow. Best from Arcadu Tonino, CS di Jerzu, Gabbas Giuseppe, Loi Alberto, SELLA & MOSCA.

Cantalupo, Antichi Vigneti di ★★→★★★ Top GHEMME wines – especially single-vineyard Breclemae and Carellae.

Cantina Cellar or winery.

Cantina Sociale (CS) Growers' coop.

Capannelle ★★★ Good producer of VDT (formerly CHIANTI CLASSICO), nr Gaiole.

Caparzo, Tenuta ★★★ MONTALCINO estate with excellent BRUNELLO La Casa; also vg ROSSO DI MONTALCINO (look for La Caduta), red blend Ca'del Pazzo and white blend Le Grance.

Capezzana, Tenuta di (or Villa) ★★→★★★ The Tuscan estate (W of Florence) of the Contini Bonacossi family. Excellent CHIANTI Montalbano and CARMIGNANO. Also vg Bordeaux-style red, GHIAIE DELLA FURBA.

Capri Cam DOC r p w ★→★★ Famous island with widely abused name. Only interesting wines are from La Caprense.

Cardizze Famous, frequently too expensive DOC PROSECCO of top vineyard nr VALDOBBIADENE.

Carema Pie DOC r ★★→★★★ 85' 88' 89' 90' (91) (92) 93' 95 Old speciality of N PIEDMONT. Best from Luigi Ferrando (or the CANTINA SOCIALE).

Carignano del Sulcis Sar DOC r p ★★→★★★ 90 91 93 94 95 Well-structured red wine with capacity for ageing. The best is Terre Brune from CANTINA SOCIALE di Santadi.

Carmignano Tus DOCG r ★★★ 85' 86 88' 90' 91 93' 94' 95 Region west of Florence. CHIANTI grapes plus 10% CABERNET S make distinctive, reliable, even excellent reds. Good producers include Ambra, ARTIMINO, CAPEZZANA, Farnete and Poggiolo.

Carpenè Malvolti Leading producer of classic PROSECCO and other sparkling wines at Conegliano, Veneto.

Carpineto Producer of CHIANTI CLASSICO in N part of region.

Carso F-VG DOC r w ★★→★★★ 90 93 94 95 DOC nr Trieste incl good MALVASIA. Terrano del C is a REFOSCO red. Top grower: Edi Kante.

Casa fondata nel... Firm founded in...

Casalte, Fattoria Le ★★★ Good VINO NOBILE DI MONTEPULCIANO; also ROSSO and white VDT Celius.

Casanova di Neri ★★★ BRUNELLO DI MONTALCINO (and vg ROSSO DI M) from the Neri family; better every year.

Case Basse ★★★ Small estate with v impressive BRUNELLO and VDT Intistieti.

Case Bianche, Le ★★ Reliable estate nr Conegliano (Ven) for PROSECCO, SAUV and surprising red Wildbacher (from ancient Austrian grape).

Castel del Monte Ap DOC r p w ★★ (r) 92 93 94 Dry fresh well-balanced southern wines. The red is RISERVA after 3 yrs. Rosé most widely known. RIVERA'S Il Falcone stands out.

Castell'in Villa ★★★ Vg CHIANTI CLASSICO estate.

Castellare ★★→★★★ Small but admired CHIANTI CLASSICO producer with first-rate SANGIOVESE VDT I Sodi di San Niccoló and sprightly GOVERNO del Castellare: old-style CHIANTI updated.

Castello Castle. (See under name: eg Albola, Castello d'.)

Castelluccio ★★→★★★ Best SANGIOVESE of Emilia-Romagna: VDT Ronco dei Cigliegi and Ronco della Simia.

Castlet, Cascina ★★→★★★ Producers of concentrated BARBERA PASSITO, VDT Passum, vg BARBERA D'ASTI.

Cavalleri ★★→★★★ Vg and reliable producer of FRANCIACORTA wines; sparkling are the best.

Cavallotto ★★→★★★ Reliable BAROLO estate: esp Barolo Vigna San Giuseppe.

Cavicchioli Large Emilia-Romagna producer of LAMBRUSCO and other sparkling: Lambrusco di Sorbara Vigna del Cristo is best.

Ca'Vit (Cantina Viticoltori) Group of quality coops near Trento. Wines include MARZEMINO, CAB, PINOTS N, BL and GR, NOSIOLA. Top wines: Brume di Monte (red and white) and sparkling Graal and Firmato.

Cerasuolo Ab DOC p ★★ The ROSATO version of MONTEPULCIANO D'ABRUZZO.

Ceretto ★★★ Vg grower of BARBARESCO (Bricco Asili), BAROLO (Bricco Rocche), top BARBERA D'ALBA (Piana), CHARD (La Bernardina), DOLCETTO and ARNEIS.

Cervaro See Castello della Sala.

Chardonnay Has recently joined permitted varieties for several N Italian DOCs (eg T-AA, FRANCIACORTA, F-VG, PIEDMONT). Some of the best (eg from ANTINORI, FELSINA, GAJA, LUNGAROTTI) are still only VDT.

To decipher codes, please refer to 'Key to symbols' on front flap of jacket, or to 'How to use this book' on page 6.

Chianti Tus DOCG r ★→★★★ 93 94' 95 The lively local wine of Florence and Siena. Fresh fruity and tangy, still sometimes sold in straw-covered flasks. Mostly made to drink young. Of the subdistricts, RUFINA (★★→★★★) and Colli Fiorentini (★→★★★) can make CLASSICO-style RISERVAS. Montalbano, Colli Senesi, Aretini and Pisani make lighter wines.

Annata Chianti Classico
The way to fame in Chianti is to make high-scoring special selections: expensive Riservas, single-vineyard wines and Super-Tuscan VDTs. But everday Annata wines can suffer in high profile cantinas. The following give excellent quality and value in standard Annata Chianti Classico: Cacchiano, Casa Emma, Fonterutoli, Isole e Olena, La Massa, Le Cinciole, Nittardi, Poggerino, Riecine, Rodano, Viticcio and Volpaia.

Chianti Classico Tus DOCG r ★★→★★★★ 88 90 91 92 93 94 95 (Riserva) 83 85 86 88 90 93 94 (95) Senior CHIANTI from the central area. Its old pale astringent style is becoming rarer as top estates opt for either darker tannic wines or softer and fruitier ones. Some are among the best wines of Italy. Members of the Consorzio use the badge of a black rooster, but several top firms do not belong.

Outstanding Chianti Classico producers include: Ama, Brolio, Cacchiano, Capaccia, Casa Emma, Castel Ruggero, Castellare, Castell'in Villa, Le Cinciole, Coltibuono, Felsina, Le Filigare, Fonterutoli, Fontodi, Isole e Olena, Querciabella, Lilliano, La Massa, Le Masse di San Leolino, Nittardi, Palazzino, Paneretta, Poggerino, Rampolla, Riecine, Rocca di Castagnoli, Rodano, San Fabiano Calcinaia, San Felice, San Giusto, Valtellina, Vecchie Terre di Montefili, Verrazzano, Viticcio, Volpaia.

Chianti Putto Tus DOCG r ★→★★ DYA From a league of producers outside the CLASSICO zone. The neck-label, a pink cherub, is now rarely seen.

Chiarli Producer of Modena LAMBRUSCO (look for Generale Cialdini label).

Chiarlo, Michele ★★ Good PIEDMONT producer. (BAROLO Cerequio and BARBERA D'ASTI are vg.)

Chiaretto Rosé (the word means 'claret') produced esp around Lake Garda. See Bardolino, Riviera del Garda.

Chiesa di Santa Restituta See Pieve di Santa Restituta.

Chionetti ★★ Makes best DOLCETTO DI DOGLIANI (look for Briccolero).

Ciacci Piccolomini ★★★ Vg BRUNELLO DI MONTALCINO (best is Vigna di Pianrosso) and ROSSO DI M.

Cigliuti, Renato ★★★ Small high quality estate for BARBARESCO.

Cinqueterre Lig DOC w dr sw pa ★★ Fragrant fruity white from steep coast nr La Spezia. PASSITO is known as SCIACCHETRA (★★→★★★). Good from De Batte, Coop Agricola di Cinquerterre, Forlini & Cappellini, F Giusti.

Cinzano Major Vermouth company also known for its ASTI from PIEDMONT and Florio MARSALA. Now owned by Grand Met.

Cirò Cal DOC r (p w) ★★→★★★ 87' 88 89 90' 91 92 93 94 (95) V strong red from Gaglioppo grapes; fruity white (DYA). Best from LIBRANDI (Duca San Felice), San Francesco (Donna Madda, Ronco dei Quattroventi), Caparra & Siciliani.

CIV&CIV Associated coops with good DOC LAMBRUSCO.

Classico Term for wines from a restricted area within the limits of a DOC. By implication, and often in practice, the best of the district. Applied to sparkling wines it denotes the classic method (as for champagne).

Clerico, Domenico ★★★ Constantly evolving PIEDMONT wines; the aim is for international flavour. Esp good for BAROLO.

Col d'Orcia ★★★ Top estate of MONTALCINO with interesting VDT. Best wine is BRUNELLO (look for Poggio al Vento).

Colle Picchioni ★★ Estate S of Rome making the best MARINO white; also red (CAB-MERLOT) VDT, Vigna del Vassallo, perhaps Latium's best.

Colli Hills. Occurs in many wine-names.

Colli Berici Ven DOC r p w ★★ Hills S of Vicenza. CAB is the best wine. Top producer is Villa Dal Ferro.

Colli Bolognesi E-R DOC r p w (w) DYA SW of Bologna. 8 wines, 5 grape varieties. TERRE ROSSE is top estate (★★★). Other good producers are Tenuta Bonzara and Santarosa; look for VDT Giò Rosso.

Colli Euganei Ven DOC r w dr s/sw (sp) ★→★★ DYA A DOC SW of Padua for 7 wines. Red is adequate; white and sparkling soft and pleasant. Best producers: Vignalta, Cà Lustra.

Colli Orientali del Friuli F-VG DOC r w dr sw ★★→★★★★ 88 90 93 94 (95) 20 different wines (18 named after their grapes) on hills E of Udine. Whites esp are vg. Top producers: ABBAZIA DI ROSAZZO, BORGO DEL TIGLIO, DORIGO, Le Viarte, LIVIO FELLUGA, LIVON, Ronchi di Cialla, RONCO DEL GNEMIZ, Torre Rosazza, Rubini, Specogna, VOLPE PASINI.

Colli Piacentini E-R DOC r p w ★→★★ DYA DOC incl traditional GUTTURNIO and Monterosso Val d'Arda among 11 types grown S of Piacenza. Good fizzy MALVASIA. Most wines FRIZZANTE. New French and local reds: La Stoppa, La Tosa, Marchese Malaspina, Villa Peirano.

Colli Romani The wooded hills S of Rome: ancient summer resort and source of FRASCATI etc.

Colli del Trasimeno Um DOC r w ★→★★ 90 91 93 94 95 Often lively wines from Perugia. Best from: La Fiorita, Marella, MARTINI & ROSSI, Morolli.

Colline Novaresi Pie DOC r w ★→★★ New DOC for old region in Novara province. 7 different wines: BIANCO, ROSSO, NEBBIOLO, BONARDA, Vespolina, Croatina and BARBERA. Incl declassified BOCA, GHEMME, FARA and SIZZANO.

Collio F-VG DOC r w ★★→★★★★ 88 90 93 94 (95) 19 wines, 17 named after their grapes, from a small area on the Slovenian border. Vg whites, esp SAUV, PINOT BIANCO and PINOT GRIGIO. Best from: BORGO DEL TIGLIO, La Castellada, GRAVNER, JERMANN, Primosic, Princic, Radikon, Ronco dei Tassi, RUSSIZ SUPERIORE, SCHIOPETTO, Venica & Venica, VILLA RUSSIZ.

Coltassala Tus r ★★★ Notable VDT red of SANGIOVESE from the ancient CHIANTI CLASSICO estate of CASTELLO DI VOLPAIA at Radda.

Conterno, Aldo ★★★★ Legendary grower of BAROLO, etc, at Monforte d'Alba. Good GRIGNOLINO, FREISA, vg CHARD 'Printanier' and 'Bussia d'Oro'. Best BAROLOS are Cicala and Colonello. Barrel-aged NEBBIOLO VDT 'Favot' vg.

Conterno, Giacomo ★★★★ Top grower of BAROLO etc at Monforte d'Alba. Monfortino Barolo is long-aged, rare, outstanding.

Conterno-Fantino ★★★ 3 young families for vg BAROLO etc at Monforte d'Alba.

Contini, Attilio ★→★★★ Famous producer of VERNACCIA DI ORISTANO; best is vintage blend 'Antico Gregori'.

Contratto ★★ PIEDMONT firm known for ASTI, BAROLO, etc.

Contucci, Conti ★★→★★★ Ancient esteemed makers of VINO NOBILE DI MONT.

Copertino Ap DOC r (p) ★★ 90 91 92 93 94 95 Savoury ageable red wine of NEGROAMARO from the heel of Italy. Look for the CANTINA SOCIALE'S RISERVA and Tenuta Monaci.

Coppo ★★ Ambitious producers of BARBERA D'ASTI (eg 'Pomorosso').

Cordero di Montezemolo-Monfalletto ★★ Tiny maker of good BAROLO.

Cortese di Gavi See Gavi. (Cortese is the grape.)

Corzano & Paterno, Fattoria di ★★→★★★ Dynamic CHIANTI Colli Fiorentini estate. Vg RISERVA, red VDT Corzano and outstanding VIN SANTO.

Costanti, Conti ★★★ Tiny estate for top quality BRUNELLO DI MONTALCINO.

D'Ambra ★★ Top producer of ISCHIA wines, esp excellent white BIANCOLELLA ('Piellero' and single-v'yd 'Frassitelli').

D'Angelo ★★→★★★ Leading producers of admirable DOC AGLIANICO DEL VULTURE. Barrel-aged Aglianico VDT Canneto also vg.

Dal Forno, Romano ★★★ Very high quality VALPOLICELLA and AMARONE from perfectionist grower, bottling only best: 14,000 bottles from 20 acres.

Darmagi Pie r ★★★★ 82' 85' 88' 89' 90' 91 92 93 94 95 CAB S from GAJA in BARBARESCO is one of PIEDMONT'S most discussed (and expensive) VDT reds.

Decugnano dei Barbi ★★ Top ORVIETO estate with an ABBOCCATO known as 'Pourriture Noble', and a good red VDT.

Di Majo Norante ★★→★★★ Lone star of Molise on the Adriatic with vg Biferno DOC MONTEPULCIANO and white Falanghina 'Ramitello'. Also lighter, more aromatic Molí. Fine value. To watch for new ideas.

Dolce Sweet.

Dolceacqua See Rossese di Dolceacqua.

Dolcetto ★→★★★ PIEDMONT's earliest ripening grape, for v attractive everyday wines: dry young-drinking fruity fresh with deep purple colour. Gives its name to several DOCs: D d'Acqui, D d'Alba, D di Diano d'Alba (also Diano DOC), D di Dogliani (CHIONETTI and Pecchenino are top growers) and D di Ovada (best from Abbazia di Vallechiara). Dolcetto is made by most BAROLO and BARBARESCO growers.

Donnafugata Si r w ★ Zesty Sicilian whites (best are Vigna di Gabri, Damaskino). Also sound red. Was VDT, now in DOC Contessa Entellina.

Donnaz VdA DOC ★★ 88 89 90 93 95 Mountain NEBBIOLO: fragrant pale, faintly bitter. Aged for a statutory 3 yrs. Now part of VALLE D'AOSTA regional DOC.

Dorigo, Girolamo ★★★ Top COLLI ORIENTALI DEL FRIULI producer for outstanding white VDT 'Ronc di Juri', CHARD, dessert VERDUZZO and PICOLIT, red Pignolo (★★★★), REFOSCO, Schioppettino, and VDT Montsclapade.

Duca Enrico See Duca di Salaparuta.

Duca di Salaparuta ★★ Popular Sicilian wines. Sound dry reds, pleasant soft whites. Excellent barrique red Duca Enrico (★★★) is one of Sicily's best. Valguarnera is premium oak-aged white.

Elba Tus r w (sp) ★ DYA The island's white is drinkable with fish. Keep a look out for the 'Acquabona'.

Enfer d'Arvier V dA DOC r ★★ 90 93 Alpine speciality; a pale pleasantly bitter light red.

Enoteca Wine library. There are many, the impressive original being the Enoteca Italiana of Siena. Also used for wine shops or restaurants.

Erbaluce di Caluso See Caluso Passito.

Eredi Fuligni ★★★ Vg producer of BRUNELLO and ROSSO DI MONTALCINO.

Est! Est!! Est!!! Lat DOC w dr s/sw ★ DYA Unextraordinary white from Montefiascone, N of Rome. Trades on its oddball name. ('Acquabona'.

Etna Si DOC r p w ★→★★ (r) 91 92 93 94 95 Wine from volcanic slopes. Red is warm, full, balanced and can age well; white is distinctly grapey.

Falchini ★★→★★★ Producer of good DOCG VERNACCIA DI SAN GIMIGNANO and the best reds of the district, eg VDT Campora (★★★).

Falerno del Massico Cam DOC r w ★★ 88 89 90 92 93 94 95 As in Falernum, the best-known wine of ancient times. Times change. Strong red from AGLIANICO, fruity white from Falanghina. Good producer: VILLA MATILDE.

Fara Pie DOC r ★★ 85' 88' 89' 90' 93 95' Good NEBBIOLO from Novara, N PIEDMONT. Fragrant; worth ageing; esp Dessilani's Caramino.

Farneta, Tenuta ★★→★★★ Nr Siena but outside CHIANTI CLASSICO, an estate for pure SANGIOVESE VDT: eg Bongoverno (★★★) and Bentivoglio (★★★).

Farnetella, Castello di ★★ Estate nr MONTEPULCIANO where Giuseppe Mazzocolin of FELSINA makes vg SAUV and Chianti Colli Senesi.

Fattoria Tuscan term for a wine-growing property, traditionally noble.

An Italian choice for 1997

Montelera spumante metodo classico, Martini & Rossi, Torino (Piedmont)

Barolo Gavarini Elio Grasso, Monforte d'Alba (Piedmont)

Brunello di Montalcino Castelgiocondo, Montalcino (Tuscany)

Chianti Classico Riserva Castello di Cacchiano, Gaiole (Tuscany)

Isonzo Sauvignon Piere Vie di Romans, Mariano del Friuli (Friuli)

Soave La Rocca Pieropan, Soave (Veneto)

Salice Salentino Riserva Candido, Sandonaci (Apulia)

Cirò Classico Duca Sanfelice Librandi, Cirò (Calabria)

Favorita Pie w ★→★★ DYA Dry fruity white making friends in BAROLO country.

Fazi-Battaglia ★★ Well-known producer of VERDICCHIO, etc. White Le Moie VDT is pleasant. Also owns Fassati (producer of VINO NOBILE DI MONTEPULCIANO).

Felluga ★★★ Brothers Livio and Marco (RUSSIZ SUPERIORE) have separate companies in COLLIO and COLLI ORIENTALI. Both are highly esteemed.

Felsina-Berardenga ★★★→★★★★ CHIANTI CLASSICO estate with famous RISERVA Vigna Rancia and VDT Fontalloro.

Ferrari Cellars making some of Italy's best dry sparkling wines nr Trento, TRENTINO-ALTO ADIGE. Giulio Ferrari RISERVA is best.

Fiano di Avellino Cam w ★★→★★★ (DYA) Considered the best white of Campania, esp MASTROBERARDINO'S Vignadora. Also good from Vadiaperti, Feudi di S Gregorio, Struzziero, Vega.

Florio The major volume producer of MARSALA, controlled by CINZANO.

Foianeghe T-AA vdt r (w) ★★ 88 89 90 93 95 Brand of Conti Bossi Fedrigotti. TRENTINO CAB-MERLOT red to age 7–10 yrs. White is PINOT BL-CHARD-TRAMINER.

Folonari Large run-of-the-mill merchant of Lombardy. See also GIV.

Fontana Candida ★★ One of the biggest producers of FRASCATI. Single-v'yd Santa Teresa stands out. See also GIV.

Fontanafredda ★★ Big historic producer of PIEDMONT wines on former royal estates, incl BAROLO from single v'yds and a range of ALBA DOCs. Also very good DOCG ASTI and SPUMANTE Brut (esp ★★★ Vigna Gattinera).

Fonterutoli Historic (★★★) CHIANTI CLASSICO estate at Castellina with noted VDT Concerto and splendid RISERVA Ser Lapo.

Le Fonti, Fattoria ★★ CHIANTI estate of 30 acres at Panzano. Still uses ancient 'promiscuo' mixed cultivation.

Fontodi ★★★→★★★★ Top Panzano CHIANTI CLASSICO estate for highly regarded RISERVA, red VDT Flacianello, white vdt 'Meriggio' (PINOT BIANCO-SAUV-TRAMINER).

Forteto della Luja ★★★ Number 1 for PIEDMONT Muscat LOAZZOLO.

Franciacorta Lom DOC w (p) sp ★★→★★★★ Some vg sparkling wines made of PINOTS BL, N or GR and CHARD; exclusively classic method. CA'DEL BOSCO estate is outstanding. BELLAVISTA, Bersi Serlini, Castelfaglia, CAVALLERI, Gatti, Lantieri de Paradico, Monte Rossa, Ricci Curbastro, Uberti and Villa also vg.

Franciacorta Rosso Lom DOC r ★★ 90 91 93 94 95 Lightish red of mixed CAB and BARBERA from Brescia.

Frascati Lat DOC w dr s/sw sw (sp) ★→★★ DYA Best-known wine of Roman hills: should be soft, limpid, golden, tasting of whole grapes. Most is disappointingly neutral today: look for Conte Zandotti, Villa Simone, or Santa Teresa from FONTANA CANDIDA. Sweet is known as Cannellino.

Freisa Pie r dr s/sw sw (sp) ★★ DYA Usually v dry (except nr Turin), often FRIZZANTE red, said to taste of raspberries and roses. With enough acidity it can be highly appetizing, especially with salami. Good wines come from CIGLIUTI, CONTERNO, Cozzo, Gilli, PARUSSO, Pecchenino, Pelissero, Sebaste, Trinchero, VAJRA and VOERZIO.

Frescobaldi ★★★ Ancient noble family, leading pioneers of CHIANTI at NIPOZZANO, E of Florence. Also white POMINO and PREDICATO SAUV BL (Vergena) and CAB (Mormoreto). See also Montesodi. Now also owns Castelgiocondo (★★★), a big MONTALCINO estate for BRUNELLO and vg VDT MERLOT Lamaione.

Friuli-Venezia Giulia The NE region on the Slovenian border. Many wines; the DOCs COLLIO and COLLI ORIENTALI include most of the best.

Friuli vintages

1995 Promising year, then heavy rains in August and September: light whites, better reds.

1994 Wet spring and September, hot between. Whites can lack acidity, reds better.

1993 A windy vintage reduced quantities but produced highly concentrated healthy grapes. Top quality whites, but harvest rains compromised the reds.

1992 August rains not so bad in Friuli: an excellent year for whites, and good reds too.

Frizzante (fz) Semi-sparkling. Used to describe wines such as LAMBRUSCO.

Gaja ★★★★ Old family firm at BARBARESCO under meteoric direction of Angelo G. Top quality – and price – PIEDMONT wines, esp BARBARESCO (single v'yds SORI Tildin, Sorì San Lorenzo, Costa Russi) and BAROLO Sperss (since '88). Also setting trends with excellent CHARD (Gaja & Rey) and CAB DARMAGI. Latest acquisition: Marengo-Marenda estate (BAROLO) commercial Gromis label, and control of PIEVE DI SANTA RESTITUTA (BRUNELLO).

Galestro Tus w ★ V light white from eponymous shaley soil in CHIANTI country. Current moves to upgrade.

Gambellara Ven DOC w dr s/sw (sp) ★→★★ DYA Neighbour of SOAVE. Dry wine similar. Sweet (known as RECIOTO DI GAMBELLARA) nicely fruity. Also VIN SANTO. Outstanding producer, LA BIANCARA (★★★).

Gancia Famous ASTI house also producing vermouth and dry sparkling. New Torrebianco estate in APULIA is making good VDT whites: CHARD, SAUV, PINOT BL, also vg single-v'yd BAROLO, 'Cannubi' (★★★), since '89.

Garganega Principal white grape of SOAVE and GAMBELLARA.

Garofoli, Gioacchino ★★→★★★ Quality leader of the Marches (nr Ancona). Notable style in VERDICCHIO Macrina and Serra Fiorese; also vg sparkling. ROSSO CONERO Piancarda and vg Grosso Agontano (★★★).

Gattinara Pie DOCG r ★★→★★★ 82' 85' 88' 89' 90' 93 95 V tasty BAROLO-type red (from NEBBIOLO, locally known as Spanna). Best are Monsecco and single-v'yd wines from Antoniolo. Others incl Nervi, Travaglini.

Gavi (or Cortese di Gavi) Pie w ★★→★★★ DYA At (rare) best, subtle dry white of Cortese grapes. LA SCOLCA is best known, vg are BANFI (watch for Vigna Regale), Castellari Bergaglio, TERRE DA VINO. La Giustiniana, Tenuta San Pietro, Castello di Tassarolo and Villa Sparina are v fair; also fair: CHIARLO, Podere Saulino, Cascina degli Ulivi, La Zerba.

Ghemme Pie DOC r ★★→★★★ 82' 85' 86 88' 89 90' 93 95 Neighbour of GATTINARA, rival in quality but scarce. Best is Antichi Vigneti di Cantalupo.

Ghiaie della Furba Tus r ★★★ 88 90 93 95 Bordeaux-style VDT CAB blend from the admirable TENUTA DI CAPEZZANA, CARMIGNANO.

Giacosa, Bruno ★★★★ Inspired loner: outstanding BARBARESCO, BAROLO and PIEDMONT wines at Neive. Remarkable ARNEIS white and PINOT N sparkling.

GIV (Gruppo Italiano Vini) Complex of coops and wineries, apparently Europe's largest (60 million bottles). Sells 12% of all Italian wine, including eg BIGI, Conti Serristori, FOLONARI, FONTANA CANDIDA, LAMBERTI, Macchiavelli, MELINI, Negri, Santi...

Goldmuskateller Aromatic ALTO ADIGE grape made into irresistible dry white, esp by TIEFENBRUNNER.

Governo Old Tuscan custom, enjoying mild revival with some producers, in which dried grapes or must are added to young wine to induce second fermentation and give a slight prickle – sometimes instead of using must concentrate to increase alcohol.

Gradi Degrees (of alcohol), ie percent by volume.

Grappa Pungent spirit made from grape pomace (skins etc after pressing).

Grasso, Elio ★★★ Hard-working, reliable quality producer at Monforte d'Alba: outstanding BAROLO (look for Gavarini and Casa Maté), potent barrel-aged BARBERA D'ALBA Vigna Martina, DOLCETTO, etc.

Grattamacco ★★★ Top Tuscan producer on coast outside classic centres (nr SASSICAIA S of Bolgheri). Vg Grattamacco SANGIOVESE-CAB blend.

Grave del Friuli F-VG DOC r w ★★ (r) 88 90 93 94 DOC covering 15 different wines, 14 named after their grapes, from nr the Slovenian border. Good MERLOT and CAB. Best producers: Borgo Magredo, Di Lenardo, Le Fredis, PIGHIN, Teresa Raiz, Vigneti Le Monde.

Gravner, Josko ★★★ Together with MARIO SCHIOPETTO, spiritual leader of COLLIO: estate with range of excellent whites, led by CHARD and SAUV.

Grechetto White grape with more flavour than the ubiquitous TREBBIANO, increasingly used in Umbria.

Greco di Bianco Cal DOC w sw ★★ An original smooth and fragrant dessert wine from Italy's toe; worth ageing. Best from Ceratti. See Mantonico.

Greco di Tufo Cam DOC w (sp) ★★→★★★ (DYA) One of the best white wines from the south of the country: fruity and slightly 'wild' in flavour. A character. MASTROBERARDINO makes single-v'yd Vignadangelo. Also vg from Vadiaperti, Di Meo, Feudi di S Gregorio.

Gresy, Marchesi de (Cisa Asinari) ★★★ Very consistent producer of fine BARBARESCO; also vg SAUVIGNON and CHARDONNAY.

Grevepesa Reliable CHIANTI CLASSICO coop.

Grignolino d'Asti Pie DOC r ★ DYA Lively standard light red of PIEDMONT.

Grumello Lom DOC r ★★ 85 88 89 90 93 95 NEBBIOLO wine from VALTELLINA. Can be delicate (or meagre).

Guerrieri-Gonzaga ★★→★★★ Top producer in TRENTINO; esp VINO DA TAVOLA San Leonardo, a ★★★ CAB-MERLOT blend.

Guerrieri-Rizzardi ★★→★★★ Top producer of AMARONE, BARDOLINO, SOAVE and VALPOLICELLA from various family estates.

Gutturnio dei Colli Piacentini E-R DOC r dr (s/sw) ★★ 90 91 93 94 95 BARBERA-BONARDA blend from the hills of Piacenza, often FRIZZANTE.

Haas, Franz ★★→★★★ Very good ALTO ADIGE MERLOT and PINOT NERO.

Hauner, Carlo ★★★ Island estate for marvellous MALVASIA DELLE LIPARI.

Hofstätter ★★★ Südtirol producer of top Italian PINOT NOIR; look for S Urbano.

Inferno Lom DOC r ★★ 85 88 89 90 93 Similar to GRUMELLO and, like it, classified as VALTELLINA SUPERIORE.

Ischia Cam DOC w (r) ★→★★ DYA Wine of the island off Naples. Slightly sharp white SUPERIORE is the best of the DOC. But top producer D'AMBRA makes better wines in the form of VINO DA TAVOLA whites BIANCOLELLA and Forestera and red PER'E PALUMMO.

ITALY

Isole e Olena ★★★ Top CHIANTI CLASSICO estate with fine red VDT Cepparello. Vg VIN SANTO, and L'Eremo Syrah.

Isonzo F-VG DOC r w ★★ (r) 88 90 93 94 DOC covering 19 wines (17 varietals) in the NE. Best whites and CAB compare with neighbouring COLLIO wines. Best from Borgo Conventi, Francesco Pecorari, Pierpaolo Pecorari, Ronco del Gelso, VIE DI ROMANS, Villanova.

Jermann, Silvio ★★★ Family estate in COLLIO: top white VDT, incl singular VINTAGE TUNINA oak-aged white blend and lighter Vinnae. Also fresh Capo Martino (91) and CHARD 'WHERE THE DREAMS HAVE NO END…'

Kalterersee German (and local) name for LAGO DI CALDARO.

Kante, Edi ★★★ Lone star of CARSO with outstanding DOC CHARD, SAUV, MALVASIA and vg red Terrano.

Lacryma (or Lacrima) Christi del Vesuvio Cam r p w dr (sw fz) ★→★★ DYA Famous but ordinary range of wines in great variety from Vesuvius. (DOC Vesuvio.) MASTROBERARDINO produces the only good example.

Lageder, Alois ★→★★★ The lion of Bolzano (ALTO A). DOCs: SANTA MADDALENA, etc. Exciting wines, incl oak-aged CHARD and CAB Löwengang. Single-v'yd SAUV is Lehenhof, PINOT BL Haberlehof, PINOT GR Benefizium Porer.

Lago di Caldaro See Caldaro.

Lagrein, Südtiroler, T-AA DOC r p ★★→★★★ 85 86 88 89 90 91 93 94 95 A Tyrolean grape with a bitter twist. Good fruity wine – at best very appetizing. The rosé is 'Kretzer', the dark 'Dunkel'. Best from Gojer, Gries, Kössler, Maddalena, Niedermayr, Rottensteiner, Schwanburg.

Lamberti ★★ Large producers of SOAVE, VALPOLICELLA, BARDOLINO, etc at Lazise on the E shore of Lake Garda. NB LUGANA and VDT Turà. See also GIV.

Lambrusco E-R DOC (or not) r p dr s/sw ★→★★ DYA Popular fizzy red, best known in industrial s/sw version. Best is SECCO, traditional is with second fermentation in bottle (yeast sediment on bottom). DOCs are L Grasparossa di Castelvetro, L Salamino di Santa Croce and, perhaps best, L di Sorbara. Best from: Barbolini, Bellei, Casali, CAVICCHIOLI, Franco Ferrari, Graziano, Rinaldo Rinaldini.

Langhe ★→★★ The hills of central PIEDMONT, home of BAROLO, BARBARESCO, etc. Has become name for recent DOC (r w ★★→★★★) for 8 different wines: ROSSO, BIANCO, NEBBIOLO, DOLCETTO, FREISA, ARNEIS, FAVORITA and CHARDONNAY. Barolo and Barbaresco can now be declassified to DOC Langhe (Nebbiolo previously only allowed VDT status).

Latisana F-VG DOC r w ★→★★ (r) 90 93 94 DOC for 13 varietal wines from 50 miles NE of Venice. Esp good TOCAI FRIULANO.

Le Salette ★★★ Small VALPOLICELLA producer: look for vg AMARONE La Marega and RECIOTO Le Traversagne.

Leone de Castris ★★ Large producer of APULIAN wines. Estate at SALICE SALENTINO, near Lecce.

Lessona Pie DOC r ★★ 85 86 88 89 90 93 Soft dry claret-like wine from the province of Vercelli. NEBBIOLO, Vespolina and BONARDA grapes.

Librandi ★★→★★★ Top Calabria producer. Vg red CIRO (RISERVA Duca San Felice is ★★★) and VDT Gravello (interesting value CAB-Gaglioppo blend).

Lilliano, Castello di ★★★ Old CHIANTI CLASSICO estate pulling its weight again.

Liquoroso Means strong and usually sweet (whether fortified or not).

Lisini ★★★ Small estate for some of the finest recent vintages of BRUNELLO.

Livon ★★★ Top producer of COLLI ORIENTALI.

Loazzolo Pie DOC w sw ★★★ 90 91 92 93 94 New DOC for MOSCATO dessert wine from botrytised air-dried grapes: expensive and sweet. Esp from Borgo Maragliano, Borgo Moncalvo, Borgo Sambui, Bricchi Mej, Luja.

Locorotondo Ap DOC w (sp) ★ DYA Pleasantly fresh southern white. To try.

Lugana Lom and Ven DOC w (sp) ★★→★★★ DYA Whites of S Lake Garda: can be fragrant, smooth, full of body and flavour. Good from Ca'dei Frati, Ottella, Roveglia, Zenato.

Lungarotti ★★★ The leading producer of TORGIANO wine, with cellars, hotel and wine museum nr Perugia. Also some of Italy's best CHARD (Miralduolo and Vigna I Palazzi) and PINOT GR. See Torgiano.

Maculan ★→★★★ The top producer of DOC BREGANZE. Also Torcolato, dessert VDT (★★★) and Prato di Canzio (CHARD, PINOT BL and PINOT GR).

Malvasia

An important underrated grape of chameleon character: white or red wines, sparkling or still, strong or mild, sweet or dry, aromatic or rather neutral, often as VDT, sometimes as DOC. White, dry to sweet, strong concentrated: **M di Cagliari** Sar DOC ★★ (eg Meloni); red fragrant grapey sweet, sometimes sparkling: **M di Casorzo d'Asti** Pie DOC ★★ (eg Bricco Mondalino); red aromatic sparkling: **M di Castelnuovo** Don Bosco Pie DOC ★★ (eg Gilli); white rich strong, long-living: **M delle Lipari** Si DOC ★★★ (eg Colosi, Hauner); white dry to semi-sweet, deep bouquet, long-lived: **M de Nus** VdA DOC ★★★ (eg La Crotta de Vignerons). Always worth trying.

Manduria (Primitivo di) Ap DOC r s/sw (dr sw fz) ★★ 88 89 90 **91** 92 93 94 Heady red, naturally strong but often fortified. From nr Taranto. Especially Vinicola Savese's.

Mantonico Cal w dr sw fz ★★ **89 90** 91 92 93 94 95 Fruity deep amber dessert wine from Reggio Calabria. Can age remarkably well. Good from Ceratti. See also Greco di Bianco.

Marchesi di Barolo ★★ Important ALBA wines: BAROLO, BARBARESCO, DOLCETTO and GAVI.

Marino Lat DOC w dr s/sw (sp) ★→★★ DYA A neighbour of FRASCATI with similar wine; often a better buy. Look for COLLE PICCHIONI brand.

Marsala Si DOC br dr s/sw sw fz ★★→★★★ NV Sherry-type wine invented by the Woodhouse Brothers from Liverpool in 1773; excellent aperitif or for dessert, but mostly used in the kitchen for zabaglione etc. The dry ('virgin'), sometimes made by the solera system, must be 5 yrs old. Top producers: FLORIO, Pellegrino, Rallo, VECCHIO SAMPERI. V special old vintages ★★★★.

Martini & Rossi Well-known vermouth and sparkling wine house (now controlled by Bacardi group), also famous for its splendid wine-history museum in Pessione, nr Turin.

Marzemino (Trentino) T-AA DOC r ★→★★ **93 94** Pleasant local red. Fruity, slightly bitter. Esp from Bossi Fedrigotti, Casata Monfort, CA'VIT, De Tarczal, Gaierhof, Letrari, Simoncelli, Vallarom, Vallis Agri.

Mascarello The name of two top producers of BAROLO etc: Bartolo M and Giuseppe M & Figli. Look for the latter's BAROLO Monprivato (★★★★).

Masi ★★→★★★ Well-known, conscientious and reliable specialist producers of VALPOLICELLA, AMARONE (★★★), RECIOTO, SOAVE etc, incl fine red Campo Fiorin. Also look for excellent new red VDT Toar.

Mastroberardino ★★★ The leading wine producer of Campania, at Avellino. Wines include FIANO DI AVELLINO, GRECO DI TUFO, LACRYMA CHRISTI and TAURASI (look for Radici).

Melini ★★ Long-est'd producers of CHIANTI CLASSICO at Poggibonsi. Good quality/price; look for single-v'yd C Classico Selvanella. See also GIV.

NB Vintages in colour are those you should choose first for drinking in 1997.

119

Meranese di Collina T-AA DOC r ★ DYA Light red of Merano, known in German as Meraner Hügel.

Merlot Adaptable red B'x grape widely grown in N (esp) and central Italy. Merlot DOCs are abundant. Best growers are: HAAS, SCHRECKBICHL and Baron Widman in T-AA, Torre Rosazza (L'Altromerlot) and BORGO DEL TIGLIO in F-VG and the Tuscan Super-vDTs of AMA (L'Apparita), AVIGNONESI, ORNELLAIA (Masseto) and FRESCOBALDI (Lamaione).

Metodo classico or tradizionale Now the mandatory terms to identify classic method sparkling wines. 'Metodo Champenois' banned since '94 and now illegal. (See also Classico.)

Mezzacorona Huge TRENTINO COOP.

Moccagatta ★★ →★★★ Specialist in impressive single-v'yd BARBARESCO: Basarin, Bric Balin (★★★) and Vigna Cole.

Moncaro MARCHES COOP: good VERDICCHIO DEI CASTELLI DI JESI.

Monferrato Pie DOC r w sw p ★★ The hills between the River Po and the Apennines give their name to a new DOC; includes ROSSO, BIANCO, CHIARETTO, DOLCETTO, Casalese and FREISA CORTESE.

Monica di Sardegna Sar DOC r ★ DYA Monica is the grape. An ordinary dry light red wine.

Monsanto ★★★ →★★★★ Esteemed CHIANTI CLASSICO estate, esp for Il Poggio v'yd.

Montalcino Small town in the province of Siena, TUSCANY, famous for its deep red BRUNELLO and younger ROSSO DI MONTALCINO.

Monte Vertine ★★★ →★★★★★ Top estate at Radda in CHIANTI. VDT Le Pergole Torte (100% SANGIOVESE) is one of TUSCANY's best. Also Sodaccio (Sangioveto plus Canaiolo) and fine VIN SANTO.

Montecarlo Tus DOC w r ★★ DYA (w) White wine area in N TUSCANY: smooth neutral blend of TREBBIANO with a range of better grapes. Now applies to a CHIANTI-style red too. Good producers: Buonamico, Carmignani (vg VDT reds 'Il Fortino' and 'For Duke'), Michi.

Montefalco (Rosso di) Umb DOC r ★★ 90 91 92 93 95 Common SANGIOVESE-TREBBIANO-SAGRANTINO blend. ADANTI's Rosso d'Arquata VDT stands out.

Montefalco Sagrantino Umb DOCG r dr sw ★★★ 90 91 92 93 95 Strong, v interesting SECCO or sweet PASSITO red from Sagrantino grapes only. Good from: ADANTI, Antano, Antonelli, Val di Maggio, Villa Antica.

Montellori, Fattoria di ★★ →★★★ Tuscan father-son team making admirable SANGIOVESE-CABERNET VDT blend 'Castelrapiti Rosso', Viognier VDT 'Bonfiglio', Chardonnay VDT 'Castelrapiti Bianco' and vg SPUMANTE.

Montepulciano An important red grape of central-east Italy as well as the famous Tuscan town (see next entries).

Montepulciano d'Abruzzo Ab DOC r p ★★ →★★★ 85 87 88 90 91 92 93 94 95 Happens rarely, but at its best one of Italy's tastiest reds, full of flavour and warmth, from the Adriatic coast round Pescara. Good from: VALENTINI (No 1), Barone Cornacchia, Filomusi-Guelfi, Illuminati, Cataldi Madonna, Masciarelli, Montori, Nicodemi, Castello di Salle, Tenuta del Priore and Zaccagnini. See also Cerasuolo.

Montepulciano, Vino Nobile di See Vino Nobile di Montepulciano.

Montescudaio Tus DOC r w ★→★★ New DOC nr Pisa. Terriccio is good producer, esp of VDT MERLOT-CAB SAUV blends Lupicaia and Tassinaia.

Montesodi Tus r ★★★ →★★★★ 85 86 88 90 91 93 94 Tip-top CHIANTI RUFINA RISERVA from FRESCOBALDI.

Montresor ★★ VERONA winehouse: good LUGANA, BIANCO DI CUSTOZA, VALPOLICELLA.

Morellino di Scansano Tus DOC r ★★ 88' 90' 91 92 93 94 95 Local SANGIOVESE of the Maremma, the S Tuscan coast; enjoying vogue. Cherry-red, lively and tasty young or matured. Fattorie Le Pupille, Moris Farms, E Banti are best.

Moscadello di Montalcino Tus DOC w sw (sp) ★★ DYA Traditional wine of MONTALCINO, much older than BRUNELLO. Sweet white fizzy, and sweet to high-octane PASSITO MOSCATO. Good producers: BANFI, POGGIONE.

> **Moscato**
> Fruitily fragrant ubiquitous grape for a diverse range of wines: sparkling or still, light or full-bodied, but always sweet. Most famous is **M d'Asti** Pie DOCG (★★→★★★): light, aromatic, sparkling and delicious from BERA, Gatti, Grimaldi, Marenco, Perrone, Redento, RIVETTI, Saracco and Vignaioli di Santo Stefano. Italy's best is from the island of Pantelleria off the Tunisian coast, with top wines from De Bartoli, Murana. And rare but prestigious is **Moscato di Trani** (sometimes fortified), best from Nugnes.

Müller-Thurgau Makes wine to be reckoned with in TRENTINO-ALTO ADIGE and FRIULI, esp TIEFENBRUNNER'S Feldmarschall.

Nasco di Cagliari Sar DOC w dr sw (fz) ★★ Sardinian speciality with light bitter taste, high alcohol content. Good from Meloni.

Nebbiolo The best red grape of PIEDMONT and Lombardy.

Nebbiolo d'Alba Pie DOC r dr (s/sw sp) ★★ 88 89 90 93 95 From ALBA (but not BAROLO, BARBARESCO). Sometimes like lightweight Barolo; can be easier to enjoy than the powerful classic wine. Best from Correggia, MASCARELLO, PRUNOTTO, RATTI, Roagna. See also Roero.

Negroamaro Literally 'black bitter'; APULIAN red grape with potential for quality. See Copertino and Salice Salentino.

Nepente di Oliena Sar r ★★ Strong fragrant CANNONAU red; a touch bitter. Good from Arcadu Tonino.

Nipozzano, Castello di ★★★ FRESCOBALDI estate east of Florence making MONTESODI CHIANTI. The most important outside the CLASSICO zone.

Nittardi ★★★ Up-coming little CHIANTI CLASSICO estate.

Nosiola (Trentino) T-AA DOC w dr sw ★★ DYA Light fruity white from dried Nosiola grapes. Also good VIN SANTO. Best from Pravis: Le Frate.

Nozzole ★★→★★★ Famous estate, owned by RUFFINO, in the heart of CHIANTI CLASSICO, N of Greve. Also good CAB.

Nuragus di Cagliari Sar DOC w ★ DYA Lively Sardinian white.

Oberto, Andrea ★★ Hardworking small La Morra producer with top BAROLO and BARBERA D'ALBA.

Oltrepò Pavese Lom DOC r w dr sw sp ★★→★★★ DOC applicable to 14 wines produced in the province of Pavia, mostly named after their grapes. PINOT NERO and METODO-CLASSICO-SPUMANTE can s'times be astonishing. Top growers incl Anteo, Cabanon, Doria, La Versa, Le Fracce, Luciano Brega, Monsupello, Montelio, Vercesi del Castellazzo.

Ornellaia Tus ★★★★ New 130-acre estate of LODOVICO ANTINORI nr Bolgheri on the Tuscan coast. Watch for VDT Ornellaia (CAB-MERLOT), vg straight VDT Masseto (MERLOT) and vg VDT SAUV Poggio delle Gazze.

Orvieto Umb DOC w dr s/sw ★→★★★ DYA The classical Umbrian golden white: smooth and substantial; formerly very dull but recently more interesting, esp in sweet versions. Orvieto CLASSICO is better. Only the finest examples (eg BARBERANI, BIGI, DECUGANO DEI BARBI) age well. But see Castello della Sala.

Pagadebit di Romagna E-R DOC w dr s/sw ★★ DYA Pleasant traditional 'payer of debts' from around Bertinoro.

Palazzino, Podere Il ★★★ Small estate with admirable CHIANTI CLASSICO and VDT Grosso Sanese.

Panaretta, Castello della ★★ An estate to follow for fine CHIANTI CLASSICO.

Panizzi ★★ Makes top class VERNACCIA DI SAN GIMIGNANO.

Pantelleria See Moscato.

Paradiso, Fattoria ★★→★★★ Old family estate near Bertinoro (E-R). Good ALBANA and PAGADEBIT and unique red Barbarossa. Vg SANGIOVESE.

Parrina Tus r w ★ 94 95 Light red and white from Maremma coast, S TUSCANY.

Parusso ★★★ Tiziana and Marco Parusso make top-level BAROLO (eg single-v'yd Bussia, Mariondino), also vg BARBERA D'ALBA and DOLCETTO etc.

Pasolini Dall'Onda Noble family with estates in CHIANTI Colli Fiorentini and Romagna, producing traditional-style wines.

Passito (pa) Strong sweet wine from grapes dried on the vine or indoors.

Paternoster ★★ Top AGLIANICO DEL VULTURE producer.

Pelaverga Pie r ★★ (DYA) Pale red with spicy perfume, from Verduno. Good producers: Alessandria, Bel Colle, Castello di Verduno.

Peppoli ★★★ Estate owned by ANTINORI, producing excellent CHIANTI CLASSICO in a full round youthful style – first vintage **85**.

Per'e Palummo Cam r ★ Appetizing light tannic red from island of ISCHIA.

Perrone, Elio ★★→★★★ Small estate for one of best MOSCATO D'ASTIS.

Piave Ven DOC r w ★→★★ (r) **90 93** 94 95 (w) DYA Flourishing DOC NW of Venice covering 8 wines, 4 red and 4 white, named after their grapes. CAB, MERLOT and RABOSO reds can all age. Good from Molon-Traverso.

Picolit (Colli Orientali del Friuli) F-VG DOC w s/sw sw ★★→★★★ 88 90 93 94 95 Delicate sweet dessert wine with exaggerated reputation. A little like Jurançon. Ages up to 6 yrs, but wildly overpriced. Best from DORIGO, Dri, LIVIO FELLUGA, Graziano Specogna.

Piedmont (Piemonte) The most important Italian region for top quality wine. Turin is the capital, ASTI and ALBA the wine centres. See Barbaresco, Barbera, Barolo, Dolcetto, Grignolino, Moscato etc.

Piedmont vintages

1995 V promising vintage, then incessant autumn rains: average quality white, Dolcetto, Barbera. Some excellent Barolos, but only where harvested mid-October or later when warm and dry.

1994 Hot summer; but vintage rains prevented excellence.

1993 Hot summer, good Dolcetto and Barbera, but September rains disrupted Nebbiolo harvest and severe selection was necessary for Barolo and Barbaresco.

1992 An extremely difficult year due to incessant rainfall. Whites good. Nebbiolo wines not so lucky.

1991 Cold April and suddenly v hot in July, harvest then interrupted by rain: some elegant Barolo, Barbaresco and Barbera. Dolcetto and whites fine.

Piemonte Pie DOC r w p (sp) ★→★★★ New all-PIEDMONT blanket-DOC incl Piemonte BARBERA, P BONARDA, P BRACHETTO, P CORTESE, P GRIGNOLINO, P CHARD, P SPUMANTE, P MOSCATO.

Pieropan ★★★ Outstanding producer of SOAVE and RECIOTO that for once deserves its fame.

Pieve di Santa Restituta ★★★ Estate for admirable BRUNELLO DI MONTALCINO, vg ROSSO DI M and red VDT Pian de Cerri. Links with GAJA.

Pigato Lig DOC w ★★ DOC under Riviera Ligure di Ponente. Often outclasses VERMENTINO as Liguria's finest white, with rich texture and structure. Good from: Anfossi, Colle dei Bardellini, Feipu, Lupi, TERRE ROSSE, Vio.

Pighin, Fratelli Solid producers of COLLIO and GRAVE DEL FRIULI.

Pinocchio Tusc r w ★ Long-established brand notable for famous nose.

Pinot Bianco (Pinot Bl) Popular grape in NE for many DOC wines, generally bland and dry. Best from ALTO ADIGE ★★ (top growers: CS St-Michael, LAGEDER, Elena Walch), COLLIO ★★ (vg from Keber, Mangilli, Picech, Princic) and COLLI ORIENTALI ★★→★★★ (best from Rodaro and VIGNE DAL LEON).

Pinot Grigio (Pinot Gr) Tasty low-acid white grape popular in NE. Best from DOCs ALTO ADIGE (LAGEDER, Kloster Muri-Gries, Schwanburg) and COLLIO (Caccese, SCHIOPETTO). AMA in TUSCANY makes vg VDT Pinot Gr.

Pinot Nero T-AA DOC r ★★→★★★ 90 91 92 94 Pinot Nero (Noir) is planted in much of northeast Italy, incl TRENTINO and esp ALTO ADIGE. Vg results from Castelfeder, HAAS, Niedrist and SCHRECKBICHL. Also fine sparkling wines. Promising trials elsewhere, eg AMA, FONTODI, HOFSTATTER, Pancrazi and RUFFINO, CS St-Michael, Schwanburg in TUSCANY. Some good also from OLTREPO PAVESE (eg La Versa, Montelio, Vercesi del Castellazzo).

Pio Cesare ★★→★★★ Long-established PIEDMONT producer. All red, incl BAROLO.

Podere Tuscan term for a wine-farm; smaller than a FATTORIA.

Poggio Antico (Montalcino) ★★★ Admirably consistent top level BRUNELLO, ROSSO and red VDT Altero.

Poggione, Tenuta Il ★★★ Perhaps the most reliable estate for BRUNELLO and ROSSO DI MONTALCINO.

Pojer & Sandri ★★★ Top TRENTINO producers: reds and whites, incl SPUMANTE.

Poliziano ★★★ Federico Carletti makes vg VINO NOBILE DI MONT (esp Asinone, Caggiole), VDT Elegia (CAB, SANGIOVESE) and wonderful VIN SANTO. Vg value.

Pomino Tus DOC w (r br) ★★★ 88' 90' 93' 94 95 Fine white, partly CHARD (as Il Benefizio), and a SANGIOVESE-CAB-MERLOT-PINOT N blend. Also VIN SANTO. Esp from FRESCOBALDI and SELVAPIANA.

Predicato Name for 4 kinds of VDT from central TUSCANY, illustrating the current headlong rush from tradition. P del Muschio is CHARD and PINOT BL; P del Selvante is SAUV BL; P di Biturica is CAB with SANGIOVESE; P di Cardisco is Sangiovese straight. Esp RUFFINO's Cabreo brand wines.

Primitivo Vg red grape of far S, now identified with California's Zinfandel. Of few producers, Coppi, Sava, Savese are best.

Primitivo di Apulia See Manduria.

Prosecco White grape making light very dry sparkling wine popular in Venice. The next is better.

Prosecco di Conegliano-Valdobbiadene Ven DOC w s/sw sp (dr) ★★ DYA Slight fruity bouquet, the dry pleasantly bitter, the sweet fruity; the best are known as Superiore di Cartizze. CARPENE-MALVOLTI is best-known producer, now challenged by ADAMI, Bisol, Bortolotti, Canevel, CASE BIANCHE, Collalto, Nino Franco, Foss Marai, Ruggeri.

Prunotto, Alfredo ★★★ Very serious ALBA company with top BARBARESCO (esp Montestefano, ★★★★), BAROLO (esp ★★★★ single-v'yd Bussia and Cannubi), NEBBIOLO, etc. Now controlled by ANTINORI.

Querciabella ★★★ Up-coming CHIANTI CLASSICO estate with excellent red VDT Camartina and a dream of a white VDT, Bâtard Pinot (P BL and GR).

Quintarelli, Giuseppe ★★★★ True artisan producer of VALPOLICELLA, RECIOTO and AMARONE, at the top in both quality and price.

Raboso del Piave (now DOC) Ven r ★★ 88 90 93 94 95 Powerful sharp interesting country red; needs age. Look for Molon-Traverso.

Ragose, Le ★★★ Family estate, one of VALPOLICELLA's best. AMARONE and RECIOTO top quality; CAB and Valpolicella vg too.

Ramandolo See Verduzzo Colli Orientali del Friuli.

Ramitello See Di Majo Norante.

Rampolla, Castello dei ★★★ Fine CHIANTI CLASSICO estate at Panzano; also excellent CAB-based VDT Sammarco.

123

Ratti, Renato ★★→★★★ Maker of vg BAROLO and other ALBA wines. The late Signor Ratti (d '88) was a highly respected local wine-scene leader.

> **Recioto**
> Wine made of half-dried grapes. Speciality of Veneto since the days of the Venetian empire; has roots in classical Roman wine, Raeticus. Always sweet, s'times sparkling: sp is to drink young; sweet, concentrated, can be kept for a long time.

Recioto di Gambellara Ven DOC w sw (sp s/sw DYA) ★ Mostly half-sparkling and industrial. Best is strong and sweet. Look for LA BIANCARA (★★★).

Recioto di Soave Ven DOC w s/sw (sp) ★★★ 87 88 90 91 92 93 95 SOAVE made from selected half-dried grapes: sweet fruity fresh, slightly almondy; high alcohol. Outstanding from ANSELMI and PIEROPAN.

Recioto della Valpolicella Ven DOC r s/sw ★★→★★★★ 80 83 85 86 88 90 93 95' Strong late-harvest red. Vg from Accordini, ALLEGRINI, BRIGALDARA, Corte Sant'Alda, DAL FORNO, Degani, Nicolis, Serègo Alighieri, LE RAGOSE, LE SALETTE, SAN RUSTICO, Speri, TEDESCHI.

Recioto della Valpolicella Amarone See Amarone.

Refosco r ★★ 88 90 93 94 95 Interesting full-bodied dark tannic red, needs ageing. The same grape as the Mondeuse of Savoie (France)? It tastes like it. Best comes from F-VG DOC COLLI ORIENTALI, GRAVE and CARSO (where known as Terrano). Vg from Bosco Romagno, Villa Belvedere, DORIGO, EDI KANTE, Le Fredis, LIVON, Villa Belvedere, VOLPE PASINI. Often value.

Regaleali ★★★ Owned by the noble family Tasca D'Almerita, perhaps the best Sicilian producer; situated between Palermo and Caltanissetta to the SE. Vg VDT red, white and pink 'Regaleali', red 'Rosso del Conte' (★★★) and CAB. Also impressive CHARD (★★★).

Ribolla (Colli Orientali del Friuli and Collio) F-VG DOC w ★→★★ DYA Thin NE white. The best comes from COLLIO. Top estates: La Castellada, GRAVNER, Krapez, Radikon, Venica & Venica, VILLA RUSSIZ.

Ricasoli ★→★★★★ Famous Tuscan family, 'inventors' of CHIANTI, whose CHIANTI CLASSICO is named after their Brolio estate and castle, now again under family direction.

Riecine Tus r (w) ★★★ First-class CHIANTI CLASSICO estate at Gaiole, created by its English owner, John Dunkley. Also VDT La Gioia SANGIOVESE.

Riesling Formerly used to mean Italian Ries (Ries Italico or Welschriesling). German (Rhine) Ries, now ascendant, is Ries Renano. Best are DOC ALTO ADIGE ★★ (esp coop Kurtatsch, Ignaz Niedrist, coop La Vis, Elena Walch) and DOC OLTREPO PAVESE Lom ★★ (Brega, Cabanon, Doria, Frecciarossa, coop La Versa), also astonishing from Ronco del Gelso (DOC ISONZO).

Ripasso VALPOLICELLA re-fermented on AMARONE grape skins to make a more complex, longer-lived and fuller wine. Best is MASI's Campo Fiorin.

Riserva Wine aged for a statutory period, usually in barrels.

Riunite One of the world's largest coop cellars, nr Reggio Emilia, producing huge quantities of LAMBRUSCO and other wines.

Rivera Reliable winemakers at Andria, near Bari (APULIA), with good red Il Falcone and CASTEL DEL MONTE rosé. Also Vigna al Monte label.

Rivetti, Giorgio (La Spinetta) ★★★ First success with MOSCATO, then with reds. Top Moscato d'Asti, vg BARBERA, v interesting VDT Pin (Barbera-NEBBIOLO).

Riviera del Garda Bresciano Lom DOC w p r (sp) ★→★★ Simple, sometimes charming cherry-pink CHIARETTO and neutral white from SW Garda. Good producers: Ca'dei Frati, Comincioli, Costaripa, Monte Cigogna.

Rocca, Bruno Young producer with admirable BARBARESCO (Rabajà).

Rocca di Castagnoli ★★→★★★ Recent producer of vg CHIANTI CLASSICO (best: Capraia, RISERVA Poggio a'Frati, also vg VDT Stielle and Buriano (blends of CAB and SANGIOVESE).

Rocca delle Macìe ★★ Large CHIANTI CLASSICO maker nr Castellina.

Rocche dei Manzoni, Podere ★★★ Go-ahead estate at Monforte d'Alba. Excellent BAROLO (best: Vigna Big), BRICCO MANZONI (outstanding NEBBIOLO-BARBERA blend VINO DA TAVOLA), ALBA wines, CHARD (L'Angelica) and Valentino Brut sparkling.

Roero Pie DOC r ★★ 93 94 95 Evolving former drink-me-quick NEBBIOLO from Roeri hills near ALBA. Can be delicious. Good from: Correggia, Deltetto, Malabaila, Malvirà.

Roero Arneis Pie DOC r ★★ DYA Mellow, light white from the hills around Roeri; usually expensive. Good from: Almondo, BRUNO GIACOSA, Correggia, Deltetto, Malabaila, Malvirà, VIETTI, Gianni Voerzio.

Ronco Term for a hillside v'yd in FRIULI-VENEZIA GIULIA.

Ronco del Gnemiz ★★★ Tiny property with outstanding COLLI ORIENTALI DOCs and VDT CHARD.

Rosa del Golfo Ap p ★★ DYA An outstanding VDT rosé of ALEZIO.

Rosato Rosé.

Rosato del Salento Ap p ★★ DYA From nr BRINDISI and v like Brindisi, COPERTINO and SALICE SALENTINO ROSATOS; can be strong, but often really juicy and good. See Brindisi, Copertino, Salice Salentino for producers.

Rossese di Dolceacqua Lig DOC r ★★ DYA Well-known fragrant light red of the Riviera. Good from Giuncheo, Guglielmi, Lupi, Perrino, Terre Bianche.

Rosso Red.

Rosso Cònero Mar DOC r ★★→★★★ 85 88 90 91 92 93 94 95 Some of the best MONTEPULCIANO (varietal) reds of Italy, eg GAROFOLI's Grosso Agontano, Moroder's RC Dorico, UMANI RONCHI's Cumaro and San Lorenzo. Also vg from Conte Dittajuti, E Lanari Leardo, Le Terrazze, Marchetti.

Rosso di Montalcino Tus DOC r ★★→★★★ 90 93 94 95 DOC for younger wines from BRUNELLO grapes. Still variable but potentially a winner if the many good producers are not greedy over prices. For growers see Brunello di Montalcino.

Rosso di Montepulciano Tus DOC r ★★ 93 94 Equivalent of the last for junior VINO NOBILE, recently introduced and yet to establish a style. For growers see Vino Nobile di M.

Rosso Piceno Mar DOC r ★★ 90 91 93 94 Stylish Adriatic red. SUPERIORE from classic zone near Ascoli. Best include Cocci Grifoni, Velenosi Ercole, Saladini Pilastri, Villamagna.

Rubesco ★★ The excellent popular red of LUNGAROTTI; see Torgiano.

Ruchè (also Rouchè or Rouchet) A rare old grape (French origin) giving fruity, fresh, rich bouqueted red wine (s/sw). Ruchè di Castagnole Monferrato is recent DOC, with Piero Bruno best producer. Rouchet Briccorosa is dry and excellent (★★★) from SCARPA.

Ruffino ★→★★★ Well known CHIANTI merchants, at Pontassieve. RISERVA Ducale Oro and Santedame are the top wines. NB new PREDICATO wines (red and white Cabreo) and CAB Il Pareto.

Rufina ★→★★★ Important subregion of CHIANTI in the hills E of Florence. Best wines from Basciano, Castello Nipozzano (FRESCOBALDI), SELVAPIANA.

Russiz Superiore (Collio) See Felluga, Marco.

Sagrantino di Montefalco See Montefalco.

For key to grape variety abbreviations, see pages 7–13.

St-Michael-Eppan Top SUDTIROL coop: look for St-Valentin (★★★), SAUV, vg SPUMANTE, PINOT N, PINOT BIANCO, Gewurz and even vg Ries Renano.

Sala, Castello della ★★→★★★ ANTINORI's estate at ORVIETO. Borro is the regular white. Top wine is Cervaro della Sala: CHARDONNAY and GRECHETTO aged in oak. Muffato della S is one of Italy's best botrytis wines.

Salice Salentino Ap DOC r ★★→★★★ 88 89 90 93 94 Resonant red from NEGROAMARO grapes. RISERVA after 2 years; not overweight, but clean and quenching. Top makers: CANDIDO, De Castris, TAURINO, Vallone.

San Felice ★★→★★★ Rising star in CHIANTI with fine CLASSICO Poggio Rosso. Also red VDT Vigorello and PREDICATO di Biturica.

San Giminiano Famous TUSCAN city of towers with potentially potent dry white VERNACCIA.

San Giusto a Rentennano One of the best CHIANTI CLASSICO producers (★★★). Delicious but v rare VIN SANTO. Excellent VDT red Percarlo.

San Guido, Tenuta ★★★★ See Sassicaia.

San Polo in Rosso, Castello di ★★★ CHIANTI CLASSICO estate with first-rate red VDT Cetinaia (aged in big casks, not barriques).

San Rustico ★★ Small VALPOLICELLA estate; vg AMARONE Vigneti del Gaso.

Sandrone, Luciano ★★★ Exponent of new-style BAROLO vogue with vg B Cannubi Boschis, DOLCETTO and BARBERA.

Sangiovese (Sangioveto) Principal red grape of Italy. Top performance only in TUSCANY, where its many forms incl CHIANTI, VINO NOBILE, BRUNELLO, MORELLINO etc. Very popular is S di Romagna (E-R DOC r ★→★★), a pleasant standard red. Vg from Cesari, Conti, PARADISO, Trerè, ZERBINA. Outstanding ★★★ VDTS Ronco dei Cigliegi, R delle Ginestre from CASTELLUCCIO. Sometimes good from ROSSO PICENO.

Santa Maddalena (or St-Magdalener) T-AA DOC r ★ DYA Typical SCHIAVA Tyrolean red, lightish with bitter aftertaste. Best from: Cantina Sociale St-Magdalena, CS Girlan, Gojer, Thurnhof.

Santa Margherita Large Veneto (Portogruaro) merchants: Veneto (Torresella), ALTO-ADIGE (Kettmeir), Tuscan (Lamole di Lamole), Lombardy (CA'DEL BOSCO).

Saracco, Paolo ★★★ Small estate with top MOSCATO D'ASTI.

Sassella (Valtellina Superiore) Lom DOC r ★★→★★★ 85 88 89 90 93 95 Considerable NEBBIOLO wine, tough when young. Known since Roman times; mentioned by Leonardo da Vinci. Neighbour to INFERNO etc.

Sassicaia Tus r ★★★★ 75' 82' 83' 85' 86 88' 89 90' 91 92 93 94 95 Outstanding pioneer CAB, Italy's best, from the Tenuta San Guido of the Incisa family, at Bolgheri nr Livorno. 'Promoted' from SUPER-TUSCAN VDT to DOC BOLGHERI in '94.

Sauvignon Sauvignon Blanc is working v well in the northeast, best from DOCs ALTO ADIGE, COLLIO, COLLI ORIENTALI, ISONZO and TERLANO.

Sauvignon (Colli Orientali del Friuli) F-VG DOC w ★★→★★★ 93 94 (95) Best from: Aquila del Torre, RONCO DEL GNEMIZ, Torre Rosazza.

Sauvignon Collio F-VG DOC w ★★→★★★ 93 94 (95) Best wines from La Castellada, GRAVNER, Renato Keber, Komjanec, Primosic, SCHIOPETTO, VILLA RUSSIZ.

Sauvignon Isonzo F-VG DOC w ★★→★★★ 93 94 (95) V full fruity white, increasingly good quality. Top producers: F and P Pecorari, VIE DI ROMANS.

Savuto Cal DOC r p ★★ 94 95 Fragrant juicy wine from the provinces of Cosenza and Catanzaro. Best producer is Odoardi.

Scarpa ★★★ Old-fashioned house with full-bodied smooth BARBERA D'ASTI (La Bogliona), rare Rouchet, vg DOLCETTO, BAROLO, BARBARESCO.

Schiava High-yielding red grape of TRENTINO-ALTO ADIGE with characteristic bitter aftertaste, used for LAGO DI CALDARO, SANTA MADDALENA etc.

Schiopetto, Mario ★★★→★★★★ Legendary COLLIO pioneer with brand-new 20,000-case winery; vg DOC SAUV, PINOT GR, TOCAI, VDT blend 'Bl de Rosis' etc.

Schreckbichl (or Colterenzio CS) No 1 Südtirol CANTINA SOCIALE. Admirable ALTO ADIGE CAB S, Gewürz, PINOT N (look for Schwarzhaus RISERVA), CHARD, PINOT BL, PINOT GR, SAUV (look for Lafoa), red VDT Cornelius etc.

Sciacchetrà See Cinqueterre.

Scolca, La ★★★ Famous estate in GAVI for top Gavi and SPUMANTE (look for Extra Brut Soldati La Scolca).

Secco Dry.

Sella & Mosca ★★ Major Sardinian growers and merchants at Alghero. Their port-like Anghelu Ruju (★★★) is excellent. Also pleasant white TORBATO and delicious light fruity VERMENTINO Cala Viola (DYA).

Selvapiana ★★★ Top CHIANTI RUFINA estate. Best wine is RISERVA Bucerchiale.

Sforzato Lom DOC r ★★→★★★ 85 86 88 89 90 93 95 VALTELLINA equivalent of RECIOTO AMARONE made with partly dried grapes. Velvety, strong, ages remarkably well. Also called Sfursat. See Valtellina.

Sizzano Pie DOC r ★★ 88 89 90 93 95 Full-bodied red from Sizzano, Novara; mostly NEBBIOLO. Ages up to 10 yrs. Esp from: Bianchi, Dessilani.

Soave Ven DOC w ★→★★★ DYA Famous mass-produced Veronese white. Should be fresh with smooth, limpid texture. Standards are rising (at last). S CLASSICO is more restricted and better. Esp from ANSELMI, PIEROPAN; also Gini, GUERRIERI-RIZZARDI, Inama, Pra, Suavia, TEDESCHI.

Solaia Tus r ★★★★ 82' 83 85' 88' 90 91 93 94 95 V fine Bordeaux-style VDT of CAB S and a little SANGIOVESE from ANTINORI; first made in '78. Extraordinarily influential in shaping VDT (and Italian) philosophy.

Solopaca Cam DOC r w ★★ 93 94 95 Rather sharp red, soft dry white from nr Benevento. Some promise: esp Antica Masseria Venditti.

Sorì Term for a high S, SE or SW oriented v'yd in PIEDMONT.

Spanna See Gattinara.

Italy's best bubbles

Italy's 12 best producers of metodo classico spumante are,
in Franciacorta: Bellavista, Bersi Serlini, Ca'del Bosco;
in Oltrepò Pavese: Anteo; in Alto-Adige: Kössler, St-Michael, Vivaldi;
in Piedmont: Bruno Giacosa, Fontanafredda, La Scolca;
in Trentino: Letrari, Pojer & Sandri.

Spumante Sparkling, as in sweet ASTI or many good dry wines, incl both METODO CLASSICO (best from TRENTINO, A ADIGE, FRANCIACORTA, PIEDMONT, some vg also from TUSCANY and Veneto) and tank-made cheapos.

Stravecchio Very old.

Südtirol The local name of German-speaking ALTO ADIGE.

Super-Tuscans Term coined for high-price novelties from TUSCANY, usually involving CAB, barriques, and frequently fancy bottles and prices.

Superiore Wine that has undergone more ageing than normal DOC and contains 0.5–1% more alcohol.

Tasca d'Almerita See Regaleali.

Taurasi Cam DOCG r ★★★ 87 88 90 92 93 94 95 The best Campanian red, from MASTROBERARDINO of Avellino. Harsh when young. RISERVA after 4 yrs. Radici (since '86) is Mastroberardino's top estate bottling.

Taurino, Cosimo ★★★ Tip-top producer of Salento-APULIA, vg SALICE SALENTINO, VDT Notarpanoro and BRINDISI Patriglione (s'times even ★★★★).

Tedeschi, Fratelli ★★★ V reliable and vg producer of VALPOLICELLA, AMARONE, RECIOTO and SOAVE. Vg Capitel San Rocco red and white VDT.

Terlano T-AA DOC w ★★→★★★ DYA DOC for 8 BOLZANO varietal whites, esp SAUV. Terlaner in German. Esp from CS Andrian, CS Terlan, LAGEDER, Niedrist.

Teroldego Rotaliano T-AA DOC r p ★★→★★★ 90 91 92 93 94 95 Attractive blackberry-scented red; slightly bitter aftertaste; can age very well. Esp Foradori's. Also good from CA'VIT, Dorigati, Sebastiani.

Terre di Ginestra Si w ★★ Good VDT from Cataratto, SW of Palermo.

Terre Rosse ★★★ Distinguished small estate nr Bologna. Its CAB, CHARD, SAUV, PINOT GR, RIES, even Viognier etc, are the best of the region.

Terre da Vino ★★→★★★ Association of 27 PIEDMONT coops and private estates selecting and selling best produce: incl most local DOCs. BARBERA D'ASTI and GAVI are best.

Teruzzi & Puthod (Fattoria Ponte a Rondolino) ★★→★★★ Innovative producers of SAN GIMIGNANO with vg VERNACCIA DI SAN G, white VDTS 'Terre di Tufi' and 'Carmen'.

Tiefenbrunner ★★ Leading grower of some of the very best ALTO ADIGE white and red wines at Schloss Turmhof, Kurtatsch (Cortaccio).

Tignanello Tus r ★★★★ 85 88 90 93 94 (95) Pioneer and still leader of the new style of Bordeaux-inspired Tuscan reds, made by ANTINORI.

Tocai Mild smooth white (no relation of Hungarian Tokay) of the northeast. DOC also in Ven and Lom (★→★★), but producers are most proud of it in F-VG (esp COLLIO and COLLI ORIENTALI): (★★→★★★). Best producers: BORGO DEL TIGLIO, Keber, Picech, Princic, Raccaro, Ronco del Gelso, RONCO DI GNEMIZ, SCHIOPETTO, Scubla, Specogna, Castello di Spessa, Toros, Venica & Venica, VILLA RUSSIZ, VOLPE PASINI.

Torbato di Alghero Sar w (pa) ★★ DYA Good N Sardinian table wine. Leading brand is SELLA & MOSCA.

Torgiano Umb DOC r w p (sp) ★★→★★★ and **Torgiano, Rosso Riserva** DOCG r ★★★ 85 87 88 90 93 94 (3 yrs ageing) 95 Creation of Lungarotti family. Excellent red from nr Perugia, comparable with top CHIANTI CLASSICO. Rubesco is standard. RISERVA Vigna Monticchio is (★★★★); keep 10 yrs. VDT San Giorgio involves CAB to splendid effect. White Torre di Giano, of TREBBIANO and GRECHETTO, also ages well. See also Lungarotti.

Toscana See Tuscany.

Tuscany vintages

1995 Much autumn rain, worse even than 1992. The top estates made good wines if they waited for a warm, dry October. Otherwise, dull quality.

1994 Dry summer, showers in September; good to very good wines.

1993 A hot summer was followed by heavy October rains; despite these Chianti Classico generally good, Brunello and Vino Nobile di Montepulciano vg.

1992 Promise of a top quality vintage dispelled for reds by rain. The whites had better luck and are vg.

1991 A difficult vintage: wines to drink quickly, without many positive surprises.

Traminer Aromatico T-AA DOC w ★★→★★★ DYA (German: Gewürztraminer) Delicate, aromatic, soft. Best from: Cantina Sociale Girlan/Cornaiano, CS St-Michael, CS SCHRECKBICHL/COLTERENZIO, Hofkellerei, HOFSTATTER, Laimburg, Plattenhof, Stiftskellerei Neustift.

Trebbiano Principal white grape of TUSCANY, found all over Italy. Ugni Blanc in French. Sadly a waste of good v'yd space, with v rare exceptions.

Trebbiano d'Abruzzo Ab DOC w ★→★★ DYA Gentle, neutral, slightly tannic white from round Pescara. VALENTINI is much the best producer (also making MONTEPULCIANO D'ABRUZZO).

Trentino T-AA DOC r w dr sw ★→★★★ DOC for as many as 20 different wines, mostly named after their grapes. Best are CHARD, PINOT BL, MARZEMINO, TEROLDEGO. The region's capital is Trento.

Triacca Vg producer of VALTELLINA; also owns estates in TUSCANY (CHIANTI CLASSICO: La Madonnina; MONTEPULCIANO: Santavenere).

Tuscany (Toscana) Italy's central wine region, incl DOCs CHIANTI, MONTALCINO, MONTEPULCIANO etc.

Umani Ronchi ★→★★★ Leading merchant of quality wines of the Marches; notably VERDICCHIO (Casal di Serra and Villa Bianchi) and ROSSO CONERO (Cumaro and San Lorenzo).

Uzzano, Castello di Famous old CHIANTI CLASSICO estate at Greve. Below par.

Vajra, Giuseppe Domenico ★★★ Vg consistent BAROLO producer, esp for BARBERA, Barolo, DOLCETTO etc. Also an interesting (not fizzy) FREISA.

Val di Cornia Tus DOC r p w ★→★★ New DOC nr Livorno; some good producers: Ambrosini, Tua Rita, Graziani, Gualdo del Re.

Valcalepio Lom DOC r w ★→★★ From nr Bergamo. Pleasant red; lightly scented fresh white. Good from Bonaldi, Il Calepino and Tenuta Castello.

Valdadige T-AA DOC r w dr s/sw ★→★★ Name for the simple wines of the ADIGE VALLEY – in German 'Etschtaler'. Best producer: Armani.

Valentini, Edoardo ★★★→★★★★ Perhaps the best traditionalist maker of TREBBIANO and MONTEPULCIANO D'ABRUZZO.

Valgella Lom DOC r ★★ 88 89 90 93 One of the VALTELLINA NEBBIOLOS: good dry red. RISERVA at 4 yrs. See Valtellina.

Valle d'Aosta VdA DOC ★★→★★★ Regional DOC for 15 Alpine wines incl DONNAZ. A mixed bag. Vg from monastery-run Institut Agricole Régional, Charrère, Crote de Vignerons, Grosjean.

Valle Isarco (Eisacktal) T-AA DOC w ★★ DYA A DOC applicable to 5 varietal wines made NE of Bolzano. Good MULLER-T, Silvaner. Top producers are CS Eisacktaler, Kloster Neustift and Kuenhof.

Vallechiara, Abbazia di ★★→★★★ Young PIEDMONT estate, owned by actress Ornella Muti, with astonishingly good wines, eg DOC Dolcetto di Ovada and DOLCETTO-based VDTS Due Donne and Torre Albarola.

Valpolicella Ven DOC r ★→★★★ 93 94 Attractive light red from nr Verona; best young. Quality improvement over last few yrs. V best can be conc, complex and merit higher prices. Delicate nutty scent, slightly bitter taste. (None of this is true of junk Valpolicella sold in litre and bigger bottles.) CLASSICO more restricted; SUPERIORE has 12% alcohol and 1 yr of age. Good esp from ALLEGRINI, Beretta, BRIGALDARA, Brunelli, Corte Sant Alda, A FERRARI, Fornaser, GUERRIERI-RIZZARDI, LE RAGOSE, MASI, LE SALETTE, SAN RUSTICO, Speri, TEDESCHI, Tommasi. DAL FORNO and QUINTARELLI make the best (★★★). Interesting VDTS on the way to a new Valpolicella style are Toar (★★★) from MASI, La Poja (★★★) from ALLEGRINI.

Valtellina Lom DOC r ★★→★★★ 88 89 90 93 (95) A DOC for tannic wines made mainly from Chiavennasca (NEBBIOLO) grapes in Alpine Sondrio province, N Lombardy. V SUPERIORE are GRUMELLO, INFERNO, SASSELLA, VALGELLA. Best from: Conti Sertoli-Salis, Fay, TRIACCA.

Vecchio Old.

Vecchio Samperi Si ★★★ MARSALA-like VDT from outstanding estate. The best is barrel-aged 20 years, not unlike amontillado sherry. The owner, Marco De Bartoli, also makes the best DOC Marsalas.

Vendemmia Harvest or vintage.

Venegazzù Ven r w sp ★★★ 88 89 90 93 94 (95) Remarkable rustic Bordeaux-style red produced from CABERNET grapes near Treviso. Rich bouquet and soft warm taste. 'Della Casa' and 'Capo di Stato' are best quality. Also makes v fair sparkling.

Verdicchio dei Castelli di Jesi Mar DOC w (sp) ★ →★★★ DYA Ancient pleasant fresh pale white from nr Ancona, dating back to the Etruscans. Also CLASSICO. Trad in amphora-shaped bottles. Esp from Belelli, Bonci-Vallerosa, Brunori, Bucci, Coroncino, GAROFOLI, Mancinelli, MONCARO, Monteschiavo, Sartarelli, UMANI RONCHI, Zaccagnini; also FAZI-BATTAGLIA.

Verdicchio di Matelica Mar DOC w (sp) ★★ DYA Similar to the last, though bigger and less well-known. Especially from Belisario, Castiglioni-Bisci and La Monacesca.

Verona Capital of the Veneto region (home of VALPOLICELLA, BARDOLINO, SOAVE etc) and seat of Italy's splendid annual April Wine fair 'Vinitaly'.

Verduzzo (Colli Orientali del Friuli) F-VG DOC w dr s/sw sw ★★ →★★★ 91 92 93 94 Full-bodied white from a native grape. The best sweet is called Ramandolo. Top makers: Dario Coos, DORIGO, Giovanni Dri.

Verduzzo (del Piave) Ven DOC w ★ DYA A dull little white wine. LIVON makes the best of them.

Vermentino Lig w DOC ★★ DYA Best seafood white wine of the Riviera: esp from Pietra Ligure and San Remo. DOC is Riviera Ligure di Ponente. See Pigato. Particularly good wines from Anfossi, Colle dei Bardellini, Lambruschi, Lupi, Cascina dei Peri.

Vermentino di Gallura Sar DOC w ★★→★★★ DYA Soft dry strong white of northern Sardinia. Especially from CS di Gallura, CS Giogantinu, CS Del Vermentino, Capichera.

Vernaccia di Oristano Sar DOC w dr (sw fz) ★→★★★ 78' 81 83 85' 87 88 91 92 93 94 95 Sardinian speciality, like light sherry, a touch bitter, full-bodied and interesting. SUPERIORE with 15.5% alcohol and 3 yrs of age. Top producer Contini also makes ancient solera wine Antico Gregori.

Vernaccia di San Gimignano Tus DOCG w ★→★★ DYA Once Michelangelo's favourite, then ordinary tourist wine. Much improvement in last few yrs, now newly DOCG with tougher production laws. Best from FALCHINI, Montenidoli, Palagetto, PANIZZI, Rampa di Fugnano, TERUZZI & PUTHOD, Vagnoni.

Vernatsch German for SCHIAVA.

Verrazzano, Castello di ★★★ Outstanding CHIANTI CLASSICO estate near Greve.

Vicchiomaggio CHIANTI CLASSICO estate near Greve.

VIDE An association of better-class Italian producers for marketing their estate wines from many parts of Italy.

Vie di Romans ★★★→★★★★ A young wine genius, Gianfranco Gallo, has built up his father's ISONZO estate to top FRIULI status within a few years. Unforgettable CHARD and SAUV; excellent TOCAI and PINOT GR.

Vietti Excellent (★★★→★★★★) producer of characterful PIEDMONT wines, including BAROLO and BARBARESCO, at Castiglione Falletto in Barolo region.

Vigna A single vineyard.

Vignamaggio ★★→★★★ Historic, beautiful and very good CHIANTI CLASSICO estate near Greve.

Vigne dal Leon ★★★ Vg producer of COLLI ORIENTALI (FRIULI).

Villa Matilde ★★ Top Campania producer: vg FALERNO and white Falanghina.

Villa Russiz ★★★ Impressive white DOC COLLIO from Gianni Menotti: eg SAUV (look for 'de la Tour'), PINOT BL, TOCAI etc.

Vin Santo or Vinsanto, Vin(o) Santo Term for certain strong sweet wines esp in TUSCANY: usually PASSITO. Can be v fine, esp in Tuscany and TRENTINO.

Vin Santo Toscano Tus w s/sw ★→★★★★ Aromatic rich and smooth. Aged in v small barrels called caratelli. Can be as astonishing as expensive, but a good one is v rare and top producers are always short of it. Best from AVIGNONESI, Cacchiano, CAPEZZANA, CONTUCCI, CORZANO & PATERNO, POLIZIANO, SAN GIUSTO A RENTENNANO, SELVAPIANA.

Vino da arrosto 'Wine for roast meat', ie good robust dry red.

Vino Nobile di Montepulciano Tus DOCG r ★★★ 85' 88' 90 91 93 94 95
Impressive SANGIOVESE red with bouquet and style, rapidly making its name
and fortune. RISERVA after 3 years. Best estates include AVIGNONESI, Bindella,
BOSCARELLI, La Calonica, Canneto, LE CASALTE, Casella, Fattoria del Cerro,
CONTUCCI, Dei, Innocenti, Macchione, Paterno, POLIZIANO, Salcheto, Talosa,
Trerose, Valdipiatta and Vecchia Cantina (look for the RISERVA). Vino nobile is
so far very reasonably priced.

Vino novello Italy's equivalent of France's primeurs (as in Beaujolais).

Vino da tavola (vdt) 'Table wine': intended to be the humblest class of Italian
wine, with no specific geographical or other claim to fame, but also category
to watch (with reasonable circumspection and a wary eye on the price) for
top-class wines not conforming to DOC regulations. New laws introduced
in '92 were for phasing out this situation (see Introduction, pages 104–105).

Vintage Tunina F-VG w ★★★ A notable blended white from JERMANN estate.

Voerzio, Roberto ★★★ Young BAROLO pace-setter: Brunate is new-style best.

Volpaia, Castello di ★★→★★★ First-class CHIANTI CLASSICO estate at Radda,
with elegant, rather light Chianti. VDT red Balifico contains CAB; COLTASSALA is
all SANGIOVESE.

Volpe Pasini ★★★ Ambitious COLLIO ORIENTALI estate, esp for good SAUV.

VQPRD Often found on the labels of DOC wines to signify Vini di Qualità
Prodotti in Regioni Delimitate.

Where the dreams have no end... ★★★ A memorable VDT CHARD from JERMANN.

Zanella, Maurizio Creator of CA'DEL BOSCO. His name is on his top CAB-MERLOT
blend, one of Italy's best.

Zardetto ★★ Vg producer of PROSECCO DI CONEGLIANO-VALDOBBIADENE.

Zerbina, Fattoria ★★→★★★ New leader in Romagna with best ALBANA DOCG
to date (a rich PASSITO), good SANGIOVESE and a barrique-aged Sangiovese-CAB
VDT called Marzeno di Marzeno.

Zibibbo Si w sw ★★ Fashionable MOSCATO from the island of PANTELLERIA. Good
producer: Murana.

Zonin One of Italy's biggest privately owned estates and wineries, based at
GAMBELLARA, with DOC VALPOLICELLA etc. Others are at ASTI and in CHIANTI, San
Gimignano and FRIULI. Also at Barboursville, Virginia (USA).

Luxembourg

Luxembourg has 3,285 acres of v'yds on limestone soils on the
Moselle's left bank. High-yielding Elbling and Rivaner (Müller-T)
vines dominate, but there are also significant acreages of
Ries, Gewürz and (usually best) Auxerrois, Pinot Bl and Pinot
Gr. These give light to medium-bodied (10.5–11.5%) dry
Alsace-like wines. The Vins Moselle coop makes 70% of the
total. Domaine et Tradition estates association, founded in
'88, promotes quality from noble varieties. The last six vintages
were all good; 89 90 92 outstanding. Best from: Aly Duhr et
Fils, M Bastian, Caves Gales, Bernard Massard (surprisingly
good Cuvée de l'Ecusson classic method sparkling),
Clos Mon Vieux Moulin, Ch de Schengen, Sunnen-Hoffmann.

To decipher codes, please refer to 'Key to symbols' on front flap of jacket,
or to 'How to use this book' on page 6.

Germany

Heavily shaded areas are the wine growing regions

North Sea

Hamburg

Bremen

Elbe

Hannover

Berlin

Rhine

Weser

Erfurt

SAALE-UNSTRUT

ELBTAL

Dresden

Bonn

AHR

MITTELRHEIN

Koblenz

RHEINGAU

Frankfurt

FRANKEN

MOSEL-SAAR-RUWER

RHEINHESSEN

Würzburg

Trier

Worms

NAHE

HESSISCHE-BERGSTRASSE

Nürnberg

PFALZ

WURTTEMBERG

Main

Stuttgart

Baden Baden

Danube

BADEN

München

Freiburg

L Bodensee

The following abbreviations of regional names are used in the text:

Bad   Baden
Frank Franken
M-M   Mittel-Mosel
M-S-R Mosel-Saar-Ruwer
Na   Nahe
Rhg   Rheingau
Rhh   Rheinhessen
Pfz   Pfalz
Würt   Württemberg

132

The finest wines of Germany today are precisely the same miracles of tension between sweetness and fruity acidity as they have always been – and almost all, as always, Riesling. What has changed in recent years is the addition to the German repertoire of a range of full-bodied dry wines from grapes not specifically associated with Germany – especially the Pinots and especially from the warmer, more southern growing regions of the Pfalz and Baden-Württemberg.

As yet these wines have scarcely been seen outside Germany, but they are the cult wines of the 1990s. There is a total polarization between these and the sugar-watery wines that still form the bulk of the export market – especially to Britain.

1995/96 was a pivotal year in the politics of German wine. The catastrophic Wine Law of 1971 came under serious challenge from the most responsible producers. The VDP – the association representing the great majority of top-quality growers – put its weight behind a long-overdue (though still unofficial) classification of the German vineyards. Most of the best are on steep land whose cultivation demands sacrifice. They are now rightly being described as National Cultural Monuments in the same way as abbeys or castles, in an attempt to force a timid and vacillating government to recognize their value.

Meanwhile the outrage of allowing great names to be used for ordinary wines from low-grade grape varieties continues.

Officially, all German wines are still only classified according to grape ripeness. Most wines (like most French) need sugar added before fermentation to make up for missing sunshine. But unlike in France, German wine from grapes ripe enough not to need extra sugar is made and sold as a separate product: Qualitätswein mit Prädikat, or QmP. Within this top category, natural sugar content is expressed by traditional terms in ascending order of ripeness: Kabinett, Spätlese, Auslese, Beerenauslese, Trockenbeerenauslese.

Qualitätswein bestimmter Anbaugebiete (QbA), the second level, is for wines that needed additional sugar before fermentation. The third level, Tafelwein, like Italian vino da tavola, is free of restraints. Officially it is the lowest grade, but impatience with outdated law makes it increasingly interesting for innovative producers who set their own high standards.

Though there is much more detail in the laws, this is the gist of the quality grading. It differs completely from the French system in ignoring geographical difference. In theory all any German vineyard has to do to make the best wine is to grow the ripest grapes – even of inferior grape varieties – which is patent rubbish.

The law distinguishes only between degrees of geographical exactness. In labelling 'quality', wine growers or merchants are given a choice. They can (and generally do) label the relatively small quantities of their best wine with the name of the precise vineyard or Einzellage. Germany has about 2,600 Einzellagen names. Obviously only a relative few are famous enough to help sell the wine. Therefore the 1971 law created a second class of vineyard name: the Grosslage. A Grosslage is a group of Einzellagen of supposedly similar character. Because there are fewer Grosslagen names, and far more wine from each, they have the advantage of familiarity – a poor substitute for hard-earned fame.

Thirdly, growers or merchants may choose to sell their wine under a regional or Bereich name. To cope with the demand for 'Bernkasteler', 'Niersteiner' or 'Johannisberger' these world-famous names were made legal for large districts. 'Bereich Johannisberg' is the whole of the Rheingau. Beware the Bereich.

Leading growers are now simplifying labels to avoid confusion and clutter. Some use the village name only, or indeed sell top wines under a brand name alone as in Italy. But before German wine can fully recover its rightful place, two things are needed: the banning of inferior grapes from top areas, and an official recognition of the vineyard classification which is now well under way. The First-class vineyards are named here and mapped in the 4th edition of The World Atlas of Wine. It is after all (in Germany above all) the vineyard and producer that count.

Recent vintages

Mosel-Saar-Ruwer

Mosels (including Saar and Ruwer wines) are so attractive young that, their keeping qualities are not often enough explored, and wines older than about 8 years are unusual. But well-made Riesling wines of Kabinett class gain from at least 5 years in bottle – often much more – Spätlese from 10 to 20, and Auslese and Beerenauslese, anything from 10 to 30 years.

As a rule, in poor years the Saar and Ruwer make sharp thin wines, but in the best years, above all with botrytis, they can surpass the whole world for elegance and thrilling steely 'breed'.

1995 Excellent vintage, mainly of Spätlese and Auslese of firm structure and long ageing potential.

1994 Another v good vintage, mostly QmP with unexceptional QbA and Kabinett, but many Auslese, BA and TBA. Rich fruit and high acidity. Try to resist: they have a glorious future.

1993 Small excellent vintage: lots of Auslese/botrytis; nr perfect harmony.

1992 A very large crop, threatened by cold and rain in October. Mostly good QbA, but 30% QmP, some exceptional, esp in the Mittelmosel. Developing quickly; start to drink.

1991 A diverse mixed vintage. Bad frost damage in Saar and Ruwer, but many fine Spätlesen. Start to drink.

1990 Superb vintage, though small. Many QmP wines were the finest for 20 years. Try to resist drinking too soon.

1989 Large and outstandingly good, with noble rot giving many Auslesen etc. Saar wines best; the Mittelmosel overproduced causing some dilution. Mostly ready to drink.

1988 Excellent vintage. Much ripe QmP, esp in Mittelmosel. For long keeping. Beginning to drink well, but will keep.

1987 Rainy summer but warm Sept/Oct. 90% QbA wines, crisp and lively, to drink soon.

1986 Fair Riesling year despite autumn rain: 13% QmP wines, mostly Kabinett. For drinking.

1985 A modest summer but beautiful autumn. 40% of harvest was QmP. Riesling vintage from best v'yds, incl Eiswein. Now drinking; will keep.

1983 The best between 76 and 88; 31% Spätlese; Auslesen few but fine. No hurry to drink.

1981 A wet vintage but some good Mittelmosels up to Spätlese quality. Also Eiswein. Drinking well.

1979 A patchy vintage after bad winter damage. But many excellent Kabinetts and better. Light but well-balanced wines should be drunk up.

1976 Vg small vintage, with some superlative sweet wines and almost no dry. Most wines ready; only the best will keep.

1971 Superb, with perfect balance. At its peak – but no hurry for best wines.

Older fine vintages: 69 64 59 53 49 45.

Rheinhessen, Nahe, Pfalz, Rheingau

Even the best wines can be drunk with pleasure when young, but Kabinett, Spätlese and Auslese Riesling gain enormously in character by keeping for longer. Rheingau wines tend to be longest-lived, improving for 15 years or more, but wines from the Nahe and Pfalz can last as long. Rheinhessen wines usually mature sooner, and dry Franken wines are best at 3–6 years.

1995 Slightly variable, but some fine Spätlese and Auslese promising to age v well – like the 90s.

1994 Good vintage, mostly QmP, with abundant fruit and firm structure. Need time to develop. Best in Pfalz where finest vintage since '90.

1993 A small vintage of v good to excellent quality. Plenty of Spätlese and Auslese wines.

1992 Very large vintage, would have been great but for October cold and rain. A third QmP wines of rich stylish quality. Start to taste.

1991 A good middling vintage in most regions, though light soils in Pfalz suffered from drought. Some fine wines are emerging. Start to taste.

1990 Small but exceptionally fine. High percentage of QmP will keep well beyond 2000 (try to resist drinking too soon).

1989 Summer storms reduced crop in Rheingau. Vg quality elsewhere, up to Auslese level. Try now.

1988 Not quite so outstanding as the Mosel, but comparable with 83. Drinking well.

1987 Good average quality: lively round and fresh. 80% QbA, 15% QmP. Now drinking well.

1986 Well-balanced Rieslings, mostly QbA but some Kabinett and Spätlese, esp in Rheinhessen and Nahe. Good botrytis-effected wines in Pfalz. Now drinking well.

1985 Sadly small crops, of variable quality, esp Riesling. Average 65% QmP. Keep the best. Best in the Pfalz.

1983 Vg Rieslings, esp in the Rheingau and central Nahe. Generally about half QbA, but plenty of Spätlesen, now excellent to drink.

1982 A colossal vintage gathered in torrential rain. All 82s should be drunk up.

1981 Rheingau poor, Nahe and Rheinhessen better, Pfalz best. Drink up.

1976 The richest vintage since 21 in places. Very few dry wines. Generally mature now.

1971 A superlative vintage, now at its peak.

Older fine vintages: 69 67 64 59 53 49 45.

Vintage notes after entries in the German section are given in a different form from those elsewhere, to show the style of the vintage as well as its quality. Three styles are indicated:

Bold type (eg 93) indicates classic, super-ripe vintages with a high proportion of natural (QmP) wines, including Spätlese and Auslese.

Normal type (eg 92) indicates 'normal' successful vintages with plenty of good wine but no great preponderance of sweeter wines.

Italic type (eg *91*) indicates cool vintages with generally poor ripeness but a fair proportion of reasonably successful wines, tending to be over-acid. Few or no QmP wines, but correspondingly more selection in the QbA category. Such wines sometimes mature more favourably than expected.

Where no mention is made the vintage is generally not recommended, or most of its wines have passed maturity.

Achkarren Bad w (r) ★★ Village on the KAISERSTUHL, known esp for RULANDER. Best site: Schlossberg. Good wines: DR HEGER and coop.

Adelmann, Graf ★★★ Aristocratic grower with 37 v'yd acres at Kleinbottwar, WURTTEMBERG. Uses the name 'Brussele'. LEMBERGER reds best. Recent yrs not so good.

Ahr Ahr r ★→★★ 85 *87* 88 89 90 91 *92* 93 94 95 Traditional specialized red wine area, south of Bonn. Very light, pale SPATBURGUNDER, esp from Deutzerhof, Kreuzberg, MEYER-NAKEL, STATE DOMAIN.

Amtliche Prüfungsnummer See Prüfungsnummer.

Anheuser, Paul Well-known NAHE grower (★★) at BAD KREUZNACH.

APNr Abbreviation of AMTLICHE PRUFUNGSNUMMER.

Assmannshausen Rhg r ★→★★★ 76 83 85 *87* 88 89 90 *91 92* 93 94 95 RHEINGAU village known for its usually pale, light reds, incl AUSLESEN. Top v'yd: Höllenberg. Grosslagen: Steil and Burgweg. Growers incl AUGUST KESSELER, Robert König, VON MUMM, and the STATE DOMAIN.

Auslese Specially selected wine with high natural sugar; the best affected by 'noble rot' (Edelfäule) and correspondingly unctuous in flavour.

Avelsbach M-S-R (Ruwer) w ★★★ 71 75 76 83 85 *87* 88 89 90 *91 92* 93 94 95 Village nr TRIER. At (rare) best, lovely delicate wines. Esp BISCHOFLICHE WEINGUTER, Staatliche Weinbaudomäne (see Staatsweingut). Grosslage: Römerlay.

Ayl M-S-R (Saar) w ★★★ 71 75 76 83 85 *87* 88 89 90 *91 92* 93 94 95 One of the best villages of the SAAR. First-class v'yd: Kupp. Grosslage: SCHARZBERG. Growers incl BISCHOFLICHE WEINGUTER, Lauer, DR WAGNER.

Bacchus Modern, perfumed, even kitsch, grape. Best for KABINETT wines.

Bacharach ★→★★★ District name for southern MITTELRHEIN v'yds down-stream from RHEINGAU. Now part of the new BEREICH 'LORELEY'. Racy RIESLINGS, some v fine. Growers include FRITZ BASTIAN, TONI JOST, Randolph Kauer, Helmut Mades, RATZENBERGER.

Bad Dürkheim Pfz w (r) ★★→★★★ 76 83 85 86 *87* 88 89 90 *91 92* 93 94 95 Main town of MITTELHAARDT, with the world's biggest barrel (it serves as a tavern) and an ancient September wine festival, the 'Wurstmarkt'. Top v'yds: Michelsberg, Spielberg. Grosslagen: Feuerberg, Hochmess, Schenkenböhl. Growers: Kurt Darting, FITZ-RITTER, Karst, Karl Schäfer.

Bad Kreuznach Nahe w ★★→★★★ 75 76 79 83 85 86 *87* 88 89 90 *91 92* 93 94 95 Agreeable spa town of many fine vineyards, First-class: Brückes, Kahlenberg and Krötenpfuhl. Grosslage: Kronenberg. Top growers include ANHEUSER, Finkenauer, PLETTENBERG.

Baden Huge SW area of scattered v'yds but rapidly growing reputation. Style is substantial, generally dry, relatively low in acid, good for meal-times. Fine Pinots, SPATBURGUNDER, RIES. Best areas: KAISERSTUHL, ORTENAU.

Badische Bergstrasse/Kraichgau (Bereich) Widespread district of N BADEN. WEISSBURGUNDER and RULANDER make best wines.

Badischer Winzerkeller Germany's (and Europe's) biggest coop, at BREISACH; 25,000 members with 12,000 acres, producing almost half of BADEN's wine: dependable unambitous.

A German wine selection for 1997

Twenty years ago most of Germany's finest wines were made by large estates, many in aristocratic ownership. Whilst some of them continue to make excellent wines – Bürklin-Wolf, Juliusspital and von Kesselstatt, for example, today many of Germany's top wines are made by small or medium-sized estates whose names were unknown a decade ago. Like the new generation of winemakers in Burgundy, these innovators have added new facets to the wines of regions with centuries of tradition. To taste these 'new' German wines look for the following producers' names:

Georg Breuer Rüdesheim, Rhg Unlike so many Rheingau wines, Breuer's elegant, full-bodied dry Rieslings live up to this region's legend.

H Dönnhoff Oberhausen, Na Helmut Dönnhoff's wines from the rocky First-class v'yds of mid-Nahe show how minerally top Riesling can be.

Gunderloch Nackenheim, Rhh Succulent Rieslings made by husband-and -wife team Fritz and Agnes Hasselbach have restored the reputation of the First-class Nackenheimer Rothenberg site to its former glory.

Reinhold Haart Piesport, M-S-R Theo Haart's rich classic Rieslings from the Great First-class Goldtröpfchen site prove that genuine Piesporter wine can be among the greatest in the entire Mosel.

Karl H Johner Bischoffingen, Bad After making wine in England for a decade, Karl Heinz Johner came home and revolutionized the wines of Baden with his new oak-aged dry whites and Spätburgunder reds.

Franz Künstler Hochheim, Rhg Rich firm subtle: Gunter Künstler's dry Rieslings show why Hochheim's wines were so beloved by the English a century ago.

Dr Loosen Bernkastel, M-S-R With his dazling wines from ancient vines Ernst Loosen has proven that low yields can result in more intense, complex wines in Germany just as elsewhere.

Müller-Catoir Neustadt, Pfz Explosively aromatic wines packed with flavour – Hans-Günther Schwarz shows that the Pfalz doesn't only excel with Riesling.

Badisches Frankenland See Tauberfranken.

Barriques Small new oak casks arrived tentatively in Germany 10 yrs ago. Results are mixed. The oak smell can add substance to the white Pinots, SPATBURGUNDER and LEMBERGER. It spoils RIESLING.

Bassermann-Jordan ★★★ 117-acre MITTELHAARDT family estate with many of the best v'yds in DEIDESHEIM, FORST, RUPPERTSBERG etc. 100% RIES. A glorious history, but currently plodding.

Bastian, Weingut Fritz ★★ 12 acre BACHARACH estate. Racy RIESLINGS with MOSEL-like delicacy, best from the First-class Posten v'yd.

Becker, J B ★★ → ★★★ Dedicated family estate and brokerage house at WALLUF. 30 acres in ELTVILLE, MARTINSTHAL, Walluf. Specialist in dry RIES.

Beerenauslese Lusciously sweet and honeyed wine from exceptionally ripe individual berries, their sugar and flavour usually concentrated by 'noble rot'. Rare and expensive.

Bensheim See Hessische Bergstrasse.

Bercher ★★★ KAISERSTUHL estate; 40 acres of white and red Pinots at Burkheim. Excellent dry whites and some of Germany's best reds.

Warning notice: Bereich

District within an Anbaugebiet (region). The word on a label should be treated as a flashing red light. Do not buy. See Introduction and under Bereich names, eg Bernkastel (Bereich).

Bernkastel M-M w ★→★★★★ 71 75 76 79 83 *84* 85 86 *87* **88** 89 90 *91* 92 93 *94* 95 Top wine town of the MITTELMOSEL; the epitome of RIES. Great First-class v'yd: Doctor, 8 acres (★★★★); First-class v'yds: Graben, Lay. Grosslagen: Badstube (★★★), Kurfürstlay (★). Top growers incl HERIBERT KERPEN, LAUERBURG, DR LOOSEN, DR PAULY-BERGWEILER, J J PRUM, Studert-Prüm, THANISCH, WEGELER-DEINHARD.

Bernkastel (Bereich) Wide area of deplorably dim quality but hopefully flowery character. Mostly MULLER-T. Includes all the MITTELMOSEL. Avoid.

Biffar, Josef ★★★ Rising star DEIDESHEIM estate. 40 acres (also WACHENHEIM) of RIES. Intense classic wines.

Bingen Rhh w ★→★★★ 76 83 85 *87* 88 89 90 *91* 92 93 94 95 Rhine/NAHE town; fine v'yds: First-class: Scharlachberg. Grosslage: St-Rochuskapelle.

Bingen (Bereich) District name for west RHEINHESSEN.

Bischöfliche Weingüter ★★★ Famous M-S-R estate at TRIER, a union of the cathedral properties with 2 other famous charities, the Bischöfliches Priesterseminar and the Bischöfliches Konvikt. 260 acres of top v'yds, esp in SAAR and RUWER. Signs of recovery to high quality after recent disappointments. Ruwer wines currently best (esp EITELSBACH, KASEL).

Blue Nun Famous but fading brand of LIEBFRAUMILCH from SICHEL.

Bocksbeutel Flask-shaped bottle used for FRANKEN wines.

Bodenheim Rhh w ★★ Village nr NIERSTEIN with full earthy wines, esp from First-class v'yds Hoch and Silberberg. Top grower: Kühling-Gillot.

Bodensee (Bereich) Idyllic district of S BADEN, on Lake Constance.

Braun, Weingut Heinrich ★★ 60-acre NIERSTEIN estate. Elegant dry and sweet RIES from First-class v'yds of Nierstein, esp Pettenthal.

Brauneberg M-M w ★★★★ 71 75 76 83 85 86 87 88 89 90 91 92 93 94 95 Top M-S-R village nr BERNKASTEL (750 acres), unbroken tradition for excellent full-flavoured RIES, 'Grand Cru' if anything on the Mosel is. Great First-class v'yd: Juffer-Sonnenuhr. First-class v'yd is Juffer. Grosslage: Kurfürstlay. Growers: Bastgen, FRITZ HAAG, WILLI HAAG, Paulinshof, M F RICHTER.

Breisach Bad Frontier town on Rhine nr KAISERSTUHL. Seat of the largest German coop, the BADISCHER WINZERKELLER.

Breisgau (Bereich) Little-known BADEN district. Good reds and pink WEISSHERBST.

Breuer, Weingut G ★★★ Family estate of 36 acres in RUDESHEIM, a CHARTA leader: 6 acres of Berg Schlossberg, also 12.5-acre monopole RAUENTHALER Nonnenberg. Superb quality in recent years, esp full-bodied elegant RIES, and new ideas, incl sparkling (87) Ries-Pinot Bl-Pinot Gr.

Buhl, Reichsrat von ★★★ Historic PFALZ family estate, returning to historic form as of '94. 160 acres (DEIDESHEIM, FORST, RUPPERTSBERG...). Leased by Japanese firm.

Bundesweinprämierung The German State Wine Award, organized by DLG (see below): gives great (Grosse), silver or bronze medallion labels.

Bürgerspital zum Heiligen Geist ★★★ Ancient charitable WURZBURG estate. 333 acres: W'bg, RANDERSACKER etc. Rich dry wines, esp SILVANER, RIES; can be vg.

Bürklin-Wolf, Dr ★★★→★★★★ Famous PFALZ family estate. 222 acres in FORST, DEIDESHEIM, RUPPERTSBERG and WACHENHEIM. Excellent 94s and 95s show the estate is back on top form.

Castell'sches, Fürstlich Domänenamt ★★→★★★★ Historic 142-acre princely estate in STEIGERWALD. SILVANER, RIESLANER, also SEKT. Noble dessert wines.

Chardonnay A small acreage of Chard has been experimentally, and sometimes illegally, planted – it is now legal in PFALZ and BADEN-WURTTEMBERG.

Charta Organization of top RHEINGAU estates making forceful dry RIES to far higher standards than dismally permissive laws require.

Christoffel, J J ★★ Tiny domain in ERDEN, URZIG. Polished RIES.

Clevner (or Klevner) Synonym in WURTTEMBERG for Blauer Frühburgunder red grape, supposedly a mutation of Pinot N or Italian Chiavenna (early-ripening black Pinot). Also ORTENAU (BADEN) synonym for TRAMINER.

Crusius ★★→★★★★ 30-acre family estate at TRAISEN, NAHE. Vivid RIES from Bastei, Rotenfels and SCHLOSSBOCKELHEIM. Top wines age v well. Also good SEKT and freshly fruity SPATBURGUNDER dry rosé.

Deidesheim Pfz w (r) ★★→★★★★ 71 76 83 85 86 87 88 89 90 91 92 93 94 95 Biggest top-quality village of PFALZ (1,000 acres). Richly-flavoured lively wines. Also Sekt. First-class v'yds: Grainhübel, Hohenmorgen, Kalkofen, Kieselberg, Langenmorgen, Leinhöhle. Grosslagen: Mariengarten (★★★), Hofstück (★★). Esp BASSERMANN-JORDAN, BIFFAR, V BUHL, BURKLIN-WOLF, DEINHARD, Kimmich.

Deinhard ★★→★★★★ Famous old Koblenz merchants and growers of high quality wines in RHEINGAU, MITTELMOSEL, RUWER and PFALZ (see Wegeler-Deinhard), also makers of vg SEKT (eg Lila). Leaders in new ideas. Their Heritage range is of single-village (DEIDESHEIM, HOCHHEIM, JOHANNISBERG etc) TROCKEN wines which are well-made but singularly austere.

Deinhard, Dr ★★ Fine 62-acre family estate: some of DEIDESHEIM's best v'yds.

Deutsche Weinstrasse Tourist road of S PFALZ: Bockenheim to SCHWEIGEN.

Deutscher Tafelwein Officially the term for v humble German wines. Now confusingly the flag of convenience for some costly novelties as well (eg BARRIQUE wines). As in Italy, the law will have to change.

Deutsches Weinsiegel A quality seal (ie neck label) for wines which have passed a statutory tasting test. Seals are: yellow for dry, green for medium-dry, red for medium-sweet. Means little; proves nothing.

Diel auf Burg Layen, Schlossgut ★★★ Fashionable 30-acre NAHE estate; known for ageing RULANDER and WEISSBURGUNDER in French BARRIQUES. Also fine traditional RIES. Impressive AUSLESE and EISWEIN.

DLG (Deutsche Landwirtschaftgesellschaft) The German Agricultural Society at Frankfurt. Awards national medals for quality – generously.

Dom German for 'cathedral'. Wines from the famous TRIER cathedral properties have 'Dom' before the v'yd name.

Domäne German for 'domain' or 'estate'. Sometimes used alone to mean the 'State domain' (STAATLICHE WEINBAUDOMANE).

Dönnhoff, Weingut Hermann ★★★ 23-acre NAHE estate with exceptionally fine RIES from NIEDERHAUSEN, Oberhausen etc.

Dornfelder New red grape making deep-coloured everyday wines in PFALZ.

Durbach Baden w (r) ★★→★★★★ 76 83 85 87 88 89 90 91 92 93 94 95 Village with 775 acres of BADEN's best v'yds. Top growers: A LAIBLE, H Männle, SCHLOSS STAUFENBERG, WOLFF-METTERNICH. Choose their KLINGELBERGERS (RIES) and CLEVNERS (TRAMINER). Grosslage: Fürsteneck.

Edel Means 'noble'. Edelfäule means 'noble rot': see page 100.

To decipher codes, please refer to 'Key to symbols' on front flap of jacket, or to 'How to use this book' on page 6.

Egon Müller zu Scharzhof ★★★★ Top SAAR estate of 32 acres at WILTINGEN. Its rich and racy SCHARZHOFBERGER RIES in AUSLESEN vintages is among the world's greatest wines. Best are given gold capsules. 89s, 90s and 93s are sublime, honeyed, immortal. Le Gallais is a second estate in WILTINGER Braune Kupp.

Eiswein V sweet wine made from frozen grapes with the ice (ie water content) discarded, thus v concentrated in flavour and sugar – of BEERENAUSLESE ripeness or more. Alcohol content can be as low as 5.5%. High acidity gives v long life. Rare and v expensive. S'times made as late as Jan/Feb of following year.

Eitelsbach Rhg (Ruwer) w ★★→★★★★ 71 75 76 83 85 87 88 89 90 *91* 92 93 94 95 RUWER village now part of TRIER, incl superb Great First-class KARTHAUSERHOFBERG estate. Grosslage: Römerlay.

Elbe The wine-river of eastern Germany. See Sachsen.

Elbling Traditional grape widely grown on upper MOSEL. Can be sharp and tasteless; but capable of real freshness and vitality in the best conditions (eg at Nittel or SCHLOSS THORN in the OBERMOSEL).

Eltville Rhg w ★★ →★★★ 71 75 76 83 85 86 87 88 89 90 *91* 92 93 94 95 Major wine town with cellars of RHEINGAU STATE DOMAIN, FISCHER and VON SIMMERN estates. First-class v'yd: Sonnenberg. Grosslage: Steinmächer.

Enkirch M-M w ★★ →★★★ 71 76 83 85 *87* 88 89 90 91 *93* 94 95 Minor MITTELMOSEL village, often overlooked but with lovely light tasty wine. Grosslage: Schwarzlay. Top v'yds: Batterieberg, Zeppwingert.

Erbach Rhg w ★★★→★★★★ 71 76 83 85 86 *87* 88 89 90 *91* 92 93 94 95 Top RHG area: powerful perfumed wines, incl superb First-class v'yds Hohenrain, MARCOBRUNN, Siegelsberg, Steinmorgen, Schlossberg. Major estates: SCHLOSS' REINHARTSHAUSEN, SCHONBORN. Also BECKER, KNYPHAUSEN, VON SIMMERN etc.

Erben Word meaning 'heirs', often used on old-established estate labels.

Erden M-M w ★★★ 71 75 76 83 *84* 85 86 *87* 88 89 90 *91* 92 93 94 95 Village between Urzig and Kröv: noble full-flavoured vigorous wine (different in style from nearby BERNKASTEL and WEHLEN but equally long-living). Great First-class v'yds: Prälat, Treppchen. Grosslage: Schwarzlay. Growers incl BISCHOFLICHE WEINGUTER, J J CHRISTOFFEL, Stefan Ehlen, DR LOOSEN, Meulenhoff, Nicolay.

Erstes Gewächs Literally 'first growth'. A new ('94) classification for the top vineyards of the RHEINGAU. Applies from '92 vintage, legal from '97.

Erzeugerabfüllung Bottled by producer. Being replaced by 'GUTSABFULLUNG'.

Escherndorf Frank w ★★→★★★ 76 83 *87* 88 *89* 90 *91* 92 93 94 95 Important wine town near WURZBURG. Similar tasty dry wine. Top v'yd: First-class Lump. Grosslage: Kirchberg. Growers incl JULIUSSPITAL, Egon Schäffer.

Eser, Weingut August ★★★ 20-acre RHEINGAU estate at OESTRICH. V'yds also in HALLGARTEN, RAUENTHAL (esp Gehrn, Rothenberg), WINKEL. Model wines.

Eser, Hans Hermann ★★★ JOHANNISBERG family estate. 45 acres. RIESLINGS that justify the great Johannisberg name.

Filzen M-S-R (Saar) w ★★→★★★ 76 83 85 *87* 88 89 90 *91* 92 93 94 95 Small SAAR village nr WILTINGEN. First-class v'yd: Pulchen. Grower to note: Piedmont.

Fischer, Weingut Dr ★★ 60-acre OCKFEN and WAWERN estate: variable quality wines (83 vg, 90 good).

Fischer Erben, Weingut ★★★ 18-acre RHEINGAU estate at ELTVILLE with highest traditional standards. Long-lived classic wines.

Fitz-Ritter ★★ Reliable BAD DURKHEIM estate. 54 acres, some fine RIES.

Forschungsanstalt See Hessische Forschungsanstalt.

Forst Pfz w ★★ →★★★★ 71 76 83 85 86 *87* 88 89 90 *91* 92 93 94 95 MITTELHAARDT village with 500 acres of Germany's best v'yds. Ripe, richly fragrant, full-bodied but subtle wines. First-class vineyards: Jesuitengarten, Kirchenstück, Pechstein, Ungeheuer. Grosslagen: Mariengarten, Schnepfenflug. Top growers incl BASSERMANN-JORDAN, DEINHARD, G MOSBACHER, Eugen Müller, Spindler, Werlé.

Franken Franconia Region of excellent distinctive dry wines, esp SILVANER, always bottled in round-bellied flasks (BOCKSBEUTEL). The centre is WURZBURG. Bereich names: MAINDREIECK, STEIGERWALD. Top producers: BURGERSPITAL, CASTELL, JULIUSSPITAL, WIRSCHING etc.

Freiburg Baden w (r) ★→★★ DYA Wine centre in BREISGAU, N of MARKGRAFLERLAND. Good GUTEDEL.

Germany's quality levels

The official range of qualities in ascending order are as follows:

1 Deutscher Tafelwein: sweetish light wine of no special character. (Unofficially, can be very special.)

2 Landwein: dryish Tafelwein with some regional style.

3 Qualitätswein: dry or sweetish wine with sugar added before fermentation to increase its strength, but tested for quality and with distinct local and grape character.

4 Kabinettwein: dry or dryish natural (unsugared) wine of distinct personality and distinguishing lightness. Can be very fine.

5 Spätlese: stronger, often sweeter than Kabinett. Full-bodied. The trend today is towards drier or even completely dry Spätlese.

6 Auslese: sweeter, sometimes stronger than Spätlese, often with honey-like flavours, intense and long. Can also be dry (and strong).

7 Beerenauslese: v sweet and usually strong, intense; can be superb.

8 Eiswein: (Beeren- or Trockenbeerenauslese) concentrated, sharpish and very sweet. Can be v fine.

9 Trockenbeerenauslese: intensely sweet and aromatic; alcohol slight. Extraordinary and everlasting.

Freinsheim Pfz w r ★★ Well-known village of MITTELHAARDT with high proportion of RIES. Aromatic spicy wines. Star grower: LINGENFELDER.

Friedrich Wilhelm Gymnasium ★★★ Important 111-acre charitable estate based in TRIER with v'yds in BERNKASTEL, GRAACH, OCKFEN, TRITTENHEIM, ZELTINGEN etc, all M-S-R. 90 91 92 93 should have been better.

Fuhrmann See Pfeffingen.

Gallais Le See Egon Müller.

Geheimrat 'J' Brand-name of good very dry RIES SPATLESE from WEGELER-DEINHARD, OESTRICH, since '83. Epitomizes new RHEINGAU thinking.

Geisenheim Rhg w ★★→★★★ 71 76 83 85 86 87 88 89 90 91 92 93 94 95 Village famous for Germany's best-known wine school and fine aromatic wines. First-class v'yds are Kläuserweg, Rothenberg. Grosslagen: Burgweg, Erntebringer. Many top growers (eg SCHLOSS SCHONBORN) have v'yds here.

Gemeinde A commune or parish.

Gewürztraminer (or Traminer) 'Spicy' grape, speciality of Alsace, used a little in Germany, esp in PFALZ, BADEN and WURTTEMBERG.

Gimmeldingen Pfz w ★★ 83 85 87 88 89 90 91 92 93 94 95 Village just S of MITTELHAARDT. At their best, similar wines. Grosslage: Meerspinne. Growers incl: Christmann, MULLER-CATOIR.

Graach M-M w ★★→★★★ 71 75 76 83 84 85 86 87 88 89 90 91 92 93 94 95 Small village between BERNKASTEL and WEHLEN. First-class v'yds: Domprobst, Himmelreich, Josephshöfer. Grosslage: Münzlay. Many top growers, eg: KESSELSTATT, DR LOOSEN, J J PRUM, WILLI SCHAEFER, SELBACH-OSTER, WEINS-PRUM.

Remember that vintage information for German wines is given in a different form from the ready/not ready distinction applying to other countries. Read the explanation at the top of page 136.

Grans-Fassian ★★ Fine 25-acre MOSEL estate at Leiwen. V'yds there and in PIESPORT and TRITTENHEIM.

Grauburgunder Synonym of RULANDER or Pinot Gris.

Grosser Ring Group of top (VDP) MOSEL-SAAR-RUWER estates, whose annual September auction regularly sets price records.

Grosslage See Introduction, pages 133–134.

Gunderloch ★★★ Excellent 30-acre NACKENHEIM estate, one of the best in RHEINHESSEN today. 80% RIES. Best from N Rothenberg, but all are vg.

Guntersblum Rhh w ★→★★ 76 83 85 88 89 90 91 92 93 94 95 Big wine town S of OPPENHEIM. First-class v'yds: Bornpfad, Himmeltal. Grosslagen: Krötenbrunnen, Vogelsgarten. Top grower: RAPPENHOF.

Guntrum, Louis ★★ Fine 164-acre family estate and reliable merchant house in NIERSTEIN, OPPENHEIM etc. Good SILVANERS and GEWURZTRAMINER as well as RIESLING.

Gutedel German word for the Chasselas grape, used in S BADEN.

Gutsabfüllung Estate-bottled. A new term limited to qualified estates.

Gutsverwaltung Estate administration.

Haag, Weingut Fritz ★★★★ 12-acre top estate in BRAUNEBERG run by Wilhelm Haag, president of GROSSER RING. MOSEL RIES of crystalline purity and racy brilliance for long ageing. Growing reputation.

Haag, Weingut Willi ★★ Tiny 7-acre BRAUNEBERG estate. Full 'old-style' RIES. Some fine AUSLESE.

Haart, Reinhold ★★★ Small estate, the best in PIESPORT, and growing in repute. Refined aromatic wines, capable of long ageing.

Halbtrocken Medium-dry (literally 'semi-dry'). Containing less than 18 but more than 9 grams per litre unfermented sugar. An increasingly popular category of wine intended for mealtimes, usually better balanced than TROCKEN.

Hallgarten Rhg w ★★→★★★★ 71 76 83 85 86 87 88 89 90 91 92 93 94 95 Small wine town behind HATTENHEIM. Robust full-bodied wines, mysteriously seldom seen. Dominated by coops (unusual for the RHEINGAU). Weingut Fred Prinz is top estate.

Hattenheim Rhg w ★★→★★★★ 71 75 76 83 85 87 88 89 90 91 92 93 94 95 Superlative 500-acre wine town. First-class v'yds are Engelmannsberg, Mannberg, Pfaffenberg, Nussbrunnen, Wisselbrunnen and most famously STEINBERG (ORTSTEIL). Grosslage: Deutelsberg. MARCOBRUNN lies on ERBACH boundary. Many fine estates incl KNYPHAUSEN, RESS, SCHLOSS SCHONBORN, VON SIMMERN, STATE DOMAIN etc.

Heger, Dr ★★★ Some of BADEN's best SPATBURGUNDER reds come from old vines on this 28-acre ACHKARREN estate. Also fine GRAUBURGUNDER. Getting better and better.

Heilbronn Würt w r ★→★★ 85 87 88 89 90 91 92 93 94 95 Wine town with many small growers and a good coop. Best wines are RIES and LEMBERGERS. Seat of DLG competition. Top growers: Amalienhof, Drautz-Able, Heinrich.

Hessen, Prinz von ★★ Famous 75-acre estate in JOHANNISBERG, KIEDRICH and WINKEL. Despite gold medals, recent wines uneven.

Hessische Bergstrasse w ★★→★★★ 76 83 85 87 88 89 90 91 92 93 94 95 Smallest wine region in western Germany (1,000 acres), N of Heidelberg. Pleasant RIES from STATE DOMAIN v'yds at Bensheim, Bergstrasser Coop, Heppenheim and Stadt Bensheim.

Hessische Forschungsanstalt für Wein-Obst-& Gartenbau Famous wine school and research establishment at GEISENHEIM, RHEINGAU. Good wines incl reds. The name on the label is Forschungsanstalt.

Heyl zu Herrnsheim ★★★ Leading 72-acre NIERSTEIN estate, 60% RIES. An excellent record, recently patchy. Now part-owned by VALCKENBERG.

Hochgewächs A superior level of QBA RIES, esp in MOSEL-SAAR-RUWER.

Hochheim Rhg w ★★ →★★★★ 71 75 76 79 83 *84* 85 86 *87* 88 89 90 91 92 93 94 95 600-acre wine town 15 miles E of main RHEINGAU area, once thought of as best on Rhine. Similar fine wines with an earthy intensity and fragrance of their own. First-class v'yds: Domdechaney, Hölle, Kirchenstück, Königin Viktoria Berg (12-acre monopoly of Hupfeld of OESTRICH, sold only by DEINHARD). Grosslage: Daubhaus. Growers incl ASCHROTT, Hupfeld, FRANZ KUNSTLER, RESS, SCHLOSS SCHONBORN, STAATSWEINGUT, WERNER.

Hock Traditional English term for Rhine wine, derived from HOCHHEIM.

Hoensbroech, Weingut Reichsgraf zu ★★★ Top KRAICHGAU estate. 37 acres. Excellent dry WEISSBURGUNDER, GRAUBURGUNDER and SILVANER wines, eg Michelfelder Himmelberg. Some of BADEN's best wines.

Hohenlohe-Oehringen, Weingut Fürst zu ★★ Noble 47-acre estate in Oehringen and WURTTEMBERG. Substantial dry RIES and powerful reds from SPATBURGUNDER and LEMBERGER grapes.

Hövel, Weingut von ★★★ Very fine SAAR estate at OBERMOSEL (Hütte is 12-acre monopoly) and in SCHARZHOFBERG. Superb wines since '93.

Huxelrebe Modern aromatic grape variety, mainly for dessert wines.

Ihringen Bad r w ★ →★★★ 83 85 86 87 88 89 90 91 92 93 94 95 One of the best villages of the KAISERSTUHL, BADEN. Proud of its SPATBURGUNDER red, WEISSHERBST and GRAUBURGUNDER. Top growers: DR HEGER, Stigler.

Ilbesheim Pfz w ★ →★★ 88 89 90 91 92 93 94 95 Base of vast growers' coop of SUDLICHE WEINSTRASSE 'Deutsches Weintor'. See also Schweigen.

Ingelheim Rhh r w ★★ 88 89 90 91 92 93 94 95 Town opposite RHEINGAU historically known for its SPATBURGUNDER. First-class v'yds are Horn, Pares, Sonnenberg and Steinacker.

Iphofen Frank w ★★ →★★★ 76 79 83 85 *87* 88 *89* 90 *91* 92 93 94 95 Village nr WURZBURG. Superb First-class v'yds: Julius-Echter-Berg, Kalb. Grosslage: Burgweg. Growers: JULIUSSPITAL, Ruck, WIRSCHING.

Jahrgang Year – as in 'vintage'.

Johannisberg Rhg w ★★ →★★★★ 71 75 76 83 85 86 *87* 88 89 90 91 92 93 94 95 260-acre village with superlative subtle RIES. Top v'yds incl Goldatzel, Klaus. First-class: Hölle, SCHLOSS JOHANNISBERG. Grosslage: Erntebringer. Many good growers. Beware 'Bereich Johannisberg' wines (next entry).

Johannisberg (Bereich) District name for the entire RHEINGAU. Avoid.

Johner, Karl-Heinz ★★★ Tiny BADEN estate at Bischoffingen, in the front line for new-look SPATBURGUNDER and oak-aged WEISSBURGUNDER.

Josephshöfer Fine v'yd at GRAACH, the sole property of VON KESSELSTATT.

Jost, Toni ★★ →★★★ Perhaps the top estate of the MITTELRHEIN. 25 acres, mainly RIES, IN BACHARACH and also in the RHEINGAU.

Juliusspital ★★★ →★★★★ Ancient WURZBURG religious charity with 374 acres of top FRANKEN v'yds and many top wines. Look for its SILVANERS and RIES.

Kabinett The term for the lightest category of natural, unsugared (QMP) wines. Low in alcohol (RIES averages 7–9%) but capable of sublime finesse. Drink young or with several yrs age.

Kaiserstuhl (Bereich) One of the top BADEN districts, with notably warm climate and volcanic soil. Villages incl ACHKARREN, IHRINGEN. Grosslage: Vulkanfelsen.

Kallstadt Pfz w (r) ★★ →★★★ 76 83 85 86 87 88 89 90 91 92 93 94 95 Village of N MITTELHAARDT. Its fine rich wines are often underrated. First-class v'yd: Saumagen. Grosslagen: Feuerberg, Kobnert. Growers include Henninger, KOEHLER-RUPRECHT, Schüster.

Kammerpreismünze See Landespreismünze.

Kanzem M-S-R (Saar) w ★★★ 71 75 76 83 85 *87* 88 89 90 91 92 93 94 95 Small neighbour of WILTINGEN. First-class v'yd: Altenberg. Grosslage: SCHARZBERG. Growers incl Othegraven, Reverchon. Best is J P Reinert.

Karthäuserhofberg ★★★★ Top RUWER estate of 46 acres at Eitelsbach. Easily recognized by bottles with only a neck-label. Recently back on top form.

Kasel M-S-R (Ruwer) w ★★→★★★ 71 75 76 83 85 86 *87* 88 89 90 91 92 93 94 95 Stunning flowery light Römerlay wines. First-class v'yds: Kehrnagel, Nies'chen. Top growers: KARLSMUHLE, VON KESSELSTATT, WEGELER-DEINHARD.

Keller Wine cellar.

Kellerei Winery.

Kerner Modern aromatic grape variety, earlier-ripening than RIES, of fair quality but without Riesling's inbuilt harmony.

Kerpen, Weingut Heribert ★★ Tiny estate in BERNKASTEL, GRAACH, WEHLEN.

Kesseler, Weingut August ★★ 35-acre estate making the best SPATBURGUNDER reds in ASSMANNSHAUSEN. Also good off-dry RIES.

Kesselstatt, von ★★★ The biggest private MOSEL estate, 600 yrs old. Some 150 acres in GRAACH, KASEL, PIESPORT, WILTINGEN etc, plus substantial rented or managed estates, producing aromatic, generously fruity MOSELS. Now belongs to Günther Reh (of Leiwen). Excellent wines made esp since '88.

Kesten M-M w ★→★★★ 71 75 76 83 85 86 87 88 89 90 91 *92* 93 94 95 Neighbour of BRAUNEBERG. Best wines (from Paulinshofberg v'yd) similar. Grosslage: Kurfürstlay. Top growers: BASTGEN, Paulinshof.

Kiedrich Rhg w ★★→★★★★ 71 76 83 85 86 87 88 89 90 91 92 93 94 95 Neighbour of RAUENTHAL; almost as splendid and high-flavoured. First-class v'yds: Gräfenberg, Wasseros. Grosslage: Heiligenstock. Growers incl FISCHER, KNYPHAUSEN, STATE DOMAIN. R WEIL now top estate.

Klingelberger ORTENAU (BADEN) term for RIESLING, esp at DURBACH.

Kloster Eberbach Glorious 12th-C Cistercian Abbey in HATTENHEIM forest. Monks planted STEINBERG. Now STATE DOMAIN-owned; HQ of German Wine Academy.

Klüsserath M-M w ★★→★★★ 76 83 85 88 89 90 *91* 92 93 94 95 Minor MOSEL village, good years are well worth trying. Best vineyard: Bruderschaft. Grosslage: St-Michael. Top growers are FRIEDRICH WILHELM GYMNASIUM and KIRSTEN.

Knyphausen, Weingut Freiherr zu ★★★ Noble 50-acre estate on former Cistercian land (see Kloster Eberbach) in ELTVILLE, ERBACH, HATTENHEIM, KIEDRICH and MARCOBRUNN. Top RHEINGAU wines, many dry.

Koehler-Ruprecht ★★★→★★★★ Highly-rated little (22-acre) estate going from strength to strength; top grower in KALLSTADT. Ultra-traditional winemaking; v long-lived dry RIESLING from K Saumagen is memorable. Now for outstanding burgundy-style Pinot N.

Kohl, Helmut Also a small producer of gd dry SEKT at Bauenheim, PFALZ.

Königin Viktoria Berg See Hochheim.

Kraichgau Small BADEN region S of Heidelberg. Top grower: HOENSBROECH.

Kreuznach District name for the entire northern NAHE, now united with SCHLOSSBOCKELHEIM to form BEREICH 'NAHETAL'. See also Bad Kreuznach.

Kröv M-M w ★→★★★ 88 89 90 91 92 93 94 95 Popular tourist resort famous for its Grosslage name: Nacktarsch, or 'bare bottom'. Be very careful.

Künstler, Franz ★★★→★★★★ Outstanding 12.5-acre HOCHHEIM estate, getting ever-better, esp for H Hölle and H Kirchenstück, model CHARTA wines and superb AUSLESEN. Rhg's No 2 after WEIL.

Laible, Weingut Andreas ★★ 10-acre DURBACH estate. Fine sweet and dry RIES, SCHEUREBE and GEWURZ from First-class Plauelrain v'yd.

Landespreismünze Prizes for quality at state, rather than national, level.

Landwein A category of better quality TAFELWEIN (the grapes must be slightly riper) from 20 designated regions. It must be TROCKEN or HALBTROCKEN. Similar in intention to France's vin de pays but without the buzz.

Lauerburg ★★★ One of the 4 owners of the famous Doctor v'yd, with 10 acres, all in BERNKASTEL. Often excellent racy wines.

Leitz, J ★★ Fine little RUDESHEIM family estate for elegant dry RIES. A rising star.

Lemberger Red grape variety imported from Austria – where it is known as Blaufränkisch. Deep-coloured, tannic wines; can be excellent. Or rosé.

Liebfrauenstift 26-acre v'yd in city of Worms; origin of 'LIEBFRAUMILCH'.

> ### Liebfraumilch
>
> Much abused name, accounting for 50% of all German wine exports – to the detriment of Germany's better products. Legally defined as a QBA 'of pleasant character' from RHEINHESSEN, PFALZ, NAHE or RHEINGAU, of a blend with at least 51% RIESLING, SILVANER, KERNER or MULLER-T. Most is mild, semi-sweet wine from Rheinhessen and Pfalz. Rules now say it must have more than 18 grams per litre unfermented sugar. S'times v cheap and of inferior quality, depending on brand or shipper. Its definition makes a mockery of the legal term 'Quality Wine'.

Lieser M-M w ★★ 71 76 83 85 86 87 88 89 90 91 92 93 94 95 Little-known neighbour of BERNKASTEL. Lighter wines. First-class v'yd: Niederberg-Helden. Grosslage: Kurfürstlay. Good grower: Schloss Liesen.

Lingenfelder, Weingut ★★★ Small, innovative Grosslkarlbach (PFALZ) estate: excellent dry and sweet SCHEUREBE, full-bodied RIES etc.

Loosen, Weingut Dr ★★★★ Dynamic 24-acre St-Johannishof estate in BERNKASTEL, ERDEN, GRAACH, URZIG, WEHLEN. Deep intense RIESLINGS from old vines in Great First-class v'yds. Superlative quality since '90.

Lorch Rhg w (r) ★→★★ 71 76 83 85 87 88 89 90 91 92 93 94 95 At extreme W of the RHEINGAU. Some fine light MITTELRHEIN-like RIESLING. Best grower: von Kanitz.

Loreley (Bereich) New BEREICH name for RHEINBURGENGAU and BACHARACH.

Löwenstein, Fürst ★★ 66-acre FRANKEN estate: classic dry powerful wines. 45-acre HALLGARTEN property is rented by MATUSCHKA-GREIFFENCLAU. V mixed quality since '91.

Maindreieck (Bereich) District name for central FRANKEN, incl WURZBURG.

Marcobrunn Historic RHEINGAU v'yd; one of Germany's v best. See Erbach.

Markgräflerland (Bereich) District S of FREIBURG, BADEN. Typical GUTEDEL wine can be delicious refreshment when drunk v young, but best wines are the -BURGUNDERS: WEISS-, GRAU- and SPATBURGUNDER. Also Sekt.

Martinsthal Rhg w ★★→★★★ 71 75 76 83 85 86 87 88 89 90 91 92 93 94 95 Little-known neighbour of RAUENTHAL. First-class v'yd: Langenberg; also gd: Wildsau. Grosslage: Steinmächer. Growers incl BECKER, Diefenhardt.

Matuschka-Greiffenclau, Graf Erwein Owner of ancient SCHLOSS VOLLRADS and tenant of WEINGUT FURST LOWENSTEIN at HALLGARTEN. A principal spokesman for German wine, esp dry, and its combination with food.

Maximin Grünhaus M-S-R (Ruwer) w ★★★★ 71 75 76 79 83 85 86 87 88 89 90 91 92 93 94 95 Supreme RUWER estate of 80 acres at MERTESDORF. Wines of firm elegance and great subtlety to mature 20 yrs+.

Mertesdorf See Maximin Grünhaus and Karlsmühle.

Meyer-Näkel, Weingut ★★ 15-acre AHR esate. Fine SPATBURGUNDERS in Dernau and Bad Neuenahr exemplify modern oak-aged German reds.

Mittelhaardt The north-central and best part of PFALZ, incl DEIDESHEIM, FORST, RUPPERTSBERG, WACHENHEIM, largely planted with RIESLING.

Mittelhaardt-Deutsche Weinstrasse (Bereich) District name for the northern and central parts of PFALZ.

Mittelheim Rhg w ★★ 76 83 85 86 87 88 89 90 91 92 93 94 95 Relatively minor village between the peaks of WINKEL and OESTRICH.

Mittelmosel The central and best part of the MOSEL, incl BERNKASTEL, PIESPORT, WEHLEN etc. Its top sites are (or should be) entirely RIESLING.

GERMANY

Mittelrhein Northern Rhine area of domestic importance (and great beauty), incl BACHARACH and Boppard. Some attractive steely RIESLING.

Morio-Muskat Stridently aromatic grape variety now on the decline.

Mosbacher, Weingut ★★★ Georg 23-acre estate for some of best dry and sweet RIES of FORST. Three stars on label indicate superior 'Reserve' bottlings.

Mosel The TAFELWEIN name of the area. All quality wines from the Mosel must be labelled MOSEL-SAAR-RUWER. (Moselle is the French – and English – spelling for this beautiful river.)

Mosel-Saar-Ruwer (M-S-R) 31,000-acre QUALITATSWEIN region between TRIER and Koblenz. Incl MITTELMOSEL, RUWER and SAAR. The natural home of RIESLING.

Moselland, Winzergenossenschaft Biggest M-S-R coop, at BERNKASTEL, incl Saar-Winzerverein at WILTINGEN. Its 5,200 members produce 25% of M-S-R wines (incl classic method SEKT), but little above average.

Müller zu Scharzhof, Egon See Egon Müller.

Müller-Catoir, Weingut ★★★★ Outstanding 40-acre NEUSTADT estate. Very aromatic powerful wines from RIESLING, SCHEUREBE, RIESLANER, GRAUBURGUNDER and MUSKATELLER grapes. Consistent quality and good value; dry/sweet always equally impressive.

Müller-Thurgau Fruity early-ripening, usually low-acid grape; commonest in PFALZ, RHEINHESSEN, NAHE, BADEN and FRANKEN; increasingly planted in all areas, incl MOSEL. Should be banned from all top v'yds by law.

Mumm, von ★★ 173-acre estate in JOHANNISBERG, RUDESHEIM etc. Under the same control as SCHLOSS JOHANNISBERG, but v variable quality.

Munchausen Rhh r w ★ Unlikely v'yd situation. Einzellagen: Märchen, Lüge. Insubstantial wines.

Münster Nahe w ★→★★★ 71 75 76 83 85 86 87 88 **89 90** 91 92 **93** 94 **95** Best village of N NAHE, with fine delicate wines. First-class v'yds: Dautenpflänzer, Kapellenberg, Pittersberg. Grosslage: Schlosskapelle. Top growers: Kruger-Rumpf, STATE DOMAIN.

Muskateller Ancient aromatic white grape with crisp acidity. A rarity in PFALZ, BADEN AND WURTTEMBERG, where it is mostly made dry.

Nackenheim Rhh w ★→★★★★ 76 83 85 86 87 88 **89 90** 91 **92 93** 94 95 Neighbour of NIERSTEIN; both have top Rhine terroir. Best wines (especially First-class Rothenberg v'yd) similar. Grosslagen: Spiegelberg (★★), Gutes Domtal (★). Best grower: GUNDERLOCH.

Nahe Tributary of the Rhine and high quality wine region. Balanced, fresh, clean but full-bodied, even minerally wines; RIES best. BEREICH: NAHETAL.

Nahetal (Bereich) BEREICH name for amalgamated KREUZNACH and SCHLOSS-BOCKELHEIM districts.

Neckerauer, Weingut Klaus ★★ Interesting, out-of-the-way 40-acre estate at Weissenheim-am-Sand, on sandy N PFALZ soil. Impressive, unpredictable.

Neef M-S-R w ★→★★ 71 76 83 85 87 88 **89 90** 91 92 **93** 94 **95** Village of lower MOSEL with one fine v'yd: Frauenberg.

Neipperg, Graf von ★★★ Noble 70-acre estate in Schwaigern, WURTTEMBERG: elegant dry RIES and TRAMINER, and trad style reds, esp from LEMBERGER.

Neumagen-Dhron M-M w ★★ Neighbour of PIESPORT: fine but sadly neglected.

Neustadt Central town of PFALZ with a famous wine school.

Niederhausen Nahe w ★★→★★★★ 71 75 76 83 85 86 *87* 88 **89 90** 91 **93** 94 95 Neighbour of SCHLOSS BOCKELHEIM and NAHE STATE DOMAIN HQ. Graceful powerful wines. First-class v'yds incl Felsensteyer, Hermannsberg, Hermannshöhle. Grosslage: Burgweg. Esp from CRUSIUS, DONNHOFF, Hehner-Kilz, STATE DOMAIN.

To decipher codes, please refer to 'Key to symbols' on front flap of jacket, or to 'How to use this book' on page 6.

Nierstein Rhh w ★→★★★★ 71 75 76 83 85 86 *87* 88 89 90 91 92 93 94 95
Famous but treacherous name. 1,300 acres incl superb First-class v'yds: Brudersberg, Glöck, Heiligenbaum, Hipping, Oelberg, Orbel, Pettenthal. Grosslagen: Auflangen, Rehbach, Spiegelberg. Ripe aromatic wines with great 'elegance'. But beware Grosslage Gutes Domtal: a supermarket deception. Growers to choose include H BRAUN, GUNDERLOCH, GUNTRUM, HEYL ZU HERRNSHEIM, ST-ANTONY, G A Schneider, Seebrich, Strub, Wehrheim.

Nierstein (Bereich) Large E RHEINHESSEN district of ordinary quality.

How strong is it?
The alcohol content of wine varies from as little as 7% by volume to as much as 16%, depending on the sugar content of the grapes (and the possible addition of sugar, or 'chaptalisation', before they are fermented).

Low strength does not mean low quality; nor vice versa. The finest Mosel Rieslings can balance alcoholic lightness with brilliant fruit-acid intensity. On the other hand a basic over-produced red at 10 or 11% will taste feeble.

Most top-quality wines, red or white, made in the French style contain between 11.5 and 13%. Above this figure the risk is an over-'heady' smell, unless it is balanced by great intensity of flavour or sweetness. Fortified wines vary from 15 to 18% (fino sherry) to about 22% (vintage ports).

Nierstein Winzergenossenschaft The leading NIERSTEIN coop, with far above average standards. (Formerly 'Rheinfront'.)

Nobling New white grape: light fresh wine in BADEN, esp MARKGRAFLERLAND.

Norheim Nahe w ★→★★★ 71 76 79 83 85 86 87 88 89 90 91 92 93 94 95
Neighbour of NIEDERHAUSEN. First-class v'yds: Dellchen, Kafels, Kirschheck; Klosterberg comes next. Grosslage: Burgweg. Growers: DONNHOFF, CRUSIUS.

Oberemmel M-S-R (Saar) w ★★→★★★ 71 75 76 83 85 86 *87* 88 89 90 *91* 92 93 94 95 Next village to WILTINGEN. V fine wines from First-class v'yd Hütte etc. Grosslage: SCHARZBERG. Esp VON HOVEL, VON KESSELSTADT.

Obermosel (Bereich) District name for the upper MOSEL above TRIER. Generally uninspiring wines from the ELBLING grape, unless v young.

Ockfen M-S-R (Saar) w ★★→★★★ 71 75 76 83 85 86 *87* 88 89 90 *91* 92 93 94 95 Superb fragrant austere wines. First-class v'yd: Bockstein. Grosslage: SCHARZBERG. Growers: DR FISCHER, Jordan & Jordan, WAGNER, ZILLIKEN.

Oechsle Scale for sugar content of grape juice (see page 272).

Oestrich Rhg w ★★→★★★ 71 75 76 83 85 86 *87* 88 89 90 *91* 92 93 94 95 Big village; variable but capable of splendid RIES AUSLESE. 1st-class v'yds: Doosberg, Lenchen. Grosslage: Gottesthal. Top growers: AUGUST ESER, WEGELER-DEINHARD.

Offene weine Wine by the glass: the way to order it in wine villages.

Oppenheim Rhh w ★→★★★ 76 83 85 86 *87* 88 89 90 *91* 92 93 94 95 Town S of NIERSTEIN; spectacular 13th-C church. First-class Herrenberg and Sackträger v'yds make top wines. Grosslagen: Guldenmorgen (★★★), Krötenbrunnen (★). Growers incl GUNTRUM, C Koch, Kühling-Gillot. Not at full potential.

Ortenau (Bereich) District just S of Baden-Baden. Good KLINGELBERGER (RIES), SPATBURGUNDER and RULANDER. Top village: DURBACH.

Ortsteil Independent part of a community allowed to use its estate v'yd name without the village name, eg SCHLOSS JOHANNISBERG, STEINBERG.

Palatinate English for PFALZ.

Pauly-Bergweiler, Dr ★★★ Fine 27-acre BERNKASTEL estate. V'yds there and in WEHLEN etc. 'Peter Nicolay' wines from URZIG and ERDEN are best.

Perlwein Semi-sparkling wine.

Pfalz 56,000-acre v'yd region S of RHEINHESSEN (see Mittelhaardt and Südliche Weinstrasse). Warm climate: grapes ripen fully. The classics are rich wines, with TROCKEN and HALBTROCKEN increasingly fashionable and well made. Biggest RIES area after M-S-R. Formerly known as 'Rheinpfalz'.

Pfeffingen, Weingut ★★★ Messrs Fuhrmann and Eymael make very good RIES and SCHEUREBE on 26 acres of UNGSTEIN.

Piesport M-M w ★→★★★★ 71 75 76 83 85 86 87 88 89 90 91 92 93 94 95 Tiny village with famous vine amphitheatre, at best glorious gentle fruity RIES. Great First-class v'yds: Goldtröpfchen and Domherr. Treppchen far inferior. Grosslage: Michelsberg (mainly MULLER-T; avoid). Esp R HAART, Kurt Hain, KESSELSTATT, Reuscher-Haart, Weller-Lehnert.

Plettenberg, von ★★→★★★ 100-acre estate at BAD KREUZNACH. Mixed quality.

Portugieser Second-rate red-wine grape now often used for WEISSHERBST.

Prädikat Special attributes or qualities. See QmP.

Prüfungsnummer The official identifying test-number of a quality wine.

Prüm, J J ★★★★ Superlative and legendary 34-acre MOSEL estate in BERNKASTEL, GRAACH, WEHLEN, ZELTINGEN. Delicate but long-lived wines, esp in WEHLENER SONNENUHR: 81 KABINETT is *still* young.

Qualitätswein bestimmter Anbaugebiete (QbA) The middle quality of German wine, with sugar added before fermentation (as in French 'chaptalisation'), but controlled as to areas, grapes, etc.

Qualitätswein mit Prädikat (QmP) Top category, for all wines ripe enough to be unsugared (KABINETT to TROCKENBEERENAUSLESE). See pages 133 and 141.

Randersacker Frank w ★★→★★★ 76 83 86 87 88 89 90 91 92 93 94 95 Leading village for distinctive dry wine. First-class v'yds: Marsberg, Pfülben. Grosslage: Ewig Leben. Growers incl BURGERSPITAL, Martin Göbel, STAATLICHER HOFKELLER, JULIUSSPITAL, Robert Schmitt, Schmitt's Kinder.

Ratzenberger, Jochen ★★ 17-acre estate making racy dry and off-dry RIES in BACHARACH; best from First-class Posten and Steeger St-Jost v'yds.

Rauenthal Rhg w ★★★→★★★★ 71 75 76 83 85 86 87 88 89 90 91 92 93 94 95 Supreme village: spicy complex wine. First-class vineyards: Baiken, Gehrn, Nonnenberg, Rothenberg, Wülfen. Grosslage: Steinmächer. Growers: BREUER, ESER, S REINHARTSHAUSEN, S SCHONBORN, VON SIMMERN, STATE DOMAIN.

Rebholz ★★★ Top SUDLICHE WEINSTRASSE grower. Many varieties on 25 acres.

Ress, Balthasar ★★→★★★ R'GAU estate (74 good acres), cellars in HATTENHEIM. Also runs SCHLOSS REICHARTSHAUSEN. Variable wines; original artists' labels.

Restsüsse Unfermented grape sugar remaining in (or more often added to) wine to give it sweetness. TROCKEN wines have v little, if any.

Rheinburgengau (Bereich) District name for MITTELRHEIN v'yds around the Rhine gorge. Wines with 'steely' acidity needing time to mature.

Rheinfront, Winzergenossenschaft See Nierstein Winzergenossenschaft.

Rheingau Best v'yd region of Rhine, W of Wiesbaden. 7,000 acres. Classic substantial but subtle RIES. BEREICH name for whole region: JOHANNISBERG.

Rheinhessen Vast region (61,000 acres of v'yds) between Mainz and Worms, bordered by the river NAHE, mostly second-rate, but incl top RIESLING wines from NACKENHEIM, NIERSTEIN, OPPENHEIM etc.

Rheinhessen Silvaner (RS) New uniform label for dry wines from SILVANER — designed to give a modern quality image to the region.

Rheinpfalz See Pfalz.

Rhodt SUDLICHE WEINSTRASSE village: esp Rietburg coop; agreeable fruity wines.

Richter, Weingut Max Ferd ★★★ Top 37-acre MITTELMOSEL family estate, based at Mülheim. Fine barrel-aged RIES from: BRAUNEBERG (Juffer-Sonnenuhr), GRAACH, Mülheim (Helenenkloster), WEHLEN (usually models).

Rieslaner Cross between SILVANER and RIES; has made fine AUSLESEN in FRANKEN, where most is grown. Also fine from MULLER-CATOIR.

Riesling The best German grape: fine, fragrant, fruity, long-lived. Only CHARDONNAY can compete as the world's best white grape.

Rosewein Rosé wine made of red grapes fermented without their skins.

Rotwein Red wine.

Rüdesheim Rhg w ★★→★★★★ 71 75 76 79 *81* 82 83 84 85 86 87 88 **89** 90 91 92 93 94 95 Rhine resort with excellent vineyards; the three best called Rüdesheimer Berg–. Full-bodied wines, fine-flavoured, often remarkable in 'off' years. Grosslage: Burgweg. Most top RHEINGAU estates own some Rüdesheim v'yds. Best growers: G BREUER, J LEITZ, Dr Nägler, SCHLOSS SCHONBORN.

Rüdesheimer Rosengarten RUDESHEIM is also the name of a NAHE village near BAD KREUZNACH. Do not be misled by the ubiquitous blend going by this name. It has nothing to do with RHEINGAU Rüdesheim. Avoid.

Ruländer PINOT GRIS: grape giving soft full-bodied wine, alias (as dry wine) GRAUBURGUNDER. Best in BADEN and southern PFALZ.

Ruppertsberg Pfz w ★★→★★★ 75 76 83 85 86 87 88 **89** 90 91 92 **93** 94 95 Southern village of MITTELHAARDT. First-class v'yds incl Hoheburg, Linsenbusch, Nussbien, Reiterpfad, Spiess. Grosslage: Hofstück. Growers incl BASSERMANN-JORDAN, BIFFAR, VON BUHL, BURKLIN-WOLF, DEINHARD.

Ruwer Tributary of MOSEL nr TRIER. V fine delicate but highly aromatic and well-structured wines. Villages incl EITELSBACH, KASEL, MERTESDORF.

Saale-Unstrut Region in former E Germany, 1,000 acres around confluence of these two rivers at Naumburg, nr Leipzig. Terraced v'yds of WEISSBURGUNDER, SILVANER, GUTEDEL etc and red PORTUGIESER and SPATBURGUNDER have Cistercian origins. Quality leader: Lützkendorf.

Saar Tributary of MOSEL S of RUWER. Brilliant austere 'steely' RIES. Villages include AYL, OCKFEN, Saarburg, SERRIG, WILTINGEN (SCHARZHOFBERG). Grosslage: SCHARZBERG. Many fine estates.

Saar-Ruwer (Bereich) District covering these 2 regions.

Sachsen Former E German region (750 acres) in ELBE VALLEY around Dresden and Meissen. MULLER-T dominant, but WEISSBURGUNDER, GRAUBURGUNDER, TRAMINER, RIES give dry wines with more character. Best growers: SCHLOSS PROSCHWITZ, Jan Ulrich, Schloss Wackerbarth, Klaus Zimmerling.

St-Antony, Weingut ★★★ Excellent 50-acre estate. Rich, intense dry and off-dry RIES from First-class v'yds of NIERSTEIN.

St-Ursula Well-known merchants at BINGEN.

Salm, Prinz zu Owner of SCHLOSS WALLHAUSEN in NAHE and Villa Sachsen in RHEINHESSEN. President of VDP.

Salwey, Weingut ★★ Leading BADEN estate at Oberrotweil, esp for RIESLING, WEISSBURGUNDER and RULANDER.

Samtrot WURTTEMBERG grape. Makes Germany's closest shot at Beaujolais.

Schaefer, Willi ★★★ The finest grower of GRAACH (but only 5 acres).

Scharzberg Grosslage name of WILTINGEN and neighbours.

Scharzhofberg M-S-R (Saar) w ★★★★ 71 75 76 83 85 86 *87* 88 89 90 91 92 93 94 95 Superlative 67-acre SAAR v'yd: austerely beautiful wines, the perfection of RIESLING. Do not confuse with the previous entry. Top estates: EGON MULLER, VON HOVEL, Jordan and Jordan, VON KESSELSTATT.

Schaumwein Sparkling wine.

Scheurebe Aromatic grape of high quality (and RIESLING parentage) esp used in PFALZ. Excellent for botrytis wine (BA, TBA).

Schillerwein Light red or rosé QBA; speciality of WURTTEMBERG (only).

Schloss Groenesteyn Formerly top-grade RHEINGAU estate (80 acres) in RUDESHEIM. Financial troubles: not on top form.

GERMANY

Schloss Johannisberg Rhg w ★★★ 76 79 83 85 86 87 **88 89 90** 91 92 **93** 94 95 Famous RHEINGAU estate of 86 acres owned by the Princess Metternich and Oetker family. The original Rhine 'first growth'. Wines incl fine SPATLESE, KABINETT TROCKEN. But more could be achieved with this truly great v'yd.

Schloss Proschwitz ★★→★★★ Resurrected princely estate at Meissen, leading former E Germany in quality, esp with dry WEISSBURGUNDER.

Schloss Reichartshausen 10-acre HATTENHEIM v'yd run by RESS.

Schloss Reinhartshausen ★★★ Fine 175-acre estate in ERBACH, HATTENHEIM, KIEDRICH, etc. Changed hands in '88. The mansion is now a hotel.

Schloss Saarstein ★★★ SERRIG estate of 25 acres with consistently fine RIES.

Schloss Salem ★★ 188-acre estate of Margrave of BADEN near L Constance in S Germany. MULLER-T and WEISSHERBST.

Schloss Schönborn ★★★ One of biggest RHEINGAU estates, based at HATTENHEIM. Full-flavoured wines, variable, at best excellent. Also vg SEKT.

Schloss Staufenberg ★★ 69-acre DURBACH estate. KLINGELBERGER is best wine.

Schloss Thorn Ancient OBERMOSEL estate, remarkable ELBLING, RIES and castle.

Schloss Vollrads Rhg w ★★★ 71 76 83 85 86 87 88 89 90 91 93 94 95 Great WINKEL estate since 1300. 116 acres. Dry austere RIES; TROCKEN and HALBTROCKEN are specialities; recently unimpressive. See Matuschka-Greiffenclau.

Schloss Wallhausen ★★★ The 25-acre NAHE estate of the PRINZ ZU SALM, one of Germany's oldest. 65% RIES. Vg TROCKEN.

Schlossböckelheim Nahe w ★★→★★★ 71 75 76 79 83 85 86 87 88 **89 90** 91 92 93 94 95 Village with top NAHE v'yds, including First-class Felsenberg, In den Felsen, Königsfels, Kupfergrube. Firm yet delicate wine. Grosslage: Burgweg. Top growers: CRUSIUS, DONNHOF, STATE DOMAIN.

Schlossböckelheim District name for the whole S NAHE, amalgamated with KREUZNACH to form BEREICH NAHETAL.

Schneider, Weingut Georg Albrecht ★★ Impeccably-run 32-acre estate. Classic off-dry and sweet RIES in NIERSTEIN, the best from First-class Hipping.

Schoppenwein Café (or bar) wine: ie wine by the glass.

Schubert, von Owner of MAXIMIN GRUNHAUS.

Schwarzer Adler, Weingut ★★→★★★ Franz Keller and his son make top BADEN GRAU-, WEISS- and SPATBURGUNDER on 35 acres at Oberbergen.

Schweigen Pfz w r ★→★★ 85 86 87 88 89 90 91 92 93 94 95 S PFALZ village. Grosslage: Guttenberg. Best is Fritz Becker, esp for SPATBURGUNDER.

Sekt German (QBA) sparkling wine, best when label specifies RIES, WEISSBURGUNDER or SPATBURGUNDER. Sekt bA is the same but from specified area.

Selbach-Oster ★★★ 15-acre ZELTINGEN estate among MITTELMOSEL leaders.

Serrig M-S-R (Saar) w ★★→★★★ 71 75 76 83 85 86 87 88 89 90 91 93 94 95 Village for 'steely' wine, excellent in sunny yrs. First-class v'yds: Herrenburg, Saarstein, Serriger Schloss, Würzberg. Grosslage: SCHARZBERG. Top growers: SCHLOSS SAARSTEIN, BERT SIMON.

Sichel, Söhne H Famous wine merchants at Alzey, RHEINHESSEN. Owners of BLUE NUN LIEBFRAUMILCH. Recently bought by Langguth of TRABEN-TRARBACH.

Silvaner The third most-planted German white grape, usually underrated; best in FRANKEN. Worth looking for in RHEINHESSEN and KAISERSTUHL too.

Simmern, Langwerth von ★★★ Top ELTVILLE family estate. Famous v'yds: Baiken, Mannberg, MARCOBRUNN. Can have some of v best, most elegant R'GAU RIES but after disastrous '93 and '94 is lacking form.

Simon, Weingut Bert ★★ One of largest SAAR estates. 80 acres: KASEL, SERRIG.

Sonnenuhr Sundial. Name of several v'yds, esp one at WEHLEN.

Spätburgunder Pinot Noir: the best red wine grape in Germany – esp in BADEN and WURTTEMBERG and, increasingly, PFALZ – generally improving quality, but most still pallid and underflavoured.

Spätlese Late harvest. One better (stronger, sweeter) than KABINETT. Wines to age at least 5 yrs. TROCKEN Spätlesen can be v fine.

Staatlicher Hofkeller ★★★ The Bavarian STATE DOMAIN. 287 acres of finest FRANKEN v'yds with spectacular cellars under the great baroque Residenz at WURZBURG. Wines currently less spectacular.

Staatsweingut (or Staatliche Weinbaudomäne) The State wine estates or domains; esp KLOSTER EBERBACH, SCHLOSS-BOCKELHEIM, TRIER.

State Domain See Staatsweingut.

Steigerwald (Bereich) District name for E part of FRANKEN.

Steinberg Rhg w ★★★ 71 75 76 79 83 85 86 87 88 89 90 91 92 93 94 95 Famous 79-acre HATTENHEIM walled v'yd, planted by Cistercians 700 yrs ago. Now owned by STATE DOMAIN, ELTVILLE. Some glorious wines; some feeble.

Steinwein Wine from WURZBURG's best v'yd, Stein.

Stuttgart Chief city of WURTTEMBERG, producer of some fine wines (esp RIES), recently beginning to be exported.

Südliche Weinstrasse (Bereich) District name for S PFALZ. Quality improved tremendously in last 25 yrs. See Ilbesheim, Schweigen, Siebeldingen.

Tafelwein Table wine. The vin ordinaire of Germany. Frequently blended with other EC wines. But DEUTSCHER TAFELWEIN must come from Germany alone and may be excellent. (See also Landwein.)

Tauberfranken (Bereich) New name for minor Badisches Frankenland BEREICH of N BADEN: FRANKEN-style wines.

Thanisch, Weingut Wwe Dr H ★★★ BERNKASTEL estate, incl part of Doctor v'yd.

Traben-Trarbach M-M w ★★ 76 83 85 86 87 88 89 90 91 92 93 94 95 Major wine town of 800 acres, 87% of it RIESLING. Top vineyards: Ungsberg, Würzgarten. Grosslage: Schwarzlay. Top grower: MAX FERD RICHTER.

Traisen Nahe w ★★★ 71 75 76 79 83 85 86 87 88 89 90 91 92 93 94 95 Small village incl superlative First-class Bastei and Rotenfels v'yds, making RIES of great concentration and class. Top grower: CRUSIUS.

Traminer See Gewürztraminer.

Trier M-S-R w ★★→★★★ Great wine city of Roman origin, on MOSEL, nr RUWER, now also incl AVELSBACH and EITELSBACH. Grosslage: Römerlay. Big Mosel charitable estates have cellars here among imposing Roman ruins.

Trittenheim M-M w ★★ 71 75 76 83 85 87 88 89 90 91 92 93 94 95 Attractive S MITTELMOSEL light wines. Top v'yds were Altärchen, Apotheke, but now incl second-rate flat land: First-class are Felsenkopf, Leiterchen. Grosslage: Michelsberg (avoid). Top growers: GRANS-FASSIAN, Milz.

Trocken

'Dry'. By law trocken on a label means with a maximum of 9 grams per litre unfermented sugar. The new wave in German winemaking upsets the old notion of sweetness balancing acidity and embraces an austerity of flavour that can seem positively Lenten. It is much harder to make dry wines in German conditions, and non-initiates should not expect to fall in love at first sip. To be good, trocken wines need substantial body or alcohol; more than most Riesling Kabinett wines have to offer. Best trocken regions are Pfalz, Baden, Württemberg, Franken. Weissburgunder trocken is more satisfying. Halbtrockens are friendlier. Spätlesen (or QbA) usually make the best trocken wines. Auslese trocken sounds like a contradiction in terms – and often tastes like one. Do not be confused by the apparent link with Trockenbeerenauslesen: they are unrelated.

For key to grape variety abbreviations, see pages 7–13.

Trockenbeerenauslese Sweetest, most expensive category of German wine, extremely rare, with concentrated honey flavour. Made from selected shrivelled grapes affected by 'noble rot' (botrytis). TBA for short. See also Edel. Edelbeerenauslese would be a less confusing name.

Trollinger Common (pale) red grape of WÜRTTEMBERG; locally v popular.

Ungstein Pfz w ★★→★★★ 71 75 76 83 85 86 *87* 88 89 90 91 92 **93** 94 95 MITTELHAARDT village with fine harmonious wines. First-class v'yds: Herrenberg, Spielberg, Weilberg. Top growers: Darting, FITZ-RITTER, PFEFFINGEN, Karl Schäfer. Grosslagen: Honigsäckel, Kobnert.

Urzig M-M w ★★★★ 71 75 76 83 85 86 87 88 **89** 90 91 **92** 93 94 95 Village on red sandstone famous for firm, full, spicy wine unlike other MOSELS. First-class v'yd: Würzgarten. Grosslage: Schwarzlay. Growers incl J J CHRISTOFFEL, DR LOOSEN, WEINS-PRUM.

Valckenberg, P J Major merchants and growers at Worms, with Madonna LIEBFRAUMILCH. Also dry Ries. Now part-owner of HEYL ZU HERRNSHEIM.

VDP Verband Deutscher Prädikats und Qualitätsweingüter. The pace-making association of premium growers. Look for their black eagle insignia. President: PRINZ ZU SALM.

Vereinigte Hospitien ★★ 'United Hospices'. Ancient charity at TRIER with large holdings in PIESPORT, SERRIG, TRIER, WILTINGEN etc; but wines recently well below their wonderful potential.

Verwaltung Administration (of property/estate etc).

Wachenheim Pfz w ★★★→★★★★ 71 75 76 79 83 85 86 *87* 88 **89** 90 *91* 92 **93** 94 95 840 acres, including exceptionally fine RIESLING. First-class v'yds are Gerümpel, Goldbächel, Rechbächel etc. Top growers: BURKLIN-WOLF, BIFFAR. Grosslagen: Mariengarten, Schenkenböhl, Schnepfenflug.

Wagner, Dr ★★★ Saarburg estate. 20 acres of RIES. Fine wines incl TROCKEN.

Waldrach M-S-R (Ruwer) w ★★ 76 83 85 88 89 90 *91* 92 93 94 95 Grosslage: Römerlay. Some charming light wines.

Walluf Rhg w ★★★ 75 76 79 83 85 *87* 88 89 90 *91* 92 93 94 95 Neighbour of ELTVILLE; formerly Nieder- and Ober-Walluf. Underrated wines. First-class v'yd: Walkenberg. Grosslage: Steinmächer. Growers incl BECKER.

Walporzheim Ahrtal (Bereich) District name for the whole AHR VALLEY.

Wawern M-S-R (Saar) w ★★→★★★ 71 75 76 83 85 *87* 88 89 90 91 92 93 94 95 Small village, fine RIES. First-class v'yd: Herrenberg. Grosslage: SCHARZBERG.

Wegeler-Deinhard ★★★ 136-acre RHEINGAU estate. Vineyards: GEISENHEIM, MITTELHEIM, OESTRICH, RUDESHEIM, WINKEL etc. Consistent quality; dry SPÄTLESE, classic AUSLESE, finest EISWEIN. Also 67 acres in MITTELMOSEL, including major part of BERNKASTELER Doctor, WEHLENER SONNENUHR etc, 46 acres in MITTELHAARDT (DEIDESHEIM, FORST, RUPPERTSBERG). Only the best sites are named on labels. See also GEHEIMRAT 'J'.

Wehlen M-M w ★★★→★★★★ 71 75 76 83 85 86 *87* 88 **89** 90 91 *92* 93 94 95 Neighbour of BERNKASTEL with equally fine, somewhat richer wine. Great First-class v'yd: SONNENUHR. Grosslage: Münzlay. Top growers: HERIBERT KERPEN, DR LOOSEN, J J PRUM, WEGELER-DEINHARD, WEINS-PRUM.

Weil, Weingut Robert ★★★★ Outstanding 95-acre estate in KIEDRICH; now financed by Suntory of Japan. Superb QmP, EISWEIN; standard wines also vg since '92. Rapidly acquiring reputation as RHEINGAU's new No 1.

Weinbaugebiet Viticultural region. For TAFELWEIN (eg MOSEL, RHEIN, SAAR).

Weingut Wine estate.

Remember that vintage information for German wines is given in a different form from the ready/not ready distinction applying to other countries. Read the explanation on page 136.

Weinkellerei Wine cellars or winery. See Keller.

Weins-Prüm, Dr ★★→★★★ Classic MITTELMOSEL estate; 12 acres at WEHLEN. WEHLENER SONNENUHR is top wine.

Weinstrasse Wine road. Scenic route through v'yds. Germany has several. The most famous is the Deutsche Weinstrasse in the PFALZ.

Weintor, Deutsches See Schweigen.

Weissburgunder Pinot Blanc. One of the better grapes for TROCKEN and HALBTROCKEN wines: low acidity, high extract. Also much used for Sekt.

Weissherbst Usually pale pink wine of QBA standard or above, from a single variety, even occasionally BEERENAUSLESE, the speciality of BADEN, PFALZ and WURTTEMBERG. Currently fashionable in Germany.

Werner, Domdechant ★★★ Fine family estate on best HOCHHEIM slopes.

Wiltingen M-S-R (Saar) w ★★→★★★★ 71 75 76 83 85 86 87 88 89 90 91 92 93 94 95 The centre of the SAAR. 790 acres. Beautiful subtle austere wine. Great First-class v'yd is SCHARZHOFBERG (ORTSTEIL); and First-class are Braune Kupp, Hölle. Grosslage (for the whole SAAR): SCHARZBERG. Top growers: EGON MULLER, LE GALLAIS, Jordan & Jordan, VON KESSELSTATT etc.

Winkel Rhg w ★★★ 71 75 76 83 85 86 87 88 89 90 91 92 93 94 95 Village famous for full fragrant wine, incl SCHLOSS VOLLRADS. First-class vineyards include Hasensprung, Jesuitengarten, Klaus, SCHLOSS VOLLRADS, Schlossberg. Grosslagen: Erntebringer, Honigberg. Growers include DEINHARD, PRINZ VON HESSEN, VON MUMM, BALTHASAR RESS, SCHLOSS SCHONBORN etc.

Winningen M-S-R w Lower MOSEL village nr Koblenz: some fine delicate RIES. Top v'yds: Röttgen, Uhlen. Top grower: Heymann-Löwenstein.

Wintrich M-M w ★★→★★★ 71 75 76 83 85 86 87 88 89 90 91 92 93 94 95 Neighbour of PIESPORT; similar wines. Top vineyards: Ohligsberg. Grosslage: Kurfürstlay. Good grower: REINHOLD HAART.

Winzergenossenschaft Wine-growers' cooperative, often making sound and reasonably priced wine. Referred to in this text as 'coop'.

Winzerverein The same as above.

Wirsching, Hans ★★★ Leading estate in IPHOFEN, and indeed FRANKEN. Wines firm, elegant and dry. 100 acres in top v'yds: Julius-Echter-Berg, Kalb etc.

Wonnegau (Bereich) District name for S RHEINHESSEN.

Wolff Metternich ★★→★★★ Noble DURBACH estate: BADEN's best RIES.

Württemberg Vast S area, little known for wine outside Germany. But some vg RIES (esp Neckar Valley). Half is red: LEMBERGER, Trollinger, SAMTROT.

Würzburg Frank ★★→★★★★ 71 76 79 81 83 85 86 87 88 89 90 91 92 93 94 95 Great baroque city on the Main, centre of FRANKEN wine: fine, full-bodied, dry. First-class vineyards: Abtsleite, Innere, Leiste, Stein. No Grosslage. See Maindreieck. Growers: BURGERSPITAL, JULIUSSPITAL, STAATLICHER HOFKELLER.

Zell M-S-R w ★→★★★ 76 83 88 89 90 91 92 93 94 95 The best-known lower MOSEL village, esp for its awful Grosslage: Schwarze Katz ('Black Cat'). RIES on steep slate gives aromatic light wines. Top grower: Albert Kallfelz.

Zell (Bereich) District name for whole lower MOSEL from Zell to Koblenz.

Zeltingen M-M w ★★→★★★★ 71 75 76 79 83 85 86 87 88 89 90 91 92 93 94 95 Top MOSEL village nr WEHLEN. Lively crisp RIES. First-class v'yd: SONNENUHR. Grosslage: Münzlay. Many estate-owned v'yds, esp PRUM, SELBACH-OSTER.

Zilliken, Forstmeister Geltz ★★★ Former estate of Prussian royal forester at Saarburg and OCKFEN, SAAR. Racy minerally RIESLINGS, incl EISWEIN.

Zwierlein, Freiherr von ★★ 55-acre family estate in GEISENHEIM. 100% RIES.

Spain & Portugal

The following abbreviations are
used in the text:

Amp	Ampurdán-Costa Brava
Alen	Alentejo
Bair	Bairrada
Cos del S	Costers del Segre
El B	El Bierzo
Est	Estremadura
La M	La Mancha
Mont-M	Montilla-Moriles
Nav	Navarra
Pen	Penedés
Pri	Priorato
Rib del D	Ribera del Duero
R Ala	Rioja Alavesa
R Alt	Rioja Alta
RB	Rioja Baja
Som	Somontano
Set	Setúbal
U-R	Utiel-Requeña
VV	Vinhos Verdes
g	vino generoso
res	reserva

MADEIRA (off west coast of Africa)

Funchal

Spain and Portugal joined the European Community (and, as far as most of their wine is concerned, the 20th century) 11 years ago. They have both made rapid progress. Grants have allowed re-equipping on a large scale. There is still much to do, but the continuing state of ferment is highly productive, and some splendid new wines are appearing both in the few traditional quality areas and in former bulk-wine regions.

Currently in Spain (apart from sherry country), the north, Rioja, Navarra, Galicia, Rueda, Somontano, Catalonia and Ribera del Duero still hold most interest; in Portugal (apart from the port vineyards and Madeira) Bairrada, the Douro, Ribatejo, Alentejo, the central coast and the north. In Portugal especially, newly delimited areas are successfully challenging such old appellations as, eg, Dão.

The following list includes the best and most interesting types and regions of each country, whether legally delimited or not. Geographical references (see map above) are to demarcated regions (DOs and DOCs), autonomies and provinces.

Bay of Biscay

Bilbao

LogroñoO *Ebro* Navarra

Rioja Somontano

jales Campo de Borja Ampurdán-Costa Brava

Valladolid *Duero* Costers del Segre Conca de Barbera

Ribera del Duero Calatayud Cariñena Priorato Alella

Rueda **Barcelona**

Madrid Penedès
O Tarragona

entrida Vinos de Madrid

Utiel- Valencia
La Mancha Requena Binassalem

OValencia Palma

Almansa Valencia

Valdepeñas Jumilla Alicante

Yecla **OAlicante**

adalquivir Heavily shaded areas are the wine growing regions

ntilla Moriles

álaga

O **Málaga**

Mediterranean Sea

Sherry, port and Madeira, still the greatest glories of Spain and Portugal, have a chapter to themselves on pages 172–179.

Spain

AGE, Bodegas Unidas R Alt r w (p) dr sw res ★→★★ 85 86 90 91 93 Large BODEGA with a wide range recently bought by BODEGAS Y BEBIDAS. Siglo red is reliable if unspectacular; avoid its white counterpart. Best are the Siglo Gran Reserva (**85**) and Azpilicueta Gran Reserva (**82**).

Agramont See Principe de Viana, Bodegas.

Albariño High-quality aromatic white grape of GALICIA, possibly descended from Alsace Riesling, and its wine. See also Rías Baixas.

Alella r w (p) dr sw ★★ Small demarcated region just N of Barcelona. Pleasantly fruity wines. (See Marfil, Marqués de Alella, Parxet.)

Alicante r (w) ★ DO. Wines still earthy and overstrong.

Alion Rib del D r ★★★ 91 92 Since discontinuing the 3-yr-old VALBUENA, VEGA SICILIA has acquired this second BODEGA to make CRIANZAS: with 100% Tempranillo; first fruits are impressive.

Almendralejo E Spain r w ★ Wine centre of Extremadura. Much of its wine is distilled to make the spirit for fortifying sherry. See Lar de Barros.

Aloque La M r ★ DYA A light (though not in alcohol) speciality of VALDEPENAS, made by fermenting red and white grapes together.

Alta Pavina, Bodegas Castilla y Léon r ★ 90 91 Non-DO Cab S and Pinot N: oak-aged, spicy, dark and dense.

Alvear Mont-M g ★★★ The largest producer of excellent sherry-like aperitif and dessert wines in MONTILLA-MORILES.

Ampurdán, Cavas del Amp r w p sp res ★→★★ Producers of big-selling white Pescador, red Cazador table wines and commercial sparklers.

Ampurdán-Costa Brava Amp r w p ★→★★ Demarcated region abutting Pyrenees. Mainly coop-made rosés, reds. See also last entry.

Año Year: 4° Año (or Años) means 4 years old when bottled. Common on labels in the past, now largely discontinued in favour of vintages, or terms such as CRIANZA.

Antaño, Bodegas Rueda w (r) DYA New BODEGA esp for clean fruity balanced whites. Labels are Viña Mocen (w) and Viña Cobranza (r). To watch.

Aragonesa, Compañia Vitivinícola Som r w p res ★★→★★★ 90 91 92 94 New SOMONTANO estate. Varietal wines under Viñas del Vero label: Chard, Ries, Gewürz, Cab... Vines still young, oak excessive: but one to watch.

Bach, Masía Pen r w p dr sw res ★★→★★★ 85 88 91 Spectacular villa-winery nr SAN SADURNI DE NOYA, owned by CODORNIU. Speciality is white Extrísimo, both sweet and dry, and dry. Also good red RESERVAS.

Barbier, René Pen r w res ★★ 87 88 89 90 Owned by FREIXENET, known for fresh white Kraliner, red RB RESERVAS.

Barón de Ley RB r (w) res ★★★ 85 86 87 Newish RIOJA BODEGA linked with EL COTO: good single-estate wines.

Barril, Masía Pri r br res ★★★ 83 86 87 88 91 93 94 Tiny family estate in DO PRIORATO: powerful fruity reds – the 83 was 18°! – and superb RANCIO.

Berberana, Bodegas R Alt r (w) res ★★ →★★★ 87 90 91 92 93 Fruity full-bodied reds best: young Carta de Plata, Carta de Oro CRIANZA, velvety RESERVAS.

Berceo, Bodegas R Alt r w p res ★★→★★★ 78 87 89 92 Cellar in HARO with vg Gonzalo de Berceo GRAN RESERVA.

Beronia, Bodegas R Alt r w res ★★→★★★ 81 82 87 89 93 Small modern BODEGA making reds in traditional oaky style and fresh 'modern' whites. Owned by Gonzalez Byass (see page 174).

Bilbaínas, Bodegas R Alt r w (p) dr sw sp res ★★ 82 87 88 89 90 Large BODEGA in HARO. Wide and usually reliable range incl dark Viña Pomal, lighter Viña Zaco, Vendimia Especial RESERVAS and Royal Carlton CAVA.

Binissalem r w ★★ Best-known MAJORCA DO. See also Ferrer, José L.

Blanco White.

Bodega Spanish term for (i) a wineshop; (ii) a concern occupied in the making, blending and/or shipping of wine; and (iii) a cellar.

Bodegas y Bebidas Formerly 'Savin'. One of largest Spanish wine companies; wineries all over Spain. Mainly good quality and value brands. Also controls various prestigious firms, eg CAMPO VIEJO, MARQUES DEL PUERTO.

Breton Rioja r res ★★ 89 90 91 Respectable Loriñon range and little-seen, expensive, concentrated Dominio de Conté (comparable with CONTINO).

Calatayud (★) Aragón DO (of 4): esp Garnacha. Coop San Isidro holds sway.

Campillo, Bodegas R Ala r (p) res ★★★ 82 85 87 88 89 Affiliated with FAUSTINO MARTINEZ, a young BODEGA with wines of consistently high quality.

Campo Viejo, Bodegas R Alt r (w) res ★→★★★ 82 87 88 89 92 94 Makes the popular and tasty young San Asensio, Beaujolais-style Albor and some big fruity red RESERVAS, esp Marqués de Villamagna. See Bodegas y Bebidas.

Can Rafols dels Caus Pen r w ★★ 87 88 89 90 Young small PENEDES BODEGA: own-estate fruity Cab, pleasant Chard-Xarel-lo-Chenin; good Cab-Merlot (93) and less expensive Petit Caus range.

Caralt, Cavas Conde de Pen r w sp res ★★ 86 88 87 90 91 CAVA wines from outpost of FREIXENET, esp good vigorous Brut NV; also pleasant still wines.

Cariñena r (w p) ★ Coop-dominated DO: large-scale supplier of strong everyday wine. Being invigorated (and wines lightened) by new technology.

Casa de la Viña Valepeñas r (w p) ★★ 88 94 BODEGAS Y BEBIDAS-owned estate, since '80s making sound range of fruity 'Cencibel' wines. Drink young.

Casar de Valdaiga El B r w ★★ Fruity red from Pérez Carames, N of LEON.

Rioja's characteristic style

To the Spanish palate the taste of luxury in wine is essentially the taste of (American) oak. Oak contains vanillin: hence the characteristic vanilla flavour of all traditional Spanish table wines of high quality – exemplified by the reservas of Rioja (red and white). Fashion swung (perhaps too far) against the oaky flavour of old Rioja whites but the pendulum is swinging back, although to subtler oak flavours than in the old days.

Castell de Remei Cos de S r w p ★★→★★★ 88 89 90 91 Historic v'yds/winery revived, re-equipped, replanted since '83. Good Cab-Tempranillo, Merlot.

Castellblanch Pen w sp ★★ PENEDES CAVA firm, owned by FREIXENET. Look for Brut Zero and Gran Castell GRAN RESERVAS (90).

Castillo Ygay R Alt r w ★★★★ (r) 25 34 42 52 59 64 68 70 75 78 82 85 87 (Current white vintage is 85) See Marqués de Murrieta.

Cava Official term for any classic method Spanish sparkling wine, and the DO covering the areas up and down Spain where it is made.

Cenalsa See Principe de Viana, Bodegas.

Cenicero Wine township in RIOJA ALTA of Roman origin.

Cepa Wine or grape variety.

Cervera, Lagar de Rías Baixas w ★★★ DYA Makers of one of best ALBARINOS: flowery and intensely fruity with subdued bubbles and a long finish.

Chacolí Pais Vasco w (r) ★ DYA Alarmingly sharp, often fizzy wine from the Basque coast, now possessing its own DO, which applies to all 141 acres! It contains only 9–11% alcohol. Best producer: Txomín Etxaníz.

Chaves, Bodegas Rías Baixas w ★★★ DYA Small firm: gd fragrant acidic ALBARINO.

Chivite, Bodegas Julián Nav r w (p) dr sw res ★★→★★★ 85 87 88 89 90 92 **94** Biggest NAVARRA BODEGA. Full red wine, flowery well-balanced white and outstanding 94 rosé. See Gran Feudo.

Cigales r p ★→★★★ Recently demarcated region north of Valladolid, esp for light reds (traditionally known as CLARETES).

Clarete Traditional term, now banned by EC, for light red wine (or dark rosé).

Codorníu Pen w sp ★★→★★★ One of the two largest firms in SAN SADURNI DE NOYA making good CAVA: v high tech, 10 million bottles ageing in cellars. Non Plus Ultra is matured. Many prefer the fresher Anna de Codorníu or premium Jaume de Codorníu RESERVA (91).

Compañía Vinícola del Norte de España (CVNE) R Alt r w (p) dr sw res ★★→★★★ 87 88 89 **90** 91 92 93 Top RIOJA BODEGA. Monopole (93) is one of the best oaky whites. Recent vintages of the red CRIANZA have not always been up to old high standards. Excellent red Imperial and Viña Real RESERVAS. CVNE is pronounced 'coonay'. See also Contino.

NB Vintages in colour are those you should choose first for drinking in 1997.

157

Conca de Barberà Pen w (r p) Catalan DO region growing Parellada grapes for making CAVA. Its best wine is TORRES MILMANDA Chard.

Condado de Huelva DO See Huelva.

Consejo Regulador Official organization for the control, promotion and defence of a DENOMINACION DE ORIGEN.

Contino R Ala r res ★★★ 85 86 87 88 89 91 Very fine single-v'yd red made by a subsidiary of COMPANIA VINICOLA DEL NORTE DE ESPANA.

Corral, Bodegas R Alt r w p ★★★ 87 90 91 Don Jacobo wines from BODEGA by the Pilgrim Way to Santiago; marked recent improvement.

Cosecha Crop or vintage.

Cosecheros Alaveses R Ala r ★★★ 90 91 92 94 Up-and-coming RIOJA coop, esp for good young unoaked red Artadi.

Costers del Segre Cos del S r w p sp Small demarcated area around the city of Lleida (Lérida) and famous for the v'yds of RAIMAT.

Criado y embotellado por... Grown and bottled by...

Crianza Literally 'nursing'; the ageing of wine. New or unaged wine is 'sin crianza' or 'joven' (young). Reds labelled 'crianza' must be at least 2 yrs old (with 1yr in oak, in some areas 6 months), and must not be released before the third yr.

Cumbrero See Montecillo, Bodegas.

De Muller Tarragona br (r w) ★★→★★★ Venerable TARRAGONA firm specializing in altar wine, gd PRIORATO, superb sumptuous v old SOLERA-aged dessert wines. Incl Priorato DULCE, PAXARETE. Also fragrant Moscatel Seco.

Denominación de Origen (DO) Official wine region (see page 154).

Denominación de Origen Calificada (DOCa) Classification for wines of the highest quality; so far only RIOJA benefits (since '91).

Diaz e Hijos, Jesús La M r w p res ★★ 86 91 92 93 The reds from this small BODEGA near Madrid win many prizes.

Domecq R Ala r (w) res ★★→★★★ 85 87 90 92 RIOJA outpost of sherry firm. Inexpensive Viña Eguia and excellent Marqués de Arienzo CRIANZAS and RESERVAS, fragrant and medium-bodied.

Don Darias/Don Hugo Alto Ebro r w ★ Huge-selling, modestly-priced wines, v like RIOJA, from undemarcated Bodegas Vitorianas. Sound red, white.

Dulce Sweet.

El Bierzo DO since '90, N of León. See Casar de Valdaiga, Palacio de Arganza.

El Coto, Bodegas R Ala r (w) res ★★ 85 86 90 BODEGA best known for light, soft, red El Coto and Coto de Imaz.

Elaborado y añejado por... Made and aged by...

Enate Somontano DO r w ★★→★★★★ 92 93 Good wines from SOMONTANO in the north: light, clean, fruity and incl Chard (93), Chard-Macabeo (94) and Cab S blends (the CRIANZA is full and juicy).

Espumoso Sparkling (but see Cava).

Evena Nav Gov't research station revolutionizing NAVARRA. Run by J OCHOA.

Fariña, Bodegas Toro r w res ★★ 87 89 92 94 Rising star of new DO TORO: good spicy reds. Gran Colegiata is cask-aged; Colegiata not.

Faustino Martínez R Ala r w (p) res ★★→★★★ 86 88 89 90 Bodega with good reds. Light fruity white Faustino V. GRAN RESERVA is Faustino I. Do not be put off by the repellent fake-antique bottles.

Ferrer, José L Majorca r res ★★ 87 89 91 93 Best-known MAJORCA BODEGA at Binissalem. RESERVAS worth finding. Second is Vinos Oliver, at Felanitx.

Fillaboa, Granxa Rías Baixas w ★★★ DYA New small firm making delicately fruity ALBARINO.

Franco-Españolas, Bodegas R Alt r w dr sw res ★→★★ Old-est'd RIOJA BODEGA now part of group controlled by Marcos Eguizabal. Bordón is fruity red. Semi-sweet white Diamante is a Spanish favourite.

Freixenet Cavas Pen w sp ★★→★★★★ Huge CAVA firm, rivalling CODORNIU in size. Range of good sparklers, notably bargain Cordon Negro in black bottles, Brut Nature (90), Reserva Real and Premium Cuvée DS (89). Also owns Gloria Ferrer in California, Champagne Henri Abelé (Reims) and a sparkling wine plant in Mexico. Paul Cheneau is low-price brand.

A Spanish choice for 1997

Fransola ('93) white from Miguel Torres
Lagar de Cervera Albariño
Marqués de Alella Chardonnay from Parxet.
Anna de Codorníu ('94) cava
Viñedos del Contino ('88) Rioja
Remellur Reserva ('91) Rioja
Viña Pedrosa ('89) Ribera del Duero from Pérez Pascuas Hermanos
Solera 1885 Málaga from Scholtz Hermanos.

Galicia Rainy NW Spain: esp for fresh aromatic, not cheap whites, eg ALBARIÑO.
Generoso (g) Aperitif or dessert wine rich in alcohol.
Gonzalez y Dubosc, Cavas Pen w sp ★★ A branch of the sherry giant GONZALEZ BYASS. Pleasant sparkling wines exported as 'Jean Perico'.
Gran Feudo Nav w res ★★→★★★★ 88 89 90 92 94 Brand name of fragrant white, refreshing rosé, soft plummy red; the best-known wines from CHIVITE.
Gran Reserva See Reserva.
Gran Vas Pressurized tanks (French cuves closes) for making cheap sparkling wines; also used to describe this type of wine.
Grandes Bodegas Rib del D r ★→★★★ 89 91 94 95 Recently reorganized and with its own extensive v'yds, this BODEGA (in a region notorious for high prices) makes affordable Marqués de Velilla quality wines. Watch this space.
Guelbenzu, Bodegas Nav r res ★★→★★★ 89 90 92 93 94 Family estate making conc full-bodied reds. Watch for new 95 Jardin from 40-yr-old Garnacha and 89 Evo Gran Reserva to keep.
Gutiérrez de la Vega Alicante r w ★★ Eccentric grower in Alicante DO. Rare expensive wines, rarely leaving Spain; sold as 'Casta Diva'. Moscatel 'Cosecha Miel' ('93) is huge sweet and apricotty.
Haro Wine centre of the RIOJA ALTA, a small but stylish old city.
Hill, Cavas Pen w r sp res ★★→★★★ 88 89 91 Old PENEDES firm: fresh dry white Blanc Cru, good Gran Civet, Gran Toc reds, delicate RESERVA Oro Brut CAVA.
Huelva Condado de Huelva (DO) r w br ★→★★★ W of Cádiz. White table wines and sherry-like GENEROSOS; formerly imp't source of 'Jerez' for blending.
Irache, SL Nav r p (w) res ★ 87 89 92 94 Well-known unpricey everyday reds.
Jean Perico See Gonzalez y Dubosc.
Joven (vino) Young, unoaked wine.
Jumilla r (w p) ★→★★ DO in mountains N of Murcia. Its overstrong (up to 18%) wines are being lightened by earlier picking and better winemaking, esp by French-owned Bodegas VITIVINO (eg Altos de Pío).
Juvé y Camps Pen w sp ★★→★★★ Family firm. Top quality CAVA, from free-run juice only, esp Reserva de la Familia (91) and Gran Juvé y Camps (90).
La Rioja Alta, Bodegas R Alt r w (p) dr (sw) res ★★★ 78 81 82 84 85 86 87 88 89 Excellent RIOJAS, esp red CRIANZA Viña Alberdi, velvety Ardanza Res, lighter Araña Reserva, splendid Reserva 904 and marvellous RESERVA 890. Lasts almost forever. Now making only RESERVAS and GRAN RESERVAS.
Laguardia Picturesque walled town at the centre of the RIOJA ALAVESA.

For key to grape variety abbreviations, see pages 7–13.

SPAIN

Lan, Bodegas R Alt r (p w) res ★★→★★★ 87 88 90 Huge modern BODEGA: aromatic red RIOJAS (good Lanciano and Lander), fresh white Lan Blanco, but recent vintages disappointing.

Lar de Lares SW r res ★★ 84 87 Meaty GRAN RESERVA from Bodegas Inviosa, in remote Extremadura (in SW). Quality of younger Lar de Barros has declined.

León r p w ★→★★ 88 91 N region to watch: fruity dry refreshing wines, esp from Vinos de León (aka VILE): eg young Coyanza, more mature Palacio de Guzman (90), full-blooded Don Suero RESERVA (91). See also El Bierzo.

León, Jean Pen r w res ★★★ 85 86 87 88 Small firm; TORRES-owned since '95. Good oaky Chard, deep full-bodied Cab that repays bottle-ageing.

Logroño First town of RIOJA region. HARO has more charm (and BODEGAS).

López de Heredia R Alt r w (p) dr sw res ★★→★★★ 76 86 87 89 Old-est'd HARO BODEGA for exceptionally long-lasting, v traditional wines. Variable since '85. Viña Tondonia (r and w) are delicate and fine; Viña Bosconia fine, beefy.

López Hermanos Málaga ★★ Large BODEGA for commercial MALAGA wines, incl popular Málaga Virgen and Moscatel Gloria.

Los Llanos Valdepeñas r (p w) res ★★ 84 87 90 One of the growing number of VALDEPENAS BODEGAS to age wine in oak. Markets a RESERVA, GRAN RESERVA and premium Pata Negra Gran Reserva (83) of 100% Cencibel (Tempranillo). Also clean fruity white, Armonioso.

Málaga br sw ★★→★★★ Demarcated region around city of Málaga. At their best its dessert wines can resemble tawny port. See Scholtz.

Majorca JOSE FERRER, Miguel Oliver and Jaume Mesquida make the island's only wines of interest (eg Chard) – otherwise, drink ROSADOS or Catalan.

Mancha, La La M r w ★→★★ Vast demarcated region N and NE of VALDEPENAS. Mainly white wines, the reds lacking the liveliness of the best Valdepeñas but showing signs of improvement. To watch.

Marfíl Alella w (p) ★★ Brand of Alella Vinícola (oldest-est'd producer in ALELLA). Means 'ivory'. Now for lively, rather pricey, new-style dry whites.

Marqués de Alella Alella w (sp) ★★→★★★ 94 95 (DYA) Light and fragrant white ALELLA wines from PARXET, some from Chardonnay (including barrel-fermented 'Allier'), made by modern methods. Also CAVA.

Marqués de Cáceres, Bodegas R Alt r p w res ★★→★★★ 82 85 86 87 89 91 Good RIOJAS made by modern French methods from CENICERO (R Alt) grapes; also surprisingly light, fragrant white (DYA) and sweet Saitinia.

Marqués de Griñón La M r w ★★★ 87 88 Enterprising nobleman making v fine Cab and a good new (93) 'Shiraz' nr Toledo, S of Madrid, a region not known for wine. Fruity wines to drink fairly young. Also an excellent white Selección Especial 91 made from Verdejo grapes in RUEDA, plus good RIOJAS (90 91 92) and Durius, a red RIBERA DEL DUERO made by BODEGAS BERBERANA.

Marqués de Monistrol, Bodegas Pen p r sp dr sw res ★★→★★★ 85 89 91 Old BODEGA now owned by Martini & Rossi. Reliable CAVAS. Fresh Merlot (91).

Marqués de Murrieta R Alt r p w res ★★★→★★★★ 34 42 52 59 62 64 68 70 78 83 85 89 90 Historic, much-respected BODEGA near LOGRONO, formerly for some of best RIOJAS. Also known for red CASTILLO YGAY, old-style oaky white and wonderful old-style RESERVA ROSADO. Except Rosado, recent quality disappointing; but currently back on form with deep brandy-scented 89.

Marqués del Puerto R Alt r (p w) res ★★→★★★ 87 88 89 Small firm, was Bodegas López Agos, now owned by BODEGAS Y BEBIDAS. Reliable.

Marqués de Riscal R Ala r (p w) res ★★★ 81 87 88 89 90 91 Best-known BODEGA of RIOJA ALAVESA. Its red wines are relatively light and dry. Old vintages are v fine, some more recent ones poor; currently are right back on form. Baron de Chirel, 50% Cab S (88) is magnificent. Whites from RUEDA, incl a vg Sauv and oak-aged RESERVA Limousin (92).

Martínez-Bujanda R Ala r p w res ★★★ 87 89 90 92 Refounded ('85) family-run RIOJA BODEGA, remarkably equipped. Excellent wines, incl fruity SIN CRIANZA, irresistible ROSADO, noble Valdemar RESERVAS and making waves with a new (89 90) 100% Garnacha.

Mascaró, Cavas Pen r p w sp 92 ★★→★★★ Top brandy maker, good sparkling, lemony refreshing dry white Viña Franca, excellent (88) Anima Cab S.

Mauro, Bodegas nr Valladolid r ★★→★★★ 87 89 90 91 92 Young BODEGA in Tudela del Duero with vg round fruity Tinto del País (Tempranillo) red. Not DO as it is made by Bodegas Sanz in RUEDA.

Méntrida La M r w ★ DO west of Madrid, source of everyday red wine.

Milmanda ★★★ See Conca de Barberá, Torres.

Monopole See Compañía Vinícola del Norte de España (CVNE).

Montecillo, Bodegas R Alt r w (p) res ★★ 86 91 RIOJA BODEGA owned by OSBORNE. Old GRAN RESERVAS (eg 73) are magnificent. Now reds are appealing young but recent vintages fragile.

Montecristo, Bodegas Mont-M ★★ Well-known brand of MONTILLA-MORILES.

Monterrey Gal r ★ Region nr N border of Portugal; strong VERIN-like wines.

Montilla-Moriles Mont-M g ★★→★★★ DO nr Córdoba. Its crisp sherry-like FINO and AMONTILLADO contain 14–17.5% natural alcohol and remain unfortified. At best, singularly toothsome aperitifs.

Muga, Bodegas R Alt r (w sp) res ★★★ 81 85 89 90 Small family firm in HARO, known for some of RIOJA's best strictly trad reds. Wines are light but highly aromatic, with long complex finish. Best is Prado Enea (81 outstanding, but 86 87 88 far below par). Whites and CAVA less good.

Navajas, Bodegas R Alt r w res ★★→★★★ 85 86 87 89 90 91 92 Small firm with bargain reds, CRIANZAS, RESERVAS, fruity and full-bodied. Also excellent oak-aged white Viura and cherry and vanilla flavoured CRIANZA ROSADO.

Navarra Nav r p (w) ★★→★★★ Demarcated region; mainly rosés and sturdy reds, now well launched on stylish Tempranillo and Cab reds, some RESERVAS up to RIOJA standards. See Chivite, Guelbenzu, Magaña, Ochoa, Príncipe de Viana.

Nuestro Padre Jésus del Perdón, Coop de La M r w ★→★★ 87 89 92 94 Look for bargain fresh white Lazarillo and more-than-drinkable Yuntero; 100% Cencibel (alias Tempranillo) aged in oak.

Ochoa Nav r p w res ★★→★★★ 88 89 90 92 Small family BODEGA now with an excellent white, but better known for well-made red and rosés, incl 100% Tempranillo. Outstanding early vintages; recently disappointing.

Olarra, Bodegas R Alt r (w p) res ★★ Vast modern BODEGA in LOGROÑO, one of the showpieces of RIOJA. Interesting 5–6 yrs ago, esp for silky, well-balanced Cerro Añón reds, but quality now disappointing.

Pago de Carraovejas Rib del D r res ★★→★★★ 91 92 94 95 New estate earning reputation for some of the region's most stylish, densely fruity Tinto Fino Cabernet.

Palacio, Bodegas R Ala r p w res ★★★ 85 87 89 90 91 94 Since this old family firm parted company with Seagram in '87 its wines have regained much of their former reputation. Esp Glorioso RESERVA and Cosme Palacio (91).

Palacio de Arganza El B r p (w) res ★★ 83 85 89 Best-known BODEGA in new EL BIERZO DO. Somewhat variable red Almena del Bierzo is worth trying.

Palacio de Fefiñanes Rías Baixas w res ★★★ Famous for atypical ALBARINO. No bubbles and oak-aged 3–5 yrs.

Palacio de la Vega Nav r p w res ★★ 91 92 New BODEGA with juicy Tempranillo JOVEN (like primeur) and much promise.

Parxet Alella w p sp ★★→★★★ Makers of excellent fresh, fruity, exuberantly fizzy CAVA (only one from ALELLA): top is Brut Nature. Also elegant white Alella, 'MARQUES DE ALELLA'.

SPAIN

Paternina, Bodegas R Alt r w (p) dr sw res ★→★★ Known for its standard red brand Banda Azul. Conde de los Andes label was fine, but the much lauded 73 is strictly for fans of oak/volatile acidity, and recent vintages, as of their other RIOJAS, are disappointing. Most consistent is Banda Dorada white (DYA).

Paxarete Traditional intensely sweet dark brown almost chocolatey speciality of TARRAGONA. Not to be missed. See De Muller.

Pazo Ribeiro r p w ★★ DYA Brand name of the RIBEIRO coop, whose wines are akin to VINHOS VERDES. Rasping red is local favourite. Pleasant slightly fizzy Pazo whites are safer; Viña Costeira has quality.

Pazo de Barrantes Rías Baixas w ★★★ 94 New ALBARIÑO from RIAS BAIXAS, from an estate owned by the Conde de Creixels of MURRIETA. Delicate exotic and of impeccable quality, but v expensive and hard to find.

Penedès Pen r w sp ★→★★★ Demarcated region including Vilafranca del Penedès, SAN SADURNI DE NOYA and SITGES (but not CAVA). See also Torres.

Perelada Amp w (r p) sp ★★ In the demarcated region of AMPURDAN on the Costa Brava. Best known for sparkling, both CAVA and GRAN VAS.

Pérez Pascuas Hermanos Rib del D r (p) res ★★★ 88 89 90 91 92 94 Immaculate tiny family BODEGA in RIBERA DEL DUERO. In Spain its fruity and complex red Viña Pedrosa is rated one of the country's best.

Pesquera Rib del D r ★★★ 87 88 89 90 91 92 Small quantities of RIBERA DEL DUERO from Alejandro Fernandez. Robert Parker has rated it level with B'x Grands Crus. Janus (86) is special (even more expensive) bottling.

Piedmonte S Coop, Bodegas Nav ★★★ 93 94 Up-and-coming coop making first-rate Oligitum Cab S-Tempranillo and Merlot.

Piqueras, Bodegas La M r ★★→★★★ 83 85 88 89 Small family BODEGA. Some of LA MANCHA's best reds: Castillo de Almansa CRIANZA, Marius GRAN RESERVA.

Principe de Viana, Bodegas Nav r w ★★ 90 91 92 93 Large firm (formerly 'Cenalsa'), blending and maturing coop wines and shipping a range from NAVARRA, incl flowery new-style white and fruity red, Agramont.

Priorato Pri br r ★★★ 87 88 89 91 92 93 94 DO enclave of TARRAGONA, known for alcoholic RANCIO, and splendidly full-bodied, almost black reds, often used for blending, but at their brambly best one of Spain's triumphs. Lighter blend is good carafe wine. See Barril, De Muller, Scala Dei.

Protos, Bodegas Rib del D r w res ★★→★★★ 86 87 89 91 92 Formerly Penafiel's coop and the region's second oldest BODEGA. Originally privatized ('91) as 'Bodegas Ribera del Duero'. Much improved by new oenologist.

Raimat Cos del S r w p sp ★★→★★★ (Cab) 85 86 87 88 89 90 91 Clean, structured wines from new DO nr Lérida, planted by CODORNIU with Cab, Chard, other foreign vines. Good 100% Chard CAVA.

Rancio Maderized (brown) white wine of nutty flavour.

Raventos i Blanc Barcelona w sp ★★→★★★ 91 Excellent CAVA aimed at top of market, also fresh El Preludi white (94).

Real Divisa, Bodegas R Alt r res ★★ 85 86 87 90 Picturesque old BODEGA; one of few growing all its own fruit. Esp Marqués de Legarda RESERVAS.

Remelluri, La Granja R Ala r res ★★★ 85 87 88 89 90 91 Small estate (since '70), making vg traditional red RIOJAS and improving all the time.

Reserva (res) Good quality wine matured for long periods. Red reservas must spend at least 1 year in cask and 2 in bottle; gran reservas 2 in cask and 3 in bottle. Thereafter many continue to mature for years.

Rías Baixas w ★★→★★★ NW DO embracing subzones Val do Salnés, O Rosal and Condado de Tea, now for some of the best (and priciest) cold-fermented Spanish whites, mainly from ALBARIÑO grapes.

Ribeiro r w (p) ★→★★★ Demarcated region on N border of Portugal: wines similar in style to Portuguese VINHOS VERDES – and others.

Ribera del Duero Rib del D 89 91 94 95 Fashionable fast-expanding DO east of Valladolid, now revealed as excellent for Tinto Fino (Tempranillo) reds. Vintages are somewhat variable and prices are high. See Pérez Pascuas, Pesquera, Torremilanos, Vega Sicilia. Also Mauro.

Ribera Duero, Bodegas See Bodegas Protos.

Rioja r p w sp 64 70 75 78 81 82 85 89 90 91 92 94 N upland region along River Ebro for many of Spain's best red table wines in some 60 BODEGAS DE EXPORTACION. Tempranillo predominates. Other grapes and/or oak included depending on fashion and vintage. Subdivided into 3 areas:

Rioja Alavesa N of the R Ebro, produces fine red wines, mostly light in body and colour but particularly aromatic.

Rioja Alta S of the R Ebro and W of LOGRONO, grows most of the finest, best-balanced red and white wines; also some rosé.

Rioja Baja Stretching E from LOGRONO, makes coarser red wines, high in alcohol and often used for blending.

> **Important note:**
> An extended range of vintages is printed for a number of Rioja bodegas. But remember that the quality of the older reservas and gran reservas is dependent on proper cellarage. Old wines kept for any period in the racks of a warm restaurant soon deteriorate. Riojas do not now last as long as their oakier predecessors – some of the 85s and 89s are already drying out – but depending upon the bodega, an older vintage from the '60s or early '70s may well be memorable. Currently 89 90 91 are the safest choices.

Rioja Santiago R Alt r (p w dr sw) res ★→★★ 87 89 90 91 94 BODEGA at HARO with brands incl the biggest-selling bottled SANGRIA. Its top reds, Condal and Gran Enologica, are respectable.

Riojanas, Bodegas R Alt r (w p) res ★★→★★★ 64 73 75 81 85 88 91 Old BODEGA for trad Viña Albina and big mellow Monte Real RESERVAS (**88**).

Rosado Rosé.

Rovellats Pen w p sp ★★→★★★ 92 Small family firm making only good (and expensive) CAVAS, stocked in some of Spain's best restaurants.

Rovira, Pedro Tar/Pen r p br w dr sw res ★→★★ Large firm with BODEGAS in the DOs TARRAGONA, Terra Alta and PENEDES. A wide range. Vintages since '95 have been much improved by Australian Nick Butler.

Rueda br w ★→★★ Small historic DO west of Valladolid. Traditional FLOR-growing, sherry-like wines up to 17% alcohol, now for fresh whites, incl MARQUES DE RISCAL, MARQUES DE GRINON. Its secret weapon is the Verdejo grape.

Ruiz, Santiago Rías Baixas w ★★★ DYA Small prestigious RIAS BAIXAS company, now owned by BODEGAS LAN: fresh lemony ALBARINO, aged on its lees, is one of v best.

Salceda, Viña R Ala r res ★★→★★★ 87 89 91 Fruity light balanced reds.

San Sadurní de Noya Pen w sp ★★→★★★ Town S of Barcelona, hollow with CAVA cellars. Standards can be v high, though the flavour (of Parellada and other grapes) is quite different from that of champagne.

San Valero, Bodega Cooperativa Cariñena r p w res ★→★★ 94 Large CARINENA coop with some modern wines. Good red CRIANZA Monte Ducay, fresh ROSADO with slight spritz, and value young unoaked Don Mendo.

Sangre de Toro Brand name for a rich-flavoured red from TORRES.

Spain entries also cross-refer to Sherry, Port & Madeira, pages 172–179.

Sangría Cold red wine cup traditionally made with citrus fruit, fizzy lemonade, ice and brandy. But too often repulsive commercial fizz.

Sanlúcar de Barrameda Centre of the Manzanilla district (see Sherry).

Santara Conc de Barbera w r ★★→★★ DYA Brand name for big-selling and v drinkable Chardonnay and Cab S-Merlot made for Concavinos by flying winemaker Hugh Ryman.

Sarría, Bodegas de Nav r (p w) res ★★→★★★ 85 86 90 Quality remains high, though the Duarte family's departure and the death of oenologist Francisco Morriones has left the lustre of this model estate's international reputation sadly dimmed.

Scala Dei, Cellers de Pri r w p res ★★→★★★ 87 88 91 92 94 One of few BODEGAS in PRIORATO. Full Cartoixa RESERVAS and lighter Novell. New: breathtaking black old-style 14% Bru de Vins (94) and savoury barrel-fermented Garnacha Blanca Blanc Prior (94).

Schenk, Bodegas Valencia r w p ★★ 88 92 Large Swiss firm and big exporter, making decent Moscatel and good Monastrell/Garnacha labelled as Cavas Murviedro, Estrella and Los Monteros.

Scholtz, Hermanos Málaga br ★★★ Makers of the best MALAGA, but future uncertain. Currently making traditional 10-yr-old Lágrima, rich old-fashioned Moscatel and bitter-sweet Solera 1885.

Seco Dry.

Segura Viudas, Cavas Pen w sp ★★→★★★ CAVA from SAN SADURNI (FREIXENET-owned). Buy the Brut Vintage, Aria or RESERVA Heredad.

Serra, Jaume Pen r w res ★★ 88 89 91 92 93 94 Refreshing varietal whites, fruity balanced reds, easy-drinking CAVA (esp 'Cristalino'). Reputation may be enhanced by '96 involvement of charismatic Chilean Ignacio Recabarren.

Sitges Pen w sw ★★ Coastal resort S of Barcelona once noted for dessert wine from Moscatel and Malvasia grapes. One maker, Celler Robert, survives.

Solis, Felix Valdepeñas r ★★ BODEGA in VALDEPENAS making sturdy oak-aged reds, Viña Albali, RESERVAS (87 88 91) and fresh white.

Somontano Som Pyrenees foothills DO. Best-known BODEGAS: old French-est'd Lalanne (esp Viña San Marcos red: Moristel-Tempranillo-Cab S; white Macabeo, Chard), Coop Somontano de Sobrarbe now privatized as Bodegas Pirineos (esp Montesierra range and oak-aged Señorío de Lazán), new COVISA (Viñas del Vero). Also Viñedos y crianza del Alto Aragón (excellent ENATE range).

Tarragona r w br dr sw ★→★★★ (i) Table wines from demarcated region (DO); of little note. (ii) Dessert wines from the firm of DE MULLER.

Tinto Red.

Toro r ★→★★ DO 150 miles NW of Madrid. Formerly for over-powerful (up to 16%) reds, now often tasty and balanced. See Bodegas Fariña.

Torremilanos Rib del D r res ★→★★★ 86 87 91 94 Label of Bodegas López Peñalba, a fast-expanding family firm nr Aranda de Duero. Tinto Fino (Tempranillo) is smoother, more RIOJA-like than most.

Torres, Miguel SA Pen r w p dr s/sw res ★★→★★★★ 87 88 89 90 92 93 World-famous family company for many of the best PENEDES wines; a flagship for all Spain. Wines are flowery white Viña Sol, Green Label Fransola Sauv (93) and Parellada, Gran Viña Sol, MILMANDA oak-fermented Chard (93), semi-dry aromatic Esmeralda, Waltraud Ries (94), red Tres Torres, Gran Sangre de Toro, vg Gran Coronas (Cabernet Sauvignon) RESERVAS (82), fresh soft Las Torres Merlot and Santa Digna Pinot. Mas Borras is 100% Pinot N. Also in Chile and California.

Utiel-Requena U-R r p (w) Demarcated region W of Valencia. Sturdy reds and chewy vino de doble pasta for blending; also light fragrant rosé.

164

Valbuena Rib del D r ★★★ 84 85 86 88 89 90 91 Made with the same grapes as VEGA SICILIA but sold when 5 yrs old. Best at about 10 yrs. Some prefer it to its elder brother. 88 is outstanding. But see Alion.

Valdeorras Gal r w ★→★★ DO E of Orense. Dry and (at best) refreshing wines.

Valdepeñas La M r (w) ★→★★ Demarcated region nr Andalucían border. Mainly red wines, high in alcohol but surprisingly soft in flavour. Best wines (eg LOS LLANOS, FELIX SOLIS and Casa la Viña) now oak-matured.

Valduero, Bodega Rib del D r 86 89 91 94 New ('84) BODEGA: vg, value RESERVAS.

Valencia r w ★ Demarcated region exporting vast quantities of clean and drinkable table wine; also refreshing whites, esp Moscatel.

Vallformosa, Masía Pen r w p s p res ★★ CAVA respectable, reds poor.

Vega Sicilia Rib del D r res ★★★★ 41 48 53 59 60 61 62 64 66 67 69 70 72 73 74 75 76 79 80 82 83 85 Top Spanish wine: full fruity piquant rare fascinating. Up to 16% alcohol. Reserva Especial is a blend, chiefly of 62 and 79(!). See also Valbuena, Alion. Now investing in Tokaji, Hungary.

Vendimia Vintage.

Verín Gal r ★ Town near N border of Portugal. Its wines are the strongest from GALICIA, without a bubble, and with up to 14% alcohol.

Viña Literally, a vineyard. But wines such as Tondonia (LOPEZ DE HEREDIA) are not necessarily made with grapes from only the v'yd named.

Viña Pedrosa See Pérez Pascuas.

Viña Toña Pen w ★★→★★★ 94 DYA Clean fresh fruity whites of Xarel-lo (100%), unoaked Chard, Parellada and Macabeo, from small Celler R Balada. Justifiably high reputation.

Viñas del Vero Som w p r res ★★→★★★ See COMPANIA VITIVINICOLA ARAGONESA.

Vinícola de Castilla La M r p w ★★ 83 84 87 89 91 92 94 One of largest LA MANCHA firms. Red and white Castillo de Alhambra are palatable. Top are Cab, Cencibel (Tempranillo), Señorío de Guadianeja (84 91) GRAN RESERVAS.

Vinícola Navarra Nav r p w res ★★ 89 90 90 91 94 Old-est'd firm, now part of BODEGAS Y BEBIDAS, thoroughly traditional. Best wines from Castillo de Tiebas, Las Campanas (91).

Vinival, Bodegas Valencia r p w ★ Huge Valencian consortium marketing the most widely drunk wine in the region, Torres de Quart (rosé best).

Vino comun/corriente Ordinary wine.

Vitivino, Bodegas Jumilla r w ★★ 89 92 French J-L Gadeau has caused a stir with lively/meaty Altos de Pío from local Monastrell grapes.

Yecla r w ★ DO north of Murcia. Decent red from Bodegas Castaño.

Yllera Rib del D r ★★ 90 91 Good value RIBERO DEL DUERO red from now privatized Los Curros coop (but bottled in RUEDA so not DO).

To decipher codes, please refer to 'Key to symbols' on front flap of jacket, or to 'How to use this book' on page 6.

Portugal

Abrigada, Quinta de Alenquer r w res ★★ 86 90 92 Family estate: characterful light whites, cherry-like Castelão Francês (PERIQUITA). Best: oaked GARRAFEIRAS.

Adega A cellar or winery.

Alenquer r w Aromatic reds, whites from IPR just N of Lisbon. Good estate wines from QUINTAS DE ABRIGADA and PANCAS.

Alentejo r (w) ★→★★★ 91 92 93 94 95 Vast tract of S Portugal with only sparse vineyards, nr the Spanish border, but rapidly emerging potential for excellent wine. To date the great bulk has been coop-made. Estate wines from HERDADE DE MOUCHAO, JOSE DE SOUSA, QUINTA DO CARMO (now part Rothschild-owned) and ESPORAO have potency and style. Best coops are at BORBA, REDONDO and REGUENGOS. Growing excitement here. Now classified as a VINHO REGIONAL subdivided into 5 DOCs: BORBA, REDONDO, REGUENGOS, PORTALEGRE, VIDIGUEIRA; and 3 IPRs: Granja-Amareleja, Moura, EVORA.

Algarve r w ★ Wines of the holiday area are covered by DOCs Lagos, Tavira, Lagoa and Portimão. Nothing to write home about.

Aliança, Caves Bair r w sp res ★★→★★★ Large BAIRRADA-based firm making classic method sparkling. Reds and whites incl good Bairrada wines and mature DAOS. Aliança Tinta Velha is the best-selling red in Portugal.

Almeirim Ribatejo r w ★ Large new IPR east of ALENQUER. Its coop makes the admirably fruity, extremely inexpensive Lezíria.

Alta Mesa See Estremadura.

Arinto White grape best from central and S Portugal where it retains acidity and produces fragrant crisp dry white wines.

Arrábida Terras do Sado r w IPR. Reds mostly from CASTELAO FRANCES (or PERIQUITA) some Cab S and Chard allowed.

Arruda, Adega Cooperative de Est r res ★ 90 91 Vinho Tinto Arruda is a best buy, but avoid the reserva. (Arruda is now an IPR.)

Aveleda, Quinta da VV w ★★ DYA Reliable VINHO VERDES made on the Aveleda estate of the Guedes family. Sold dry in Portugal but sweetened for export.

Azevedo, Quinta de VV w ★★ DYA Superior VINHO VERDE from SOGRAPE. 100% LOUREIRO grapes.

Bacalhoa, Quinta da Set r res ★★★ 88 89 90 91 92 American-owned estate nr SETUBAL, famous for harmonious fruity mid-weight Cab vinified by J P VINHOS.

Bairrada Bair r w sp ★→★★★ 83 85 86 87 88 89 90 91 92 94 DOC for excellent red GARRAFEIRAS. Also good classic method sparkling. Now an export hit.

Barca Velha Douro r res ★★★★ 78 81 82 83 85 Perhaps Portugal's best red, made in v limited quantities in the high DOURO by the port firm of FERREIRA (now owned by SOGRAPE). Powerful resonant wine with deep bouquet, but being challenged by younger rivals (see Redoma).

Beiras VINHO REGIONAL including DAO, BAIRRADA and granite mt ranges of central Portugal. MATEUS ROSE is now classified as Vinho Regional Beiras. IPRs: CASTELO Rodrigo, COVA DE BEIRA, LAFOES, PINHEL.

Borba Alen r ★→★★★ Small DOC area near Evora producing some of the best ALENTEJO wine.

Borba, Adega Cooperativa de Alen r (w) res ★→★★ 84 88 89 90 91 92 93 Leading ALENTEJO coop modernized with stainless steel and oak by EC funding. Big fruity vinho de año red and vg reserva.

Borges & Irmão Merchants of port and table wines at Vila Nova de Gaia, incl GATAO and (better) Gamba VINHOS VERDES, sparkling Fita Azul.

Branco White.

Brejoeira, Palacio de VV w (r) ★★★ Outstanding estate-made VINHO VERDE from MONCAO, with astonishing fragrance and full fruity flavour. 100% Alvarinho grapes used.

Bright Brothers The gifted Australian Peter Bright, formerly with VINHOS, has teamed up with his brother to make several attractive RIBATEJO wines: Chard, Sauv, 'Early Release' Cab (93), Merlot (93), also pleasant (92 94) DOURO reds.

Buçaco Beiras r w (p) res ★★★★ (r) 51 53 57 58 60 63 67 70 72 75 77 78 82 (w) 56 65 66 70 72 75 78 82 84 85 86 Legendary speciality of the Palace Hotel at Buçaco nr Coimbra, not seen elsewhere. At best incredible quality, worth the journey. So are the palace and park.

A choice of Portuguese wines
Dry Muscat J P Vinhos white
Palacio de Brejoeira Vinho Verde
Red and White Vinho Verde Cooperativa de Ponte de Lima
Dão ('85) Porta dos Cavalheiras red
Quinta da Bacalhoa ('91) Cabernet Sauvignon
Barca Velha ('85) A A Ferreira (Sogrape) red
Quinta do Carmo ('88) red
Moscatel de Setúbal (6-year-old) José Maria da Fonseca

Bucelas Est w ★★★ Tiny demarcated region N of Lisbon in the hands of 3 producers. Quinta da Romeira make attractive wines from the ARINTO grape.

Camarate, Quinta de Est r ★★ 85 86 87 89 90 Notable red from JOSE MARIA DA FONSECA, S of Lisbon, incl detectable proportion of Cab S.

Campos da Silva Olivera, JC Dão r res ★★ 84 85 Small ADEGA with v fruity estate DAO, Sete Torres Reserva.

Carcavelos Est br sw ★★★ Normally NV. Minute DOC W of Lisbon. Excellent but rare sweet aperitif or dessert wines average 19% alcohol and resemble honeyed MADEIRA. The only producer is now Quinta dos Pesos, Caparide.

Carmo, Quinta do Alen r w res ★★★ 86 87 88 89 92 Beautiful small ALENTEJO ADEGA, partly bought '92 by Rothschilds (Lafite). 125 acres, plus cork forests. Fresh dry white, better fruity harmonious red. 2nd wine: Dom Martinho (90).

Cartaxo Ribatejo r w ★ District in RIBATEJO N of Lisbon, now an IPR area making everyday wines popular in the capital.

Cartuxa, Herdade de Alen r w ★ 89 90 91 94 Vast estate nr EVORA with nearly 500 v'yd acres. Big ripe flavoured reds; soft creamy whites.

Carvalho, Ribeiro & Ferreira N Lisbon r w res ★★→★★★ Large merchants for SERRADAYRES and excellent GARRAFEIRAS from the RIBATEJO and elsewhere (74 78 85 91). Have now ceased trading but wines are still seen.

Casa da Insua Dão r w ★★ One of the v few single-estate wines of DAO (but not DOC), made with a proportion of Cab for the proprietors by FONSECA.

Casa de Sezim VV w ★ DYA Estate-bottled VINHO VERDE from a member of the association of private producers, APEVV.

Casal García VV w ★★ DYA Big-selling VINHO VERDE, made at AVELEDA.

Casal Mendes VV w ★★ DYA The VINHO VERDE from CAVES ALIANCA.

Casaleiro Trademark of Caves Dom Teodosio-João T Barbosa, who make a variety of standard wines: DAO, VINHO VERDE etc.

Castelão Francês Red grape widely planted throughout S Portugal. Good firm-flavoured reds, often blended with Cab S. Aka PERIQUITA.

Castelo Rodrigo Beiras r w IPR reds resembling DAO.

Cepa Velha VV w (r) ★★★ Brand name of Vinhos de Monção. Their Alvarinho is one of the best VINHOS VERDES.

Chaves Trás-os-Montes r w IPR. Sharp pale fizzy reds from granite soils. Rounder ones from schist.

Portugal entries also cross-refer to Sherry, Port & Madeira, pages 172–179.

PORTUGAL

Colares r ★★★ Small DOC on the sandy coast W of Lisbon. Its antique-style dark red wines, rigid with tannin, are from vines that have never suffered from phylloxera. They need ageing, but TOTB (the older the better) no longer. See Paulo da Silva.

Conde de Santar Beiras r (w) res ★★→★★★ 78 85 86 Estate-grown DAO, matured and sold by port firm CALEM. Reserva wines are fruity, full-bodied, v smooth.

Consumo (vinho) Ordinary wine.

Coruche Ribatejo r w Large IPR of Sorraia River basin NE of Lisbon.

Côtto, Quinta do Douro r w res ★★★ 82 85 90 Pioneer table wines from port country; vg red Grande Escolha and also Q do Côtto are dense fruity tannic. Wines for long keeping. Also port.

Cova da Beira Beiras r w Largest of the IPRs nr Spanish border. Light reds best.

Crasto, Quinta do Douro r dr sw (★) 94 95 Top class PINHEL estate where Australian David Baverstock makes port and excellent oak-aged table wine.

Dão r w res ★★ 85 86 87 88 89 90 91 92 94 DOC region round town of Viseu. Produces some of Portugal's best-known but often dull table wines: solid reds of some subtlety with age; substantial dry whites. Most sold under brand names. But see Duque de Viseu, Casa da Insua, J M da Fonseca, Porta dos Cavalheiros, etc.

DOC (Denominacâo de Origem Controlada) Official wine region. There are 18 in Portugal, including BAIRRADA, COLARES, DAO, DOURO, SETUBAL, VINHO VERDE; and new in '95: BORBA, PORTALEGRE, REDONDO, REGUENGOS, VIDIGUEIRA in the ALENTEJO. See also IPR, Vinhos Regionals.

Doce (vinho) Sweet (wine).

Dom Ferraz Brand name for v drinkable wines from DAO, BAIRRADA etc, shipped to Great Britain.

Douro r w 82 83 84 85 86 87 88 89 90 91 92 94 Northern river whose valley produces port and some of Portugal's most exciting new table wines. See Barca Velha, Quinta do Côtto etc. Watch this space.

Duque de Viseu Dão r 90 91 92 High quality branded red DAO from SOGRAPE.

Esporão, Herdade do Alen w r ★★→★★★ 89 90 91 92 93 94 Owners Finagra SA spent US $10 million on space-age winery surrounded by 900 new v'yd acres. Wines are made (since '92) by Australian David Baverstock: light fresh Roupeiro white, fruity young red Alandra, superior (91 92) Cab S – Esporão, with a touch of Cab S, is one of ALENTEJO's best reds. Also incl Monte Velho gently oaked reds and fruity whites.

Espumante Sparkling.

Esteva Douro r ★ 92 V drinkable DOURO red from port firm FERREIRA.

Estremadura VINHO REGIONAL on Portugal's W coast, s'times called 'Oeste'. Large coops. Alta Mesa from São Marmade de Ventosa coop is good. IPRs: ALENQUER, ARRUDA, Encostas d'Aire, Obidos, TORRES VEDRES.

Evelita Douro r ★★ Reliable middle-weight red made near Vila Real by REAL COMPANHIA VINICOLA DO NORTE DE PORTUGAL. Ages well.

Evora Alen r w 86 87 88 89 90 91 Large new IPR south of Lisbon.

Fernão Pires White grape making ripe-flavoured slightly spicy whites in RIBATEJO. (Known as Maria Gomes in BAIRRADA.)

Ferreirinha Douro r res ★★★ 80 84 Reserva Especial. Second wine to BARCA VELHA, made in less than ideal vintages.

Fonseca, José Maria da Est r w dr sw sp res ★★→★★★ Venerable firm in Azeitão nr Lisbon with one of the longest and best ranges in Portugal, incl dry white PASMADOS, PORTALEGRE and QUINTA DE CAMARATE; red PERIQUITA, PASMADOS, TERRAS ALTAS, DAO, several GARRAFEIRAS; and famous dessert SETUBAL. Fonseca also owns JOSE DE SOUSA and makes the wines for CASA DA INSUA.

Fonseca Internacional, JM da nr Lisbon p sp ★ Formerly part of the last, now owned by Grand Metropolitan. Produces LANCERS rosé and a surprisingly drinkable sparkling Lancers Brut made by a continuous process of Russian invention.

Foz de Arouce, Quinta de Beiras r ★ Big, cask-aged red from heart of BEIRAS.

Franqueira, Quinta de VV w ★ Typically dry, fragrant VINHO VERDE made by Englishman Piers Gallie.

Fuiza Bright Ribatejo r w ★ 94 95 Joint venture with Peter Bright (BRIGHT BROS). Good Chard, Sauv, Merlot and Cab S.

Gaivosa, Quinta de Douro r ★ 92 94 Important estate near Regua. Deep concentrated cask-aged reds from port grapes. Quinta do Vale da Raposa (95) is lighter fruity red from same producer.

Garrafeira Label term. The 'private reserve' wine of a merchant, aged for a minimum of 2 years in cask and 1 in bottle, but often much longer. Usually their best, though traditionally often of indeterminate origin. Now have to show origin on label.

Gatão VV w ★★ DYA Standard BORGES & IRMAO VINHO V; fragrant but sweetened.

Gazela VV w ★★ DYA VINHO VERDE made at Barcelos by SOGRAPE since the AVELEDA estate went to a different branch of the Guedes family.

Generoso Aperitif or dessert wine rich in alcohol.

Grão Vasco Dão r w res ★★ 83 87 88 89 91 92 94 One of the best and largest brands of DAO, from a new high-tech ADEGA at Viseu. Fine red GARRAFEIRA (90); fresh young white (DYA). Owned by SOGRAPE.

IPR Indicações de Proveniência Regulamentada. See below.

> Thirty-one new Portuguese wine regions came into play in 1990; there are now 47. These 'IPRs' (Indicações de Proveniência Regulamentada) are on a six-year probation for DOC status. In EC terminology they are VQPRDs. Those which really perform are included in this edition. 1992 saw nine new broader 'Vinhos Regionais' introduced: Alentejo, Algarve, Beiras, Estremadura, Ribatejo, Rios do Minho, Terras Durienses, Terras do Sado, Trás os Montes.

José de Sousa Alen r res ★★ 83 86 87 88 90 91 (was Rosado Fernandes) Small firm recently acquired by JOSE MARIA DA FONSECA, making the most sophisticated of the full-bodied wines from the ALENTEJO, fermenting them in earthenware amphoras and ageing them in oak.

J P Vinhos Set r w sp res ★★→★★★ One of best-equipped and best-run wineries. Delicious João Pires Branco (Moscato), Catarina (with Chard), dry red and white Santa Marta, red Santo Amaro made by macération carbonique, Meia Pipa TINTO DE ANFORA, QUINTA DA BACALHOA, dessert SETUBAL, classic sparkling J P Vinhos Bruto and Cova da Ursa oak-fermented Chard.

Lafões Beiras r w IPR between DAO and VINHO VERDE.

Lagosta VV w ★ DYA VINHO VERDE white from the REAL COMPANHIA VINICOLA DO NORTE DE PORTUGAL.

Lancers Est p w sp ★ Sweet carbonated rosé and sparkling white extensively shipped to the US by FONSECA INTERNACIONAL.

Lagoaloa de Cima, Quinta da r w ★→★★ RIBATEJO estate of 125 aces.

Lezíria See Almeirim.

Loureiro Best VINHO VERDE grape variety: crisp fragrant white wines.

Madeira br dr sw ★★→★★★★ Atlantic island belonging to Portugal, making famous fortified dessert and aperitif wines. See pages 172–179.

PORTUGAL

NB Vintages in colour are those you should choose first for drinking in 1997.

Maduro (vinho) A mature table wine – as opposed to a VINHO VERDE.

Mateus Rosé Bair p (w) ★ World's biggest-selling medium-sweet carbonated rosé, from SOGRAPE at Vila Real and Anadia in BAIRRADA. Now a VINHO REG 'BEIRAS'.

Monção N subregion of VINHO VERDE on River Minho: best wines from the Alvarinho grape. See Palacio de Brejoeira.

Morgadio de Torre VV w ★★ DYA Top VV from SOGRAPE. Largely Alvarinho.

Mouchão, Herdade de Alen r res ★★★ 74 82 89 90 91 92 Perhaps the best ALENTEJO estate, ruined in the '74 revolution; since replanted.

Palmela Terras do Sado r w Sandy soil IPR. Reds esp long-lived.

Pancas, Quinta de Est r w res ★★ 90 91 92 94 Red and white Cab S and Chard from estate with NAPA connections nr ALENQUER (NW of Lisbon). 80% Cab has been much praised, but is somewhat heavy and closed. Quinta Dom Carlos is vg white made here from ARINTO grapes.

Pasmados V tasty JOSE MARIA DA FONSECA red from SETUBAL peninsula (88 90).

Pato, Luis Bair r sp ★★→★★★ 80 85 89 90 91 92 92 94 Luis Pato makes some of the best estate-grown BAIRRADA incl tremendous red QUINTA DE RIBEIRINHO and João Pato. Also fresh classic method sparkling.

Paulo da Silva, Antonio Bernardino Colares r (w) res ★★→★★★ 79 80 83 84 85 87 88 His COLARES Chita is one of the v few of these classics still made.

Pedralvites, Quinta de Bair w ★→★★ 93 95 Pleasant BAIRRADA white with apple and apricot flavours from the Maria Gomes grape, by SOGRAPE.

Periquita Est r ★★ 85 86 87 88 90 91 94 One of Portugal's most enjoyable robust reds, made by JOSE MARIA DA FONSECA at Azeitão S of Lisbon. Periquita is an alias of CASTELAO FRANCES, a grape much grown in the RIBATEJO.

Pinhel Beiras w (r) sp ★ IPR region E of DAO: similar white, mostly sparkling.

Pires, Vinhos João See J P Vinhos.

Planalto Douro w ★★ 95 Good white wine from SOGRAPE.

Planalto Mirandês Trás-os-Montes r w Large IPR NE of DOURO. Port grapes in reds. Verdelho in whites.

Ponte de Lima, Cooperativa de VV r w ★★ Maker of one of the best bone-dry red VINHOS VERDES, and first-rate dry and fruity white.

Porta dos Cavalheiros Dão ★★ 80 83 85 One of the best red DAOS, matured by CAVES SAO JOAO in BAIRRADA.

Portalegre Alen r w 88 89 90 91 92 94 New DOC on Spanish border. Strong fragrant reds with potential to age. Alcoholic whites.

Quinta Estate.

Ramada Est r w ★ 93 94 Modestly-priced red from the São Mamede coop: fruity and v drinkable.

Ramos-Pinto, Adriano Douro r ★★ 91 92 94 Rich red Duas Quintas from go-ahead port house.

Raposeira Douro w sp ★★ Well-known fizz made by the classic method at Lamego. Ask for the Bruto. An outpost of Seagram.

Real Companhia Vinícola do Norte de Portugal Giant of the port trade (see page 177); also produces EVELITA, LAGOSTA etc.

Redoma ★★ Amazing mouthfilling red from port-shippers NIEPOORT (91).

Redondo Alen r w Nr Spanish border. One of Portugal's best large coops. Newly granted DOC status.

Reguengos Alen r (w) res Important DOC nr Spanish border. Incl JOSE DE SOUSA and ESPORAO estates, plus large coop for good reds.

Ribatejo r w 86 87 88 89 90 91 92 94 VINHO REGIONAL on R Tagus north of Lisbon. Good GARRAFEIRAS and younger wines from ALMEIRIM coop, FUIZA BRIGHT and BRIGHT BROS. IPRs: ALMEIRIM, CARTAXO, Chamusca, Coruche, Santarém, Tomar.

A general rule for Portugal: chose youngest vintages of whites, oldest of red.

Ribeirinho, Quinta de Bair r sp ★★→★★★ 80 85 92 Vg tannic and concentrated reds from LUIS PATO. Limited edition Vinhos Velhas (94) is magnificent.

Rios do Minho VINHO REGIONAL covering NW – similar area to VINHO VERDE.

Roques, Quinta dos Dão r ★ 92 Promising estate for big solid oaked reds.

Rosa, Quinta de la Douro r ★★ 91 92 94 Firm oak-aged red from old port v'yds and young peppery Quinta das Lamelas, from Australian David Baverstock.

Rosado Rosé.

Rosado Fernandes See José de Sousa.

Saima, Casa de Bair r ★ 90 Promising estate: firm reds (from Baga grapes).

São Domingos, Comp dos Vinhos de Est r ★ 95 Reds (Espiga, Palha-Canas), from estate managed by José Neiva, maker of ALTA MESA.

São João, Caves Bair r w sp res ★★→★★★ 78 80 82 83 85 One of top BAIRRADA firms, known for fruity and full reds, PORTA DOS CAVALHEIROS DAOS. Also fizz.

Seco Dry.

Serradayres Ribatejo r (w) res ★ 92 94 Blended RIBATEJO table wines from CARVALHO, Ribeiro & Ferreira. Recently much improved.

Setúbal Set br (r w) sw (dr) ★★★ Tiny demarcated region S of the River Tagus, where FONSECA make a highly aromatic Muscat-based dessert wine (80 81 82 83 84 85 86 87 88 89 90 91 92 93) sold at 6 and 20 yrs old.

Sogrape Sociedad Comercial dos Vinhos de Mesa de Portugal. Largest wine concern in the country, making VINHOS VERDES, DAO, BAIRRADA, ALENTEJO, MATEUS ROSE, Vila Real red etc, and now owners of FERREIRA and OFFLEY port.

Tamariz, Quinta de VV w ★ Fragrant VINHO VERDE from Loureiro grapes only.

Terra Franca Bair r res ★★ 85 87 88 90 91 Good red BAIRRADA from SOGRAPE, available also as a GARRAFEIRA (85 89).

Terras Altas Dão r w res ★★ 90 91 92 Good DAO from FONSECA.

Terras do Sado VINHO REGIONAL covering sandy plains around Sado estuary. IPRs: ARRABIDA and PALMELA.

Tinta Roriz Major port grape (red) making good DOURO table wines and increasingly planted elsewhere for similarly full-bodied reds.

Tinto Red.

Tinto da Anfora Est r ★★ 85 86 87 89 90 91 Deservedly popular juicy and fruity red from J P VINHOS.

Torres Vedras Est r w ★ IPR area N of Lisbon famous for Wellington's 'lines'. Major supplier of bulk wine; one of biggest coops in Portugal.

Touriga Nacional Top red grape used for port and DOURO table wines; now increasingly elsewhere, esp DAO, ALENTEJO, ESTREMADURA.

Trás-os-Montes VINHO REGIONAL covering mountains of NE Portugal. Light reds and rosés. IPRs: CHAVES, PLANALTO-MIRANDES, Valpacos.

Trincadeira Vg red grape in ALENTEJO for spicy single-varietal wines.

Velhas, Caves Bucelas r w res ★★→★★★ Until very recently the only maker of BUCELAS; also good DAO and (80) Romeira GARRAFEIRAS.

Verde Green (see Vinhos Verdes).

Vidigueira Alen w r Famous DOC for traditionally-made unmatured whites from volcanic soils and some plummy reds.

Vinhos Regionals Larger provincial wine region, with same status as French vin de pays: they are: ALGARVE, ALENTEJO, BEIRAS, ESTREMADURA, RIBATEJO, RIOS DO MINHO, TRAS OS MONTES, TERRAS DO SADO. See also DOC, IPR.

Vinhos Verdes VV w ★→★★★★ r ★ DOC between R Douro and N frontier with Spain, for 'green wines' (which may be white or red): made from grapes with high acidity and (originally) undergoing a special secondary fermentation to leave them with a slight sparkle. Today the fizz is usually just added CO_2. Ready for drinking in spring after harvest.

Sherry, Port & Madeira

Sherry, Port and Madeira are the world's great classic fortified wines: reinforced with alcohol up to between 16 percent (for a light sherry) and 22 (for vintage port). No others have ever supplanted them for quality or value – despite many attempts.

1996 was a historic year for sherry in Great Britain. At last its name was legally recognized as belonging to Spain alone. The Cape, Cyprus and other imitators of this great wine must now find other names.

The map on pages 154–55 locates the port (Douro) and sherry (Jerez) districts. Madeira is an island 400 miles out in the Atlantic off the coast of Morocco, a port of call for west-bound sailing ships: hence its historical market in North America.

Shippers (that is producers, blenders and bottlers) are still far more important than growers in these industries. This section lists both types of wines and shippers names with the names and vintages (if any) of their best wines.

Abad, Tomas Small sherry BODEGA owned by LUSTAU. Vg light FINO.

Almacenista Individual matured but unblended sherry; usually dark dry wines for connoisseurs. Often superb quality and value. See Lustau.

Amontillado A FINO which has been aged in cask beyond its normal span to become darker, more powerful and pungent. The best are natural dry wines. In general use merely means medium sherry.

Amoroso Type of sweet sherry, v similar to a sweet OLOROSO.

Barbadillo, Antonio Much the largest SANLUCAR firm, with a range of 50-odd MANZANILLAS and sherries mostly excellent their type, including Sanlúcar FINO, superb SOLERA manzanilla PASADA, Fino de Balbaina, austere Principe dry AMONTILLADO. Also young Castillo de San Diego table wines.

Barbeito One of the last independent MADEIRA shipping families, now Japanese controlled. Wines incl rare vintages, eg MALMSEY 1901 and the latest, BUAL 1960.

Barros Almeida Large family-owned port house with several brands (incl Feist, Feuerheerd, KOPKE): excellent 20-yr-old TAWNY and many COLHEITAS.

Blandy One of two top names used by MADEIRA WINE CO. Duke of Clarence Rich Madeira is their most famous wine. 10-year-old reserves (VERDELHO, BUAL, MALMSEY) are good. Many glorious old vintages, now mostly seen at auctions.

Blázquez Sherry BODEGA at PUERTO DE SANTA MARIA owned by DOMECQ. Outstanding FINO, Carta Blanca, v old SOLERA OLOROSO Extra, and Carta Oro AMONTILLADO al natural (unsweetened).

Bobadilla Large JEREZ BODEGA, recently bought by OSBORNE and best known for v dry Victoria FINO and Bobadilla 103 brandy, esp among Spanish connoisseurs. Also excellent sherry vinegar.

Borges, H M Independent MADEIRA shipper of old repute.

Brown sherry British term for a style of budget dark sweet sherry.

Bual One of the best grapes of MADEIRA, making a soft smoky sweet wine, usually lighter and not as rich as MALMSEY. (See panel on page 179.)

Burdon English-founded sherry BODEGA owned by CABALLERO. Puerto FINO, Don Luis AMONTILLADO and raisiny Heavenly Cream are top lines.

Burmester Old, small, family port house with fine soft sweet 20-yr-old TAWNY; also vg range of COLHEITAS. Vintages: 48 55 58 60 63 70 77 80 84 85 89 91 94.

Caballero Important sherry shippers at PUERTO DE SANTA MARIA, best known for Pavón FINO, Mayoral Cream OLOROSO, excellent BURDON sherries and PONCHE orange liqueur. Also owners of LUSTAU.

Cálem Old family-run Portuguese house with fine reputation, esp for vintage wines. Owns excellent Quinta da Foz (82 84 86 87 88 89 90 92). Vintages: 50 55' 58 60 63' 66 70 75 77' 80 83 91 94. Good light TAWNY; exceptional range of COLHEITAS: 48 50 52 57 60 62 65 78 84 86.

Casa dos Vinhos da Madeira Vg house (long-time market leader in Canada): fine basic, 5 yr-olds, reserves and 10 yr-olds.

Churchill The only recently founded port shipper, already highly respected for excellent vintages 82 and 85, also 91 94. Vg traditional LBV. Quinta da Agua Alta is Churchill's single-QUINTA port: 83 87 90 92.

Cockburn British-owned (Allied-DOMECQ) port shippers with a range of good wines incl the v popular fruity Special Reserve. Fine VINTAGE PORT from high v'yds can look deceptively light when young, but has great lasting power. Vintages: 55 60 63' 67 70' 75 83 91 94.

Colheita Vintage-dated port of a single yr, but aged at least 7 winters in wood: in effect a vintage TAWNY. The bottling date is also shown on the label. Excellent examples come from KOPKE, CÁLEM, NIEPOORT and Krohn.

Cossart Gordon At one time the leading firm of MADEIRA shippers, founded 1745, with BLANDY now one of the two top-quality labels of the MADEIRA WINE CO. Wines slightly less rich than Blandy's. Best known for Good Company Finest Medium Rich but also producing 5-yr-olds reserves, old vintages (latest 74) and SOLERAS (esp BUAL 1845).

Cream Sherry A style of amber sweet sherry made by sweetening a blend of well-aged OLOROSOS. It originated in Bristol, England.

Croft One of the oldest firms shipping VINTAGE PORT: since 1678. Now owned by Grand Met Co. Well-balanced vintage wines tend to mature early (since 66). Vintages: 55 60 63' 66 67 70' 75 77' 82 91 94; and lighter vintage wines under the name of their Quinta da Roeda in several other years (78 80 83 87). Distinction is their most popular blend. MORGAN is a small separate company (see also Delaforce). Also in the sherry business with Croft Original (PALE CREAM) and Particular (medium), Delicado (FINO, also medium), and good PALO CORTADO.

Crusted Term for vintage-style port, usually blended from several vintages not one. Bottled young, then aged so it forms a 'crust'. Needs decanting. Specifically for UK market – not recognized in Portugal.

Cruz Huge brand and market leader in France. (The French take 40% of all port exports.) Standard TAWNY in French style – not brilliant quality. Owned by French co La Martiniquaise.

Delaforce Port shippers owned by CROFT, best known in Germany. His Eminence's Choice is a v pleasant TAWNY; VINTAGE CHARACTER is also good. Vintage wines are v fine, among the lighter kind: 55 58 60 63' 66' 70 74 75 77' 82 83 85' 94; Quinta da Côrte in 78 80 84 87 91.

Delgado, Zuleta Old-established SANLUCAR sherry firm best known for marvellous La Goya MANZANILLA PASADA.

Diez-Merito SA Sherry house famous for FINO Imperial and Victoria Regina OLOROSO. Bought by Rumasa and incorporated into BODEGAS INTERNACIONALES. Control passed to Marcos Eguizabal (of PATERNINA in RIOJA). Now apparently exists as little more than a name. Its excellent DON ZOILO sherry has been sold to the MEDINA group, and Gran Duque de Alba brandy to WILLIAMS & HUMBERT.

Domecq Giant family-run sherry BODEGAS at JEREZ, recently merged with Allied-Lyons as Allied-Domecq, famous also for Fundador and other brandies. Double Century Original OLOROSO, their biggest brand, now replaced by Pedro Cream Sherry, La Ina is excellent FINO. Other famous wines incl Celebration CREAM, Botaina (old AMONTILLADO) and magnificent Rio Viejo (v dry amontillado) and Sibarita (PALO CORTADO). Recently: a range of wonderful old SOLERA sherries (Sibarita, Amontillado 51-1a and Venerable Oloroso). Also in RIOJA and Mexico.

Don Zoilo Luxury sherries, including velvety FINO, recently sold by BODEGAS INTERNACIONALES to the MEDINA group (Luis Paez).

Dow Old port name, well-known for relatively dry but splendid vintage wines, said to have a faint 'cedarwood' character. Also vg VINTAGE CHARACTER and Boardroom, a 15-year-old TAWNY. Quinta do Bomfim is single-QUINTA port (78 79 82 84 86 87 88 89 90 92). Vintages: 55 60 63' 66' 70' 72 75 77' 80 83 85' 91 94. Dow, GOULD CAMPBELL, GRAHAM, QUARLES HARRIS, SMITH WOODHOUSE, WARRE all belong to the Symington family.

Dry Fly A household name in the UK. A crisp nutty AMONTILLADO made in JEREZ for its British proprietors Findlater Mackie Todd & Co.

Dry Sack See Williams & Humbert.

'All wine would be port if it could.' – old English saying

Duff Gordon Sherry shippers best known for El Cid AMONTILLADO. Also good FINO Feria and Nina Medium OLOROSO. Owned by OSBORNE.

Eira Velha, Quinta da Small port estate with old-style vintage wines shipped by MARTINEZ. Vintages: 78 82 87 92 94.

Ferreira One of the biggest Portuguese-owned port growers and shippers (since 1751). Largest selling brand in P. Well-known for old TAWNIES and juicily sweet, relatively light vintages: 60 63' 66 70' 75 77' 78 80 82 85' 87 91 94. Also Dona Antónia Personal Reserve, splendidly rich tawny Duque de Bragança and single-QUINTA wines Quinta do Seixo (83) and Q do Leda (90).

Fino Term for lightest, finest sherries, completely dry, v pale, delicate but pungent. Fino should always be drunk cool and fresh: it deteriorates rapidly once opened. TIO PEPE is the classic. Use half bottles if possible.

Flor A floating yeast peculiar to FINO sherry and certain other wines that oxidize slowly and tastily under its influence.

Fonseca Guimaraens British-owned port shipper with a stellar reputation; connected with TAYLOR'S. Robust deeply coloured vintage wine, among the v best. Vintages: Fonseca 60 63' 66' 70' 75 77' 80 83 85' 92 94; Fonseca Guimaraens 76 78 82 84 86 87 88 91 94. Quinta do Panascal 78 is a single-QUINTA wine. Also delicious VINTAGE CHARACTER Bin 27.

Forrester Port shippers and owners of the famous Quinta da Boa Vista, now owned by SOGRAPE. Their vintage wines tend to be round 'fat' and sweet, good for relatively early drinking. Baron de Forrester is vg TAWNY. Vintages: (Offley Forrester) 55 60 62' 63' 66 67 70' 72 75 77' 80 82 83 85' 87 89 94.

Garvey Famous old sherry shippers at JEREZ, now Danish-owned. Their finest wines are deep-flavoured FINO San Patricio, Tio Guillermo Dry AMONTILLADO and Ochavico Dry OLOROSO. San Angelo Medium amontillado is the most popular. Also Bicentenary PALE CREAM.

Gonzalez Byass Enormous family-run firm shipping the world's most famous and one of v best FINO sherries: TIO PEPE. Brands include La Concha medium AMONTILLADO, Elegante dry fino and new El Rocío Manzanilla Fina, San Domingo PALE CREAM, Nectar CREAM and Alfonso Dry OLOROSO. Amontillado del Duque is on a higher plane, as are Matusalem and Apostoles: respectively sweet and dry old olorosos of rare quality. Also makers of top-selling Soberano and exquisite Lepanto brandies. Now linked with Grand Metropolitan.

Gould Campbell See Smith Woodhouse.

Graham Port shippers famous for some of the richest, sweetest and best of VINTAGE PORTS, largely from their own Quinta dos Malvedos (52 57 58 61 65 68 76 78 79 82 84 86 87 88 90 92). Also excellent brands, incl Six Grapes RUBY, LBV, and 10- and 20-yr-old TAWNIES. Vintages: 55' 60 63' 66' 70' 75 77' 80 83 85' 91 94.

Guita, La Famous old SANLUCAR sherry BODEGA noteworthy for its particularly fine MANZANILLA PASADAS.

Hartley & Gibson See Valdespino.

Harvey's Important pillar of the Allied-Domecq empire, along with DOMECQ and TERRY. World-famous Bristol shippers of Bristol Cream and Bristol Milk (sweet), Club AMONTILLADO and Bristol Dry (medium), Luncheon Dry and Bristol FINO (not v dry). More to the point is their very good '1796' range of high quality sherries comprising Fine Old Amontillado, PALO CORTADO and Rich Old OLOROSO. Harvey's also control COCKBURN and have been MADEIRA shippers since 1796 (vg range).

Henriques & Henriques The biggest independent MADEIRA shippers at Câmara de Lobos, now with the largest, most modern cellars on the island: wide range of well-structured rich, toothsome wines – the 10 year-olds are gold and platinum medal winners. Also a good extra-dry aperitif, Monte Seco, and v fine old reserves and vintages.

Hildalgo, Vinícola Old family firm based in SANLUCAR DE BARRAMEDA, best known for high quality sherries: pale MANZANILLA La Gitana, fine OLOROSO Seco and Jerez CORTADO.

Sherry: which to choose
The sherry industry has been so badly depleted in recent years that a list of truly excellent wines still being made is needed to keep it in focus. They include: Barbadillo manzanillas; Blázquez Carta Blanca fino; Domecq La Ina fino, Rio Viejo oloroso, Sibarita palo cortado; Gonzalez Byass Tio Pepe fino, Amontillado del Duque, Matusalem and Apostoles dry and sweet olorosos; Hildago La Gitana manzanilla fino; Lustau Almacenista range; Osborne Fino Quinta and 'Rare' range (esp Alonso del Sabio); Páez Don Zoilo fino; Sandeman Don fino, Royal Corregidor sweet oloroso; de Soto Soto fino; Valdespino Inocente fino, Don Tomás amontillado; Williams & Humbert Pando fino and palo cortado.

Internacionales, Bodegas Once the pride of the now-defunct Rumasa and incorporating such famous houses as BERTOLA, VARELA and DIEZ-MERITO, the company was taken over by the entrepreneur Marcos Eguizabal. The building, one of the largest in Jerez, and remaining stocks of sherry, have recently been sold to the MEDINA group.

Jerez de la Frontera Centre of the sherry industry, between Cádiz and Seville in southern Spain. The word 'sherry' is a corruption of the name, pronounced in Spanish 'hereth'. In French, Xérès.

Kopke The oldest port house, founded by a German in 1638. Now belongs to BARROS ALMEIDA. Fair quality vintage wines (55 58 60 63 65 66 67 70 74 75 77 78 79 80 82 83 85 87 89 91 94) and excellent COLHEITAS.

Late-bottled vintage (LBV) Port from a single vintage kept in wood for twice as long as VINTAGE PORT (about 5 years), therefore it is lighter when bottled and ages more quickly. Traditional late-bottled vintage will 'throw a crust' like VINTAGE PORT (WARRE, SMITH WOODHOUSE, NIEPOORT, CHURCHILL, FERREIRA LBVs all qualify).

Leacock One of the oldest MADEIRA shippers, now a label of the MADEIRA WINE company. Basic St-John range is v fair; 10-yr-old Special Reserve MALMSEY and 15-yr-old BUAL are excellent.

Sherry, Port & Madeira entries also cross-refer to Spain and Portugal sections, respectively pages 154–165 and 166–171.

Lustau One of the largest family-run sherry BODEGAS in JEREZ (now controlled by CABALLERO), making many wines for other shippers, but with a vg Dry Lustau range (esp FINO and OLOROSO) and Jerez Lustau PALO CORTADO. Pioneer shippers of excellent ALMACENISTA and 'landed age' wines; AMONTILLADOS and olorosos aged in elegant bottles before shipping. See also Abad.

Macharnudo One of the best parts of the sherry v'yds, N of JEREZ, famous for wines of the highest quality, both FINO and OLOROSO.

Madeira Wine Company Formed in 1913 by two firms as the Madeira Wine Association, subsequently to include all the British MADEIRA firms (26 in total) amalgamated to survive hard times. Remarkably, three generations later the wines, though cellared together, preserve their house styles. BLANDY and COSSART GORDON are top labels. The company is now controlled by the Symington group (see Dow).

Malmsey The sweetest and richest form of MADEIRA; dark amber, rich and honeyed yet with Madeira's unique sharp tang. (See panel on page 179.)

Manzanilla Sherry, normally FINO, which has acquired a peculiar bracing salty character from being aged in BODEGAS at SANLUCAR DE BARRAMEDA, on the Guadalquivir estuary nr JEREZ.

Manzanilla Pasada A mature MANZANILLA, half-way to an AMONTILLADO-style wine. At its best (eg LA GUITA) one of the most appetizing of all sherries.

Marqués del Real Tesoro Old sherry firm, famous for its MANZANILLA and AMONTILLADO, bought by the enterprising José Estévez. Shrugging off the current slump in sales he has built a spanking new BODEGA – the first in years. Tío Mateo, for which the SOLERA was acquired from the now defunct Palomino & Vergara via HARVEY'S, is a vg FINO.

Martinez Gassiot Port firm, subsidiary of COCKBURN, known esp for excellent rich and pungent Directors 20-yr-old TAWNY, CRUSTED and LBV. Vintages: **55 60 63 67 70 75** 82 85 87 91 94.

Medina, José Originally a SANLUCAR family BODEGA, now a major exporter, especially to the Low Countries. By taking over the buildings and huge sherry stocks of the former BODEGAS INTERNACIONALES and by the more recent acquisition of WILLIAMS & HUMBRECHT, the Medina group, which also embraces Pérez Megia and Luis Paez, has probably become the biggest sherry grower and shipper, with some 25% of total volume.

Miles Formerly Rutherford & Miles. MADEIRA shippers famed for Old Trinity House Medium Rich etc. Latest vintage 73 VERDELHO. Now a MADEIRA WINE CO label.

Niepoort Small (Dutch) family-run port house with long record of fine vintages (42 45 55 60 63 66 70 75 77 78 80 **82** 83 87 91 92 94) and exceptional COLHEITAS. Also excellent SINGLE QUINTA port, Quinta do Passadouro (91 92).

Noval, Quinta do Historic port house now French- (AXA) owned. Intensely fruity structured and elegant VINTAGE PORT; a few ungrafted vines still at the QUINTA make a small quantity of Nacional – extraordinarily dark, full, velvety, slow-maturing wine. Also vg 20-yr-old TAWNY. Vintages: **55' 58 60 63 66' 67 70' 75 78 82** 85' 87 91 94.

Offley Forrester See Forrester.

Oloroso Style of sherry, heavier and less brilliant than FINO when young, but maturing to greater richness and pungency. Naturally dry, but frequently sweetened, for sale.

Osborne Enormous Spanish firm with well-known brandies but also good sherries including Fino Quinta, Coquinero dry AMONTILLADO, 10 RF (or Reserva Familiale) Medium OLOROSO. Also a range of v fine 'Rare' sherries, top quality with numbered bottles. See also Duff Gordon.

Pale Cream Popular style of pale sherry made by sweetening FINO, pioneered by CROFT's Original.

Palo Cortado A style of sherry close to OLOROSO but with some of the character of an AMONTILLADO. Dry but rich and soft. Worth looking for.

Pasada Style of FINO or MANZANILLA which is close to AMONTILLADO: a stronger drier wine without FLOR character.

Passing the Port

Vintage port is almost as much a ritual as a drink. It always needs to be decanted with great care (since the method of making it leaves a heavy deposit in the bottle). All except very old ports can safely be decanted the day before drinking. A week may not be too long. At table the decanter is traditionally passed from guest to guest clockwise. Vintage port can be immensely long-lived. Particularly good vintages older than those mentioned in the text include 1904 08 11 20 27 34 35 45 50. Bottles over 25 years old usually have very fragile corks. The answer is to cut the neck with red-hot 'port tongs'.

Pereira D'Oliveira Vinhos Family-owned MADEIRA co est'd 1850. V good basic range as well as 5 and 10 yr-olds; fine old reserve VERDELHO 1890, BUAL 1908 and Malvasia 1895.

Pinhel Small town at the heart of port country, in the upper DOURO.

Poças Junior Family port firm specializing in TAWNIES and COLHEITAS.

Ponche An aromatic digestif made with old sherry and brandy, flavoured with herbs and presented in eye-catching silvered bottles. See Caballero, de Soto.

Puerto de Santa María Second city and former port of the sherry area, with important BODEGAS.

PX Short for Pedro Ximénez, the grape part-dried in the sun used in JEREZ for sweetening blends.

Quarles Harris One of the oldest port houses, since 1680, now owned by the Symingtons (see Dow). Small quantities of LBV, mellow and well-balanced. Vintages: **60 63' 66' 70' 75** 77' 80 83 85' 91 94.

Quinta Portuguese for 'estate'. Also used to denote VINTAGE PORTS which are usually (legislation says 100%) from the estate's v'yds, made in good but not exceptional vintages.

Rainwater A fairly light, Medium Dry blend of MADEIRA – traditionally popular in N America.

Ramos-Pinto Dynamic small port house specializing in single-QUINTA TAWNIES of style and elegance; now owned by champagne house Louis Roederer.

Real Companhia Vinícola do Norte de Portugal Aka Royal Oporto Wine Co and Real Companhia Velha; large port house, with a long political history. Many brands and several QUINTAS, incl Quinta dos Carvalhas which makes TAWNIES and COLHEITAS. Vintage wines generally dismal.

Rebello Valente Name used for the VINTAGE PORT of ROBERTSON. Light but elegant and well-balanced, maturing rather early. Vintages: **55' 60 63' 66' 67 70' 72 75** 77' 80 83 85' 94.

Robertson Subsidiary of SANDEMAN, shipping (almost only to Holland) REBELLO VALENTE VINTAGE, LBV, Robertson's Privateer Reserve, Game Bird TAWNY, 10-yr-old Pyramid and 20-yr-old Imperial. Vintages: **63' 66' 67 70' 72 75** 77' 80 83 85' 94.

Rosa, Quinta de la Fine single-QUINTA port from the Bergqvist family at Pinhão. Recent return to traditional methods and stone lagares. Look for 85 88 90 vintages.

Rozes Port shippers controlled by Moët-Hennessy. RUBY v popular in France; also TAWNY. Vintages: **63 67 77'** 78 83 85 87 91 94.

Ruby Youngest (and cheapest) port style: simple, sweet and red. The best are vigorous, full of flavour; others can be merely strong and rather thin.

Sanchez Romate Family firm in JEREZ since 1781. Best known in Spanish-speaking world, esp for brandy Cardenal Mendoza. Good sherry: FINO Cristal, OLOROSO Don Antonio, AMONTILLADO NPU ('Non Plus Ultra').

Sandeman A giant of the port trade and a major figure in the sherry one, owned by Seagram. Founder's Reserve is their well-known VINTAGE CHARACTER; TAWNIES are much better. Partners' RUBY is new (94). Vintage wines are at least adequate – some of the old vintages were superlative (**55' 57 58 60' 62' 63' 65 66 67 68 70' 72 75 77 78 80 82 88 94**). Of the sherries, Medium Dry AMONTILLADO is top-seller, Don FINO is vg; also two excellent CREAM SHERRIES: Armada, and rare de luxe Royal Corregidor. Also shippers of MADEIRA since 1790 (elegant RAINWATER, fine Rich).

Sanlúcar de Barrameda Seaside sherry town (see Manzanilla).

Sercial MADEIRA grape for driest of the island's wines – a supreme aperitif. (See panel on the next page.)

Smith Woodhouse Port firm founded in 1784, now owned by the Symington family (see Dow). Gould Campbell is a subsidiary. Relatively light and easy wines incl Old Lodge TAWNY, Lodge Reserve VINTAGE CHARACTER (widely sold in USA). Vintages (v fine): **60 63' 66' 70' 75** 77' 80 83 85' 91 92 94. Gould Campbell Vintages: **60 63 66 70 75** 77 80 83 85 91 94.

Solera System used in making both sherry and (in modified form) MADEIRA, also some port. It consists of topping up progressively more mature barrels with slightly younger wine of the same sort, the object being to attain continuity in the final wine. Most sherries when sold are blends of several solera wines.

Soto, José de Best known for inventing PONCHE, this family firm, which now belongs to the former owner of RUMASA, José María Ruiz Mateos, also makes a range of good sherries, esp the delicate FINO.

Tawny Style of port aged for many yrs in wood (VINTAGE PORT is aged in bottle) until tawny in colour. Many of the best are 20-yrs-old. Low-price tawnies are blends of red and white ports. Taste the difference.

Taylor, Fladgate & Yeatman (Taylor's) Often considered the best of the port shippers, esp for full rich long-lived VINTAGE wine and TAWNIES of stated age (40-yr-old, 20-yr-old etc). Their VARGELLAS estate is said to give Taylor's its distinctive scent of violets. Vintages: **55' 60' 63' 66' 70' 75** 77' 80 83' 85' 92' 94. QUINTA DE VARGELLAS is shipped unblended in certain (lesser) years (**67 72 74** 76 78 82 84 86 87 88 91). Also now Terra Feita single-QUINTA wine (82 86 87 88 91). Their LBV is also better than most.

Terry, Fernando A de Magnificent BODEGAS at PUERTO DE SANTA MARIA, now part of Allied-Domecq. Makers of Maruja MANZANILLA and a range of popular brandies. The blending and bottling of all HARVEY'S sherries is carried out at the vast modern El Pino plant.

Tío Pepe The most famous of FINO sherries (see Gonzalez Byass).

Valdespino Famous family BODEGA at JEREZ, owner of the Inocente vineyard and making the excellent aged FINO of that name. Tío Diego is their dry AMONTILLADO, Solera 1842 an OLOROSO, Don Tomás their best amontillado. Matador is the name of their popular range. In the US, where their sherries rank No 3 in sales volume, they are still sold as 'Hartley & Gibson'.

Vargellas, Quinta de Hub of the TAYLOR'S empire, giving its very finest ports. The label for in-between vintages. See Taylor Fladgate & Yeatman.

Verdelho MADEIRA grape for fairly dry but soft wine without the piquancy of SERCIAL. A pleasant aperitif and a good all-purpose wine. Some glorious old vintage wines. (See panel on next page.)

Vesuvio, Quinta de Enormous 19th-C FERREIRA estate in the high DOURO. Bought '89 by Symington family. 130 acres planted. Esp 89 90 91 92.

Vintage Character Somewhat misleading term used for a good quality, full and meaty port like a premium RUBY. Lacks the splendid 'nose' of VINTAGE PORT.

Vintage Port The best port of exceptional vintages is bottled after only 2 yrs in wood and matures very slowly for up to 20 or more in bottle. Always leaves a heavy deposit and therefore needs decanting.

> Since 1993, Madeiras labelled Sercial, Verdelho, Bual or Malmsey must be at least 85% from that grape variety. The majority, made using the chameleon Tinta Negra Mole grape, which vinified similarly easily imitates each of these grape styles, may only be called Seco (Dry), Meio Seco (Medium Dry), Meio Doce (Medium Rich) or Doce (Rich) respectively. Meanwhile replanting is building up supplies of the (rare) classic varieties.

Warre The oldest of all British port shippers (since 1670), owned by the Symington family (see Dow) since 1905. Fine elegant long-maturing vintage wines, a good TAWNY (Nimrod), VINTAGE CHARACTER (Warrior), and excellent LBV. Their single-v'yd Quinta da Cavadinha is a new departure (78 79 82 84 86 87 88 89 90 92). Vintages: 55' 58 60 63' 66' 70 75 77' 80 83 85' 91 94.

White Port Port made of white grapes, golden in colour. Formerly made sweet, now more often dry: a fair aperitif but a heavy one.

Williams & Humbert Famous first-class sherry BODEGA, now owned by the MEDINA group. Dry Sack (medium AMONTILLADO) is its best-seller; Pando an excellent FINO; Canasta CREAM and Walnut BROWN are good in their class; Dos Cortados is its famous dry old OLOROSO. Also the famous Gran Duque de Alba brandy acquired from DIEZ-MERITO.

Wisdom & Warter Not a magic formula for free wine, but an old BODEGA (controlled by GONZALEZ BYASS) with good sherries, especially AMONTILLADO Tizón and v rare Solera. Also FINO Olivar.

Switzerland

Heavily shaded areas are the wine growing regions

S witzerland is handicapped by expensive money and the fact that her top wines come from tiny estates – hence are all drunk locally. Yet almost all Swiss wines (especially whites) are enjoyable and satisfying – if dear. Switzerland has some of the world's most efficient and productive vineyards; costs are high and nothing less is viable. All the most important (28,000 out of 37,000 acres) are in French-speaking areas: along the south-facing slopes of the upper Rhône Valley and Lake Geneva, respectively the Valais and the Vaud. Wines from German- and Italian-speaking zones are mostly drunk locally. Wines are known by place, grape names and legally controlled type names and are usually drunk young. 1988 saw the establishment of a Swiss cantonal and federal appellation system: established in Geneva first (1988, revised 1993), then the Valais (1991), Neuchâtel (1993) and Vaud (1995); others are still under discussion.

Aargau Wine-growing canton in E Switz (963 acres). Best for fragrant RIES-SILVANER and rich BLAUBURGUNDER.
Aigle Vaud r w ★★→★★★★ Well-known for elegant whites and supple reds.
Aligoté White Burgundy variety doing well in the VALAIS and GENEVA.
Amigne Trad VALAIS white grape, esp of VETROZ. Full-bodied tasty, often sweet.
Ardon Valais r w ★★→★★★★ Wine commune between SION and MARTIGNY.
Arvine Old VALAIS white grape (also 'Petite Arvine'): dry and sweet, elegant long-lasting wines with characteristic salty finish. Best in SIERRE, SION.

Auvernier NE r p w ★★ Old wine village on Lake NEUCHATEL and biggest wine-growing commune of the canton.

Basel Second-largest Swiss town and canton with many vines: divided into Basel-Stadt and Baselland. Best wines: RIES-SYLVANER, BLAUBURGUNDER, CHASSELAS.

Beerliwein Originally wine of destemmed BLAUBURG'R (E). Today name for wine fermented on skins traditionally rather than SUSSDRUCK.

Bern Swiss capital and canton of same name. V'yds in W (BIELERSEE: CHASSELAS, PINOT, SPECIALITIES) and E (Thunersee: BLAUBURGUNDER, RIES-SYLVANER); 635 acres. Prized by Germanic Swiss.

Bex Vaud r w ★★ CHABLAIS appellation, esp for red wines.

Bielersee r p w ★→★★ Wine region on N shore of the Bielersee (dry light CHASSELAS, PINOT N) and at the foot of Jolimont (SPECIALITIES).

Blauburgunder German-Swiss name for PINOT N. (Aka Clevner.)

Bonvillars Vaud r p w ★→★★ Characterful red AC of upper end of L Neuchâtel.

Bündner Herrschaft Grisons r p w ★★→★★★★ Best German Swiss region incl top villages: Fläsch, Jenins, Maienfeld, Malans. Serious BLAUB'R ripens esp well due to warm Foehn wind, cask-aged vg. Also CHARD, SPECIALITIES.

Recent vintages

1995 Variable year: humid June, hot dry July, wet September; very sunny harvest led to very good wines.

1994 Summer close to perfect; but rainy harvest.

1993 Classic year: wines better than expected.

1992 A hot summer with particularly high yields in the east; a rainy harvest in the south.

Calamin Vaud w ★★→★★★ LAVAUX v'yds next to DEZALEY: lush fragrant whites.

Chablais Vaud r w ★★→★★★★ Wine region on right bank of Rhône and upper-end of L Geneva, incl VILLAGES: AIGLE, BEX, Ollon, VILLENEUVE, YVORNE. Robust full-bodied reds and whites

Chamoson Valais r w ★★→★★★ Largest VALAIS wine commune, esp for SYLVANER.

Chardonnay Long-est'd in French Switzerland, now also in other parts.

Chasselas (Gutedel) Top white grape of French cantons: neutral in flavour, so takes on local character: elegant (GENEVA), refined and full (VAUD), potent and racy (VALAIS), pleasantly sparkling (lakes Bienne, Neuchâtel, Murtensee). In east only in BASEL.

Completer Native white grape, only in GRISONS. Aromatic generous wines which keep well. ('Complet' was a monk's final daily prayer, hence his night cap glass of something strong.)

Cornalin Local VALAIS speciality; dark spicy v strong red. Best: SALGESCH, SIERRE.

Cortaillod Neuchâtel r (w) ★★ Small village south of Lake: esp PINOT N, OEIL DE P.

Côte, La Vaud r p w ★→★★★ Largest VAUD wine area between Lausanne and Geneva (N shore of Lake). Whites with elegant finesse; fruity harmonious reds. Esp from MONT-SUR-ROLLE, Vinzel, Luins, Féchy, Morges etc.

Côtes de l'Orbe Vaud r p w ★→★★ N VAUD appellation between Lake Neuchâtel and Lake Geneva esp for light fruity reds .

Dézaley Vaud w (r) ★★★ Famous LAVAUX v'yd on slopes above L Geneva, once tended by Cistercian monks. Unusually potent CHASSELAS, develops esp after ageing. Red Dézaley is a GAMAY-PINOT N-MERLOT-SYRAH rarity.

Dôle Valais r ★★→★★★★ Appellation for PINOT N, can also be blend of PINOT, GAMAY and other varieties (at least 85% PN): full, supple, often vg. Lightly pink Dôle Blanche is pressed immediately after harvest. Eg from MARTIGNY, SIERRE, SION, VETROZ etc.

Epesses Vaud w (r) ★★→★★★★ LAVAUX appellation: supple full-bodied whites.

Ermitage Alias the Marsanne grape; a VALAIS SPECIALITY. Concentrated full-bodied dry white, s'times with residual sugar. Esp from FULLY, SION.

Féchy Vaud ★★→★★★ Famous appellation of LA COTE, esp elegant whites.

Federweisser German Swiss name for white wine from BLAUBURGUNDER.

Fendant Valais w ★→★★★ VALAIS appellation for CHASSELAS. Wide range of wines. Better ones now use village names only (FULLY, SION etc).

Flétri/Mi-flétri Late-harvested grapes from which sweet and slightly sweet wine (respectively) is made; SPECIALITY in VALAIS.

Fribourg Smallest French Swiss wine canton (279 acres, nr Jura). Esp for CHASSELAS, PINOT N, GAMAY, SPECIALITES from VULLY, L Murten, S Lake Neuchâtel.

Fully Valais r w ★★→★★★ Village nr MARTIGNY: excellent ERMITAGE and GAMAY.

Gamay Red Beaujolais grape abounds in French cantons but is forbidden in German. Fairly thin wine mostly used for blends. (See Salvagnin, Dôle).

Geneva Capital of, and French Swiss wine canton; the third largest (3,312 acres). Key areas: MANDEMENT, Entre Arve et Rhône, Entre Arve et Lac. Mostly CHASSELAS, GAMAY. Also lately CHARD, Cab, PINOT and good ALIGOTE.

Gewürztraminer Grown in Switzerland as a SPECIALITY variety.

Glacier, Vin du (Gletscherwein) Fabled oxidized wooded white from rare Rèze grape of Val d'Anniviers; offered by the thimbleful to visiting dignitaries.

Goron Valais r ★ AC for pleasant reds and DOLE that fails to make the grade.

Grand Cru Quality designation. Implication differs by canton: in VALAIS, GENEVA and VAUD used where set requirements fulfilled.

Grisons (Graubünden) Mountain canton, mainly in German Switz (BUNDNER HERRSCHAFT, Churer Rheintal; esp BLAUBURGUNDER) and partly S of Alps (Misox, esp MERLOT). 921 acres, primarily for red, also RIESLING-SYLVANER and SPECIALITIES.

Heida (Païen) Old VALAIS white grape (Jura's Savagnin) for country wine of upper V (v'yds of Visperterminen at 1,000 m+). Successful now in lower V too.

Humagne Strong native white grape (VALAIS SPECIALITY). Humagne Rouge (unrelated, from Aosta Valley) also. Esp from CHAMOSON, LEYTRON.

Landwein (Vin de pays) Traditional light easy white and esp red BLAUB'R from E.

Lausanne Capital of VAUD. No longer with v'yds in town area, but long-time owner of classics: Abbaye de Mont, Château Rochefort (LA COTE); Clos des Moines, Clos des Abbayes, Dom de Burignon (LAVAUX). Pricey.

Lavaux Vaud w (r) ★→★★★ Scenic region on N shore of L Geneva between Montreux and Lausanne. Delicate refined whites, good reds. Best: CALAMIN, Chardonne, DEZALEY, EPESSES, Lutry, ST-SAPHORIN, VEVEY-MONTREUX and Villette.

Leytron Valais r w ★★→★★★ Commune nr SION/MARTIGNY, esp Le Grand Brûlé.

Mandement r w ★→★★ Geneva wine area incl Satigny, the largest wine commune of Switzerland. Wines of local interest only.

Martigny Valais r w ★★ Lower VALAIS commune esp for HUMAGNE ROUGE.

Merlot Grown in Italian Switzerland (TICINO) since 1907 (after phylloxera destroyed local varieties): aromatic, soft. Also used with Cab.

Mont d'Or, Domaine du Valais w s/sw sw ★★→★★★ Well-sited property nr SION: rich concentrated demi-sec and sweet wines, notable SYLVANER.

Mont-sur-Rolle Vaud w (r) ★★ Important appellation within LA COTE.

Morges Vaud r p w ★→★★ Largest LA COTE/VAUD AOC: CHASSELAS, fruity reds.

Muscat Grown in VALAIS as a SPECIALITY.

Neuchâtel City and canton. V'yds (1,500 acres) from L Neuchâtel to BIELERSEE. Mainly CHASSELAS: fragrant lively (sur lie, sp). Also (increasingly) good PINOT N (esp OEIL DE PERDRIX), PINOT GR, CHARD.

Nostrano Word meaning 'ours', applied to red wine of TICINO, made from native and Italian grapes (Bondola, Freisa, Bonarda etc).

For key to grape variety abbreviations, see pages 7–13.

Oeil de Perdrix Pale PINOT rosé. Esp (originally) NEUCHÂTEL's; also VALAIS, VAUD.

Pinot Blanc (Weissburgunder) Recent, full-bodied and elegant Swiss wines.

Pinot Gris (Malvoisie) Widely planted white grape for dry and residually sweet wines. Makes v fine late-gathered wines in VALAIS (called Malvoisie).

Pinot Noir (Blauburgunder) Top red grape. Esp: BÜNDNER H, NEUCHÂTEL, VALAIS.

Rauschling Old white ZURICH grape; esp for discreet fruit, elegant acidity.

Riesling (Petit Rhin) Mainly in the VALAIS. Excellent botrytis wines.

Riesling-Sylvaner Swiss for Müller-THURGAU (top white of E; a SPECIALITY in W). Typically elegant wines with nutmeg aroma and some acidity.

St-Gallen E wine canton nr L Constance (540 acres). Esp for BLAUBURG'R (full-bodied), RIES-SYLVANER, SPECIALITIES. Incl Rhine Valley, Oberland, upper L Zürich.

St-Leonard Valais r w ★★→★★★ Wine commune between SIERRE and SION.

St-Saphorin Vaud w (r) ★★→★★★ Famous appellation of LAVAUX producing fine light whites.

Salquenen Valais r w ★→★★★ Village nr SIERRE. First to use 'GRAND CRU'.

Salvagnin Vaud r ★→★★★ GAMAY and/or PINOT N appellation. (See also Dôle.)

Schaffhausen German-Swiss canton and wine town on River Rhine. Esp BLAUBURGUNDER; also some RIESLING-SYLVANER and SPECIALITIES.

Schafis Bern r p w ★→★★ Top BIELERSEE village and name for wines of its N shore.

Schenk Europe-wide wine giant, founded and based in Rolle (VAUD). Owns firms in Burgundy, Bordeaux, Germany, Italy, Spain.

Sierre Valais r w ★★→★★★ Sunny resort and famous wine town. Known for Fendant, PINOT N, ERMITAGE, Malvoisie. Vg DOLE.

Sion Valais r w ★★→★★★ Capital/wine centre of VALAIS. Esp Fendant de Sion.

Sylvaner (Johannisberg, Gros Rhin) White grape esp in warm VALAIS v'yds. Heady, spicy: some with residual sweetness.

Spezialitäten (Spécialités/Specialities) Wines of unusual grapes: vanishing local Gwäss, Elbling, Bondola, etc, or modish Chenin Bl, Sauv, Cab (first grown experimentally). Eg VALAIS: 43 of its 47 varieties are considered 'specialities'.

Süssdruck Dry rosé/bright red wine: grapes pressed before fermentation.

Thurgau German Swiss canton beside Bodensee (632 acres). Wines from the valley of Thur: Weinfelden, Seebach, Nussbaume and Rhine. S shore of the Untersee. Esp BLAUBURGUNDER, also good RIES-SYLVANER (ie Müller-Thurgau: Herr Müller was born in the region).

Ticino Italian-speaking S Switzerland (with Misox), growing mainly MERLOT (good from mountainous Sopraceneri region) and SPECIALITIES. Trying out Cab (cask-matured Bordeaux style), Sauv, Sém, Chard, Merlot rosé.

Valais Rhône Valley from German-speaking upper-V to French lower-V. Largest and most varied wine canton in French Switz (13,000 acres). Near perfect climatic conditions. Wide range: 47 grape varieties including FENDANT, SYLVANER, GAMAY, PINOT N, plus many SPECIALITES. Esp white.

Vaud Region of L Geneva and the Rhône. French Switzerland's second largest wine canton (9,430 acres) incl CHABLAIS, LA COTE, LAVAUX and Bonvillars, Côtes de l'Orbe, VULLY, CHASSELAS stronghold. Also GAMAY, PINOT N etc.

Vétroz Valais w r ★★→★★★ Top village nr SION, esp famous for AMIGNE.

Vevey-Montreux Vaud r w ★★ Up-coming appellation of LAVAUX. Famous wine festival held about every 30 years; next in 1999.

Villeneuve Vaud w (r) ★★→★★★ Nr L Geneva: powerful yet refined whites.

Vispertal Valais w (r) ★→★★ Upper VALAIS v'yds esp for SPECIALITES.

Vully Vaud w (r) ★→★★★ Refreshing white from L Murten/FRIBOURG area.

Yvorne Vaud w (r) ★★★ Top CHABLAIS appellation for strong fragrant wines.

Zürich Capital of largest German-speaking wine canton (same name). Mostly BLAUBURGUNDER; also PINOT GRIS and GEWURZTRAMINER, and esp RIESLING-SILVANER and RAUSCHLING.

Austria

KAMPTAL
KREMSTAL
WACHAU
WEINVIERTEL
DONAULAND
VIENNA ○ Vienna
Danube
CARNUNTUM
THERMENREGION
NEUSIEDLERSEE
Neusiedler See
NEUSIEDLERSEE-
HUGELLAND
Mur
BURGENLAND
SOUTHWEST
STYRIA
SUDBURGENLAND
WEST ○ Graz
STYRIA
STYRIA

Heavily shaded areas
are the wine
growing regions

During the last decade Austria has emerged as a vigorous, innovative producer of dry white and dessert wines up to the very finest quality. Her red wines (20 percent of vineyards) are starting to make an international reputation too. New laws, passed in 1985 and revised for the 1993 vintage, include curbs on yields (Germany please copy) and impose higher levels of ripeness for each category than their German counterparts. Many regional names, introduced under the 1985 law, are still unfamiliar outside Austria. This is a country to explore.

Ausbruch PRADIKAT wine (v sweet) between Beerenauslese and Trockenbeeren-auslese in quality. Traditionally produced in RUST.

Ausg'steckt ('hung up') HEURIGEN are not open all year. To show potential visitors wine is being served, a green bush is hung up above the door.

Bergwein Legal classification for wines made from grapes grown on slopes with an incline of over 26%.

Blauburger Austrian red grape variety. A cross between BLAUER PORTUGIESER and BLAUFRANKISCH. Dark-coloured but light-bodied; simple wines.

Blauer Burgunder (Pinot Noir) A rarity. Vintages fluctuate greatly. Best in BURGENLAND, KAMPTAL, THERMENREGION (from growers BRUNDLMAYER, STIEGELMAR and UMATHUM).

Blauer Portugieser Light, fruity wines to drink slightly chilled when young. Mostly made for local consumption. Top producers: Fischer, Lust.

Blauer Wildbacher Red grape used to make SCHILCHER wines.

Blauer Zweigelt BLAUFRANKISCH-ST-LAURENT cross: high yields and rich colour. Top producers (especially Heinrich, Pittnauer, Pöckl, UMATHUM) are making it a reputation.

Blaufränkisch (Lemberger in Germany, Kékfrankos in Hungary) Austria's most widely planted red grape, especially in MITTELBURGENLAND: wines with good body, peppery acidity and a fruity taste of cherries. Often blended with Cabernet Sauvignon. Best from GESELLMANN, Iby, IGLER, Krutzler, Nittnaus, Tibor Szemes, E TRIEBAUMER and WENINGER.

Bouvier Indigenous grape, producing light wines with low acidity but plenty of aroma, esp good for Beeren- and Trockenbeerenauslese.

Bründlmayer, Willi r w sp ★★→★★★★ 90 92 93 94 95 Leading LANGENLOIS-KAMPTAL estate. Vg wines: both local (RIES, GRUNER V) and international (CHARD, red) styles. Also Austria's best Sekt.

Recent vintages

1995 Rain threatened to ruin the harvest, but late pickers and dessert winemakers hit the jackpot.

1994 Unusually hot summer and fine autumn resulted in v ripe grapes. An excellent vintage.

1993 Frost damage caused a smaller-than-average yield which produced excellent wines.

1992 Extremely hot summer may have led to acidity problems in some areas. Very good wines from the Wachau, Kamptal-Donauland and Styria. Good red wine year (esp Burgenland).

1991 Good to average quality along with a few top class wines from Burgenland.

1990 One of the best vintages of the last 50 yrs.

Burgenland Province and wine area (50,000 acres) in E next to Hungarian border. Warm climate. Ideal conditions, esp for botrytis wines near NEUSIEDLER SEE, also reds. Four wine regions: MITTELBURGENLAND, NEUSIEDLERSEE, NEUSIEDLERSEE-HUGELLAND and SUDBURGENLAND.

Buschenschank The same as HEURIGE; often a country cousin.

Cabernet Sauvignon Increasingly cultivated in Austria; used esp in blends.

Carnuntum r w Wine region since '94, E of Vienna, bordered by the Danube to the north. Best producers: Glatzer, Pitnauer.

Chardonnay Increasingly grown, mainly barrique-aged. Also trad in STYRIA as 'MORILLON' (unoaked): strong fruit taste, lively acidity. Esp BRUNDLMAYER, Loimer, MALAT, SATTLER, STIEGELMAR, TEMENT, Topf, WIENINGER.

Deutschkreutz r (w) MITTELBURGENLAND red wine area, esp for BLAUFRANKISCH.

Donauland (Danube) w (r) Wine region since '94, just W of Vienna. Includes KLOSTERNEUBURG and Wagram regions south of Danube. Mainly whites, esp GRUNER VELTLINER. Best producers include: Chorherren Klosterneuburg, Leth, Neumayer, Wimmer-Cerny, R Zimmermann.

Dürnstein w Wine centre of the WACHAU with famous ruined castle. Mainly GRUNER V, RIES. Top growers are FREIE WEINGARTNER WACHAU, KNOLL, Mittelbach, PICHLER, Schmidl.

Eisenstadt r w dr sw Capital of BURGENLAND and historic seat of Esterházy family. Top producer: Esterházy.

Falkenstein w Wine centre in eastern Weinviertel nr Czech border. Good GRUNER VELTLINER. Best producers: Jauk, Luckner, Salomon.

Federspiel Medium quality level of the VINEA WACHAU categories, roughly corresponding to Kabinett. Fruity, elegant wines.

Feiler-Artinger r w sw ★★★ 90 91 92 93 94 95 Vg RUST estate: top PRADIKATS.

Fels am Wagram r w Large wine region with loess terraces in DONAULAND. Best producers: Leth, Wimmer-Cerny.

Forstreiter Good KREMS grower; president of local growers' association.

Freie Weingärtner Wachau w (r) ★★→★★★ 91 92 93 94 95 Important and vg wine-growers' cooperative in DURNSTEIN. Excellent GRUNER VELTLINER, RIES.

Gamlitz w Largest, oldest region of southern STYRIA. Growers incl Lackner-Tinnacher, SATTLER.

Gemischter Satz A blend of grapes (mostly white) grown, harvested and vinified together. Traditional wine, still served in HEURIGEN.

Gesellmann, Engelbert r (w) ★★→★★★ 90 92 93 94 95 Estate in DEUTSCH-KREUTZ. Vg red and white: both traditional and international styles.

Gols r w dr sw Largest BURGENLAND wine commune (N shore of NEUSIEDLER SEE). Best producers: Beck, HEINRICH, Leitner, Nittnaus, Renner, STIEGELMAR.

Grüner Veltliner Austria's national white grape (over a third of total v'yd area). Fruity, racy, lively young wines. Distinguished age-worthy Spätlesen. Best producers: BRUNDLMAYER, FREIE WEING'R WACHAU, HIRTZBERGER, Högel, KNOLL, MANTLER, NIKOLAIHOF, Pfaffl, F X PICHLER, PRAGER, Schmelz, Walzer.

G'spritzer Popular refreshing summer drink, usually white wine-based; made sparkling by adding soda or mineral water. Esp in HEURIGEN.

Gumpoldskirchen w r dr sw Resort village S of Vienna, famous for HEURIGEN. Centre of THERMENREGION. Distinctive, tasty wines from ZIERFANDLER and ROTGIPFLER grapes. Best producers: Biegler, Schellmann.

Heinrich Gernot r w dr sw ★★→★★★ 90 91 92 93 94 Young modern estate in GOLS with Pannobile and (esp) red Gabarinza labels.

Heurige Wine of the most recent harvest, called 'new wine' for one yr, then classified as 'old'. Heurigen are wine houses where growers-cum-patrons serve wine by glass/bottle with simple local food – an institution, esp in VIENNA.

Hirtzberger, Franz w ★★★★ 90 91 92 93 94 95 Leading producer with 22 acres at Spitz an der Donau, WACHAU. Esp RIES and GRUNER VELTLINER.

Horitschon MITTELBURGENLAND region for reds. Best: Anton Iby, WENINGER.

Igler, Hans r ★★→★★★ 90 92 93 94 Top DEUTSCHKREUTZ estate; pioneer reds.

Illmitz w (r) dr sw SEEWINKEL region famous for Beeren- and Trockenbeeren-auslese. Best from KRACHER, Haider, Alois and Helmut Lang, Opitz.

Jamek, Josef w ★★ 91 92 93 94 95 Well-known estate and restaurant at Joching in the WACHAU. Pioneer of dry whites since the '50s.

Jurtschitsch/Sonnhof w (r) dr (sw) ★→★★★ 92 93 94 95 Domaine run by three brothers: vg whites (RIES, GRUNER VELTLINER, CHARD).

Kamptal r w Wine region since '94, along R Kamp N of Wachau. Top v'yds: LANGENLOIS, STRASS, Zöbing. Best growers: BRUNDLMAYER, Dolle, Ehn, Hiedler, Hirsch, JURTSCHITSCH, Loimer, METTERNICH-SANDOR, Topf.

Kattus ★→★★★ Producer of traditional Sekt in VIENNA.

Kellergassen Picturesque alleyways lined with wine presses and cellars, devoted exclusively to the production, storage and consumption of wine, situated outside the town, typical of the WEINVIERTEL region.

Klöch w W STYRIA wine town famous for Traminer. Best from Stürgkh.

Kloster Und Wine tasting centre in a restored Capuchin monastery near KREMS, run by ERICH SALOMON.

Klosterneuburg r w Wine district rich in tradition, N of VIENNA, with a famous Benedictine monastery and a wine college founded in 1860. Best producers: Chorherren Klosterneuburg, Zimmermann.

KMW Abbreviation for 'Klosterneuburger Mostwaage' (must level), the unit used in Austria to measure the sugar content in grape juice.

Knoll, Emmerich w ★★★→★★★★ 91 92 93 94 95 V traditional, highly regarded estate in Loiben, WACHAU, producing showpiece wines from GRUNER VELTLINER and RIESLING grapes.

Kollwentz-Römerhof w r dr (sw) ★★→★★★★ 90 92 93 94 95 Innovative wine producer in Grosshöflein nr EISENSTADT: Sauv Bl, Eiswein and reds.

Kracher, Alois w (r) dr (sw) ★★→★★★★ 81 89 90 92 93 94 95 First class small ILLMITZ producer; speciality: PRADIKATS, some barrique-aged, others not.

Krems w (r) dr (sw) Ancient town, W of VIENNA. Capital of KREMSTAL. Best from FORSTREITER, SALOMON, Weingut Stadt Krems, Walzer.

Kremstal w (r) Wine region since '94 esp for GRUNER V and RIES. Top growers: MALAT, MANTLER, Nigl, SALOMON, W Stadt Krems.

Langenlois r w ★★→★★★ Wine town and region in KAMPTAL with 5,000 acres. Best producers: BRUNDLMAYER, Ehn, Hiedler, JURTSCHITSCH.

Lenz Moser ★★→★★★ Major producer nr KREMS, now in 5th generation. Lenz Moser III invented a high vine system. Also incl wines from Schlossweingut Malteser Ritterorden (wine estate of the Knights of Malta) in Mailberg, WEINVIERTEL and Klosterkeller Siegendorf in BURGENLAND.

Loiben w Wine region in lower, wider part of Danube Valley (WACHAU) where conditions are ideal for RIES and GRUNER VELTLINER. Best from Alzinger, FREIE WEINGARTNER, KNOLL, FRANZ X PICHLER.

Malat, Gerald w r sp ★★→★★★ 90 91 92 93 94 95 Modern producer in Furth, S of KREMS; vg trad and 'international' wines. Good classic sparkling.

Mantler, Josef w ★★→★★★ 86 90 92 93 95 Leading trad estate in Gedersdorf nr KREMS. Vg RIES, GRUNER VELTLINER, CHARD, and rare Roter Veltliner (synonym for Malvasia grape, white wine).

Mayer, Franz w With 60 acres, the largest producer in VIENNA. Traditional jug wines (at picturesque HEURIGE Beethovenhaus – yes, he drank here), plus excellent 'older-vintage' (20–30 yrs) RIESLING.

Messwein Mass wine: must have ecclesiastical approval and natural must.

Metternich-Sándor, Schlossweingüter w (r) ★→★★ Large wine estate in STRASS; 173 acres of vineyard jointly run with Adelsgütern Starhemberg, Abensberg-Traun and Khevenhüller-Metsch estates.

Mittelburgenland r (w) dr (sw) Wine region on Hungarian border protected by three hill ranges. Makes large quantities of appellation-controlled red (esp BLAUFRANKISCH). Producers: GESELLMANN, Iby, IGLER, Szemes, Weninger.

Mörbisch r w dr sw Region on W shore of NEUSIEDLER SEE. Schindler is good.

Morillon Name given in STYRIA to CHARDONNAY.

Müller-Thurgau See Riesling-Sylvaner.

Muskat-Ottonel Grape for fragrant, often dry whites, interesting PRADIKATS.

Muskateller Rare aromatic grape, recently popular again as aperitif. Best from STYRIA and WACHAU. Top growers: Gross, HIRTZBERGER, Lackner-Tinnacher, F X PICHLER, POLZ, SATTLER.

Neuburger Indigenous white grape: nutty flavour; mainly in the WACHAU (delicate, flowery), in the THERMENREGION (mellow, well-developed) and in N BURGENLAND (strong, full). Best from FREIE WEINGARTNER, HIRTZBERGER.

Neusiedler See V shallow (max 1.5m deep) BURGENLAND lake on Hungarian border. Warm temperatures, autumn mists encourage botrytis. Gives name to wine regions of NEUSIEDLERSEE-HUGELLAND and NEUSIEDLERSEE.

Neusiedlersee r w dr sw Region N and E of NEUSIEDLER SEE. Best growers: Beck, HEINRICH, KRACHER, Nittnaus, Opitz, Pöckl, UMATHUM, Velich.

Neusiedlersee-Hügelland r w dr sw Wine region W of NEUSIEDLER SEE based around OGGAU, RUST and MORBISCH on the lake shores, and EISENSTADT in the foothills of the Leitha Mts. Best producers: FEILER-ARTINGER, KOLLWENTZ, Mad, Prieler, Schröck, ERNST TRIEBAUMER.

Niederösterreich (Lower Austria) With 58% of Austria's v'yds: CARNUNTUM, DONAULAND, KAMPTAL, KREMSTAL, THERMENREGION, WACHAU, WEINVIERTEL.

Nikolaihof w ★★★ 90 91 92 93 94 95 Mautern-Wachau estate: top RIES, GRUNER V.

Nussdorf VIENNA district famous for HEURIGEN and vg Ried Nussberg.

Oggau Wine region on the W shore of NEUSIEDLER SEE.

Pichler, Franz Xavier w ★★★★ 90 91 92 93 94 95 Top WACHAU producer with v intense rich RIES, GRUNER VELTLINER (esp Kellerberg) and MUSKATELLER of great breed. Widely recognized as Austria's No 1 grower.

Polz, Erich and Walter w ★★★ 91 92 93 94 95 S STYRIAN (Weinstrasse) growers: top Hochgrassnitzberg label for SAUV, CHARD. Building international reputation.

Prädikatswein Quality graded wines from Spätlese upwards (Spätlese, Auslese, Eiswein, Strohwein, Beerenauslese, AUSBRUCH and Trockenbeerenauslese). See Germany, page 141.

Prager, Franz w ★★★→★★★★ 90 91 92 93 94 95 Together with JOSEF JAMEK, pioneer of top quality WACHAU dry white. His son-in-law Anton Bodenstein carries on the tradition developing new varieties and great PRADIKAT wines.

Renomierte Weingüter Burgenland Wine estates association founded in '55 by 9 top producers in the state of BURGUNDELAND to promote region's top wines. Members incl KRACHER, TRIEBAUMER, UMATHUM.

Retz r w Important region in W WEINVIERTEL. Esp Weinbauschule Retz.

Ried Single v'yd: when named on the label it is usually a good one.

Riesling On its own always means German RIES. WELSCHRIES (unrelated) is labelled as such. Top growers: BRUNDLMAYER, FREIE W WACHAU, HIRTZBERGER, Högl, KNOLL, Nigl, NIKOLAIHOF, F X PICHLER, PRAGER, Salomon.

Riesling-Sylvaner Name used for Müller-T, which accounts for about 10% of Austria's grapes. Best producers: HIRTZBERGER, JURTSCHITSCH.

Rotgipfler Fragrant indigenous grape of THERMENREGION. With ZIERFANDLER makes lively, interesting wine. Esp Biegler, Schellmann, Stadelmann.

Rust w r dr sw BURGENLAND region, famous since 17th C for super-sweet AUSBRUCH. Now also for red and dry white. Esp from FEILER-ARTINGER, Schandl, Heidi Schröck, ERNST TRIEBAUMER, Paul Triebaumer, Wenzel. The Cercle Ruster Ausbruch is a group of a dozen producers set on reestablishing the preeminence of their powerful Sauternes-like dessert wines, from a wide range of grapes. Standards are already very high.

St-Laurent Traditional red wine grape, potentially vg, with cherry aroma, believed to be related to Pinot N. Esp from Fischer, Mad, STIEGELMAR, UMATHUM.

Salomon-Undhof w ★★★ Vg producer of RIES, WEISSBURGUNDER, Traminer in KREMS. Erich Salomon also owns/runs KLOSTER UND wine tasting centre.

Sattler, Willi w ★★→★★★ 90 92 93 94 95 Top south STYRIA grower. Esp for Sauvignon, MORILLON.

Schilcher Rosé wine from indigenous BLAUER WILDBACHER grapes (sharp, dry: high acidity). Speciality of W STYRIA. Vg: Klug, Lukas, Reiterer, Strohmeier.

Schlumberger Largest sparkling winemaker in Austria (VIENNA); wine is bottle-fermented by unique 'Méthode Schlumberger'. Delicate fruity.

Seewinkel ('Lake corner'.) Name given to the southern part of NEUSIEDLERSEE incl Apetlon, ILLMITZ and Podersdorf. Ideal conditions for botrytis.

Servus w BURGENLAND everyday light and mild white wine brand.

Smaragd Highest quality category of VINEA WACHAU, similar to Spätlese.

Spätrot-Rotgipfler Typical THERMENREGION (Spätrot and ROTGIPFLER) wine.

Spitz an der Donau w W WACHAU region: vg individual microclimate: esp from Singerriedel (by far the best), HIRTZBERGER, Hochrain, Högl, Lagler, Steinborz.

Steinfeder VINEA WACHAU quality category for light fragrant dry wines.

Stiegelmar, Georg w r dr sw ★→★★★ 90 91 92 93 94 95 GOLS grower: consistent for CHARD, Sauv Bl, red wine and unusual specialities.

Strass w (r) Wine centre in the KAMPTAL region for good Qualität white wines. Best producers: Dolle, METTERNICH-SANDOR, Topf.

To decipher codes, please refer to 'Key to symbols' on front flap of jacket, or to 'How to use this book' on page 6.

Styria (Steiermark) The southernmost wine region of Austria bordering Slovenia. Its Qualitätswein are gaining real prestige. Incl SUDSTEIERMARK, SUD-OSTSTEIERMARK and WESTSTEIERMARK (S, SW and W Styria).

Süd-Oststeiermark (SW Styria) w (r) STYRIAN region with islands of v'yds. Best producers: Neumeister, Winkler-Hermaden.

Südburgenland r w Small S BURGENLAND wine region: good red wines. Best producers: Krutzler, Wachter, Wiesler.

Südsteiermark (S Styria) w Best wine region of STYRIA: makes v popular whites (MORILLON, MUSKATELLER, WELSCHRIESLING and Sauv Bl). Top producers: Gross, Lackner-Tinnacher, Muster, POLZ, SATTLER, TEMENT, Wohlmuth.

Tement, Manfred w ★★★→★★★★ 90 92 93 94 95 Vg and renowned estate on S STYRIA Weinstrasse for beautifully made traditional ('Steirisch Klassik') and international whites.

Thermenregion r w dr sw Wine/hot-springs region, S of VIENNA. Indigenous grapes (eg ZIERFANDLER, ROTGIPFLER) and good reds. Main centres: Baden, GUMPOLDSKIRCHEN Tattendorf, Traiskirchen. Top producers: Alphart, Biegler, Fischer, Reinisch, Schafler, Schellmann, Stadelmann.

Traditionsweingüter Association of wine estates in KAMPTAL and KREMSTAL, committed to qualty and v'yd classification. Members include BRUNDLMAYER, G MALAT, SALOMON-UNDHOF.

Triebaumer, Ernst r (w) dr sw ★★★ 90 91 92 93 94 One of the best red wine producers in Austria (RUST). Top label: Mariental. Top wines: BLAUFRANKISCH and CAB-Merlot.

Umathum, Josef w r dr sw ★★→★★★ 90 91 92 94 Distinguished NEUSIEDLERSEE producer for vg reds; whites also from Burgunder grapes.

Vienna w (r) ('Wien' in German and on wine-labels.) The Austrian capital is a wine region in its own right (1,800 v'yd acres in suburbs). Simple lively wines served in HEURIGEN are increasingly well-made: esp from Bernretter, MAYER, Schilling, WIENINGER.

Vinea Wachau WACHAU appellation started by winemakers in '83 with three categories of dry wine: STEINFEDER, FEDERSPIEL and SMARAGD.

Wachau w Danube wine region W of KREMS: some of Austria's best wines, incl RIES, GRUNER V. Top producers: Alzinger, FREIE WEINGARTNER, HIRTZBERGER, Högl, JAMEK, KNOLL, NIKOLAIHOF, F X PICHLER, Pichler, PRAGER.

Weinviertel (Wine Quarter) w (r) Largest Austrian wine region, between the Danube and the Czech border. Mostly light refreshing whites esp from Falkenstein, Poysdorf, RETZ. Best producers: Hardegg, Jauk, Luckner, Lust, Malteser Ritterorden, Pfaffl, Taubenschuss, Zull.

Weissburgunder (Pinot Bl) Ubiquitous: good dry wines and PRADIKATS. Esp Beck, Fischer, Gross, HEINRICH, HIRTZBERGER, Jement, POLZ.

Welschriesling White grape, not related to RIESLING, grown in all wine regions: light, fragrant, young-drinking dry wines and good PRADIKATS.

Weststeiermark (West Styria) p Smallest Austrian wine region specializing in SCHILCHER. Esp from Klug, Lukas, Reiterer, Strohmeier.

Wien See Vienna.

Wieninger, Fritz w r ★★→★★★ 90 91 92 93 94 95 Vg VIENNA-Stammersdorf grower: HEURIGE, CHARD, reds and esp good GRUNER VELTLINER and RIES.

Winzer Krems Wine growers' cooperative in KREMS: dependable solid whites.

Zierfandler (Spätrot) White grape variety grown almost exclusively in the THERMENREGION. With the ROTGIPFLER produces robust lively wines which age well. Best producers: Biegler, Schellmann, Stadlmann.

Central & Southeast Europe

Prague O

CZECH REPUBLIC

Heavily shaded areas are
the wine growing regions

Bratislava O

Da

Ljubljana
O
SLOVENIA   Zagreb
O

Drava

CROATIA

Sava

**BOSNIA-
HERZEGOVIN**

Split   Sarajev
O
Adriatic Sea

Dubrovnik
O

To say that parts of the region covered by this map are somewhat
provisional these days is an understatement. But new regional
autonomies and new statehoods are frequently followed by
higher aspirations in winemaking and new international interest
and/or investment.

In several much-publicized cases this takes the form of
international 'flying winemakers' pitching their tents at vintage-time,
usually to make wines acceptable to Western supermarkets from
predictable grape varieties. But the change of style this brings has
its effect on indigenous winemaking, too; often with happy results,
making fresher and fruiter wines of intriguingly different flavours.

So far Hungary and Bulgaria, and perhaps Moldova, as well as
Czechoslovakia, have taken the lead in what has become an area to
follow with fascination. The potential of other ex-Communist
states is still on hold.

In this section references are arranged country by country,
each shown on the map on this page. Labelling in all the countries
involved, except Greece and Cyprus, is broadly based on the
international pattern of place name and grape variety. Main grape
varieties are therefore included alongside areas, producers and
other terms in the alphabetical listings.

Hungary

Hungary is the unquestioned regional leader in terms of tradition, although neighbouring Austria is now far ahead in quality. Magyar taste is for fiery, hearty, full-blooded wines, which their traditional grapes (mainly white) perfectly provide, but which are being superseded in many cases by 'safer' international varieties. Since the end of Communism several French, German and other concerns have bought land or entered into joint ventures, especially in Hungary's most famous region, Tokay. Expect to hear much more of this. Meanwhile visitors to the country will find plenty of original wines in the old style.

Alföld Hungary's Great Plain: much everyday wine (mostly Western grapes) and some better, esp at HAJOS, HELVECIA, KECSKEMET, KISKUNHALAS, Szeged.

Asztali Table wine.

Aszú Botrytis-shrivelled grapes and the sweet wine made from them, as in Sauternes (see page 100). Used to designate both wine and rotten berries.

Aszú Eszencia Tokaji br sw ★★★★ 57 63 Second commercial TOKAY quality: superb amber elixir, like a great Sauternes with a hint of fino sherry.

Badacsony Balaton w dr sw ★★→★★★ Famous 426-m hill on the N shore of LAKE BALATON whose basalt soil can give rich high-flavoured white wines, among Hungary's best, esp SZURKEBARAT and KEKNYELU.

Balaton Balaton r w dr sw ★→★★★ Hungary's inland sea and Europe's largest freshwater lake. Many good wines take its name. The ending 'i' (eg Balatoni, Egri) is the equivalent of -er in Londoner.

Balatonboglár Balaton r w p ★→★★ Newer progressive area south of Lake Balaton: sound wines, esp whites (Chard, Sémillon, Muscat). Also cuve close sparkling.

Balatonfüred Balaton w (r) dr sw ★★ Town on N shore of LAKE BALATON. Softer, less fiery wines from Western and OLASRIZLING grapes.

Bársonyos-Csàszàr Northern area for traditional dry whites.

Bikavér Eger r ★ 'Bull's Blood', the historic name of the best-selling red wine of EGER: at best full-bodied and well-balanced, but dismally variable in its export version today. A three-variety (minimum) blend, mostly KEKFRANKOS and Cab, some Merlot. Now also made in SZEKSZARD.

Bór Wine. Vörös is red, Fehér is white, Asztali is table.

Csárfás Royal vineyard, still state-owned, at Tarcal; this is the finest site in TOKAJI.

Csopák Village next to BALATONFURED, with similar wines but drier whites.

Debrö Mátraalja w sw ★★ Town famous for mellow aromatic HARSLEVELU.

Dinka Widespread but ordinary white grape.

Disznókö Important French insurance (AXA) investment in first-rate TOKAY land at Szombor. 100+ acres. To date mainly table wines.

Edes Sweet (but not as luscious as ASZU) wine.

Eger Eger district r w dr sw ★→★★ Best-known red wine centre of N Hungary; a baroque city of cellars full of BIKAVER. Also fresh white LEANYKA (perhaps its best product today), OLASZRIZLING, Chard and Cab.

Eszencia ★★★★ The fabulous quintessence of TOKAY (Tokaji): intensely sweet and aromatic from grapes wizened by botrytis. Properly grape juice of v low, if any, alcoholic strength, reputed to have miraculous properties: its sugar content can be over 750 grams per litre.

Etyek Nr Budapest. Source of modern standard wines, esp Chard, Sauv Bl.

Ezerjó The grape grown at MOR to make one of Hungary's best dry white wines; potentially distinguished, fragrant and fine.

Felsöbabad Regional cellar S of Budapest with authentic (but in Hungary unauthorized) fragrant Pinot N.

François President French founded (1882) sparkling wine producer at Budafok, nr Budapest. Vintage wine: President.

Furmint The classic grape of TOKAY (Tokaji), with great flavour and fire, also grown for table wine at LAKE BALATON and in SOMLO.

Gyöngyös Mátraalja w (r) ★★ Region with promising dry white SZURKEBARAT, Chardonnay, MUSKOTALY and Sauvignon Blanc wines, and recent French and Australian investment.

Hajós Alföld r ★ Village in S Hungary known for good lively Cab S reds of medium body and ageing potential. Also good (if unpermitted) Pinot N.

Hárslevelü 'Lime-leaved' grape used at DEBRO and as the second main grape of TOKAY (cf Sém/Sauv in Sauternes). Gentle mellow wine: aromatic and full.

Helvécia (Kecskemét) Historic ALFOLD cellars. V'yds ungrafted: phylloxera bugs cannot negotiate sandy soil. Whites and rosés modernist; reds traditional.

Hétszölö Noble first-growth 116-acre estate at TOKAJI bought by Grands Millésimes de France and Suntory. Second label: Dessewffy.

Hungarovin Traders/producers with huge cellars at Budafok nr Budapest: mainly 'Western varietals', also cuve close, transfer and classic sparkling. Now owned by German Sekt specialists, Henkell.

Izsák Major sparkling wine producer; the majority by cuve close.

Kadarka Red grape for vast quantities of everyday wine in the south, but capable of producing ample flavour and interesting maturity (eg esp at SZEKSZARD and VILLANY).

Kecskemét Major town of the ALFOLD. Much everyday wine, some better.

Kékfrankos Hungarian for Blaufränkisch; reputedly related to Gamay. Good light or full-bodied reds, esp at SOPRON. Used in BIKAVER at EGER.

Kéknyelü High-flavoured, low-yielding white grape making the best and 'stiffest' wine of MT BADACSONY. It should be fiery and spicy stuff.

Kékoporto Kék means blue, so this grape could be the German Portugieser. Makes concentrated oakable red; esp from VILLANY, s'times in BIKAVER.

Kisburgundi Kék German Spätburgunder: Pinot Noir.

Kiskunhalas Huge-scale plains winery, good esp for KADARKA.

Különleges Minöség Special quality: highest official grading.

Lang and Lauder Partnership of famous international Hungarians to make TOKAY at Mád. Also v'yds at EGER.

Leányka or Király Old Hungarian white grape also grown in Transylvania. Makes admirable aromatic faintly Muscat dry wine in many areas. Kiraly ('Royal') Leányka is supposedly superior.

Mátraalja Wine district in the foothills of the Mátra range in N Hungary, incl DEBRO, GYONGOS and NAGYREDE. Esp for white wines.

Mecsekalja S Hungary district (the warmest), known for good whites of PECS.

Médoc Noir The Merlot grape.

Mezesfehér Widely planted 'white honey' grape; sweet, soft wine esp from EGER and GYONGYOS.

Minöségi Bor Quality wine. Hungary's appellation contrôlée.

Mór N Hungary w ★★→★★★ Region long famous for fresh dry EZERJO. Now also Riesling and Sauvignon.

Muskotály The yellow Muscat. Makes light, though long-lived, wine in Tokaji and EGER. A little goes into the TOKAY blend (cf Muscadelle in Sauternes). V occasionally makes an ASZU wine solo.

Nagyburgundi Literally 'great burgundy': indigenous grape, not Pinot N as sometimes thought. Sound solid wine esp around VILLANY and SZEKSZARD.

Nagyréde Mátraalja Foothill winery. Competent and modern.

OBI Official laboratory based in Budapest, responsible for labelling, quality control and export licence. Old notions being modernized.

Olaszrizling Hungarian name for the Italian Riesling or Welschriesling.

Oportó Red grape increasingly used for soft jammy wines to drink young.

Oremus Ancient TOKAJI v'yd of founding Rakóczi family at Sárospatak, being reconstituted by owners of Spain's Vega Sicilia.

Pécs Mecsek w (r) ★→★★ Major southern wine city. Esp for OLASZRIZLING and Pinot Bl wines etc.

Pezsgö Sparkling wine, mostly made by the transfer method, can often be very palatable.

Pinot Noir Normally means NAGYBURGUNDI. But see Felsöbabad.

Puttonyos

The measure of sweetness in TOKAY Aszú. A 'putt' is a 20–25 kilo measure (traditionally a hod) of Aszú grapes. The number of 'putts' added per barrel (136 litres) of dry base wine determines the richness of the final product, from 3 putts to 7. 3 = 60 grams of sugar per litre, 4 = 90, 5 = 120, 6 = 150. Aszú Eszencia must have 180 gpl. But see Eszencia for the really sticky stuff.

Royal Tokaji Wine Co Early Anglo-Danish-Hungarian joint venture at Mád (TOKAJI). 150 acres, mainly first or second growth. First wine (90) a revelation: 91 and (esp) 93 are making waves.

Siklós Southern district known for its white wines: esp HARSLEVELU, also Chard, TRAMINI, OLASZRIZLING.

Somló N Hungary w ★★ Isolated small v'yd district N of BALATON: white wines (formerly of high repute) from FURMINT and ancient Juhfark grapes.

Sopron W Hungary r ★★ Historic enclave S of Neusiedler See (see Austria): light KEKFRANKOS, Austrian-style sweet wines, but now mostly for Cab etc.

Szamorodni Word meaning 'as it comes'; used to describe TOKAY without the addition of ASZU grapes. Can be dry or (fairly) sweet, depending upon proportion of Aszú grapes naturally present. Sold as an aperitif.

Száraz Dry, esp of TOKAJI SZAMORODNI.

Szekszárd r ★★ District in south-central part of Hungary with investment from Germany and Italy's Antinori. KADARKA red wine which needs age (say 3–4 yrs); can also be botrytised ('Nemes Kadar'). Also good organic wines (reintroduced), BIKAVER and good Chard too, 'Agrar Coöp'.

Szürkebarát Literally means 'grey friar': Pinot Gr, which makes rich (not necessarily sweet) wine in the BADACSONY v'yds and elsewhere.

Tokay (Tokaji) Tokaji w dr sw ★★→★★★★ The ASZU is Hungary's famous liquorous sweet wine (since c1660), comparable to a highly aromatic and delicate Sauternes, from hills in the NE close to the Russian (Belarus) border. The appellation covers 13,500 acres. See Aszú, Eszencia, Furmint, Puttonyos, Szamorodni. Also dry table wine of character.

Tramini Gewürztraminer, esp in SIKLOS.

Villány Siklós r p (w) ★★ Southernmost town of Hungary and well-known centre of red wine production. Villányi Burgundi is largely KEKFRANKOS and can be good. Cabs S and F are v promising. See also Nagyburgundi.

Villány-Siklós Wine region named after the two towns.

Zweigelt Indigenous (S) red grape: deep-coloured spicy flavoursome wine.

To decipher codes, please refer to 'Key to symbols' on front flap of jacket, or to 'How to use this book' on page 6.

Bulgaria

Since 1978 Bulgaria has come from nowhere to be the world's second-largest exporter of bottled wines after France, trading 90 percent of production. Enormous new vineyards and wineries have overwhelmed an old, if embattled, wine tradition. The formerly state-run and state-subsidized wineries learnt almost everything from the New World and offer Cabernet, Chardonnay and other varieties at bargain prices. Controlled appellation ('Controliran') wines, introduced in 1985, have been joined by wood-influenced 'Reserve' bottlings, simpler wines of Declared Geographical Origin and Country Wines. Bulgaria's main wine regions are the northern Danube Valley, the eastern Black Sea region, southwest Struma Valley, southern Maritsa River and Stara Planina.

The recent drop in sales to Russia has led to new emphasis on quality, somewhat higher prices and a ban on planting outside the 27 Controliran regions. There are 410,000 acres of vines in all.

In 1990 the organizing monopoly, Vinprom, was disbanded to give wineries autonomy (30 at first; then increasingly more, along with privatization). A brisk air of competition provokes even greater efforts.

Assenovgrad Main MAVRUD-producing cellar on the outskirts of PLOVDIV – stainless steel being introduced. Mavrud and CAB can last well.

Boyar, Domaine Bulgaria's first independent wine merchants for almost 50 yrs: based in Sofia, set up '91, now marketing in the UK.

Burgas Black Sea resort and source of rosé (the speciality), easy whites (incl MUSCAT blend) and increasingly reds too.

Cabernet Sauvignon Highly successful (with four times California's acreage). Dark vigorous fruity wine, v drinkable young; top qualities good with age.

Chardonnay Rather less successful (than CABERNET). Many wines appear to be blends with less exalted varieties. V dry but full-flavoured wine, can improve with a yr in bottle. Some recent oaky examples are promising.

Controliran Top quality wines (single grape variety) of AC-style status. The system was begun in '78: 27 regions were est'd by late '80s.

Country Wines Regional wines (cf French vins de pays), often 2-variety blends.

Damianitza MELNIK winery with good Stambolovo MERLOT and Melnik CAB.

Danube Cool northern region, mostly for reds: incl SUHINDOL and SVISHTOV.

Dimiat The common native white grape, grown in the E towards the coast. Agreeable dry white without memorable character.

Euxinograd (Château) Ageing cellar on the coast, in a once-royal palace.

Gamza Good red grape, the Kadarka of Hungary. Aged wines, esp from LOVICO SUHINDOL, can be delicious.

Han Krum Company near VARNA: modern whites, esp oaked CHARD, lighter Chard and SAUV.

Harsovo Southwest region, esp for MELNIK.

Haskovo S region, principal source of MERLOT for export. Incl ASSENOVGRAD, ORIACHOVITSA, PLOVDIV, STAMBOLOVO, SLIVEN and other areas.

Iskra Sparkling wine, normally sweet but fair quality. Red, white or rosé.

Kadarka Widespread (Albanian) red grape; spicy in good yrs (see Hungary).

Karlovo Town famous for its 'Valley of Roses' and pleasant white MISKET.

Korten Subregion of SLIVEN. Korten CAB is more tannic than most.

Lovico Suhindol Neighbour of PAVLIKENI, site of Bulgaria's first coop (1909). Good GAMZA (CONTROLIRAN), CAB, MERLOT, PAMID, blends. First to declare independence after collapse of state monopoly ('90). Privatized '92. Now B's most important winery/coop, giving guidance to contributing v'yds.

BULGARIA

Mavrud Grape variety and darkly plummy red from S Bulgaria, esp ASENOVGRAD. Can mature 20 yrs. Considered the country's best.

Melnik City of SW and highly prized grape. Dense red; locals say it can be carried in a handkerchief. Needs at least 5 yrs; lasts 15. Also ripe age-worthy CAB.

Merlot Soft red grape variety grown mainly in HASKOVO in the south.

Misket Indigenous Bulgarian grape: mildly aromatic wines; white and red Misket often used to fatten up white blends.

Muscat Ottonel Normal Muscat grape, grown in E for mid-sweet fruity white.

Novi Pazar Controlled appellation CHARD winery nr VARNA with finer wines.

Novo Selo Controliran red GAMZA from the north.

Oriachovitza Major S area for Controliran CAB-MERLOT. Rich savoury red best at 4–5 yrs. Recent RESERVE Cab releases have been good, esp **84 86**.

Pamid The light soft everyday red of the southwest and northwest.

Pavlikeni Northern wine town with a prestigious estate specializing in GAMZA and CAB of high quality. Also light COUNTRY WINE MERLOT and Gamza blend.

Peruschitza PLOVDIV's winery, nr ASSENOVGRAD, esp for reds.

Petrich Warm SW area for soft fragrant MELNIK, also blended with CAB.

Pinot Noir One of B's three main red grapes, along with CAB and MERLOT.

Pleven N cellar for PAMID, GAMZA, CAB. Also Bulgaria's wine research station.

Plovdiv Southern HASKOVO wine town and region, source of good CAB and MAVRUD. Winemaking mostly at ASSENOVGRAD.

Preslav Bulgaria's largest white wine cellar, in NE region. Esp for SAUV BL and RESERVE CHARD. Also makes rather good brandy.

Provadya Another centre for good white wines, esp dry CHARD.

Reserve Used on labels of selected and oak-aged wines. Usually with 2–4 yrs in oak vats (often American), may or may not be CONTROLIRAN.

Riesling In Bulgaria normally refers to Italian Riesling (Welschriesling). Some Rhine Riesling is grown: now made into Germanic-style white.

Rkatziteli One of Russia's favourite white grapes for strong sweet wine. Produces bulk dry or medium whites in NE Bulgaria.

Russe NE wine town on Danube. Fresh high-tech whites: Welschries-MISKET, med-dry Welschries, CHARD, MUSCAT, gd Aligoté. Also reds, esp YANTRA V CAB.

Sakar SE wine area for CONTROLIRAN MERLOT, some of Bulgaria's best.

Sauvignon Blanc Grown in E Bulgaria, recently released for export.

Schumen Eastern region, especially for whites.

Sliven Big producing S region, esp for CAB. Also MERLOT and Pinot N (Merlot is blended with Pinot in a COUNTRY WINE), Silvaner, MISKET and CHARD.

Sofia The country's capital with large pace-setting winery, but no v'yds.

Sonnenkuste Brand of medium-sweet white sold in Germany.

Stambolovo Wine area esp for CONTROLIRAN MERLOT from HASKOVO.

Stara Planina Balkan mountain region of central Bulgaria, incl KARLOVO.

Stara Zagora S region of ORIACHOVITZA: CAB and MERLOT to RESERVE quality.

Suhindol N Red CONTROLIRAN from between DANUBE and Balkan Mountains.

Sungarlare E town giving its name to a dry CONTROLIRAN MISKET; also CHARD.

Svishtov CONTROLIRAN CAB-producing winery by the Danube in the north. A front-runner in Bulgaria's controlled appellation wines.

Tamianka Sweet white wine of eponymous aromatic grape. (Aka Tamîîoasa.)

Targovichte Independent cellar nr SCHUMEN. Esp medium and sweet whites.

Tirnovo Strong sweet dessert red wine.

Varna Major coastal appellation for CHARD (buttery or unoaked, Ch Euxinograd promising), SAUV. Also Aligoté, Ugni Bl (s'times blended).

Yantra Valley DANUBE region, CONTROLIRAN for CABERNET SAUVIGNON since '87.

For key to grape variety abbreviations, see pages 7–13.

The Former Yugoslav States

Before its disintegration in 1991 Yugoslavia was well-established as a supplier of wines of international calibre, if not generally of exciting quality. Now all newly-formed states are again working on export. Current political disarray and competition from other East European countries makes commercial contacts difficult (except in Slovenia, whose 'Riesling' was the pioneer export, since followed by Cabernet, Pinot Blanc, Traminer and others). All regions, except the central Bosnian highlands, make wine, almost entirely in giant cooperatives, although many small private producers are emerging with the '90s. the Dalmatian (Croatian) coast and Macedonia have good indigenous wines whose roots go deep into the ancient world.

Slovenia

Barbera Vg sparkling from Janez Istenic and family.

Bela Krajina SAVA area, esp 'Ledeno Laski Ries' (late-harvest frozen grapes).

Beli Pinot The Pinot Bl, a popular grape variety. Belo is white.

Bizeljsko-Sremic In SAVA district. Full-flavoured local variety reds and LASKI R.

Brda Slovene upper part of Collio DOC (Italy). Many estates on both sides.

Crno vino Red (literally 'black') wine.

Curin-Prapotnik Pioneer Slovenian white wine trader.

Cvicek Traditional pale red or dark rosé of the SAVA VALLEY. ('Schilcher' in Austria.)

Dolenjska SAVA region: CVICEK, LASKI RIZLING and Modra Frankinja (dry red).

Drava Valley (Podravski) Slovene wine region. Mainly whites from aromatic (WELSCHRIES, Muscat Ottonel) to flamboyant (RIES and SAUV); also Eisweins and Beerenauslesen as in neighbouring Austria.

Drustvo Vinogradnikov BRDA assoc of 45 growers/winemakers (with SAVA, DRAVA and Morava equivalents).

Gorna Radgona Winery for sparkling, late-harvest sweet and Eiswein. Many grape varieties used, mostly in blends.

Grasevina Slovenian for Italian RIES. The normal 'Riesling' of the region.

Hlupic Juruj Producer of fine whites from around Haloze.

Jerusalem Slovenia's most famous v'yd, at LJUTOMER. Its best wines are late-picked RAJNSKI RIZLING and LASKI RIZLING. Also makes tank fermented sparklers.

Kakovostno Vino Quality wine (one step down from VRHUNSKO).

Kontrolirano poreklo Appellation. Wine must be 80% from that region.

Koper Hottest area of LITTORAL between Trieste and Piran. Full rich MERLOTS.

Kmetijska Zadruga Wine farmers' cooperative.

Kraski Means grown on the coastal limestone or Karst. A region famous for REFOSCO wines eg Kraski Teran and oak-aged Teranton.

Laski Rizling Yet another name for Italian RIES. Best-known Slovene wine, not best quality. Top export brand: 'Cloburg' from Podravski (DRAVA) region.

Littoral (Primorski) Coastal region bordering Italy (Collio) and the Med. Esp reds: Cab, Merlot (aged in Slovene oak), Barbera and REFOSCO.

Ljutomer (or Lutomer) -Ormoz Slovenia's best-known, probably best white wine district, in NE (DRAVA); esp LASKI RIZLING, at its best rich and satisfying. Ormoz winery also has sparkling and late-harvest wines.

Malvazija Ancient Greek white grape for luscious (now also lively fresh) wine.

Maribor Important centre in NE (DRAVA). White wines, mainly from VINAG, incl LASKI RIZLING, RIES, SAUV, Pinot Bl and Traminer.

Merlot Reasonable in Slovenia. Comparable with neighbouring NE Italian.

Metlika BELA KRAJINA wine centre with warm Kolpa River v'yds.

Namizno Vino Table wine.

Pozna Trgatev Late harvest.

Ptui Historic wine town with trad-based coop: wines clean, mostly white.

Radgona-Kapela DRAVA district next to Austrian border, esp late-harvest wines, eg RADGONSKA RANINA, also classic method sparkling.

Radgonska Ranina Ranina is Austria's Bouvier grape. Radgona is nr MARIBOR. The wine is sweet. Trade name is Tigrovo Mljeko (Tiger's Milk).

Rajnski (or Renski) Rizling Rhine RIES: rare here, but a little in LJUTOMER-ORMOZ.

Refosk Vg Italian red ('Refosco') grape in E and in ISTRIA (Croatia) as TERAN.

Riesling Formerly meant Italian Ries. Now legally limited to real Rhine Riesling.

Sauvignon Blanc Vg with the resources to make it well; otherwise horrid.

Sava Valley Central Slovenia: light dry reds, eg CVICEK. Northern bank is for whites, eg LASKI RIZLING, Silvaner and recent Chard and SAUV BL.

Sipon Name for Furmint of Hungary – locally prized, p'haps has a future.

Slamnak A late-harvest LJUTOMER estate RIES.

Slovenijavino Slovenia's largest exporter. Wines (esp WELSCHRIES) bought in and blended with care for Slovin, Ashewood and Avia brands.

Tigrovo Mljeko See Radgonska Ranina.

Tocai The Pinot Gr, making rather heavy white wine.

Vinag Huge production cellars at MARIBOR. Top wine: Cloburg LASKI RIZLING.

Vinakras Sezana v'yds for deep purple fresh-tasting TERAN.

Vipava LITTORAL region with tradition of export to Austria and Germany: good Cab, MERLOT, Barbera, Chard. Vipava winery is the most modern.

Vrhunsko Vino Top quality wine.

Welschriesling Alias LASKI RIZLING.

Croatia

Babi Standard red of DALMATIA, ages better than ordinary PLAVAC.

Badel Top négociant of Croatian wines.

Banat Region partly in Romania: up-to-date wineries making adequate RIES.

Baranjske Planote SLAVONIA area for RIES and BIJELI BURGUNDAC.

Benkovac Town and wine cellar: wines look good as it emerges from war.

Bogdanusa Local white grape of the DALMATIAN islands, esp Hvar and Brac. Pleasant, refreshing faintly fragrant wine.

Bolski Plavac Top quality vigorous red from Bol on the island of Brac.

Burgundac Bijeli Chard, grown in SLAVONIA.

Dalmacijavino Coop at Split: full range of DALMATIAN coastal/island wines.

Dalmatia The coast of Croatia, from Rijeka to Dubrovnik. Has a remarkable variety of characterful wines, most of them potent.

Dingac Heavy sweetish PLAVAC red, speciality of steep mid-DALMATIAN coast.

Faros Substantial age-worthy PLAVAC red from the island of Hvar.

Grasevina Local name for ubiquitous LASKI RIZLING. Best from Kutjevo.

Grk White grape, speciality of the island of Korcula, giving strong, even sherry-like wine, and also a lighter pale one.

Istravino Rijeka Oldest wine négociant of Croatia.

Istria Peninsula in the N Adriatic, Porec its centre: a variety of pleasant wines, Merlot as good as any. V dry TERAN is perfect with local truffles.

Kontinentalna Hrvatska Inland Croatia. Mostly for whites (GRASEVINA).

Marastina Strong herbal dry DALMATIAN white, best from Lastovo.

Opol Pleasant light pale PLAVAC red from Split and Sibenik in DALMATIA.

Plavac Mali DALMATIA red grape; wine of body, strength, ageability. Current thinking has it as Zinfandel. See Dingac, Opol, Postup. Also white, Plavac Beli.

Plenkovic Tough new private grower: good Zlatan PLAVAC reds from Hvar Island.

Polu Semi... Polu-slatko is semi-sweet, polu-suho is semi-dry.

Portugizac Austria's Blauer Portugieser: plain red wine.

Posip Pleasant white of the DALMATIAN islands, notably Korcula.

Postup Soft heavy DALMATIAN red of Peljesac peninsula. Highly esteemed.

Prosek Dessert wine from ISTRIA and DALMATIA: 15% (can be almost port-like).

Slavonija N Croatia, on Hungarian border between Slovenia and Serbia. Big producer. Standard wines, esp white, incl most of former 'Yugoslav RIES'. Well-known for its oak forests.

Stolno vino Table wine.

Teran Stout dark red of ISTRIA. See Refosk (Slovenia).

Vrhunsko Vino New origin-based designation for quality wines.

Vugava Rare white variety of Vis in DALMATIA. Linked (at least in legend) with Viognier of the Rhône Valley.

Bosnia and Herzegovina

Blatina Ancient MOSTAR red grape and wine from pebbled W bank of Neretva.

Kameno Vino White wine of unique irrigated desert v'yd in Neretva Valley.

Mostar Means 'old bridge'. Was Herzegovina's Islamic-looking wine centre, but cellars destroyed during the civil war. Ljubuski and Citluk are rebuilding. Potentially admirable ZILAVKA white and BLATINA red.

Samotok Light red (rosé/'ruzica') wine from run-off juice (and no pressing).

Zilavka White grape of MOSTAR, making wines rather neutral when exported, but can be dry pungent and memorably fruity with a faint flavour of apricots.

Serbia

Amselfelder Reds from KOSOVO POLJE (once top cellars). Disagreeably sweet.

Bijelo (Beli) White.

Burgundac Crni Local widely-planted equiv of Pinot N – like German version.

Cabernet Sauvignon Now introduced in many places with usually pleasant, occasionally exciting results. See Kosovo.

Crno Black, ie red wine.

Fruska Gora Hills in VOJVODINA, on the Danube NW of Belgrade, with modern v'yds and a wide range of wines incl Traminer and Sauv Bl.

Game Pronounced 'Gamay'. Pleasant red wines from KOSOVO.

Kameno Vino White from unique (irrigated) v'yd at Medugorje-Caplina in Neretva Valley.

Kosovo (or Kosmet) Region in the S between SERBIA and MACEDONIA. Source of AMSELFELDER and some lively Cab. Kos means blackbird.

Kosovo Polje Pinot N-covered Mediterranean-warm polder surrounded by mts. Was base for German AMSELFELDER; post-war sees more Spanish interest.

Leskovac Region in Serbia for good whites, eg Sauv Bl.

Kratosija Much-praised local red grape for good quality, drinkable wines.

Montenegro Small southwest region known for VRANAC red wines.

Muscat-Ottonel The E European Muscat, grown in VOJVODINA.

Oplenac Cab-producing region in Serbia.

Plovdina Native dark-skinned red grape of Macedonia grown here too.

Prokupac Native sturdy red grape and wine. Best from ZUPA.

Ruzica Rosé. Usually from PROKUPAC. Darker than most, and better.

Smederevka Major white grape of Serbia and Kosovo. Fresh dry wines.

Stono Vino Table wine.

Suvarak Late-harvested dessert wine (15%) from PROKUPAC grapes.

Velika Morava Area of Serbia famous for Laski Riesling.

Vojvodina Big plain (also Hungary, Romania). Sandy soil vg esp for white vines.

Zupa Central Serbian district giving its name to above average red and rosé (dark and light red) wines from PROKUPAC, PLOVDINA grapes: respectively Zupsko CRNO, Z RUZICA.

Montenegro

13 July State-controlled coop (mainly, but not just grapes) with high-tech Italian equipment, outside PODGORICA. VRANAC is high quality.

Cemovsko Polje Vast pebbled semi-desert plain; esp VRANAC. Awaits discovery.

Crmnica Lake-side/coastal v'yds esp for Kadarka grape (see Macedonia).

Crna Gora Black Mountains.

Duklja Late-picked semi-sweet version of VRANAC.

Krstac Montenegro's top white grape and wine; esp from CRMNICA.

Merlot Since '80: good wood-aged results.

Podgorica Ancient name reintroduced for capital Titograd.

Vranac Local vigorous and abundant red grape and wine. Value.

Macedonia

Belan White Grenache. Makes neutral Gemischt wine.

Crna Reka River with many artificial lakes for irrigation.

Crveno suvo vino Red dry wine.

Kadarka Major red grape of Hungary; here closer to its origins around L Ohrid.

Kratosija Locally favoured red grape; sound wines.

Plovdina Native (S) grape for mild red, white; esp blended with tastier PROKUPAC.

Prokupac Serbian and Macedonian top red grape. Makes dark rosé (RUZICA) and full red of character, esp at ZUPA. PLOVDINA often added for smoothness.

Rkaciteli Russian (white) grape making a home close to the Bulgarian border.

Temjanika Grape for spicy semi-sweet whites. (Tamianka in Bulgaria.)

Teran Transferred from ISTRIA, but Macedonia's version is less stylish.

Tikves Much favoured hilly v'yd region (20,000 acres). Esp for pleasant dark red Kratosija, fresh dry Smederevka (see Serbia) – locally mixed with soda.

Traminac The Traminer. Also grown in Vojvodina and Slovenia.

Vardar Valley Brings the benefits of the Aegean Sea to inland v'yds (just as the Rhône Valley channels Mediterranean warmth into France).

Vranec Local name for Vranac of Montenegro (qv).

Vrvno Vino Controlled origin designation for quality wines.

Former Czechoslovakia

The country was re-established in January '93 as the Czech (Moravia and Bohemia) and Slovak republics. While there was little or no tradition of exporting from this mainly white wine region, good wines have emerged since 1989. Labels will say whether they are blended or single varietal. All are worth trying for value. Privatization and foreign investment bode well for future developments.

Moravia Favourite wines in Prague: variety and value. V'yds situated along Danube tributaries. Many wines from Austrian border: similar grapes, Grüner Veltliner, Müller-T, Sauv, Traminer, St-Laurent, Pinot N, Blauer Portugieser, Frankovka etc; and similar wines, eg from **Mikulov** (white, red, dry, sweet classic-method sparkling; especially popular Valtice Cellars, est'd 1430, and traditional Vino Mikulov), **Satov** (modern, mostly white – incl Sauv, Grüner Veltliner, Müller-Thurgau – grapes from local farms and coops) and **Znojmo** (long-est'd, ideal limestone soil; local white grapes, Grüner-V, Müller-T, Sauv, 'Tramín' and sweetish prize-winning 'Rynsky Ryzlink' (82) from Znovín). Other regions: Jaroslavice (oak-aged reds), Prímetice (full aromatic whites), Blatnice, Hustopece, sunny Pálava, Saldorf (esp Sauv, 'Rynsky' Ries) and Velké Pavlovice (good Ruländer, Traminer, St-Laurent and award-winning Cab 92, still expanding). Moravia also has sparkling.

Bohemia Winemaking since 9th C. Same latitude and similar wines to eastern Germany. Best: N of Prague, in Elbe Valley, and (best known) nr Melník (King Karel IV bought in Burgundian vines in 15th C; today Ries, Ruländer and Traminer predominate). 'Bohemia Sekt' is growing, eg increasingly popular from Stary Plzenec: tank-fermented (mostly), some oak used, with grapes from SLOVAKIA and MORAVIA too; French advice. Top wineries: **Lobkowitz** (at Melnik), **Roudnice**, **Litomerice**, **Karlstein**.

Slovakia Warmest climatic conditions and most (as much as 65%) of former Czechoslovakia's wine. Best in eastern v'yds neighbouring Hungary's Tokay region. Slovakia uses Hungarian varieties and makes a little Tokay too. Key districts: Malo-Karpatská Oblast (largest region, in foothills of the Little Carpathians, incl Ruländer, Ries, Traminer, Limberger etc), Malá Trna, Nové Mesto, Skalice (small area, mainly reds), and (in Tatra foothills) Bratislava, Pezinok, Modra. Best recent vintages: 71 79 81 83 89 92 94.

Romania

Romania has a long winemaking tradition and good potential for quality, wasted during decades of supplying the Soviet Union with cheap, sweet wine. The present political situation sadly allows little progress. Quantity is still the goal (domestic wine consumption is large). But with cleaner winemaking and earlier bottling, there is certainly the potential to rival the success of Bulgaria. There are 500,000 acres of vines.

Aiud TIRNAVE region with wine school, quality and a 'flor sherry'-style wine.

Alba Iulia Town in warm TIRNAVE area of TRANSYLVANIA, known for off-dry white (Italian RIES, FETEASCA, MUSKAT-OTTONEL), bottle-fermented sparkling.

Aligoté The junior white burgundy grape makes pleasantly fresh white.

Băbească Traditional red grape of the FOCSANI area: agreeably sharp wine tasting slightly of cloves. (Means 'grandmother grape'.)

Banat Plain on border with Serbia. Workaday Italian RIES, SAUV BL, MUSKAT-OTTONEL; light red CADARCA, CABERNET and Merlot.

Baratca Gentle slopes around PAULIS for good Merlot and Cabernet.

Burgund Mare 'Big Burgundian'. A clone of Pinot N, not the real thing.

Buzav Hills Good red wines (CABERNET, Merlot, BURGUND M) from continuation of DEALUL MARE region.

Cabernet Sauvignon Increasingly grown, esp at DEALUL MARE, to make dark intense wines, though sometimes too sweet for Western palates.

Cadarca Romanian spelling of the Hungarian Kadarka.

Chardonnay Used at MURFATLAR to make sweet dessert wine. Dry and oak-aged styles.

Cotesti Warmer part of the FOCSANI area making deep-coloured reds (PINOT N, Merlot etc), and dry whites claimed to resemble Alsace wines.

Cotnari Region at Moldavia's N v'yd limit; good botrytis. Famous (rarely seen) historical wine: light dessert white from local GRASA, FETEASCA ALBA, TAMAIOASA, rather like v delicate Tokay, gold with tints of green.

Crisana Western region including historical Miniş area (since 15th-C: reds, especially CADARCA, and crisp white Mustoasa), Silvania (esp FETEASCA), Diosig, Valea lui Mihai.

Dealul Mare Important up-to-date vineyard area in southeast Carpathian foothills. Red wines from FETEASCA NEAGRA, CAB, Merlot, PINOT etc. Whites from TAMIIOASA etc.

201

Dobrudja Sunny dry Black Sea region. Incl MURFATLAR. Quality is good.

Drăgăşani Region on River Olt south of the Carpathian Mountains, since Roman times. Both traditional and 'modern' grapes (esp Sauv). Good MUSKAT-OTTONEL, reds.

Fetească Romanian white grape with spicy, faintly Muscat aroma. Two types: F Albă (same as Hungary's Leányka, considered more ordinary, but base for sparkling wine and sweet COTNARI) and F Regala (F Albă x Furmint cross, good acidity and good for sparkling).

Fetească Neagră Red Feteasca. Light wines, made coarse by clumsiness, good when aged (blackcurranty and deep red).

Focsani Important MOLDAVIA region incl COTESTI, NICORESTI and ODOBESTI.

Grasă A form of the Hungarian Furmint grape grown in Romania and used in, among other wines, COTNARI. Prone to botrytis. Grasa means 'fat'.

Iaşi Region for fresh acidic whites (F ALBA, also Welschries, ALIGOTE, spumante-style MUSKAT O): Bucium, Copu, Tomesti. Reds: Merlot, CAB; top BABEASCA.

Istria-Babadag Newish wine region N of MURFATLAR (CAB S, Merlot, F ALBA etc).

Jidvei Winery in the cool Carpathians (TIRNAVE) among Romania's N-most v'yds. Good whites: FETEASCA, Furmint, RIES, SAUV BL.

Lechinta Transylvanian wine area. Wines noted for bouquet (local grapes).

Moldavia NE province. Largest Romanian wine area with 12 subregions incl IASI, FOCSANI, PANCIU. Temperate, with good v'yd potential.

Murfatlar V'yds nr Black Sea, 2nd-best botrytis conditions (see Cotnari): esp sweet CHARD, late-harvest CAB. Now also full dry wines and sparkling.

Muskat Ottonel The E European Muscat, a speciality of Romania, esp in cool climate TRANSYLVANIA and dry wines in MOLDAVIA.

Nicoreşti Eastern area of FOCSANI, best known for its red BABEASCA.

Odobeşti The central part of FOCSANI; white wines of FETEASCA, RIES etc.

Oltenia Wine regions including DRAGASANI. Sometimes also a brand name.

Panciu Cool MOLDAVIA region N of ODOBESTI. Good still and sparkling white.

Paulis Small estate cellar in town of same name. Barrique-aged Merlot is one of its treasures.

Perla The speciality of TIRNAVE: a pleasant blended semi-sweet white of Italian RIES, FETEASCA and MUSKAT-OTTONEL.

Pinot Noir Grown in the south: can surprise with taste and character.

Piteşti Principal town of the Arges region S of Carpathians. Trad whites.

Premiat Reliable range of higher quality wines for export.

Riesling Actually Italian Riesling. V widely planted. No exceptional wines.

Sadova Town in the SEGARCEA area exporting a sweetish rosé.

Sauvignon Blanc Romania's tastiest white, esp blended with FETEASCA.

Segarcea Southern wine area near the Danube. Rather sweet CAB.

Tamîioasa Traditional white grape known as 'frankincense' for its exotic scent and flavour. Pungent sweet wines often affected by botrytis.

Tirnave Important Transylvanian wine region (Romania's coolest), known for its PERLA and much FETEASCA R. Well-situated for dry and aromatic wines, eg JIDVEI'S. Also bottle-fermented sparkling. Germanic-style.

Trakia Export brand. Better judged for Western palates than most.

Transylvania See Alba Iulia, Lechinta, Tirnave.

Valea Călugărească 'Valley of the Monks', part of DEALUL MARE with go-ahead research station. Currently proposing new AC-style rules. CAB (esp Special Reserve 85), Merlot, PINOT are admirable, as are Italian RIES, Pinot Gr.

Vin de Mesa Most basic wine classification – for local drinking only.

VS and VSO Higher quality wines; VSO requires specified grapes and region.

VSOC Top range wines: CMD is late harvest, CMI late harvest with noble rot, CIB is from selected nobly rotten grapes (like Beerenauslese).

Greece

Since Greece's entry into the EC in 1981 its antique wine industry has started moving into higher gear. Much is still fairly primitive, but a new system of appellations is in place and the past seven years have seen much investment in equipment and expertise. Modern, well-made, but still authentically Greek wines are well worth tasting.

Achaia-Clauss Well-known wine merchant with cellars at PATRAS, IN north PELOPONNESE. Makers of DEMESTICA etc.

Agiorgitiko Widely planted red-wine grape in the NEMEA region.

Agioritikos (Appellation) Good medium white and rosé from Agios Oros or Mt Athos, Halkidiki's monastic peninsula. Source of Cab etc for TSANTALI.

Amintaion Light red or rosé, often pétillant, from MACEDONIA.

Ankiralos Fresh white from the Aegean-facing v'yds of Thessaly.

Attica Region round Athens, the chief source of RETSINA.

Autocratorikos New semi-sparkling medium-dry white from TSANTALI.

Botrys Old-established Athenian wine and spirits company.

Boutari Merchants and makers with high standards in MACEDONIAN and other wines, esp NAOUSSA and SANTORINI. Grand Réserve is excellent (84).

Caïr Label of the RHODES coop. Makes Greece's only classic sparkling wine.

Calliga Modern winery with 800 acres on CEPHALONIA. ROBOLA white and Monte Nero reds from indigenous grapes are adequately made.

Cambas, Andrew Important wine-growers and merchants in ATTICA.

Carras, John Estate at Sithoniá, Halkidiki, N Greece. Interesting COTES DE MELITON wines. Ch Carras is a claret-style oak-aged red (75 79 81 83 84 85 87 90) worth 10–20 yrs in bottle. Also non-appellation, eg Ambelos.

Cava Legal term for blended aged red and white. Eg, Cava Boutari (NAOUSSA-NEMEA blend) and Cava Tstantalis (NAOUSSA-Cab).

Cephalonia (Kephalonia) Ionian island: good white ROBOLA, red Thymiatiko.

Château Lazaridis Family-owned estate NE of Salonika for fine red, white and rosé (mainly from international varieties).

Corfu Adriatic island with wines scarcely worthy of it. Ropa is traditional red.

Côtes de Meliton Appellation (since '81) of CARRAS estate: red (esp Cab and Limnio) and white (again, Greek and French grapes), incl Ch Carras.

Crete Island with potential for excellent wine but current phylloxera problems. Best now from BOUTARI, Kourtaki and indigenous grapes.

Danielis One of the best brands of dry red wine, from ACHAIA-CLAUSS.

Demestica A reliable brand of dry red and white from ACHAIA-CLAUSS.

Emery Maker of good CAVA Emery red and vg Villare white on RHODES.

Epirus Central Greek region with high-altitude vines (1,200 metres): 'Katoyi' Cab is celebrated expensive, 'Zitsa' is dry, demi-sec and sparkling white.

Gentilini Up-market white from CEPHALONIA; a ROBOLA blend, soft and very appealing. Now also a v promising oak-aged version. To watch.

Goumenissa (Appellation) Oak-aged red from W MACEDONIA. Esp BOUTARI.

Hatzimichali Small Atalanti estate. Greek-grape whites; reds incl Cab, Merlot.

Ilios Very drinkable standard RHODES wine from CAIR.

Kokkineli The rosé version of RETSINA: like the white. Drink cold.

Kosta Lazaridis, Domaine Not to be confused with CHATEAU LAZARIDIS, but also for quality red, white, rosé from local and international grapes.

Kouros Highly rated white from KOURTAKIS; also red from NEMEA.

Kourtakis, D Athenian merchant with mild RETSINA and good dark NEMEA.

Kretikos White wine made by BOUTARI from CRETAN varieties.

Lemnos (Appellation) Aegean island: sweet golden Muscat RETSINA, KOKKINELI.

Lindos Higher quality RHODES wine (from Lindos or not). Acceptable, no more.

Macedonia Quality wine region in the north, for XYNOMAVRO, esp NAOUSSA.

Malvasia White grape said to be from Monemvasia (south PELOPONNESE).

Mantinia (Appellation) Fresh aromatic PELOPONNESE white, now widely made.

Mavro Black – the word for dark (often sweet) red wine.

Mavrodaphne (Appellation) 'Black laurel'. Dark, sweet, port/recioto-like conc red; fortified to 15–22%. Speciality of PATRAS, N PELOPONNESE. To age.

Mavroudi Red wine of Delphi and N shore of Gulf of Corinth: dark, plummy.

Mercouri Family estate in PELOPONNESE for v fine Refosco red. (Refosco grapes brought to Greece in 1870 and known locally as Mercouri.)

Metsovo Town in Epirus (north) producing Cab blend called Katoi.

Minos Popular CRETAN brand; the Castello red is best.

Moscophilero Lightly spicy grape that makes MANTINIA.

Naoussa (Appellation) Above average strong dry XYNOMAVRO red from MACEDONIA in the north, esp from BOUTARI, the coop and TSANTALI.

Nemea (Appellation) Town in E PELOPONNESE famous for its lion (a victim of Hercules), fittingly forceful MAVRO, AGIORGITIKO grapes (unique spicy red).

Oenoforos PELOPONNESE estate for top white Asprolithi from local Roditis grape.

Patras (Appellation) White wine (eg plentiful dry Rhoditis and rarer Muscats) and wine town on the Gulf of Corinth. Home of MAVRODAPHNE.

Pegasus, Château NAOUSSA estate for superior red (esp 81 86 88).

Peloponnese Southern landmass of mainland Greece, with half of the country's v'yds, incl NEMEA and PATRAS; vines mostly used for currants.

Rapsani Interesting oaked red from Mt Ossa. Rasping until rescued by TSANTALI.

Retsina White wine with Aleppo pine resin added, tasting of turpentine and oddly appropriate with Greek food. ATTICA speciality. Much modern retsina is disappointingly mild. (So is commercial Taramasalata.)

Rhodes Easternmost Greek island. Chevalier de Rhodes is a pleasant red from CAIR. Makes Greece's best sparkling. See also Caïr, Emery, Ilios.

Robola (Appellation) Dry CEPHALONIA white: pleasant, soft, quite characterful.

Samos (Appellation) Island nr Turkey with ancient reputation for sweet pale golden Muscat and Malvasia. Esp (fortified) Anthemis, (sun-dried) Nectar.

Santorini Dramatic volcanic island N of CRETE: sweet Visanto (sun-dried grapes, once Orthodox church communion wine), v dry white. Potential.

Semeli, Château Estate nr Athens making good white and red, incl Cab S.

Strofilia Brand of 'boutique' winery at Anavissos. Good whites; reds incl Cab.

Tsantali Producers at Agios Pavlos with wide range of country and appellation wines, incl MACEDONIAN and wine from the monks of Mt Athos, NEMEA, NAOUSSA, RAPSANI and Muscat from SAMOS and LIMNOS. CAVA is a blend.

Vaeni Good red from NAOUSSA producers' coop.

Xynomavro The tastiest of many indigenous Greek red grapes – though its name means acidic-black. Basis for NAOUSSA and other northern wines.

Zitsa Mountainous N Epirus appellation. Delicate Debina white, still or fizzy.

Cyprus

Cyprus exports 75 percent of its production, mostly strong red wines of reasonable quality and low-price Cyprus 'sherry', though treacly old Commandaria is the island's finest product. As with Bulgaria, the fall of the old USSR as a major wine market was a serious blow. Quality now has to compete with that in the rest of Europe. Until recently only two local grapes were grown; now another 12 have been discovered. The international standards are inevitably being planted, but many growers still believe in the individuality of their own varieties. The island has never had phylloxera.

Afames Village at the foot of Mt Olympus, giving its name to dry tangy red (MAVRO) wine from SODAP.

Alkion A smooth light dry KEO white (XYNISTERI grapes from Akamas, Paphos). Grapes harvested just before ripeness.

Aphrodite Consistent medium-dry XYNISTERI white from KEO.

Arsinöe Dry white wine from SODAP, named after an unfortunate female whom the last entry turned to stone.

Bellapais Fizzy medium-sweet white from KEO, named after the famous abbey nr Kyrenia. Essential refreshment for holiday-makers.

Commandaria Good quality brown dessert wine since ancient times in hills N of LIMASSOL, from 15 specified villages; named after a crusading order of knights. Made by solera maturation of sun-dried XYNISTERI and MAVRO grapes. Best (as old as 100 yrs) is superb, of incredible sweetness, fragrance, concentration. Most is just standard Communion wine.

Domaine d'Ahera Modern-style lighter estate red from KEO. (From Grenache – recent on the island – and local Lefkas grapes.)

Emva Brand name of well-made fino, medium and cream SHERRIES.

ETKO See Haggipavlu.

Haggipavlu Wine merchant at LIMASSOL since 1844. Trades as ETKO.

Heritage A KEO rich dry red from rare indigenous Pambakina grape; matured in new oak.

KEO The biggest and most go-ahead firm at LIMASSOL. Standard KEO Dry White and Dry Red are vg value. See also Othello, Heritage and Aphrodite.

Khalokhorio Principal COMMANDARIA village, growing only XYNISTERI.

Kokkineli Rosé: the name is related to 'cochineal'.

Kolossi Crusaders' castle nr Limassol; gives name to table wines from SODAP.

Laona The largest of the small independent regional wineries at Arsos, now owned by KEO. Good range incl an oak-aged red and a fruity dry white.

Limassol 'The Bordeaux of Cyprus'. Southern wine port (and its region): location for all four main Cyprus wineries.

Loel Major producer, with Amathus and Kykko brands, Command Cyprus SHERRY and good Negro red.

Mavro The black grape of Cyprus (and Greece) and its dark wine.

Monte Roya Modern regional winery at Chryssoroyiatissa Monastery.

Muscat All major firms produce pleasant low-price (15% alcohol) Muscats.

Opthalmo Black grape (red/rosé): lighter, sharper than MAVRO. Not native.

Othello A good standard dry red wine (made with MAVRO and OPTHALMO grapes from the PITSILIA region). Solid and satisfying version from KEO. Best drunk at 3–4 years.

Palomino Soft dry white made of this (sherry) grape by LOEL. V drinkable ice-cold. Imported to make Cyprus SHERRY.

Pitsilia Region south of Mount Olympus for some of the best white and COMMANDARIA wines.

Rosella Light dry fragrant rosé from KEO. OPTHALMO from PITSILIA.

St-Panteleimon Brand of medium-sweet white from KEO.

Semeli Good traditional red from HAGGIPAVLU. Best at 3–4 years old.

Sherry Sherry-style wine is an island staple. The best is dry. But the name will have to change.

SODAP Major wine coop at LIMASSOL.

Thisbe Fruity medium-dry light KEO wine (of XYNISTERI grapes from LIMASSOL).

Xynisteri The native aromatic white grape of Cyprus.

Asia & North Africa

Algeria As a combined result of Islam and the EC, once massive v'yds have dwindled in the last decade from 860,000 acres to under 200,000 (still nearly as many as Germany); many vines are 40+ yrs old and won't be replaced. Red, white and esp rosé wines of some quality are still made in coastal hills of Tlemcen (powerful), Mascara (good red and white), Haut-Dahra (strong red, rosé), Zaccar, Tessala, Médéa and Ain-Bessem (Bouira esp good). Sidi Brahim is a drinkable red brand. These had VDQS status in French colonial days. Wine is still the third largest export. Algeria is also a cork producer.

China Germans and Russians started making wine on Shantung (now called Shandong) peninsula late 1800s. Since 1980 a modern industry, initiated by Rémy Martin, has made adequate white Dynasty and Tsingtao wines (T is on same latitude as S France). New plantings of better varieties in Shandong and Tianjin (further north) promise more interest. Basic table wines are made of the local Dragon Eye and Muscat Hamburg grapes (esp in Tianjin). In Qingdao (with China's only maritime climate) Huadong winery (since '86, now Allied-Lyons owned) has made very palatable Welschries and Chard and is experimenting with Cab S, Syrah and Gewürz. Dragon Seal Wines (nr Peking, since '87) have Dragon Eye grapes, recent Chard (with oak), and more planned. Other foreign investors and innovators are Seagram (Summer Palace), Pernod Ricard (Beijing Friendship Winery since '87). As of '92 Rémy Martin are making 'Imperial Court', China's first classic method sparkling, nr Shanghai. Further big investments in N will revolutionize the industry.

India In 1985 a Franco-Indian firm launched a Chard-based sparkling wine, Omar Khayyám, made at Náráyangoan, nr Poona, SE of Bombay. It sets an astonishing standard. Plans are to export up to 2M bottles and to add still Chard and Cab. Sweeter Marquise de Pompadour followed, also slightly drier Princess Jaulke, with advice from Charbaut of Champagne – still improving. Now nr Bangalore there is Cab, from Grover V'yds in Dodballapur Hills.

Japan Japan has a small wine industry, mostly in Yamanashi Prefecture, W of Tokyo, but extending as far as cool Hokkaidò (N island). Most wine is blended with imports from S America, Eastern Europe, etc. But premium Sémillon, Chardonnay, Cabernet and local white Kôshû, are the new surprise. Top producers are Manns, Sanraku (Mercian label) and Suntory. Château Mercian and Suntory lead with quality Chard, Cabernet etc.

The most interesting (and expensive) are Suntory's Ch Lion red B'x-blend and vg botrytis Sém; Mercian's Kikyogahara Merlot (since '85), and esp Jyonohira Cab of extraordinary denseness and quality. Manns not only have Chard, Cab (French oaked) but emphasize local varieties (Kôshû, Zenkôji – China's Dragon Eye) and local-Euro crosses (adapted to Japan's rainy climate) too. 2nd-rank are Sapporo (Polaire label), Kyowa Hakko Kogyo (Ste-Neige), Marufuji (big-selling Rubaiyat), Shirayuri Winery (L'Orient label), Ch Lumière.

Regrettably, labelling laws have been so lax that misrepresentation of imported wines as 'Japanese' has been rule rather than exception. Law now stipulates that if imported wine in bottle is above 50% it must be indicated on label (larger percentage printed before the smaller). But local wines are now attracting interest, and Katsunuma district is capitalizing by introducing Certificate of Origin labels.

For key to grape variety abbreviations, see pages 7–13.

Lebanon The small Lebanese industry, based in Ksara in Bekaa Valley NE of Beirut, makes wines of vigour and quality. Three wineries of note. Ch Musar (★★★), the heroic survivor of yrs of civil war, produces splendid claret-like matured reds, largely of Cab; a full-blooded oaked white, from indigenous Obaideh grapes (like Chard), surprisingly capable of ageing 10–15 yrs; and recently a lighter red wine, 'Tradition', which is 75% Cinsaut, 25% Cab S. Ksara is the largest, oldest (Jesuit-founded) winery (vg fresh white blend). Kefraya makes: 'Rouge de K' Cinsaut-Carignan, 'Château Kefraya' is fragrant and from best yrs only; there is rosé and white too; all early-drinking.

Morocco Morocco makes North Africa's best wine (85% red, from Cinsaut, Grenache, Carignan), from v'yds along Atlantic coast (Rabat to Casablanca, light, hopefully fruity with speciality white – 'Gris' – from red grapes) and around Meknès and Fèz (solid full-bodied, best-known). Also further east around Berkane and Angad (tangy, earthy) and in the Gharb and Doukkalas regions. But in 10 years v'yds have declined from 190,000 to 35,000 acres. Main producers are Dom de Sahari (nr Meknès, French investment, a new winery in '93, Cab S and Merlot vines, along with local grapes), Celliers de Meknés (dominating state-owned coop), Chaudsoleil, and Sincomar. Chantebled, Tarik and Toulal are drinkable reds. Vin Gris (10% of production), esp de Boulaoune, is the best bet for hot-day refreshment. Cork production is also important.

Tunisia Tunisia now has 22,000 v'yd acres (there were 120,000 10 yrs ago). Her speciality is sweet Muscat, but most wines are reasonable reds and light rosés from Cap Bon, Carthage, Mornag, Tébourba and Tunis. Trying to improve quality; state and coop best. A third is exported.

Turkey Most of Turkey's 1.5 million acres of v'yds produce table grapes; only 3% are for wine. Wines from Thrace, Anatolia and the Aegean are very drinkable. Indigenous varieties (there are over 1,000: 60 are commercial) such as Emir, Narince (for white) and Bogazkere, Oküzgözü (for red) are used along with Ries, Sém, Pinot N, Grenache, Carignan and Gamay. Trakya (Thrace) white (light Sém) and Buzbag (E Anatolian) red are the well-known standards of Tekel, the state producer (with 21 state wineries). Diren, Doluca, Karmen, Kavaklidere and Taskobirlik are private firms of fair quality. Doluca's Villa Neva red from Thrace is well made, as is Villa Doluca. Kavaklidere makes good light Primeurs (white 'Cankaya' and red 'Yakut') from local grapes. But Buzbag remains Turkey's most original and striking wine.

The old Russian Empire

Over 3 million acres of vineyards make the 16 republics of the former USSR collectively the world's fourth-biggest wine producer. Russia is the largest of the 12 producing wine, followed by Moldova, the Ukraine (including top Crimea region) and Georgia. Soviet consumers have a sweet tooth, for both table and dessert wines, also sparkling.

Russia Makes fair Riesling (Anapa, Arbau, Beshtau) and sweet sparkling Tsimlanskoye 'Champanski. Abrau Durso is classic sparkling (since 1870) from Pinot, Chard and Cab F in similar climate to Champagne's. Also Chard, Sauv, Welschriesling (heavy, often oxidized), processed in state wineries nr Moscow, St-Petersburg etc. Best are Don Valley v'yds (Black Sea Coast of the Caucasus), for Ries, Aligoté, Cab.

Moldova The most temperate climate (as in N France) and now most modern outlook, Moldova has high potential: esp whites from centre, reds from S, red and fortified nr Black Sea (W), making more wine than Australia. Grapes incl Cab, Pinot N, Merlot, Saperavi (fruity), Ries, Chard, Pinot Gr, Aligoté, Rkatsiteli. Former Moscow bottling was disastrous. But the 63 Negru de Purkar released in '92 gave a startling glimpse of potential (4 yrs oak, and v best from Cab-Saperavi-Rara Negre (like 63)). Purkar may be top winery. Krikova also good: esp Kodru 'Claret' blend, Krasny Reserve Pinot-Merlot-Malbec, sp. Romanesti winery (since '82) has French varieties; Yavloveni, fino- and oloroso-style 'flor sherries'. Good old-vine Cab from Tarakliya. German, Italian, UK, Australian (Penfolds since '93) investment at Hincesti enables local clean bottling, better winemaking, future improvements: Ryman's Chard is vg. Half v'yds still state farmed: progress (and privatization) not smooth, but worth watching. Appellation system being planned.

Crimea (Ukraine) Crimea produces first-class dessert wines. Sotheby's auction house disclosed as much in '90, with sales of old wines from the Tsar's Crimean cellars at Massandra, nr Yalta (top-quality Muscats, port-, Madeira-like wines). Alupka Palace fortified (European grapes, since 1820s), classic sparkling from Novi Svet and Grand Duchess (the latter from Odessa Winery founded by Henri Roederer in 1896) also adequate. Reds have potential (eg Alushta from Massandra). All still made under state monopoly. Ukraine also has Aligoté and Artemosk sparkling (Romanian grapes). Full potential yet to be realized.

Georgia Uses antique methods for v tannic wines for local drinking, slightly newer techniques for export blends (Mukuzani, Tsinandali); Georgians are disinclined to modernize. Kakhetià (E) is famed for weighty red, acceptable white. Imeretia (W) makes milder, highly original, earthenware-fermented wines. Kartli is central area. Sparkling is v cheap, drinkable. When equipment (incl bottles, stoppers), techniques improve, Georgia will be an export hit.

Israel

Israeli wine, since the industry was re-established by Baron Edmond de Rothschild in the 1880s, has been primarily of kosher interest until recently, when Cab, Merlot, Sauv, Chard were introduced. Traditionally vines were planted in coastal Samson and Shomron but new cooler Golan Heights vineyards (N) have resulted in great improvements. Sixty percent of the annual 25 million bottle production is white.

Barkan Newish winery with promising Emerald Ries, Sauv Bl and Cab S.

Baron Small family grower. Vg whites, esp dry Muscat and Sauv Bl.

Binyamina (Formerly Eliaz) Medium-sized winery for light-style wines.

Carmel Coop, est 1882, with Israel's 2 largest wineries. Top wines are Carmel Rothschild, Chard, Selected Vineyards Cab, Emerald Ries. Also new Merlot.

Galil/Galilee Region incl Golan Heights (Israel's top v'yd area).

Gamla & Golan Both labels of the Golan Heights winery. Soft fruity Cab S, oaky Chard and grassy Sauv Bl. (See Yarden.)

Samson Central coastal plain v'yds (SE of Tel Aviv to W of Jerusalem).

Segal Family winery (aka Askalon). Cab S-Carignan Segal and Ben Ami labels.

Shomron V'yds in the valleys around Zichron-Yaacov, nr Haifa.

Yarden Young ('83) modern Golan Heights winery, with California oenologists setting highest standards. Full-bodied oaky Cab (85 89 90), complex Merlot, barrel-fermented Chard, crisp Sauv; recently classic method sparkling.

England & Wales

Well over a million and a half bottles a year are now being made from over 430 vineyards, amounting in total to some 2,600 acres. Almost all are white and are developing a new and distinctive crisp English style, many from new German varieties designed to ripen well in cool weather. Acidity is often high, which means that good examples have a built-in ability (and need) to age. Four years is a good age for many, and up to eight for some. Experiments with both oak-ageing and bottle-fermented sparkling are promising; especially the latter. The English Vineyards Association seal is worn by tested wines (the EVA is about to become the United Kingdom Vineyards Association). Since 1991 non-hybrid English wines may be labelled as 'Quality Wine', taking them into the European Community quality bracket for the first time although the English criteria are higher than those of the EC. But as the (excellent) hybrid Seyval Blanc is so important here, few growers apply. NB Beware 'British Wine', which is neither British nor indeed wine, and has nothing to do with the following.

Adgestone nr Sandown (Isle of Wight) Prize-winning 8.5-acre v'yd on chalky hill site. Est'd '68. Wines with good structure and longevity.

Astley Stourport-on-Severn (Hereford and Worcester) 4.5 acres; some fair wines. Madeleine Angevine and Kerner are prize-winning.

Avalon Shepton Mallet (Somerset) Organically grown grapes. 2.3 acres.

Bagborough Shepton Mallet (Somerset) New v'yd to note. 3 acres.

Bardingley Staplehurst (Kent) 2.5-acres. Interesting red (some oak-aged).

Barkham Manor E Sussex 34 acres since '85. Wide range. Modern winery.

Barton Manor East Cowes (Isle of Wight) 15.5-acre v'yd: trophy-winning, consistently interesting wines incl barrel-matured and bottle-fermented sparkling. Considerable recent investment. New owners since '91.

Bearstead Maidstone (Kent) 4 acres planted '86. Improving, esp Bacchus.

Beaulieu Abbey Brockenhurst (Hampshire) 4.6-acre v'yd, established '58 by Gore-Browne family on old monastic site. Good rosé.

Beenleigh Manor Totnes (Devon) Esteemed Cab S and Merlot grown under 0.5 acres of polythene. Wine made at SHARPHAM. 90 is trophy winner.

Biddenden nr Tenterden (Kent) 20-acre v'yd planted '69: wide range includes Ortega, Huxelrebe, Bacchus, bottle-fermented sparkling. Good cider too.

Bishops Waltham Southampton (Hampshire) 13 acres: fair Würzer, Schönburger.

Bookers Bolney (E Sussex) 4 acres of Müller-T; other varieties planted '92.

Bothy Abingdon (Oxfordshire) Just 3 acres so far, for esp good Huxelrebe-Perle and fragrant Ortega-Optima (**90 91**).

Boyton Stoke-by-Clare (Suffolk) Small 2-acre v'yd: Huxelrebe (90), Müller-T.

Boze Down Whitchurch-on-Thames (Oxfordshire) 5.8 acres. Wide range; red and sweet now looking good. Worth watching.

Breaky Bottom Lewes (Sussex) 5.5-acre v'yd. Semi-cult following. Good dry wines, esp award-winning Seyval (**89 90**), Müller-T. Sparkling is next.

Brenchley Tonbridge (Kent) 17 acres: Seyval, Schönburger, Huxelrebe. To watch.

Bruisyard Saxmundham (Suffolk) 10 acres Müller-T: oaked, sparkling. Since '76.

Cane End Reading (Berkshire) 12 acres; mixed vines. Good sweet late-harvest Bacchus in '90. Interesting style.

Carr Taylor Vineyards Sussex 21 acres, planted '73. Esp for Reichensteiner. Pioneer of classic method sparkling wine in UK: Kerner-Reichensteiner (vintage, NV), Pinot N rosé. Some lively, intense, balanced wines.

Chapel Down Winery Tenterden (Kent) New winery venture, blending from bought-in grapes, esp classic-method sparkling. Barrel-fermented 'Epoch I' red is good, as are 'sur lie' still and sparkling.

Chiddingstone Edenbridge (Kent) 28-acre v'yd with stress on dry French-style wines, esp good Pinot Bl de Noir. Some barrique-ageing.

Chilford Hundred Linton (Cambridgeshire) 18 acres: fairly dry wines since '74.

Chiltern Valley Henley-on-Thames (Oxfordshire) 3 acres of own v'yds high up on chalk, plus neighbouring growers': incl prize-winning oak-aged unusual sweet late-harvest Noble Bacchus, Old Luxters Dry Reserve.

Crickley Windward Little Witcombe (Gloucestershire) 5.5 acres beginning to show well, esp 91 Schönburger Reserve.

Denbies Dorking (Surrey) 250-acre v'yd (England's biggest); first harvest '89. Impressive winery: gd tour facilities, improving wines, esp 92 dessert Botrytis.

Elham Valley Canterbury (Kent) Boutique winery/2-acre v'yd: impressive hand-crafted medium-dry Müller-T, and sparkling Kerner-Seyval Bl.

Elmham Park East Dereham (Norfolk) 4.5-acre v'yd, est '66. Light flowery wines, Madeleine Angevine esp good. Also apple wine.

Gifford's Hall Bury St-Edmunds (Suffolk) 12 acre-v'yd for interesting wines (incl oak-aged) and visitor facilities.

Hagley Court Hereford 7.5 acres planted '85, wines now worth watching.

Halfpenny Green W Midlands 28 v'yd-acres; esp good Madeleine Angevine.

Hambledon nr Petersfield (Hampshire) The first modern English v'yd, planted in '51 on a chalk slope with advice from Champagne.

Harden Farm Penshurst (Kent) 18 acres. Member of Winegrowers coop.

Headcorn Maidstone (Kent) 5-acre medal-winning v'yd: Seyval Bl etc.

Helions Helion's Bumpstead, Haverhill (Suffolk) One acre, 50:50 Müller-T and Reichensteiner; good aromatic dry wine.

Hidden Spring Horam (E Sussex) 9 acres. Esp oaked Dry Reserve, Dark Fields red.

Highfield Tiverton (Devon) 1.5 acres. Good wines, esp Siegerrebe.

La Mare Jersey (Channel Islands) Only (but long-est'd) CI v'yd. Fair wines.

Lamberhurst (Kent) One of the best: 11 acres est'd '72. Consistent range of award winners (83 85 90), reds, sparkling, oak-aged. Medium-dry 91 Bacchus esp good. Winemaker for many other growers.

Leeford nr Battle (Sussex) 25-acre v'yd; more planned. Various labels incl Saxon Valley, Battle, Conquest. New very modern winery.

Llanerch S Glamorgan (Wales) 5.5 acres est'd '86. Wines sold under Cariad label. Individual style developing, worth its awards. Good rosé.

Loddiswell Kingsbridge (Devon) 6 acres plus one under plastic tunnels.

Lymington Hampshire 6 acre-v'yd est'd '79.

Manstree Exeter (Devon) 3-acres; esp sparkling: 'Essling' (90) is a winner.

Meon Valley Southampton (Hampshire) 25 acres: variable, reds interesting.

Mersea Colchester (Essex) Small v'yd. Wine quality gets better and better.

Monnow Valley Monmouth (Wales) 4 acres. Wines attracting increasing attention, esp 92 Huxelrebe-Seyval Bl.

Moorlynch Bridgewater (Somerset) 15 acres of an idyllic farm. Good wines: have been variable, now improving.

New Hall nr Maldon (Essex) 87 acres of mixed farm planted with Huxelrebe, Müller-T and Pinot N etc. Some vinified elsewhere.

Northbrook Springs Bishops Waltham (Hampshire) 13 acres of young vines and improving wines. Gold medal in English Wine of Year competition '95.

Nutbourne Manor nr Pulborough (W Sussex) 18.5 acres: elegant and tasty Schönburger and Bacchus.

Nyetimber West Chiltington (W Sussex) 12-acre v'yd of Chard, Pinot N, Pinot Meunier specializing in bottle-fermented sparkling. First vintage 95.

Oatley Bridgewater (Somerset) 4.5 acres new vines. Esp good 92 Kernling.

Partridge Blandford (Dorset) 5 acres. 92 dry Bacchus is trophy-winning.

Penshurst Tunbridge Wells (Kent) 12 acres since '72, incl good Seyval Bl and Müller-T. Fine modern winery.

Pilton Manor Shepton Mallet (Somerset) 15-acre hillside v'yd (est'd '66). Wines regaining form, esp Westholme Late Harvest, a '92 and '94 prize-winner.

Plumpton Agricultural College nr Lewes (Sussex) 1-acre experimental v'yd.

Priory Vineyards Little Dunmow (Essex) 10 acres; now some good wines.

Pulham Diss (Norfolk) 12.6-acre v'yd planted '73; Müller-T is top wine.

Queen Court Faversham (Kent) Brewery-owned: esp Müller-T, Schönburger.

Rock Lodge nr Haywards Heath (Sussex) 8-acre v'yd since '65. Fumé (oak-aged Ortega-Müller-T blend) and Impresario sparkling recommended.

St-George's Waldron, Heathfield (E Sussex) 15 acres, planted '79. Müller-T etc. Well-publicized; wide range, popular styles.

St-Nicholas Ash (Kent) 5 acres. Esp good for Schönburger.

Sandhurst Cranbrook (Kent) Mixed farm with 16 acres of vines. Improving wines, esp 91 Seyval, 92 Bacchus (both oak-aged). Sparkling Pinot N-Seyval.

Scott's Hall Ashford (Kent) Boutique v'yd: oak-aged white, sparkling rosé.

Seddlescombe Organic Robertsbridge (E Sussex) The UK's main organic v'yd. 6 acres for range of wines with quite a following.

Sharpham Totnes (Devon) 5 acres. Now own winery: getting interesting.

Shawsgate Framlingham (Suffolk) 17 acres: good Seyval-Müller-T. Wins awards.

South Ridge Pace-setting Pinot N-Chard, classic method sparkling from consultant winemaker Kit Lindlar.

Staple Saint James nr Canterbury (Kent) 7 acres planted '77. Excellent quality. Müller-T and Huxelrebe especially interesting.

Staplecombe Taunton (Somerset) 2.5 acres for some good wines.

Staverton (Woodbridge) Suffolk 1.5 acres of improving v'yds, esp Bacchus.

Tenterden Tenterden (Kent) 12 acres, planted '79. Wines very dry to sweet, Müller-T, oak-aged Seyval (vg 81, 91 Trophy winner), rosé, sparkling.

Thames Valley Twyford (Berkshire) 25-acre v'yd: all styles of wine. Serious oak-matured white, red; classic method sparkling; also late harvest sweet.

Three Choirs Newent (Gloucestershire) 60 acres (more planned), est'd '74. Müller-Thurgau, Seyval Bl, Schönburger, Reichensteiner, and esp Bacchus Dry, Huxelrebe. Recent new £1-million winery. English 'Nouveau' is popular.

Throwley Faversham (Kent) 4.5 acres. Excellent bottle-fermented sparkling from Pinot N and Chard. 91 Ortega also vg.

Wickham Shedfield (Hampshire) 9.5-acre v'yd (since '84): starting to show some style. Vintage Selection is worth trying, esp 91.

Wissett Halesworth (Suffolk) 10 acres beginning to show up well. Esp for Auxerrois-Pinot blends and Müller-T.

Wooldings Whitchurch (Hampshire) Young 7-acre v'yd. Vg Schönburger.

Wootton Shepton Mallet (Somerset) 6-acre v'yd of Schönburger, Müller-T, Seyval Bl, Auxerrois, etc. Consistently good fresh fruity wines since '71.

Wyken Bury-St-Edmunds (Suffolk) Range starting to look good, esp dry Bacchus white and full dark red. Good restaurant too.

> The trend towards 'low-alcohol' wines and beers, from which most alcohol has been removed artificially, should be a golden opportunity for wines naturally lower in alcohol than usual. Germany is the prime exponent; England another. Their best wines, with plenty of fruity acidity, do not need high alcohol to make an impact. Today's logical choice – at least at lunch-time.

North America

WASHINGTON

OREGON

CALIFORNIA

EASTERN STATES

California

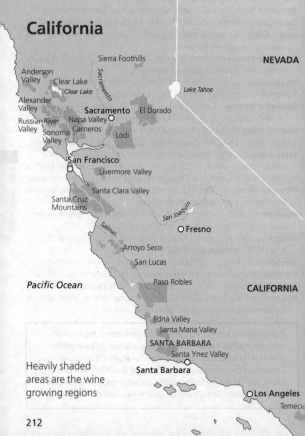

NEVADA

Sierra Foothills

Anderson Valley

Clear Lake

Clear Lake

Sacramento

Alexander Valley

Russian River Valley

Sonoma Valley

Napa Valley

Carneros

Sacramento

El Dorado

Lake Tahoe

Lodi

San Francisco

Livermore Valley

Santa Clara Valley

Santa Cruz Mountains

Salinas

San Joaquin

○ Fresno

Arroyo Seco

San Lucas

Pacific Ocean

Paso Robles

CALIFORNIA

Edna Valley

Santa Maria Valley

SANTA BARBARA

Heavily shaded areas are the wine growing regions

Santa Ynez Valley

Santa Barbara

○ Los Angeles

Temecu

The wine boom carried California to dizzy heights in the 1970s and 1980s. The 1990s have seen retrenchment – and a very expensive plague of phylloxera which will cause the replanting of many of the vineyards of the west. In the long run its effect will be beneficial: more of the right grapes in the right places. Meanwhile finer tuning is producing even better-balanced, easier and more harmonious wines.

At the same time America's old puritanical streak allied to the country's not-so-latent hypochondria and the 1992–93 recession badly frightened bankers. Expansion may be on hold for the moment, but progress continues; not to mention changes of ownership, management, style…. This edition records some 280 of the 600-odd wineries now operating. Brevity is not dismissive; it is intended to be practical. Vintages given reflect the probable maturity of wines kept in, say, reasonable restaurant conditions. Some considerably older bottles kept in ideal cellars will still be excellent. Chardonnays can sometimes mature for 10 years with ease, Cabernets for 20. But this is the exception, not the rule.

Appellation areas (AVAs) are now an important fact of life. They are being registered thick and fast: the current total is well over 50, with nine in Napa alone. But it is still much too soon to use them as a generally applicable guide to style. Listed below are the regions usually referred to. Grapes and makers' names, though, remain the key to California wine.

Principal vineyard areas

Central Coast
A long sweep of coast with scattered though increasing wine activity, from San Francisco Bay south to Santa Barbara.

Carmel Valley Tiny coastal area; sometimes impressive Cab and Chard.

Hecker Pass Pass through the SANTA CRUZ MTS S of San Francisco Bay; dwindling cluster of small old-style wineries.

Livermore Valley E of San Francisco Bay long famous for white wines (esp Sauvignon Blanc). Though area largely built over, v'yds and wineries are surprisingly resilient.

Monterey See Salinas Valley.

Salinas Valley/Monterey The Salinas Valley runs SE inland from Monterey. After frenzied expansion in the '70s interest shifted sharply south to warmer zones. Currently refining its internal divisions: Arroyo Seco AVA (esp Chard and Ries), Santa Lucia Highlands AVA (Chard, has hopes for Pinot N), San Lucas AVA (steady commercial wines).

San Luis Obispo Biggest, warmest district is Paso Robles (6,000 acres of esp Zin, Cab S); finest is Edna Valley (1,000 acres, esp Chard); newest is Arroyo Grande (500 acres, esp Pinot N and sparkling).

Santa Barbara Santa Maria Valley is dominant, esp for vg Chardonnay and distinctive Pinot N. The smaller Santa Ynez Valley also has cool foggy conditions: good for Burgundian varieties at seaward end, B'x varieties in warmer inland areas.

Santa Cruz Mts Wineries (though few v'yds) are scattered round the Santa Cruz Mts S of San Francisco Bay, from Saratoga down to HECKER PASS.

Temecula (Rancho California) Small area in S California, 25 miles inland, halfway between San Diego and Riverside. Mainly whites.

NORTH AMERICA

213

North Coast
Encompasses Lake, Menodocino, Napa and Sonoma counties, all north of San Francisco.

Carneros, Los Important cool region N of San Francisco Bay, shared between NAPA and SONOMA counties. Esp for Chard and Pinot N.

Lake Clear Lake AVA: warm climate, most impressive for Sauv Bl, good for Cab S. Small Guenoc Valley AVA similar.

Mendocino North of SONOMA. A varied climate, coolest in Anderson Valley nr the coast, warm inland around Ukiah (Zin, Barbera).

Napa The Napa Valley, N of San Francisco Bay. The oldest and most-honoured of California wine valleys busily fragmenting itself: Stag's Leap AVA (Cab), CARNEROS AVA (shared with SONOMA, good Chard, Pinot N and sparkling), Mt Veeder AVA (Cab), Howell Mountain AVA (Cab, Zinfandel, Chard), Atlas Peak AVA (Sangiovese) and new AVAs on the valley floor, Rutherford, Oakville and St-Helena.

Sonoma County N of San Francisco Bay, between rival NAPA and the sea. California's most divided wine area. Has a dozen AVAs in two separate drainage basins: (1) tipped to SF Bay: Sonoma Valley AVA ('Valley of the Moon', versatile, includes Sonoma Mountain and part of CARNEROS, see Napa); (2) orientated to ocean: Russian River drainage: includes warmer inland valleys Alexander (Cab, Italian varieties), Dry Creek (Zin, Rhône varieties), Knights – and cooler seaward AVAs of Russian River Valley (Chalk Hill, Sonoma-Green Valley, all for Pinot N, Chard, sparkling).

The Interior
Amador County E of Sacramento. Vg Zinfandel, esp Shenandoah Valley AVA.

Lodi Town and district at the N end of the SAN JOAQUIN VALLEY, its hot climate modified by a westerly air-stream.

San Joaquin Valley The great central valley of California, fertile and hot, the source of most of the jug and dessert wines in the state. (Incl LODI AVA and the Clarksburg AVA on the Sacramento River delta.)

Sierra Foothills Encompasses AMADOR (Shenandoah Valley, Fiddletown AVAs), El Dorado (AVA of the same name), Calaveras counties, among others. Zin is universal grape; Rhône and Italian varieties seen more and more.

Recent vintages

California's climate is far from being as consistent as its reputation. Although, on the whole, grapes ripen regularly, they are subject to spring frosts in many areas, sometimes a wet harvest-time and too often drought.

Wines from the San Joaquin Valley tend to be most consistent year by year. The vintage date on these, where there is one, is more important for telling the age of the wine than its character.

Vineyards in the Central Coast region are widely scattered; there is little pattern. The Napa and Sonoma valleys are the areas where comment can usefully be made on the last dozen or more vintages of the top varietal wines: Cabernet Sauvignon and Chardonnay.

Chardonnay
NB These ageing assessments are based on well-balanced wines with fruit flavours dominant. Very rich and oaky examples tend to be v short-lived: 2 yrs at most. Marker wines for good ageing qualities incl eg Acacia, Bouchaine, Chappellet, Clos du Bois-Calcaire, Cuvaison, Dehlinger, Freemark Abbey, Navarro, Silverado, Sonoma-Cutrer, Trefethen.

1995 After a spotty spring and erratic summer, a benign harvest season led to all-round optimism.

1994 Finer balance, more profound flavours than excited first reports. Best vintage to cellar since '91s.

1993 Attractive early, many still on upward path.

1992 Softly agreeable, at peak in '96 and likely to fade fast.

1991 Balanced, firm; showing evolution but still on top of game.

1990 Useful vintage now as well developed as it can expect to be.

1989 Edging onto downslope in many cases, but quite a few are excellent and holding well.

1988 Pretty well past it.

1987 The most durable of the marker wines are good, the rest fading.

1986 Drink up the best; should have drunk the rest.

1985 Drink up the best; the rest should have been drunk by now.

1983 Only Trefethen, Navarro are left.

Cabernet Sauvignon

NB As with Chardonnays, over-rich and over-oaky wines usually collapse quickly. The markers for the assessments below are not Reserves, but fine standard Cabernets from eg Beringer (Knights Valley), Caymus, Chappellet, Clos du Val, Freemark Abbey, Hafner, Jordan, Laurel Glen, Louis M Martini (Monte Rosso), Parducci, Pine Ridge, Raymond, Shafer, Silverado.

1995 After a spotty spring and erratic summer, a benign harvest season led to all-round optimism.

1994 In barrel rivals 91 for focus and length, though less austere than that year. Probable textbook demo of California capacity to charm early, impress later.

1993 As the first major players come to market, still looking approachable early.

1992 Beginning to look desolately like the '88s.

1991 After latest harvest ever, leanest, raciest, best focussed wines in years. Still slightly reticent.

1990 Picture-perfect California vintage: ripe, enveloping, still showing more fruit than maturity.

1989 Many beautifully dark, flavoury wines with solid structure for ageing; some got caught in rains.

1988 Bland, lacking focus and structure.

1987 Evolving as perhaps the best of the decade overall.

1986 Quickly approachable vintage. Baby fat is now fleshy.

1985 Lean, firm to hard, deep-flavoured. Slow-maturing but impressive (frailer ones with some decline).

1984 Showy early: ripe and fragrant. Still in good form.

1983 Still awkward, hard. Many now fading.

1982 Long written off, yet many Napas now wonderfully harmonious, complex. However, even best v fragile. Hurry.

1981 Best at peak, most slightly past.

1980 High reputation but merely good and solid. Over-tannic. Should drink up.

1979 Apparently lightish, but the best kept going sturdily. Drink up.

1978 Wonderful early; most faded now. Drink up.

1977 Attractive wines now mainly crumbling. Drink up.

1976 Drought made v concentrated wines. Good ones are v ripe and potent now. Drink up.

1975 Delicate, charming; mature. Still in good form and able to wait.

1974 Blockbuster wines: some flopped, the best are ripe and ready. Drink up.

1970 Wonderful vintage, but has about run its course. Drink up.

California wineries

Acacia Napa ★★★ (Chard) 89 91 92 93 94 95 (Pinot N) 87. 88 89 90 91 92 93 94 95 Long-time specialist in durable, deep CARNEROS Chard and Pinot on a quality run with both; former single-v'yd wines now blended into extra-oaky Reserves due to depredations of phylloxera.

Adelaida Cellars San Luis Obispo ★★ Supple Cab, vigorous Zin the standbys, now joined by Sangiovese and Rhône varieties.

Alderbrook Sonoma ★★ (Chard) 89 90 91 92 93 94 95 New owner, new winemaker in '94; expanding volume and softening style of Chard, Sauv, Sém. Zin and other reds newly added.

Alexander Valley Vineyards Sonoma ★★ Cab S mostly likely of 6 wines to live up to promise of fine v'yd. Whites quirky at best.

Almaden San Joaquin ★ Famous pioneer name, now a CANANDAIGUA-owned everyday brand, operated from Madera. 1 million+ cases.

S Anderson Vineyard Napa ★★→★★★ (Cab) 89 90 91' 92 95 (Brut) 90 91 95 Top Chardonnay classic sparkling as new CARNEROS v'yd kicks in. Cab (from neighbouring Stag's Leap) is stunning.

Arrowood Sonoma ★★→★★★ (Chard) 91 92 93 94 95 (Cab) 85 87 90 91 92 95 Long-time CHATEAU ST JEAN winemaker Dick A on peak form with supple, age-worthy Cab S. Chard (esp Res) for oak-lovers.

Araujo Napa ★ Eisele v'yd, now estate: dark, brooding Cab S.

Artisans and Estates Diverse specialist winery group collected by KENDALL-JACKSON: incl CAMBRIA, Camelot, LA CREMA, Edmeades, Hartford Court, R PEPI, J Stonestreet.

Atlas Peak Napa ★★ From Antinori-owned v'yds in E hills. Allied-Hiram Walker-owned winery makes ever-improving Sangiovese and Sangiovese-Cab 'Consenso'.

Au Bon Climat Sta Barbara ★★★ (Chard) 91 92 93 94 95 (Pinot N) 87 88 89 90 91 92 93 94 95 Jim Clendenen listens to his private drummer: ultra-toasty Chard, flavourful Pinot N, light-hearted Pinot Bl. Italian varietals under Podere dellos Olivos label. Also for QUPE and VITA NOVA (Santa Maria Valley) wines.

Barnett Napa ★ Tiny producer. Intriguing Cab from estate high on Spring Mtn.

Beaucanon Napa ★★ Bordeaux owners Lebègue turning out consistently supple stylish Cab S, Merlot and improving Chard from own 250 acres. LaCrosse is Second label.

Beaulieu Vineyard Napa ★★ (Cab) 36 45 49 58 65 80 83 85 87 89 90 91 92 95 Long-time growers and makers of famous age-worthy Georges Delatour Private Reserve Cab. Best value: lean oak-free Sauv and polished CARNEROS Chard. HEUBLEIN-owned.

Belvedere Sonoma ★★ William Hambrecht uses mostly his own grapes for Alexander Valley Cab S, Dry Creek Valley Zin, Russian River Chard.

Benziger Family Winery Sonoma ★★ Called Benziger of Glen Ellen until Proprietors Reserve sold to HEUBLEIN. Now all SONOMA grapes and dotty for oak in everything in a wide range.

Beringer Napa ★★★ (Chard) 92 93 94 95 (Cab S) 78 79 80 81 84 87 89 90 91 92 95 Century-old winery restored to front rank. Well-defined Cabs (NV Private Reserve, Knights Valley) far outshine fat, ultra-oaky Chardonnays; Zin more than just worthy. Also own CHATEAU SOUVERAIN, MERIDIAN, NAPA RIDGE and (as of '96) CH ST JEAN.

Boeger El Dorado ★★ Mostly estate wines. Attractive Merlot, Barbera, Zin – all less bold than many neighbours.

Bonny Doon Sta Cruz Mts ★★★ Literary, adventurous Rhône-pioneer makes fascinating Le Sophiste (white), red Cigare Volant and Old Telegram; delicious Vin Gris de Cigare. Italian varieties are now claiming equal attention.

Bouchaine Carneros ★★★ (Chard) 89 90 91 92 93 94 95 (Pinot) 91 92 93 94 95
Long somnolent, recently inspired or close to it. Chard and Pinot N both in
upper ranks of region. Renovated cellars may have helped.

Brander Vineyard Sta Barbara ★★ More interest in power, less in finesse
during recent vintages in both impressive intense Sauv from regional leader
of Sta Ynez Valley and MERITAGE-type Bouchet.

Bronco Wine Company San Joaquin ★→★★ Umbrella label for varietal wines:
LAURIER (cream of crop), Forest Glen, Grand Cru, Hacienda, Napa Creek,
RUTHERFORD VINTNERS. C C Vineyard and J F J Bronco are labels for penny-saver
generic wines.

In 1970, California Chardonnay plantings produced roughly
370,000 cases of wine. In 1995 the potential was approximately
18,600,000 cases.

Bruce, David Sta Cruz Mts ★★★ (Pinot N) 85 87 88 89 90 91 92 93 95 Long-
time source of eccentric bruiser (now moderated) Chard. Pinot N (from own
SONOMA vines is forte).

Buehler Napa ★★ (Chard) 92 93 95 (Cab S) 89 90 91 92 95 In E hills: has
turned a sharp corner: flavoury Cabs and Zins. Vg Russian River fruit-first
Chard has finesse.

Buena Vista Carneros ★★ (Chard) 90 91 94 95 (Cab S) 82 85 86 87 89 89 90
91 95 Back on form after a few stumbling yrs with delicious taste-the-
grapes CARNEROS Chard, Lake County Sauv, Merlot, and (well kept secret)
intense, ageless Cab S from biggest property in the AVA.

Burgess Cellars Napa ★★ (Zin) 85 87 88 90 91 92 Emphasis on dark weighty
well-oaked reds; Cab rather plain-faced, Zin more compelling.

BV Abbreviation of BEAULIEU VINEYARD used on its labels.

Bynum, Davis Sonoma ★★ (Chard) 90 91 92 93 94 95 (Pinot N) 90 91 92 93
94 95 Steady for years. Now turning to single-v'yd wines and gaining
added depth: especially Russian River Valley Chard, Pinot N, vg Sauv Bl
and Gewürz.

Byron Vineyards Sta Barbara ★★★ (Chard) 89 91 92 93 95 (Pinot) 84 85 88
89 90 91 92 93 95 Prospering under R MONDAVI-ownership; estate Pinot N
leads with Chard not far behind.

Cain Cellars Napa ★★★ (Cain Five) 85 86 87 89 90' 91 92 95 Focal point is
increasingly stylish supple Cain Five, blended from Cab varieties grown in
estate v'yd on Spring Mt. Cain Cuvée is declassified C Five that s'times rivals
it; white is (also fine) MONTEREY Sauv Musqué.

Cafaro Napa ★★ Winemaker label for sturdy to stolid Cab and Merlot.

Cakebread Napa ★★★ (Chard) 92 93 95 (Cab S) 80 81 85 86 87 88 89 90 91 95
Bold well-oaked style rules in Sauv, Chard and Cab.

Calera San Benito ★★★ (Chard) 91 92 93 95 (Pinot) 82 84 85 87 89 90 91 92 95
Dry sunny chalky hills nr Chalone lead to booming Rhône-weight estate
Pinot Ns named after individual v'yd blocks (Reed, Selleck, Jensen). Also for
perfumiest Viognier.

Callaway Temecula ★★ (Chard) 87 88 89 90 91 92 93 94 95 Oak-free, lees-aged
Chard is a triumph from this warm dry region; Fumé Blanc also good.

Cambria Sta Barbara ★★ Part of KENDALL-JACKSON'S ARTISANS AND ESTATES group.
Watch for Chard and enticing Pinot N.

Canandaigua Huge NY firm with major role in California; now No 2 to GALLO
and growing. Today includes INGLENOOK, DUNNEWOOD, Paul Masson, COOKS.

NB Vintages in colour are those you should choose first for drinking in 1997.

Carey Cellars Sta Barbara ★★ (Chard) 89 90 91 92 93 95 Impressive since acquisition by FIRESTONE: vg tropical Chard, also Sauv and Cab and Merlot of the capsicum persuasion.

Carmenet Sonoma ★★→★★★ (Cab S blend) 87 89 90 91 92 95 CHALONE-owned mountain v'yd and winery above SONOMA town: classy plummy Cab-based blends (Dynamite, Moon Mountain, Vin de Garde etc). Also MONTEREY Sauv blend and CARNEROS Chard.

Carneros Creek Carneros ★★→★★★ (Chard) 91 92 93 94 95 (Pinot N) 85 90 91 92 93 95 Resolute explorer of climates and clones in CARNEROS focuses on Pinot N. Well-oaked Reserve, lightheartedly fruity Fleur and split-the-difference estate bottlings. Also deftly oaked Chard. 25,000 cases.

Castoro San Luis Obispo ★★ Paso Robles estate, as substantial as its wines (Cab S and Zin).

Caymus Napa ★★★→★★★★★ (Cab S) 73 74 75 78 79 81 85 87 89 90 91 92 95 Dark firm textbook American-oaked Cab 'Special Selection' is the celebrated core; slightly lighter regular bottling not far behind. Developing v'yds in MONTEREY, SONOMA for other varieties. Second label: Liberty School.

Cedar Mountain Livermore ★★ One of most ambitous in new wave of estate wineries: Cab and Chard.

Chalk Hill Sonoma ★★ From large estate nr Windsor, me-too Chard, similarly oaky Sauv. Still groping for a style for Cab. New winemaker in '96.

Chalone Monterey ★★★ (Chard) 86 87 88 89 90 91 92 93 95 Unique hilltop estate high in Gavilan Mts; source of smoky woody flinty Chard and dark tannic Pinot N, both slow-to-open burgundy-imitations. Also Pinot Bl and Chenin styled after Chard. 25,000 cases. Also owns ACACIA, CARMENET, EDNA VALLEY VINEYARD, Gavilan and Canoe Ridge (Washington). Has links with (Lafite) Rothschilds.

Chappellet Napa ★★★ (Cab S) 75 76 78 82 84 86 87 89 90 91' 92 95 Beautiful amphitheatrical hill v'yd: lean racy Cab to age. Chard and California's best dry Chenin Bl no longer the sure agers they once were. 25,000 cases.

Chateau De Baun Sonoma ★★ Young winery doing well by Chard and Pinot N from Russian River estate v'yd. Esp value Pinot-based Ch Rouge. Sparkling Symphony a curiosity.

Chateau Montelena Napa ★★★ (Chard) 89 90 91 92 93 95 Understated age-worthy Chard and recently modified (91 92) but still tannic potent Calistoga-estate Cab to age forever.

Château Potelle Napa ★★ French-owned new producer of balanced quietly impressive Chard (with toasty Reserve version). Also Cab S and luxury-priced Mt Veeder Zin.

Château St Jean Sonoma ★★→★★★ (Chard) 90 91 92 93 94 95 Intensely flavoured, richly textured, individual-v'yd Chards (Robert Young, Belle Terre, McCrea), Fumé Bl (Petite Etoile), and sweet botrytised Ries and Traminers (Robert Young, Belle Terre). Small lots of red. Suntory negotiating to sell to new owners of BERINGER.

Château Souverain Sonoma ★★ (Cab S) 85 87 89 90 91 92 95 Reliable Chard, Alexander Valley Cab S and Dry Creek Zin, all lately with lots of oak. 150,000 cases. Same owner as BERINGER.

Château Woltner Napa ★★→★★★ Howell Mountain estate Chards (incl expensive 'Frederique') from ex-owners of Ch La Mission Haut Brion. Tasty young but have yet to find the secret of long life.

Chimney Rock Napa ★★ (Cab S) 86 87 88 89 90 91 92 95 Supple mannerly Cab and Sauv from Stag's Leap district. Chard, newly CARNEROS, on upswing.

The Christian Brothers Madera (San Joaquin Valley) ★ One-time NAPA VALLEY institution, now shrunk to brandy-only label for HEUBLEIN.

Christopher Creek Sonoma ★★ Expat Briton pouring heart and soul into Syrah and Petite Sirah in small lots from the Russian River Valley.

Cline Cellars Carneros ★★ Originally Contra Costa (imp't v'yds still there), now in SONOMA/CARNEROS and still dedicated mostly to husky Rhône Rangers (blends and varietals), eg Côtes d'Oakley, Mourvèdre.

Clos du Bois Sonoma ★★→★★★ (Chard) 91 92 93 94 95 (Cab) 85 87 89 90 91 92 93 95 Sizeable (400,000-case) Allied-Hiram Walker firm at Healdsburg. Winemaker Margaret Davenport hitting impressive stride with Cab S, Cab blends, Chard, Sauv. Top are single-v'yd incl Cab 'Briarcrest', Chard 'Calcaire'.

Clos Pegase Napa ★★★ (Chard) 87 89 90 91 92 93 94 95 (Cab S) 85 87 89 90 91 92 95 Post-modernist winery-cum-museum (or vice versa) improving on already good reputation esp with CARNEROS Chard and Calistoga Cabs.

Clos du Val Napa ★★★ (Chard) 89 90 91 92 93 95 (Cab) 72 73 74 75 77 78 79 80 81 82 83 84 85 86 87 88 89 90 91 92 95 French-run. Cab S, Cab-based Reserve from Stag's Leap district perhaps NAPA's best agers of all, yet accessible early. Merlot also sure-footed. Understated silky CARNEROS Chard is best white. 55,000 cases.

Codorníu Carneros ★★★ California arm of great Catalan cava co is competing well with local Champenois. Style improving.

Cohn, B R Sonoma ★★→★★★ Widely praised SONOMA estate Cab S: oaky young, oaky old and oaky in between.

Concannon Livermore ★★ WENTE BROS now own this historically famous source of Sauv. Starting to specialize in Rhône varieties.

Conn Creek Napa ★★ (Cab S) 83 85 86 87 88 89 90 91 92 95 Best known for supple, almost juicy Cab: as of '93 concentrating on this and 'Anthology' blend. Owned by Château Ste Michelle (see Washington).

Cooks Penny-saving 'Cooks Champagne' and others from San Joaquin; belongs to CANANDAIGUA.

Corbett Canyon San Luis Obispo ★★ (Chard) 91 92 93 94 95 (Pinot N Res) 85 86 89 90 91 92 93 95 Large Central Coast producer with often memorable Reserve Pinot N. Good value attractive wines, especially abundant Coastal Classics line.

Corison Napa ★★→★★★ (Cab) 87 90 91 92 95 Long-time winemaker at CHAPPELLET on her own making supple flavoury Cab promising to age well.

Cosentino Napa ★★ (Pinot N) 92 93 94 95 Irrepressible winemaker-owner always full-tilt. Results s'times odd, sometimes brilliant, never dull. CARNEROS Pinot Ns are to seek first.

Crichton Hall Napa ★★ Ambitious estate launched Chard label; now also CARNEROS Merlot, Pinot.

Cronin Sta Cruz Mtns ★★ Lilliputian cult producer of Brobdignagian buttered toast Chards from varied sources.

Culbertson Temecula ★★ Specialist in classic sparkling: labelled Thornton.

Cuvaison Napa ★★★ (Chard) 90 91 92 93 94 95 (Merlot) 85 86 87 88 89 90 91 92 95 Lean crisp CARNEROS Chard is steadily top rank. Dark ripe Merlot and up-valley Cab following suit. Recent CARNEROS Pinot begins to shine.

Dalla Valle Napa ★★→★★★ Larger-than-life founder Gustave DV died in '95; his widow continues with epically-scaled estate Cab, Cab-based 'Maya'.

Dehlinger Sonoma ★★★ (Pinot) 87 89 90' 91 92 93 95 Focus ever stronger on estate Russian River Valley Pinot Noirs, and rightly. Chard good too. Family-owned.

DeLoach Vineyards Sonoma ★★★ (Chard) 89 90 91 92 93 94 95 (Zin) 81 87 88 90 91 92 93 95 Fruit-rich Chard still the mainstay of reliable 80,000-case Russian River Valley winery. Pinot N even better, and gargantuan single-v'yd Zins (Papera, Pelletti) finding an audience.

de Lorimier Sonoma ★★ Alexander Valley estate winery: worthy Sauv-Sém and Cab family blends; also Chard.

Diamond Creek Napa ★★★ (Cab S) 76 77 78 79 80 81 82 83 84 85 86 87 89 90 91 95 Austere long-ageing Cabs from hilly v'yd nr Calistoga go by names of v'yd blocks, eg Gravelly Meadow, Volcanic Hill. 3,000 cases.

Domaine Carneros Carneros (★★★) Showy US outpost of Taittinger in CARNEROS echoes austere style of its parent in Champagne. Recent Blanc de Blancs leads the way. 25,000+ cases.

Domaine Chandon Napa ★★→★★★ Maturing v'yds, maturing style, broadening range taking Moët & Chandon's California arm to new heights. Look esp for NV Reserve, Brut Rosé. 350,000 cases.

Domaine Napa Napa Sadly, now defunct.

Domaine Saint-Gregory Mendocino ★ Companion label to MONTE VOLPE, for wines from French grapes.

Dominus Napa ★★★★ 83 84 85 86 87 88 89 90 91 95 Christian Moueix of Pomerol is now sole owner of v fine v'yd. Massively tannic Cab-based blend up to 88, now looks amazingly like fine B'x (tannins softer in 90 91). Dave Ramey is new winemaker.

Dry Creek Vineyard Sonoma ★★ Unimpeachable source of dry tasty whites, esp Chard and Fumé Blanc, but also Chenin Bl. Cab S and Zinfandel rather underrated. 110,000 cases.

Duckhorn Vineyards Napa ★★★ (Merlot) 81 82 83 84 85 86 87 88 89 90' 91 92 93 95 Known for dark, tannic, almost plummy-ripe single-v'yd Merlot (Three Palms, Vine Hill). Now also Cab-based blend 'Howell Mountain'. Also vg Sauv. 18,000 cases.

Dunn Vineyards Napa ★★★ (Cab) 80 81 84 85 86 87 89 90 91 92 95 Owner-winemaker Randall Dunn makes dark tannic austere Cab from Howell Mt, slightly milder from valley floor. 4,000 cases.

Dunnewood Mendocino ★→★★ Canandaigua-owned producer of reliably good value North Coast varietals.

Durney Vineyard Monterey ★★→★★★ (Cab) 83 95 New owners reviving estate after death of eponymous founder. Esp dark robust Carmel Valley Cab, rich Chard. Cachagua line is ★★.

Eberle Winery San Luis Obispo ★★ Burly ex-footballer makes Cab and Zin in his own image. Also look for their polar opposite: Muscat Canelli.

Edna Valley Vineyard San Luis Obispo ★★ (Chard) 89 90 91 92 93 95 Decidedly toasty Chard from a joint venture of local grower and CHALONE. Pinot N best drunk soon after vintage. 48,000 cases.

Estancia MONTEREY white (good value Chard, Sauv) and Alexander Valley red (Cab and Sangiovese) made at FRANCISCAN.

Etude Napa ★★★ (Pinot N) 87 89 90 91 92 93 95 Winemaker-owned cellar of respected consultant Tony Soter. Burnished CARNEROS Pinot (87 89 90 91 95), equally polished NAPA Cab, plus experiments such as Pinots Gris and Meunier.

Far Niente Napa ★★★ (Chard) 93 94 95 (Cab S) 85 87 89 90 91 92 95 Opulence appears to be the goal in both Cab S and Chard from luxury mid-NAPA estate.

Farrell, Gary Sonoma ★★→★★★ (Pinot) 90 91 92 93 94 95 Winemaker's label for brilliant well-oaked toasty Russian River Pinots, also Chard, berryish Zin.

Ferrari-Carano Sonoma ★★→★★★ (Chard) 93 94 95 (Cab) 87 89 90 91 95 Shifting styles make wines hard to track: show-case winery drawing on SONOMA v'yds for toasty Chard, sturdy Cab S, intriguing Sangiovese.

Fetzer Mendocino ★★ Consistently good value from least expensive (Sun Dial, Valley Oaks) to expensive (Reserve) ranges. 1.5M cases. From organic v'yds.

Ficklin San Joaquin ★★ First in California to use Douro grapes. Since 1948, Tinta California's best 'port'. Sometimes vintages.

Field Stone Sonoma ★★ Flavourful estate-grown Alexander Valley Cab S too often overlooked. Old vine Petite Sirah can be impressive.

Firestone Sta Barbara ★★→★★★ (Chard) 90 91 92 93 94 95 (Merlot) 86 89 90 91 92 93 95 Fine Chard overshadows but does not outshine delicious Ries. Merlot good; Cab one of region's best. New investment in Sta Maria Pinot Noir v'yd. Owns CAREY.

Fisher Sonoma ★★ Hill-top SONOMA grapes for often fine Chard; NAPA grapes dominate steady Cab. 10,000 cases.

California wines to try in 1997

Domaine Chandon Napa Valley (Brut) rosé (notably delicious)

Kunde Sonoma Valley Sauvignon Blanc 'Magnolia Lane' (with a whiff of Viognier)

Buena Vista Carneros Chardonnay (the essence of Chardonnay)

Freemark Abbey Napa Valley Cabernet Sauvignon 'Sycamore Vineyard'

Lane Tanner Santa Maria Valley Pinot Noir 'Sierra Madre Hills' (acknowledges burgundy but isn't trying to imitate it)

Monte Volpe Mendocino Barbera (a tart flavoury California secret weapon)

Niebaum-Coppola Napa Valley Rubicon (...shaped by the vineyard)

Try **Nalle** for Zinfandel

Flora Springs Wine Co Napa ★★→★★★ (Chard) 91 92 93 95 (Trilogy) 87 89 90 91 95 Old stone cellar. Fine Sauvignon Soliloquy parallels oak-fermented Chard, flavoury Reserve Cab and luxury Cab blend Trilogy. Sangiovese to be watched. 18,000 cases.

Fogarty, Thomas Sta Cruz Mts ★★ Fine Gewürz from VENTANA sets the pace; whole line is well made.

Folie à Deux Napa ★ Veteran winemaker Dr Richard Peterson heads the revival of a small winery once known for fine Chard.

Foppiano Sonoma ★★ Long-est'd wine family annually turns out fine reds, esp transcendent Petite Sirah. Reserve label for Cab is Fox Mountain; second label is Riverside Vineyards.

Forman Napa ★★★ The winemaker who brought STERLING its first fame in the '60s now makes excellent Cab and Chard on his own. 15,000 cases.

Foxen Sta Barbara ★★★ (Pinot N) 89 90 91 92 93 95 Tiny winery nestled between the Santa Ynez and Santa Maria valleys. Always bold, frequently brilliant Pinot N.

Franciscan Vineyard Napa ★★ (Cab) 74 79 85 87 89 90 91 92 95 Big v'yd at Oakville: increasingly stylish Chard, Cab, Zin. Sister labels: MOUNT VEEDER, ESTANCIA, Pinnacles (MONTEREY).

Franzia San Joaquin ★ Penny-saver wines (eg Franzia label); varietals under many labels. All say 'Made and bottled in Ripon'. 5M cases.

Freemark Abbey Napa ★★★ (Chard) 87 89 90 91 92 93 95 (Cab S) 70 72 73 74 75 77 78 79 80 81 82 83 85 87 88 89 90 91 92 95 Underrated today, but consistent for inexhaustible stylish Cabernet Sauvignons (esp single-v'yd Sycamore and Bosché) of great depth. Vg deliciously true-to-variety Chardonnay. Also late-harvest Riesling Edelwein, infrequent but always among California's finest.

Fritz, J Sonoma ★★ V'yd-first Chard and Sauv are the anchors; small winery also offers startlingly fine Dry Creek Zin (88 90 91 92 95). 8,000 cases.

To decipher codes, please refer to 'Key to symbols' on front flap of jacket, or to 'How to use this book' on page 6.

Frog's Leap Napa ★★→★★★ (Cab S) 82 84 85 87 89 90 91 92 93 95 Small winery, charming as its name (and T-shirts) and organic to boot. Lean racy Sauv, Zin, Cab, Merlot usually understated; toasty Chard quite the reverse.

Gainey Vineyard, The Sta Barbara ★★ Steadily attractive Chard, Sauv, Cab and esp Pinot N 'Sanford & Benedict V'yd'. 12,000 cases.

Gallo, E & J San Joaquin ★→★★★ (Chard) 93 (Cab S) 80 81 82 90 91 95 Having mastered the world of commodity wines (Hearty 'Burgundy', Pink Chablis etc) this 40M-case family firm (the world's biggest) is turning ever sharper focus on SONOMA holdings for single-v'yd wines and specialities. Top estate Cab, Zin are excellent; Chard closing the gap.

Gan Eden Sonoma ★★ Kosher producer of traditional single-varietals has won substantial praise for Chards.

Geyser Peak Sonoma ★★ Since brief marriage with Penfolds of Australia, extensive v'yds of Henry Trione in Alexander and Russian River valleys (lovely grapes) make Penfolds-style wine. Well-oaked Chard, Cab now joined by Shiraz, all mostly from winery-owned v'yds. Also: superb new-mown Sauv. Second label: Canyon Road.

Glen Ellen Proprietor's Reserve HEUBLEIN widely-sourced penny-saver varietal brand purchased '94 from BENZIGER.

Gloria Ferrer Carneros ★★ Substantial classic sparkling winery of Spain's Freixenet has scored well, esp for Cuvée Royale and Cuvée Carneros. Smoky, silky CARNEROS Pinot N commands attention.

Green and Red Napa ★★ Tiny winery. Vigorous Tuscan-tasting Zin and rustic Chard worth a hunt.

Greenwood Ridge Mendocino ★★ (Pinot) 89 90 91 92 95 Est'd specialist in racy Anderson Valley Ries more recently appreciable for melony Sauv, herby Merlot. Pinot N begins to convince, too. 4,000 cases.

Grgich Hills Cellars Napa ★★★ (Chard) 89 90 91 92 93 95 (Cab S) 80 81 83 84 85 86 87 89 90 91 95 Winemaker Grgich and grower Hills join forces on a stern deftly-oaked Chard, impressively long-ageing rich Cab, Sauv Bl, and – too little noticed – Spätlese-sweet Ries. Also plummy thick SONOMA Zin. 40,000 cases.

Groth Vineyards Napa ★★→★★★ (Chard) 92 93 94 95 (Cab S) 82 85 86 87 88 90 91 92 95 Estate at Oakville challenges leaders among NAPA Cab and Sauv Bl. Also vg Chard. 30,000 cases.

Guenoc Vineyards Lake County ★★ Ambitious winery/v'yd venture just N of NAPA county line. Property once Lillie Langtry's challenge to Bordeaux. Now best known for surprisingly fine Chard. Also vg Cab, Zin.

Guild Long-time cooperative and its many labels, esp COOKS, DUNNEWOOD, bought by and absorbed into CANANDAIGUA.

Gundlach-Bundschu Sonoma ★★→★★★ (Chard) 92 93 95 (Cab) 82 85 86 87 89 90 91 92 95 Pioneer name solidly revived by fifth generation. Versatile Rhinefarm v'yd signals memorably individual Gewürz, Merlot, Zin, Pinot N. 50,000 cases.

Hafner Sonoma ★★ (Cab S) 82 85 87 89 90 91 92 95 Semi-secretive Alexander V winery for flavourful ageable Cab. Also agreeable Chard. 8,000 cases.

Hagafen Napa ★★ First and perhaps still finest of the serious kosher producers. Esp Chard and Johannisberg Ries. 6,000 cases.

Handley Cellars Mendocino ★★ (Chard) 89 90 91 92 93 94 95 Winemaker-owned producer of excellent Anderson Valley classic sparklers. Also still Pinot N (91 92) and Gewürz, and, from family v'yd in Dry Creek Valley, superior Chard and Sauv.

Hanna Winery Sonoma ★★ 600 acres of Russian River and Alexander valleys with sound middle-of-the-road Chard, Cab, Sauv. New winemaker in '96.

Hanzell Sonoma ★★★ (Chard) **90 91 92** 93 95 (Pinot N) 86 87 88 89 90 91 92 95 The late founder revolutionized California Chards, Pinot Ns with new oak in late '50s. Three owners later Hanzell remains a throwback source of original ripe full-flavoured wines from SONOMA estate v'yd.

> The vigorous strain of phylloxera that is forcing Napa and Somona to replant about half of their 60,000 acres of vineyard on new rootstocks is being combated: Napa is expected to pass its planting halfway mark in 1997, Sonoma about two years later.

Haywood Vineyard Sonoma ★★ BUENA VISTA-owned SONOMA vineyards esp good for Chard, Zin. Vintner Select line for bought-in wine.

Heitz Napa ★★★→★★★★ (Cab) 74 75 77 78 79 80 84 89 90 91 95 Individualist winemaker set lofty standards for his peers in '60s and '70s with dark deep emphatic Cabs, esp Martha's Vineyard. Newer Trailside Vineyard in similar league. Bella Oaks one step back. Whites can be eccentric but dry Grignolino Rosé brilliant. 40,000 cases.

Hess Collection, The Napa ★★→★★★ (Chard) **91 92** 93 94 (Cab S) 85 87 89 90 91 92 95 A Swiss art collector's winery-cum-museum in former Mont La Salle winery of CHRISTIAN BROTHERS. Steady Cab, Chard on Mount Veeder. Non-Napa Hess Selection label is vg value. 40,000 cases.

Heublein Vast drinks firm with ambivalent interest in wine. (See Beaulieu, Christian Bros, Glen Ellen Proprietor's Reserve, M G Vallejo).

Hidden Cellars Mendocino ★★ Ukiah producer of Sauv Bl, Zin often from single v'yds.

Hill Winery, William Napa ★★ (Chard) 92 93 94 95 (Cab S) 81 84 85 87 90 91 92 95 Since '94 a Wine Alliance stablemate to ATLAS PEAK, CLOS DU BOIS. Good Chard, Cab, but Sauv, Merlot have shown greater promise. Jill Davis, ex-BUENA VISTA, the new winemaker.

Hop Kiln Sonoma ★★ Source of sometimes startlingly fine 'Valdiguie' (aka Napa Gamay). Russian River Gewürz is full-flavoured and large-scale.

Husch Vineyards Mendocino ★★ Reliable Ukiah Chard, Sauv, Cab; sometimes outstanding Pinot N and Gewürz from Anderson Valley. 15,000 cases.

Inglenook Napa ★★→★★★ (Chard) 86 90 91 95 (Cab) 55 56 62 68 78 81 87 88 89 95 History-rich NAPA name (but not property) purchased by CANANDAIGUA. Inglenook Navalle label active, Napa not at present. V'yd and splendid old cellars now part of NIEBAUM-COPPOLA.

Iron Horse Vineyards Sonoma ★★★ (Chard) 92 93 94 95 (Cab) 89 90 91 92 95 Substantial Russian River property increasingly focussed on classic ageworthy sparklings that hover between finesse and boldness, but continues with Chard and Pinot from same estate v'yd, plus Cab and Sauv from affiliated Alexander V vines.

Jade Mountain Napa (★★) Sharing winery with WHITE ROCK and pursuing lofty goals using Rhône varieties, esp Syrah.

Jekel Vineyards Monterey ★★ (Chard) 91 92 93 94 95 Jekel's ripe juicy Ries is most successful wine from SALINAS v'yds. Also good Chard, intensely regional (capsicum-flavoured) Cab. 60,000 cases.

Jepson Vineyards Mendocino ★★ Sound steady Chard, Sauv Bl and classic sparkling from estate in Ukiah area. Also pot-still brandy.

Jordan Sonoma ★★★ (Chard) 92 93 94 95 (Cab S) 80 81 84 85 86 87 89 90 91 92 95 Extravagant Alexander Valley estate models its Cab on supplest Bordeaux. And it lasts. (Chard is less successful.) Separate classic sparkling called simply 'J' is deft, soft, luxurious (**89 90 91**). 75,000 cases.

Karly Amador ★★ Among more ambitious sources of SIERRA FOOTHILLS Zin.

Keenan Winery, Robert Napa ★★ (Cab) 81 85 86 87 88 89 90 91 95 Winery on Spring Mountain producing supple, restrained Cab, Merlot under new winemaker Nils Venge; also Chard.

Kendall-Jackson Lake County ★★→★★★ Staggeringly successful with style aimed at widest market: esp broadly sourced off-dry toasty Chard. Even more noteworthy for the development of a diversity of wineries under the umbrella of 'ARTISANS AND ESTATES'.

Kenwood Vineyards Sonoma ★★→★★★ (Chard) 90 91 92 93 95 (Cab S) 87 88 89 90 91 95 Substantial producer of reliable Chard and Cab S (incl single-v'yd Jack London). Esp worth seeking for stellar v'yd-first Sauv, single-v'yd Zin (Nuns Canyon, Mazzoni).

Kistler Vineyards Sonoma ★★★ (Chard) 88 89 90 91 92 93 95 Chards much in smoky buttery style (esp single v'yd). Pinot N and Cab more recent.

Konocti Cellars Lake County ★★ Excellent value Sauv, good Chard, but intrigue is refreshing Cab Franc.

Korbel Sonoma ★★ Long-established classic sparkling specialists source widely and place extra emphasis on fruit flavours. Lots of fizz; Natural, Brut and Blanc de Blancs are best. Currently making one of episodic dips into still wines.

Krug, Charles Napa ★★ (Chard) 92 93 94 95 (Cab S) 73 74 78 79 81 84 85 89 90 91 92 95 Historically important winery with generally sound wines. Cabs at head of list, CARNEROS Chards, Pinot Ns not far behind. CK-Mondavi is jug brand.

Kunde Estate Sonoma ★★→★★★ (Chard) 92 93 94 95 Long-time large growers emerging as winemaking force with buttery Chard, flavoury Sauv (lightly touched with Viognier). Cab, Cab Reserve, Merlot and Zin still finding a footing.

La Crema Sonoma ★★ (Chard) 91 92 93 94 95 (Pinot N) 89 90 91 92 93 95 Part of K-J's ARTISANS AND ESTATES group, turning ever-more to Russian River Valley AVA as a source for Chardonnay and Pinot N wines of vg and improving quality.

La Jota Napa ★★ Pricey Cab S from small estate on Howell Mountain.

Lakespring Napa ★★ Label of one-time NAPA winery bought '95 by Frederick Wildman; wines being custom-made by assoc v'yd group.

Lambert Bridge Sonoma ★★ New owners have resurrected briefly defunct cellar with Dry Creek Valley v'yd: fine track record for Chard, Cab S.

Landmark Sonoma ★★ (Chard) 89 92 93 94 95 Long-time Chard specialist moving from crisp and fresh to me-too toasty-buttery.

Laurel Glen Sonoma ★★★ (Cab S) 81 82 85 86 89 90 91 92 93 95 Big-scale firm, distinctly regional Cab from steep hilly v'yd in Sonoma Mountain sub-AVA. Counterpoint is good value second label. 5,000 cases.

Laurier Sonoma ★★ (Chard) 91' 92' 93 94 95 Crown-jewel label of BRONCO WINE CO. Currently aiming high with Chard. Pinot N began with 93.

Lava Cap El Dorado ★★ Where bold styles rule, these are understated, intriguing. Zins, Cabs and others.

Lazy Creek Mendocino ★★ 'Retirement hobby' of a long-time restaurant waiter yields serious Anderson Valley Gewürz and Chard. Also Pinot N.

Leeward Winery Ventura ★★ (Chard) 91 92 93 94 95 Ultra-toasty Central Coast Chards are the mainstay. 18,000 cases.

Liparita Napa ★★ Estate on Howell Mt making Chard, Cab, Merlot in leased winery pending contruction of own. Merry Edwards (of MERRY VINTNERS) consults. Chard best so far.

Lockwood Monterey ★★ Huge v'yd in S SALINAS VALLEY supplying show-case winery. Terroir is foremost throughout range.

Lohr, J Central Coast ★→★★ Large wide-reaching firm at peak with Paso Robles Cab S 'Seven Oaks'. Mainstream line subtitled Cypress.

Long Vineyards Napa ★★★ (Chard) 89 90 91 92 93 95 (Cab) 80 81 82 83 84 85 86 87 90 91 92 95 Tiny neighbour of CHAPPELLET: lush Chard, flavoury Cab, luxury prices.

Lyeth Vineyard Sonoma ★★ Former winery/estate, now a négociant label for Burgundian J C Boisset's California arm. Good red, excellent white MERITAGE types. Also Chard. Christophe is second label. Boisset also own WHEELER.

Lytton Springs Sonoma ★★ Now RIDGE-owned: ink-dark hard heady Zins.

MacRostie Carneros ★★ Buttered-toast Chards are the flagship. Recent Pinot Noir and Merlot coming along.

Madrona El Dorado ★★ Loftiest v'yds in SIERRA FOOTHILLS, good for steady Chards (among others). 10,000 cases.

Maison Deutz San Luis Obispo ★★→★★★ California arm of Champagne Wm Deutz shows a firm sense of style: grapes from Arroyo Grande AVA.

Mark West Vineyards Sonoma ★★ V satisfactory Gewürztraminer, sturdy to rustic Chard, Pinot and Bl de Noirs sparkling. Now owned by Associated Vintners Group.

Markham Napa ★★ (Chard) 92 93 94 95 (Cab S) 89 90 91 92 95 Recently good to excellent, esp Merlot and Cab S grown in own v'yds. ('Laurent' label discontinued.)

Martin Bros San Luis Obispo ★★ Entirely dedicated to Italian varieties (Nebbiolo, Sangiovese), or styles ('Vin Santo', chestnut-aged Chard). Bros recently split.

Martini, Louis M Napa ★★→★★★ (Cab S) 52 55 59 64 68 70 74 78 79 80 83 85 87 88 89 90 91 92 93 95 Historic family-owned winery with high standards, esp single v'yd Cab (Monte Rosso), Merlot (Los Vinedos del Rio) and reserve Cab. Zins s'times surpassing.

Masson Vineyards Monterey ★→★★ This is the 'Fighting varietal' spoke in CANANDAIGUA's growing wheel of California wineries and labels. Taylor California Cellars is companion label.

Matanzas Creek Sonoma ★★★ (Chard) 91 92 93 94 95 (Merlot) 89 90 91 92 93 95 Fine ripe toasty-oaky Chard, Sauv, and renowned ultra-fleshy Merlot. Once-clear style drifting just a bit late.

Maurice Car'rie Temecula ★★ Setting standards for its region with reliable, approachable Chard, Sauv and others.

Mayacamas Napa ★★★ (Chard) 85 87 90 91 92 93 95 (Cab S) 69 73 78 81 85 87 88 89 90 91 95 Vg small v'yd with rich Chard and firm (but no longer steel-hard) Cab. Some Sauv, Pinot. 5,000 cases.

Mazzocco Sonoma ★★ Good and improving Chard, Cab from Alexander and Dry Creek valley estate v'yds.

McDowell Valley Vineyards Mendocino ★★ Grower-label for family with hearts set on Rhône varieties, esp ancient-vine Syrah and Grenache.

Meridian San Luis Obispo ★★ Fast-growing sibling to BERINGER making mark with single-vineyard Edna Valley Chard, Paso Robles Syrah. Also Sta Barbara Chard, Pinot N, Paso Robles Cab S. 300,000 cases.

Meritage Trademarked name for reds or whites using Bordeaux grape varieties. Aiming for 'varietal' status and gaining ground.

Merry Vintners Sonoma (★★) Busy consulting winemaker Merry Edwards has temporarily put her small winery in mothballs to concentrate on eg LAURIER, LIPARITA.

Merryvale Napa ★★ Sauv-Sém white MERITAGE is best. Middle-of-the-road are Chard, Cab S and red Meritage.

For key to grape variety abbreviations, see pages 7–13.

Michael, Peter Sonoma ★★→★★★★ Partly Knights Valley estate-v'yd, partly bought-in Howell Mt: larger-than-life, Frenchified Chard, Merlot, Cab.

Michel-Schlumberger Sonoma ★★ Dry Creek Valley winery with reinvigorating Alsace input; esp evident with newly subtle Cab S.

Mill Creek Sonoma ★★ Oft-overlooked reliable producer of Dry Creek Valley Cab, Merlot, Chard, Sauv.

Mirassou Central Coast ★★ Fifth-generation grower and pioneer in Monterey (SALINAS) gets highest marks for Pinot Bl classic sp. Chard, Pinot worth a look.

Mondavi, Robert Napa ★★→★★★★ (Chard) 92 93 94 95 (Cab) 71 73 74 75 79 81 82 84 85 87 89 90 91 92 95 Winery with brilliant quarter-century record of innovation in styles, equipment, technique. Famous successes: Sauv ('Fumé Bl'), Cab, Chard, even Pinot N. 'Reserves' are marvels, regularly among California's best. New are expensive district wines eg CARNEROS Pinot N, Oakville Cab S, Stag's Leap Sauv. Mid-price is Coastal line (vg début Sauv). Less pricey California appellation varietals: Mondavi-Woodbridge. 500,000 cases. See also Opus One.

Mont St John Carneros ★★ Old NAPA wine family makes good value Pinot N, Chard from own v'yd; buys in for solid Cab.

Monte Volpe Mendocino ★★ Greg Graziano looks to his heritage and wins with brisk Pinot Bianco, tart Barbera, juicy Sangiovese. French varieties separately labelled as DOM ST-GREGORY.

Monterey Peninsula Monterey ★★ Now part of group owning QUAIL RIDGE in NAPA; making same bold MONTEREY, Amador wines as before.

Monterey Vineyard, The Monterey ★★ Seagram-owned label for good-value Salinas Valley Chard, Pinot N, Cab. Classic and more costly Limited Release.

Monteviña Amador ★★ Owned by SUTTER HOME. Turning more to Italian varieties (30 trial plantings) but hearty SIERRA Zin still the foundation stone.

Monticello Cellars Napa ★★ (Chard) 93 94 95 (Cab S) 87 88 89 90 91 92 95 Basic line under Monticello label, reserves under Corley. Both incl Chard, Cab S. Reserve Pinot is the most intriguing.

Morgan Monterey ★★→★★★ (Pinot) 89 90 91 92 93 95 Winemaker-owner. Basic Pinot N blends MONTEREY, CARNEROS but deep earthy possibly age-worthy Reserve is all Monterey now. Also toasty Chard, herby SONOMA Sauv.

Mount Eden Vineyards Sta Cruz Mts ★★ (Chard) 88 90 91 92 93 95 Expensive big-scale Chard from old Martin Ray v'yds and gentler one from MONTEREY. Also Pinot N, Cab.

Mount Veeder Napa ★★ (Cab) 87 89 90 91 92 95 Once steel-hard Mt Veeder Cab now merely austere, as is more recent red MERITAGE. FRANCISCAN-owned.

Mumm Napa Valley Napa ★★★ G H Mumm-Seagram joint venture out of the box fast with fine leanish Vintage Reserve (85 87 89). Still expanding range includes cheery Blanc de Noir, distinctive single-v'yd Winery Lake and opulent luxury DVX.

Murphy-Goode Sonoma ★★ Large Alexander V estate. Whole range lavishly oaked, esp reserves. Pinot Bl, Sauv Merlot to explore.

Nalle Sonoma ★★→★★★ (Zin) 85 86 88 90 91 92 93 95 Winemaker-owned Dry Creek cellar getting to the very heart of Zin: wonderfully berryish young; that and more with age. 2,500 cases.

Napa Ridge Sonoma(!) ★ BERINGER affiliate ensconced in old Italian Swiss colony winery, churning out solid, attractive, broadly-sourced Chard, Cab, others.

Navarro Vineyards Mendocino ★★→★★★ (Chard) 85 86 88 89 90 91 92 93 95 From Anderson Valley, splendidly age-worthy Chard, perhaps the grandest Gewürz in state. Even more special: late-harvest Ries, Gewürz. Pinot N not to be ignored. Only self-deprecating prices keep this from being cult favourite of big-shot collectors.

Newton Vineyards Napa ★★ (Chard) **92** 95 (Cab S) **83 85 86 88** 89 90 91 95 Luxurious estate growing more so; formerly ponderous style now reined back to the merely opulent for Chard, Cab, Merlot.

Niebaum-Coppola Estate Napa ★★→★★★ Movie-man Coppola's luxuriously wayward hobby much invigorated by new winemaker (Tony Soter of ETUDE) and acquisition of INGLENOOK winery and 220-acre v'yd (but not name). Flagship (Cab-based) Rubicon beginning to take form; more accessible Coppola Family single-varietals show the up-turn better.

Opus One Napa ★★★★ (Cab S) **80 81 83 84 85 87 89** 90 91 92 95 Joint venture of R MONDAVI and Baronne Philippine de Rothschild. Spectacular new winery opened '92. Wines are showpieces too. 10,000 cases.

Parducci Mendocino ★★ (Cab S) **87 90** 91 92 92 93 95 Long-est'd Ukiah v'yds and winery: reliable Cab, Cab-Merlot, Zin, Barbera. Characterful off-dry Sauv.

Pecota, Robert Napa ★★ Drink-young Cab, Sauv, Chard, Gamay.

Pedroncelli Sonoma ★★ (Chard) **92 93 94** 95 (Cab S) **83 85 89** 90 91 92 93 95 Old-hand in Dry Creek turns out honest, fairly-priced Cab, Zin. Chard and Sauv often show a turn of speed.

Pepi, Robert Napa ★★ Purchased '95 by K-J and put under ARTISANS AND ESTATES banner where new role is to focus on the Sauv and Sangiovese wines that built its reputation.

Phelps, Joseph Napa ★★★ (Chard) **91 92 93 94** 95 (Cab S) **75 81 82 84 85 86 87** 89 90 91 92 95 Deluxe winery and beautiful vineyard: impeccable standards. Vg Chard, Cab S (esp Backus) and Cabernet-based Insignia. Splendid late-harvest Ries and Sémillon. Promising Rhône series under Vin du Mistral label.

Philips, R H Yolo, Sacramento Valley ★→★★ Pioneer in Dunnigan Hills NW of Sacramento trying everything on huge property, succeeding best with Syrah, Viognier and pretty good Chard.

Pine Ridge Napa ★★→★★★ (Chard) **92 93 94** 95 (Cab S) **80 81 82 85 87 89** 90 91 92 95 At growing winery in Stag's Leap district, gentlemanly Cabs are best (Stag's Leap, Rutherford etc), Merlot not bad either. Dry oak-aged Chenin 'Petite Vigne' is intriguing and there is Chard too, of course.

Piper Sonoma Sonoma ★★→★★★ Venture of Piper-Heidsieck hit a bump in '80s, now returning to vigorous life. Mostly Russian River grapes in classic sparklers that benefit from bottle-age.

Preston Sonoma ★★ One of California's pioneer 'terroiristes' concentrating on wines best suited to his Dry Creek v'yds: esp top Sauv and Zin, with promising Barbera, Syrah and Marsanne experiments.

Quady Winery San Joaquin ★★ Imaginative Madera Muscat dessert wines, including celebrated orangey 'Essencia', dark 'Elysium' and Moscato d'Asti-like 'Electra'. 'Starboard' is a play on port; a better name than wine.

Quartet See Roederer Estate.

Quail Ridge Napa ★★ Third owner has installed winery at Rutherford (ex-DOMAINE NAPA); still worthy toasty Chard, rich Sauv. Also Cab, Merlot.

Quivira Sonoma ★★ Sauv, Zin, others, from Dry Creek Valley estate. More enamoured of oak than v'yd in recent vintages.

Qupé Sta Barbara ★★→★★★ Never-a-dull-moment cellar-mate of AU BON CLIMAT. Marsanne, Pinot Bl, Syrah are all well worth trying.

Rafanelli, A Sonoma ★★ (Cab) **84 87 89** 90 91 92 95 Hearty, fetchingly rustic Dry Creek Zin; Cab of striking intensity.

Rancho Sisquoc Sta Barbara ★★ Long-time friends-and-family winery edging onto larger stage with toasty Chard, lean Ries from sizeable estate.

Ravenswood Sonoma ★★★ Major critical success for (or despite) great bruiser single-v'yd Zins of skull-rattling power.

Raymond Vineyards and Cellar Napa ★★ (Chard) 90 91 92 93 94 95 (Cab S) 82 84 85 87 89 90 91 92 93 95 Old NAPA wine family now with Japanese partners. Emphatically fruity whites; polished Cabs. Amberhill is consistent drink-young value-for-money line.

Renwood Amador ★ Old Santino winery. Ambitious new player in SIERRA FOOTHILLS Zin game. Several single-v'yd bottlings.

Ridge Sta Cruz Mts ★★★★ (Cab S) 83 85 86 87 88 89 90 91 92 95 Winery of highest repute among connoisseurs. Drawing from NAPA (York Creek) and its own mountain v'yd (Monte Bello) for concentrated Cabs, worthy of long maturing in bottle but needing less than formerly (MB 90 91 more approachable than 80). But power remains in SONOMA (Geyserville) and San Luis Obispo (Dusi) Zinfandels and other red wines. Also v pleasant Chardonnays from Santa Cruz.

Rochioli, J Sonoma ★★★ (Pinot N) 89 90 91 92 93 95 Long-time Russian River grower making vg Pinot N, Sauv from own vines, long-celebrated under other labels.

> Count on typical Napa Valley and other North Coast Cabernet Sauvignons to last eight years in good form. Do not expect any but famously durable ones to stay at their peak beyond 15.

Roederer Estate Mendocino ★★★ Anderson Valley branch of champagne house (est '88). Resonant Roederer style apparent esp in luxury cuvée l'Ermitage. Still stuns the Champenois. 25,000 cases, poised to triple. Sold as 'Quartet' in Europe.

Rombauer Vineyards Napa ★★ Well-oaked Chard, dark Cab S (esp reserve-style 'Meilleur du Chai'). Now also owners of the revived Hanns Kornell sparkling wine cellars.

Roudon-Smith Sta Cruz Mts ★★ Chard, Cab. 10,000 cases.

Round Hill Napa ★★ Formerly diverse range now narrowed to Cab, Chard, Merlot, Sauv, but in 3 price ranges: basic, reserve and top-of-the-line Rutherford Ranch.

Rutherford Hill Napa ★★ (Cab) 82 85 89 90 91 92 95 Aims to dominate NAPA Merlot market but finer Chard XVS and Cab XVS (the reserves) rather undercut the plan.

Rutherford Ranch Top ROUND HILL wine (see above). Value.

Rutherford Vintners Napa ★★ One time NAPA winery, now BRONCO label.

St Clement Napa ★★→★★★ (Chard) 91 92 93 94 95 (Cab) 86 87 88 90 91 92 95 Firm CARNEROS Chard, NAPA Cab, Merlot. Ageable Pope Valley Sauv the star. Japanese-owned.

St Francis Sonoma ★★ (Chard) 91 92 93 94 95 (Cab S) 86 87 88 90 91 92 95 Firm v tasty SONOMA VALLEY estate Chard. Steady Merlot. Also Cab.

St Supery Napa ★★ French-owned; supplied by 500-acre estate v'yd in Pope Valley. Easy Sauv Bl, accessible Cab, Merlot. Also Chard. 50,000 cases, able to expand tenfold.

Saintsbury Carneros ★★★ (Chard) 85 89 90 91 92 93 94 95 (Pinot N) 85 86 87 89 90 91 92 93 95 Contends as AVA's finest and longest-lived Pinot N. Lighter Pinot Garnet and oaky Chard also vg. 45,000 cases.

Sanford Sta Barbara ★★★ (Pinot N) 84 86 87 89 90 91 92 93 95 Specialist in intense, firmly tannic, age-worthy Pinot Noir (esp Barrel Select). Also exceptionally bold Chard, firmly regional long-lived Sauv Bl. 40,000 cases.

Santa Barbara Winery Sta Barbara ★★ (Chard) 91 92 93 94 95 (Pinot) 91 92 93 95 Former jug-wine producer, now among regional leaders, esp for Reserve Chard. Also Pinot N, Cab. 28,000 cases.

Santa Cruz Mountain V'yd Sta Cruz Mts ★★ Huge, tannic, heady Pinot N and subtler Rhône-variety reds. 2,500 cases.

Sausal Sonoma ★★ Steady large-scale Alexander Valley estate esp notable for its Zin and Cabs.

Scharffenberger Mendocino ★★ First to try MENDOCINO for serious classic sparkling. Now Clicquot-owned and doing well. 25,000 cases.

Schramsberg Napa ★★★★ Dedicated specialist: California's best sparkling. Historic caves. Reserve splendid; Bl de Noir outstanding, deserves 2–10 yrs. Luxury cuvée J Schram is America's Krug.

Schug Cellars Carneros ★★ (Chard) **90 91 92** 93 94 95 (Pinot N) 91 92 93 95 German-born and trained owner-winemaker developing refined Chard and Pinot N from CARNEROS after relocating from NAPA in '91. 10,000 cases.

Sebastiani Sonoma ★→★★ Substantial old family firm working low end of market (August Sebastiani Country, Vendange, Talus) but, esp Sonoma Creek, can compete above their price level. 4 million cases.

Seghesio Sonoma ★★ (Zin) **85 86 88 89 90** 91 92 93 95 Able family of long-time growers turning away from Cab, Chard wars to focus on wines they grow best: exceptional Zins, Alexander Valley Sangiovese 'Vitigno Toscano', value Russian River Pinot N.

Sequoia Grove Napa ★★→★★★ (Chard) 93 94 95 (Cab) **82 87 89 90 91 92 95** NAPA Cabs (Napa, Estate): dark and firm. Same, alas, can be said of Chards.

Shadow Creek DOMAINE CHANDON label for non-NAPA/CARNEROS classic sparkling.

Shafer Vineyards Napa ★★★ (Chard) **90** 91 92 93 95 (Cab S) **80 84 85 86 87 89 90 91 92 95** Polished Chard (new 80 acres in CARNEROS), stylish Cab (esp Hillside Select) and Stag's Leap District Merlot.

Sierra Vista El Dorado ★★ Steady SIERRA FOOTHILLS Chard, Cab, Zin, Syrah.

Silver Oak Napa/Sonoma ★★★ Cabs, very American-oaked; same story for separate bottling Alexander Valley wine.

Silverado Vineyards Napa ★★→★★★ (Chard) 87 **90** 91 92 93 94 95 (Cab S) **82 83 85 87 89** 90 91 92 95 Showy hilltop Stag's Leap District winery. Cab, Chard, Sauv and newer Sangiovese all consistently refined.

Simi Sonoma ★★★ (Chard) 80 84 85 88 **90** 91 92 93 95 (Cab) **74 81 85** 87 90 91 95 Restored historic winery has flowered under dedicated direction of Zelma Long. Long-lived Cab. Chard, Sauv and new Sauv-Sém Sendal. Reserves, like most, try too hard. Seductive Cab rosé for picnics.

Sinskey Vineyards, Robert Napa ★★ Winery in Stag's Leap, v'yds in CARNEROS for boldly oaked, firm Chard, red MERITAGE, Pinot N.

Smith & Hook Monterey ★★ (Cab S) **86 88 90** 91 92 95 Specialist in dark age-worthy SALINAS VALLEY Cabs. Regional flavour so herbaceous you can taste dill (fades with time).

Smith-Madrone Napa ★★ Chard from Spring Mt estate has had ups and downs; now up (**91 92 93**). Ries always superior.

> Current thinking on Zinfandel, after many interim theories, is again that it originated somewhere between southern Hungary, Slovenia and Croatia.

Sonoma-Cutrer Vineyards Sonoma ★★★→★★★★ (Chard) 87 88 **90** 91 92 93 94 95 Ultimate specialist in Chard. Advanced techniques display characters of individual v'yds, as in Burgundy. Les Pierres is No 1 ager; Russian River Ranches is quickly accessible. 75,000 cases.

Spottswoode Napa ★★★→★★★★ (Cab S) **85 86 87** 89 90 91 92 95 Firm resonant luxury Cab from small estate v'yd in St Helena town. Also supple polished Sauv. 3,500 cases.

Stag's Leap Wine Cellars Napa ★★★★ (Chard) 91 92 93 95 (Cab S) 75 77 78 83 84 86 87 89 90 91 92 95 Celebrated v'yd for silky, seductive Cabs (SLV, Fay, top-of-line Cask 23), Merlots; non-estate vg; also Chard, Sauv, Ries. 50,000 cases.

Staglin Napa (★★★) (Cab S) 90 91 92 93 95 From small Rutherford v'yd designed by the late André Tchelistcheff, consistently superior, startlingly silky Cabs. 1,000 cases made annually.

Stags' Leap Winery Napa ★★ Neighbour to above with more tannic, austere Cab and muscular Petite Syrah. 25,000 cases.

Steele Wines Lake (★★→★★★) Long-time K-J winemaker patrols whole coast for sources of big, boldly-oaked Chard, Pinot N, Cab, Zin. Pricey.

Stemmler, Robert Sonoma ★★ Soft easy Pinot N made at BUENA VISTA by RS.

Sterling Napa ★★→★★★ (Chard) 85 88 90 91 92 93 95 (Cab S) 78 80 81 85 87 88 89 90 91 95 Scenic Seagram-owned winery with extensive v'yds and inexplicable ups and downs. Tart Sauv and firm basic bottling of Cab most reliably attractive. Also to be watched for Chard, Three Palms Merlot, Winery Lake Pinot Noir.

Stony Hill Napa ★★★ (Chard) 75 81 85 90 91 92 93 95 Hilly v'yd and winery for many of California's v best whites over past 30 yrs. Founder Fred McCrea died in '77, widow Eleanor in '91; son Peter carries on powerful tradition. Chard (both estate and non-estate SHV) is less steely, more fleshy than before. Oak-tinged Riesling and Gewürz are understated but age-worthy. 6,000 cases.

Storybook Mountain Napa ★★ NAPA's only dedicated Zin specialist with a heartily-oaked model from Calistoga v'yds.

Strong Vineyard, Rodney Sonoma ★★ (Chard) 91 92 93 94 95 (Cab) 87 90 91 92 93 95 Formerly Sonoma V'yds; produces good basic bottlings, better single-v'yd ones (Alexander's Crown Cab, Chalk Hill Chard, Charlotte's Home Sauv, River East Pinot N).

Sutter Home Napa ★★ (Zin) 73 77 83 85 89 90 91 92 93 95 Best known for sweet white Zin; most admired for sometimes heady Amador Zin. Also bargain-priced Cab, Chard. 3 million cases.

Swan, Joseph Sonoma ★★ (Zin) 77 78 79 80 81 82 83 84 85 86 87 90 91 92 95 Ultra-bold Zins, Pinots of late Joe Swan, now directed by his son-in-law.

Swanson Napa ★★→★★★ Beginnng to emerge from over-oaked phase. Estimable age-worthy Chards lead list; Cab and Merlot are worth note. Sangiovese and Syrah gaining.

Taft Street Sonoma ★★ After muddling along, has hit an impressive stride with esp good value Russian River Chards, Merlots. 18,000 cases.

Talbott, R Monterey Wealthy owner doing well with big toasty Chards from Santa Lucia Highlands AVA, Carmel Valley.

Tanner, Lane Santa Barbara ★★→★★★ Owner-winemaker with often superb single-v'yd Pinot Noirs (Sanford & Benedict, Sierra Madre Plateau) to drink immediately or to keep.

Torres Estate, Marimar Sonoma ★★★ Sister of Catalan hero makes ultra-buttery Chard, lovely Pinot from Russian River Valley estate.

Trefethen Napa ★★★ (Chard) 79 81 82 83 84 85 86 87 90 91 92 93 95 (Cab) 75 78 79 80 84 85 87 88 89 90 91 92 95 Respected family winery. Vg dry Ries, tense Chard for ageing (late-released Library wines show how well). Cab shows increasing depths. Low-priced wines sub-titled 'Eschcol'.

Truchard Carneros ★★→★★★ From warmer, inner-end of CARNEROS comes one of the flavoury, firmly-built Merlots that give the AVA identity. Also Chard, Cab.

Turley Napa ★ Former partner in FROG'S LEAP, now, with winemaker sister, focussed on Rhone varieties. Style leans heavily on oak.

Tudal Napa ★★ (Cab S) **80 84 86 87 89** 90 91 92 95 Tiny estate winery N of St Helena; steady source of dark firm ageable Cabs.

Tulocay Napa ★★ (Pinot N) **82 85 89 90** 91 92 93 95 Tiny winery at Napa City. Pinot esp can be v accomplished. Cab is also worth attention.

Turnbull Wine Cellars Napa ★★ (Cab) **81 83 84 85 86 87** 89 90 91 92 95 Rich full minty Cab from estate facing ROBERT MONDAVI winery.

Ventana Monterey ★★ '78 winery, showcase for owner's v'yds: watch for Chard and esp Sauv from Musqué clone.

Viader Napa ★★ 90 91 95 Argentine Delia Viader fled to California to do her own thing: dark Cab-based blend from estate in hills above St Helena.

Viansa Carneros ★★ Sam SEBASTIANI's reliable label for Italianate varietals: Nebbiolo, Sangiovese; also Sangio-Cab ('Thalia') from SONOMA, NAPA.

Vichon Winery Napa ★★ (Chard) **91 92 93** 94 95 (Cab) **82 87 89** 90 91 92 95 MONDAVI-owned. Subtle agreeable Chard and Chevrignon (Sauv-Sém). Stern oaky NAPA and sterner oakier Stag's Leap District Cabs. Coastal Selection is value second line.

Villa Mt Eden Napa ★★ (Chard) **91 92 93 94** 95 (Cab) **75 85 86 88** 90 91 92 95 Owned by Washington's Ch Ste Michelle, which has it doing two jobs: 'Grand Reserve' wines from carefully-chosen v'yds the length and breadth of state (NAPA Cab, Sta Barbara Pinot N top the list), 'Cellar Select' line useful for modest-priced varietals.

Vine Cliff Napa (★★★) New well-heeled family winery in E hills above Oakville. V ambitious with estate Chard, Cab S. Shows promise.

Vita Nova Sta Barbara ★★ Label from stable of AU BON CLIMAT. To watch esp for regionally distinctive Bordelais red blend.

Wente Bros Livermore and Monterey ★★ Historic specialists in whites, esp LIVERMORE Sauv and Sém. MONTEREY sweet Ries can be exceptional. A little classic sparkling. Also owns CONCANNON. 300,000 cases.

Whaler Mendocino ★★ Family-owned estate winery producing deep dark Zin from E hills of Ukiah Valley.

Wheeler Sonoma ★★ Was William Wheeler until bought by J C Boisset (see France). Steady source of middle-of-the-road Chard, Cab.

White Rock Napa ★★★ French owner placing faith in impressive vineyard-foremost, finessy Cab-based red called simply 'Claret'. Also Chard.

White Oak Sonoma ★★ (Zin) **87 88** 90 91 95 Vibrant Zin dominates; fruit-rich ALEXANDER VALLEY Chard and Sauv underrated.

Whitehall Lane Napa ★★ Recently bought from Japanese owners by San Francisco family. Heady and boldly oaked obligatory Chard, Cab.

Wild Horse Winery San Luis Obispo ★★→★★★ (Pinot) **86 87 89 90** 91 92 95 Owner-winemaker has a particular gift for Pinot N (mostly San Louis Obispo and Sta Barbara grapes). Also worthy Chard, Merlot.

Williams & Selyem Sonoma ★★★→★★★★ (Pinot) **87 88** 89 **90** 91 92 95 Intense smoky Russian River Pinot esp Rochioli and Allen v'yds. Followers gladly pay high prices for emphatic individuality.

Zaca Mesa Sta Barbara ★★ Turning away from Chard and Pinot to concentrate on Rhône varieties (especially Viognier and Syrah) and blends (Cuvée Z) grown on estate.

ZD Napa ★★→★★★★ (Pinot) **86 87 90** 91 92 93 95 Lusty Chard tattooed by American oak is the ZD signature wine. Pinot N is often finer. 18,000 cases.

CALIFORNIA

NB Vintages in colour are those you should choose first for drinking in 1997.

The Pacific Northwest

America's main quality challenge to California lies in Oregon and Washington, on the same latitudes of the Pacific Coast as France is on the Atlantic. As in California, the modern wine industry started in the 1960s. Each of the northwestern states (Oregon, Washington, Idaho) has developed a distinct identity. The small production of Canada's British Columbia fits in here too.

Oregon's vines (6,050 acres) lie mainly in the cool temperate Willamette and warmer Umpqua valleys between the Coast and Cascade ranges, in sea-tempered climates giving delicate flavours.

Washington's vineyards (11,300 acres) are mostly east of the Cascades in a dry, severe climate scarcely curbed by the Yakima and Columbia rivers. Idaho's are east of Oregon along the Snake River. Both regions have hot days and cool nights which preserve acidity and intensify flavours.

Most of Oregon's 96 wineries are small and highly individual. Vintages are as uneven as in Burgundy, whose Pinot Noir is the state's most celebrated (also controversial) grape. Pinot had a rare run of good vintages with '88, '89, '90 and '91; '92 was hot and heady; '93 again was excellent, and '94 is exceptional.

The Washington industry, with 95 wineries, is remarkably consistent over a wide range. Cabernet and Merlot grow excellently, as well as all the classic white varieties. A run of fine vintages, '88, '89, '90, '91, '92, '94 has coincided with maturing winemaking talent. '93 was a record crop. Value remains good.

Oregon

Adelsheim Vineyard Willamette ★★★ (Chard) 90 93 94 (Merlot) 88 92 93 94 (Pinot) 88 90 91 92 93 94 Nicely oaked Pinot Noir, Chard best early. Pinots Gris and Blanc are clean, bracing.

Amity Willamette ★★ (w) 90 91 92 93 94 Excellent Gewürz and Riesling, patchy Pinot Noirs.

Archery Summit Yamhill Country ★★ Flashy new operation of NAPA owner Gary Andrus. First releases of Pinot N (92 93), were made in California; competent wines.

Argyle (Dundee Wine Co) ★★→★★★ Willamette (w) 90 93 94 (sp) 88 Since '87, Australia's NW outpost, led by Brian Croser of Petaluma (qv). Dry Ries, Chard; vg classic sparkling.

Beaux Freres Willamette ★★★ Big, extracted, oaky, somewhat controversial Pinot Noirs (91 92 93 94), now also Chard (92). Partly owned by wine critic Robert Parker.

Bethel Heights Willamette ★★★ (Pinot N) 88 90 91 92 93 94 Deftly made, rising-star Pinot N ('Early Release', Vintage and Selected) from estate nr Salem; top quality. Chard vg since '93.

Brick House Vineyards ★★ Tiny, Pinot N-focussed property with TV-star owner/winemaker. Good early efforts.

Bridgeview Vineyards Rogue Valley ★ (w) 91 93 94 (Pinot N) 91 92 93 94 To watch; esp whites: good Gewürz, also Chard and Pinot.

Cameron Willamette (Pinot) ★★ 91 Nr KNUDSEN-ERATH. Eclectic producer of Pinot N, Chard: some great, others conversation pieces. Vg Pinot Bl.

Château Benoit Willamette ★ Most consistent successes Müller-T and Ries. Pioneer sparkling wines. Currently solid, unexciting.

Chehalem N Willamette ★★ (Pinot N) 90 91 92 93 94 Small premium estate winery, established since '90. Makes Pinot N and also Chard, Pinot Gr and 'Cerise' (Passe-Tout-Grains-style Gamay-Pinot Noir). To watch, esp for Burgundy-influenced, first-release 94 Pinot N.

Cristom N Willamette ★★★ r 92' 93 94 First vintage 91. Vg Pinot N and Chard. Rising star.

A choice of Pacific Northwest wines for 1997

Argle Brut (Oregon)

Leonetti Cabernet Sauvignon (Washington)

The Hogue Cellars Sauvignon Blanc (Washington)

Domaine Drouhin Pinot Noir (Oregon)

Chateau Ste Michelle Chardonnay Cold Creek (Washington)

Tyee Wine Cellars Gewürztraminer (Oregon)

Chehalem Pinot Gris Reserve (Oregon)

Columbia Cabernet Sauvignon Red Willow Vineyard (Washington)

Domaine Drouhin Willamette ★★★★ Bold enterprise of great Beaune name; superb quality. The best Oregon Pinot N (88 89 90 91 92' 93 94), tiny amount of estate Chard.

Domaine Serene Willamette ★★ New as of 92 vintage. Meaty Pinot N from former PANTHER CREEK winemaker.

Elk Cove Vineyards Willamette ★★ Pinot N was somewhat erratic; steadier now and can rival best (esp estate 'La Bohème', 90 91 92 93 94). Also fresh Ries (and late-harvest 86 92), well-oaked Chard and Pinot Gr.

Eola Hills Nr Salem (Willamette) ★★ Consistently good Chardonnay (4-acre v'yd-designated) and Pinot Noir.

Erath Vineyards Willamette ★★→★★★ (Pinot) 91 92 93 94 Formerly Knudsen-Erath and Oregon's second-largest winery (est '72). Ever-improving: increasingly fine (and expensive) Pinot and Chard, dry Ries and Gewürz v fine. Pinot Gr 93 is among O's best.

Evesham Wood Willamette ★★★ Tiny family winery nr Salem showing talent. Esp for Pinot Gris and Gewürztraminer (92 93 94); Pinot N (91 92 93 94) is often vg too.

Eyrie Vineyards, The Willamette ★★★ Pioneer ('65) winery with Burgundian convictions. Oregon's most famous Pinot (recent vintages wavering) and v oaky Chard (91). Also Pinot Gr (irreplaceable with salmon), Pinot Meunier and dry Muscat.

Firesteed ★★ Light, no-oak Pinot N. Delicious, early-drinking and vg value.

Foris Vineyards S Oregon ★ Pinot N, Chard etc from warmer Rogue Valley. Oustanding Merlot and Gewürz in 92.

Henry Estate Umpqua Valley ★ Distinctive Pinot (American oak), good Gewürz.

Hinman Vineyards S Willamette ★→★★ Eugene winery focussing on quality: Pinot Gr, Gewürz, Ries all vg. Sliven Ridge is the premium label.

Ken Wright Cellars Yamhill County (Willamette) ★★★ New venture by former PANTHER CREEK owner. Makes extracted, textured, luscious-style Pinot N that has a cult following.

King Estate S Willamette ★★ Huge by Oregon standards. First wines: 92 93 Pinot Gr (vg), Chard and Pinot N.

Knudsen-Erath See (new name) Erath Vineyards.

Lange Winery Yamhill County (Willamette) ★ Small family winery, occasionally brilliant Pinot N and Pinot Gr. Inconsistent.

Laurel Ridge Winery Willamette ★→★★ Washington County winery with v'yds in Yamhill. Reliable classic method sparkling and Sauv Bl.

THE PACIFIC NORTHWEST

Montinore Vineyards Willamette ★★★ Ambitious winery with, for Oregon, huge 465-acre v'yd nr Forest Grove. New French winemaker since '92. Chard and Pinot N improving (Pinot N **91** 93 94).

Nicolas Rolin Portland (Willamette) ★★ V small producer of consistent Pinot N.

Oak Knoll Willamette ★★ Started with fruit wines; now one of Oregon's larger Pinot N producers. Recently inconsistent.

Panther Creek Willamette ★★ (Pinot N) 89 **90 91** 92 93 94 Tiny McMinnville winery: excellent beefy Pinot N, luscious Melon de Bourgogne.

Ponzi Willamette Valley ★★★ (Pinot N) **90 91** 92 93 94 Small winery almost in Portland, well-known for Ries. Also Pinot Gr (**85** still good), Chard, and delicate full, (French) oaky, cellarable Pinot N.

Rex Hill Willamette ★★★ (Pinot N) 88 **90 91** 92' 93 94 Well-financed successful assault on top Pinots, Chards. Esp single v'yd. Ries too.

St-Innocent Willamette ★★ Up-and-coming Eola Hills winery: Chard, Pinot N.

Shafer Vineyard Cellars Willamette ★★ Small producer of frequently good Pinot N, delicate Chard. Currently rather inconsistent.

Sokol Blosser Willamette ★★★ (Pinot N) **90 91** 92' 93 94 One of the larger Oregon wineries. Aim is popular taste: producing easy, accessible Chard and Redland Pinot N (vg 91 92); also Ries, Sauv and Merlot (seldom grown in Oregon). Recently rough.

Tualatin Vineyards Willamette ★★ (Pinot) **92** 93 94 (Chard) **91** 92 93 94 Large estate winery: v consistent Chard best, plus Gewürz, Ries. Pinot improving.

Tyee Willamette ★★ Recent arrival: family-owned and run, now well-established. Early vintages of Gewürz, Chard, Pinot N are well made.

Valley View Vineyards S Oregon ★★ Rogue Valley estate since '90. Focus is top Cabernet (**90 91** 92), Merlot, Chard (**91 92 93 94**) and Sauv (**92 93 94**): always improving.

Van Duzer Eola and Amity Hills (N Willamette) ★★ William Hill-owned (see California). Exciting Ries, vg Pinot N, Chard since '90.

Willamette Valley Vineyards Willamette ★★ New, large, nr Salem. Moderate to high quality Chard, Ries, Pinot N. Founders' Reserve wines best.

Yamhill Valley Vineyards Willamette ★ Young estate near college town of McMinnville focusses on Pinot Gr, Chard and Pinot N (avoid 91 92).

Washington & Idaho

Arbor Crest Spokane (Washington) ★★ Expanding winery has had ups and downs. Ups are Chard, Sauv Bl and late-harvest Ries.

Barnard Griffin Prosser (Washington) ★★★ Small producer of well-made Merlot (91), Chard (esp barrel-fermented, 93) and Sauv.

Canoe Ridge Walla Walla ★★★ New winery owned by Chalone Group (California). Impressive **93 94** Chard and Merlot.

Caterina NE Wash ★ Spokane wines (Cab, Merlot, Chard, Sauv) to watch.

Château Ste Michelle (ubiquitous in Washington) ★★★ Regional giant growing ever larger. Château Ste M and COLUMBIA CREST made 750,000 cases before '91 acquisition of SNOQUALMIE, then the state's second-largest producer. Major v'yd holdings, first-rate equipment and skilful winemakers keep Chard (**91 92 93 94**), Sém, Sauv Bl, Ries, Cab (83 85 86 87 89 91 92 **93** 94) and Merlot in the front ranks. Serious efforts at sparkling are attractive. Newest reds and Chards v exciting.

Chinook Wines Yakima Valley (Washington) ★★★ Owner-winemakers Kay Simon and Clay Mackey buying in Yakima Valley grapes for sturdy Chard, Sauv and Merlot. Excellent Sém too (**92**).

For key to grape variety abbreviations, see pages 7–13.

Columbia Crest Columbia Valley (Washington) ★★★ Separately run CHATEAU STE MICHELLE label for delicious well-made accessible wines priced one cut lower – most of them from big River Run v'yd. Reserve line is best Cab, Merlot (86 88 90 91 92 93 94) and Chard. Value.

Columbia Winery Woodinville (Washington) ★★★→★★★★ (Cab) 79 85 86 87 88 89 92 93 94 Pioneer ('62, as Associated Vintners): still a leader. Balanced stylish understated single-v'yd wines, esp Merlot (Milestone), Cabernets (Otis, Red Willow), Syrah (Red Willow). Oak-fermented Woodburne Chard, elegant Pinot, vg fruity long-lived Sém. Reds consistently among finest.

Covey Run Yakima Valley (Washington) ★★(Chard) 91 92 93 94 Mostly estate. Intriguing Aligoté and Caille de Fumé; intense heady Merlot, Cab.

De Stefano ★ Small winery for classic sparkling wines. Has been called De Stefano since late '94.

DeLille Cellars Woodinville (Washington) ★★★ Exciting new winery for vg red 'Bordelais' blends: Chaleur Estate (needs 5 yrs age), 'D2' (more forward, affordable). Massive expertise and potential. Another LEONETTI?

Gordon Brothers Columbia Valley (Washington) ★★ Tiny cellar for consistent Chard (Reserve 91), Merlot and Cab (89).

Hedges Cellars Puget Sound (Washington) ★★★ Esp for Washington's first (vg) Cab-Merlot blend. Began as négociant label, now with own v'yd, château-style winery and delicious wines.

Hogue Cellars Yakima Valley (Washington) ★★★ (Cab) 85 87 88 89 90 91 92 93 94 Leader in region, known for off-dry whites (esp Ries, Chenin, Sauv), but recently for stylish balanced Chard, Merlot, Cab. Value.

Kiona Vineyards Yakima Valley (Washington) ★★ (Cab) 83 85 Good v'yd for substantial Cabs and (Austrian) Lembergers; fruity Chard and Ries. Also v fine late-harvest Ries (88) and Gewürz.

Latah Creek Spokane (Washington) ★ Small cellar, mainly for off-dry Chenin Bl, Ries. Erratic, esp with drier oak-aged types and reds.

Leonetti Walla Walla (Washington) ★★★★ (r) 83 85 87 88 91 92 93 94 The top Washington estate. Harmonious individualistic Cab, fine big-scale Merlot: bold, ageworthy.

Matthews Cellars W Washington New winery for promising blended whites and Merlot.

McCrea Seattle (Washington) ★★ Small winery for delicious Chard and Grenache. Experiments with Rhône blends are in progress.

Neuharth W Washington ★ Olympic Peninsula winery uses Yakima Valley grapes for supple balanced Cab (Chard fair, though not equal to reds).

Preston Wine Cellars Columbia Valley (Washington) ★ Wide range. Some eccentric, some conventional/sound. Occasionally wonderful Cab, Merlot.

Quilceda Creek Vintners Puget Sound (Washington) ★★★ (Cab) 83 85 87 88 89 90 91 92 93 94 Leading ripe well-oaked Cab S from Columbia Valley grapes is the speciality.

Ste Chapelle Caldwell (Idaho, nr Boise) ★★→★★★ Top-drawer winemaking keeps intensely flavoured, impeccably balanced Chard, Ries (Washington and local v'yds) in forefront. Reds on the rise. Attractive sparkling.

Salishan Vancouver (Washington) ★ Promising Pinot N and occasionally brilliant dry Ries from nr Willamette Valley.

Silver Lake nr Seattle (Washington) ★★ Fine regular and reserve Chard and Sauv; also fine Cab, Merlot.

Snoqualmie ★★ Consistent quality. Whites best.

Staton Hills Yakima Valley (Washington) ★★ Recently inconsistent, s'times excellent Cab; good off-dry white (Ries, Chenin, Gewürz). Also sparkling.

Stewart Vineyards Yakima Valley (Washington) ★★ Estate v'yds well-suited to whites, esp Chard and Ries. Latterly some promising Cabs.

Thomas, Paul Yakima Valley (Washington) ★★ Started as (and still is in part) a fruit winery; now makes full-flavoured Chard, Sauv Bl and Chenin Bl. Reds also show promise.

Thurston Wolfe Yakima Valley (Wash) ★★★ Tiny eclectic Yakima-based winery: excellent Lemberger (red), late-harvest Sauv, Black Muscat.

Washington Hills Cellars Yakima Valley (Washington) ★★ Newly est'd. Winemaker Brian Carter making solid attractive Sém, Fumé and Cab. Value. Apex label is premium line for Sauv, Cab, late-harvest white.

Waterbrook Walla Walla (Wash) ★★ (r) 85 87 89 90 91 92 93 94 Young winery has now hit its stride: stylish big and oaky Cab, Merlot, Sauv.

Will, Andrew Seattle ★★★ Exciting Cabernet Sauvignon and Merlot from east Washington grapes.

Woodward Canyon Walla Walla (Washington) ★★★ (r) 81 82 83 84 85 87 88 89 90 91 92 93 94 Small top-notch cellar: well-oaked ultra-bold Cab, buttery Chard. Also Charbonneau blends (Merlot-Cab, Sauv-Sém).

British Columbia

A small but locally significant wine industry has developed since the '70s in Canada's Okanagan Valley, 150 miles east of Vancouver, in climatic conditions not very different from eastern Washington.

Blue Mountain ★★ 95 Small property for vg Pinot Gris, v fair Pinot Noir wines and sparkling.

Gray Monk ★★ 92 94 Good Okanagan Auxerrois, Gewürz and Pinot Blanc.

Lang Vineyards 94 Juicy Pinot Meunier.

Mission Hill ★→★★★ 93 94 95 Caused a gold medal stir in '94. Esp for Reserve Chard, Pinot Blanc.

Quails' Gate ★★ 94 95 Producing Chard, Chenin Bl, Pinot N, Ries Ice Wine.

Sumac Ridge ★★ 94 95 Gewürz and Pinot Bl from improving property.

East of the Rockies & Ontario

Producers in New York (there are now 108 in 6 AVAs) and other eastern states, as well as Ohio (44 in 4 AVAs) and Ontario (35), traditionally made wine from hardy native grapes, varieties of Vitis labrusca whose wine has strong 'foxy' flavour, off-putting to non-initiates. To escape the labrusca flavour, growers then turned to more nuanced French-American hybrids. Today consumer taste plus cellar and vineyard technology have largely bypassed these, although Seyval Blanc and Vidal keep their fans. Chardonnay, Riesling, Cabernet Sauvignon and Merlot are now firmly established. Success is mixed (the winter of 1993/94 took its toll), but progress, from Virginia to Ontario, is accelerating, particularly on Long Island.

Northeastern grape varieties

Aurora (Aurore) One of the best white French-American hybrids; the most widely planted in New York. Good for sparkling.

Baco Noir One of the better red French-American hybrids: high acidity but clean dark wine which usually needs ageing.

Catawba Old native American grape, perhaps the second most widely grown. Pale red and 'foxy' flavoured. Appears in crowd-pleasing dry, off-dry and sweet wines, still and sparkling.

Cayuga White Hybrid created at Cornell Uni. Delicate fruity off-dry wine.

Chambourcin Red grape of French origin: under-appreciated Loire-like reds and agreeable rosé.

Chelois Popular red hybrid. Dry medium-bodied burgundy-style wine.

Concord Labrusca variety, by far the most widely planted grape in New York. Heavy 'foxy' sweet one-dimensional red wines, but mostly grape juice and jelly. Long a staple of kosher wines.

De Chaunac Red wine hybrid found in New York and Canada. Avoid.

Maréchal Foch Workmanlike red French hybrid. Depending on vinification yields boldly flavoured or nouveau-style wines.

Niagara Quintessential labrusca greenish-white grape, s'times called 'white Concord': lovely aromatic sweet wine; wants to be gobbled right from vine.

Ravat (Vignoles) French-American white hybrid of intense flavour and high acidity, often made in yummy prize-winning 'late harvest' style.

Vidal Mainstay French-American hybrid grape for full-bodied personable dry white wines.

Wineries and vineyards

Allegro ★★ 91 92 94 95 Est Pennsylvania maker of noteworthy Chard, Cab.

Bedell ★★★ 93 94 95 LONG ISLAND winery known for excellent Merlot and Cabernet Sauvignon.

Biltmore Estate ★★ 93 94 95 North Carolina winery on 8,500-acres with 253-room mansion, America's largest. Chard and sparkling.

Canandaigua Wine Co ★→★★ FINGER LAKES winery with many California properties. Major producer (second largest in the US, behind Gallo) of labrusca, and table and sparkling wines. Owns Manischewitz, the best-selling kosher sweet wine. See California.

Cave Spring ★★★ 95 Ontario boutique: sophisticated Chard and Ries.

Chaddsford ★★ 93 94 95 Pennsylvania producer since '82: esp for burgundy-style Chard.

Chamard ★★ 93 94 95 Connecticut's best winery, owned by Tiffany's chairman. Top Chard. AVA is Southeastern New England.

Château des Charmes ★★→★★★ 91 93 94 95 Show-place château-style Ontario winery (opened '94). Fine Chard, Aligoté, Cab, sparkling.

Clinton Vineyards ★★ 92 93 Hudson River winery known for clean dry Seyval Bl and spirited Seyval sparkling.

Debonné Vineyards ★★ 93 94 Popular Ohio estate (in Lake Erie AVA): hybrids, eg CHAMBOURCIN and VIDAL; and vinifera, eg Chard, Ries.

Finger Lakes Beautiful historic upstate New York cool-climate vineyard region, source of most of the state's wines (from 52 producers), and the seat of its 'vinifera revolution'. GLENORA and WAGNER are the outstanding wineries. To watch.

Firelands ★★ 91 93 95 Ohio estate on Isle St George in LAKE ERIE AVA, growing Chard and Cab.

Frank, Dr Konstantin (Vinifera Wine Cellars) ★★ 93 94 95 Small, influential winery. The late Dr F was a pioneer in growing European vines in the FINGER LAKES. Vg Chateau Frank sparkling.

Glenora Wine Cellars ★★★ 91 93 94 95 Aggressive FINGER LAKES producer of outstanding sparkling wine and good Chard and Ries.

Gristina ★★ 93 94 95 Promising young winery on LONG ISLAND'S N FORK AVA with Chard, Cab and Pinot N.

Hamptons (Aka South Fork) LONG ISLAND AVA. The top winery is moneyed SagPond. Duck Walk is up and coming.

Hargrave Vineyard ★★★ 93 94 95 LONG ISLAND's pioneering winery, v'yds since '72 on NORTH FORK. Good Chard, Cab S and Cab F.

Henry of Pelham ★★★ 94 95 Elegant Ontario Chard, Ries; distinctive Baco Noir.

Hillebrand Estates ★→★★ 94 95 Aggressive Ontario producer attracting attention with Chard and Bordeaux-style red blend.

Hudson River Region America's oldest winegrowing district (21 producers) and New York's first AVA. Straddles the river, two hours' drive N of Manhattan.

Inniskillin ★★★ 93 94 95 Outstanding (VINCOR-owned) producer that spearheaded birth of modern Ontario wine industry. Skilful burgundy-style Chard and Pinot N. Vg Riesling, Vidal ice wine, Pinot Gris and Auxerrois. Interesting winery tours.

Knapp ★★ 93 94 95 Versatile FINGER LAKES winery. Tasty Bordeaux-style blend, Cab, Ries, Bl de Bls sparkling.

Lake Erie The biggest grape-growing district in the east; 25,000 acres along the shore of Lake Erie, incl portions of New York, Pennsylvania and Ohio. 90% is CONCORD, most heavily in New York's Chautauqua County. Also the name of a tristate AVA: NY's sector has 7 wineries, Pennsylvania's 5, Ohio's 22.

Lakeridge ★★ Popular Florida winery nr Disneyland. Esp for Muscadine. Spumante-like sparkling from local Carlos grapes flies off the shelf. Rarely uses vintage dates.

Lamoreaux Landing ★★→★★★ 94 95 Young, stylish, talented FINGER LAKES house: promising Chard and Ries from striking Greek-revival winery.

Lenz ★★★ 93 94 95 Classy winery of NORTH FORK AVA. Fine austere Chard in the Chablis mode, also Gewürz, Merlot and sparkling wine.

Long Island The most exciting new wine region E of the Rockies and a hothouse of experimentation. Currently 1,300 acres all vinifera (47% Chard) and 2 AVAs (NORTH FORK and HAMPTONS). Most of its 17 wineries are on the North Fork. Best varieties: Chard, Cab, Merlot. A long growing season; relatively little frost.

Michigan Potentially America's finest cool-climate Ries area. Ch Chantal's can be stunning, Ch Grand Traverse's vg. Watch Fenn Valley, Good Harbor, Tabor Hill, Bowers Harbor (for sparkling version).

Millbrook ★★★ 91 93 95 The No 1 HUDSON RIVER REGION winery. Money-no-object viticulture and savvy marketing has lifted spiffy, whitewashed Millbrook in big old barn into New York's firmament. Burgundian Chards are splendid, Cab F can be delicious.

North Fork LONG ISLAND AVA (of 2). Top wineries: BEDELL, GRISTINA, HARGRAVE, LENZ, PALMER, PAUMANOK, PELLEGRINI, PINDAR. 2½ hrs drive from Manhattan.

Ontario Main E Canada wine region, on Niagara Peninsula: 35 producers. Heavy investment and glimmerings of great future. Ries, Chard, even Pinot N, show incipient longevity. Ice wine is flagship.

Palmer ★★★ 93 94 95 Superior LONG ISLAND (N FORK) producer and byword in the Darwinian metropolitan market. High profile due to perpetual-motion marketing; fast growth. Flavourful Chard, Sauv and Loire Chinon-like Cab F.

Paumanok ★★ 93 94 95 Rising LONG ISLAND (NORTH FORK) winery, with promising Cab, Merlot, Ries, and savoury late-harvest Sauv Bl.

Pellegrini ★★★ 93 94 95 LONG ISLAND's most enchantingly designed winery (on NORTH FORK), opened '93. Opulent Merlot, stylish Chard, B'x-like Cab. Inspired winemaking. Exceptionally flavourful wines.

Pindar Vineyards ★★→★★★ 93 94 95 Huge 287-acre mini-Gallo winery of NORTH FORK, LONG ISLAND. Wide range of toothsome blends and popular varietals, incl Chard, Merlot, and esp good Bordeaux-type red blend, Mythology.

Sakonnet ★★ **94 95** Largest New England winery, based in Little Compton, Rhode Island (Southeastern New Eng AVA). Its regional reputation, resting on Chard, VIDAL and dry Gewürz, has blossomed since '85.

Tomasello ★★ **93 94** Progressive New Jersey winery. Good Blanc de Noirs sparkling and CHAMBOURCIN. Promising Cab S.

Unionville Vineyards ★★→★★★ **93 95** New Jersey's best winery, est '91. Lovely Ries, French-American hybrids elevated to nr-vinifera status.

Vincor International ★→★★ Canada's biggest winery (formerly Brights-Cartier), in Ontario, BC, Quebec, New Brunswick. Mass-market and premium wines; varietals, blends, Canadian and imported grapes. Owns INNISKILLIN. Also Jackson-Triggs and Sawmill Creek labels.

Vineland Estates ★★ **92 93 94 95** Good Ontario producer whose VIDAL ice wine, dry and semi-dry Ries and Ries ice wine are much admired.

Wagner Vineyards ★★★ **93 95** Jewel of a winery in the FINGER LAKES – arguably New York's best – for succulent barrel-fermented Chard, dry and sweet Ries, RAVAT ice wine and NIAGARA. Charming to visit.

Westport Rivers ★★ **93 94 95** Massachusetts house est'd '89. Good Chard and fledgling sparkling. (Southeastern New England AVA.)

Wiemer, Hermann J ★★→★★★ **93 94 95** Creative German-born FINGER LAKES winemaker. Interesting Ries incl vg sparkling and 'late harvest'.

94 Wollersheim ★★ Wisconsin winery specializing in variations of Maréchal Foch. 'Prairie Fumé' (Seyval Bl) is a commercial success.

Southern and central states

Virginia Ambitious young wine state (since '72). Acquiring status. Whites, esp Chard, lead. 47 wineries (in 6 AVAs) produce good Ries, Viognier, Cabs and Merlot from 1,394 acres of grapes. Monticello has some of the top producers: Prince Michel (though its good 'Le Ducq' B'x blend is made mostly with Napa grapes) and its second property, Rapidan River, Barboursville (inspired Malvaxia Reserve), Montdomaine. Others are Horton (for Viognier), Ingleside Plantation, Linden, Naked Mountain, Meredyth, Oasis (for 'champagne'), Piedmont, Tarara and Williamsburg Winery. Ch Morrisette and Wintergreen bear watching.

Missouri A blossoming industry with 36 producers in 3 AVAs: Augusta (first in the US), Hermann, Ozark Highlands. In-state sales catching fire. Best wines are Seyval Bl, Vidal, Vignoles (sweet and dry versions). Top estate is Stone Hill, in Hermann (since 1847), with rich red from the Norton (or Cynthiana) grape variety; Hermannhof (1852) is drawing notice for the same. Mount Pleasant, in Augusta, makes rich 'port' and nice sparkling wine. To watch are Augusta Winery, Blumenhof, Les Bourgeois, Montelle, Röbller, St James.

Maryland 9 wineries and 2 AVAs. Basignani makes good Cabernet Sauvignon, Chard, Seyval. Catoctin, a mountain-v'yd boutique-winery, is developing solid, modest-priced Riesling and Chard. Elk Run's Chard and Cab can be delicious. Best-known Boordy Vineyards gets good marks for Seyval Bl (esp Reserve) and sparkling. Woodhall understands Seyval and Cab. Fiore's Chambourcin is interesting. Catoctin AVA is the main Cab and Chard area. Linganore is Second AVA.

EAST OF THE ROCKIES & ONTARIO

To decipher codes, please refer to 'Key to symbols' on front flap of jacket, or to 'How to use this book' on page 6.

The Southwest

Texas

In the past 15 years a brand-new Texan wine industry has sprung noisily to life. It now has 450 growers, 26 wineries (10 in Hill Country) and five AVAs. The best wines (nearly all single varietals) are comparable with northern California's.

Bell Mountain Vineyards Bell Mountain AVA winery at Fredericksburg. 52 acres. Erratic but known for Cab S, Chard next.

Cap*Rock (Lubbock) Since '90. Cab, Chard, Chenin, Sauv, Ries, sparkling all doing well for local medals.

Fall Creek Vineyards Consistent TEXAS HILL COUNTY estate: fine Sauv, Chard. Also Cab S. Watch for Emerald Ries, Chenin and Carnelian.

Grape Creek Vineyards Small winery nr Fredericksburg for Chardonnay and Muscat Canelli.

Hill County Cellars Nr Austin: exemplary Chard and Sauv.

Llano Estacado The pioneer (since '76): nr Lubbock with 220 acres (210 leased). Known for Chard and Cab S; good Signature red.

Messina Hof Wine Cellars Winning with Muscat Canelli grape and late-harvest Johannisberg Ries 'Angel'. Also has Pinot N.

Pheasant Ridge Lubbock estate founded '78. Now 36 acres. State leader esp for reds and now Chenin and Chard.

Sainte-Genevieve Largest Texas winery, linked with Cordier (France). V'yds (1,000 acres) owned by University of Texas. Well-made, mostly NV wines.

Slaughter-Leftwich Tiny amount of Chard from Lubbock vineyards; the winery is near Austin.

Texas Hill Country One of 3 Hill Country AVAs (S of Lubbock, W of Austin).

New Mexico etc

New Mexico is still known for one wine, Rio Grande Valley's remarkable Gruet sparkling, but other sparklers (Dom Cheurlin) and Anderson Valley Winery varietals have proved the potential. La Chiripada is another winery doing very well, with French hybrids and port-style wine. Gruet also has good Chard. There are now three AVAs and 19 wineries.

Colorado and **Arizona** are both focussing on vinifera grapes. Colorado (16 wineries) is growing rapidly, with Chard and Merlots leading the planting. Plum Creek Cellars (the largest winery, good Chard) and Grande River V'yds (recent success with Viognier) among others at Palisade are both vg. Arizona (8 wineries) is highlighting Rhône varieties (eg at Callaghan V'yds) and Pinot N and Cab from hot, high altitude, terra rossa v'yds. **Oklahoma** and **Utah** will be the next to emerge – Utah's one winery (Arches Vineyard) sets the pace with Ries, Oklahoma's two suit sweet-toothed locals better.

South America

Argentina

The world's fifth biggest producer is at last turning a serious eye to the outside world, though poor communications and strong domestic demand still provide obstacles to export-drives. Nicolas Catena's revolutionary steps with Cabernet and Chardonnay in Mendoza will hopefully act as a catalyst for positive changes in vineyard management and winemaking, and not just a promotion for these two varieties. Malbec, Syrah and Torrentes have far more potential. Ninety percent of fine wine production is in Mendoza, with irrigation and altitude essential elements in combating the scorching dry heat. Most promising developments are in the subregion of Tupungato Valley up in the Andes. Denomination of Origin regulations currently only exist for Lujan de Cuyo and San Rafael, although Maipu is soon to follow. In regions north of Mendoza (San Juan and La Rioja) temperatures soar and only the high altitude vineyards of Salta have achieved decent quality. To the south, the cooler climate of Rio Negro shows promise for whites. High yielding Criolla and Pedro Gimenez still dominate the Argentine crop, but classic varieties are now being widely planted.

Star-ratings are local, and provisional.

Arizu, Leoncio ★★★ Makers of Luigi Bosca wines: Malbec, Cab and Syrah from small Mendoza (Maipu) bodega; all vg. Also interesting Chard, Sauv, Pinot N and Riesling.

Bianchi, Bodegas ★→★★ Well-known producer at San Rafael owned by Seagram. Don Valentin Cab, Bianchi Borgoña and Malbec-Barbera blend are best-sellers. 'Particular' is their top Cab. Also Sauv.

Canale, Bodegas ★★→★★★ Premier Rio Negro winery: 95 Sauv Bl and Pinot N excellent. Also improved Merlot and Malbec.

Catena ★★★★ Argentina's export pioneer with best work coming from Bodega Esmerelda. Cab and Chard reach international standards; second label Alamos Ridge equally impressive. 94 Malbec is refreshingly Argentine.

Etchart Salta and Mendoza wineries. Delicate aromatic but dry Torrontes white and sound range of reds (mainly Cab S).

Finca Flichman ★★ Old Mendoza co now owned by bank investing heavily in wine. Top Caballero de la Cepa Cab, Chard; also Syrah, Merlot, varietals.

Goyenechea, Bodegas ★→★★★ Basque family firm in San Rafael known for old-style wines (esp Cab, Syrah, Malbec, Merlot and Aberdeen Angus red), but now modernizing.

Lagarde ★→★★★ Old bodega revived. Good Cabs and Malbecs.

Lopez, Bodegas ★★→★★★ Family firm best known for Château Montchenot red and white and Château Vieux Cab.

M Chandon ★★★→★★★★★ Makers of Baron B and M Chandon sparkling under Moët & Chandon supervision. Also still reds and whites incl vg Castel Chandon, less exciting Kleinburg (w); smooth Comte de Valmont, Beltour and Clos du Moulin (r). Chard Renaud Poirier is first of varietal range.

Martins ★★ Recent notable Merlot and Malbec from Mendoza.

Nacari, Bodegas ★★ Small La Rioja cooperative. NB its Torrontes white.

Navarro Correas ★★★ 3 wineries: vg Malbec, notable Syrah, sparkling and Spätlese-style Ries.

Norton, Bodegas ★★→★★★ Old firm, was English, now Austrian-owned, being thoroughly updated. Esp reds: Sangiovese, Barbera, Malbec, Merlot.

Orfila, José ★→★★ Long-established bodega at St Martin, Mendoza. Top wines: Cautivo Cab and white Extra Dry (Pinot Bl). Also making sparkling wine in France for sale in Argentina.

Peñaflor ★ Argentina's biggest wine co, reputedly the world's third largest. Bulk wines for top jugs, but see Trapiche (esp Medalla), Andean V'yds, Fond de Cave (Chard, Cab). Aim is to export. Also 'Sherry': Tio Quinto.

H Piper ★★→★★★ Sparkling wine made under licence from Piper-Heidsieck.

Rural, Bodegas La ★★→★★★ ('San Filipe' is label.) Recently acquired by Nicholas Catena and recipient of much-needed capital injection. Good Chard, Merlot, Malbec. To watch.

San Telmo ★★→★★★ Modern winery with a California air and outstanding fresh full-flavoured Chard, Chenin Bl, Merlot and esp Malbec and Cab 'Cruz de Piedra-Maipu'. 568 acres.

Santa Ana, Bodegas ★→★★★ Said to be S America's biggest. Old-est'd family firm at Guaymallen, Mendoza. Wide range incl good Syrah, Merlot-Malbec, Pinot Gr 'blush' and sparkling (Chard-Chenin) 'Villeneuve'.

Suter, Bodegas ★ Swiss-founded firm (distributed by Seagram) famous for Etiquetta Marron white and good classic 'JS' red.

Toso, Pascual ★★→★★★ Old Mendoza winery at San José, making one of Argentina's best reds, Cabernet Toso. Also Ries and sparkling wines (incl one classic method).

Trapiche ★★→★★★ Premium label of PENAFLOR now with French consultant Michel Rolland. Single-grape wine range incl Merlot, Malbec, Cab, Pinot N, Chard and Torrontes and an excellent Sauv Bl from Tupungeto Valley.

Vistalba, Viña y Cava ★★★→★★★★ (Ex Perez Cuesta) Small bodega for outstanding reds, esp Syrah and Malbec.

Weinert, Bodegas ★★★★ Small winery. Classic reds led by good Cab-Merlot-Malbec Cavas de Weinert. Also promising Sauv Carrascal.

Chile

Chile is now firmly on the international scene and learning fast. At last a few fine wines are emerging from a mass of good ones – and plenty of poor. Foreign investors, especially French, are highly optimistic. Conditions are ideal for wine growing in central Chile, the Maipo Valley near Santiago, and in places for 300 miles south. Cabernets led the way with easy-drinking flavours, rapidly gaining in quality. Merlot is now hot on its heels. Other varieties are beginning to emerge from behind strict quarantine regulations – Syrah and Viognier are two. Stainless steel and new oak have brought international standards. Casablanca leads the way with whites: citrusy Chardonnays and crisp Sauvignons in distinctly regional style. Many long-time grape-growers are no longer supplying large bodegas but branching out, even exporting, alone. Principal regions, from north to south, are Aconcagua, Maipo, Rapel, Curicó, Maule and southern Itata and Bio-Bio.

Aconcagua Northernmost quality wine region. Incl CASABLANCA, Panquehue.

Agrícola Aquitania 60-acre joint venture of Bordeaux's Paul Pontallier and Bruno Prats with Felipé de Solminihac. Their label is Paul Bruno. Cabernet only, from '93. 93 94 disappointing; 95 looks good.

Bio-Bio Southernmost 'quality' wine region. V rainy.

Bisquertt Colchagua (RAPEL) family-winery (350 acres) with bulk reputation but now investing heavily for export success. Vg Merlot.

Caliterra New joint venture with Mondavi in US will doubtless bring changes of style. Vg Curicó (MAULE).

Canépa, José Big modern bodega, of Italian origin, in Isla de Maipo producing in large quantity. Talented winemaker Andrés Ilabaca is now also making stunning premium Cabs, good Merlot and Zin and simple crisp Sauv Bl.

Carmen, Viña One of the oldest Chilean wineries, dating from 1850 and acquired by Ricardo Claro (also owner of SANTA RITA) in '88. Extensive v'yds and new MAIPO winery make good Sauv, Chard and Cab and Merlot. Viognier and Petite Syrah on the way.

Carta Vieja 1,160 rejuvenated acres in Maule. Del Pedregal family-owned for 6 generations. Top selection Cab, Merlot and Chard are good (reds better).

Casa Lapostolle Moneyed (Grand Marnier) new French winery in Colchagua, MAULE with Michel Rolland at the helm. Excellent oak-aged Merlot and promising Sauv.

Casablanca, Viña Second bodega of VINA SANTA CAROLINA. For premium wines. Top Sauv, Chard, Gewürz and new vg low-yield Cab and Merlot.

Chateau Los Boldos Label of French-owned Santa Amalia winery at the foot of the Andes in MAULE. Cab, Sauv and some Chard for export only.

Concha y Toro Biggest, most outward-looking wine firm with bodegas and v'yds all over Chile, mainly in MAIPO and RAPEL, totalling 4,210 acres. New Cab-Syrah is good, as is Casablanca Chard, premium 'Trio' red and white, and Don Melchor Cab. Watch out for Alicanté Bouchet.

Cono Sur Chimbarongo-based winery owned by CONCHA Y TORO for Chile's top Pinot and value Isla Negra label. Talented winemaker recently departed to ERRAZURIZ.

Cousiño Macul Distinguished and beautiful old estate nr Santiago (MAIPO). V dry Sém and Chard. Don Luis light red, Don Matias dark and tannic, are good Cabs. Antiguas Reservas is top export Cab.

Domaine Oriental French-owned modern winery in Maule Valley, Talca.

Domaine Rabat Since 1927 in MAIPO and Colchagua (RAPEL); offers Cab, Chard, Sauv Bl. Different labels from each estate incl Domaine Rabat, Santa Adela. Joined forces with Grand Marnier in '94.

Echeverría Boutique Curicó (MAULE) winery producing intense complex Reserve Cabs and Chard.

Errázuriz Historic firm in Aconcagua Valley, N of Santiago, modernized and making v rich full-bodied wines, esp Merlot and Cabernet Don Maximiano.

La Fortuna, Viña Old-established winery in the Lontué Valley now exporting good Sauv, Chard, Merlot, Cab S and esp Malbec (95) all grown without fertilizer or herbicides.

La Rosa, Viña Massive investment and consultation from Ignacio Recabarren have produced spectacular first vintages from this RAPEL winery. Unoaked Chard and Merlot are superb.

Luís Felipé Edwards Impressive Puguillay boutique winery. Esp Cab, Chard.

Maipo Oldest wine region, nr Santiago. Relatively warm. Many good v'yds.

Maule S'most top quality region. Incl Claro, Loncomilla and Tutuven valleys.

Mont Gras New state-of-the-art winery in Colchagua Valley. Reds more impressive than whites. Top Merlot Reserve and Cabernet.

Montes Label of Discover Wines 250-acre estate, nr Curicó, emerging as quality leader with fresh Sauv, fine Chard, fruity Merlot, good Montes Cab, excellent Montes Alpha (90, French oak). Reds are generally best, incl recent Malbec.

Paul Bruno See Agrícola Aquitania.

Porta Viña, Premium Cab and Chard specialists with Cachapoal Valley v'yds. New Merlot is good.

Portal del Alto, Viña Small bodega with excellent Cab-Merlot blend. 250 acres: half in Maipo, half in San Fernando (RAPEL).

Rapel Central quality region divided into Colchagua and Cachapoal valleys.

Robles, Los Label of coop of Curicó. Wines include Cab and Merlot. 'Flying winemaker' Peter Bright is consultant.

San Carlos, Viña New Colchagua bodega with good range. Esp full-bodied Sém, Cab-Malbec blend.

San Pedro Long established at Molina, Curicó. One of the biggest exporters, with 2,250 acres in the Lontué Valley. Gato Negro and Gato Blanco are top sellers. Best are Castillo de Molina and Santa Helena Seleccíon de Director. Jacques Lurton of Bordeaux is consultant.

Santa Carolina Viña, Architecturally splendid old Santiago bodega with 'Reserva Especial'. Recent modernization. Concentrating on Casablanca Valley (ACONCAGUA) and quality. Other labels: CASABLANCA.

Santa Ema 550-acre MAIPO estate in family since 1955. Esp Cab, Merlot (90), Sauv and Chard. Reserva Cab (French oak) is their pride.

Santa Emiliana A division of CONCHA Y TORO. V'yds in RAPEL and CASABLANCA. Second label popular in Canada and USA: Walnut Crest.

Santa Inés Successful small family winery in Isla de MAIPO. Labels are De Martino, Santa Inés.

Santa Mónica Rancagua (RAPEL) winery; the best label is Tierra del Sol. Good Ries and Merlot under Santa Mónica label.

Santa Rita, Viña Long-established bodega in the MAIPO Valley south of Santiago. Medalla Real Cab and '120' are best-sellers abroad. Top wine is excellent Casa Real Cab.

Segu Ollé Linares (MAULE) estate owned by two Catalan families. Labels: Caliboro and Doña Consuelo: Cab (92), and vg Merlot (94).

Tarapacá Ex-Zavala Santiago producer rated in Chile for red wines. New investment in Isla del Maipo and conversion to imported oak underway should increase quality.

Terra Noble Talca winery with Loire wizard Henry Marionnet consulting: grassy Sauv and light Merlot.

Torreón de Paredes Recent family-owned RAPEL bodega (253 acres). Modern; no expense spared. Good Reserva Cab.

Torres, Miguel Enterprise of Catalan family firm (see Spain) at Curicó sets a modern pace. Good Sauv, Chard; vg Ries. Cab, formerly leaner than most of Chile's, is now achieving lovely harmony.

Undurraga Famous MAIPO family winery; first to export to the USA. Old and modern styles: good clean Sauv, oaky yellow Viejo Roble, fruity Pinot.

Valdivieso An old household word in Chile for sparkling wines. New Lontué winery. French winemaker and new consultant are creating an impressive range: good Chard, Reserve Pinot N, Merlot and Grange-like red wine project called 'Loco'.

Vascos, Los Family estate in Colchagua Province, RAPEL. 550 acres. Some of Chile's better Cab (B'x- and California-influenced). Also stylish Sauv-Sém. Link with Lafite-Rothschild (50% owners) ensures quality (and exposure).

Villard Recent Casablanca venture of Frenchman Thierry Villard. Big buttery Chard, intenese Sauv Bl, good Cab and Merlot from RAPEL.

Vinícola Mondragón CANEPA'S Second bodega. Labels: Rowan Brook, Peteroa, Montenuevo etc.

For key to grape variety abbreviations, see pages 7–13.

Other Southern American wines

Brazil New plantings of better grapes are transforming a big and booming industry. International investments, esp in Rio Grande do Sul and Santana do Liuramento, esp from France (eg Moët & Chandon) and Italy (Martini & Rossi), are significant. The new sandy Frontera region (neighbouring Argentina and Uruguay) and the Sierra Gaucha hills (for Italian-style sparkling) are some to watch. Exports are beginning. Large home market increasing too. Equatorial v'yds (eg nr Recife) can have two crops a year – or even five in two years. This is not a recommendation.

Mexico Oldest American wine industry is reviving, with investment from abroad (eg Freixenet, Martell, Domecq) and California influence via UC Davis. Best in Baja California (85% of total), Querétaro and on the Aguascalientes and Zacatecas plateaux. Top Baja C producers are L A Cetto (Valle de Guadaloupe, the largest, esp for Cab, Nebbiolo, Syrah), Bodegas Santo Tomas (since 1888, Mexico's oldest), Monte Xanic (with Napa-award winning Cab), Bodegas San Antonio, and Cavas de Valmar. Marqués de Aguayo is the oldest (1593), now only for brandy.

Peru Viña Tacama near Ica (top wine region) exports some promising wines, esp the Gran Vino Blanco white; also Cab S and classic method sparkling. Chincha, Moquegua and Tacha regions are slowly making progress. But phylloxera is a serious problem.

Uruguay Winemaking since 1700s, influenced along the way by France, Spain, Germany and Italy. Great efforts currently being made, with French advice and grapes, to improve wine from the 30,000 acres of warm, humid v'yds (eg along Rio de la Plata and the Brazilian border, esp Bella Unión). 50% is planted with hybrids. Regions with promise are Cerro Chapeau, Carpinteria, El Carmen, Montevideo (incl classic method sparkling). Simple varietals (mainly white) have been sighted in European supermarkets.

Australia

Heavily shaded areas are the wine growing regions

SOUTH AUSTRALIA

NEW SOUTH WALES

Upper Hunter

Mudgee

Hunter Valley

Sydney

Clare Valley

Riverland

Darling

Murray

Mildura
Mildura

Murray River

Adelaide
Barossa Valley

Adelaide Hills
Southern Vales

Murrumbidgee Irrigation Area

Cowra

Canberra

Wagga Wagga

Murrumbidgee

Corowa

Murray

VICTORIA

Padthaway

Great Western

Pyrenees

Goulburn Valley

Macedon

Coonawarra

Melbourne

Geelong
Geelong

Yarra Valley

Mornington Peninsula

Indian Ocean

TASMANIA

Hobart

The influence of Australia in the modern wine world is out of all proportion to the size of its vineyards. They represent less than two percent of global production, yet Australian ideas and names are on all wine-lovers' lips. In nine years her exports have grown from 8 to 140 million litres and the number of wineries has climbed to over 800. It is not just the climate that has done this, but radical research, uninhibited experiment and generous pooling of techniques. Even growers in the south of France are listening carefully. Australia has mastered easy-drinking wine and is well on the way to making some of the world's very best.

Her long-term classics are Shiraz, Semillon and Riesling wines. In the seventies they were joined by Cabernet Sauvignon and Merlot, Chardonnay, Pinot Noir and other varieties. Then in the nineties Grenache and Mourvèdre were rediscovered and embraced with the enthusiasm of a lost lover. At the same time, cool fermentation and the use of new barrels accompanied a general move to cooler areas. For a while excessive oak flavour was a common problem. Moderation is now the fashion – and sparkling wine of startling quality is a new achievement.

A massive planting programme is underway with the aim of doubling production and trebling exports. Value for money is generally high. Long may the boom continue.

Wine regions

Adelaide Hills (SA) Spearheaded by PETALUMA: 22 wineries at v cool, 450-metre sites in the Mt Lofty ranges.

Adelaide Plains (SA) Small area just north of Adelaide, formerly known as Angle Vale. The top Adelaide Plain winery is PRIMO ESTATE.

Barossa (SA) Australia's most important winery (though not v'yd) area; grapes from diverse sources (local, to MURRAY VALLEY; high quality cool regions: from adjacent hills, to COONAWARRA far S) make diverse wines. Local specialities: SHIRAZ, SEMILLON, GRENACHE etc. 46 wineries.

Bendigo/Ballarat (Vic) Widespread small v'yds, some of vg quality, re-creating glories of the gold rush. 21 wineries incl BALGOWNIE, JASPER HILL, HEATHCOTE.

Canberra District (ACT) 16 wineries now sell 'cellar door'. Quality is variable, as is style.

Clare Watervale (SA) Small, high quality area 90 miles north of Adelaide, best for Riesling; also SHIRAZ and CABERNET. 26 wineries spill over into new subdistrict, Polish Hill River.

Coonawarra (SA) Southernmost and finest v'yd of state: most of Australia's best CAB, successful CHARD, RIES and SHIRAZ. Newer arrivals incl Balnaves, Majella, PARKER ESTATE, PENLEY ESTATE. 23 wineries.

Geelong (Vic) Once-famous area destroyed by phylloxera, re-established mid-'60s. Very cool dry climate: firm table wines from good quality grapes. Names incl BANNOCKBURN, IDYLL, SCOTCHMAN'S HILL. 15 wineries.

Goulburn Valley (Vic) Very old (eg CHATEAU TAHBILK) and relatively new (eg MITCHELTON) wineries in temperate mid-Victoria region; full-bodied table wines. 12 wineries.

Granite Belt (Qld) High altitude, (relatively) cool region just N of NSW border; 16 wineries. Esp spicy SHIRAZ and rich SEM-CHARD.

Great Western (Vic) Temperate region in central W of state. High quality (esp sparkling). 9 wineries, 7 of relatively recent origin.

Hunter Valley (NSW) Great name in NSW. Broad soft earthy SHIRAZ and SEMILLON that live for 30 years. CABERNET not important; CHARD increasingly so. 52 wineries.

Margaret River (WA) Temperate coastal area with superbly elegant wines 174 miles S of Perth. 45 operating wineries; others planned for Australia's most vibrant tourist wine region.

Mornington Peninsula (Vic) Exciting wines in new cool coastal area 25 miles south of Melbourne. 400 acres. 37 commercial wineries including DROMANA, STONIERS, T'GALLANT.

Mount Barker/Frankland River (WA) New remote cool area in S of state; GOUNDREY and PLANTAGENET are biggest/best wineries, from 38 in all.

Mudgee (NSW) Small isolated area 168 miles NW of Sydney. Big reds, full CHARDS; from 21 wineries.

Murray Valley (SA, Vic & NSW) Vast irrigated vineyards near Mildara, Swan Hill (Vic and NSW), Berri, Loxton, Morgan, Renmark and Waikerie (S Aus). Principally making 'cask' table wines. Forty percent of the total Australian wine production.

AUSTRALIA

NE Victoria Historic area incl Corowa, Rutherglen, Wangaratta. Weighty reds and magnificent sweet dessert wines. 30 wineries.

Padthaway (SA) Large vineyard area (no wineries) developed as an over-spill of COONAWARRA. Cool climate; some good PINOT N is produced and excellent CHARDONNAY (esp LINDEMANS and HARDY'S), also Chard-Pinot N sparkling wines.

Perth Hills (WA) Fledgling area 19 miles E of Perth with 11 wineries and a larger number of growers on mild hillside sites.

Pyrenees (Vic) Central Vic region with 8 wineries: rich minty reds and some interesting whites, esp Fumé Bl.

Riverina (NSW) NV Large-volume irrigated zone centred around Griffith; good quality 'cask' wines (especially white), great sweet botrytised SEM. There are 12 wineries.

Southern Vales (SA) Covers the energetic McLaren Vale and Reynella in southern outskirts of Adelaide. Big reds now rapidly improving; also vg CHARD. 52 wineries.

Swan Valley (WA) The birthplace of wine in the west, on the N outskirts of Perth. Hot climate makes strong low-acid table wines but good dessert wines. Declining in importance viticulturally. 16 wineries.

Tasmania 50 vineyards now offering wine for commercial sale: over 700,000 litres in all. Great potential for CHARDONNAY, PINOT NOIR and RIESLING grapes in cool climate.

Upper Hunter (NSW) Est'd in early '60s; irrigated vines (mainly whites), lighter and quicker-developing than Lower Hunter's. Often value.

Yarra Valley ('Lilydale') Superb historic area nr Melbourne: 45 wineries. Growing emphasis on v successful PINOT NOIR and sparkling.

Grape varieties in Australia

In 1996 Australia crushed a record 800,000 tonnes of grapes which produced some 600 million litres of wine. The most important varieties are the following (tonnages from the very small 1995 vintage):

Cabernet Sauvignon (53,000 tonnes) Grown in all of Australia's wine regions, best in COONAWARRA. Flavour ranges from herbaceous, green pepper in coolest regions to blackcurrant and mulberry in Coonawarra, and dark chocolate and redcurrant in warmer areas such as SOUTHERN VALES and BAROSSA. Used both as single varietal and blended with Merlot or more traditionally with SHIRAZ. Reaching 72,000+ tonnes in '96.

Chardonnay (57,000 tonnes) Has come from nowhere since '70, with production forecast to top 89,000+ tonnes in '96. Best known for fast-developing buttery, peachy, at times syrupy, wines, but cooler regions such as PADTHAWAY, southern Victoria and the ADELAIDE HILLS can produce more elegant, tightly structured, ageworthy examples. Oak, too, is becoming less heavy-handed.

Grenache (20,400 tonnes) As everywhere, produces thin wine if over-cropped but given half a chance can do much better. Growing interest in old Dryland BAROSSA plantings, with increasing amounts being diverted from fortified to table wine making.

Mourvèdre (7,800 tonnes) Called Mataro in Australia. Has fulfilled the same role and has a similar destiny to GRENACHE.

Muscat Gordo Blanco (60,000 tonnes) An up-market version of Sultana: scented spicy wine v useful in cheap table and sparkling blends.

For key to grape variety abbreviations, see pages 7–13.

Pinot Noir (13,500 tonnes) Mostly used in sparkling. Growing awareness of exciting quality of table wines from S Victoria, TASMANIA and ADELAIDE HILLS; plantings are increasing rapidly.

Riesling (33,000 tonnes) For long the mainstay of the quality Australian wine industry, with a special place in the BAROSSA, Eden and CLARE valleys. Usually made bone-dry; can be glorious with up to 20 years bottle-age. Newer Botrytis Rieslings sparingly made but can be superb. Will hold its place in the sun.

Sauvignon Blanc (12,000 tonnes) Another recent arrival, with strong growth forecast. Usually not as distinctive as that of New Zealand, and made in many different styles from bland to pungent.

Semillon (31,300 tonnes) Before the arrival of CHARDONNAY, Semillon was the HUNTER VALLEY's answer to South Australia's RIESLING. Traditionally made without oak and extraordinarily long-lived, but now unfortunately often an oaky Chard substitute. Far from passé; production was projected to increase to 54,000+ tonnes in '96.

Shiraz (65,400 tonnes) Until the arrival of CABERNET in the '60s, Shiraz was unchallenged as Australia's red grape. Hugely flexible, with styles ranging from velvety/earthy in the HUNTER, spicy peppery and Rhône-like in central and southern Victoria; and brambly rummy sweet and luscious in BAROSSA and environs (eg PENFOLDS Grange). Recently discovered by overseas markets, with demand exceeding supply.

Wineries

Alkoomi Mt Barker ★★→★★★ (Ries) 86' 87' 88' 90' 92' 93' 94 ' 95' (Cab S) 80' 83' 84' 86' 87' 90' 91 94' 25-year veteran producing 25,000 cases of fine steely RIES and potent long-lived reds, incl rare Malbec.

All Saints NE Vic ★★→★★★ Once famous old family winery bought in '92 by BROWN BROTHERS: excellent Muscat and 'Tokay'.

Allandale Hunter Valley ★→★★ Small winery without v'yds, buying selected local grapes. Quality variable; can be good, esp CHARD.

Allanmere Hunter Valley ★★→★★★ (Chard) 85' 86' 88' 90' 91 '93' 94 Expat English doctor's small winery: excellent SEM, CHARD; smooth reds.

Amberley Estate Margaret River ★★→★★★ Highly successful and rapidly expanding maker of a full range of regional styles with Chenin Blanc the commercial engine, driving sales to 24,000 cases.

Angove's Riverland (SA) ★→★★ Large long-established MURRAY VALLEY family business in Adelaide and Renmark. Value-for-money whites, especially CHARD, also Colombard.

Arrowfield Upper Hunter ★★ Light CABERNET, succulent Reserve CHARDONNAY from large irrigated vineyard; also wooded SEMILLON. Majority owned by Japanese firm.

Ashbrook Estate Margaret River ★★★ Minimum of fuss; consistently makes 8,000 cases of exemplary SEM, CHARD, SAUV, Verdelho and CAB S.

Bailey's NE Vic ★★→★★★★ Rich old-fashioned reds of great character, esp SHIRAZ (formerly Hermitage) and magnificent dessert Muscat (★★★★) and 'Tokay'. Now part of ROTHBURY group.

Balgownie Bendigo/Ballarat ★★ Once fine pioneer now owned by MILDARA BLASS: recent vintages v disappointing. Look for pre-'91 CABS.

Bannockburn Geelong ★★★ (Chard) 89' 90' 91' 92' 94' (Pinot N) 84' 86' 88' 89' 91' 92' 94 Intense complex CHARD and PINOT N made using Burgundian techniques. 6,000 cases.

Basedow Barossa Valley ★★ Reliably good range of red and white wine; especially SEMILLON 'White Burgundy'. Acquired by GRANT BURGE in '94 but resold '96. (NB 94 CHARD.)

Bass Phillip Gippsland (Vic) ★★★→★★★★ (Pinot) 89 91 92 93 94' Tiny amounts of stylish, eagerly sought PINOT NOIR in three quality grades; very Burgundian in style.

Berri-Renmano Coop Riverland (SA) ★→★★ See Renmano.

Best's Great Western ★★→★★★ (Shiraz) 85' 87' 88' 90' 91' 92' 94 Conservative old family winery in GREAT WESTERN with very good mid-weight reds, and CHARD not half bad.

Blass, Wolf (Bilyara) Barossa ★★★ (Cab blend) 75 78 80 82 83 84 86 87 88 90 91' 92 Founded by BAROSSA's ebullient German winemaker, Wolf Blass, but now merged with MILDARA. Dazzling labels, extraordinary wine-show successes, mastery of blending varieties and areas, and lashings of new oak all continue, though indications/hopes are that less extreme sensations are on the way.

Botobolar Mudgee ★★ Marvellously eccentric little organic winery which exports successfully to the UK.

Bowen Estate Coonawarra ★★★ (Shiraz) 84 87 90 91 92 (Cab) 84 86 90' 91' 92 Small winery; intense CAB and spicy SHIRAZ.

Brand Coonawarra ★★→★★★ (Shiraz) 82 84 85 87 90 91 92 (Cab S) 79 81 82 84 87 90 91 92 Family estate now owned by MCWILLIAMS. Fine bold and stylish CHARD, CAB and SHIRAZ under Laira label.

Brookland Valley Margaret River ★★→★★★ Superbly sited 8,000-case winery and restaurant doing great things with SAUV, amongst others.

Bridgewater Mill Adelaide Hills ★★→★★★ Second label of PETALUMA; suave wines, SAUV BL and SHIRAZ best.

BRL Hardy See Hardy's.

Brokenwood Hunter Valley ★★★ (Shiraz) 86 87 89' 91' 93 94' (Cab) 75 77 80 81 83 86 87 89 91 Exciting CAB, SHIRAZ since '73 – Graveyard SHIRAZ outstanding. New winery ('83) added quality CHARD, SEM.

Brown Brothers Milawa (Vic) ★→★★★★ (Chard) 90 91 92 94 (Noble Ries) 78 82 84 85 88 90 Old family firm with new ideas: v wide range of delicate single-grape wines, many from cool mountain districts. CHARD, RIES. Dry white Muscat outstanding. CAB blend is best red. See also All Saints.

Buring, Leo Barossa ★★→★★★ (Ries) 71 73 75 79 82 84 86 87 88 90 91 92 94 'Chateau Leonay', old RIES specialists, now owned by LINDEMANS. Steady Reserve Bin is great with age (even great age), esp show reserve releases.

Campbells of Rutherglen NE Vic ★★ Smooth ripe reds and good dessert wines, the latter in youthful fruity style.

Cape Mentelle Margaret River ★★★→★★★★ (Zin) 87 88 90 91 92 93 (Cab) 78 81 82 83 86 88 90 91 92 Idiosyncratic robust CAB can be magnificent, CHARD even better; also Zin and v popular SAUV-SEM. David Hohnen also founded Cloudy Bay, NZ. Both bought in '90 by Veuve Clicquot.

Capel Vale SW (WA) ★★★ (Ries) 86 90 91 93 94 95' (Chard) 86 87 91 93 95' Outstanding whites, incl RIES, Gewürz. Also vg CAB.

Cassegrain Hastings Valley (NSW) ★★ Relatively new winery on NSW coast: grapes from local plantings. CHARD is best, Chambourcin striking.

Chambers' Rosewood NE Vic ★★→★★★ Good cheap table and great dessert wines, esp 'Tokay'.

Charles Melton Barossa ★★★ Tiny winery with bold luscious reds, esp Nine Popes, an old-vine GRENACHE and SHIRAZ blend. To watch.

Chapel Hill McLaren Vale (SA) ★★★→★★★★ (r) 90' 91' 92' 93' Once tiny, now a booming estate: extra-rich fruity-oaky CHARD, SHIRAZ and CABERNET; big show successes.

NB Vintages in colour are those you should choose first for drinking in 1997.

Chateau Hornsby Alice Springs (N Territory) ★ A charming aberration and magnet for tourists to Ayer's Rock.

Chateau Rémy Great Western/Avoca ★★ (Cab S) 84 86 88 90 91 92 94 Owned by Rémy Martin. Sparkling based on CHARD and PINOT N is much improved. Also good Blue Pyrenees CAB S.

Chateau Reynella S Vales ★★→★★★★ ('Vintage Port') 71 72 75 77 79 81 82 87 88 Historic winery serving as HQ for BRL HARDY group. VG 'Basket pressed' red table wines, superb vintage 'Port'.

Chateau Tahbilk Goulburn Valley ★★→★★★ (Marsanne) 70 72 74 75 80 82 86 88 89 90 92 94 (Shiraz) 68 71 76 79 80 81 84 86 88 91 92 (Cab) 62 64 65 66 71 76 79 81 83 86 88 90 92 Beautiful historic family estate: reds for long ageing, also RIES and Marsanne. Private Bins outstanding; value for money ditto.

> Australia aspires to become one of the major players in the international wine world, with a vision of exporting 540 million litres a year by 2010, and 820 million litres a year by 2025. If world exports were to remain at their 1993 level, this would place Australia fourth (not far behind Spain, and within spitting distance of France and Italy), with 17% of the world market by volume, and more by value. A tall order? Yes, but Australians have always been prepared to have a go, as the national saying goes.

Chateau Yaldara Barossa ★→★★ A plethora of brands incl Acacia Hill, Ch Yaldara, Lakewood and The Farms: oaky, slightly sweet, cheap – apart from eccentrically expensive The Farms.

Coldstream Hills Yarra Valley ★★★ (Chardonnay) 86 88 90 91 92 93' 94' (Pinot N) 87 88 90 91 92' 94' (Cab S) 85 86 88 90 91' 92' 93' Estate winery est'd '85 by wine critic James Halliday. Delicious PINOT N to drink young and Reserve to age lead Australia. Vg CHARD (esp Reserve wines), delicate CAB and Cab-Merlot.

Conti, Paul Swan Valley ★→★★ One of the doyens of the SWAN VALLEY, s'times exceptionally elegant SHIRAZ and intensely grapey Frontignac.

Coriole S Vales ★★→★★★ (Shiraz) 84 88 89 90 91 92 94' To watch especially for old-vine SHIRAZ Lloyd Reserve; best when nicely balanced by oak. Other wines are worthy.

Craiglee Macedon (Vic) ★★★ (Shiraz) 86 88 90 91 92 93 94 Recreation of famous 19th-C estate: fragrant peppery SHIRAZ, CHARD.

Croser Adelaide Hills ★★★→★★★★ 88 90 92 93 Now Australia's top sparkling CHARD-PINOT N blend. Offshoot of PETALUMA with Bollinger as partner. Lean, fine, with splendid backbone from Pinot N.

Cullens Willyabrup Margaret River ★★★ (Chard) 86 87 88 90 92 93 94 95' (Cab S-Merlot) 82 84 86 87 89 90 91 92 Mother-daughter team pioneered the region with strongly structured (esp Reserve) CAB-Merlot, substantial but subtle SAUV and bold CHARD: all real characters.

Dalwhinnie Pyrenees ★★→★★★ (Chard) 88 90 91 92 94 (Cab S) 82 85 86 88 90 91 92 93 94' 3,500-case producer of concentrated rich CHARD, SHIRAZ and CAB S, arguably the best in PYRENEES.

d'Arenberg S Vales ★★→★★★ Old firm now with a new lease of life; sumptuous SHIRAZ and GRENACHE, fine CHARDONNAY and sound RIESLING, all at misleadingly low prices.

De Bortoli Griffith (NSW) ★→★★★ (Noble Sem) 87 88 90 91 92 93' Irrigation-area winery. Standard reds and whites but magnificent sweet botrytised Sauternes-style Noble Sem. See also next entry.

De Bortoli Yarra Valley ★★→★★★ (Chard) 91 92 93 94 (Cab S) 88 90 91 92 94' Formerly Chateau Yarrinya: bought by DE BORTOLI and now YARRA VALLEY'S largest producer. Main label is more than adequate; second label, Windy Peak, vg value.

Delatite Central Vic ★★★ (Ries) 90 92 93 94 Winemaker Rosalind Ritchie makes appropriately willowy and feminine RIES, Gewurz, PINOT N and CAB from this v cool mountainside v'yd.

Devil's Lair Margaret River ★★→★★★ 100 acres of estate vineyards for opulently concentrated CHARDONNAY, PINOT NOIR and CABERNET-MERLOT. Production is 10,000 cases annually.

Diamond Valley Yarra Valley ★★→★★★ (Pinot) 88 90 91 92 93 94 Outstanding PINOT N in significant quantities; other wines good.

Domaine Chandon Yarra Valley ★★★ The showpiece of the YARRA VALLEY, leading Oz in fizz. Classic sparkling wine from grapes grown in all the cooler wine regions of Australia, with strong support from owner Moët & Chandon in France. Immediate success in United Kingdom under Green Point label.

Drayton's Bellevue Hunter Valley ★★ ('Hermitage') 81 85 86 87 91 93 94 Traditional 'Hermitage' and SEM, occasionally good CHARD; recent quality improvements after a lapse.

Dromana Estate Mornington Peninsula ★★→★★★ (Chardonnay) 90 91 92 94 (Cab S-Merlot) 88 90 92 94 Led energetically by Gary Crittenden: light fragrant CABS, Pinots, CHARDS. Second label: Schinus Molle.

Eaglehawk Clare ★→★★ Formerly Quelltaler. Once known for Granfiesta 'Sherry'. Recently good RIES and SEM. Owned by MILDARA BLASS.

Evans Family Hunter Valley ★★★ (Chard) 82 84 86 87 88 91 93 94 95' Excellent CHARD from small vineyard owned by family of Len Evans and made at ROTHBURY ESTATE. Fermented in new oak. Repays cellaring.

Elderton Barossa ★★ Old v'yds are base for flashy rich American-oaked CAB and SHIRAZ.

Evans and Tate Swan Valley ★★★ (Sem) 84 88 89 91 92 93 94 95' (Cab) 86 88 90 91 92 Fine elegant SEM, CHARD, CAB, Merlot from MARGARET RIVER, Redbrook. Going from strength to strength

Freycinet Tasmania ★★→★★★ (Pinot N) 90 91 93 94 East coast winery producing voluptuous rich PINOT N, good CHARD.

Geoff Merrill S Vales ★→★★★ (Sem-Chard) 87 88 89 90 91 (Cab) 85 86 88 90 91 92 Ebullient maker of Geoff Merrill, Mount Hurtle and Cockatoo Ridge wines. A questing enthusiast; the best wines are excellent, others can miss the mark.

Giaconda Central Vic ★★★ (Chard) 88 90 91 92 93 94 (Pinot N) 88 89 91 92 93 94 Very small ultra-fashionable winery near Beechworth: popular CHARDONNAY and PINOT N.

Goundrey Wines Great Southern (WA) ★★★ (Ries) 88 90 91 93 94 95' (Cab S) 85 87 88 89 90 91 Recent expansion and quality upgrade. Now in top rank: esp good CABERNET, CHARD and SAUV BL.

Grant Burge Wines Barossa ★★→★★★ Rapidly expanding output of silky-smooth reds and whites (vg CHARD 93) from the best grapes of Burge's large v'yd holdings. Burge was founder of KRONDORF. 70,000 cases.

Green Point See Domaine Chandon.

Grosset Clare ★★★→★★★★★ (Ries) 82 84 86 88 90 92 93 94 95' (Gaia) 86 90 91 92 93' Fastidious winemaker: very elegant RIES, recent spectacular Gaia CAB-Merlot.

Hanging Rock Macedon (Vic) ★→★★★ (Shiraz) 87 88 90 91 92 Eclectic range: budget Picnic wines; huge Heathcote SHIRAZ; complex sparkling.

Hardy's S Vales, Barossa, Keppoch etc ★→★★★ (Eileen Chard) **90 91 92 93' 94** ('Vintage Port') **45' 51' 54 56 69 71 73 75' 81' 87 88'** Historic company using and blending wines from several areas. Best are Eileen Hardy and Thomas Hardy series and (Australia's greatest) 'Vintage Ports'. Hardy's bought HOUGHTON and CHATEAU REYNELLA and, more recently, STANLEY. Chateau Reynella's beautifully restored buildings are now group headquarters. '92 merger with BERRI-RENMANO and public ownership (BRL Hardy) makes this Australia's second-largest wine co.

Heemskerk Tasmania ★★★ A major commercial operation; concentrating on high profile Jansz sparkling wine, sold to Tasmanian JAC group in '94.

Heggies Adelaide Hills ★★ (Ries) **86 88 90 91 92 93 94** (Chard) **90 91 92 93 94** (Botrytis Ries) **84 86 88 90 91 92** Vineyard at 500 metres in eastern Barossa Ranges owned by S SMITH & SONS. Excellent RIESLING and Botrytis Ries are separately marketed.

Henschke Barossa ★★★★ (Shiraz) **52 56 59 61 62 66 67 72 78 80 82 84 86 88 90 91' 92' 93'** (Cab S) **78 80 81 84 85 86 88 90 91 92 93'** 125-year-old family business, perhaps Australia's best, known for delectable SHIRAZ (especially Hill of Grace), vg CABERNET and red blends, but Eden Valley RIESLING and SEMILLON also excellent. New high-country Lenswood v'yds on ADELAIDE HILLS add excitement.

Hill-Smith Estate Adelaide Hills ★★→★★★ Another separate brand of S SMITH & SONS, perhaps best of all; CHARD, SAUV and CAB-SHIRAZ can be vg value.

Hillstowe Adelaide Hills ★★ Recent small winery using excellent fruit for intense vivid CHARD, PINOT N; also CAB-Merlot, SAUV BL.

Hollick Coonawarra ★★ (Chard) **90 91 92 93 94** (Cab-Merlot) **86 90 91 92'** Hollick family plus former TOLLANA maker: gd CHARD, RIES; much-followed reds, esp Ravenswood. Terra is trendy Second label.

Houghton Swan Valley ★→★★★ (Supreme) **84 86 87 89 91 93 94 95** The most famous old winery of WA. Soft ripe Supreme CHARD is top wine; a national classic. Also excellent CAB, Verdelho etc. See Hardy's.

Howard Park Mount Barker ★★ (Ries) **86 87 88 90 91 93' 94' 95'** (Cab S) **86 88 89 90 91 92' 93'** John Wade (formerly of WYNNS, now PLANTAGENET'S winemaker) handcrafts tiny quantities of scented RIESLING, CHARDONNAY and spicy CABERNET SAUVIGNON. Major winery expansion is under way. Second label: Madfish Bay.

Huntington Estate Mudgee (Cab S) **81 83 84 86 89 91' 92' 93'** Small winery; best in MUDGEE. Fine CABS, vg SHIRAZ. Invariably under-priced.

Idyll Geelong ★→★★ Small winery making Gewürz and CAB in v individual style. A pioneer exporter.

Jasper Hill Bendigo ★★★ (Shiraz) **80 82 85 86 90 91 92' 94'** Emily's Paddock SHIRAZ-Cab F blend and George's Paddock Shiraz from dryland estate v'yds are intense, long-lived and much admired; BENDIGO's best maker.

Jim Barry Clare Valley ★→★★★★ Some great v'yds provide good RIES, McCrae Wood SHIRAZ and convincing Grange pretender The Amagh.

Katnook Estate Coonawarra ★★★ (Chard) **86 90 92 94** (Cab S) **80 81 82 85 86 90' 91' 92** Excellent and pricey CAB and CHARD; also SAUVIGNON.

Krondorf Wines Barossa ★★→★★★ Part of MILDARA BLASS group with niche market brands: Show Reserve wines are best, esp CHARD.

Lake's Folly Hunter Valley ★★★★ (Chard) **85 86 87 89 91 92 93 94** (Cab S) **69 72 75 77 78 81 83 85 87 89 91 92 93** Small family winery of Max Lake. The pioneer of HUNTER CABERNET. Cab is v fine, complex. CHARDONNAY exciting and age-worthy.

Lark Hill Canberra District ★★ Most consistent CANBERRA producer, making esp attractive RIES, pleasant CHARD.

Leasingham Clare ★→★★★ Important medium-sized quality winery bought by HARDY's in '87. Good RIES, SEM, CHARD and CAB-Malbec. Various labels.

Leconfield Coonawarra ★★→★★★ (Ries) 90 91 92 94 (Cab S) 80 82 84 88 90' 91' 92' 94' COONAWARRA CAB of great style. RIES and CHARD well made by former TYRRELL winemaker.

Leeuwin Estate Margaret River ★★★★ (Chard) 82 83 85 86 87' 89 90 91 92' (Cab) 79 81 82 84 85 87 88 89 90 91' Leading W Australia estate, lavishly equipped, making superb (and v expensive) CHARD; vg RIES, SAUV and CAB.

Lindemans originally Hunter Valley, now everywhere ★→★★★ (Hunter Sem) 66 67' 70' 72 75 79' 86 87 91 92 94 (Hunter Shiraz) 59' 65' 66' 70 73 75 79 82 83 86 87 91 93 (Padthaway Chard) 85 86 87 88 90 91 92 93 94 (Coonawarra Red) 78 80 82 85 86 88 90 91 92 94 One of the oldest firms, now a giant owned by PENFOLDS. Owns BURING in BAROSSA, ROUGE HOMME in COONAWARRA, and important v'yds at PADTHAWAY. Vg CHARD and Coonawarra reds (eg Limestone Ridge, Pyrus). Pioneer of new styles, yet still makes fat, old-style 'Hunters'. Bin-number Classics can be vg. Dominant performer at wine shows.

Little's Hunter Valley ★→★★ Popular little tourist-trap winery producing very ordinary wines.

Marsh Estate Hunter Valley ★★ Substantial producer of good SEM, SHIRAZ and CAB of steady quality.

McWilliams Hunter Valley and Riverina ★→★★★ (Elizabeth Sem) 79' 80 81 82 84' 86 87' 88 89 91 94 Famous family of HUNTER VALLEY winemakers at Mount Pleasant: 'Hermitage' and SEMILLON – 'Elizabeth' is the only bottle-aged (6 yrs) Sem sold, vg value. McWilliams are also pioneers in RIVERINA with CABERNET SAUVIGNON and sweet white Lexia. Recent show results demonstrate high standards.

Mildara Coonawarra and Murray Valley ★→★★★ (Coonawarra Cab) 63' 64 70 71 78 79 80 82 85 86 88 90 91 92 'Sherry' and brandy specialists at Mildara on the Murray River, also make fine CAB S and RIESLING at COONAWARRA. Now own BALGOWNIE, BLASS, KRONDORF and YELLOWGLEN too.

Miramar Mudgee ★★ Some of MUDGEE's best white wines, especially CHARD and long-lived CAB.

Mitchells Clare ★★★ (Ries) 78 84 86 90 92 93 94 95 (Cab S) 78 80 82 84 85 90 92 Small family winery for excellent CAB and v stylish dry RIES.

Mitchelton Goulburn Valley ★★→★★★ Big modern winery, acquired by PETALUMA in '92. A wide range incl a vg wood-matured Marsanne, SHIRAZ; classic Blackwood Park RIES from GOULBURN VALLEY is one of Australia's v best value wines. Many enterprising blends and labels.

Montrose Mudgee ★★ Reliable underrated producer of CHARD and CAB blends. Now part of the ORLANDO group.

Moondah Brook Estate Gingin (WA) ★★ HOUGHTON v'yd 80km NW of Perth: v smooth flavourful CHARD, Chenin Bl, Verdelho and CAB.

Moorilla Estate Tasmania ★★→★★★ (Ries) 88 89 90 91 93 94' 95' Senior winery on outskirts of Hobart on Derwent River: vg RIESLING (94' superb), Traminer and CHARD; PINOT N rather disappointing. Several recent unsettling changes of ownership.

Morris NE Vic ★★→★★★★ Old winery at Rutherglen for Australia's greatest dessert Muscats and 'Tokays'; also recently vg low-price table wine.

Moss Wood Margaret River ★★★★ (Sem) 83 85 86 87 88 91 92 93 94 95' (Chard) 80 85 89 90 92 93 95' (Cab S) 74 77 80 81 83 86 87 90 91 92 93 To many the best MARGARET RIVER winery (only 29 vineyard acres). SEMILLON, CABERNET, Pinot and CHARD, all with rich fruit flavours, not unlike some of the top California wines.

Mount Hurtle See Geoff Merrill.

Mount Langi Ghiran Great Western ★★★ (Shiraz) 85 **86** 88 89 90 91' 92 93 94' Esp for superb rich peppery Rhône-like SHIRAZ wine, one of Australia's best cool-climate versions.

Mount Mary Yarra Valley ★★★★ (Pinot N) 78 79 82 83 85 **86** 87 89 90 91 92 94 (Cab S-Cab F-Merlot) 76 78 **79** 80 82 **84** 85 **86 88 90** 91 92 Dr John Middleton is a perfectionist making tiny amounts of suave CHARD, vivid PINOT N, and (best of all) CAB S-Cab F-Merlot. All age impeccably.

The taste of oak

The fashion of deliberately flavouring wine with oak began in California in the '60s and has been widely exaggerated and misused ever since. Formerly, barrels were used for their virtues as strong movable containers with enough porosity to allow very gradual oxidation of their contents. New barrels were needed for transport, but were used for storage only for the very finest, most concentrated wines, whose expected life was decades – by which time any oak flavour would be lost. The slower oak grows, the better its physical properties and the less pungent its aroma/flavour. American oak is very pungent; Baltic oak the opposite. Of the famous French oak forests, 'Limousin' (western) is relatively pungent and coarse, usable only for red wines; central 'Allier', 'Nevers', 'Tronçais' (top-grade), are most delicate, best for white or red wines; 'Bourgogne', 'Champagne', 'Vosges' (eastern) are intermediate. Barrels are put together over a fire which helps bend the staves. How much this burns (or 'toasts') the oak affects the wine as much as its origin.

Mountadam Barossa ★★★ (Chard) **82** 84 87 **89** 90 91 92 93 High Eden Valley winery of David and Adam Wynn. CHARDONNAY is rich, voluptuous and long. Other labels include David Wynn, Eden Ridge.

Normans McLaren Vale (Southern Vales) ★→★★★ Public listing in late '94 lifted the profile of this winery, but premium Chais Clarendon has always been excellent.

Orlando (Gramp's) Barossa ★★→★★★ (St Hugo Cab) 80 **82** 84 85 86 88 90 91 92 94 Great pioneering company, bought by management in '88 but now owned by Pernod Ricard. Full range from huge-selling Jacob's Creek 'Claret' to excellent Jacaranda Ridge CABERNET from COONAWARRA. See Wyndham Estate.

Paringa Estate Mornington Peninsula ★★★ Maker of quite spectacular CHARD, PINOT N and (late-picked) SHIRAZ winning innumerable trophies with tiny output of 2,000 cases.

Parker Estate Coonawarra ★★★→★★★★ Young estate making exceptional CAB, esp Terra Rossa First Growth.

Penfolds orig Adelaide, now everywhere ★★→★★★★ (Grange) 52 **53** 55 62 **63** 66 67 71 75 76 80 82 83 85 86' 88' 90' 91' (Bin 707) **64** 65 66 78 80 **83** 84 86 **88** 90' 91' 92' (Bin 389) 66 **70** 71 **82** 83 86 87 88 90 91 92 Ubiquitous and excellent: in BAROSSA VALLEY, CLARE, COONAWARRA, RIVERINA etc. Consistently Australia's best red wine company. Bought LINDEMANS in '90. Its Grange (was called 'Hermitage') is deservedly ★★★★. Bin 707 CABERNET not far behind. Other bin-numbered wines (eg Cab-SHIRAZ 389, Kalimna Bin 28 Shiraz) can be outstanding. Grandfather 'Port' is often excellent. The Penfolds/Lindemans group was taken over by SOUTHCORP, already owner of SEPPELT, in '90.

Penley Estate Coonawarra ★★★ High profile, no-expense-spared new-comer winery: rich, textured, fruit-and-oak CAB; also SHIRAZ-Cab blend and CHARD.

Petaluma Adelaide Hills ★★★★ (Ries) 79 80 82 84 86 88 90 91 93 94 95' (Chard) 77 80 81 86 90 92 93 (Cab S) 79 82 85 86 88 90 91 92 A rocket-like '80s success with COONAWARRA CAB S, ADELAIDE HILLS CHARDONNAY, CLARE VALLEY RIESLING, all processed at winery in Adelaide Hills. Red wines have become richer from '88 on, most recent vintages are outstanding. Also: BRIDGEWATER MILL. Now owns TIM KNAPPSTEIN and MITCHELTON. See also Croser.

Peter Lehmann Wines Barossa ★★→★★★ Defender of BAROSSA faith, Peter Lehmann, makes vast quantities of wine (some sold in bulk), with v fine 'special cuvées' under own label; now public listed and flourishing. NB Stonewell SHIRAZ (tastes of blackberries and rum) and dry RIESLING.

Pierro Margaret River ★★★ (Chard) 87 89 90 91 93 94 95' Highly rated maker of expensive, tangy SEM, SAUV BL and sophisticated barrel-fermented CHARD.

Piper's Brook Tasmania ★★★ (Ries) 79 82 84 85 89 91 92 93 94 (Chard) 82 84 86 87 88 91 92 93 Cool-area pioneer with vg RIES, PINOT N, excellent CHARD from Tamar Valley. Lovely labels. Second label: Ninth Island.

Plantagenet Mount Barker ★★★ (Chard) 86 88 89 90 91 93 95' (Shiraz) 77 79 82 83 85 86 88 90 91 92 (Cab S) 77 81 82 85 86 88 90 91 92 The region's largest producer: wide range of varieties, especially rich CHARDONNAY, SHIRAZ and vibrant potent CABERNET SAUVIGNON.

Primo Estate Adelaide Plains ★★★ Joe Grilli is a miracle worker given the climate; successes incl vg botrytised RIES, tangy Colombard, rich Joseph CAB and Merlot. Latest potent red: Moda Amarone.

Quelltaler See Eaglehawk.

Redman Coonawarra ★→★★★ (Cab S) 69' 70 71 76 79 87 90' 91' 92 93' 94' The most famous old name in COONAWARRA; makes two wines: 'Claret' and CABERNET. Quality reviving after a disappointing period.

Renmano Murray Valley ★→★★ Huge coop now part of BRL HARDY (see Hardy's). 'Chairman's Selections' value. Exceedingly voluptuous CHARD.

Reynold's Yarraman Estate Upper Hunter ★★ Former stone prison building to watch: winery of ex-HOUGHTON/WYNDHAM winemaker Jon Reynolds.

Rockford Barossa ★★→★★★ Small producer, wide range of thoroughly individual wines, often made from v old low-yielding v'yds; reds best. Sparkling Black Shiraz has super-cult status.

Rosemount Upper Hunter, McLaren Vale, Coonawarra ★★→★★★ Rich and unctuous HUNTER 'Show' CHARDONNAY is international smash. This, McLaren Vale Show Syrah and COONAWARRA CABERNET lead the wide range, which gets better every year.

Rothbury Estate Hunter Valley ★★★ (Cowra Chard) 81' 86 90 91 92 93 94 (Shiraz) 73' 75' 79' 80 81 83' 89 91 93 94' Now a public listed company under chairmanship of Len Evans. Traditional HUNTER Reserve SHIRAZ and SEMS to keep for ever. Rich buttery COWRA CHARD is vg and value too. Hunter Chard now oak-fermented. New: Chard and SAUV v'yds in Marlborough, NZ. Also owns BAILEY'S, ST HUBERTS, SALTRAM.

Rouge Homme Coonawarra ★★ (Shiraz-Cab S) 80 81 85 86 90' 91' 92 94' Separately branded and promoted arm of LINDEMANS with keenly priced CHARD and SHIRAZ-CAB leaders.

Rymill Coonawarra ★★→★★★ Descendants of John Riddoch carrying on the good work of the founder of COONAWARRA. Strong dense SHIRAZ and CABERNET esp noteworthy.

To decipher codes, please refer to 'Key to symbols' on front flap of jacket, or to 'How to use this book' on page 6.

St Hallett Barossa ★★★ (Old Block) 80 82 83 84 86 87 88 90' 91' 92' 93 Rejuvenated winery. 100-yr-old vines give splendid Old Block SHIRAZ. Rest of range (eg CHARD, SAUV-SEM) is smooth and stylish.

St Huberts Yarra Valley ★★→★★★ (Chard) 86 87 88 90' 91 92' 93 94' (Cab) 77 79 82 84 86 88 90 91 92 Acquired by ROTHBURY in late '92; accent on fine dry CHARD and smooth 'berry' CAB. Second label: Rowan.

St Leonards NE Vic ★★ Excellent varieties sold only 'cellar door' and by mailing list, incl exotics, eg Orange Muscat.

St Sheila SA p sw sp 36 22 38 Full-bodied fizzer. Ripper grog.

Saltram Barossa ★→★★★ Merged with ROTHBURY in '94. Pinnacle Selection is best label (esp COONAWARRA CAB); also good are Mamre Brook wines. Metala is assoc Stonyfell label for old-style Langhorne Creek Cab-SHIRAZ.

Sandalford Swan Valley ★→★★ Fine old winery with contrasting styles of red and white single-grape wines from SWAN and MARGARET RIVER areas. Wonderful old fortified Verdelho.

Scotchman's Hill Geelong ★★ Newcomer making significant quantities of v stylish PINOT N and good CHARD at modest prices.

Seaview S Vales ★★→★★★ Old winery now owned by SOUTHCORP. CHARD, SHIRAZ-CABERNET and single-varietal CAB s frequently rise above their station in life, while the sparkling wines are among Australia's best – now based on PINOT N and Chard.

Seppelt Barossa, Great Western, Keppoch etc ★★★ ('Hermitage') 70 78 81 84 85 86 89 90 91 92 (Salinger) 88 90 91 92 Far-flung producers of Australia's most popular sparkling (Great Western Brut); also good dessert and new range of Victoria-sourced table wines, from PADTHAWAY and BAROSSA (in South Australia). Top sparkling is highly regarded 'Salinger'. Part of SOUTHCORP, Australia's biggest wine company.

Sevenhill Clare Valley ★★ Owned by the Jesuitical Manresa Society since 1851; consistently good wine; reds (esp SHIRAZ) can be outstanding.

Seville Estate Yarra Valley ★★★ (Chard) 90 91 92 94 (Shiraz) 85 86 88 90 91 92 93 94' Tiny winery with CHARD, SHIRAZ, PINOT N and vg CAB. Sadly, Botrytis RIES is no more.

Shaw & Smith S Vales ★★★ Trendy young venture of flying winemaker Martin Shaw and Australia's first MW, Michael Hill-Smith. Crisp SAUV, vg unoaked CHARD, complex barrel-fermented Chard are the 3 wines.

Southcorp The giant of the industry, despite its naff name: owns PENFOLDS, LINDEMANS, SEPPELT, SEAVIEW, WYNNS, etc, etc.

Having languished in the wilderness, but as recently as the early 1960s having accounted for 80% of all red wine production, Mourvèdre, Grenache and Shiraz (in sharply ascending order of importance) are now receiving the care and attention they deserve. Old low-yielding vines, warm summers, skilled winemaking and judicious oak usage are producing wines of unique character, great quality and in increasing profusion.

S Smith & Sons (alias Yalumba) Barossa ★★→★★★ Big old family firm with considerable verve, using computers, juice evaluation etc, to produce full spectrum of high-quality wines, incl HILL-SMITH ESTATE. HEGGIES and Yalumba Signature Reserve are best. Angas Brut, a good value sparkling wine, and Oxford Landing CHARD are now world brands.

Stafford Ridge Adelaide Hills ★★→★★★ 20-acre estate of former HARDY's winemaker, Geoff Weaver, at Lenswood. V fine SAUV, CHARD, RIES and CAB-Merlot blend.

Stoniers Mornington Peninsula ★★★ (Chard) 90 91 92 93 94 (Pinot) 91 92 93 94 Has overtaken DROMANA ESTATE for pride of place on the Peninsula. CHARD, PINOT are consistently vg; Reserves outstanding.

Taltarni Great Western/Avoca ★★★ (Shiraz) 78 79 81 82 84 86 88 89 90 91 92 (Cab S) 79 81 82 84 86 88 89 90 91 92 Dominique Portet, brother of Bernard (Clos du Val, Napa), makes huge but balanced reds for long ageing, good SAUV and adequate sparkling.

Tarrawarra Yarra Valley ★★★ (Chard) 87 88 89 91 92 93 94 (Pinot N) 88 91 92 94 Multimillion dollar investment: limited quantities of idiosyncratic expensive CHARDONNAY and robust long-lived PINOT NOIR. Tunnel Hill is their second label.

Taylors Wines Clare ★→★★★ Large inexpensive range of table wines, now on the improve.

Tim Knappstein Wines Clare ★★★ Tim Knappstein make RIESLING, Fumé Blanc, CABERNET S-Merlot and Cab Franc wines; now wholly owned (and managed) by PETALUMA.

Tisdall Wines Goulburn Valley ★★ Went into hibernation after its recent acquisition in '93 by MILDARA BLASS; now is cautiously being revived with low-key re-launch.

'Tokay' Speciality of northeast Victoria. An aged intense sweet strong Muscadelle wine; less aromatic than Muscat but at best superb. Under EC rules the name will have to go.

Tollana Barossa ★★→★★★ Old company once famous for making brandy. Has latterly made some fine CABERNETS, CHARDONNAY and RIESLING. Acquired by PENFOLDS in '87.

Tulloch Hunter Valley ★ Old name at Pokolbin with reputation for dry red wines, CHARDONNAY and Verdelho. Now part of the PENFOLDS group but a shadow of its former self.

Tyrrell Hunter Valley ★★★ (Sem Vat 1) 70 75 76 77 79 86 87 89 90 92 94 (Chard Vat 47) 72 73 77 79 82 84 85 89 90 92 93 94 95 (Shiraz Vats) 73 75 77 79 80 81 83 85 87 89 91 92 Some of the v best traditional HUNTER VALLEY wines, 'Hermitage' and SEM. Pioneered CHARD with big rich Vat 47 – still a classic. Also delicate Pinot.

Vasse Felix Margaret River ★★★ (Cab S) 79 83 85 88 89 91 92 With CULLENS, pioneer of the MARGARET RIVER. Elegant CABERNETS, notable for mid-weight balance. Second label: Forest Hills (esp RIES, CHARD).

Virgin Hills Bendigo/Ballarat ★★★★ 74 75 78 79 80 82 83 85 87 88 90 91' 92' Tiny supplies of one red (a CABERNET-SHIRAZ-Malbec blend) of legendary style and balance.

Wendouree Clare ★★★★ 78 79 83 86 89' 90' 91' 92' Treasured maker (in tiny quantities) of some of Australia's most powerful and concentrated reds based on SHIRAZ, CAB S and Malbec; immensely long-lived.

Westfield Swan Valley ★→★★★ John Kosovich's CAB, CHARD and Verdelho show particular finesse for a hot climate, but he is now developing a new v'yd in the much cooler Pemberton region.

Wignalls Great Southern (WA) ★★→★★★ In the far southwest corner of Austalia (near Albany), Bill Wignall makes sometimes ethereal, always stylish PINOT NOIR.

Wirra Wirra S Vales ★★★ (Ries) 84 86 89 91 92 93 94 (Chard) 88 90 91 92 93 (Cab S) 77 80 84 87 90 91 92 High quality, beautifully-packaged wines making a big impact. Angelus is superb, top of range CAB.

Woodleys Barossa ★ Well-known for low-price 'Queen Adelaide'.

For key to grape variety abbreviations, see pages 7–13.

Woodstock McLaren Vale (Southern Vales) ★★ Ever-reliable maker of chunky, high-flavoured reds in regional style and luscious botrytis wines from esoteric varieties. 20,000 cases.

Wyndham Estate Branxton (NSW) ★→★★ Aggressive large HUNTER and MUDGEE group with brands: CRAIGMOOR, Hunter Estate, MONTROSE, Richmond Grove and Saxonvale. Acquired by ORLANDO in '90.

Wynns Coonawarra ★★★ (Shiraz) 53 54 55 63 65 70 82 85 86 88 **90** 91 92 (Cab S) **57** 58 59 60 62 82 85 86 88 **90** 91 92 PENFOLDS-owned COONAWARRA classic. RIES, CHARD, SHIRAZ and CAB are all very good, esp John Riddoch Cab, and Michael 'Hermitage'.

Yalumba See S Smith & Sons.

Yarra Burn Yarra Valley ★★ Estate making SEM, SAUV, CHARD, sparkling Pinot, PINOT N, CAB; acquired by BRL HARDY in '95, with changes in store.

Yarra Ridge Yarra Valley ★★→★★★ Expanding young (50,000 case) winery, v successful CHARD, CAB, SAUV BL, Pinot, all with flavour and finesse at modest prices. Now fully owned by MILDARA BLASS.

Yarra Yering Yarra Valley ★★★→★★★★ (Dry Reds) 78 79 **80 81 82** 83 84 85 87 90 91 92 93 Best-known Lilydale boutique winery. Esp racy powerful PINOT N, deep herby CAB (Dry Red No 1) and SHIRAZ (Dry Red No 2). Luscious daring flavours in red and white.

Yellowglen Bendigo/Ballarat ★★→★★★ High-flying sparkling winemaker owned by MILDARA BLASS. Recent dramatic improvement in quality, with top end brands like Vintage Brut, Cuvée Victoria and 'Y'.

Yeringberg Yarra Valley ★★★ (Marsanne) 83 84 86 88 **90** 91 92 93 94 (Cab) **74** 75 76 79 80 **81** 82 84 86 87 88 90 91 92 94' Dreamlike historic estate still in the hands of the founding family, now again producing very high quality Marsanne, Roussanne, CHARDONNAY, CAB and PINOT N, in minute quantities.

Zema Estate Coonawarra ★★→★★★ One of the last bastions of hand-pruning and picking in COONAWARRA making silkily powerful, disarmingly straightforward reds. 6,000 cases.

New Zealand

Heavily shaded areas are
the wine growing regions

Northland
Auckland O
Waiheke Island
Waikato
Gisborne
Hawke's
Bay
Wairarapa and
Nelson Martinborough
Nelson O
Marlborough
O Wellington
Blenheim
Canterbury
O Christchurch
Central Otago
O
Dunedin

Tasman Sea   *Pacific Ocean*

In the last 12 years or so New Zealand has made a world-wide name for wines (mainly white) of startling quality, well able to compete with those of Australia or California. In 1982 it exported 12,000 cases; in 1994 some 867,000. There are now over 18,000 vineyard acres.

White grapes prevail. Formerly dominant Müller-Thurgau has now been overtaken by the best varieties: in 1993 Chardonnay supplanted it as number one; in 1994 Sauvignon Blanc overtook Chardonnay. Next in line are Cabernet Sauvignon and Pinot Noir respectively, with Riesling, happily, gaining ground.

Intensity of fruit flavours and crisp (often too crisp) acidity are the hall-marks of New Zealand. No region on earth can match Marlborough Sauvignon Blanc for pungency. Barrel fermentation and/or ageing add to its complexity (or at least flavour). Marlborough also makes very fine sweet Rieslings with botrytis, and has proved its worth with excellent sparkling. 1989 was perhaps the first vintage to produce worthy reds: most are green/stalky. The principal areas and producers follow.

Allan Scott Blenheim ★→★★ Established '90. Ries, Chard and good Sauv Bl. Neighbour of famous CLOUDY BAY.

Ata Rangi Martinborough ★★★ V small but respected winery, est '80 primarily for reds. Outstanding Pinot N, also Cab-Merlot-Petit Syrah (Célèbre). Now also good Chard.

Auckland (r) 89 90 91 93 94 95 (w) 92 93 94 95 Largest city in NZ. Location of head offices of major wineries; many medium and small in outskirts, many bringing in fruit from other regions. Incl Henderson, Huapai, Kumeu and Waiheke Island wine regions.

Babich Henderson (nr Auckland) ★★ Large old Auckland family firm, highly respected in NZ for consistent quality and value. Also uses MARLBOROUGH, GISBORNE and HAWKE'S BAY grapes. Good Chards (esp Irongate, Stopbank), Sauv Bl (92 is big medal-winner, vg and value), Sém-Chard blend, Gewürz, Cab S and Cab-Merlot. Pinot N less good.

Brajkovich See Kumeu River.

Brookfields Hawke's Bay ★★ One of the area's top v'yds: outstanding Cab-Merlot, good Chard, Sauv Bl, Cab S, Pinot Gris.

Cairnbrae Wines (Marlborough) ★ Small winery producing quality range of Sauv Bl, Sém, Chard and Ries.

Canterbury (r) 89' 90 91 92 94 95 (w) 89' 90 91 94 95 Promising smallish South Island region. Long dry summers favour Pinot N, Chard and Riesling.

Central Otago (r) 90 93 94 95 (w) 90 93 94 95 Smallest and coolest region, in S of South Island, Chard and Pinot are best.

Cellier Le Brun Renwick, nr Blenheim ★★→★★★ Small winery est'd by son of Champagne family: some of NZ's best classic method sparkling incl NV, rosé (vg 90 91), Blanc de Blancs (90 91 exceptional).

A Choice for 1997 from New Zealand

Cabernet-Merlot blends: Stoneyridge Larose, Brookfields Reserve, Te Mata Coleraine

Pinot Noir from Ata Rangi (**94**), Fromm Reserve (**94**)

Chardonnays of Kumeu River (**94**), Babich Irongate (**94**), Collards Rothesay (**94**)

Sauvignon: Cloudy Bay (**94**), Hunters oak-aged (**94**), Nga Waka (**94**)

Chenin Blanc: The Milton Vineyard (**94**)

Riesling: Coopers Creek (**95**)

Blanc de Blancs classic sparkling: Daniel le Brun (**91**)

Chard Farm Central Otago ★★ Scenically NZ's No 1 winery, producing Pinot N, Chard, Ries. Also NZ's only ice wine.

Chifney Wines Martinborough ★ Promising Cab S and good Chard.

Church Road See MacDonald Winery.

Clearview Estate Hawke's Bay ★ New '92. Small producer of intense wines. Chard, Cab Franc and Merlot.

Cloudy Bay Blenheim ★★★★ Offshoot of W Australia's Cape Mentelle, with Veuve Clicquot a major shareholder. Top name worldwide for Sauv, Chard. Richly subtle Cab-Merlot 89 shows equal promise, as does Pelorus classic sparkling: rich and dense (87 88 89 90 91).

Collard Brothers Henderson (nr Auckland) ★★→★★★ Well-est'd small family winery using grapes of four main areas: top-award Chard from each, Sauv (esp Rothesay), Chenin, Ries, Cab-Merlot, Sém. Consistent (esp HAWKE'S B).

Cooks Hawke's Bay ★★ Large firm merged with CORBANS and McWilliams in '85. Good steady Chard (esp Winemakers Reserve). Also Cab-Merlot and late-harvest Sauv Bl-Sém.

Coopers Creek Huapai Valley (NW of Auckland) ★★ Small winery augmenting own grapes with GISBORNE, HAWKE'S BAY and MARLBOROUGH fruit. Exporting good Chard, Sauv Bl, Ries, dry and late-harvest. Also Cab S-Merlot and popular blends: Coopers Dry (white), Coopers Red.

Corbans Henderson (nr Auckland) ★★ Old-established, now one of biggest. Incorporates COOKS, McWilliams and (new premium brands) STONELEIGH (at MARLBOROUGH) and Longridge (HAWKE'S BAY). Vg Sauv, Chard, Ries, Cab. Corbans White Label collection is good low-priced. Additional premium wines: Robard & Butler label, classic Amadeus sparkling.

NEW ZEALAND

Crab Farm Hawke's Bay Small winery with good restaurant: Cab S (**91** vg) and Chard best.

Cross Roads (Hawke's Bay) Small winery with good Chard and Riesling as well as Sauv Bl and Cab S.

De Redcliffe Mangatawhiri (SE Auckland) ★→★★ Small progressive winery and resort 'Hotel du Vin'; good Chard, Ries, Sauv, Sém, Cab-Merlot.

Delegat's Henderson (nr Auckland) ★★ One of NZ's largest family-owned/ run wineries: v'yds in HAWKE'S BAY. Good Chard, Sauv; Proprietor's Reserve Cab-Merlots (**89 91 93 94 95**) outstanding. Also Chard and Sauv from MARLBOROUGH sold under successful Oyster Bay label.

Deutz Auckland ★★★ The Champagne firm in a pioneer joint venture with MONTANA. 'Classic method' is brisk, lively and vg.

Domaine Chandon (Blenheim) ★★ Start-up of Moët & Chandon in NZ. Still tiny.

Dry River (Martinborough) ★★→★★★ V small winery, but a perfectionist over a wide range: Ries, Chard, Pinot Gr, Gewürz, Pinot N etc.

Esk Valley Bayview (Hawke's Bay) ★★ Former large family firm, now merged with VILLA MARIA/VIDAL. Small range incl vg dry Chenin, Chard, Sauv and some of NZ's best reds, esp 90 91 Merlot and Merlot-Cab F, Cab-Merlot Private Bin.

Eskdale (Hawke's Bay) ★★ Boutique winery for v tasty Cab, Chard, Gewürz.

Fromm Blenheim New winery with highly promising Pinot N Reserve (95). Also Chard and Cab S.

Gibbston Valley (Otago) ★★ Pioneer Alan Braay was Otago's first viticulturist. Now successfully makes Pinot, Gewürz, Pinot Gr, Sauv, Chard.

Giesen Estate Canterbury (S Island) ★★★ German family winery. Main grapes are Ries, Chard, Sauv Bl and Gewürz. Great success with botrytised Riesling.

Gisborne (r) 89' 90 91 92 94 95 (w) 91 92 94 95 Site of 3 large wineries (CORBANS, MONTANA, PENFOLDS) and centre of large viticultural area incl MATAWHERO and Tolaga Bay. Good for Müller-T, Sém and esp Chard and Gewürz. Replanting due to '86 phylloxera led to improved grapes.

Gladstone Martinborough Small winery consistently producing top quality Sauv Bl, also Chard and Cab S.

Glenmark Wines (Waipara) ★★ Small, consistent medal-winner, esp Ries.

Glover's (Nelson) ★ Tiny winery for excellent Pinot N, Cab S and Sauv Bl.

Goldwater Waiheke I ★★ Small v'yd at sea edge, esp for drink-soon Cab-Merlot; also MARLB'H Chard (outstanding own-grown 92 93 Delamore).

Grove Mill Blenheim ★★ Excellent new winery bursting onto the scene with 89 Chard; Lansdowne in 90 91 93 94 even better. Vg Riesling, Blackbirch Cab, Drylands botrytis Sauv. Also Gewürz, Sauv, Pinotage.

Hawke's Bay (r) 89 90 91' 94 95 (w) 89 91' 92 94 95 Long-est'd, expanding wine region on east coast of N Island. Known for high quality grapes: some of NZ's best reds (esp Cab, Merlot), also big meaty Chards.

Heron's Flight Matakana (nr Auckland) Up-and-coming winery producing Cab-Merlot (**91 94** vg) and Chard.

Highfield Estate Marlborough ★→★★ Bought by international partnership in '91. Sauv, Chard, Ries, Merlot all promise well. Sparkling planned.

Hunters Marlborough ★★★ Well-est'd small progressive winery using only MARLBOROUGH grapes. Highly reputed for outstanding Sauv Bl (oaky 'Fumé' style), and reliably good Chard. Ries since '89. Also Cab S and Pinot N. Links with DOMAINE CHANDON.

Jackson Estate Blenheim ★★ Large private v'yd. First vintage 91: impressive Sauv (**91 92 94**), also Chard, Ries (esp sweet botrytis, one of NZ's best). New sparkling vg.

Johannesburg Cellars Blenheim Underground cellar and production of quality wines: Chard, Gewürz, Sauv Bl, Ries.

Kumeu River Kumeu (NW of Auckland) ★★★ Family-run winery (son Michael is NZ's first MW). Bold rich Chard and Sauv Bl, vg Cab-Merlot. Second label under family name, Brajkovich.

Landfall Wines Gisborne ★ New organically-run winery with good Chard (Revington Vineyard, 89 90), Sauv Bl and Pinot N.

Lawson Dry Hills Blenheim New small v'yd making intense Sauv and Ries.

Lincoln Vineyards Henderson (nr Auckland) ★ Medium-sized family winery; esp for Chard, Chenin and Cab. Other varietals: Sauv, Ries, Müller-T, Merlot.

MacDonald Winery Hawke's Bay (was 'Church Road') Owned by MONTANA, which, with Bordeaux producer Cordier, helped in making the reds. Chard and Cab S vg still sold under Church Road label.

Marlborough (r) 89 91 94' 95 (w) 89 91' 94 95 Now NZ's largest (and sunniest) wine region: at N end of South Island on stony plain formed by Wairau River. Well-suited to white varieties Chard, Sauv Bl and Ries. Promising Pinot N; Cab tends to greenness. Potential here for vg sparkling. Many top growers.

Martinborough (r) 89' 90 91 94 95 (w) 89' 90 91 94' 95 New smallish quality appellation in S Wairarapa (North Island). Stony soils, similar to MARLBOROUGH. Home of some of NZ's best Pinot Noir.

Martinborough Vineyards Martinborough ★→★★ Noted for Pinot N (89 91 94). Also good Chard, Sauv, Ries, Gewürz.

Matawhero nr Gisborne ★★ Small winery known esp for Gewürz. Also conc aromatic Chard, Sauv-Sém. Reds are Cab-Merlot, Pinot N, Syrah.

Matua Valley NW of Auckland ★★→★★★ One of NZ's best, most consistent wineries. Wide range incl Chard (from Ararimu & Judd Estate, GISBORNE), Sauv Bl and Fumé Blanc. Top-class Cab S (v fine Ararimu). Vg MARLBOROUGH wines under Shingle Peak label.

Merlen Wines Marlborough ★→★★ German-born Almuth Lorenz makes excellent Chard and Ries (90 91 92 94). Also Sauv, Gewürz.

Mills Reef Bay of Plenty ★★ Producer (since '89) of ripe fat Chard (Elspeth), also Sauv Bl from HAWKE'S BAY grapes, Ries, Cab, Merlot.

Millton nr Gisborne ★★ Small organic producer. Good Chard (Clos de Ste-Anne 89 outstanding) and Ries (dry and late harvest, vg 91). Splendid barrel-fermented Chenin Bl (87 90 92) like fine Anjou.

Mission Greenmeadows (Hawke's Bay) ★★ Oldest continuing wine estate in NZ, French mission-founded and still run by the Society of Mary. Good Sém-Sauv, Ries and Cab-Merlot; Reserve Cab much best wine.

Montana Auckland and Hawke's Bay ★★ NZ's largest wine enterprise: wineries in GISBORNE, MARLBOROUGH; incorporating Penfolds label (in NZ only). Pioneer vineyards in Marlborough, also uses Gisborne and HAWKE'S BAY grapes. Marlborough labels: Sauv, Chard (vg, outstanding Show Reserves), Ries, Cab and Pinot. Gisborne Chard also big-selling and sound. Original Lindauer sparkling joined by vg cuvée DEUTZ. An input of French know-how in recent Cordier joint venture should improve Hawke's Bay reds.

Morton Estate Tauranga (Bay of Plenty) ★★→★★★ Expanding winery bought by Mildara (of Australia) in '89: excellent Chard (range is best black label, white then yellow labels). Also Fumé Bl, Gewürz, Ries and good classic method sparkling (89 90 91).

Nautilus (Marlborough) ★→★★ Owned by Australia's Yalumba: young winery with vg Chard (92 93 94) from MARLBOROUGH, Sauv from HAWKE'S BAY.

Nelson (r) 89' 90 91 93 94 95 (w) 91' 93 94 95 Neighbour of MARLBOROUGH, with v'yds hilly not flat, wineries boutique, not large: quality excellent.

Neudorf Nelson ★ Outstanding Chard and Ries, also good Sauv and Pinot N.

Nga Waka Martinborough Relatively new winery consistently producing top quality Ries, Chard and vg Sauv Bl.

Ngatarawa nr Hastings (Hawke's Bay) ★★ Boutique winery in old stables of est'd HAWKE'S BAY family. Well-made, elegant Glazebrook label Cab-Merlot. Also vg Chard (Alwyn) and good Sauv Bl.

Nobilo NW of Auckland ★→★★ NZ's largest family winery: own plus GISBORNE, HAWKE'S BAY, MARLBOROUGH fruit. Good Chard (Marlborough and Dixon V'yd), vg pungent Sauv, Sém; long recognized for ageable red: eg Cab, Pinotage. White Cloud is off-dry commercial line.

Oyster Bay See Delegats.

Palliser Estate Martinborough ★ Ambitious new winery: first vintage '89. Good Chard, Sauv Bl, Ries; also promising Pinot N (**91**).

Pask, C J Hawke's Bay ★★ Rising star of the area; outstanding Chard, and Sauv Bl since 91. Also good Cab S, Pinot N and Cab-Merlot.

Pegasus Bay N Canterbury ★★→★★★ New 100-acre estate venture in warm Waipara sub-region. Pinot N, Cab F, Chard, Ries show great promise.

Robard & Butler See Corbans. NB Amberley Riesling.

Rongapai Waikato (S of Auckland) ★★ German-influenced winery esp for botrytised Ries and Chard. Now with Pinot, Merlot, Cab and Cab-Merlot.

Rothbury NZ ★★ Off-shoot of Australia's Rothbury Est. Ries, Chard both good.

Sacred Hill (Hawke's Bay) ★★ Up and coming for Chard; also first-class Cab.

St Jerome Estate Henderson (nr Auckland) Small winery growing Cab-Merlot and maturing in French oak for two yrs (90 vintage esp good).

St Nesbit Karaka (S of Auckland) ★★→★★★ A lawyer's passion. One barrique-matured red blend: Cab S-Cab F-Merlot (vg **91**). Also rosé (when main vintage below standard).

Seifried Estate Upper Moutere (nr Nelson) ★→★★ Small winery started by an Austrian: esp Chard, Sauv, Ries (dry and late-harvest).

Selak's Kumeu (NW of Auckland) ★★ Small stylish winery. Esp Chard (Founders Selection best), vg Sauv, classic sparkling. Grapes: local, MARLBOROUGH, GISBORNE, HAWKE'S BAY. Reds less good.

Stoneleigh See Corbans.

Stonyridge Waiheke Island ★★★→★★★★ Boutique winery concentrating on two reds in Bordeaux style: Larose is exceptional, one of NZ's best (esp 87 93 94, also good **91**); Airfield is second label (**92**).

Te Kairanga Martinborough ★★ Largest winery in region, with underground facilities. Chard, Sauv Bl, Pinot N coming together.

Te Mata Havelock North (Hawke's Bay) ★★★→★★★★★ Image-leader for HAWKE'S BAY; consistently fine Chard (esp Elston), plus Sauv from nearby v'yds, plus one of NZ's v best Cab blends, 'Coleraine' Cab-Merlot (**85 88 89 90 91 94 95**) from proprietor's home v'yd. Awatea is second label, also quite outstanding.

Vavasour nr Blenheim ★★★ First vintage 89. 91 Chards top quality; Dashwood Chard also good. Vg Fumé Bl, Sauv, Cab S-Merlot, Cab S-Cab F Reserve.

Vidal Hastings (Hawke's Bay) ★★ Atmospheric old winery, merged with VILLA MARIA. Vg HAWKE'S BAY Chards (**90 91 92 94**), Cab S, Cab-Merlot, Fumé Bl. Reserves best; Private Bin fair value.

Villa Maria Mangere (S Auckland) ★★ Important company including VIDAL and ESK VALLEY. Ihumatao (nr Auckland airport), GISBORNE and HAWKE'S BAY grapes. Very wide range; esp Reserve oak-fermented Chard, Sauv (and wooded 'Fumé'), Gewürz, Cab and Cab-Merlot.

Waipara Springs N Canterbury ★★ Recent producer of model Sauv Bl, Chard (**93**) and Pinot N (**90 91** good). To follow (most is exported).

Wairau River Marlborough ★ Small winery, full-flavoured Sauv and Chard.

Wellington (r) 89 90 91 93 94 95 (w) 91 94 95 Capital city and official name of the region which includes Wairarapa, Te Horo and MARTINBOROUGH.

South Africa

Since the relaxation of the apartheid boycotts in 1994 exports of Cape wine have risen dramatically, converting a chronic 20-year local surplus into a shortage within two years. Quality is rising in response to international demand and tastes, but most exported wine is still shipped in bulk (the UK is the largest market) at low prices. However, the end of a quota system which confined the vineyards of some 4,500 growers to traditional, irrigated and warm areas has encouraged exploration of virgin land in cooler regions, promising an altogether new look to Cape wine by the turn of the millenium. New vineyard patterns and overseas tastes will also change South Africa's plantings, currently about 250,000 acres and 80% bulk varieties such as Cinsaut, Chenin Blanc and Colombard – a legacy of South Africa's big brandy industry. New vineyards are mainly of new clones: imported Cabernet Sauvignon, Merlot, Shiraz, Chardonnay and Sauvignon Blanc. Fairly low per capita wine consumption (in the world's eighth-largest producer) has begun to rise and there are signs that South Africa's Black majority, always beer drinkers, may begin to take more to wine the future.

Allesverloren r ★→★★ (Cab) 89 91 Old 395-acre family estate, best known for 'Port' (86 88 90). Also hefty well-oaked but not always long-lived CAB and Shiraz (89) from hot wheatlands district of Malmesbury.

Alphen ★ Gilbeys brand name for wines.

Alto r ★★→★★★ (Cab) 89 Atlantic-facing mountain v'yds S of S'BOSCH. Solid CAB, Cab-Merlot, Shiraz. Best since mid-'80s (with new French oak).

Altydgedacht r w ★→★★ (Cab S) 89 Durbanville estate, best for CAB; also gutsy Tintoretto blend of Barbera and Shiraz.

Avontuur r w ★★ (r) 89 90 91 93 200-acre ST'BOSCH v'yd, bottling since '87. Soft B'x-style blend, Avon Rouge; CAB, Merlot, promising CHARD.

Backsberg r w ★★→★★★ (r) 89 91 92 (Merlot) 90 92 93 (Chard) 91 92 93 Prize-winning 395-acre PAARL estate. Pioneered oak-fermented CHARD in mid-'80s, with US advice. Delicious B'x blend Klein Babylonstoren is best (91 92); also vg oaked SAUV John Martin.

Bellingham r w ★★★ Big-selling, improving brand of DGB. Sound reds (93), popular whites (94), especially sweet soft CAPE RIES-based Johannisberger wines (exported as Cape Gold), CHARDONNAY, SAUVIGNON BLANC and Chard-Sauv blend 'Sauvenay'.

Bergkelder Big STELLENBOSCH company, member of Oude Meester group, making/distributing many brands (FLEUR DU CAP, GRUNBERGER), 12 estate wines. First to use French oak (now 10,000 barrels), top for fine oaked reds.

Bertrams r ★★ (Cab) 89 90 91 94 (Shiraz) 89 Gilbeys brand of varietals, esp Shiraz, PINOTAGE. Also Robert Fuller Reserve B'x-style blend.

Beyerskloof r ★★★ (Cab S) 89 90 91 93 New small STELLENBOSCH property, devoted to vg tannic deep-flavoured CAB S. Also now PINOTAGE 95.

Blaauwklippen r w ★★→★★★ (r) 89 90 91 STELLENBOSCH winery with some of the Cape's best bold reds, esp CAB Reserve. Also S Africa's top Zin (89 90 91); patchy but improving CHARD; good off-dry RIES.

Bloemendal r w ★→★★ (Chard) 90 91 92 Sea-cooled Durbanville estate. Fragrant CAB; still CHARD no more. Now good Chard Cap Classique.

Boberg Controlled region for fortified wines, comprising PAARL and TULBAGH.

Bon Courage W SW ★→★★ ROBERTSON estate; vg dessert GEWURZ and CHARD.

Boplaas r w ★★ Estate in dry hot Karoo. Earthy deep 'Vintage Reserve Port' esp since '87 (**91 94**), fortified Muscadels. Links with Grahams in Portugal.

Boschendal w sp ★★ (Chard) 89 91 94 617-acre estate in PAARL area. Good CHARD and METHODE CAP CLASSIQUE (Chard and Pinot); also Cape's first 'blush' off-dry Blanc de Noirs. Improving Merlot (91).

Bouchard-Finlayson r w ★★★ (Chard) 93 94 95 (Pinot) 93 First French-Cape partnership (Paul Bouchard of Burgundy, Peter Finlayson at Hermanus, Walker Bay). Maiden release 91. PINOT N firm, even hard. Also outstanding Sauv 95.

Breede River Valley Fortified and white wine region E of Drakenstein Mts.

Buitenverwachting r w sp ★★★ (Chard) 91 93 94 Exceptional, German-financed, recently replanted CONSTANTIA v'yds. Vg SAUV (plain, oaked Bl Fumé) 95, CHARD, B'x blend (89 90 92 95), Merlot (91). Lively clean METHODE CAP CLASSIQUE (Pinots Gr and Bl). Restaurant worthy of a Michelin star.

Cabernet Sauvignon Most successful in COASTAL REGION. Range of styles: sturdy long-lived to elegant fruity. More use of new French oak since '82 giving great improvements. Best recent vintages: 84 86 87 89 91.

Cabrière Estate ★★→★★★ Franschhoek growers of good NV CAP CLASSIQUE under Pierre Jordan label (Brut Sauvage, CHARDONNAY-PINOT N and Belle Rose Pinot N). Now also bottling v promising 'new clone' Pinot N 94.

Cap Classique, Méthode Term used for classic method sparkling wine in South Africa.

Cape Independent Winemakers Guild Young group of winemakers in the vanguard of quality. Holds an annual auction of progressive-style wines.

Cavendish Cape ★★ Range of remarkably good 'Sherries' from the KWV.

Chardonnay S Africa came to Chard relatively late, beginning mid-'80s. Now offering many styles, incl unwooded and blended – with SAUV, among others. Currently nearly 200 labels, and growing; a decade ago, 3.

Chateau Libertas ★ Big-selling CAB S brand made by SFW.

Chenin Blanc Workhorse grape of the Cape; one vine in three. Adaptable, sometimes vg. KWV makes good value example. See also Steen.

Cinsaut The principal bulk-producing French red grape in S Africa; formerly known as 'Hermitage'. V seldom seen with varietal label.

Claridge r w ★★→★★★ (r) 91 92 (Chard) 91 92 93 94 Good barrel-fermented CHARD and CAB-Merlot from small new winery at Wellington nr PAARL.

Clos Malverne r ★★ 89 90 91 93 Small STELLENBOSCH winery. Individual dense CAB S, PINOTAGE (92) from own v'yds and purchased grapes.

Colombard French white grape, as popular in Cape as in California. Crisp lively flowery, usually short-lived wine; often in blends, or for brandy.

Constantia Once the world's most famous sweet Muscat-based wine (both red and white), from the Cape. See Klein Constantia.

Craighall Brand for successful new CHARD-SAUV (94), CAB-MERLOT, by Gilbeys.

De Wetshof w sw ★★→★★★ (Chard) 91 93 94 Pioneering ROBERTSON estate. Powerful CHARD (varying oakiness: Finesse lightly, Bateleur heavily) and fresh dry RHINE RIES. Also dessert GEWURZ, Rhine Ries under Danie de Wet label and own-brand Chards for British supermarkets.

Delaire Vineyards r w ★★ (Chard) 92 93 94 (r) 90 91 92 93 Full-flavoured CHARD, Bordeaux blend named Barrique (91 92), and elegant off-dry RHINE RIES, from young winery at Helshoogte Pass above STELLENBOSCH.

Delheim r w d sw ★★→★★★ Big winery with mountain v'yds nr STELLENBOSCH. Elegant barrel-aged CAB S-Merlot-Cab F Grand Reserve (91). Value Cab (89 91 92), PINOTAGE, Shiraz; variable PINOT N; improving CHARD, SAUV. Sweet wines: GEWURZ, outstanding botrytis STEEN.

NB Vintages in colour are those you should choose first for drinking in 1997.

266

Die Krans Estate ★★ Karoo semi-desert v'yds making rich full Vintage Reserve 'Port'. Best are 93 93. Also traditional fortified sweet Muscadels.

Dieu Donné Vineyards r w ★★→★★★ Franschhoek CO: CHARD 92 94, CAB 93.

Douglas Green ★→★★ Cape Town merchants marketing range of sound wines incl 'Sherries' and 'Ports' mostly from KWV.

Drostdy ★ Good range of 'Sherries' from BERGKELDER.

Drostyhof r w ★ Well-priced range incl CHARD made at TULBAGH cellars.

Edelkeur ★★★★ Excellent intensely sweet noble rot white by NEDERBURG.

Eikendal Vineyards r w ★★ (red, Merlot) 90 91 92 93 (Chard) 91 92 93 94 Swiss-owned 100-acres v'yds and winery in STELLENBOSCH. Vg CHARD; CAB S-Merlot blend Classique. Fresh whites incl semi-sweet CHENIN BL.

Estate Wine Official term for wines grown and made (not necessarily bottled) on registered estates. Regulations relaxed in '94; estates may now buy in up to 40% of their production. Estate status is not lost if bottling is off property.

Fairview Estate r w dr sw ★★→★★★ (r) 90 91 (Chard) 90 91 92 93 94 Enterprising PAARL estate with wide range. Best are Reserve Merlot (89 91 93), Bordeaux blend Charles Gerard Reserve (90 94), Shiraz Reserve (90 91 93 94). Also lively Gamay, good CHARD, plus sweet CHENIN BL. Experiments in progress to obtain softer, fruitier wines. Also v interesting Sémillon and Shiraz-Merlot blend.

Fleur du Cap r w sw ★★→★★★ (r) 90 91 92 Value range from BERGKELDER at STELLENBOSCH: vg CAB (89 91) esp since '86. Also Merlot (90 91 92), Shiraz (86 88 91), fine GEWURZ, botrytis CHENIN.

Gewürztraminer The famous spicy grape of Alsace. Naturally low acidity makes it difficult to handle at the Cape.

Glen Carlou r w ★★→★★★ (r) 89 90 91 93 (Chard) 90 91 92 93 94 PAARL property. Good B'x blends Grande Classique (90 91 93), Les Trois, Merlot; gd CHARD Res (91 92 93). V promising 'new clone' PINOT N from '94.

Graça ★ Huge-selling slightly fizzy white blend in Portuguese-style bottle.

Graham Beck Winery w sp ★★ Avant-garde ROBERTSON winery (57 acres); first METHODE CAP CLASSIQUE Brut Royale NV and CHARD well-received.

Grand Cru (or Premier Grand Cru) Term for a totally dry white, with no quality implications. Generally to be avoided.

Grangehurst Wines (★★★) Among a crop of new STELLENBOSCH wineries, buying grapes from range of suppliers. Specializing in PINOTAGE (93 94), and concentrated CAB-Merlot Res (93).

Groot Constantia r w ★★→★★★ Historic gov't-owned estate nr Cape Town. Superlative Muscat in early 19th C. Renaissance in progress; so far fine CAB (esp CAB-Merlot blend Gouverneur's Reserve 89 91 90 92), Weisser (Rhine) Ries-Gewürz Botrytis blend (92), dessert Muscat.

Grünberger ★ BERGKELDER brand: range of dry and semi-sweet STEEN whites.

Hamilton Russell Vineyards r w ★★★ (Pinot N) 90 91 93 (Chard) 92 93 95 The pioneer. Good PINOT N 'Burgundy' vineyards and cellar. Small yields, French-inspired vinification in cool Walker Bay. Many awards. Vg Sauv Bl 95 and Southern Right label (incl PINOTAGE).

Hanepoot Local name for the sweet Muscat of Alexandria grape.

Hartenberg r w ★★ STELLENBOSCH estate, recently modernized; rich Shiraz.

Haute-Cabrière ★★★ Franschhoek hillside estate run jointly with valley-floor Clos Cabrière, now making outstanding Pinot N (since 94) from recently imported new clone (deeper colours, luscious fruit). V'yd planted with Burgundian density.

Jordan Vineyards ★★→★★★★ New property in southwest STELLENBOSCH hills: vg SAUV BL 94, CHARD 93 94 95 and Cab S 93. Husband and wife team is California-trained.

J P Bredell ★★★ Stellenbosch v'yds. Rich dark deep Vintage Reserve 'Port' from Tinta Barocca and Souzão grapes.

Kanonkop r ★★★ (r) 89 90 91 94 Outstanding N STELLENBOSCH estate. Individual powerful CAB (**89 91**) and B'x-style blend Paul Sauer (**86 89 91**). Benchmark PINOTAGE (**89 91 94**), oak-finished since '89 (v improved).

Klein Constantia r w sw ★★★ (r) 89 90 (Chard) 92 93 95 Old subdivision of famous GROOT CONSTANTIA neighbour. Emphatic CHARD, SAUV (**95** is outstanding), fine powerful CAB, B'x-style blend Marlbrook first released in '88 (**89 90 91**). From 86, Vin de Constance revives the 18th-C Constantia legend (annual release, now **91**). Revamped since early '80s.

KWV The Kooperatieve Wijnbouwers Vereniging, S Africa's national wine coop created in 1917: vast premises in PAARL, a range of good wines, esp Cathedral Cellars reds, RIES, 'Sherries', sweet dessert wines. In '92 gave up widely criticized quotas, freeing growers to plant v'yds at will.

La Motte r w ★★★ (r) 89 91 92 Lavish new Rupert family estate nr Franschhoek. Lean but stylish, intensely flavoured reds: Merlot, B'x-style blend Millennium (**90 91**), among top three for Cape Shiraz (**89 91 92**). Racy SAUV.

L'Avenir ★★ Well-appointed new STELLENBOSCH property, promising CAB (**93**), PINOTAGE (**94**) and Chard (**95**).

Laborie r w ★★ KWV-owned showpiece PAARL estate. White and red blends.

Landgoed Afrikaans for 'estate': on official seals and ESTATE WINE labels.

Landskroon r w ★→★★ Family estate owned by Paul and Hugo de Villiers. Good dry reds, esp Shiraz, CAB S, Cab F.

Late Harvest Term for a mildly sweet wine. 'Special Late Harvest' must be naturally sweet. 'Noble Late Harvest' is highest quality dessert wine.

Le Bonheur r w ★★★ (r) 89 91 STELLENBOSCH estate often producing classic tannic minerally CAB; big-bodied SAUV BL revived with 93.

Leroux, JC ★★ Old brand revived as BERGKELDER's sparkling wine house. SAUV (charmat), PINOT (top METHODE CAP CLASSIQUE is well-aged). Also CHARD.

Lievland r w ★★→★★★ (r) 89 90 STELLENBOSCH estate for top Cape Shiraz (**89 90 92**), vg CAB S, Merlot, Cab S-F-Merlot (outstanding **92**) and Cab S-Merlot 'DVB' 92. Also whites incl intense RIES, off-dry promising Sauternes-style wine.

Long Mountain ★→★★ New Pernod-Ricard label, buying grapes from coops under Australian direction (Robin Day, formerly of Orlando). Cab, Chard, Chenin.

Longridge Winery ★★ New ('95) STELLENBOSCH winery, purchasing grapes and wines from many sources. Incl CHARD, CAB, Shiraz. Also good CAP CLASSIQUE sp.

L'Ormarins r w sw ★★→★★★ (r) 89 91 (Chard) 89 90 One of two Rupert family estates nr Franschhoek. CAB (**86 89**) and vg claret-style Optima (**89**), also Shiraz (**89**). Fresh lemony CHARD, forward oak-aged SAUV, outstanding GEWURZ-Bukketraube botrytis dessert wine.

Louisvale w ★★→★★★ (Chard) 90 91 92 93 95 STELLENBOSCH winery. Attractive CHARD, now also good Cab and Cab-Merlot (from '94) and SAUV BL-Chard.

Meerlust r w ★★★ (r) 89 90 91 Old family estate nr STELLENBOSCH; Cape's only Italian winemaker. Outstanding Rubicon (Médoc-style blend **89 91**), Cab (**91**), Merlot (**89 91 93**), PINOT (**89 91**). Now CHARD too: 1st release leesy, oaky **95**.

Middelvlei r ★★ 89 90 STELLENBOSCH estate: good PINOTAGE (**90 91**), CAB (**89 90 91**), Shiraz (**90**) and Chard (**95**).

Monis ★→★★ Well-known wine co of PAARL, with fine 'Special Reserve Port'.

Morgenhof r w dr s/sw ★★ Fresh start at elaborately refurbished S'BOSCH estate. New French owner and change of winemaker (from '92). Improving reds (**93** Cab, Merlot); dry white (excellent **93 95** Sauv, Chard); s/sw whites; 'Port'.

To decipher codes, please refer to 'Key to symbols' on front flap of jacket, or to 'How to use this book' on page 6.

Mulderbosch Vineyards w ★★★ Penetrating consistently impressive SAUV from mountain v'yds nr s'BOSCH: one oak-fermented, the other fresh bold. Also CHARD and B'x-style blend Faithful Hound (93).

Muratie Ancient STELLENBOSCH estate, esp 'Port'. Recent revival incl excellent CAB (93 94) and B'x blend 94.

Nederburg r w p dr sw s/sw sp ★★→★★★★ (r) 89 91 92 93 (Chard) 92 93 94 95 Well-known large modern PAARL winery (producing 650,000 cases pa; 50 different wines). Bicentenary in '92. Own grapes and suppliers'. Sound CAB, Shiraz, CHARD, RIES, blends in regular range. Limited Vintages, Private Bins often outstanding. Fresh approach with late '80s top reds: emphasis on richer fruitier flavour, more barrel-ageing. '80s pioneer of botrytis dessert wines, now benchmarks: CHENIN, GEWURZ, SAUV, Muscat, even Chard consistently good. Stages Cape's biggest annual wine event, the Nederburg Auction. See Edelkeur.

Neethlingshof r w sw ★★→★★★ (r) 89 90 91 93 (Chard) 91 Estate: replanted with classic grapes, cellar revamped at huge cost since '85. Run jointly with nearby STELLENZICHT. Vg CAB S (89 90 93), Merlot, CHARD joining fresh SAUV BL, excellent GEWURZ (91 93) and blush Bl de Noir. Consistently judged national champion botrytis wines from RIES (92 93), and Sauv Bl. New B'x-blend Lord Neethling Res 93.

Neil Ellis Wines r w ★★★ (r) 89 90 91 92 (Chard) 93 94 95 Good wines from Jonkershoek Valley nr STELLENBOSCH (16 widely spread coastal v'yds). Spicy structured CAB S; excellent SAUV (94 95); full bold CHARD.

Nuy Cooperative Winery r w dr sw sp ★★ Small Worcester Coop, frequent local-award winner. Outstanding dessert wines; fortified Muscadels (91), regularly excellent Cape COLOMBARD. Good S African RIES.

Oak Village Wines ★ Export brand, blend of good coop cellar wines from STELLENBOSCH, incl CAB-Shiraz, SAUV-CHENIN BL blends.

Overgaauw r w ★★ (r) 89 90 91 Old family estate nr STELLENBOSCH; CHARD, CAB S, Merlot (90 91 92), and Bordeaux-style blend Tria Corda (89). Also 'Vintage Port' 85 and excellent 86 from 5 Portuguese varieties.

Paarl Town 30 miles northeast of Cape Town and the surrounding demarcated district, among the best in the country, particularly for 'Sherry'.

Paul Cluver w ★★ Label launched '92. Good SAUV, RHINE RIES, CHARD (93): grapes from cool upland Elgin Coastal region. Wines made by NEDERBURG.

Pinot Noir Like counterparts in California and Australia, Cape producers struggle for fine, burgundy-like complexity. They are getting closer. Best are HAUTE-CABRIERE, BOUCHARD FINLAYSON, HAMILTON RUSSELL, MEERLUST. Very promising from CABRIERE ESTATE and GLEN CARLOU, both 'new clone' growers.

Pinotage S African red grape cross of PINOT N and CINSAUT, useful for high yields and hardiness. Can be delicious but overstated flamboyant esters often dominate. Experiments/oak-ageing show potential for finesse.

Plaisir de Merle r w ★★★ New SFW-owned cellar nr PAARL producing its first reds from own v'yds in '93: Cab-Merlot is outstanding, supple, also CHARD (93). Paul Pontallier of Château Margaux is consultant.

Pongracz ★★→★★★ Successful value non-vintage sp METHODE CAP CLASSIQUE from PINOT N (75%) and CHARD, produced by the BERGKELDER, named after the exiled Hungarian ampelographer who upgraded many Cape vineyards.

Premier Grand Cru See Grand Cru.

Rhebokskloof r w ★→★★ (r) 90 92 (Chard) 92 200-acre estate behind PAARL mountain: sound small range. CAB is promising.

Rhine Riesling Produces full-flavoured dry and off-dry wines but reaches perfection when lusciously sweet as 'Noble Late Harvest'. Generally needs 2 yrs or more of bottle-age. Also called Weisser Riesling.

Riesling S African Ries (actually Crouchen Bl) is v different from RHINE RIES, providing neutral easy-drinking wines. Known locally as Cape Ries.

Robertson District inland from Cape. Mainly dessert wines (notably Muscat); white table wines on increase. Few reds. Irrigated v'yds.

Roodeberg ★→★★ Red KWV blend: equal PINOTAGE-Shiraz-Tinta Barocca-CAB. Can age well (76 in '96!): sweetish porty, 'typical old Cape red style'.

Rooiberg Cooperative Winery ★ Successful big-selling ROBERTSON range of more than 30 labels. Good CHENIN BL, COLOMBARD.

Rozendal r ★★★ (r) 89 91 92 93 Small STELLENBOSCH v'yd: excellent CAB-Merlot.

Ruiterbosch ★★ Individual wines from outside traditional Cape vine area nr Indian Ocean. Striking SAUV BL, RHINE RIES. Made at BOPLAAS cellars.

Rust en Vrede r ★★★ Well-known estate just E of STELLENBOSCH: red only. Good CAB (89 90 91), Shiraz (89 90 91), vg Rust en Vrede blend (89 91).

Rustenberg r w ★★★ (red except Pinot N) 82 84 86 89 91 92 93 The most beautiful old STELLENBOSCH estate, founded 300 yrs ago, making wine for last 100. Grand reds, esp Rustenberg Gold CAB (89 91 92), Médoc-style blend. Also lighter Cab-CINSAUT-Merlot and Cab (89 91 92). Variable PINOT (91 92).

Sauvignon Blanc Adapting well to warm conditions. Widely grown and marketed in both wooded and unwooded styles. Also v sweet.

Saxenburg Wines r w dr sw ★★ (r) 91 92 STELLENBOSCH v'yds and winery; recently prize-winning. Distinctive powerful reds: robust deep-flavoured PINOTAGE (92); Cab (91 92), Shiraz (91 92 93). Also Merlot, Chard and Sauv Bl.

Simonsig r w sp sw ★★→★★★ (r) 89 90 91 92 93 (Chard) 91 92 95 Malan family s'BOSCH estate with a wide range: vg CAB, Shiraz (89 91), CHARD, PINOTAGE (89 92 93), dessert-style GEWURZ (90 92). First release in '92 of widely acclaimed Cab-Merlot Tiara (90 91 92 93). Also popular oak-matured white Vin Fumé and first Cape METHODE CAP CLASSIQUE (esp 91).

Simonsvlei r w p sw sp ★ One of S Africa's best-known coop cellars, just outside PAARL. A prize-winner with PINOTAGE.

Steen S Africa's commonest white grape, said to be a clone of CHENIN BL. It gives strong tasty lively wine, sweet or dry: short-lived if dry, lasts better when off-dry or sweet. Normally better than S African RIES.

Stein Name often for commercial blends of s/sw white. Not to be despised.

Stellenbosch Town and demarcated district 30 miles E of Cape Town (oldest town in S Africa). Heart of wine industry, with the 3 largest companies. Most top estates, esp for red wine, are in mountain foothills.

Stellenbosch Farmers' Winery (SFW) The world's fifth largest winery, South Africa's biggest after KWV: equivalent of 14M cases pa. Range incls NEDERBURG; top is ZONNEBLOEM. Wide selection of mid-/low-price wines.

Stellenryck Collection r w ★★★ Top quality BERGKELDER range. RHINE RIES, Fumé Blanc, CAB (89 91) among S Africa's best.

Stellenzicht ★★★ Recently replanted STELLENBOSCH v'yds; outstanding wines now, across wide range: B'x blend (94), Cab (93), Shiraz (94), Sauv (95).

Swartland Wine Cellar r w dr s/sw sw sp ★ Vast range of wines from hot, dry wheatland: big-selling and low-price, esp CHENIN dry, off-dry or sweet, but (recently) penetrating, SAUV, also big no-nonsense PINOTAGE.

Talana Hill r w ★★ (r) 88 89 (Chard) 91 92 93 New STELLENBOSCH winery: good CHARD and Bordeaux-style blend Royale (91 92).

Tassenberg ★ Popular PINOTAGE blend by SFW, fondly called 'Tassies'. Trad student and braaivleis (barbecue) wine. Oom Tas, a dry Muscat, is white equivalent.

Thelema r w ★★★★ (Cab S) 89 90 91 92 93 (Chard) 93 94 95 Prize-winning, vogue v'yds and winery at Helshoogte, above s'BOSCH. Impressive, individual fruity-minty CAB and B'x blend (starting with vg 91), now Merlot too (92). Excellent CHARD, and unoaked SAUV.

Theuniskraal w ★ TULBAGH estate: whites incl S Afrian RIES, GEWURZ.

Tulbagh Demarcated district N of PAARL best known for white THEUNISKRAAL, TWEE JONGEGEZELLEN and dessert wines from DROSTDY. See also Boberg.

Twee Jongegezellen w sp ★★ Old TULBAGH estate, helped pioneer cold fermentation in '60s, night harvesting in '80s; still in Krone family (18th-C founder). Esp whites, best known: popular dry TJ89 (mélange of a dozen varieties), Schanderl off-dry Muscat-GEWURZ. Recently METHODE CAP CLASSIQUE Cuvée Krone Borealis Brut (CHARD, PINOT N) with Champagne's Mumm.

Uiterwyk r w ★ Old estate W of s'BOSCH. CAB 'Carlonet' (**89 90**), Merlot, whites.

Uitkyk r w ★★ (r) 89 90 92 Old estate (400 acres) W of STELLENBOSCH esp for Carlonet (big gutsy CAB, **89 90**), Carlsheim (SAUV) white. Recently CHARD.

Van Loveren r w sw sp ★★ Go-ahead ROBERTSON estate: range incl muscular CHARD (**93 94 95**), good Pinot Gr (**92 93**); scarcer Fernão Pires, Hárslevelü.

Veenwouden ★★ Promising Merlot (**93**) from new PAARL property owned by Geneva-based opera tenor, Deon Van der Walt.

Vergelegen w (★★★) One of Cape's oldest wine farms, founded 1700. Long neglected, now spectacularly restored. Les Enfants series marked '92 re-launch with wine from bought-in grapes; good CHARD (**93 94**) and SAUV. Impressive CABERNET and now new deep complex 94 Merlot.

Vergenoegd r w sw ★→★★ Old family estate in S s'BOSCH supplying vg 'Sherry' to KWV and bottling CAB S, Shiraz. New B'x-style blend 'Reserve' (**89 90**).

Villiera r w ★★→★★★ PAARL estate with popular NV METHODE CAP CLASSIQUE 'Tradition'. Top SAUV BL (**93 94 95**), good RHINE RIES, fine B'x-style blend CAB-Merlot 'Cru Monro' (**90 91 92**). Recently exceptional Merlot (**91 92**).

Vredendal Cooperative r w dr sw ★ S Africa's largest coop winery in hot Olifants River region. Big range: mostly white, reds incl Ruby Cab.

Vriesenhof r w ★★→★★★ (Cab) 89 91 92 (Chard) 93 94 95 Highly rated CAB and B'x blend Kalista (**89 91**). Since '88, vg CHARD. Also Pinot Bl.

Warwick r w ★★→★★★ (r) 89 90 92 STELLENBOSCH estate run by one of Cape's few female winemakers. CAB and vg Médoc-style blend Trilogy (**89 90 92**), Cab F (**89 90 92**) and Chard (**92 94**). New in '96 was PINOTAGE from 22-yr-old untrellised bush vines.

Weisser Riesling See Rhine Riesling.

Welgemeend r ★★→★★★ (r) 89 90 92 Boutique PAARL estate: Médoc-style blends (**90 92**), delicate CAB, and Amadé (Grenache-Shiraz-PINOTAGE).

Weltevrede w dr sw ★→★★ (Chard) 93 94 Progressive ROBERTSON estate. Blended, white, fortified. Vg CHARD, Gewürz (**93 94**), White Muscadel (**91**).

Wine of Origin The Cape's appellation contrôlée, but without French crop yield restrictions. Demarcated regions are described on these pages.

Woolworths Wines Best S African supermarket wines, many specially blended. Top are CHARDS, young reds incl Merlot, B'x-style blends.

Worcester Demarcated wine district round BREEDE and Hex river valleys, E of PAARL. Many coop cellars. Mainly dessert wines, brandy, dry whites.

Yonder Hill ★★ Small new STELLENBOSCH mountainside property, launching with vg Merlot and CAB-Merlot blend (**93**).

Zandvliet r ★→★★ (Shiraz) 89 94 Estate in the ROBERTSON area making fine light Shiraz and recently a CAB S and Chard and a cap classique sparkler.

Zevenwacht r w ★★ (Cab S) STELLENBOSCH wines Sound CAB (**91**), Rhine Ries (**93**). Also one-off Pinot N (**94**). New winemaker from '96 should revive.

Zonnebloem r w ★★ (Cab S) 91 Good quality range from SFW incl CAB S, Merlot (**88 91 92 93**), Bordeaux-style blend Laureat (**89 90 91**) launched '92, Shiraz, PINOTAGE (**87 89 91 92**), SAUV BL and CHARD (**91 93 95**) and, new '94, a Sauv-Chard blend. Bl de Bl is among best dry Chenins of the Cape – drink young.

A little learning…

A few technical words

The jargon of laboratory analysis is often seen on back-labels of New World wines. It has crept menacingly into newspapers and magazines. What does it mean? This hard-edged wine-talk, unsympathetic as it is to most lovers of wine, is very briefly explained below.

The most frequent technical references are to the ripeness of grapes at picking; the resultant alcohol and sugar content of the wine; various measures of its acidity; the amount of sulphur dioxide used as a preservative; and occasionally the amount of 'dry extract' – the sum of all the things that give wine its character.

The **sugar** in wine is mainly glucose and fructose, with traces of arabinose, xylose and other sugars that are not fermentable by yeast, but can be attacked by bacteria. Each country has its own system for measuring the sugar content or ripeness of grapes, known in English as the '**must weight**'. The chart below relates the three principal ones (German, French and American) to each other, to specific gravity, and to the potential alcohol of the wine if all the sugar is fermented.

Sugar to alcohol: potential strength

Specific Gravity	°Oechsle	Baumé	Brix	% Potential Alcohol v/v
1.065	65	8.8	15.8	8.1
1.070	70	9.4	17.0	8.8
1.075	75	10.1	18.1	9.4
1.080	80	10.7	19.3	10.0
1.085	85	11.3	20.4	10.6
1.090	90	11.9	21.5	12.1
1.095	95	12.5	22.5	13.0
1.100	100	13.1	23.7	13.6
1.105	105	13.7	24.8	14.3
1.110	110	14.3	25.8	15.1
1.115	115	14.9	26.9	15.7
1.120	120	15.5	28.0	16.4

Residual sugar is the sugar left after fermentation has finished or been artificially stopped, measured in grams per litre.

Alcohol content (mainly ethyl alcohol) is expressed in percent by volume of the total liquid. (Also known as 'degrees'.)

Acidity is both fixed and volatile. **Fixed acidity** consists principally of tartaric, malic and citric acids which are all found in the grape, and lactic and succinic acids which are produced during fermentation. **Volatile acidity** consists mainly of acetic acid, which is rapidly formed by bacteria in the presence of oxygen. A small amount of volatile acidity is inevitable and even attractive. With a larger amount the wine becomes 'pricked' – to use the graphic Shakespearian term. It starts to turn to vinegar.

Total acidity is fixed and volatile acidity combined. As a rule of thumb for a well-balanced wine it should be in the region of one gram per thousand for each 10°Oechsle (see above).

pH is a measure of the strength of the acidity, rather than its volume. The lower the figure the more acid. Wine usually ranges from pH 2.8 to 3.8. Winemakers in hot climates can have problems getting the pH low enough. Lower pH gives better colour, helps stop bacterial spoilage and allows more of the SO_2 to be free and active as a preservative.

Sulphur dioxide (SO_2) is added to prevent oxidation and other accidents in winemaking. Some of it combines with sugars etc and is known as '**bound**'. Only the '**free**' SO_2 that remains in the wine is effective as a preservative. **Total SO_2** is controlled by law according to the level of residual sugar: the more sugar, the more SO_2 needed.

A few words about words

In the shorthand essential for this little book (and often in bigger books and magazines as well) wines are often described by adjectives that can seem irrelevant, inane – or just silly. What do 'fat', 'round', 'full', 'lean' and so on mean when used about wine? Some of the more irritatingly vague and some of the more common 'technical' terms are expanded in this list:

Acid
To laymen often a term of reproval, meaning 'too sharp'. But various acids are vital to the quality and preservation of wine (especially white) and give it its power to refresh. For those on the advanced course, malolactic, or secondary, fermentation is the natural conversion of tart malic (apple) acid to lactic, replacing the immediate bite of a wine with milder, more complex tastes. The undesirable acid is acetic, smells of vinegar and is referred to as 'volatile'. Too much and the wine is on the way out.

Astringent
One of the characters of certain tannins, producing a mouth-drying effect. Can be highly appetizing, as in Chianti.

Attack
The first impression of the wine in your mouth. It should 'strike' positively, if not necessarily with force. Without attack it is feeble or too bland.

Attractive
Means 'I like it, anyway'. A slight put-down for expensive wines; encouragement for juniors. At least refreshing.

Balance See Well-balanced.

Big
Concerns the whole flavour, including the alcohol content. Sometimes implies clumsiness, the opposite of elegance. Generally positive, but big is easy in California and less usual in, say, Bordeaux. So the context matters.

Bitterness
Another tannic flavour, usually from lack of full ripeness.
Much appreciated in N Italy but looked on askance in most regions.

Body
The 'weight', the volume of flavour and alcohol in wine. See Big and Full.

Botrytis See page 100.

Charming
Rather patronizing when said of wines that should have more impressive qualities. Implies lightness and possibly a slight sweetness. A standard comment regarding Loire Valley wines.

Corky
A musty taint derived (far too often) from an infected cork. Can be faint or blatant, but is always unacceptable.

Crisp
With pronounced but pleasing acidity on the palate; fresh and eager.

Deep/depth
This wine is worth tasting with attention. There is more to it than the first impression; it fills your mouth with developing flavours as though it had an extra dimension. (Deep colour simply means hard to see through.) All really fine wines have depth.

Earthy
Used of a sense that the soil itself has entered into the flavour of the wine. Often positive, as in the flavour of red Graves.

Easy
Used in the sense of 'easy come, easy go'. An easy wine makes no demand on your palate (or your intellect). The implication is that it drinks smoothly, doesn't need maturing, and all you remember is a pleasant drink.

Elegant
A professional taster's favourite term when he or she is stuck to describe a wine whose proportions (of strength, flavour, aroma), whose attack, middle and finish, whose texture and whose overall qualities call for comparison with other forms of natural beauty.

Extract
The components of wine (apart from water, alcohol, sugar, acids etc) that make up its flavour. Usually the more the better, but 'over-extracted' means harsh, left too long extracting matter from the grape skins.

Fat
Wine with a flavour and texture that fills your mouth, but without aggression. Obviously inappropriate in eg a light Moselle, but what you pay your money for in Sauternes.

Finesse See Elegance.

Finish See Length.

Firm
Flavour that strikes the palate fairly hard, with fairly high acidity or tannic astringency giving the impression that the wine is in youthful vigour and will age to gentler things. An excellent quality with high-flavoured foods, and almost always positive.

Flesh
Refers to both substance and texture. A fleshy wine is fatter than a 'meaty' wine, more unctuous if less vigorous. The term is often used of good Pomerols, whose texture is notably smooth.

Flowery
Often used as though synonymous with fruity, but really meaning floral, like the fragrance of flowers. Roses, violets etc are some of those specified.

Fresh
Implies a good degree of fruity acidity, even a little nip of sharpness, as well as the zip and zing of youth. All young whites should be fresh: the alternative is flatness, staleness. . . ugh.

Fruity
Used for almost any quality, but really refers to the body and richness of wine made from good ripe grapes. A fruity aroma is not the same as a flowery one. Fruitiness usually implies at least a slight degree of sweetness. Attempts at specifying *which* fruit the wine resembles can be helpful. Eg grapefruit, lemon, plum, lychee. On the other hand writers' imaginations frequently run riot, flinging basketfuls of fruit and flowers at wines which could well be more modestly described.

Full
Interchangeable with full-bodied. Lots of 'vinosity' or wineyness: the mouth-filling flavours of alcohol and 'extract' (all the flavouring components) combined.

Heady
The sense that the alcohol content is out of proportion.

Hollow
Lacking a satisfying middle flavour. Something seems to be missing between the first flavour and the last. Characteristic of wines from greedy proprietors who let their vines produce too many grapes. A very hollow wine is 'empty'.

Honey
A smell and flavour found especially in botrytis-affected wines, but often noticeable to a small and seductive degree in any mature wine of a ripe vintage.

Lean
More flesh would be an improvement. Lack of mouth-filling flavours; often astringent as well. Occasionally a term of appreciation of a distinct and enjoyable style.

Length
The flavours and aromas that linger after swallowing. In principle the greater the length, the better the wine. One second of flavour after swallowing = one 'caudalie'. Twenty caudalies is good; 50 terrific.

Light
With relatively little alcohol and body, as in most German wines. A very desirable quality in the right wines but a dismissive term in eg reds where something more intense/ weighty is desired.

Maderized
Means oxidized until it smells/tastes like Madeira. A serious fault unless intentional.

Meaty
Savoury in effect with enough substance to chew. The inference is lean meat; leaner than in 'fleshy'.

Oaky
Smelling or tasting of fresh-sawn oak, eg a new barrel. Appropriate in a fine wine destined for ageing in bottle, but currently often wildly overdone by winemakers to persuade a gullible public that a simple wine is something more grandiose. Over-oaky wines are both boring and tiring to drink.

Plump
The diminutive of fat, implying a degree of charm as well.

Rich
Not necessarily sweet, but giving an opulent impression.

Robust
In good heart, vigorous, and on a fairly big scale.

Rough
Flavour and texture give no pleasure. Acidity and/or tannin are dominant and coarse.

Round
Almost the same as fat, but with more approval.

Structure
The 'plan' or architecture of the flavour, as it were. Without structure wine is bland, dull, and won't last.

Stylish
Style is bold and definite; wears its cap on its ear.

Supple
Often used of young red wines that might be expected to be more aggressive. More lively than 'easy' wine, with good quality implications.

Well-balanced
Contains all the desirable elements (acid, alcohol, flavours etc) in appropriate and pleasing proportions.

The Options Game

Like-minded wine-lovers who enjoy discussing wines together to improve their knowledge cannot do better than to play the Options Game. The game was devised by the MC of the wine world, Australian Len Evans of Rothbury Estate. It is played during a meal and needs only a chairman who knows what the wine is, and any number of players who don't. Each player is given a glass of the same wine. The chairman asks a series of questions: one choice is the truth.

For example: 'Is this wine from California, France or Australia?' France is correct. Any player who has said France collects a point. 'Is it from Bordeaux, the Rhône or Provence?' Bordeaux is correct; another point. 'Is it from St-Emilion, Graves or the Haut-Médoc?' Haut-Médoc is correct; another point. 'Is it from Pauillac, St-Julien or Margaux?' Pauillac is right; another point. 'Is it a first, second or fifth growth?' Fifth is right; another point. 'Is it Grand-Puy-Lacoste, Lynch-Bages or Batailley?' Grand-Puy-Lacoste is right. 'Is it from 1982, 1983 or 1985?' The answer is 1985: the wine is identified.

Each time a player answers correctly he or she scores a point. There is no penalty for being wrong. So you can start by believing it was a California wine and still be in at the kill. There are many possible variations, including a knock-out version which can be played with a ballroom full of guests, who stand so long as they are answering correctly, and sit when they drop out. 'Options' is a great game for the competitive, and a wonderful way to learn about wine.

What to drink in an ideal world

Wines approaching their peak in 1997

Red Bordeaux
Top growths of 87, 85, 83, 81, 79, 78, 75, 70, 66, 61, 59
Other crus classés of 89, 88, 87, 86, 85, 83, 82, 81, 79, 70, 66, 61
Petits châteaux of 95, 94, 93, 90, 89, 88, 86, 85, 82

Red Burgundy
Top growths of 92, 90, 89, 88, 87, 85, 83, 82, 80, 79, 78, 71, 69, 66, 64
Premiers Crus of 92, 90, 89, 88, 87, 85, 83, 78
Village wines of 94, 93, 92, 90, 89

White Burgundy
Top growths of 93, 92, 90, 89, 88, 86, 85, 83, 79, 78...
Premiers Crus of 94, 93, 92, 91, 90, 89, 88, 86, 85, 83, 78...
Village wines of 95, 94, 93, 92, 90, 89, 88

Rhône reds
Hermitage/top northern Rhône reds of 88, 86, 85, 83, 82, 79, 78, 71, 70, 69...
Châteauneuf-du-Pape of 90, 89, 88, 86, 85, 83, 82, 81

Sauternes
Top growths of 88, 86, 85, 83, 82, 81, 79, 78, 76, 75, 71, 70, 67...
Other wines of 90, 89, 88, 86, 85, 83, 82, 81, 79, 76, 75...

Alsace
Grands Crus and late-harvest wines of 90, 89, 88, 86, 85, 83, 81, 78, 76, 67...
Standard wines of 94, 93, 92, 91, 90, 89, 88, 85...

Sweet Loire wines
Top growths (Anjou/Vouvray) of 93, 90, 88, 86, 85, 78, 76, 75, 71, 64...

Champagne
Top wines of 86, 85, 83, 82, 81, 79, 78, 76, 75...

German wines
Great sweet wines of 90, 89, 88, 86, 85, 83, 76, 71, 67...
Auslesen of 92, 90, 89, 88, 86, 85, 83, 79, 76, 71...
Spätlesen of 93, 92, 91, 90, 89, 88, 86, 85, 83, 79, 76...
Kabinett and QbA wines of 93, 92, 91, 90, 89, 88, 85, 83...

Italian wines
Top Tuscan reds 91, 90, 88, 86, 85, 82, 79, 78
Top Piedmont reds 90, 89, 88, 87, 86, 85, 83, 82, 79...

California wines
Top Cabernets/Zinfandels of 91, 87, 86, 85, 84, 82, 81, 80, 79, 78, 77, 76, 75
Most Cabernets etc of 93, 90, 89, 87, 86, 85...
Top Chardonnays of 94, 91, 90, 89, 87, 83...
Most Chardonnays of 94, 93, 91, 90, 89...

Australian wines
Top Cabernets and Shiraz of 91, 89, 88, 86, 84, 82, 80, 79, 75...
Most Cabernets etc of 91, 90, 89, 88, 87, 86...
Top Chardonnays of 94, 92, 90, 89, 88, 87, 86
Most Chardonnays of 94, 93, 92, 91...
Top Semillons and Rieslings of 92, 91, 90, 88, 86, 82, 79...

Vintage Port
83, 82, 80, 70, 66, 63, 60, 55, 48, 45...

The right temperature

No single aspect of serving wine makes or mars it so easily as getting the temperature right. White wines almost invariably taste dull and insipid served warm and red wines have disappointingly little scent or flavour served cold. The chart below gives an indication of what is generally found to be the most satisfactory temperature for serving each class of wine.

		°F	°C	
		68	20	
		66	19	
Room temperature		64	18	Best red wines especially Bordeaux
		63	17	
	Red burgundy	61	16	
	Best white burgundy	59	15	Chianti, Zinfandel Côtes du Rhône
	Port, madeira	57	14	
		55	13	*Ordinaires*
		54	12	Lighter red wines eg Beaujolais
Ideal cellar	Sherry	52	11	
	Fino sherry	50	10	Rosés Lambrusco
	Most dry white wines	48	9	
	Champagne	46	8	
Domestic fridge		45	7	
		43	6	Most sweet white wines
		41	5	Sparkling wines
		39	4	
		37	3	
		35	2	
		33	1	
		32	0	

Masters of Wine

The Institute of Masters of Wine was founded in London in 1953 to provide an exacting standard of qualification for the British wine trade. A small minority pass its very stiff examinations, even after rigorous training, both theoretical and practical. (They must be able to identify wines 'blind', know how they are made, and also know the relevant EC and Customs regulations.) In all, only 193 people have qualified to become Masters of Wine. Thirty-two 'Masters' are women.

In 1988 the Institute, aided by a grant from the Madame Bollinger Foundation, opened its examinations for the first time to non-British candidates. The first to pass was a New Zealander (see Kumeu River, page 263). Now candidates come from the USA, Australia, Germany, France, etc. 'Master of Wine' (MW) should eventually become the equivalent of a Bachelor of Arts degree in the worldwide wine trade.

And the score is...

It seems that Europe and America will never agree about the idea of scoring wines. America is apparently besotted with the 100-point scale devised by the critic Robert Parker, based on the strange US school system in which 50 = 0. Arguments that taste is too various, too subtle, too evanescent, too wonderful to be reduced to a pseudo-scientific set of numbers fall on deaf ears. Arguments that the accuracy implied by giving one wine a score of 87 and another 88 is a chimera don't get much further.

America likes numbers (and so do salesmen) because they are simpler than words. When it comes to words America like superlatives. It likes gurus. It likes a system that creates stars (as in film). In short, Robert Parker's approach to wine suits it fine.

The Johnson System

Very cautiously, therefore, I offer an alternative way of registering how much *you* like a wine. The Johnson System is based on many years of self-sacrifice in tasting every wine that comes to hand, then painstakingly analysing the experience in the slightly doubtful piece of software between my ears. It is a system that reflects the enjoyment (or lack of it) that each wine offered at the time it was tasted or drunk with inescapable honesty. Here it is:

> **The minimum score is 1 sniff**
>
> **One step up is 1 sip**
>
> **2 sips = faint interest**
>
> **A half glass = slight hesitation**
>
> **1 glass = tolerance, even general approval**

Individuals will vary in their scoring after this (they do with points systems, too). You should assume that you are drinking without compunction – without your host pressing you or the winemaker glowering at you.

> **Two glasses means you quite like it**
>
> (or there is nothing else to drink);
>
> **three glasses – you find it more than acceptable;**
>
> **four – it tickles your fancy;**
>
> **one bottle means thorough satisfaction;**
>
> **two, it is irrisistable.** The steps grow higher now:
>
> **a full case means you are not going to miss out on**
>
> **this one...** and so on.
>
> **The logical top score in the Johnson System is,**
>
> **of course, the whole vineyard.**

Quick reference vintage charts

These charts give a picture of the range of qualities made in the principal 'classic' areas (every year has its relative successes and failures) and a guide to whether the wine is ready to drink or should be kept.

I	drink now	—	needs keeping
/	can be drunk with pleasure now, but the better wines will continue to improve	穴	avoid
		0	no good
		10	the best

France

	Red Bordeaux		White Bordeaux		Alsace	
	Médoc/ Graves	Pom/ St-Em	Sauternes & SW	Graves & dry		
95	6–9 —	6–9 —	6–9 —	5–9 V	5–8 K	95
94	5–8 —	5–9 —	4–6 —	5–8 V	4–8 K	94
93	4–7 ∠	5–8 ∠	2–5 /	5–7 /	6–8 V	93
92	3–7 K	3–5 V	3–5 ∠	4–8 V	7–9 V	92
91	3–6 V	2–4 V	2–5 V	6–8 /	5–7 V	91
90	7–10 K	8–10 K	7–10 ∠	7–8 V	7–9 V	90
89	6–9 K	7–9 K	7–9 V	6–8 V	7–10 V	89
88	6–9 ∠	7–9 K	6–10 ∠	7–9 V	8–10 V	88
87	3–6 I	3–6 I	2–5 穴	7–10 V	7–8 穴	87
86	6–9 K	5–8 V	7–10 ∠	7–9 I	7–8 I	86
85	7–9 K	7–9 K	6–8 V	5–8 I	7–10 V	85
84	3–5 I	2–5 ∠	4–6 穴	5–7 穴	4–6 穴	84
83	6–9 V	6–9 I	6–10 ∠	7–9 I	8–10 穴	83
82	8–10 K	7–9 I	3–7 V	7–8 I	6–8 穴	82
81	5–8 V	6–9 I	5–8 V	7–8 I	7–8 I	81
79	5–8 V	5–7 I	6–8 V	4–6 穴	7–8 穴	79
78	6–9 V	6–8 I	4–6 I	7–9 穴	6–8 I	78
76	6–8 I	7–8 I	7–9 V	4–8 V		76

	Burgundy			Rhone		
	Cote d'Or red	Cote d'Or white	Chablis	Rhone (N)	Rhone (S)	
95	4–8 —	4–7 ∠	5–8 /	6–8 —	6–8 —	95
94	5–7 ∠	5–8 ∠	6–8 V	6–9 ∠	5–7 K	94
93	6–9 ∠	4–6 V	4–7 V	3–6 I	4–9 K	93
92	4–7 V	6–8 V	5–8 V	4–6 I	3–6 V	92
91	5–7 /	4–6 I	4–6 I	6–9 V	4–5 I	91
90	7–10 K	7–9 K	6–9 V	6–9 K	7–9 K	90
89	6–9 K	6–9 V	7–10 V	6–8 ∠	6–8 K	89
88	7–10 K	7–9 V	7–9 V	7–9 V	5–8 V	88
87	6–8 V	4–7 穴	5–7 I	3–6 V	3–5 I	87
86	5–8 I	7–10 V	7–9 I	5–8 V	4–7 V	86
85	7–10 V	5–8 V	6–9 I	6–8 V	6–9 I	85
83	5–9 V	6–9 I	7–9 I	7–10 K	7–9 I	83
82	4–7 I	6–9 I	6–7 I	5–8 穴	5–8 穴	82

Beaujolais 95, 94 and 93 Crus will keep, 92 was vg, 91 superb. **Mâcon-Villages** (white) Drink 94, 93, 92 now or can wait. **Loire** (Sweet Anjou and Touraine) best recent vintages: 93, 90, 89, 88, 85, 84, 83, 82, 79, 78, 76. **Upper Loire** (Sancerre and Pouilly Fumé): 95 vg; 94, 93 and 90 are good now. **Muscadet** DYA.

Germany | Italy | USA (California)

	Rhine	Mosel	Tuscan reds	Cabs	Chards	
95	7–10 /	8–10 /	4–6 —	4–6 —	4–6 —	95
94	5–7 /	6–10 K	5–7 ∠	6–9 —	4–7 V	94
93	5–8 K	6–9 K	7–9 V	6–8 V	5–8 V	93
92	5–9 V	5–9 V	3–6 V	7–9 V	6–8 I	92
91	5–7 V	5–7 V	4–6 V	8–10 ∠	5–7 I	91
90	8–10 K	8–10 K	7–10 V	8–9 K	5–9 I	90
89	7–10 V	8–10 K	5–8 V	6–9 I	5–9 I	89
88	6–8 V	7–9 V	6–9 I	6–8 V	7–8 穴	88
87	4–7 I	5–7 I	4–7 I	7–10 /	7–9 I	87
86	4–8 I	5–8 I	5–8 I	5–8 V	6–8 穴	86
85	6–9 I	5–8 I	7–10 I	7–9 V	7–9 穴	85
83	6–9 I	7–10 V	5–7 I	4–8 V	4–7 I	83
82	4–6 穴	4–7 穴	5–8 I	5–8 I	5–6 穴	82